2001 INTERNATIONAL Travel Health Guide

Stuart R. Rose, M.D.

CONTRIBUTING EDITORS
Jay Keystone, M.D. – Phyllis Kozarsky, M.D.
Frank J. Bia, M.D. – Bradley A. Connor, M.D. – Mark S. Fradin, M.D.
Karl Neumann, M.D. – Richard Thompson, M.D.

Travel Medicine, Inc. 1-800-872-8633
369 Pleasant Street, Northampton, MA 01060

IMPORTANT NOTICE

Information in the *2001 International Travel HealthGuide* is not intended to replace professional medical advice or treatment. If such advice or treatment is required or recommended, either before, during, or after travel, the reader is advised to consult his or her own physician or other competent licensed health professionals, agencies, or facilities.

International Travel HealthGuide – 2001 Edition
Copyright © 2001 by Travel Medicine, Inc.
Published by:
Travel Medicine, Inc.
369 Pleasant Street
Northampton, MA 01060
Tel: 413-584-0381
Fax: 413-584-6656
E-mail: travmed@travmed.com
Web site: www.travmed.com

Printed in the United States of America by McNaughton and Gunn.
ISBN 0-923947-01-9

ACKNOWLEDGMENT

The *International Travel HealthGuide*—12th Edition—has been funded, in part, through an educational grant provided by the Merck Vaccine Division. Chris Page provided assistance with computer graphics and text layout. I am again thankful to Laura Simmons, my layout editor, for her meticulous review of the manuscript.

Special thanks goes to my editors. Continued publication of the *International Travel HealthGuide* would not be possible without their expertise, enthusiasm, encouragement, and assistance.

ABOUT THE AUTHOR

Stuart Ramage Rose, M.D., is Director of the International Travel Clinic at Noble Hospital in Westfield, Massachusetts. He is a graduate of Amherst College and Columbia University, College of Physicians and Surgeons.

Dr. Rose, Founder and President of Travel Medicine, Inc., is a member of the American Society of Tropical Medicine and Hygiene and the International Society of Travel Medicine.

CONTRIBUTING EDITORS

Jay Keystone, M.D., FRCPC, M.Sc. (CTM), Professor of Medicine, University of Toronto, is a world-recognized authority in the field of tropical and travel medicine. Dr. Keystone sits on the Editorial Board of the American Journal of Tropical Medicine & Hygiene and is a past president of the International Society of Travel Medicine.

Phyllis Kozarsky, M.D., is Assistant Professor of International Health at the Emory University School of Public Health. Dr. Kozarsky serves on the Executive Board of the International Society of Travel Medicine and is on the Editorial Board of both the American Journal of Tropical Medicine & Hygiene and the Journal of Travel Medicine.

ASSISTANT EDITORS

Frank J. Bia, M.D., M.P.H, is Professor of Medicine and Laboratory Medicine, and Co-Director, the International Health Program, Department of Medicine, Yale University School of Medicine. Dr. Bia is an authority on diabetes and travel.

Bradley A. Connor, M.D. is Associate Clinical Professor of Medicine, Columbia-Cornell Medical School, and the author of numerous publications in the field of gastroenterology, parasitic diseases and travel medicine. He is a charter member of the International Society of Travel Medicine.

Mark S. Fradin, M.D., is Clinical Associate Professor of Dermatology at the University of North Carolina. He is an expert in the field of insect-bite prevention and insect repellents.

Karl Neumann, M.D., is the editor of the *Traveling Healthy Newsletter* and is a world-recognized authority and lecturer on the subject of children and travel. He is Associate Professor of Pediatrics at Columbia-Cornell Medical School.

Richard Thompson, M.D., is Director of Occupational Medicine at Camino Medical Group in Encino, California. He is the author of the annually published *Travel & Routine Immunizations—A Practical Guide for the Medical Office.*

Contents

Introduction	1
1 Trip Preparation	13
2 Vaccines	31
3 Jet Lag & Motion Sickness	55
4 Food & Drink Safety Water Purification	67
5 Travelers' Diarrhea & Rehydration Therapy	77
6 Malaria	93
7 Insect-Bite Prevention	117
8 Insect-Borne Diseases	129

9	Travel Related Diseases	151
10	Lyme Disease	173
11	Hepatitis	179
12	Diabetes	189
13	AIDS, HIV & Sexually Transmitted Diseases	197
14	Altitude Sickness	205
15	Medical Care Abroad	219
16	Travel Health Insurance	227

17 Emergency Medical Transport — 233

18 Business Travel & Health — 239

19 Travel & Pregnancy — 251

20 Traveling with Children — 267

World Medical Guide — 281
Disease Risk Summaries
Mexico and C. America	282
The Caribbean	284
South America	286
Europe, Russia, CIS	289
North Africa	292
Sub-Saharan Africa	293
The Middle East	296
China & Southern Asia	297
Southeast Asia	299
Japan, Korea, Taiwan	301
Australia and Oceania	302

Index — 491

INTRODUCTION
Travel Abroad: What are the risks?

How risky is foreign travel? People tend to exaggerate unlikely dangers such as terrorism and disregard or minimize more common perils such as motor vehicle accidents or malaria.

The Risk of Illness While Traveling

The chances of acquiring certain diseases or having an accident depends largely on where you travel and what you do while traveling. Out of 30 million Americans who go abroad each year, about eight million will be go to lesser-developed countries where the incidence of tropical and infectious diseases is high. Almost seven million U.S. citizens travel to countries where there is risk of malaria. Here's what health surveys show about your risk of getting sick while traveling:

- There is a 60%–70% chance that you will have an illness when traveling in lesser-developed countries for up to 90 days (median trip duration—19 days).
- There is a 8% chance you will seek medical care.
- Your chance of being hospitalized will be less than 1%.
- The greatest risks to travelers overall are: diarrhea (34%); a respiratory disease (26%); a skin disorder (8%); acute mountain sickness (6%); motion sickness (5%); an accident and injury (5%); an illness with fever (3%).
- On return home, there is a 26% chance that you will have a bout of diarrhea, a respiratory illness, a skin problem, or a fever.

Your individual degree of risk, however, may vary from the above risks for many reasons. These include (1) the countries you visit—some are much more disease-ridden than others (2) the duration of your trip, (3) your use (or nonuse) of prophylactic antimalarial drugs, (4) your use of personal protection measures against insect bites, (5) which vaccinations you received, (6) your personal risk-taking behavior, and (7) your own health status.

Bear in mind, however, that traveling might also reduce your risk of illness or injury! Perhaps your trip abroad will temporarily remove you from a high-crime neighborhood, a dangerous or stressful job, or a harsh climate.

Prevention of Illness

Most travel-related diseases can be prevented. Schistosomiasis and sexually transmitted diseases, including HIV, can be avoided by behavior modification. Hepatitis, rabies, yellow fever, and many other diseases can be prevented by vaccination. Chemoprophylaxis, combined with the proper use of protective measures against mosquito bites, can prevent virtually all cases of malaria, as well as most other insect-transmitted diseases.

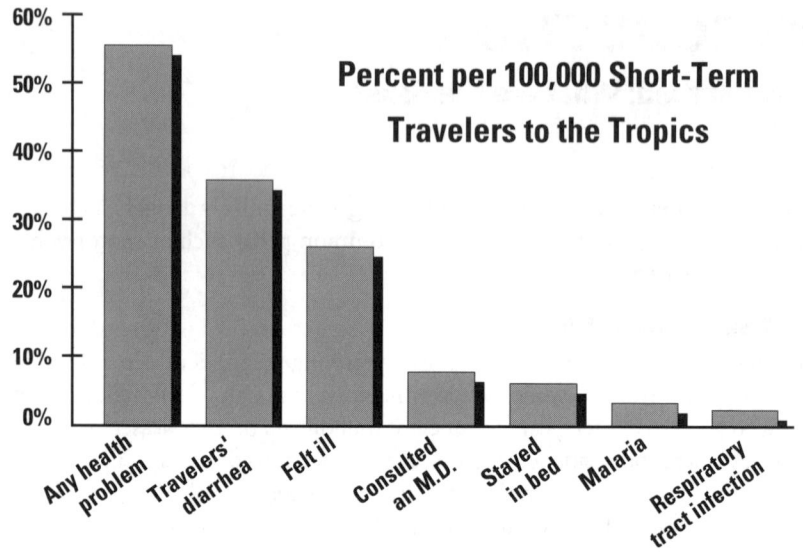

Types of Illnesses

Diarrhea (see Chapter 4)—This is the most common malady affecting travelers. There's a 35%–60% chance that you will get a bout of travelers' diarrhea during a month-long trip to a lesser-developed country. Pay careful attention to safe food and drink guidelines—this will reduce your risk. Prompt treatment with antibiotics and loperamide stops most cases of diarrhea.

Malaria (see Chapter 5)—This mosquito-transmitted illness, which can be fatal, is the most important parasitic disease to avoid overseas. Malaria is a serious health problem in many tropical and subtropical countries. Check your itinerary carefully to assess your risk of exposure.

Hepatitis (see Chapter 10)—Hepatitis is the most important viral illness you need to avoid. Although rarely fatal, hepatitis A can ruin a carefully planned vacation and result in weeks or months of disability. You can prevent it with the hepatitis A vaccine. You can prevent hepatitis B with vaccination and/or avoidance of exposure to potentially contaminated blood and secretions. Although there are no vaccines against hepatitis C and E, Chapter 10 outlines measures you can take to reduce your risk of these illnesses.

Other illnesses—The bar graph above illustrates the frequency of various symptoms and illnesses you may encounter.[1] Viral diseases and colds, respiratory infections, constipation, skin rashes, ear infections and sunburn (very common among swimmers and divers in the tropics), sprains, contusions, and superficial injuries account for the majority of less-serious problems.

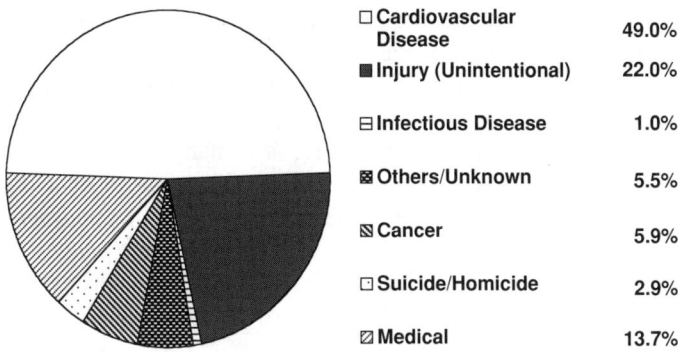

Causes of Death While Traveling (all ages)

FATALITIES DURING TRAVEL

While it's quite possible you will have some type of minor illness while abroad, the chance that your illness will be fatal is reassuringly small. In 1984, out of 30 million travelers overseas, just 1,298 deaths were recorded. Mortality abroad is due mainly to heart attacks and accidents. Infections cause relatively few deaths. Although heart attacks are the greatest overall cause, almost all of these deaths occur in older travelers who already have preexisting cardiovascular disease. Accidental deaths, however, unlike heart attacks, are directly travel related—and often preventable.

Overseas Fatalities of U.S. Travelers—An Overview
- Fatalities abroad are due mainly to heart attacks and accidental injuries.
- Heart attacks are the most common cause of death in older travelers of both sexes. Cardiovascular death rates, however, are not increased by travel.
- Injuries are the most common cause of death in younger travelers. Fatal injuries are mostly due to motor vehicle crashes or drownings. The number of accidental deaths in 15- to 44-year-old travelers is higher by a factor of two to three as compared with rates among the same age group back home.
- "Excess mortality" abroad, therefore, is mainly due to accidental injuries, not heart attacks.
- Infections cause only 1% of deaths among travelers.

ACCIDENTS AND TRAVEL

Accidents are the leading cause of death among travelers under the age of 55. Death rates from motor vehicle accidents, according to The Association for Safe International Road Travel, are 20 to 80 times higher in some countries than in the United States (see table on page 4), illustrating one reason why "excess mortality" abroad is primarily injury related.

The majority of deaths in younger travelers are motor vehicle and motorcycle related; drownings, aircraft crashes, homicides, and burns are lesser causes. Each year, an estimated 750 Americans die of injuries on foreign roads, and at least 25,000 are injured.

One study has revealed an interesting fact: many road accidents involving tourists do not involve a collision between two vehicles but are often due to loss of driver control caused by fatigue, alcohol, unfamiliar road conditions, or other factors.

In many developing countries, vehicles are in disrepair, drivers are inexperienced, roads are not well maintained, and common-sense rules of the road are disregarded.

The Bethesda-based **Association for Safe International Road Travel** (ASIRT; Tel: 301-983-5252; Fax: 301-983-3663; Web site www.asirt.org) can provide you with a report on road safety conditions in 70 foreign countries. Their Road Travel Reports also contain information about seasonal hazards; city, rural, and interstate traffic; and the most dangerous roads in various countries. ASIRT currently cites Egypt, Kenya, India, South Korea, Turkey, and Morocco as some of the most dangerous countries. (A small donation to this nonprofit organization is requested for information received.)

Preventing Traffic Accidents and Injury

If you follow the recommendations below, you will decrease your chances of having an accident or being injured while driving overseas.

- Always wear a seat belt (if one is present).
- Bring a car seat for infants.
- Consider hiring a qualified guide or driver.
- Do not be afraid to tell your driver to slow down or use more caution.
- Rent a larger rather than a smaller vehicle.
- Know the meaning of all road sign symbols.

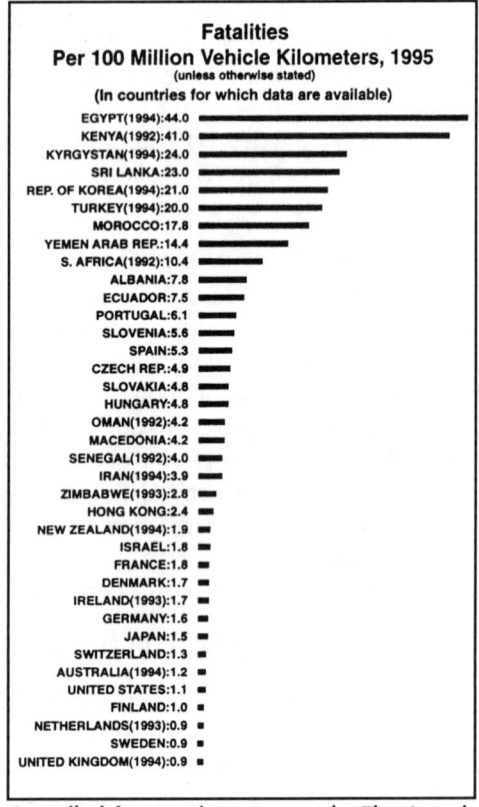

Fatalities Per 100 Million Vehicle Kilometers, 1995 (unless otherwise stated) (In countries for which data are available)

EGYPT(1994):44.0
KENYA(1992):41.0
KYRGYSTAN(1994):24.0
SRI LANKA:23.0
REP. OF KOREA(1994):21.0
TURKEY(1994):20.0
MOROCCO:17.8
YEMEN ARAB REP.:14.4
S. AFRICA(1992):10.4
ALBANIA:7.8
ECUADOR:7.5
PORTUGAL:6.1
SLOVENIA:5.6
SPAIN:5.3
CZECH REP.:4.9
SLOVAKIA:4.8
HUNGARY:4.8
OMAN(1992):4.2
MACEDONIA:4.2
SENEGAL(1992):4.0
IRAN(1994):3.9
ZIMBABWE(1993):2.8
HONG KONG:2.4
NEW ZEALAND(1994):1.9
ISRAEL:1.8
FRANCE:1.8
DENMARK:1.7
IRELAND(1993):1.7
GERMANY:1.6
JAPAN:1.5
SWITZERLAND:1.3
AUSTRALIA(1994):1.2
UNITED STATES:1.1
FINLAND:1.0
NETHERLANDS(1993):0.9
SWEDEN:0.9
UNITED KINGDOM(1994):0.9

Compiled from various sources by The Association for Safe International Road Travel, 1997.

- Be sure you have collision/liability insurance.
- Know that a driver approaching a traffic circle must yield the right of way to those already in the circle.
- Know the route to your destination. Study road maps thoroughly.

The two most important rules to follow are:
- Do not drive at night in rural areas.
- Do not ride a motorcycle, moped, or bicycle (even if you are experienced).

PERSONAL SAFETY GUIDELINES

Although you can't escape from the remote possibility that some nasty, unlucky incident might happen, you can take steps to lessen that possibility: plan your trip carefully, be reasonably cautious, obey common sense rules of behavior, and don't panic! Remember that the vast majority of travelers arrive home unscathed.

The following guidelines will be helpful in ensuring your travel safety:

- Carefully select swimming areas. Don't swim alone, intoxicated, or at night.
- Avoid small, nonscheduled airlines in lesser-developed countries.
- Don't travel by road at night outside urban areas. If you are out at night, stay in a group.
- Don't go out alone on beaches at night.
- Don't hitchhike or pick up hitchhikers.
- Don't sleep in your car or RV at the roadside at night.
- Camp only in legal campsites.
- If you are drinking alcohol, don't relax by sitting on the railing of your hotel balcony. Falls and serious injuries often occur this way.
- Review hotel fire safety rules. Locate nearest exits.
- If possible, book a room between the second and seventh floors—high enough to prevent easy entrance by an intruder and low enough for fire equipment to reach.
- Lock your hotel room at all times.
- Keep valuables and travel documents in your room or hotel safe.
- Avoid countries or regions where there is drug-related violence and drug trafficking. Avoid excursions into certain remote areas of countries such as Mexico, Colombia, or Peru, where you might be mistaken for a drug agent or a rival drug dealer.
- Never purchase, transport, or use illegal drugs.

Personal Security Information/Advisories

Security problems in many countries mandate that you take precautions to reduce your risk of being involved in a terrorist act or a political kidnapping. When traveling to a politically unstable country, you should read publications that provide specific advice on how to reduce these risks. Some of the more useful publications are listed below.

The Safe Travel Book, a Guide for the International Traveler by Peter Savage (MacMillan Publishing Co., 1999; 800-257-5755; $12.95). Covers every possibility from plane hijacking, kidnapping, and terrorism to how to prevent your passport from being stolen. Extensive pretravel checklists and information sources.

TRAVEL SAFELY: Don't Be A Target! (published by Uniquest Publications. Available from Magellan's, Box 5485, Santa Barbara, CA 93150; 805-568-5400 or 800-962-4943; item #BB654A: $12.95). A 75-page pocket manual with precautions, helpful hints, strategies, and tactics (1150 solid tips in all) on how to make your trip a safe one.

Risk-Reduction Services

The companies listed below provide travelers and corporations, for a fee, with detailed reports that analyze the risks of terrorism, crime, and political instability in trouble spots worldwide—and how personal risks can be reduced.

The Ackerman Group, 1666 Kennedy Causeway, Miami Beach, FL 33141; Tel: 305-865-0072.

Air Security International, 2925 Briarpark Drive, 7th floor, Houston, TX 77042; Tel: 800-503-5814.

Pinkerton Global Intelligence, 200 N. Glebe Road, Suite 1011, Arlington, VA 22203-3728; Tel: 800-824-7502.

Kroll Information Services, 100 East Street SE, Vienna, VA 22180; Tel: 800-824-7502.

HOW THE U.S. GOVERNMENT CAN HELP

American Citizens Services (202-647-5225;) offices are set up at U.S. embassies and consulates throughout the world. ACS has six geographical divisions with case officers who assist in all matters involving protective services for Americans abroad, including arrests, death cases, financial or medical emergencies, and welfare and whereabouts inquiries. The office provides travel warnings by telephone and also provides guidance on nationality and citizenship determination, document issuance, judicial and notarial services, estates and property claims, third-country representation, and disaster assistance.

Emergency Services to U.S. Citizens Abroad

The **Overseas Citizens Services** (travel.state.gov/acs.html#emr) works with embassies to keep you (or your family) informed and advised when hospitalization occurs overseas. If emergency medical transport is needed, they will refer you (or the people helping you) to an assistance company; in some cases, the Overseas Citizens Services (working with the embassy or consulate) will coordinate stretcher transport on a commercial airliner to bring a sick traveler home to the United States. In event of death, they will assist with returning the remains. They will also give assistance with legal problems such as arrest/detention of an American citizen, robbery of an American citizen, property matters, citizenship, marriage overseas, or missing persons.

State Department Travel Warnings & Consular Information Sheets

Tel: 202-647-5225; Fax: 202-647-3000
Bureau of Consular Affairs Home Page: *http://travel.state.gov/index2.html*

The U.S. State Department, Bureau of Consular Affairs, issues travel warnings, consular information sheets, and public announcements on over 200 countries. These may be obtained by **telephone, fax,** or the **Internet**. Travel warnings are issued when the State Department believes travel to a particular country should be avoided. The Consular Information Sheets are available for every country in the world. They give the location of every embassy and consulate, and information on health conditions, minor political disturbances, currency, entry regulations, crime and security information, and penalties for being caught with illegal drugs. The Public Announcements provide information on terrorist threats and other conditions posing significant risks to the security of American travelers. This includes information on bomb threats to airlines and the anniversary dates of specific terrorist events. Using the Internet you can easily get all this information from the Bureau of Consular Affairs Home Page (listed above). The fax service provides the same information, but to receive the fax, your telephone and fax must be on the same phone line.

Other information available from the Bureau of Consular Affairs includes (1) travel publications (below), (2) passport and visa information, (3) international legal assistance, and (4) links to the Centers for Disease Control and prevention (*http://www.cdc.gov/*) and Department of State (*http://www.state.gov/index.html*) Web sites.

Personal security advisories—In-depth advice about specific security issues in any particular country is available from an embassy's Regional Security Officer (RSO). Here is what to do:

- Contact the Department of State at 202-647-4000 and ask to be connected to the Country Desk covering the destination country.
- Request the name and overseas telephone number of the RSO stationed at the embassy. This information is also available on the Department of State Web site *(http://www.state.gov/www/about_state/contacts/keyofficer_index.html)*.
- Telephone the RSO during Embassy business hours in the destination country and inquire about the following:

    – The safest taxi cab/route to take from the airport.
    – Street crime or terrorism problems.
    – Neighborhoods to avoid.
    – Recent incidents involving tourists or corporate executives.
    – Safety of public transportation.

TRAVEL HEALTH SERVICES AND INFORMATION

Before you depart you'll want to consult with a health care provider if you have chronic medical problems or cardiac risk factors, take medication, or are traveling to a country where immunizations are recommended or required. Although your own doctor may be able to administer routine childhood or adult immunizations, most physicians' offices don't stock specialized vaccines such as typhoid or yellow fever. More importantly, your health care provider may not have the expertise to give you accurate, up-to-date pretravel advice. Also, most physicians in the United States are unfamiliar with tropical diseases, such as malaria. Providing travelers with accurate health information can be quite complex and time-consuming, and many physicians are not prepared to give this type of consultation.

Fortunately, the specialty of travel medicine is rapidly growing, and there are now many health care providers who either specialize in this field or who have developed a professional interest in it.

Physicians who belong to travel medicine organizations have elected to devote time and energy to this field and can provide up-to-date recommendations based on current information from scientific journals, conferences, public health agencies, computer databases, and other sources of travel health information.

Most travel medicine physicians belong to the International Society of Travel Medicine (ISTM) and/or the American Society of Tropical Medicine & Hygiene (ASTMH). Some of these physicians have also obtained additional formal training in tropical medicine and have received a Diploma of Tropical Medicine & Hygiene (DTM&H). Recently, the American Society of Tropical Medicine & Hygiene (ASTMH) has developed a certification examination that awards a Certificate of Knowledge in Clinical Tropical Medicine and Travelers' Health.

Types of travel clinics—Travel clinics vary in their range of services, hours of operation, and professional staffing. A travel clinic is sometimes a free-standing facility, but more often it is a service offered by an ambulatory care facility, a doctor's private practice, an HMO, an occupational health clinic, or the infectious disease department of a medical center or a university teaching hospital. Physicians in these facilities provide pre- and post-travel advice and counseling, but in more and more travel clinics nurses now provide most of the services, with physicians being available primarily for consultation.

Travel clinics that are staffed by health care providers who have received specialty training in infectious diseases and/or tropical medicine can provide a broader range of services involving the diagnosis and treatment of travel-related diseases. These clinics are often, but not invariably, associated with a university hospital or a medical school. If you need an in-depth predeparture consultation, or you suspect that you have acquired an exotic illness abroad and need to see a specialist, check on the capabilities of the clinic when you make an appointment.

Finding a Travel Clinic

If you don't know of a travel clinic in your area, check the listing of travel clinics in Appendix II. The Internet has several Web sites with extensive lists of travel clinics detailing hours of operation, services provided, and training of staff.

Finding a Travel Clinic on the Internet

Travel Medicine, Inc.
(www.travmed.com)
Lists over 1,200 travel clinics.

Shoreland's Travel Health Online
(http://www.tripprep.com)

International Society of Travel Medicine (ISTM)
(www.istm.org/clinidir/clinidir.html)

American Society of Tropical Medicine & Hygiene (ASTMH)
Directory of Travel Clinics and Consulting Physicians
(http://www.astmh.org/clinics/clinindex.html)
The directory lists physicians who offer extensive consultation services in tropical medicine, medical parisitology, and travelers' health.

TRAVEL HEALTH INFORMATION

Knowledge is the key to successful travel. Good trip preparation involves a variable amount of "required" reading and data gathering, but a single source may not give you all the necessary health information you will need for your trip. Multiple sources are usually necessary, and the *HealthGuide* lists many of these. To get more specific information, you can (1) consult the **World Medical Guide** of this book, (2) make an appointment at a travelers' clinic (see previous page), (3) contact the CDC or WHO Web site (see below and page 12), or (4) read one or more of the publications also listed below.

CDC Travelers' Health Information

The U.S. Public Health Service **Centers for Disease Control and Prevention (CDC)** has expanded its **International Fax Information Service** and **Internet** information systems. You can get current malaria advisories, immunization schedules, disease risk and prevention information by region of the world, bulletins on disease outbreaks, guidelines for the HIV-infected traveler, lists of countries where yellow fever and choleras are active, and much more. For fax information, call toll-free (888-232-3299) to get a directory sheet. The directory lists a six-digit number for each document. You then call back and order, by number, as many as five documents at once. For voice information, call toll-free 888-232-3228.

The Internet, however, is probably the best and easiest way to get the information you want. The Web address of the **CDC's Travel Information Home Page** is *http://www.cdc.gov/travel/travel.html*

On this site you can get not only the latest information on disease outbreaks, vaccination recommendations, and geographic health information, but also the complete text of the CDC publication *Health Information for International Travel* (Yellow Book). Countries where cholera and yellow fever are active are also listed.

Canadians can obtain health information produced by the Committee to Advise on Tropical Medicine and Travel (CATMAT), Health Canada, on the Health Canada Web site (*www.hwc.ca/hpb/lcdc*), or by fax (613-941-3900).

Culturgrams give useful information on over 160 countries. Each four-page Culturgram gives detailed information about a country's geography and climate, history, general attitudes, customs and courtesies, eating and dietary customs, greetings, gestures, personal appearance codes, dating and marriage customs, etc. Contact the David M. Kennedy Center for International Studies at Brigham Young University; 800-528-6279; Fax: 801-378-5882; Web site: *http://fhss.byu.edu/kenncent/publications/* ($6 per copy).

Travel Medicine Publications

Textbook of Travel Medicine and Health by Herbert L. DuPont, M.D., and Robert Steffen, M.D. (B.C. Decker Inc. 2000. 370 pages; ISBN: 1-55009-037-2). An authoritative resource edited by two of the best known experts in the field. Covers the entire spectrum of travel medicine. Highly recommended.

Manual of TRAVEL MEDICINE and HEALTH by DuPont and Steffen (B.C. Decker Inc. 1999. 515 pages; $28.95; ISBN: 1-55009-078-X) is a quick-reference companion to the *Textbook of Travel Medicine and Health*. To order either publication, call B.C. Decker at 800-568-7281 or send e-mail to info@bcdecker.com.

Travel Medicine Advisor. A comprehensive source of travel health information for physicians, travel clinics, corporations, health departments, and others who counsel travelers. Includes bimonthly updates, prepared by recognized travel medicine experts. $328 annual subscription. American Health Consultants, P.O. Box 740060, Atlanta, GA 30374; 800-688-2421.

Health Hints for the Tropics published by the American Society of Tropical Medicine & Hygiene. Contact: Karl A. Western, M.D., ASTMH, 8000 Westpark Drive, Suite 130, McLean, VA 22102; 703-790-1745.

The Travel and Tropical Medicine Manual, edited by Elaine C. Jong, M.D., and Russell McMullen, M.D. (W.B. Saunders Company, 1998). A comprehensive source of information on tropical medicine and travel-related infectious diseases.

Traveller's Health—How to Stay Healthy Abroad by Dr. Richard Dawood (Oxford University Press, 1998; Fifth Edition). A 600-page source of travel health information compiled by British experts.

Health Information for International Travel from Superintendent of Documents Government Printing Office, Washington, D.C. 20402. Call 202-512-1800 to order. Price: $20. Published annually. The complete text is also available on the **CDC's World Wide Web Home Travel Information Page:** *http://www.cdc.gov/travel/travel.html*

Physicians Overseas

The International Association for Medical Assistance to Travellers (**IAMAT**) publishes a booklet listing English-speaking physicians and health clinics worldwide. IAMAT also provides information on tropical diseases such as malaria and schistosomiasis. IAMAT is a tax-free foundation, and officially there is no charge for their publications; however, a $15 donation is suggested. In the United States, contact 417 Center Street, Lewiston, NY 14092; 716-754-4883. In Canada: 40 Regal Road, Guelph, Ontario, N1K 1B5; 519-836-0102.

Wilderness Medicine

Wilderness Medicine—Management of Wilderness and Environmental Emergencies, 3rd Edition. Paul S. Auerbach, M.D., editor (Mosby, 1995. ISBN 0-8016-7044-6). An outstanding book and *the* required reference for anyone seriously interested in outdoor and wilderness medicine.

Underwater Medicine/Decompression Chambers

For a guide to hyperbaric and decompression chamber facilities worldwide, contact the Undersea and Hyperbaric Medical Society, 9650 Rockville Pike, Bethesda, MD; 301-571-1817.

First Aid

A Comprehensive Guide to Wilderness and Travel Medicine by Eric A. Weiss, M.D. 198 pages with illustrations, $6.95. (Adventure Medical Kits, 1997. P.O. Box 43309, Oakland, CA 94624; 800-324-3517.)

Travel Medicine Databases

TRAVAX (Travel Health Information Service), 10625 W. North Ave., Milwaukee, WI 53226; 800-433-5256. Extensive travel health information on over 200 countries. Shoreland's "Travel Health Online" address is *http://www.tripprep.com.*

Newsletters

T*raveling Healthy* by Karl Neumann, M.D. and Senior Editor Jay Keystone, M.D. (Published by Travel Medicine, Inc., 369 Pleasant St., Northampton, MA 01060; 1-800-TRAVMED; $45/year for print version).

Kids on the Go! Edited by Karl Neumann, M.D. and Senior Editor Jay Keystone, M.D. (Published by Travel Medicine, Inc., 369 Pleasant St., Northampton, MA 01060; 1-800-TRAVMED; $45/year for print version). First issue March 2001.

Kidney Dialysis Abroad

Dialysis and Transplantation: The List (Creative Age Publications: 800-442-5667 or 818-782-7328; $10). Dialysis clinics worldwide.

Dialysis Worldwide for the Traveling Patient (American Association of Kidney Patients, 1 Davis Blvd., Suite LL1, Tampa, FL; 813-251-0725).

USEFUL TRAVEL INFORMATION

CDC Malaria Hotline for Physicians   **770-488-7788**

Passports made simple
(http://travel.state.gov/passport_services.html)—The Department of State has established this site to help people apply for passports. You can download printable passport applications, as well as find a list of where and how to apply. Can't find your birth certificate? This site has a list of where to obtain certified birth certificates, and includes an application form for you.

Should you even go?
(http://travel.state.gov.travel_warnings.html)—U.S. State Department updates on areas with civil unrest, terrorist bombings, and disease outbreaks, plus Consular Information Sheets and travel warnings for every country in the world.

Business Security Advisories
(www.ds-osac.org/) The Overseas Security Advisory Council (OSAC) was established in 1985 by the U.S. Department of State to foster the exchange of security related information between the U.S. Government and American private sector operating abroad.

Embassy tip sheets
(http://travel.state.gov/links.html)—Links to United States Embassies and Consulates worldwide. Here you can learn about visas, emergency services, consulate office hours, and more. For instance, the Emergency Services section provides specific information on what you need to do if a theft occurs, if you are arrested, if you become ill, or even if you are in need of money.

Electronic Embassy
(www.embassy.org/embassies)—The Electronic Embassy provides information on each of the embassies in Washington D.C.

Air Ambulance/Med-Evac/Travel Insurance with Assistance
(http://travel.state.gov/medical.html)—Listing of national and international air ambulance companies, as well as a listing of companies that sell travel insurance with medical assistance hotlines.

Global Weather
http://weather.yahoo.com

Hargarten, S, Baker SP. Fatalities in the Peace Corps. *JAMA*. 1985;254:1326–29.
Hill DR. Health problems in a large cohort of Americans traveling to developing countries; J Trav Med 2000;7:259.

1 Trip Preparation

When preparing for your trip, list the countries you will be visiting (in order) and the length of time you plan to spend in each one. Then, there are five categories of questions you need to answer about your trip. Your answers will determine the degree of detail needed in planning ahead.

Where Am I Going?

You should ask yourself the following questions: What illnesses are prevalent in the region I will be visiting? What is the general level of sanitation? How competent, and close by, is medical care? How harsh is the climate? How safe are the roads? Is the country politically stable?

Also, remember that a trip to Western Europe, for example, doesn't require as much preparation as an extended stay in a remote village in a lesser-developed country. Because some countries and cities are much safer than others, be careful not to overdo precautions. You don't need a typhoid shot if you are going to London or Tokyo, nor do you necessarily need a whole series of immunizations if you're taking a brief trip to a lesser-developed country but staying exclusively in a first-class hotel in a large city. For updated information on country-by-country disease risks, consult the World Medical Guide section of this book.

What Will I Be Doing?

Staying in rural areas of lesser-developed countries puts you at greater risk of contact with unsanitary food and drink and usually brings greater exposure to disease-carrying insects. (However, some diseases, such as dengue fever, are also transmitted in urban areas. There is also the risk of malaria in most cities in sub-Saharan Africa.) You should answer these questions: Will I be traveling on a tour and staying only in air-conditioned, first-class hotels, or traveling in rural areas off the usual tourist routes? Planning an adventure or wilderness itinerary with exposure to extremes of heat, cold, or altitude? Trekking or camping in a remote area far from medical care? Driving a car, motorcycle, or moped in a lesser-developed country? *(Be aware that motor vehicle accidents account for most reported accidental fatalities among travelers.)* Swimming in unfamiliar, possibly treacherous, waters, or wading in freshwater ponds, lakes, or streams? Having sexual or close physical contact with the indigenous population? A close analysis of your potential activities is critical to helping you avoid illness and injury.

How Long Will I Be There?

A brief trip usually means less exposure to diseases and less opportunity for an accident. Longer trips increase the likelihood of side trips and excursions that may place you at an unforeseen risk, perhaps for a mosquito-transmitted disease such as malaria. Longer travel may also cause you to discontinue prophylactic antimalarial medication, abandon safe food and drink practices, or neglect insect protection measures. Long-stay travel also brings with it the risk of "culture shock" and the need to know more about local customs, traditions, and history. Therefore, if you will be working overseas, you must also consider what psychological stresses you, and perhaps your family, will experience while adjusting to life abroad and what resources you will need beforehand to help make a smooth adjustment.

What Should I Bring?

Your itinerary, the climatic conditions you expect to encounter, the duration of your trip, and the disease risks in the countries you will be visiting all influence what you should bring. Your health status may also require you to take additional precautions.

For example, many travelers to tropical and subtropical regions neglect to take insect precautions necessary to prevent malaria and other insect-transmitted diseases. Be sure you have the necessary supplies (e.g., DEET repellents, permethrin, mosquito netting) described in Chapter 7.

When traveling overseas, take an ample supply of any medication that you use regularly. Don't carry a mixture of pills in unmarked vials. To avoid problems with customs officers who might suspect that your pills are recreational drugs or narcotics, keep each medication in its labeled original container. Exception: HIV-positive travelers may want to disguise the labeling of their medications because immigration officials at border checkpoints in certain countries may deny entry to any person suspected of being HIV positive.

Carry legally prescribed narcotics and controlled drugs (tranquilizers, sleeping pills, etc.) only if medically necessary. Get a letter from your doctor certifying the need for these medications. If you are a diabetic taking insulin and carrying needles and syringes, you may arouse suspicion at customs checkpoints. Also get a letter from your doctor certifying your diagnosis and treatment. The same applies if you will be carrying needles and syringes in an AIDS/hepatitis prevention kit.

Preparation Checklists

Use the following checklists as general guidelines and modify them according to your itinerary and specific travel and health needs. A nylon or canvas pack (e.g., the Wallaby Trip Kit by Eagle Creek) or a first aid kit (see page 17 for list of suppliers of medical kits) are useful for carrying medications and other health care items. Any medical kit containing medications should be in your "carry-on" baggage so access during travel is not a problem.

Medical and Personal Care Items

- ❏ Adequate supply of your prescription medications. Carry copies of your prescriptions by generic names. How much of each medication will you need for the duration of your trip? If you will be living abroad, or traveling extensively, will you need to refill prescriptions? Check local availability of medications, but also remember this: in some developing countries, regionally manufactured drugs may be substandard. Therefore, it may be necessary to carry a full supply of crucial medications, such as heart drugs, for the entire trip—or make arrangements for additional drugs to be shipped to you.
- ❏ Antibiotics for treating travelers' diarrhea—Quinolone antibiotics are the most effective and include ofloxacin (Floxin), levofloxacin (Lēvaquin), ciprofloxacin (Cipro) and nalidixic acid (Negram). Azithromycin (Zithromax), furazolidone (Furoxone), and cefixime (Suprax) are the best alternatives; the last four are available in liquid form and thus more easily taken by children (see also Chapter 20—Travel and Children).
- ❏ Antibiotics for emergency self-treatment of other infections—Levofloxacin is effective against sinusitis, some pneumonias, acute bacterial exacerbations of chronic bronchitis, urinary tract infections, typhoid fever, uncomplicated skin infections, and uncomplicated pelvic inflammatory disease due to gonorrhea and chlamydia. If you have to carry only one antibiotic, levofloxacin is the best choice because of its broader spectrum of activity. Azithromycin is a good alternative multi-purpose antibiotic for travel.
- ❏ Loperamide (Imodium-AD)—Use to treat mild travelers' diarrhea, or use in combination with an antibiotic to treat more severe diarrhea.
- ❏ Antimalarial drugs (depending on itinerary, length of stay, etc.)—chloroquine (Aralen), mefloquine (Lariam), atovaquone/proguanil (Malarone), primaquine, or doxycycline.
- ❏ Medical kit—Carry at least a basic kit that contains a thermometer, Band-Aids and wound dressings, an antibiotic ointment, scissors, tape, and other supplies to treat an abrasion, minor laceration, minor burn, etc.
- ❏ Water filtration/purification supplies.
- ❏ Oral rehydration salts (e.g., CeraLyte) to prevent or treat dehydration caused by diarrhea.
- ❏ 1-liter plastic water bottle—for storing water or oral rehydration solution.
- ❏ Epinephrine kit—If you have a history of severe bee sting reactions or severe food or drug allergies, have your doctor prescribe an emergency epinephrine self-injection kit (Epi-Pen®). Be sure you learn how to use it *before* you travel.
- ❏ Sterile needle/syringe kit—recommended for travel to countries where hepatitis B and C and HIV transmission are potential threats and where local medical care is substandard and the sterility and safety of medical supplies are questionable. (Available from the suppliers listed on page 17.)

- Analgesics—such as ibuprofen or acetaminophen, or the newer antiinflammatory drugs, rofecoxid (Vioxx) and celecoxib (Celebrex). Tylenol with codeine is an effective pain medication and also has anti-diarrheal properties. Aspirin can lose potency when exposed to humidity and heat. Acetaminophen (Tylenol) is not affected by these conditions.
- Antacids—such as Maalox or Mylanta.
- Cathartics and/or stool softeners since constipation is not uncommon, especially in the elderly.
- Pepto-Bismol—can be used to prevent or treat diarrhea (see Chapter 5).
- Motion/sea sickness drugs—TransDerm Scōp patch (for sea sickness), SCOPACE (scopolamine tablets), Dramamine, Phenergan.
- Drugs for acute mountain sickness (acetazolamide, dexamethasone) should be considered for all trekkers to Nepal and other high-altitude destinations.
- Jet lag—Melatonin and sleeping pills (e.g., triazolam) are helpful for some people, but are considered controversial by others (see Chapter 3). Temazepan (Restoril), zolpidem (Ambien), and zaleplon (Sonata) may have fewer side effects than Halcion (triazolam).
- Antibiotic eye drops (e.g., Ciloxan) should be carried by contact-lens wearers. An untreated infected corneal ulcer can cause serious eye damage.
- Nasal decongestant spray—Afrin or Neo-Synephrine (short-term use only).
- EarPlanes—Pressure-regulating ear plugs will reduce pain associated with air travel. Especially recommended if you have trouble clearing your nasal passages.
- Antihistamine tablets—for allergic reactions and rhinitis (hay fever). Consider Zyrtec or Claritin-D—they are long-acting and nonsedating.
- Vōsol solution—to prevent or treat swimmer's ear.
- Corticosteroid cream—such as Cortaid, or Topicort by prescription.
- Antifungal skin and foot cream—Lotrisone and Nizoral are good choices.
- Antifungal tablets—A single, oral 150-mg tablet of fluconazole (Diflucan) will eradicate a vaginal yeast infection.
- Extra pair of prescription glasses or contact lenses. Copy of lens prescription.
- Tweezers (good for tick removal), small knife, scissors, or Swiss Army knife (best to keep out of carry-on luggage). Large safety pins are very useful.

For Rain, Sun, Heat, and Insects

- ❏ Hat, sunglasses
- ❏ Sunscreens. SPF 30 or higher. Use a broad spectrum product that blocks both UVA and UVB.
- ❏ Insect repellent (minimum 30% DEET)—such as Ultrathon or Sawyer's Gold. The EPA no longer allows low-concentration (<15% DEET) repellents to be labelled "child-safe." (See Chapter 7)
- ❏ Clothing insecticide—permethrin aerosol or pump spray (Sawyer's Permethrin Spray or Permanone) and/or permethrin solution (PermaKill from Coulston Products). Use in combination with DEET repellent.
- ❏ Mosquito bed net (preferably permethrin-treated)
- ❏ Insecticide spray (e.g., Raid Flying Insect Spray) to rid sleeping quarters of night-biting insects

Medical kits and supplies: Sources of supplies include Travel Medicine, Inc., 369 Pleasant Street, Northampton, MA 01060, 800-TRAVMED (800-872-8633); on-line catalog *www.travmed.com* and Chinook Medical Gear, 2805 Wilderness Place, Boulder, CO 80301 (800-766-1365).

Checking the Weather at Your Destination

The *World Weather Guide* by E.A. Pearce and Gordon Smith (Times Books: ISBN 0-81291881-9) is available directly from Random House Inc. 800-733-3000; $17.95 plus $2.50 shipping.

American Express 1-900-WEATHER (1-900-932-8437)

Gives you up-to-the-minute current weather and 3-day forecasts for 900 cities worldwide. Cost: 95 cents a minute. Use a touch-tone phone.

Global Weather Information: *http://www.weather.yahoo.com*

Wilderness Travel

If you're on an adventure itinerary, determine what exposure you will have to heat, cold, or altitude. This may require complex pretrip planning. Most tour organizers will advise you of what to bring, but you may need to consult experts in outdoor/wilderness travel to determine if it's adequate. *A Comprehensive Guide to Wilderness & Travel Medicine* by Eric A. Weiss, M.D. (ISBN 0-9659768-0-7), is an excellent resource and can be ordered from booksellers or through the Internet.

Checklist for campers, hikers, and trekkers—You need to anticipate sudden changes in weather, in particular, high winds, rain, and temperature drops. For your comfort and safety, be sure always to carry a windbreaker or parka (Gore-Tex-type preferred), wool cap or balaclava, and gloves. Layers of clothing should be worn in more extreme conditions. Review the checklist for additional items your trip may require.

- ❏ Sleeping bag and pad
- ❏ Bivouac bag
- ❏ Ground cloth and pad
- ❏ Vapor barrier
- ❏ Tent
- ❏ Thermal blanket
- ❏ Radiant heat barrier
- ❏ Fuel, firestarter
- ❏ Fire and camping permits
- ❏ Stove
- ❏ Matches
- ❏ First-aid kit
- ❏ Cooking supplies, dehydrated food
- ❏ Candle and candle lantern
- ❏ Maps and guides
- ❏ Compass/GPS
- ❏ Binoculars
- ❏ Altimeter
- ❏ Flashlight
- ❏ Extra batteries and bulbs
- ❏ Rope
- ❏ Trowel and shovel
- ❏ Chemical hand and feet warmers
- ❏ Washcloth, soap, toilet kit

Travel Documents You May Need

Passports—The Bureau of Consular Affairs' Passport Agency Web site (http://travel.state.gov/passport_services.html) provides comprehensive information about applying for, or renewing, a passport. Passport application forms can be downloaded from this site.

What if I need a passport in a hurry?—Normally, it takes about six weeks to get your passport—or two weeks if you pay an extra fee to the Passport Agency. A passport/visa service company, however, can obtain documents for you in 1–4 working days. Contact one of the following:

- American Passport Express, 800-841-6778 (www.americanpassport.com)
- Instant Passport, 401-274-4002 (www.instantpassport.com)
- Passport Plus, New York, NY, 212-759-5540 or 800-367-1818 (www.passportplusny@aol.com)
- Passport & Visa Expeditors, Washington, D.C.; 800-237-3270
- Travisa, Washington, D.C., 202-463-6166 or 800-222-2589 (www.travisa.com)
- Passport Now, 1-888-FAST-PASS (www.passportnow.com)

Lost passport overseas—Go to the nearest American consulate and bring the following:

- A police report that documents the loss or theft
- Four (4) passport-size photos (must be 2" x 2" size)
- Application fee in U.S. currency, traveler's checks, or local currency. Bring the exact amount of currency.

If you have a photocopy of the lost passport showing the passport number and the date and place of issue, it will expedite the process. With the right information, a replacement passport can often be obtained in 20 minutes. Otherwise, you might wait up to two days.

- **Visas**—The best source to obtain up-to-date visa requirements for travel to other countries is the Web site of the **Bureau of Consular Affairs** (*http://travel.state.gov/foreignentryreqs.html*).

  After verifying the need for a visa, contact the embassy or consulate of the country or countries of your destination to verify information regarding the documents you will need and the processing time required.

- **Extra photos**—Get at least eight (8) additional 2" x 2" photos when applying for your passport or visa(s). These extra photos will come in handy if you need additional visas or an international driver's permit or if you need to replace a lost passport or other document.

- **Personal health records**—Consider carrying photocopies of your health and hospital records, recent electrocardiogram (ECG), laboratory test results, list of current medications, allergies, etc. Or, you may wish to subscribe to a service that can assemble all of your pertinent medical records, store them in a computer, and fax them anywhere in the world within minutes. Contact **Global Med-Net** (800-650-0434) for further information.

- **Travel health insurance**—See Chapters 15, 16 and 17. If you don't buy separate travel health insurance, check your existing health insurance policy to see what benefits are provided in case of illness overseas. Basic medicare usually does not pay for out-of-country illnesses or accidents. If you are over 65, you should purchase medi-gap coverage or a travel health insurance policy.

- **Doctors and hospitals abroad**—The International Association for Assistance to Travelers (**IAMAT**) publishes a booklet listing hospitals and English-speaking physicians overseas. 417 Center Street, Lewiston, NY 14092; 716-754-4883.

- **Medic Alert bracelet**—If you have a serious or chronic medical condition, a history of severe drug allergy, etc., you should consider wearing a Medic Alert bracelet. Call 1-800-ID-ALERT to order.

- **Prescription drugs abroad**—Worldwide emergency delivery of noncontrolled drugs via Federal Express or DHL. Contact: **International Pharmacy Organization**, 85 Station Road, Edgware, London, England; tel: (44) 181-381-1911; fax: (44) 181-952-2063; e-mail: *ipo@aapi.co.uk*

- **Divers Alert Network (DAN)**—For non-emergency medical questions and general information, scuba divers can call (919) 684-2948 for DAN'S Dive Safety and Medical Information Line. (Web site: *www.diversalertnetwork*). For scuba diving emergencies, DAN'S Diving Emergency Hotline is (919) 684-4DAN (4326) or (919) 684-8111. These lines are open to all divers.

- **Telephone number and e-mail address of your personal physician in the United States or Canada.**

- **Foreign language telephone assistance**—When dealing with medical problems long distance, there may be language barriers. Call **AT&T's Language Line** at 800-628-8486 for assistance. The service costs $4.15 to $7.25 per minute, depending on the language being interpreted.
- **Traveler's checks**—Make a photocopy of the numbers. Leave the photocopy at home but carry the list of numbers with you that you get with the checks. Copy the date and place of purchase. To replace lost traveler's checks, call collect to the following numbers in the United States from abroad:
  - American Express: 801-968-8300
  - VISA: 415-574-7111
  - MasterCard: 212-974-5696
  - Bank of America: 415-622-3800
  - Citibank: 813-879-7701
  - Thomas Cook: 212-974-5696
- **Credit cards**—Know your charge card credit limits. U.S. citizens have been arrested in some countries for exceeding credit limits. Keep a copy of your card numbers in case they are lost or stolen. Report the loss immediately.
- **Money**—To have emergency funds sent overseas, call the **American Express MoneyGram** (800-926-9400) or the **Western Union Money Transfer** service (800-325-6000). The State Department's **Overseas Citizens Service** (202-647-5225) can also arrange money transfers abroad. **ATM** facilities in other countries are becoming more prevalent; they offer convenience and usually the best exchange rates. **Foreign banks** usually will advance cash against your credit card. Be sure you remember your PIN number.
- **Birth certificate and photo ID**—These documents can sometimes be used in lieu of a passport for entry into certain countries. They're also useful to have if you lose your passport. If you are living overseas or getting married in a foreign country, be sure to have these documents with you.
- **Green card for resident aliens**—Don't leave home without it.
- **International Certificate of Vaccination**—A validated *International Certificate of Vaccination* (yellow card) is needed when the yellow fever immunization is required to enter a country. This document is obtained at an authorized Yellow Fever Vaccination Center, usually a travelers' clinic or a State Health Department immunization clinic. You should carry the yellow card with your passport. The yellow card has useful sections where you can list all of your other vaccinations. There is a section that your doctor can fill out if you are unable to receive a required vaccination for medical reasons.
- **HIV testing requirements for entry into foreign countries**—Go to the State Department's Bureau of Consular Affairs Web site: *http://travel.state.gov/HIVtestingreqs.html* to check country requirements. The HIV test is usually required only for those applying for a foreign work permit, prolonged residence, or immigration—not for tourist visits of less than 1–3 months. Tests done in the United States or Canada may not be accepted.

- **Doctor's letter**—You may want a doctor's letter describing and authorizing the prescription medications you will be taking on your trip, including needles/syringes if you are a diabetic. The letter should contain the generic names of the medications and the dosage.
- **International driver's permit**—This is available at any AAA office. When applying you'll need two passport-size photos, your driver's license, and $10 for the fee. Permits can also be obtained through **Passport Plus, Inc.**, 677 Fifth Ave. (5th floor), New York, NY 10022; 800-367-1818 or 212-759-5540. Passport Plus provides nationwide service. The international driver's permit is printed in 9 languages and serves as a translation for your license, which is valid in many countries. A few countries (China, Egypt, Nepal) don't allow tourists to drive.
- **Notarized parental consent**—Necessary when a minor child is traveling with the noncustodial parent. You may not be able to board the aircraft or enter a country (e.g., Mexico) without this document.

VACCINATIONS

See Chapter 2 for travel vaccination guidelines.

TRAVELERS WITH SPECIAL NEEDS

Heart Disease

Travelers with diagnosed heart disease—If you have a history of heart disease, and especially if you have had coronary artery bypass surgery or angioplasty, you may be wondering "Should I travel?" If your medical condition is stable, travel should not represent any significant additional risk unless (1) you will be going to a remote location where the medical care that you might ordinarily receive in an emergency is not available and/or (2) you will be subjecting yourself to unusual physical stress (e.g., trekking at high altitudes). Under these circumstances you should have a pretravel medical consultation and possibly undergo testing to assess your exercise capacity. If you do travel, you should have with you:

- An adequate supply of your current medications
- A copy of your most recent ECG
- A list of your medications and drug allergies (if any)
- The telephone numbers of your personal physician and nearest relative

Travel after heart attack—If you have had a heart attack, a convalescence of 2–6 weeks is usually recommended prior to travel, but your case should be considered individually.

Travel after angioplasty—Following coronary artery angioplasty, travel is generally not restricted if the procedure has been successful.

Travel after coronary artery bypass grafting (CABG) surgery—Routine screening by exercise testing is generally not recommended for people who are symptom free after CABG surgery. Recently, however, exercise-thallium-201 SPECT testing has been shown to be a strong independent predictor of subsequent death or nonfatal heart attack when there are thallium-perfusion defects and impaired exercise capacity. An abnormal thallium-201 SPECT test might weigh against your going to a medically underserved area.

Pacemakers—A pacemaker or an implanted defibrillator is not a contraindication to air travel, and these devices are not affected by walk-through airport security magnetometers. However, the handheld security magnetometers should never be used on someone with an implanted defibrillator. Electronic telephone checks of pacemaker function cannot be transmitted by international satellite.

Chronic Lung Disease and Air Travel

If you have chronic obstructive pulmonary disease (COPD), air travel is considered safe if you can walk a block or climb a flight of stairs without becoming breathless. In-flight oxygen may be indicated if your sea level arterial oxygen level (PaO_2) is 72 mm Hg or less because this would correspond to an in-flight PaO_2 of 55 mm Hg when the cabin is pressurized to 8,000 feet.

If your doctor advises in-flight oxygen, contact the airline medical department at least 48–72 hours prior to departure. There is a $50–$75 charge for oxygen for each flight/plane change. The airline will request a physician's letter stating your medical condition and a prescription for the oxygen. Be sure to carry copies of these documents with you. Unlike foreign airlines, U.S. carriers must legally supply all in-flight oxygen. You will not be allowed to use your personal oxygen supply enroute, and if you have a portable unit, it must be empty when checked in. Unfortunately, on-board oxygen delivery systems (mask or nasal cannulae) are not standardized, and you may need to use a system other than your own. In addition, the airline won't provide oxygen for ground use. You'll need to make arrangements yourself if you need ground oxygen between flights.

If you have hypoxemic, hypercapnic COPD, acetazolamide, 250 mg twice daily, will stimulate breathing and improve your blood gas values. This drug may be useful prior to and during air flight or going to higher elevations.

Peptic Ulcer Disease

The antiulcer drugs Zantac and Tagamet, which are H2 receptor antagonists, probably do not increase your risk of enteric infection. The stronger proton pump inhibitors Prilosec and Prevacid, however, more effectively reduce stomach acid and probably do increase your risk of travelers' diarrhea. If getting diarrhea is a major concern, you may wish to discuss with your physician switching to Carafate (sucralfate). This stomach-coating antiulcer drug does not decrease the stomach's acid secretion and, in fact, may even reduce your chance of getting travelers' diarrhea due to its intrinsic antibacterial activity. Carafate, however, does not afford as much antiulcer protection as the other drugs mentioned.

Diabetes (Chapter 12)

- If you take pills to control blood sugar, no time zone adjustment of dosage is necessary when flying. Take your medication according to the local time.
- If you are a diabetic using insulin, take enough insulin and U-100 syringes to last the entire trip. (Many countries still use U-80 syringes.)
- If traveling by airliner, call 72 hours before departure to order a diabetic menu.
- Hand carry your insulin at airport security checkpoints.
- Keep your insulin in your carry-on baggage to protect it from temperature extremes. Consider carrying all your diabetic supplies in a specially designed case, such as the DIA-PAK®. Insulin will keep its full potency for several months even if it's not refrigerated, but its temperature should be kept below 86°F. The DIA-PAK has optional refreezable cold Gel Packs for keeping insulin cool in hot climates. The DIA-PAK is available from **Mercury Marketing**, P.O. Box 8223—RW, Stamford, CT 06905; 203-327-5832.
- Test blood glucose at six-hour intervals or before each meal during the flight.
- Carry sugar cubes or a snack in case an insulin reaction (hypoglycemia) occurs.

Figure 1.1

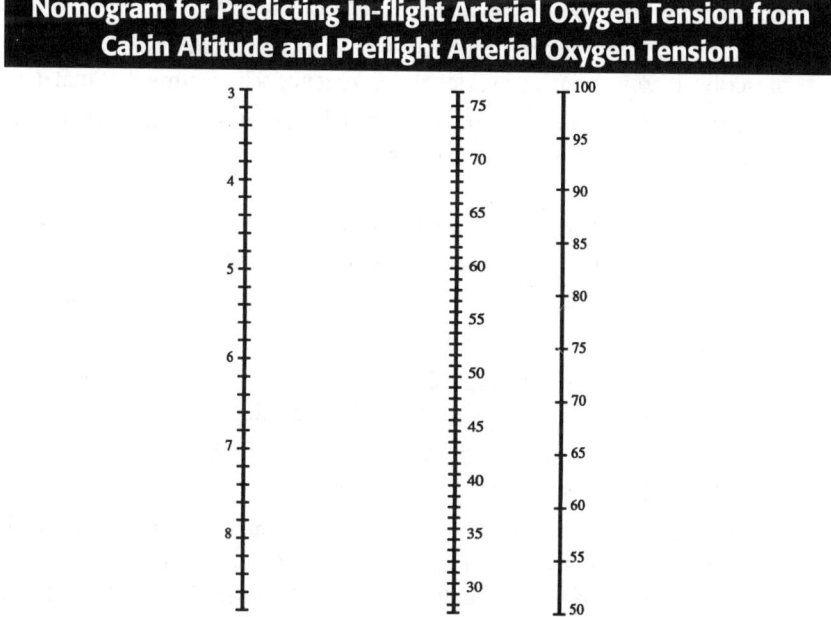

Nomogram for Predicting In-flight Arterial Oxygen Tension from Cabin Altitude and Preflight Arterial Oxygen Tension

To predict the in-flight arterial oxygen tension, draw a line between the estimated cabin altitude and the traveler's preflight PaO_2. If the line crosses the middle bar at less than 55 mm Hg, in-flight oxygen should be considered.

THE PRETRAVEL MEDICAL CHECKLIST

The following checklist will help you avoid travel-related medical problems. Travelers who are pregnant, or who plan to be pregnant while they are abroad, should consult Chapter 19.

The Pretravel Medical Consultation

Before departure, your doctor should do the following, where appropriate:

- ❑ Review your medical history and current medications, and alter current therapy for travel when necessary.
- ❑ Review your travel itinerary in order to advise you regarding the prevention of medical problems.
- ❑ Administer immunizations, as indicated, and complete the International Certificate of Vaccination for yellow fever (if administered) and for cholera (if necessary) to avoid possible border crossing problems.
- ❑ Review measures to prevent travelers' diarrhea, hepatitis, motion sickness, and acute mountain sickness.
- ❑ Review methods to prevent insect bites, emphasizing the use of DEET repellents, permethrin, bednets, and insecticide room sprays.
- ❑ Prescribe drugs for malaria prophylaxis, review the symptoms of malaria, and prescribe, if appropriate, drugs for the emergency self-treatment of malaria.
- ❑ Prescribe medication to treat travelers' diarrhea, motion sickness, mountain sickness, jet lag, and other possible problems. Treat ear or sinus problems prior to air flight.
- ❑ Perform a physical examination, if there are underlying health concerns for which an examination would be appropriate. Perform appropriate testing.
- ❑ Advise you about health issues if you are pregnant or traveling with children.
- ❑ Help with referral to overseas physicians.
- ❑ Screen for exposure to tuberculosis by administering a PPD skin test if you are traveling for a prolonged period to a risk area. Repeat PPD on return.
- ❑ Suggest where you can arrange transport if you are disabled or chronically ill. The following companies can assist:
  - ➤ **MedEscort International** provides medically trained health professionals to accompany disabled travelers worldwide. Contact: ABE International Airport, P.O. Box 8766, Allentown, PA 18105; 800-255-7182. Worldwide call collect at 215-791-3111.
  - ➤ **Traveling Nurses' Network** provides registered nurses for worldwide escort. Contact Helen Hecker, RN, P.O. Box 129, Vancouver, WA 98666; 360-694-2462.

Teeth, Eyes, and Feet

- Schedule a dental checkup—Allow enough time for corrective work. Avoid dental work and injections in countries where HIV and hepatitis B infections are threats. Consider carrying an emergency dental kit to treat broken or lost fillings—a Dentemp Kit, for example (photo right).
- Check your feet—Proper foot care is essential, especially for hikers and diabetics. Carefully trim nails, corns, and calluses. Use foot powder to keep feet dry and fungus free. Be sure shoes and hiking boots are broken in and fit properly. Thin liner socks should be worn by hikers. Don't let a painful, infected blister or another preventable foot problem ruin your trip or jeopardize your health.
- Schedule an eye examination. Carry an extra set of eyeglasses. Contact-lens wearers should also carry a pair of eyeglasses. Keep a copy of your eyeglass prescription with you. Also, if you wear contact lenses, carry antibacterial eye drops (Ciloxan®, containing ciprofloxacin, is recommended). Contact-lens wearers, especially those who wear their lenses overnight, are at increased risk for developing bacterial keratitis (infected corneal ulcers, usually caused by pseudomonas or serratia bacteria). This infection may cause permanent corneal scarring or perforation if not treated promptly. NOTE: Even daily-wear soft contact lenses are three times more likely to cause bacterial keratitis as are the daily-wear rigid gas-permeable lenses.

The HIV-Positive Adult Traveler

Pretravel evaluation—Pretravel medical screening should include (just as with all travelers) a brief medical history, immunization history, allergy history, and a history of any problems during previous travel. Those whose CD4+ cell counts are normal or >500/µL are usually at no greater risk than noninfected travelers for travel-related problems, but those whose CD4+ cell counts are <200 cells/µL, or who are symptomatic, are at a greater risk of acquiring some infections.

Travelers' diarrhea—In HIV-positive travelers, this disorder can occur more frequently, be more severe, and be more difficult to treat. Infections with salmonella, shigella, and campylobacter are more protracted and more often associated with bacteremia. The usual 1- to 3-day course of antibiotic treatment for travelers' diarrhea may need to be extended to 7 days.

Cryptosporidium, a common cause of diarrhea in the tropics, produces severe chronic diarrhea, malabsorption, and, occasionally, inflammation of the gallbladder (cholecystitis). Cyclospora parasites cause similar symptoms. *Isospora belli* infections are also common and cause malabsorption and weight loss. There is no apparent increased risk for gastrointestinal infections caused by viruses, *E. histolytica*, *Giardia lamblia*, or enterotoxigenic *E. coli* (the most common cause of travelers' diarrhea).

Other infections—Respiratory illnesses, such as bacterial pneumonia and fungal infections (e.g., histoplasmosis and coccidiomycosis), cause greater mortality in HIV-positive patients. Tuberculosis is a serious risk for those living or working with lower socioeconomic populations in the developing world. Short-term business travelers and tourists are at low risk for this infection. Visceral leishmaniasis is difficult to diagnose and treat, and the mortality is high. Even short-term travelers to Spain, southern Europe, and other risk areas have acquired this illness. Increased severity of malaria has not been demonstrated conclusively in HIV-infected patients, but this infection must be prevented by chemoprophylaxis and personal protection measures.

Preventive measures—Food and drink precautions should be carefully followed. This includes avoidance of undercooked meat, fish, shellfish, eggs, raw and unpeeled fruits, raw vegetables and salads, tap water, and unpasteurized dairy products. Consideration should be given to giving prophylactic antibiotics to short-term travelers with low CD4+ cell counts to prevent travelers' diarrhea. A standby self-treatment course of a quinolone antibiotic should be carried by all other travelers, including those travelers taking prophylactic sulfa drugs to prevent pneumocystis pneumonia. Taking precautions against insect bites is important to prevent diseases such as malaria, dengue, and leishmaniasis.

Sexually transmitted diseases—HIV-infected travelers should be counseled against engaging in sexual behavior that might infect others or that will increase their own risk of acquiring infections such as syphilis, herpes simplex, or an enteric pathogen. Hepatitis B is likely to be more severe as is the chance of becoming a chronic carrier of the virus.

Immunization (vaccination)—All HIV-positive travelers should be appropriately immunized, but the antibody response to immunization may be impaired, especially when the CD4+ cell counts are <200 cells/µL. Because the antibody response to vaccines is higher in individuals with early HIV disease and higher CD4+ counts, it is best to immunize such individuals at the earliest opportunity. This applies to any HIV-positive person who contemplates possible future travel, as well as any person who has imminent travel plans.

POST-TRAVEL ILLNESS

Evaluation of Illness Acquired Abroad

This is a very important topic. If you have traveled abroad, especially to rural tropical areas, you may be at risk for developing a serious illness—or for harboring a bacterial or parasitic organism in your intestine that could later cause medical problems and possibly infect others who have close contact with you. If you have any of the following post-travel symptoms, you should consult a physician.

Important Post-Travel Symptoms

The most common symptoms of a tropical or infectious disease are the following:
- Fever
- Abdominal pain
- Diarrhea
- Weight loss
- Fatigue
- Cough
- Skin rash

It is beyond the scope of this book to consider every diagnostic possibility, but fever, which is the most important post-travel symptom, should always be carefully and promptly evaluated.

Your doctor must determine if your fever is caused by a travel-related illness or is due to an illness that you might have acquired after coming home. However, in about 25% of travelers, no cause of the fever can be found, and it is assumed in these instances that the fever is due to a self-limited viral infection.

POST-TRAVEL FEVER

Evaluation of Fever

Time may be critical. Some diseases, such as malaria, may be fatal if not promptly treated—therefore, don't delay seeing a doctor if you develop a post-travel fever.

Second, you and/or your physician must have some suspicion that your illness might be travel related. If you don't tell your doctor you were abroad, or if he/she doesn't ask, the proper tests might not be done, and you may not be given appropriate treatment.

Important Causes of a Travel-Related Fever

Malaria is the most important cause of fever in the returned traveler. Once malaria has been excluded, the following infections should be considered:

- Bacterial enteritis/enterocolitis due to (a) shigella, (b) salmonella, and (c) campylobacter
- Dengue fever • Viral hepatitis • Typhoid fever
- Rickettsial infections (tick or scrub typhus, Q fever)

Approach to Diagnosis

How long after you returned (or how long after your possible exposure to disease) did you develop the fever? This question has diagnostic implications because diseases vary in how quickly they cause symptoms. Although there is often considerable overlap, some diseases become symptomatic only a few days after exposure, whereas others take weeks to months before symptoms occur. Table 1.1 below lists many travel-related diseases with fever and their incubation periods.

Consult the **World Medical Guide** section of this book to see which diseases are common to your itinerary. Combining the knowledge of which diseases are found on your itinerary with the incubation period data in Table 1.1 will narrow the diagnostic possibilities.

Certain diseases can immediately be eliminated if they don't exist in any of the countries you visited—for example, African trypanosomiasis (sleeping sickness) or hemorrhagic fever resulting from Lassa, Ebola, or Marburg viruses would not be diagnostic considerations unless you had traveled in Africa.

THE POSTTRAVEL MEDICAL CHECKLIST

Although you might have traveled in countries where certain diseases exist, this doesn't necessarily mean you had any exposure; therefore, a detailed history of your actual activities is essential to assess your risks. Your immunization status is also important. The important questions are the following:

- ❏ Your itinerary: What countries did you visit and for how long? Were you in a disease-endemic area in that country?
- ❏ What were your arrival and departure dates?
- ❏ Which vaccinations did you receive prior to departure? For example, if you were given the hepatitis A or yellow fever vaccines, these diseases can virtually be eliminated as diagnostic possibilities. The typhoid fever vaccine, however, is not 100 percent effective so vaccination will not entirely eliminate the risk of this disease.
- ❏ Did you travel in rural areas of tropical/semitropical countries?
- ❏ Did you take measures to prevent insect/mosquito bites?
- ❏ Did you adhere to your malaria prophylaxis schedule (if prescribed) and was the drug appropriate?
- ❏ Did you adhere to safe food and drink guidelines?
- ❏ Did you have contact with sick people while abroad?
- ❏ Did you develop any illness while abroad? Were you treated by a doctor? What medications were you given? Any injections or blood transfusions?
- ❏ When was the onset of post-travel symptoms—days, weeks, months, after return?
- ❏ What was your exposure to the following?
  – Unsafe food and drink—Did you eat undercooked or raw meat or fish (e.g., sushi); cold food from salad bars; street vendor food not piping hot?
  – Insect and animals bites—Were you bitten by mosquitoes, flies, or ticks? Were you bitten by a dog or other animal?
  – Walking barefoot on beaches or moist soil
  – Freshwater swimming, wading, or bathing
  – Unprotected sex with a new partner
  – Recreational drugs (especially by injection), tatooing, or body piercing

It is only after a detailed history has been taken that a physical examination should be performed and selected laboratory tests obtained.

Table 1.1

Incubation Periods for Selected Infections with Fever

(Source: Wiselka MJ, et al. *Travel Medicine International*, October 1992.)

	Acute (0–14 days)	**Subacute** (2 weeks–6 months)	**Chronic** (Over 6 months)
Protozoal	Malaria Trypanosomiasis	Malaria Amebic colitis/abscess Leishmaniasis Trypanosomiasis	Malaria Amebic abscess Leishmaniasis
Bacterial	Typhoid fever Leptospirosis Meningitis Legionellosis Bacterial enteritis	Brucellosis Tuberculosis	Brucellosis Tuberculosis
Rickettsial	Boutonneuse fever* Rocky Mt. spotted fever Typhus		
Viral	Dengue Other arboviruses Viral hemorrhagic fever	Hepatitis A, B, E HIV seroconversion CMV, E-B virus	HIV
Helminths (Worms)	Schistosomiasis	Schistosomiasis Filariasis	Filariasis

*Also known as Mediterranean spotted fever and African tick typhus. Other tick-borne rickettsial diseases include North Asian tick-borne rickettsiosis and Queensland tick typhus.

——— Important Alert ———

Malaria is the most important illness to consider if you develop a fever after having been in a malaria endemic area, especially one in sub-Saharan Africa. If you develop a fever after returning home, be sure to tell your doctor that you have traveled abroad and that a tropical illness, especially malaria, must be considered. If malaria is a consideration, request thick and thin blood films and have them repeated 2–3 times if the initial one(s) are negative. You should have the results back within 24 hours.

Table 1.2

Physical Findings in Selected Tropical Infections with Fever

Physical finding	Disease
Rash	Dengue fever, typhoid, typhus, syphilis, HIV, cutaneous leishmaniasis, brucellosis, Lyme disease
Jaundice	Malaria, hepatitis, yellow fever, leptospirosis, relapsing fever
Lymphadenopathy	Dengue fever, brucellosis, visceral leishmaniasis, HIV, rickettsial infections, mononucleosis, CMV, EBV
Hepatomegaly	Malaria, typhoid, hepatitis, leptospirosis, amebiasis
Splenomegaly	Malaria, brucellosis, typhoid, relapsing fever, visceral leishmaniasis, typhus, dengue fever, trypanosomiasis
Eschar	Rickettsial diseases, e.g., tick typhus or scrub typhus, cutaneous anthrax

Table 1.3

Laboratory Tests

The basic laboratory tests that should be done to evaluate fever include the following:

- Complete blood count to screen for anemia, eosinophilia, elevated white blood cell count and/or low platelets
- Thick and thin blood films to screen for malaria (3 times, 12–24 hours apart)
- OptiMAL malaria assay, if available
- Stool culture to test for bacteria
- Liver function tests, including hepatitis serology
- Blood culture x 2
- Serology (for dengue, brucella, typhus, etc.)
- Chest X-ray
- Urinalysis and urine culture

Mileno MD, Bia FJ. The Compromized Traveler. Inf. Dis. Clin. N. Am 1998; 12:369–412.

Suh KN, Kozarsky PE, Keystone JS. Evaluation of fever in the returned traveler. Med. Clin. N. Am. 1999; 83: 997–1017.

Van Gompel A, Kozarsky P, Colebunders R. Adult travelers with HIV infections. J Trav Med 1997;4:136–141.

2
VACCINES FOR TRAVEL

Being up-to-date on your "shots," or completing a vaccination (immunization) schedule before departure, is one of the most important steps you can take to prevent a travel-related disease. Immunizing travelers, however, has become increasingly complex as new vaccines are being brought to market, while others (e.g., cholera) are being phased out; and as some vaccine-preventable diseases are brought under control (such as polio), others (e.g., diphtheria) have flared up.

Travelers often complicate the situation by not allowing enough time to be immunized according to established vaccination schedules. Although some vaccines can be administered on an accelerated schedule, some travelers could be forced to delay their trip or forego essential protection. Ideally, travelers should begin immunizations up to eight weeks before departure in case multiple doses of one or more vaccines are necessary.

Planning Vaccinations

In the real world, practical—and affordable—vaccination recommendations must reflect a host of factors:

- The traveler's age, medical history, vaccination history, travel history, country of birth, and country where he or she was raised.
- Duration of travel, lifestyle activities during travel, occupation during travel (e.g., health-care or relief worker).
- The traveler's present health status. Individuals who have immunodeficiency diseases (such as AIDS) or who are taking immunosuppressive medications require an individualized approach to vaccinations. Such individuals may be more susceptible to vaccine-preventable diseases, are at increased risk of uncontrolled virus replication due to their inability to produce antibodies, or may have a less than optimal immune response to vaccines.
- Current disease patterns in the *specific localities* of the country to be visited.
- Types of accommodations and restaurants to be frequented.
- Planned association with local people.
- The traveler's budget for vaccines. Unfortunately, for "budget" travelers, the cost of vaccines can approach the budget for the entire trip. However, some vaccines recommended for travelers may be reimbursed by insurance coverage, but that is the exception, not the rule.

Vaccinating pregnant women requires expertise regarding the effect of the vaccine, if any, on the fetus, and the magnitude of the risk of exposure to the disease. In rare cases, such as yellow fever, the risk of exposure may outweigh the remote risk to the fetus.

To complicate matters further, vaccine recommendations continue to change, and will likely continue to do so at an ever more rapid rate. Salient points to consider include the following:

- Some travelers are susceptible to diseases (e.g., measles, diphtheria) that they assume that they are protected against.
- Some vaccines have been made more effective and with fewer side effects (such as typhoid)—or can be given over a shorter period of time (e.g., hepatitis B), making them useful in more travel scenarios.
- New vaccines give providers more options—and sometimes, more headaches.
- One-hundred percent protection against all vaccine-preventable diseases is not practical or possible.

Vaccines for routine use, and specialized vaccines for international travel, are described below. Table 2.2 contains specific information on dosing schedules, indications, booster doses, and precautions. Table 2.3 is a schedule of recommended childhood immunizations in the United States. HIV immunization guidelines are found in Table 2.4. Immunization during pregnancy is discussed in Chapter 19.

VACCINE & DISEASE SUMMARY

Chickenpox (Varicella)

Chickenpox vaccine is a routine immunization for all children in the United States. All children should receive one dose of chickenpox vaccine between 12 and 18 months of age, or at any age after that, if they have never had chickenpox. Adults and adolescents 13 years of age or older should receive two doses of the vaccine, 4–8 weeks apart. Chickenpox vaccine, which is a live virus vaccine, should not be given during pregnancy, and female patients should not become pregnant for at least 1 month after immunization.

International travelers of any age who have neither had the disease nor the vaccination should receive this vaccine prior to departure. This applies especially to female travelers of childbearing age who may become pregnant. Varicella can cause as serious damage to the fetus as rubella, albeit, apparently less often.

Chickenpox is a viral infection that is highly contagious and usually quite mild, but it can be serious, especially in young infants and adults. Any person who has ever had chickenpox in the past has lifelong immunity and does not need this vaccine. Once otherwise healthy people contract chickenpox, the disease rarely ever occurs a second time.

See Table 2.2 for a summary of the varicella vaccine schedule, indications, precautions and booster recommendations.

Cholera

The manufacture and availability of the injectable cholera vaccine in the United States ceased in June 2000. This vaccine had numerous shortcomings: frequent and unpleasant side effects (particularly high fever); variable immunity for only about six months—with most of that protection in the first few months; and incomplete protection against all strains of cholera. Moreover, since cholera so rarely affects healthy travelers, and is easily treated, a vaccine for international travelers, especially one that was not very effective, made little sense. When it was available in the United States, the CDC recommended it only for travelers at high risk who worked and lived in high-risk areas under less than adequate sanitary conditions.

Cholera vaccine is no longer listed in a separate section in the *International Certificate of Vaccination* and is not "officially" required for entry into, or exit from, any country. Despite this, some countries (e.g., Tanzania, Kenya, Egypt, and Saudia Arabia during the Hajj or Umra) are known to require, on occasion, proof of cholera vaccination from travelers coming from cholera-infected countries. Anticipating such a situation, travelers may need a medical exemption letter, containing the Official Stamp, from their health-care provider. It may be advisable to contact the embassy or consulate at a destination country to confirm the requirement for cholera vaccination and the acceptability of a medical exemption letter. In some cases, a traveler and health-care provider may consider stamping the *International Certificate of Vaccination* with the Uniform Stamp, even though the vaccine was not administered. In Canada, where an oral cholera vaccine is available, travelers still have the option of being immunized as a way of satisfying an unlikely request for proof of vaccination.

Oral cholera vaccine—Two oral cholera vaccines are available in some countries outside the United States. Both vaccines appear to provide somewhat better immunity and fewer side effects than the previously available injectable vaccine. The oral vaccines require only a single dose for protection.

- Mutachol is a live vaccine that is available in Canada and Europe. This vaccine—compared to the injectable vaccine—is more efficacious (100% protection against severe diarrhea for six months and 86% against any diarrhea due to classical strains of *V. cholerae*) and has fewer side effects. However, in 1998, the U.S. Food and Drug Administration (FDA) decided not to approve it for the U.S. market.
- Dukoral is based on an inactivated, whole cell/recombinant B-subunit of cholera toxin and is made in Sweden and available in some European countries. It appears to provide about 50%–60% protection for at least three years and also appears to provide some protection against enterotoxigenic *E. coli*, the most common bacterial cause of travelers' diarrhea.

Cholera vaccine is generally not recommended for any international traveler; however, it may be beneficial for some small subgroups of travelers:

- Travelers with increased susceptibility to the disease due to decreased stomach acidity—the result of medication, disease, or previous surgery.
- Relief workers in refugee camps, who live and work under less than adequate sanitary conditions in a high-risk environment.
- Individuals with blood group O. People with this blood group have a higher incidence and more severe disease than people with other blood groups.

Diphtheria

The DTaP vaccine (which protects not only against diphtheria, but also tetanus and pertussis) is a routine childhood immunization in the United States. This is a 5-dose series starting at 2 months of age and finishing at 4–6 years of age. It is frequently given in combination with the *Haemophilus influenzae* (Hib) vaccine. It is never administered after the seventh birthday. Following completion of the DTaP series (by age 7), the Td vaccine (tetanus-diphtheria) is given at 11–12 years of age if at least 5 years have elapsed since the last dose of DTaP. Booster doses of Td vaccine are recommended every 10 years thereafter to maintain immunity against diphtheria (and tetanus).

Diphtheria still exists in many developing countries, especially the former Soviet Union, Albania, Haiti, Dominican Republic, Ecuador, Brazil, Philippines, Indonesia, and many countries in Africa and Asia—the result of failure to vaccinate all children, use of low-quality vaccines, and failure to give booster doses to older children and adults. The disease spreads from infected individuals via airborne respiratory excretions—in exhaled air, coughs, and sneezes—to susceptible persons in close proximity.

Diphtheria is characterized by a very sore throat, difficulty breathing, paralysis, and heart failure. It is very rare in the United States and Canada because of the high immunization rates in children and young adults. However, more than one-half of U.S. adults over the age of 60, and many adults under that age, have no measurable antibodies against diphtheria and are at potential risk when traveling to lesser-developed countries.

Ideally, travelers to areas where the disease still exists should have adequate immunity. Yet present recommendations for establishing or maintaining diphtheria immunity in adults—a booster dose every 10 years regardless of the time interval since the last dose—may not even restore protective levels of antibodies, let alone demonstrable ones. Also, 10-year scheduling assumes that the primary (pediatric) series—usually given early in childhood—was given, and was given correctly, which is not always the case. Many persons born before 1940 did not receive the primary series.

The primary (pediatric) series of diphtheria vaccinations (see above) contains 6 to 25 Lime flocculation (Lf) units of diphtheria toxoid per dose of vaccine. This is the amount necessary to establish immunity. Virtually all children in the developed world are well-protected.

Protection gradually wanes over the years. The adult diphtheria formulation (combined with tetanus toxoid as the Td vaccine) contains a much smaller amount of diphtheria toxoid, only 2 Lf units of toxoid per dose—the larger pediatric dosage being contraindicated for adults because of possible adverse side effects in those adults with high titers of diphtheria antibodies. Adult booster doses (Td) are recommended every 10 years. In fact, few adults receive booster doses as recommended. Furthermore, the recommended adult formulation may be insufficient to establish immunity in those individuals who were not correctly "primed" in childhood and in those who have not had a booster dose in several decades. Moreover, the present recommended three doses over a 6-month period for adults who may not be immune may not be sufficient to establish immunity. Recommendations for diphtheria vaccination are presently under review.

See Table 2.4 for diphtheria schedule recommendations.

Haemophilus influenzae Type b (Hib)

Hib vaccine is a routine childhood immunization in the United States. This is a four-dose series (it may be a three-dose series depending on the brand of Hib vaccine used) starting at 2 months of age and finishing at 12–15 months of age. Many pediatricians give this vaccine in combination with DTaP vaccine. Because infection with *Haemophilus influenzae* is rare after five years of age, older children and adults do not routinely need this vaccine. *Haemophilus influenzae* type b disease is common in many countries of the world. Every child should be vaccinated against this disease prior to international travel.

Hib bacteria can cause serious, contagious infections. Before the availability of the Hib vaccine in 1987, *Haemophilus influenzae* was the leading cause of bacterial meningitis among children under five years of age in the United States. In addition to meningitis, *Haemophilus influenzae* type b bacteria can cause a variety of serious illnesses such as pneumonia and epiglottitis.

NOTE: *Haemophilus influenza* type b disease and influenza ("the flu") are different illnesses. The similarity of their names acknowledges their historical association. The *haemophilus influenzae* bacterium was isolated in 1889 from the sputum of a patient dying of influenza, which in 1933 was discovered to be a viral disease.

See Table 2.4 for Hib vaccine schedule recommendations.

Hepatitis A

Hepatitis A vaccine is recommended for all nonimmune international travelers over 2 years of age going to lesser-developed countries. It is also a routine immunization for some children (in selected states) in the United States who are 2–18 years of age. Studies are underway to evaluate the use of hepatitis A vaccine for children younger than 2 years of age; in Canada, Havrix is licensed for children above 1 year of age.

Hepatitis A is the most frequent vaccine-preventable disease of travelers, and there are two vaccines available in the United States: VAQTA (Merck) and Havrix (GlaxoSmithKline). In Canada AVAXIM (Aventis), EPAXAL (Berna), and Havrix are also available. They all give rise to measurable antibody levels within two weeks after a single injection. A second dose, recommended 6–12 months later, dramatically boosts antibody levels and provides virtually 100% immunity, probably for life. If a person's hepatitis A immune status is unknown, he or she can be vaccinated or their blood can be tested for antibodies. People who have had the disease do not need vaccination, but vaccinating people already immune causes no harm.

When a traveler is departing immediately for a hepatitis A endemic area, it has been recommended that the traveler receive either immune globulin (see below) or a combination of hepatitis A vaccine and immune globulin. Most travel physicians, however, now believe that giving immune globulin is unnecessary because the hepatitis A vaccine becomes effective in about two weeks—which is soon enough to give protection.

See Table 2.2 for hepatitis A vaccine schedule, indications, precautions, and booster recommendations.

Hepatitis B

Hepatitis B vaccine is a routine immunization for all children and adolescents in the United States who are 18 years of age and younger. The vaccines currently available in the United States are produced by recombinant DNA technology using baker's yeast that has been genetically modified to synthesize hepatitis B surface antigen. The original vaccine prepared from the plasma of hepatitis B surface antigen carriers is no longer available in the United States, but plasma-derived vaccines are still used in other countries.

The duration of protection, no matter what schedule is used, is many years, and there is no specific booster recommendation at this time. The length of immunity has not been determined, but individuals vaccinated 15 years ago still have adequate protective antibodies. Protection may be lifelong.

International travelers who have increased risk of exposure to hepatitis B include the following:

- Frequent travelers to areas with a high incidence of hepatitis B such as sub-Saharan Africa, the Balkans, the Middle East, China, Southeast Asia, Haiti, the Dominican Republic, and the interior Amazon Basin
- Travelers who plan to reside for six months or more in endemic areas
- Travelers likely to engage in sexual or recreational drug sharing activities
- Travelers, especially children, exposed to open skin lesions from the local population
- Travelers with underlying health problems who may require health care abroad (and the need for injections).
- Health-care workers
- Recipients of blood transfusions, medical procedures, or dental procedures.

Immune Globulin (IG)

Immune globulin (also known as IG, immune serum globulin, ISG, or gamma globulin) is not a vaccine. Although IG contains pooled human blood products, it has never been shown to transmit infectious disease, such as HIV. It is effective for the prevention of hepatitis A for international travelers (for 3–5 months, depending on the amount given), and it is also effective if used for the prevention of measles or hepatitis A immediately after a known exposure. Since the introduction of hepatitis A vaccine in 1995, the use of IG has markedly decreased.

Travelers younger than 2 years of age who need protection against hepatitis A should receive a single dose of IG. NOTE: Most children under 2 years will remain asymptomatic when they become infected with hepatitis A; the main threat is that they can transmit the infection to others.

IG can interfere with replication of live viruses in vaccines. Experience has shown that this occurs only with measles, mumps, and rubella vaccine (MMR) and with the varicella vaccine. Therefore, these vaccines should not be administered in the period from two weeks before IG is administered until several months after the IG. If IG must be given soon after MMR or varicella, these vaccines must be repeated at a later date.

See Table 2.2 for immune globulin schedule, indications, precautions, and booster recommendations.

Influenza

Influenza is a contagious viral disease that occurs worldwide, and travel increases exposure. Because the influenza viruses change continually and vary geographically, vaccines need to be reconstituted each year to reflect this change, and there is now a vaccine for the Northern Hemisphere and one for the Southern Hemisphere (below).

Effective October 2000, influenza vaccine has become a routine immunization in the United States for adults 50 years of age and older. The optimum time to receive this vaccine is annually from October 1 until mid-November. Other persons who are candidates for the flu vaccine include the following:

- Travelers of any age going to countries where influenza activity is reported
- Pregnant women in their second and third trimester
- Health-care workers
- Persons at high risk of severe consequences of contracting influenza
- Presence of a chronic health condition including: asplenia, asthma, chronic pulmonary disease, diabetes, heart disease, HIV infection, immunosuppression, metabolic disease, kidney disease
- Persons on long-term aspirin therapy
- Travelers aboard cruise ships along the western coast of the U.S. and Canada during summer months.

Southern Hemisphere vaccine—Travelers to the Southern Hemisphere between April and September, or those traveling to the tropics any time, should consider influenza vaccination. A vaccine formulated for the Southern Hemisphere is a slightly different formulation, but it is only available in the Southern Hemisphere (it is not licensed in the United States). Travelers to the Southern Hemisphere between May and October should consider obtaining this vaccine at their destination site.

See Table 2.2 for influenza vaccine schedule, indications, precautions, and booster recommendations.

Japanese Encephalitis (JE)

Three doses of JE vaccine, administered over a 30-day period (0, 7, 30), are recommended for travelers who will be at risk (see chapter 8). A two-dose schedule (0, 14 days) can be used when the 30-day schedule is impractical. Two doses will give you about 80% protection. If you find that neither schedule is possible, two doses of vaccine, administered one week apart, will offer some protection. It is advisable to receive your last injection of vaccine a minimum of 10 days prior to departure to (1) allow time for immunity to develop and (2) see if any side effects occur.

There is a 20% chance that you'll have localized arm tenderness, redness, or swelling. Less common symptoms include headache, itching (pruritus), fever, myalgia (muscle aches), nausea, abdominal pain, urticaria (hives), vasodilatation (flushing), and dizziness. The most severe side effects include widespread urticaria, angioedema (edema of the face or other body parts), and hypotension. These more severe symptoms are quite rare (less than 6 cases /100,000 doses of vaccine) and usually occur within a few days following immunization, but can be delayed 7–10 days. Because of the chance of delayed side effects, you should not embark upon international travel within 10 days of your last dose of JE vaccine.

The adverse effects of immunization need to be weighed against the risk of infection, which can be fatal in 10%–25% of symptomatic people.

See Table 2.2 for Japanese encephalitis vaccine schedule, indications, precautions, and contraindications.

Lyme Disease

Lyme disease vaccine was licensed in the United States in 1998. It should be considered for persons from 15–70 years of age who have frequent or prolonged exposure to outdoor, wooded areas infested with deer ticks. The highest risk of Lyme disease in the United States occurs in just eight states: Connecticut, Delaware, Maryland, New Jersey, New York, Pennsylvania, Rhode Island, and Wisconsin.

Because it is not protective for strains of Lyme disease found outside the United States, it is not an appropriate vaccine for international travelers.

Lyme disease vaccine is a three-dose series: one dose initially, followed by a second dose 1 month later, and a third dose 12 months after the initial dose. An accelerated, equally effective schedule can also be used: three doses of vaccine at 0,

Table 2.1 - Antiviral Agents for Influenza

Generic Name	Trade Name	Indications	Dosage	Comments
M2 Inhibitors—Influenza A				
Amantadine	Symmetrel	Treatment > age 1 Prophylaxis > age 1	100 mg bid x 7 days 100 mg qd	CNS side effects > age 65—dose decreased to 100 mg qd If CrCl>80 mL/min—decrease dose
Rimantidine	Flumadine	Treatment > age 14 Prophylaxis > age 1	100 mg bid x 7 100 mg qd	If CrCl>80 mL/min—decrease dose
Neuraminidase Inhibitors—Influenza A and B				
Zanamivir	Relenza	Treatment > age 7	2 blisters bid x 5 days	Diskhaler inhalation device Pending indication: Prophylaxis > age 7 Caution with history of bronchospasm
Oseltamivir	Tamiflu	Treatment > age 18 Prophylaxis	75 mg bid x 5 10 mg daily x 10	Pending indications: treatment > age 1 prophylaxis > age 1 Mid GI side effects

NOTE: The CDC states that antiviral drugs are not substitutes for vaccination, but, nevertheless, may be useful. Recent studies show that a once-daily standard dose of Relenza may also be effective for prophylaxis.

Source: *Emergency Medicine Reports* Oct. 23, 2000

1, and 2 months. At this time there is no recommendation for additional, or booster doses, after the initial three-dose series. The vaccine is considered about 75% to 80% effective against clinical disease.

See Table 2.2 for Lyme disease vaccine schedule, indications, precautions, and booster recommendations.

Measles

WHO expects measles to be eradicated worldwide by the year 2010. All cases now occurring in the United States originate abroad, brought in by travelers, many of them foreign students attending U.S. secondary schools and colleges. Measles continues to be a major health problem in many developing countries, especially in sub-Saharan Africa and on the Indian subcontinent. In some areas, fewer than one-half of the children are immunized. In poor areas of the world, the case-fatality rate for measles is far higher than it is/was in the developed world, probably the result of poor nutrition.

Travelers to lesser-developed countries should be immune to measles, either by having had the disease, or by immunization. Occasionally, there are reports of measles in developed countries: recent outbreaks have occurred in Holland and Ireland. The outbreak in Holland occurred in a semi-isolated religious community that refuses immunizations. Such outbreaks present little risk to travelers to the involved country. However, several thousand cases, with several deaths, were reported this year in Ireland in the general population, suggesting that all travelers should be immune, regardless of destination.

Many adult travelers, however, may not be immune to measles. Measles vaccination in the United States began in the late 1950s. People born before 1957 (before 1970 in Canada) are assumed to have had the disease during childhood and therefore have lifelong immunity. In fact, even when measles was prevalent and "everyone got it," some individuals, by chance, escaped the disease and remain susceptible. This number is higher than is generally appreciated. The same is true for mumps, rubella, and varicella (chickenpox.) It should be noted that all of these diseases are far more severe when they occur in adults, therefore making immunity especially important for older people.

Measles vaccines used in the late 1950s and early 1960s were poorly immunogenic, and sometimes immune globulin was given simultaneously to reduce side reactions. This also reduced the effectiveness of the vaccine. Between 1963 and 1967, killed virus vaccine was used, resulting in short-term immunity. In the mid-60s, when effective live virus vaccines were introduced, experts believed that one dose would provide lifelong immunity. But experience has shown that immunity from measles vaccine is all or none—a "take" or a "no take"—and one dose immunizes only about 90% of vaccinees; the second dose immunizes most of the rest.

Measles vaccine (given as MMR—measles, mumps, rubella combination) is a two-dose series given on or after the first birthday and again at 4–6 years of age, but it is acceptable to give the two doses any time with as little as 1 month between them. The MMR vaccine should not be given during pregnancy, and female patients should not become pregnant for at least 3 months after immunization. NOTE: It is not contraindicated to give MMR to a breast-feeding mother. For babies age 6–11 months traveling to countries where measles is endemic (e.g., India), a single dose of monovalent measles (MMR is acceptable) is recommended. If the vaccine is given at age 6–11 months, a routine MMR is still recommended at age 1 year or as soon after as practical. Infants less than 6 months of age are protected by maternal-derived antibodies.

See Table 2.2 for measles vaccine schedule, indications, precautions, and booster recommendations.

Meningococcal

The meningococcal vaccine is a single-dose injection. It is recommended for international travelers to the "meningitis belt" countries of Africa, from December through June, and required for pilgrims traveling to the Hajj or Umra in Saudi Arabia. Vaccination is also recommended for travel to areas when sporadic outbreaks occur. In recent years, there have been outbreaks in India, Nepal, and southern Africa, but these are now under control; therefore, vaccination is no longer recommended for travel to these areas.

Vaccination should also be considered for college students, particularly those living in dormitories. All persons who have had a splenectomy, or have an nonfunctioning spleen, should be immunized against meningococcal disease.

The vaccine currently available in the United States is effective against meningococcal groups A, C, Y, and W135, but not against group B, the cause of some epidemics. Protection lasts 3 years. Most vaccines available outside of North America are only effective against groups A and C.

The effectiveness of the vaccine for children is dependent on the age of the child. Infants and children between 3 months and 2 years may not receive complete protection with a single dose. For travelers over age 2 years, a booster dose, when indicated, is recommended 2–5 years later.

See Table 2.2 for meningococcal vaccine schedule, indications, precautions, and booster recommendations.

Pertussis (whooping cough)

Pertussis vaccine is administered to children as the DTaP vaccine. However, the vaccine is not 100% protective, and vaccinated children may still become infected (albeit, the disease tends to be milder), making it important to limit exposure to the disease. Immunity from vaccination lasts about 10 years, making older teenagers and adults susceptible, but for a generally milder form of the disease.

Pertussis infects an estimated 60 million people worldwide annually, causing 600,000 deaths, mostly children in developing countries. It can be a serious disease, especially in infants, and it is highly contagious. Pertussis is characterized by choking and coughing—often prolonged for many weeks.

See Table 2.4 for DTaP vaccine schedule, indications, precautions and booster recommendations.

Polio (poliomyelitis)

According to the CDC, persons who have received a complete series of polio vaccine (either IPV or OPV) should receive an additional single dose of vaccine if they are 18 years of age or older and are traveling to any of the developing countries of Africa (southern, central, East, West, and North), Asia (east and Southeast), the Middle East, the Indian subcontinent, and the New Independent States of the former Soviet Union. This additional (booster) dose of polio vaccine is necessary only once in adulthood. Only inactivated polio vaccine (IPV) should be used for this dose.

Although the Western Hemisphere was declared polio-free in the 1990s, an outbreak of polio was reported in July 2000 in the Dominican Republic (16 cases) and Haiti (one case). Currently, no travel restrictions to these countries are being recommended, but all travelers to these countries should be fully immunized, as outlined above. This recommendation should probably apply for travel to other Western Hemisphere countries, but the CDC has not yet addressed this issue.

OPV can—very rarely—cause paralytic polio in the recipient, or nonimmune persons close to the recipient. Therefore, OPV is no longer manufactured or administered in the United States—only injectable polio vaccine (IPV) is used. OPV, however, is still widely used in the rest of the world. The only circumstances in which OPV should be used are the following:

1. For an unvaccinated child who will be traveling in less than 4 weeks to areas of the world where wild poliovirus still exists (south Asia and Africa).
2. For the third or fourth dose of polio vaccination series for children whose parents will not accept the additional number of injections required to complete the series with IPV.
3. In mass vaccination campaigns to control outbreaks.

See Table 2.2 for polio vaccine schedule, indications, precautions, and booster recommendations.

Rabies

Rabies vaccine is recommended for long-stay travelers to endemic areas, particularly children, who are often attracted to animals and who are less likely to report a bite or scratch.

The primary series of rabies vaccine is a total of three injections given at 0, 7, and 21 or 28 days. Accelerated schedule: 2 doses, one week apart (intramuscular route only) when time does not allow three doses to be administered over 21–28 days. Veterinarians and spelunkers should receive a booster every 2–3 years.

If you are taking chloroquine or mefloquine for malaria prevention, rabies intradermal vaccine is not recommended. The intramuscular formulation should be used. Intradermal rabies vaccine, when used, should be started 30 days prior to departure to allow for its completion before beginning chloroquine or mefloquine.

Three types of rabies vaccine, all equally effective, are available in the United States. Pre-exposure vaccination eliminates the need of administering rabies immune globulin (RIG), reduces the number of doses of post-immune vaccine, and possibly lengthens the safe interval between animal exposure and the onset of treatment. It does not preclude proper wound care.

See Table 2.2 for rabies vaccine schedule, indications, precautions and booster recommendations.

Rubella (German measles)

Most Americans are immune to rubella, either by having had the disease, or by vaccination with the measles-mumps-rubella (MMR–Merck) vaccine. Large-scale vaccination programs began in the early 1970s and included most children in school at the time. For the past two decades, nearly all children have been receiving two doses of MMR vaccine.

The only travelers who realistically need the rubella component of the vaccine are women who may become pregnant and whose rubella immunity status is unknown. (If rubella is contracted during pregnancy, the fetus can be severely damaged.) These women should consider receiving one dose of MMR. One dose of the rubella component immunizes virtually 100% of recipients for life.

Rubella vaccine and arthritis—About 10%–25% of postpubertal women report joint pain after receiving rubella vaccine, and about 10% report arthritis-like signs and symptoms. When joint symptoms occur, they generally begin 1–3 weeks after vaccination, persist for 1 day to 3 weeks, and rarely recur. Chronic joint symptoms attributable to rubella vaccine are very rare, if they occur at all.

Tetanus/diphtheria (Td)

The Td vaccine is a routine childhood immunization in the United States for those 7 years of age and older. Following completion of the DTaP series (by the seventh birthday), Td is given at 11–12 years of age if at least 5 years have elapsed since the last dose of DTaP. Subsequent Td boosters are recommended every 10 years.

Tetanus, or lockjaw, is a very serious disease that may follow a cut, burn, or wound. It causes serious muscle spasms and frequently ends in death if not treated. Tetanus is a global health problem, occurring particularly among infants and young children in developing countries. In the United States, it is a very rare disease because almost all children and young adults have received the vaccine; most infections are seen in the elderly population who have never received a primary series of injections.

The tetanus bacillus inhabits soil worldwide, especially soil contaminated by animal excreta, and survives particularly well in tropical climates. Infected wounds need not be deep or obvious to allow tetanus bacteria to multiply and secrete toxin.

The schedule for tetanus immunization is identical to that for diphtheria, and the two vaccines are generally combined in one product. (One way to increase diphtheria protection in the population is to give tetanus/diphtheria injections whenever tetanus is administered.)

See Table 2.2 for Td vaccine schedule, indications, precautions, and contraindications.

Tuberculosis (BCG-Bacille Calmette Guerin)

BCG vaccine is used very rarely in travelers; the risk for acquiring the disease while traveling is small. The CDC states: "To become infected, a person usually would have to spend a long time in a closed environment where the air was contaminated by a person with untreated tuberculosis (TB) who is coughing and has numerous TB bacteria in secretions from the lung." BCG is routinely given to children in many countries, both developed and developing. In the United States, TB control is based on identifying and treating infected individuals and BCG is not given.

BCG may be appropriate for travelers, chiefly children, who have prolonged and close contact with local populations in remote areas of developing countries with high incidences of TB (children of missionaries, for example). BCG may be more effective in preventing complications (meningitis, for example) than preventing the disease itself. In the United States, current recommendations for individuals at risk are not to use BCG vaccine but to perform TB skin testing before and after exposure (including travel) and to treat individuals who convert their skin test from negative to positive.

Typhoid

Oral typhoid vaccine is no longer available in the United States but may be reintroduced in 2001. Injectable typhoid vaccine (Wyeth) for children 6 months to 2 years of age is no longer available in the United States.

Typhoid fever vaccine has at least four formulations (oral suspension, oral capsule, and two injectable formulations) worldwide, but only the injectable Typhim Vi is currently available in the United States. Typhim Vi is a single-dose vaccine used in persons 2 years of age or older. A booster dose is recommended every 2 years in the U.S. and every 3 years in Canada. Oral typhoid vaccine (Vivotif) is taken on alternate days for a total of four capsules, and in Canada as a sachet in water on alternate days for a total of 3 doses. It is only approved for persons 6 years of age or older. A booster dose is recommended every 5 years. The capsules must be refrigerated and taken with a cool liquid approximately 1 hour before eating.

Typhoid fever is an acute, life-threatening bacterial disease introduced into the body from contaminated food and water. It presents typically as a prolonged fever with headache, cough, and constipation.

Since the majority of cases of typhoid fever in the U.S. originate in immigrants, the vaccine is strongly recommended for VFR's (immigrants returning the their home country to visit family, friends, and relatives), particularly those returning to Latin America, Asia, and Southeast Asia.

See Table 2.2 for typhoid vaccine schedule, indications, precautions, and booster recommendations.

Yellow Fever

Yellow fever is the only vaccine that may be required for entry into certain countries. (Go to *http://www.cdc.gov/travel/yelfever.htm* or *http://www.catis.org/immunization/_yelpro_e.htm* for a comprehensive listing of vaccination certificate requirements worldwide.) After vaccination (by a travel clinic or your local health department) an *International Certificate of Vaccination* is issued which will meet entry requirements for all persons traveling to or arriving from countries where there is active, or a potential for, yellow fever transmission. The certificate is good for 10 years. If there is a medical reason (e.g., infants less than 4 months old, pregnant women, persons hypersensitive to eggs, or those with a immunosuppressed condition) not to receive the vaccine, most countries will accept a medical waiver. The CDC recommends obtaining the waiver from a consulate or embassy before departure.

Yellow fever vaccine is a live attenuated viral vaccine. A single dose confers immunity lasting 10 years or more.

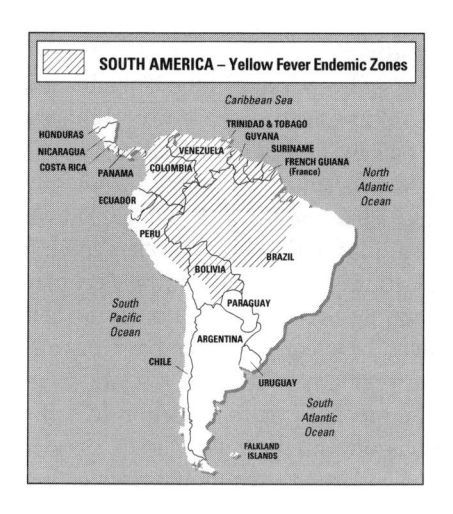

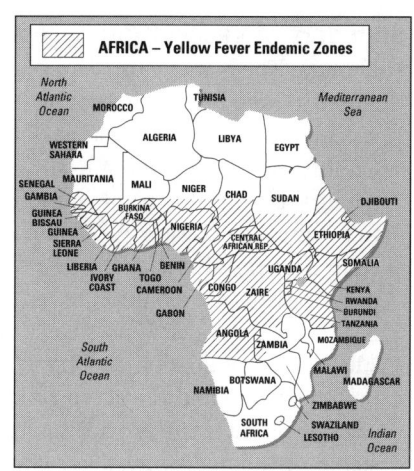

Vaccine Precautions

The vaccine generally is associated with few side effects: fewer than 5% of vaccines develop mild headache, muscle pain, or other minor symptoms 5 to 10 days after vaccination. However, three groups of individuals should not receive the vaccine, and a fourth group should be closely evaluated.

The vaccine is contraindicated for three groups:

1. Yellow fever vaccine should never be given to infants under 4 months of age due to a risk of developing viral encephalitis. In most cases, vaccination should be deferred until 9 to 12 months of age.
2. Pregnant women should not be vaccinated because of a theoretical risk that the developing fetus may become infected from the vaccine.
3. Persons hypersensitive to eggs should not receive the vaccine because it is prepared in embryonated eggs.

Other groups that should be closely evaluated before administering the vaccine:

- Persons with an immunosuppressed condition associated with AIDS or HIV infection, or those with their immune system altered by other diseases, such as leukemia and lymphoma, or receiving drugs and/or radiation. People with asymptomatic HIV infection may be vaccinated if they are at risk.
- Elderly travelers (>65 years of age). Recent studies have shown that this group may be at significantly greater risk of severe adverse reactions to the vaccine. Therefore, a careful risk/benefit assessment should be carries out in this group.

Summary of Vaccination Recommendations

- **Cholera:** The manufacture and availability of this vaccine in the United States ceased in June 2000. Many countries, including Canada, license an oral cholera vaccine. The oral cholera vaccine is not available in the United States.

  Cholera vaccine is not "officially" required for entry into, or exit from, any country. Despite this, some countries (e.g., Tanzania, Kenya, Egypt) are known to require, on occasion, proof of cholera immunization from travelers coming from cholera-infected countries. Anticipating such a situation, travelers may need a medical exemption letter, containing the official stamp, from their health-care provider. If possible, it is advisable to contact the embassy or consulate at the destination country to confirm the requirement for cholera vaccination (if any) and the acceptability of a medical exemption letter. In some cases, the health-care provider, in consultation with the traveler, may consider stamping the *International Certificate of Vaccination*, even though vaccination was not administered.

  Because it is an extremely rare disease in international travelers from developed countries, such as the United States and Canada, and the injectable vaccine may have significant side effects and is probably not more than 50% effective, it is not recommended by WHO. When it was available in the United States, the CDC recommended it only for travelers at high risk who worked and lived in highly endemic areas under less than adequate sanitary conditions.

- **Hepatitis A:** This vaccine is recommended for all nonimmune travelers over age 2 (over age 1 in Canada) going to areas of intermediate or high risk for hepatitis A transmission, especially frequent short-term travelers or persons staying for extended periods. This recommendation does not include travelers to Japan, Australia, New Zealand, or developed countries in northern and Western Europe (except Spain, Portugal, and southern Italy).

- **Hepatitis B:** This vaccine is recommended for: frequent short-term travelers; persons living for prolonged periods (more than 3 months) in high-risk areas; adventure travelers; travelers with chronic diseases, such as chronic liver disease due to hepatitis C or other causes; people who will have close, prolonged contact with the local population, such as health-care workers, missionaries, and relief workers; travelers who might have sexual contact with the local population. It should be considered for any risk-averse traveler desiring maximum pre-travel preparation, especially if they are traveling in a country where the sterility of needles and syringes for medical injections cannot be guaranteed.

- **Immune globulin:** Most travelers' clinics have discontinued immune globulin for the prevention of hepatitis A and rely solely on the hepatitis A vaccine, regardless of time before departure. NOTE: Immune globulin is still recommended for travelers under 2 years of age since the hepatitis A vaccine is not approved for use under age 2 in the U.S. In Canada the hepatitis A vaccine (Havrix) is approved down to 1 year of age.

- **Influenza:** Influenza is transmitted year-round in the tropics. The vaccine is recommended for all travelers over age 50; all travelers of any age with any chronic or immunocompromising conditions; any traveler wishing to decrease the risk of influenza; shipboard travelers along the coast of the U.S. and Canada; all pregnant women after the first trimester.
- **Japanese encephalitis (JE):** Recommended for stays of more than one month in rural endemic areas, especially during the peak transmission season; hikers, bicyclists, or others with extensive outdoor exposures in endemic area; repeated short visits to rural farming areas of all islands, such as may occur with long-term expatriates.
- **Measles/Mumps/Rubella:** All travelers to endemic or epidemic areas should be vaccinated if they have not had these illnesses or have not been appropriately immunized.
- **Meningococcal (meningitis):** Recommended for all travelers staying longer than 1 month during the dry season in the meningitis belt countries of sub-Saharan Africa; consider for all travelers during dry season if prolonged contact with the local populace is anticipated; all travelers into epidemic regions. The vaccine is required for travelers to Saudi Arabia for purpose of pilgrimages to Mecca.
- **Pneumococcal (PPV-23):** Advised for travelers over 65, those with chronic illnesses, or people who have had a splenectomy.
- **Polio:** Immunized travelers over age 18 should receive a one-time polio booster prior to international travel.
- **Rabies:** Recommended for all stays of over 30 days in risk areas, especially children; shorter stays at locations that are more than 24 hours in travel time from a reliable source of postexposure rabies vaccine; occupational exposure; all adventure travelers and backpackers to risk areas. Consider for shorter stays in risk-averse travelers desiring maximum protection.
- **Tetanus/Diphtheria:** Booster every 10 years, for adults. Diphtheria protection is important, especially for adults, 60% of whom have no little or immunity to this disease.
- **Typhoid:** Recommended for travelers going to endemic areas, especially lesser-developed countries, who will be staying for a prolonged period of time, eating adventurously, or venturing off the usual tourist routes into small cities, villages, and rural areas. Consider for short-term travel in those desiring maximum protection.
- **Varicella (chickenpox):** Adolescents and adults who have never been immunized, or have not had the disease, should be vaccinated. Immigrants from developing countries are at particular risk.
- **Yellow fever:** Vaccination may be required for entry into certain countries in the yellow fever endemic zones, and/or recommended for protection in certain yellow fever endemic zone countries with active disease.

Immunization Tables

Table 2.2 Immunizations for International Travel

Vaccine	Type	Schedule	Booster	Indications for Travelers	Precautions and Contraindications
Cholera*	Inactivated bacterial	Two-dose series, at least 1 wk apart	6 mos	High-risk travelers, i.e. living in highly endemic areas, compromised gastric defense mechanisms	Age < 6 mos
Hepatitis A	Inactivated viral (VAQTA®) (Havrix®) (AVAXIM®) (EPAXAL®)	Two-dose series, at 0 and 6-12 mos	None	Travelers to areas of intermediate or high-risk, especially frequent short-term travelers or persons staying for long time periods	Age < 2 yrs; Age < 1 year in Canada (Havrix®)
Hepatitis B	Inactivated viral (RECOMBIVAX HB®) (Engerix-B®)	Three-dose series, at 0, 1, and 6 mos; Engerix-B® may be given at 0, 1, 2 mos; booster at 12 mos	None	Routine immunization for children 0-18 years; high-risk international travelers, especially those working in health care or residing more than 6 mos	None
Immunoglobulin (IG)	Pooled human immunoglobulins	One dose 0.02 mL/kg IM/for 3-month protection; 0.06 mL/kg IM for 5-mo protection	3- 5-mo intervals, depending on initial dose	Single visit < 5 mos to endemic area, used when immediate protection is needed	Give measles > 2 wks before or > 3 mos after IG; give varicella > 3 wks before or > 5 mos after IG
Influenza	Inactivated viral whole and split	One dose	Annual	Routine immunization for persons ≥50 yrs; high-risk travelers should receive the most current vaccine	Anaphylactic reaction to eggs

*No longer manufactured or available in the United States; An oral 3-dose vaccine is available in Canada.

Vaccine	Type	Schedule	Booster	Indications for Travelers	Precautions (major)
Japanese B encephalitis	Inactivated viral	Three doses at 0, 7, and 30 days	3 yrs	>30 days to rural SE Asia, especially rice paddies and pig farms	Pregnancy; age <1 yr
Measles, mumps, rubella	Live viral monovalent or combined MMR	Two doses, at least one mo apart	None	Routine childhood immunization; travelers to endemic countries	Immunocompromised; pregnancy; immunoglobulins; anaphylactic reation to eggs or gelatin
Meningococcal	Inactivated bacterial	One dose	3–5 yrs	Travel to meningitis belt of Africa from Dec- June; absence of spleen; travel to Saudi Arabia for Hajj	None
Pneumococcal (PPV-23)	Inactivated bacterial	One dose (polysaccharide)	Consider booster dose if > 5 yrs since primary vaccination	Routine immunization age ≥ 65; absence of spleen; immunocompromised	None
Poliomyelitis, oral* (OPV)	Live viral	Three-dose series; 2nd dose 6-8 wks after 1st, 3rd dose 8-12 mos after 2nd	None	Unvaccinated children traveling in <4 weeks to countries where polio is endemic	Immunocompromised; nonimmune close contacts; pregnancy
Poliomyelitis, injectable (IPV)	Inactivated viral	Routine childhood immunization; three dose series, 2nd dose 4-8 wks after 1st, 3rd dose 6-12 mos after 2nd	One-time booster for foreign travel if >18 yrs	Travel to countries where polio is epidemic or endemic	Pregnancy

Vaccine	Type	Schedule	Booster	Indications for travelers	Precautions (major)
Rabies	Inactivated viral HCDV (available in ID & IM formulations); PCEC; RVA	Three-dose series at 0, 7, and 21-28 days	2 yrs if antibodies decline	> 30 days in risk areas	If ID rabies vaccine is not completed prior to starting chloroquine or mefloquine, use IM vaccine
Tetanus-diphtheria	Bacterial toxoid	Three-dose series, 2nd dose 4-8 wks after 1st dose, 3rd dose 6-12 mos later	10 yrs	Routine immunization; nonimmune	Age < 7 yrs
Typhoid, oral	Attenuated live bacterial Ty21a (Vivotif)	One capsule at 0, 2, 4, and 6 days (3 sachets at 0, 2, 4 days in Canada)	5 yrs	Travel in a developing country	Immunocompromised; pregnancy; concurrent antibiotic use; age
Typhoid, injectable	Bacterial polysaccharide (Typhim Vi)	One dose	2 yrs	Travel in a developing country	Pregnancy; age < 2 yrs
Varicella	Live viral	One dose at 12 mos -12 yrs; two doses 4-8 wks apart age ≥ 13 yrs	None	Routine childhood immunization < 13 yrs old; likely exposure in non-immune adolescent or adult	Immunocompromised; pregnancy; concurrent aspirin use; neomycin; immunoglobulins
Yellow fever	Live viral	One dose	10 yrs	Travel to equatorial Africa and South America; required by some countries	Immunocompromised; pregnancy; age < 9 mos; anaphylactic reaction to eggs; age over 75

Table 2.3

Immunizations for the HIV-Positive Traveler

Vaccine	Recommendation	Comments
Cholera	Probably safe	Use only for travel to epidemic areas. Rarely indicated.
H. influenza type b	Recommended	Consider one dose of conjugated vaccine.
Hepatitis A	Recommended	The expected immune response may not be obtained.
Hepatitis B	Recommended	Test for pre-existing immunity
Influenza	Recommended	Administer annually.
Japanese encephalitis	Recommended	Mosquito-bite prevention.
Lyme disease	Recommended	The expected immune response may not be obtained.
Measles (MMR)	Recommended for persons not severely compromised	Not recommended for persons. severely compromised
Meningococcal	Recommended	Booster in 3 years.
Pneumococcal (PPV-23 vaccine)	Recommended	Booster after 5 years.
Polio	Use only inactivated vaccine (IPV)	The live oral polio vaccine (OPV) is contraindicated.
Rabies	Recommended	Administer by IM route only.
Tetanus/diphtheria	Booster every 10 years	Diphtheria immunity may be diminished or absent.
Typhoid	Use Typhim Vi	Avoid live oral typhoid vaccine.
Varicella	Recommended for some asymptomatic individuals	Not recommended for symptomatic persons.
Yellow fever	Recommended for asymptomatic patients if risk of disease is unavoidable.	Letter of waiver if vaccine not administered. Strict mosquito-bite protection advised.

Medical waivers—Most countries will accept a medical waiver for persons with a health reason for not receiving the yellow fever vaccination. The CDC recommends obtaining written waivers from consular or embassy officials before departure, but travel clinics hardly ever recommend doing this. Instead, a physician's letter that states the reason for withholding the vaccination and that is written on letterhead stationery usually suffices. The letter should bear the stamp used by a health department or official immunization center to validate the *International Certificate of Vaccination* (Yellow Card).

Table 2.4
Recommended Childhood Immunization Schedule[1], January–December 2001

Vaccines[1] are listed under routinely recommended ages. Bars indicate range of recommended ages for immunization. Any dose not given at the recommended age should be given as a "catch-up" immunization at any subsequent visit when indicated and feasible. Ovals indicate vaccines to be given if previously recommended doses were missed or given earlier than the recommended minimum age.

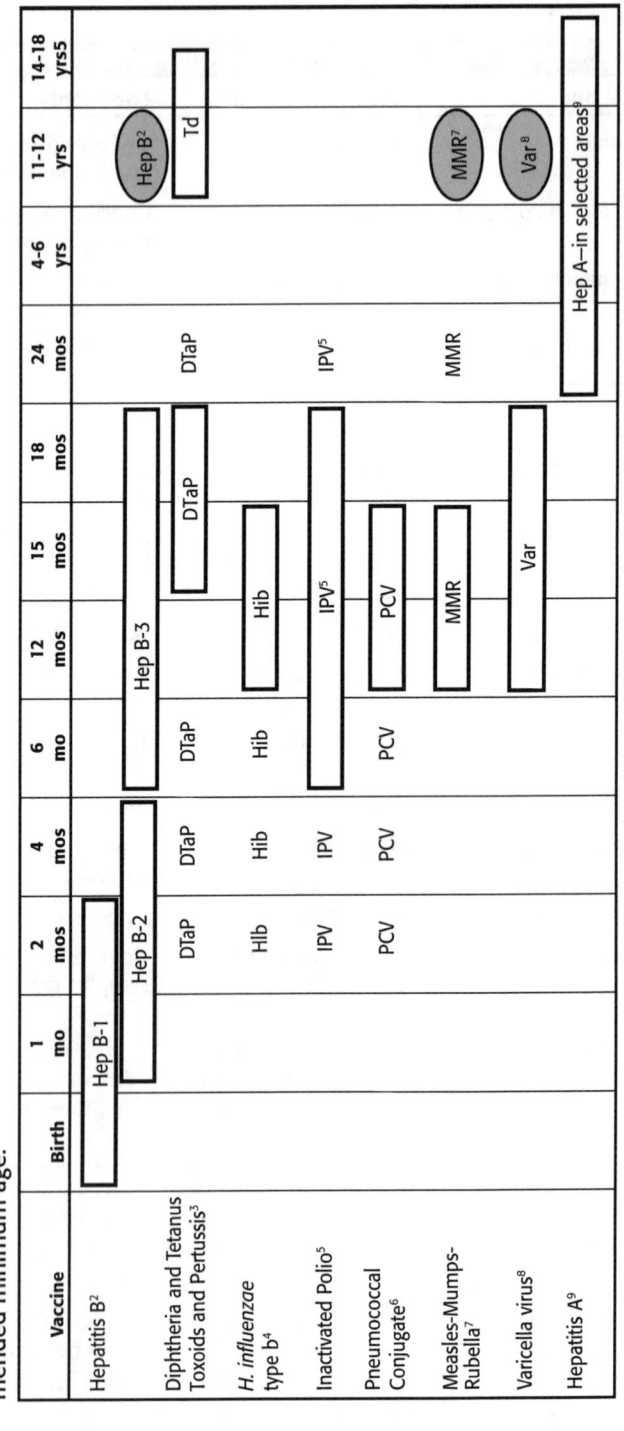

Vaccine	Birth	1 mo	2 mos	4 mos	6 mo	12 mos	15 mos	18 mos	24 mos	4-6 yrs	11-12 yrs	14-18 yrs[5]
Hepatitis B[2]		Hep B-1	Hep B-2			Hep B-3					Hep B[2]	
Diphtheria and Tetanus Toxoids and Pertussis[3]			DTaP	DTaP	DTaP			DTaP	DTaP		Td	
H. influenzae type b[4]			Hib	Hib	Hib	Hib						
Inactivated Polio[5]			IPV	IPV	IPV[5]	IPV[5]						
Pneumococcal Conjugate[6]			PCV	PCV	PCV	PCV						
Measles-Mumps-Rubella[7]						MMR	MMR		MMR		MMR[7]	
Varicella virus[8]						Var	Var				Var[8]	
Hepatitis A[9]										Hep A—in selected areas[9]		

52 Vaccines

1. This schedule indicates the recommended ages for routine administration of currently licensed childhood vaccines, as of 11/01/00, for children through 18 years of age. Additional vaccines may be licensed and recommended during the year. Licensed combination vaccines may be used whenever any components of the combination are indicated and its other components are not contraindicated. Providers should consult the manufacturers' package inserts for detailed recommendations.

2. Infants born to HBsAg-negative mothers should receive the 1st dose of hepatitis B (Hep B) vaccine by age 2 months. The 2nd dose should be at least one month after the 1st dose. The 3rd dose should be administered at least 4 months after the 1st dose and at least 2 months after the 2nd dose, but not before 6 months of age for infants.

   Infants born to HBsAg-positive mothers should receive hepatitis B vaccine and 0.5 mL hepatitis B immune globulin (HBIG) within 12 hours of birth at separate sites. The 2nd dose is recommended at 1-2 months of age and the 3rd dose at 6 months of age.

   Infants born to mothers whose HBsAg status is unknown should receive hepatitis B vaccine within 12 hours of birth. Maternal blood should be drawn at the time of delivery to determine the mother's HBsAg status; if the HBsAg test is positive, the infant should receive HBIG as soon as possible (no later than 1 week of age).

   All children and adolescents who have not been immunized against hepatitis B should begin the series during any visit. Special efforts should be made to immunize children who were born in, or whose parents were born in, areas of the world with moderate or high endemicity of hepatitis B virus infection.

3. The 4th dose of DTaP (diphtheria and tetanus toxoids and acellular pertussis vaccine) may be administered as early as 12 months of age, provided 6 months have elapsed since the 3rd dose and the child is unlikely to return at age 15-18 months. Td (tetanus and diphtheria toxoids) is recommended at 11-12 years of age if at least 5 years have elapsed since the last dose of DTP, DTaP or DT. Subsequent routine Td boosters are recommended every 10 years.

4. Three *Haemophilus influenzae* type b (Hib) conjugate vaccines are licensed for infant use. If PRP-OMP (PedvaxHIB® or ComVax® [Merck]) is administered at 2 and 4 months of age, a dose at 6 months is not required. Because clinical studies in infants have demonstrated that using some combination products may induce a lower immune response to the Hib vaccine component, DTaP/Hib combination products should not be used for primary immunization in infants at 2, 4 or 6 months of age, unless FDA-approved for these ages.

5. An all-IPV schedule is recommended for routine childhood polio vaccination in the United States. All children should receive four doses of IPV at 2 months, 4 months, 6-18 months, and 4-6 years of age. Oral polio vaccine (OPV) should be used only in selected circumstances. (See Chapter 2 "Vaccines").

6. The heptavalent conjugate pneumococcal vaccine (PCV) is recommended for all children 2-23 months of age. It also is recommended for certain children 24-59 months of age. (See MMWR Oct.6, 2000/49(RR- 9);1-35).

7. The 2nd dose of measles, mumps, and rubella (MMR) vaccine is recommended routinely at 4-6 years of age but may be administered during any visit, provided at least 4 weeks have elapsed since receipt of the 1st dose and that both doses are administered beginning at or after 12 months of age. Those who have not previously received the second dose should complete the schedule by the 11-12 year old visit.

8. Varicella (Var) vaccine is recommended at any visit on or after the first birthday for susceptible children, i.e., those who lack a reliable history of chickenpox (as judged by a healthcare provider) and who have not been immunized. Susceptible persons 13 years of age or older should receive 2 doses, given at least 4 weeks apart.

9. Hepatitis A (Hep A) is shaded to indicate its recommended use in selected states and/or regions, and for certain high-risk groups; consult your local public health authority. (See MMWR Oct.1, 1999/48(RR-12);1-37).

For additional information about the vaccines listed above, please visit the National Immunization Program Home Page at http://www.cdc.gov/nip/ or call the National Immunization Hotline at 800-232-2522.

MMWR 1998

Thompson RF. Travel & Routine Immunizations 2001 Edition. Shoreland, Inc. P.O. Box 13795 Milwaukee, WI 53213.

3 Jet Lag & Motion Sickness

Most travelers have experienced jet lag. The common symptoms—insomnia, fatigue, change in appetite, irritability—are due in part to your body's cyclical hormone production being temporarily out of synch with your activities. After several days at your destination, your body's biological clock (circadian rhythm) becomes reset, and the symptoms subside. In general, it takes the body one day to adjust for each time zone crossed.

Like many disorders that have no cure, there are lots of proposed jet lag remedies and preventatives. Numerous travelers have tried jet lag "diets." More recently, exposure to artificial light sources and melatonin have been touted as being effective in resetting the body's clock.

NOTE: For short stays of three days or less, adjustment of the body clock is not possible and should not be attempted.

Jet Lag Diets
Despite their apparent popularity, there is no scientific evidence that jet lag diets do any good. Many travelers find these diets too complex and tedious to follow. Any claimed benefits may be purely psychological, due to a placebo effect.

Light Exposure
Light exposure seems to play a role in resetting circadian rhythms. The mechanism involves suppression of the hormone melatonin, which is secreted by the brain's pineal gland.

The current dogma is that for eastward travel additional morning sunlight (whether cloudy or not) is beneficial, whereas for westward travel, afternoon light is important. Special high intensity lights (>10,000 lux) are available to help accomplish this end. Regardless of travel destination and arrival time, recent studies suggest that exposure to outdoor light *at any time of day* assists in readjustment of your circadian rhythm.

Melatonin
Ten years of placebo-controlled studies have shown that the hormone melatonin can reset your body's internal clock. In one study, travelers were given 3 to 5 mg of melatonin at the "destination nighttime" for three days before travel, then for three days after arrival. They experienced much less fatigue, required less time to normalize their sleep patterns, and scored better on a visual analog scale. Some

other studies, however, have shown no significant beneficial effect in about 25% of recipients, and up to 10% of travelers taking melatonin have adverse side effects, e.g., headache and excessive drowsiness. In summary, melatonin appears to be somewhat beneficial, but there's much individual variation in response to this hormone. Although there is little evidence of toxicity, concerns have been raised about melatonin's safety since the drug's strength, quality, and purity are not standardized. Also, there are little data on optimal dosing and timing of administration.

Researchers point out that little is known about melatonin's long-term safety, its effects on reproduction, and its possible dangers to people with autoimmune diseases. Since melatonin is a hormone, it is not recommended for children or during pregnancy. It should also be noted that unidentified chemical impurities have been detected in some melatonin preparations.

Sleeping Pills

Insomnia is one of the most troublesome symptoms of jet lag. While you're trying to fall asleep, your internal clock is saying "wake up."

If you need to adapt more rapidly to the new time zone, and insomnia is a significant problem for you, ask your doctor to prescribe a short-acting sleeping pill. Halcion (triazolam) is a drug that acts rapidly, is quickly eliminated from the body, and is only rarely associated with next-day sedation. There have been reports, however, of next-day memory impairment/amnesia following the use of Halcion. To help avoid the possibility of this side effect, don't exceed the recommended dose of 0.25 mg (elderly travelers should not exceed a dose of 0.125 mg). In addition, you should (1) not take Halcion during your flight, but reserve it for bedtime use after arrival, and (2) not drink alcohol when taking Halcion. Also, rebound insomnia may occur if the drug is taken for more than 1–2 weeks.

Halcion is considered a safe, effective drug if used properly. In fact, a panel of the National Academy of Sciences reached the same conclusion that an FDA task force did in 1996: "Halcion is beneficial and safe for adults, but only if it's taken at the recommended dose for seven to 10 days."

For travelers wishing to avoid Halcion, other efficacious sleep inducers to consider are the following:

- Ambien (zolpidem tartrate): 5 to 10 mg for adults
- Pro-Som (estazolam): 1 to 2 mg for adults
- Restoril (temazepam): 15 to 30 mg for adults
- Sonata (Zaleplon): 10 to 20 mg for adults

There have been fewer reports of adverse side effects associated with use of the above drugs; however, if you use one of these drugs, take the lowest effective dose and discontinue the medication after 3–5 nights. NOTE: Ambien and Sonata are non-benzodiazepine drugs and therefore chemically unrelated to Halcion, Pro-Som, and Restoril.

Another alternative: Consider Tylenol PM or Excedrin PM. These are mild soporifics that contain an antihistamine (diphenhydramine) plus acetaminophen.

Are sleeping pills safe? Generally yes, if they are used for only a short time and in the lowest effective dose. According to the *Harvard Medical School Health Letter* (May 1990), "Taking sleeping pills for a short period—perhaps a few days—can be quite helpful . . . and there is little controversy about prescribing them to help people through a crisis."

Jet Lag Formulas

These vitamin–amino acid formulas or homeopathic preparations supposedly help reset your biorhythms, but no scientific studies have been done and they are most likely ineffective. Jet lag formulas previously contained the amino acid L-tryptophan, which has mild sedative qualities, but the purified substance is now banned. Other amino acids have been substituted but may be less effective.

So What to Do?

Before taking medication or using techniques to prevent jet lag, consider the following:

- Is the treatment safe? Are there side effects?
- Is the treatment effective?
- Is the treatment practical and cost-effective?

What Really Causes Jet Lag Anyway?

Feeling tired and irritable after a long trip is not due entirely to changes in your circadian rhythms. The issue is more complex. Consider the typical scenario:

For several days prior to departure, you are frantically taking care of what seems like a thousand and one last minute errands and details • You are probably too keyed up to get enough sleep • Your normal eating and drinking patterns are disrupted • You are somewhat apprehensive about flying • You are anxious about leaving home and/or your family • You fight heavy traffic getting to the airport • You park your car, but wonder if it will be safe • You carry a heavy suitcase half a mile to check in and hope it won't get lost • You catch a connecting flight • You stand in line again at check-in • You clear security checkpoints • Then you wait in a crowded, smoky airport lounge because your overseas flight is delayed by hours.

It's no surprise that you're feeling stressed out even before takeoff. Add to this a lack of sleep enroute, cramped seating, further dehydration—even constipation. Then, after arrival in a foreign country, you face still more hassles simply getting to your hotel. No wonder you've got jet lag.

The *HealthGuide* takes the following view—Jet lag is not a single entity and the symptom complex will probably never be completely alleviated by a single treatment. The symptoms you experience are usually a combination of travel-related physical and emotional stress, sleep deprivation, plus the biological effect of your circadian rhythm being out of synch.

Enroute Strategies to Reduce Jet Lag
- Don't drink too much alcohol—If you are a drinker, there's no reason not to have a cocktail or two, but remember that alcohol is a depressant drug, and larger amounts can cause rebound nervous stimulation and restlessness, interfering with your sleep. Contrary to popular belief, a few drinks won't dehydrate you.
- Don't drink too much coffee—Excess caffeine may cause nervousness and insomnia. Caffeine also stimulates gastric acid production, which can lead to heartburn. However, if you habitually drink many cups of coffee each day, missing your "caffeine fix" during your flight may not be a good idea—you might get symptoms of caffeine withdrawal and feel even worse (e.g., severe headache)! Coffee-drinker strategy: Reset your watch to destination time when you board the aircraft. Drink your coffee enroute at the destination time that corresponds to your regular "caffeine fix" time at home.
- Do drink water and fruit juices. They are good substitutes for (or complements to) alcoholic drinks and coffee. You may be somewhat dehydrated at the beginning of the flight due to disrupted eating and drinking habits prior to departure. Also, breathing low-humidity cabin air during a long flight will dry the mucous membranes of your throat and make you thirsty. Water and fruit juices are the best drinks to quench your thirst.
- Sleeping enroute—Avoid, unless it coincides with nighttime at your destination.

After Arrival at Your Destination
- The most important principle is to begin all activities, including eating and sleeping, at destination time as soon as possible. If you have an evening arrival, have a light dinner and go to bed late. The next day try to eat and sleep according to the local time.
- If you have a morning arrival, stay active during the day and get as much exposure to natural light as possible, if your schedule and the weather permit. If possible, don't nap, but overpowering fatigue should not be resisted. If you do nap, keep it under 45 minutes to avoid Stage IV (REM) sleep, which causes grogginess upon awakening. NOTE: For trips less than 3 days, short naps *should* be taken when you feel most tired.
- Take a sleeping pill if you have troubling insomnia (see below). Discontinue sleeping medication after three to five nights.

The Myth of Dehydration
For many years it has been touted by the travel media that dry cabin air in jet airliners causes dehydration—which presumably could aggravate jet lag. The recommended remedy has always been to drink extra fluids enroute—and avoid certain beverages, such as caffeinated drinks, that would "dehydrate" you. This advice appears to be misleading. According to a new study from the University of

Nebraska Medical Center, healthy adults showed the same "hydration status" (as determined from urine analysis and other tests) when they drank caffeinated beverages, such as coffee or caffeinated colas as when they drank only water and/or fruit drinks. Also, the Medical Director of British Airways Aviation Medical Services has stated (in the medical journal *Lancet*) that low cabin humidity causes, at most, only a 3 oz. water loss during an 8-hour trip. (In fact, the stress of travel may cause your body to retain water.) Therefore, dehydration from dry cabin air, aggravated by certain beverages, appears to be a myth, and compulsively drinking extra water or other fluids enroute is unnecessary.

Keep the Problem of Jet Lag in Perspective

Enjoying your vacation is more important than fighting jet lag. Don't waste your time following complex jet lag diets and cures that have not been shown to work. Try not to worry too much about jet lag. Less than one-half of travelers report significant symptoms.

Business travelers—If you are traveling on important business, you probably have more need than others to reduce the symptoms of jet lag. Consider the following strategies: (1) reserve a sleeperette (reclining airline seat) to improve the chances of sleeping enroute, (2) budget, if possible, one or two extra days after arrival to rest and recuperate prior to business activities, or (3) break up a long trip (>6 time zones) along the way for a day or two.

MOTION SICKNESS

Strictly speaking, motion sickness is neither an illness nor "sickness" but a normal, albeit exaggerated, response to unfamiliar motion of increased intensity and duration. Nausea, sweating, salivation, and vomiting are the usual symptoms. If vomiting does occur, it is frequently followed by drowsiness and lethargy.

Risk Factors

- Sea > Air > Car > Train
- Women > Men
- Inexperienced travelers > Experienced travelers
- Young age > Older age
- Passengers > Crew
- Passengers > Driver

Motion sickness occurs in about 1% of airline passengers. Symptoms are rare below age 2 and peak between the ages of 3 and 12. The elderly are less susceptible.

Preventing/Treating Motion Sickness

Don't travel on an empty stomach; this seems to promote symptoms. If you feel yourself becoming nauseated, keep your head stationary. Don't read, but do listen to music if you have a Walkman™ or airline headset. A stable head position is very important in controlling motion sickness because your inner ears contain the balance "gyroscopes" that monitor and coordinate motion and body position.

Increasing ventilation, decreasing food intake, and avoiding alcohol are other techniques to reduce motion sickness. For those interested in natural remedies, ginger root may offer some benefit.

Body position—On a boat, try to stay amidships. Lie supine with your head supported on pillows. Keep your head still and your eyes closed. If on deck, look out at the horizon. One trick: pretend you are "dancing with the ship." On airliners, either (1) press your head against the seat in front of you, or (2) lean back in the seat, keep your head still, and look straight ahead. In cars, sit in the front seat. Look forward at the horizon, rather than out the side windows.

Acupressure bands (Sea-Bands)—Some people swear by these wrist bands with the plastic beads, but a study conducted by *Conde Nast Traveler* magazine (October 1991) found no effect on seasickness.

Drugs

Stimulation of nerve fibers in the balance center of the inner ear (the labyrinth) causes the symptoms of motion sickness. The drugs used to control motion sickness not only reduce the activity of these nerve fibers but also appear to act directly on the body's vomiting center located in the brain stem.

The drugs commonly used to prevent motion sickness are the scopolamine preparations and the antihistamines.

Scopolamine

Scopolamine is a belladonna plant alkaloid with significant anticholinergic activity. The most frequent side effect is dryness of the mouth, but blurred vision and drowsiness can also occur.

TRANSDERM SCōP—The Transderm Scōp System (Figure 2.1) is a circular flat patch that delivers 1.0 mg of scopolamine at a constant rate over 3 days. Because of its prolonged action, it is especially useful for seasickness. Travelers may want to try it for a few days before departure to identify any adverse effects.

SCOPACE™ (scopolamine hydrobromide)—This drug is an oral form of scopolamine with a duration of 6–8 hours. It acts more rapidly than the scopolamine patch. The more rapid onset and shorter action makes it better suited for airline or automobile travel. The dosage range is 0.4 to 0.8 mg. You should take it on an empty stomach one hour prior to departure. The dosage can be titrated for best effect.

Ginger—This natural motion sickness remedy is safe and moderately effective and is readily available in health food stores.

Antihistamines

Although scopolamine is considered to be the more effective drug for the treatment of motion sickness, many physicians prefer antihistamines because they produce fewer adverse effects (e.g., dry mouth, blurred vision) than does scopolamine. Drowsiness is the most common antihistamine side effect, which can be troublesome if you need to drive a car. Drowsiness on the other hand can help you sit or lie quietly and thus may be beneficial on a boat or a plane.

Antivert (meclizine)—The initial adult dose is 25 to 50 mg. Take one hour prior to departure. Repeat every 12–24 hours, as needed, for the duration of the journey. Available by prescription only.

Dramamine (dimenhydrinate)—Available without prescription. This drug has a rapid onset of action, and you can use it for either prevention or treatment of symptoms. Adults and children over 12 should take one or two tablets every four to six hours, as needed. Start one hour before embarkation. Follow package instructions for younger children.

Phenergan (promethazine)—The average adult dose is 25 mg taken twice daily. Take the first dose one-half to one hour prior to embarkation and repeat in 8–12 hours, as necessary. Suppositories are quite helpful. For children: Phenergan tablets, syrup, or rectal suppositories, 12.5 to 25 mg (for larger children), twice daily may be administered. This drug, available by prescription, may be the most effective of the antihistamines for the treatment of motion sickness.

Combination therapy—If motion sickness is a serious problem for you, try a combination therapy, using Phenergan and ephedrine. British travel experts often prescribe drugs together. The adult dosage is Phenergan 25 mg, plus ephedrine 50 mg, every 12 hours.

Which one to choose?—Given the choice of motion sickness medications, how is one to choose? A recent comparative trial of seven commonly used agents to prevent motion sickness showed that they all performed equally well.

SINUSES AND EARS

When traveling by commercial airliner, you will be cruising at an altitude of 30,000 to 45,000 feet above sea level. Your cabin will be pressurized to an altitude of 6,000 to 8,000 feet above sea level. The air contained within your middle ear and si-

Figure 2.1. The small patch placed behind the ear releases minute amounts of scopolamine that permeate the intact skin at a preprogrammed rate over a 72-hour period. The scopolamine is directly absorbed into the bloodstream.

Scopolamine acts on the nerve fibers of the inner ear and brainstem to reduce nausea and vomiting.

The transdermal patch should not be used by children, travelers with glaucoma, or men with prostate enlargement. Confusion in the elderly may occur.

nuses will expand by about 25% and will usually escape without causing any symptoms. During descent, however, cabin air pressure starts to increase and exceeds the pressure within the middle ear. To allow equalization of pressure on either side of the eardrum, the eustachian tube must open to allow air to enter from the back of your nose. If necessary, clearing the tube can usually be accomplished by yawning or swallowing. Pinching your nostrils closed and gently forcing air from your lungs into the nasopharynx can assist this process. Chewing gum can also help contract the muscles at the end of the tube to allow passage of air up into the middle ear.

If the pressure difference between your middle ear and the nasopharynx becomes too great during descent, the end of the eustachian tube might collapse completely, making further ventilation of the middle ear impossible (Figure 2.2). If this occurs, pressure will continue to rise outside the eardrum (tympanic membrane), causing painful stretching and inward bulging of this structure. You might experience dizziness, vertigo, and decreased hearing. There could be bleeding into the middle ear from ruptured blood vessels. More commonly, you might experience several hours, rarely days, of pain and pressure in the ear. During this period of inadequate middle ear ventilation, an acute middle ear infection requiring antibiotics might develop.

If your sinus openings are blocked, pressure symptoms will develop over that particular sinus which air is trying to enter. You may feel a headache over the lower forehead or eyebrows, or over your cheek and around your eyes.

Prevention and treatment—Your ear structure may be such that you may have difficulty adapting to the pressure changes described. (You would probably also note similar symptoms when scuba diving, traveling in high speed elevators, or even driving in the mountains.) In this case, you may benefit from a decongestant. A recent study concluded that taking the oral decongestant (pseudoephedrine—Sudafed) decreases the incidence of ear pain and discomfort associated with air travel, but that using a popular decongestant nasal spray (oxymetazoline-Afrin) is only minimally effective. The *HealthGuide*, however, sees no reason why these drugs shouldn't be taken together.

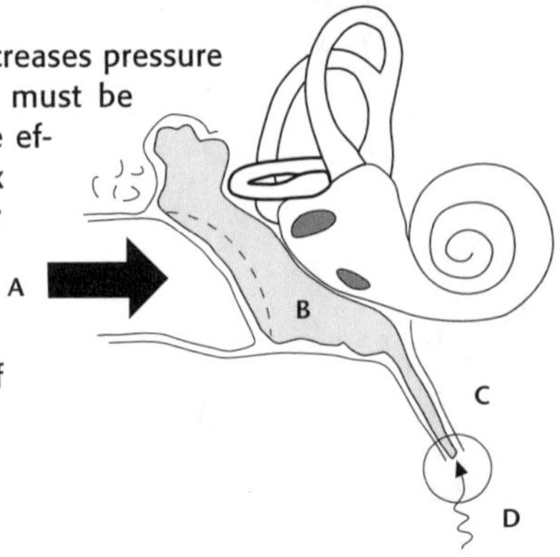

Figure 2.2 Descent from cruising altitude increases pressure on the canal side of the drum (A), which must be equalized in the middle ear (B). This can be effected only by airflow via the nasopharynx through the eustachian tube (C). If the latter is not open, airflow is impeded (D), and the relative negative pressure in the middle ear sets in motion a chain of damaging effects, beginning with pain due to the stretching of the tympanic membrane.[1]

EarPlanes (Figure 2.3) regulate the air flowing into and out of the ear thereby alleviating ear pain caused by rapid changes in cabin pressure. Inside, porous ceramic elements slow down rapid pressure changes, giving the Eustachian tubes more time to equalize pressure between your middle ear and the cabin.

If you are suffering from an acute ear infection, sinusitis, or an upper respiratory infection, you might have too much swelling and edema of the nasal mucous membranes to allow equalization of pressure during air travel. You probably should not fly under these conditions. If in doubt, consult with your physician or an ear-nose-throat specialist.

Figure 2.3. EarPlanes are recommended for travelers who must fly with colds, allergies, or sinus conditions.

Here is a summary of steps you can take to reduce ear and sinus discomfort when traveling by air:

- If you are suffering from hay fever (allergic rhinitis), have your doctor prescribe a nasal steroid spray such as Vancenase or Beconase plus the nonsedating antihistamine Zyrtec. In addition, take an oral decongestant such as pseudoephedrine (Sudafed). Start treatment several days prior to departure.
- If your problem is simple congestion from a head cold, or if you have a history of trouble equalizing middle ear pressure, start decongestants. Use Sudafed plus oxymetazoline (Afrin) or phenylephrine (Neosynephrine) nasal spray. Start Sudafed at least one day prior to departure. Use the nasal spray 1–2 hours prior to landing.
- If you have a sinus infection, you should also be on an antibiotic.
- Blow your nose frequently to remove mucous.
- Remain awake during descent in order to keep up with pressure changes. Pinch your nose and blow air up into the Eustachian tube, as necessary.
- Infants: During descent, they should be in a sitting position only when given their bottles, which should contain only water.

CABIN AIR

Contrary to popular belief, the cabin air in airliners is not a major source of contamination. Although cabin air contains varying amounts of carbon dioxide, ozone, volatile organic compounds, respirable particles, and microbial aerosols, the risk of contamination (especially the risk of acquiring an infectious disease) is practically eliminated by the filtering and air exchange mechanisms used in today's airliners. According to Thomas Bettes, M.D., M.P.H., southwestern area medical director for American Airlines, there are fewer microbial aerosols in an airliner than in any other public location. In fact, the heating and filtration to which cabin air is subjected maintains its quality to that of an operating room with the exception of increased carbon dioxide.

The risk of airborne illness is not related to inadequate filtration of cabin air but rather to being in close proximity to a passenger who happens to have a communicable disease (such as tuberculosis, or the flu) that can be transmitted directly to you when that person coughs in your direction and you happen to inhale the infected droplets.

TRAVELER'S THROMBOSIS

A transcontinental or transoceanic airline flight subjects you to prolonged sitting, usually where you can't fully extend or elevate your legs. Sitting in an airliner (or a car, bus or train, for that matter) with the seat cushion pressing against the back of your bent knees and legs may result in stagnant blood flow—a situation that can potentially promote the formation of a blood clot in the veins of your legs (deep vein thrombosis—DVT). The clot can break off and lodge in your lungs, sometimes with fatal results. Physicians report that journeys as short as three to four hours have been associated with DVT, but the risk to travelers is not known.

There are reports (British medical journal *Lancet* 1988) of young, healthy travelers developing DVT after a trip, but most people who develop DVT have one or more risk factors. Risk factors include the following:

- Older age
- Immobility or recent prolonged bed rest
- Obesity
- Smoking
- Pregnancy—especially third trimester and first postpartum month
- Recent surgery
- Cast on a broken leg
- High-estrogen contraceptives and hormone replacement therapy
- History of phlebitis or previous DVT
- Recent serious illness, especially heart failure or cancer
- Abnormal blood clotting factors. Up to 5% of Europeans carry factor V Leiden and another 2% carry a prothrombin variant that predisposes to DVT. Less common inherited DVT risks include deficiency of antithrombin III, or protein C or S, or an abnormal fibrinogen molecule.

Over 90% of travelers who develop DVT will become symptomatic within three days of travel. Symptoms include leg or ankle swelling, followed by pain, usually in one of your calves or thighs. This pain may be intense. See a doctor immediately. A Doppler ultrasound exam should be done. If DVT causes a pulmonary embolus, and the clot is large, you'll have shortness of breath and chest pain.

To prevent DVT, the medical journal advises frequent leg and body exercises such as regular walks from the aisle seat (avoiding the inside seat, if possible), particularly by passengers in the more cramped economy class. They also advise avoiding dehydration, which they say can promote blood clotting—but there are no studies that prove this.

If you are on anticoagulants, be sure your physician has your medication dosage properly adjusted prior to departure. If you have severe varicose veins, have your doctor order you some graduated compression stockings.

It's not scientifically proven how best to prevent DVT. It would seem prudent, however, to do the following:

- Take frequent walks in the aisles. This is easy to recommend but often impractical to do.
- Reserve a bulkhead seat so you have more room to stretch out.
- Fly in a business- or first-class sleeperette if full extension and elevation of your legs is desired or medically indicated. (DVT related to air travel has been dubbed the "economy-class syndrome." The problem, however, does not appear to be confined to any one section of the aircraft.)
- Do isometric exercises while seated. Point foot downward, clench toes, and hold for three seconds. Point foot upward, clench toes and hold for three seconds. Do 10 repetitions with each foot every half hour.
- Wear fitted support stockings. Don't wear knee socks that have a tight elastic band around the upper calf.
- Aspirin has been recommended by some as a blood thinner, but there is no evidence it prevents this type of blood clot. A more effective preventive measure would be an injection of low molecular weight heparin (e.g., Lovenox) before departure, but this would be a very special situation, reserved for a very small number of travelers at special high risk for DVT.

But does travel significantly increase the risk for DVT? A report in *Lancet* (October 2000) downplays the risk. Seven hundred and eighty eight patients with DVT were studied and compared to a control group. There was no association of travel (by air, bus, motorcar, train, or boat) with DVT. The authors concluded that "these results do not lend support to the widely accepted assumption that long travelling time is a risk factor for venous thrombosis. Even for journeys lasting more than 5 hours no association was apparent."

Dramatic cases, however, tend to override the nuances of clinical studies. In October 2000, a 28-year-old woman collapsed at London's Heathrow Airport after debarking from a 20-hour Qantas flight from New Zealand. Enroute to the hospital, she died from a massive pulmonary embolus resulting from a deep vein thrombosis.

1. Adapted from Schley, WS: Airflight and the middle ear. HOSPITAL MEDICINE, March 1988, pp. 85, 86, and 95. Copyright Hospital Publications, Inc.

Arendt J, Deacon S. Treatment of circadian rhythm disorders–melatonin. Chronobiol Int 1997;**14**:185–204.

Bettes T. Trends in Travel Medicine 1999. ©Merck and Co., Inc.

Cruickshanks JM, Gorlin R, Jennett B. Air travel and thrombotic episodes: The economy class syndrome. Lancet 1988:2:497–98.

Ferrari E et al. Travel as a risk factor for venous thrombembolic disease: A case-control study. Chest 1999;115:440–444.

Kozarsky PE. Prevention of Common Travel Ailments. Inf Dis Clinics of N America 1998;**12**:305–324.

Kraaijenhagen RA, et al. Travel and risk of venous thrombosis. Lancet 2000;356:1492-1493.

James PB. Jet "leg," pulmonary embolism, and hypoxia. Lancet 1996;**347**:1697.

Morris HH, Estes ML. Travelers' amnesia: Transient global amnesia secondary to triazolam. JAMA 1987;**258**:945–946.

Penev PD, Zee PC. Melatonin: A clinical perspective. Ann. Neurol. 1997;**42**:545–55.

Rees DC et al. Born to clot: The European burden. British J Hematology 1999;105:564–566.

Waterhouse J, Reilly T, Atkinson G. Jet-Lag. Lancet 1997;**350**:1611–15.

4 Food & Drink Safety

Most Americans take for granted the safety of their food and water. If we do worry, we usually focus on sugar, salt, cholesterol, saturated fat—and food additives. We forget that modern methods of food preparation, packaging, refrigeration, and the use of preservatives—combined with efficient municipal water purification and sanitation—have resulted in the United States and other developed countries having unparalleled safety and freedom from infectious diseases transmitted by contaminated food and water. Probably the main health hazard we face from food in this country is its abundance. We eat *too much*. Obesity, not travelers' diarrhea, is the greater health threat.

Food and Drink in the United States and Canada

Despite our excellent safety record, hundreds of outbreaks of food- and waterborne illnesses are officially reported each year in the United States. Undercooked bacteria-contaminated eggs, meat, and chicken transmit most cases of disease. The most common illnesses are enterocolitis (usually caused by salmonella and campylobacter bacteria) and hepatitis A. These illnesses often affect hospital patients, nursing home residents, or school children. Recently, cases of hemolytic-uremic syndrome (HUS), associated with the consumption of undercooked hamburger meat containing *E. coli* bacteria, have received extensive publicity, but cases of HUS have also been associated with raw cider, person-to-person contact, as well as bathing in the "kiddie pool" at water parks. Gastroenteritis caused by various *Vibrio* species of bacteria is occasionally reported from the Gulf of Mexico; most cases are related to the consumption of raw shellfish. Botulism, caused by improperly canned food, is sporadically reported, and giardiasis, a water-borne parasitic illness, sometimes afflicts hikers and wilderness campers who drink from contaminated ponds, lakes, or streams. Giardiasis and cryptosporidiosis outbreaks have also been traced to chlorinated but inadequately filtered municipal water supplies. In addition, because seasonally over 50% of our fresh fruits and vegetables are imported from developing countries, we can suffer from "travelers' diarrhea" without even traveling! (Multistate outbreaks of cyclosporiasis in 1995–1997, for example, have been traced to raspberries and mesclun lettuce imported from Central America.)

Food and Drink Overseas

Outside of the United States, Canada, Europe, Australia, and parts of Asia, the situation is far more serious. Most third world countries don't have our standard of living, our sanitation technology, nor our cultural attitudes toward the disposal of human fecal material. Toilets may drain into the sources of drinking water, and agricultural fields may be contaminated with various bacteria, viruses, and parasites because human feces (night soil) are often used as fertilizer.

Many countries have only rudimentary water treatment facilities and water distribution systems, and where these facilities do exist there are often breakdowns in the system. Public health regulations and inspections may be unenforced or nonexistent. The hygiene of restaurant personnel is usually below Western standards. The importance of handwashing may not be emphasized to kitchen workers. Refrigeration of food in restaurants may be inadequate, or totally lacking, and countertops and cutting surfaces may not be cleaned as required.

Such practices not only promote the transmission of diarrheal diseases caused by bacteria and viruses, but also help spread hepatitis A, typhoid fever, poliomyelitis, trichinosis, tapeworm, and other bacterial and parasitic diseases rarely found in this country.

FOOD SAFETY

When you choose foods to eat, evaluate each item in terms of its ability to harbor dangerous organisms or harmful toxins. Eating undercooked, raw, or unpasteurized products is especially hazardous. Remember that thorough cooking will destroy harmful bacteria, parasites, and viruses. Food contamination can result from any of the following:

- Contamination at the source: Shellfish, for example, may be harvested from polluted water containing hepatitis A virus, aeromonas, salmonella, or cholera bacteria; chicken and beef can be fecally contaminated during slaughter, picking up salmonella or *E. coli* bacteria; lettuce and other uncooked vegetables may be contaminated in the field from contact with fecally contaminated soil and transmit a variety of bacteria and parasites; unpasteurized dairy products, made from milk produced by sick cattle, can cause brucellosis, listeriosis, and tuberculosis.
- Contamination from handling: Foods that require a lot of touching during preparation and that are not cooked afterward, especially vegetables, are risky. Salads may have also been washed with contaminated water during preparation.
- Contamination from bacterial growth: Foods that are prepared moist and warm and that are allowed to sit unrefrigerated are risky. Under these conditions, bacteria, such as staphylococci, can rapidly multiply, producing enterotoxins that cause sudden, severe vomiting and diarrhea. This is often called "food poisoning." Reheated foods are particularly dangerous in this regard.

- Contamination from parasitic larvae: Beef, pork, fish, and shellfish may contain parasitic larvae encysted in their flesh. Aquatic plants (watercress, water chestnuts) may have parasitic cysts attached to their shoots. Examples of illness transmitted by encysted parasites include trichinosis, beef and pork tapeworm disease, anisakiasis, and clonorchiasis, paragonimiasis, and fascioliasis (liver fluke and lung fluke diseases).

No matter where you decide to eat, if you follow the guidelines below, you'll improve your chances of staying healthy.

- Eat only meat and fish that have been thoroughly and recently cooked, not rewarmed. Beef and pork should be well done without any pink areas.
  CAUTION: Microwaving may not completely destroy surface bacteria. Microwave thoroughly.
- Eat only cooked fruits and vegetables or fruits that can be peeled by you.
- Wash the surface of melons before slicing. Bacteria can otherwise be carried onto the cut surface.
- Foods that require little handling are safer.
- Order hard-boiled eggs served in the shell.
- Choose dairy products from large, commercial dairies. Boiled milk is safe.
- Milk and dairy products in Canada, Western Europe, Australia, and Japan are considered safe. Canned milk is safe.
- NOTE: Commercially prepared mayonnaise is safe. The combination of vinegar, lemon juice, and salt in mayonnaise actually helps kill bacteria, such as salmonella, that can cause infectious diarrhea.

Foods to Avoid
- Rare or raw meat; raw fish, shellfish, crayfish, and sushi. (Japan and Scandinavia have higher safe food standards regarding sushi and raw fish.)
- Raw vegetables, especially leafy salads served in restaurants.
- Fruits not peeled by you and fruits with punctured skins. Watermelons, for example, are often injected with tap water to increase their market weight.
- Aquatic plants in the Orient (e.g., watercress, water chestnuts).
- Raw eggs, undercooked eggs, unpasteurized milk and cheese. Some cooking techniques (sunny-side up, "soft" scrambled) won't kill salmonella bacteria.
- Street vendor food unless it is hot and well cooked.
- All food that has been left out in the sun, especially dairy products.
- Buffet food that has been rewarmed or recycled (e.g., the same cheeses brought out at each meal).
- Food prepared in some lesser-developed countries for airlines requires the same scrutiny as food served in restaurants in those countries.

Street Vendor Guidelines
- Choose food that is cooked, boiled, steamed, or grilled directly in front of you. These items are safe if served fresh and hot.
- Avoid food handled excessively by the vendor after cooking.
- Avoid juices and other drinks unless they are commercially bottled.
- Eat only food that is served in a clean container.

Wash Your Hands
If possible, wash your hands before you eat. You could have picked up diarrhea-causing germs from touching objects or shaking hands. These germs can then be transferred directly to your mouth or to the food that you touch and then eat. Hand Sanitizer Gel™ (available from Magellan's 800-962-4943) destroys skin bacteria without soap and water and is convenient to carry.

If you have travelers' diarrhea, or if you are caring for someone with this problem, be sure to wash your hands with soap and water after using the toilet, or after having personal contact with the patient. Shigellosis and giardiasis, in particular, can be spread directly between people, and personal hygiene is important to prevent such person-to-person spread.

"Safe" Restaurants
Appearances can be deceiving. It's not always possible to tell if a particular restaurant serves safe food. While the big, established restaurants and hotels may have better safety records, even their kitchens can have lapses in sanitation. As for eating in local restaurants, ask for a recommendation from business contacts, hotel managers, tour guides, etc. When in doubt, don't hesitate to eat in a deluxe hotel restaurant. Some travelers say that Chinese restaurants are often the safest. These restaurants use fresher ingredients, cooked at high temperature (not reheated), which are served immediately. Mexican-style restaurants are riskier because many dishes require more handling to prepare and often contain eggs, lettuce, and uncooked vegetables.

The following checklist will also help you decide which restaurants may be safer than others.

- Are the silverware, tablecloths, glasses, and plates clean?
- Are the toilets clean? Are soap and hot water provided for handwashing?
- Are there many flies inside? (Flies can carry disease germs.)
- Is there adequate screening to keep out flies and other insects?
- Is there excess/uncovered garbage outside?
- Are the waiters well groomed?
- Is the restaurant recommended by knowledgeable people?

Remember that the enjoyment of eating is partly what travel is all about. Eating well will also help you stay well, provided you use common sense. Be sure you have enough to eat and drink to avoid fatigue and dehydration. Within reason, you can often eat what the locals eat. For example, if you're traveling in Europe, choose a tasty but well-cooked specialty such as Wiener schnitzel and pass up the risky, uncooked, steak tartare. In the Orient, enjoy the Peking duck but skip the raw sushi.

WATER AND BEVERAGES

In all lesser-developed countries, water from streams, ponds, wells, and irrigated areas should be considered unsafe. Tap water, however, is sometimes unfairly maligned. Properly filtered and chlorinated tap water is perfectly safe and is available in many cities, hotels, and resorts worldwide. The problem, however, is that you cannot tell when there are lapses in appropriate purification/chemical treatment. It is therefore wisest to treat the water as outlined below.

Safe Beverages
- Boiled water
- Chemically treated water
- Filtered water is generally safe for older children and adults in most countries. It should be avoided by infants, children, and pregnant women in lesser-developed countries unless the water filter also employs a virus-killing iodine resin purifier (see discussion below about water filters and viruses).
- Hot beverages such as tea or coffee are generally safe. Even if the water was never actually boiled during preparation, heating water over a period of time is similar to pasteurizing it, and most, if not all, harmful bacteria, parasites, and viruses will be eliminated. Be sure the cup you drink from is clean.
- Commercially bottled or canned beverages, carbonated water, soft drinks, fruit juices, beer, and wine.

Beverages to Avoid
- Untreated tap water by the glass, in mixed drinks, or in the form of ice cubes. Commercial ice in blocks should be suspect.
- Locally bottled water. Be suspicious. These bottles are sometimes refilled with local tap water.
- Uncapped bottled water. These bottles may also have been refilled locally and are best avoided.
- Sea water is always unfit to drink because of the salt content, but it can be used for cooking.
- Pristine-looking water in wilderness lakes and streams in the United States and Canada may be contaminated with giardia parasites or campylobacter.

Planning Your Water Needs
Review your itinerary to determine what your water needs and sources will be. Will you be vagabond traveling, wilderness trekking, living in tropical countries,

touring the third world? All present different problems and require different strategies. You may be faced with preparing quantities of safe drinking water from polluted sources or simply disinfecting small amounts of tap water in your hotel room. When planning your water needs, consider the following:

- Will you be in an urban, rural, desert, mountain, or jungle environment?
- For how long will you be there?
- Will you be hiking or trekking? Need to disinfect water enroute?
- Will you be staying at a fixed base camp?
- Will you be storing drinking water on a boat or vehicle?
- How many people will be in your group?
- How much water (maximum amount) will you need to disinfect at one time?
- How close will you be to rivers, lakes, streams? Will you be using that water to drink? How safe is that water to drink?
- What illnesses are common at your destination?
- What type of disinfection equipment or chemicals are you planning to take on your trip?
- What type and how many water containers will you carry?

Wilderness hiking and camping in the USA and Canada expose you mainly to giardia, whereas drinking water in lesser-developed countries is potentially more dangerous—especially near population centers where raw sewage may contaminate the drinking water. In lesser-developed countries, additional protection against bacteria and viruses (especially for certain groups) is essential. See "Recommendations" on the following page.

Except in resorts, first-class hotels, and cities that properly filter and chlorinate their water, you should disinfect tap water.

What About Viruses?

In wilderness areas in the USA and Canada, where giardiasis is the main threat, water filters alone can be used. They are an acceptable alternative to iodine or boiling for ridding water of parasites and bacteria. When traveling or trekking overseas, however, you may be advised not to rely upon filters because they may not eliminate viruses. The Wilderness Medical Society states, "Filtration may be used for giardia and . . . bacteria, but for field use, filtration is not practical for viruses (although many are removed by adhering to larger particles)."

Should everyone drinking unsafe water in third world countries use iodine, chlorine, or boiling to guarantee protection against viruses? Or rely on bottled water? Just what illnesses do viruses cause that we must guard against? Consider:

➢ The most dangerous water-borne virus to avoid is polio, but this disease is effectively prevented by immunization. Hepatitis A, also caused by a virus, can be prevented by the hepatitis A vaccine.

➢ The most common illness-causing viruses are the Norwalk and Rotaviruses. These cause vomiting and watery diarrhea, but except for dehydration in

children, and sometimes the elderly, viral gastroenteritis is usually not considered a serious problem. In 1999, a Rotavirus vaccine will be available.
➢ Water-borne viral hepatitis E is common in Asia, northern and sub-Saharan Africa, and the eastern Mediterranean. Most people recover completely. In pregnant women, however, the fatality rate is 15%–20%.

Recommendations

The considerations above lead the *HealthGuide* to recommend the following:

1. All travelers should be fully immunized against polio and hepatitis A.
2. Pregnant women in regions endemic for the hepatitis E virus should drink only commercially bottled or boiled water, or water treated with chlorine or iodine. A water purifier with a demand-release iodine-matrix attachment can be used, but these units should not be employed for more than three weeks continuously as the sole source of drinking water because of the high levels of residual iodine in the treated water. Iodine tablets can be used short-term to purify water.
3. Infants, young children, and the elderly should take the above precautions in order to avoid intestinal viral infections that cause dehydration.

In reality, many travelers may want to have both a water filter and a chemical disinfectant to use as local sanitary conditions, itinerary, length of stay, convenience, and personal preference dictate. One technology doesn't necessarily exclude the other. Each method has advantages and disadvantages. You may not have your filter or purifier with you at all times. It may clog or break, or you may not have a replacement filter element. Likewise, you may lose your taste for iodine, or perhaps you may run out of chlorine or iodine. Whatever the scenario, you may need a backup method of water disinfection.

Remember that no matter what system you use to disinfect water, travelers' diarrhea is still a threat because it is also caused by the consumption of contaminated food and by the person-to-person transmission of microorganisms. Water disinfection, therefore, only reduces your risk of illness—it doesn't eliminate it entirely.

WATER DISINFECTION

Obtaining Clear Water

If you are drawing water from a polluted source, it may be grossly contaminated with organic material. For aesthetic reasons alone, you wouldn't want to drink cloudy, scummy water. Furthermore, cloudy water requires more time and bigger doses of chemicals to disinfect, especially if it is cold. Chlorine, in particular, reacts with, and is neutralized by, organic material such as rotting vegetation. Unless you are literally dying of thirst, you should take enough time to clarify your drinking water before it is treated. Here are some techniques:

Sedimentation—Let the turbid water stand undisturbed for several hours, then pour off the upper, clear portion. This works best if the cloudiness is due to sand, silt, or other inorganic material.

Flocculation—Organic impurities may not sediment out with gravity alone. Add a pinch of alum (available over the counter in drug stores) and mix. Flocculation (clumping) of suspended organic impurities will occur, and these clumped particles will settle to the bottom of the container. Pour off the clarified water. To save time, pour the water through a coffee filter, commercial filter paper, fine cloth, or a canvas filter bag to remove the flocculated sediment more rapidly.

Filtering—Ceramic and glass fiber filters that filter bacteria and parasites also filter out turbidity, but clogging will occur. Ceramic filters can be cleaned many more times than glass fiber filters. Prefilters on the intake hose should be used to eliminate large particles.

Methods of Disinfecting Water

Boiling water—Water that is brought just to a boil and then allowed to cool is safe to consume. Boiling water for 10 to 20 minutes, even at high altitudes, is unnecessary and wastes time and fuel. Some people even question the need to boil water at all—they just "pasteurize" it by heating it for a period of time at a subboiling temperature. To kill cholera germs, for example, boiling is not necessary. Heating contaminated water to 144°F (62°C) for 10 minutes is sufficient to eliminate completely all strains of this bacterium.

NOTE: Boiling water at 10,000 feet raises its temperature to an adequate 194°F (90°C).

Advantages of boiling—Boiling water completely eliminates bacteria, cysts of parasites (amoebic, giardia, cryptosporidia), worm larvae that cause schistosomiasis, and viruses (the cause of hepatitis, polio, and viral gastroenteritis). Briefly boiling water won't eliminate the spores of certain bacteria; hence, the water can't be considered absolutely sterile. However, bacterial spores, should they be in the water, don't cause intestinal illness and can be consumed without harm.

Disadvantages of boiling—Boiling is easier said than done. Heating the water is time-consuming, often inconvenient, and may require you to carry a source of fuel with you. Boiling is usually most easily done at a base camp, not on the trail. Other technologies of water disinfection now make the tedious process of boiling water often unnecessary.

Iodine and chlorine—Under proper conditions, both iodine and chlorine are excellent water disinfectants for eliminating bacteria and viruses; they are less effective, or even ineffective, against parasites, especially when contact time is brief and/or the water is cloudy and cold.

Iodine has been used to disinfect water since the turn of the century and is still the lightest, cheapest, simplest method of water purification. U.S. Army studies have demonstrated that under field conditions (dirty, cold water; a 10-minute contact time) iodine completely kills bacteria, parasites, viruses, and worm larvae. However, that was before *Cryptosporidium* came along. The one serious drawback to iodine is that it does not kill crypto. Unlike all other microorganisms (bacteria, viruses, giardia) that iodine effectively eliminates, cryptosporidium is a supercyst with an extremely durable shell. The only way to eliminate it is by either boiling or filtering the water.

Iodine tablets—Tablets usually have a long shelf life, even under adverse conditions, and they won't stain your pack or clothing if spilled. Tablets are also convenient and quite safe even if swallowed.

Disadvantage: Many people object to the iodine taste. Travelers should avoid prolonged use (more than 3 weeks) of iodine-treated water (as the sole source of drinking water) to avoid potential suppression of thyroid function. This limitation of iodine intake is especially important during pregnancy because of the potential adverse effects on fetal thyroid gland development. However, iodine should be used by pregnant women if there is no other short-term alternative to purifying water, especially in areas endemic for hepatitis E.

Liquid chlorine bleach (4% to 6% Clorox)—Household bleach is easily available and cheap, but doesn't kill crypto and may not kill giardia or cyclospora cysts, especially if the water is cloudy or cold. Add 2–3 drops of chlorine bleach to each quart of water if it is clear and from the tap; add 4–6 drops if the water is cloudy or not from the tap. Wait at least 30 minutes before drinking.

Pristine—This unique water treatment system can provide safe water anywhere in the world. Pristine uses chlorine dioxide (not chlorine) to eliminate bacteria, viruses, and protozoa, including Giardia and Cryptosporidium. Chlorine dioxide is widely used as a disinfectant and sanitizer by municipal water treatment facilities.

The Pristine Water Treatment System

Water Filters and Purification Devices

A filter's basic task sounds deceptively simple: Remove organisms and other particles larger than a specified size from water. This mission isn't so easy, given the small size and variety of pathogenic microorganisms that can be encountered, and a variety of filters has therefore evolved: ceramic filters, depth filters, surface filters, and depth filters with an attached iodine element. These filters all come with a rating of their pore size, which determines what size particles can be physically removed. Pore sizes are measured in microns, and the period at the end of this sentence is about 600 microns across. In commercial terms, the most important number is the "absolute" pore size rating, which means the filter element will pass no particle above a certain size. These absolute ratings are much more meaningful than the vaguely defined "nominal" ratings that filter manufacturers sometimes use.

To strain out common parasites, such as giardia, a pore size no larger than 4.0 microns is necessary. (Protozoa range in size from 5 to 15 microns.) For bacteria that range in size from 0.2 microns to 10 microns an absolute pore size of 0.2 microns is understandably desirable. Unfortunately, a filter this fine is subject to more rapid clogging and will require more frequent cleaning. (A prefilter will help reduce clogging.) Because viruses can be as small as 0.0004 microns, no field device that relies entirely on filtration will remove them.

Some filters have been designed to filter out only larger organisms such as parasites and worm larvae. These devices are sold primarily to backpackers who want to avoid giardiasis. Many international travelers, however, now opt for complete protection and choose a unit that will also remove bacteria and viruses. Because a filter alone won't take out viruses, many of them now come with an attached demand-release iodine-resin element. The filter is then turned into what is called a purification device.

How the demand-release iodine system works—Iodide ions are bound to an anion exchange resin, creating an electrically charged structure. When negatively charged microorganisms contact the resin, iodine is instantly released, penetrating the microorganism. By this process, bacteria and viruses, and some parasites, are killed. However, the residual iodine in the water may have a concentration of 10 mg/liter, which is significant considering that the RDA (recommended daily allowance) of iodine is only 0.15 mg/day.

NOTE: A Peace Corps study published in 1998 in the medical journal *Lancet* described a group of Peace Corps volunteers in Niger who used two-stage iodine-resin filters for more than 24 months as the sole source of potable water. Forty-six percent developed enlarged thyroid glands (goiter) and 34% had abnormalities of thyroid function, primarily elevated thyrotropin (TSH) levels. The authors' recommendation (personal communication) is not to use an iodine-resin filter as the sole source of potable water for more than 3 weeks in any 6-month period. In view of this recent finding, the *HealthGuide* also recommends that travelers, especially if they are pregnant, attach a carbon cartridge third stage to any iodine-resin two-stage filter/purifier in order to reduce residual iodine in the treated water.

Choosing a filter/purification device—Aside from removal of microoganisms, you need to consider the following factors in choosing one of these devices: (1) rated output in liters/minute, (2) life of filter/purifier element before replacement, (3) the size and weight of unit with accessories, (4) cost, not only of the device but also of the replacement filter, and (5) whether a carbon cartridge can be attached to reduce residual iodine and other chemicals in the filtered water.

NOTE: There are some purification units that contain only an iodine-resin matrix, which is fine for eliminating bacteria and viruses, but these units won't necessarily kill parasites, such as crypto or giardia. By the same token, filters that remove bacteria and parasites won't eliminate viruses. However, depending upon your itinerary, and the degree of potential exposure to various waterborne diseases, either of these types of devices might be appropriate.

Khan LK, Li R, Gootnick D, et al. Thyroid abnormalities related to iodine excess from water purification units. Lancet 1998;352:1519.
Backpacker Magazine. March 1994.

5 Travelers' Diarrhea
and Rehydration Therapy

Diarrhea is by far the most common medical problem among people traveling to lesser-developed tropical and semitropical countries. Travelers' diarrhea, however, is not a specific disease. The term describes the symptoms of an intestinal infection caused by certain bacteria, parasites, or viruses that are transmitted by the consumption of contaminated food or water. The severity and duration of symptoms depend upon which microorganism is causing the illness.

Your Risk of Getting Travelers' Diarrhea
Your risk is related to which countries you visit, the month or season of your visit, the duration of your visit, and possibly how often you eat in restaurants. (In fact, some studies show that poor restaurant hygiene may be the source of most cases of travelers' diarrhea.)

There is little risk (attack rate about 4%) when visiting North America, northern and central Europe, Australia, and New Zealand. Intermediate attack rates (8%–20%) are found in travelers to most destinations in the Caribbean, southern Europe, Israel, Japan, and South Africa. High-risk destinations (attack rates up to 60% during the first two weeks) include Mexico and the developing countries of Africa, South and Central America, the Middle East, and Asia.

One attack of travelers' diarrhea won't "immunize" you against further episodes. In fact, the attack rate in long-term travelers and expatriates remains unchanged for the first two years after arrival.

Symptoms of Travelers' Diarrhea
In general, travelers' diarrhea presents in one of three ways: (1) as an acute, watery diarrhea, (2) as dysentery, or (3) as chronic diarrhea.

1. Watery diarrhea—This is the most common form of travelers' diarrhea, affecting up to 60% of travelers. Most cases of watery diarrhea, worldwide, are caused by a bacterium called enterotoxigenic (toxin-producing) *E. coli.* Other bacterial causes of watery diarrhea include salmonella, campylobacter, and vibrio bacteria. About 5%–10% of cases are caused by intestinal viruses.

The symptoms range from several loose or watery stools per day to a more explosive illness with profuse, but nonbloody, diarrhea. Associated symptoms often include nausea, vomiting, abdominal cramps, and a low-grade fever. These symptoms, if untreated, usually last three to five days. For travelers, this is a major cause of inconvenience and discomfort, potentially ruining a carefully planned vacation or business trip.

The main medical danger from profuse diarrhea is dehydration, especially in children and the elderly. Early treatment with fluids and antibiotics is usually successful.

2. Dysentery (bloody diarrhea)—Up to 15% of travelers are affected by dysentery. Dysentery results from a more serious intestinal infection caused by certain bacteria (and sometimes parasites) that invade and inflame the wall of the intestine. The most common type of dysentery is bacillary dysentery, also called shigellosis, which is caused by certain species of shigella bacteria. Other bacterial microorganisms that can cause dysentery include salmonella, campylobacter *(C. jejuni)*, yersinia, and *E. coli* serotype 0157:H7. A rare form of dysentery is amebic dysentery (amebiasis), caused when *E. histolytica* parasites invade the colon wall.

Dysentery is typically recognized by the presence of bloody diarrhea (or bloody stools mixed with mucus), fever, abdominal pain and tenderness, and prostration.

If you get the symptoms of dysentery, you should start antibiotic treatment (as described below), drink sufficient fluids to prevent dehydration, and seek medical attention. If your symptoms are severe, or if you don't improve with antibiotics, you should see a doctor immediately—you may need to be hospitalized.

3. Chronic diarrhea—3% to 5% of travelers develop chronic diarrhea, defined as diarrhea lasting more than one month. Chronic diarrhea may be accompanied by vague abdominal pain, bloating, nausea, loss of appetite, fatigue, weight loss, and low-grade fever.

If there is an infectious cause, chronic travelers' diarrhea is usually due to giardiasis, a parasitic disease discussed in Chapter 9. A recent Belgian study reported that giardia and campylobacter (*C. jejuni*) are the two most commonly found infectious causes of chronic diarrhea. Other unusual causes of chronic diarrhea include amebiasis, cryptosporidiosis, and cyclosporiasis, caused by the recently discovered parasite, *Cyclospora cayetanensis*.

However, diagnosed infections account for a minority of the causes of chronic travelers' diarrhea. Postinfectious lactose intolerance and irritable bowel syndrome appear to be the most common causes of chronic bowel symptoms in returning travelers.

If you develop chronic diarrhea, consult with your physician or an infectious disease specialist. Testing should be done to try to establish a precise diagnosis, but in many cases all diagnostic tests are negative, and no definite diagnosis can be made. If medical consultation is not available, assume that you may have giardiasis and self-treat with metronidazole (Flagyl) or tinidazole (Fasigyn is available overseas). Also consider furazolidone (Furoxone)—this antibiotic is effective against both bacterial and parasitic causes of diarrhea.

NOTE: Giardiasis, unlike amebiasis, does not cause bloody diarrhea.

Causes and Geographic Variations of Travelers' Diarrhea

The four principal bacterial microorganisms causing travelers' diarrhea in most high-risk areas are *E. coli*, shigella species, salmonella species, and campylobacter.

Temperature; annual rainfall; presence or absence of rivers, lakes, or seacoasts; dry and rainy seasons (monsoons); and other geographic and climatic factors—as well as agricultural, eating, and sanitary practices—will determine which diarrhea-causing bacteria are most common in any particular country, or part of a country. For example, in Thailand, after *E. coli*, salmonella and campylobacter bacteria are most prevalent; in Nepal, after *E. coli*, shigella and campylobacter are the most common diarrhea-causing bacteria. In Mexico, *E. coli*, salmonella, and shigella predominate in the rainy summer season, whereas campylobacter is more common in the drier winter season.

These studies show that globally the causes of infectious diarrhea are not fixed and that each region has a unique pattern of disease.

Travelers' Diarrhea Facts

- Bacteria cause about 80% of travelers' diarrhea.
- Contaminated food causes more illness than contaminated water.

PREVENTING TRAVELERS' DIARRHEA

Food and Drink Precautions—Do They Work?

It is commonly believed that your chances of gastrointestinal illness will be reduced by being counseled to "boil it, cook it, peel it, or forget it." Surveys of returning travelers, however, have shown that receiving advice about food and drink safety appears to have no significant effect on rates of diarrhea. In fact, the overwhelming majority of travelers will commit a food and beverage indiscretion within 72 hours after arrival in a developing country, despite predeparture counseling. Why is this? In some cases, the choice of food may not be under the traveler's control, but it may also be that many people just can't overcome the temptation to sample delicacies in exotic locations. Most travelers find it difficult, impractical, or impossible to resist well-presented, mouth-watering buffets or to eat only piping-hot foods. Perhaps then, to the adage quoted above, should be added the words "easy to remember . . . impossible to do!"

Does this mean that travelers should throw caution to the wind and simply forget about prudent dietary habits? Not at all. The medical literature shows a definite correlation between dietary indiscretions and the frequency of travelers' diarrhea. If you can overcome temptation and stick to safe eating habits, you can significantly reduce your chance of illness. For many, though, this can be a difficult task.

NOTE: An important benefit of prudent eating habits is also the prevention of diseases other than travelers' diarrhea. Depending on your itinerary, you could be at risk for acquiring food- and drink-transmitted diseases such as hepatitis A and E, typhoid fever, trichinosis, tapeworm disease, anisakiasis, clonorchiasis, paragonimiasis, and fascioliasis. These are souvenirs you don't want to bring home!

The impracticality of following rigid dietary precautions during international travel is a compelling argument for all travelers to carry standby antimotility drugs and antibiotics for self-treatment of diarrhea and for a minority of high-risk travelers to take prophylactic antibiotics.

Handwashing

Before eating, always wash your hands with soap and water (or use an antibacterial towelette). This helps prevent diarrhea-causing bacteria or parasites being transferred to your food or mouth.

Drug Prophylaxis for Travelers' Diarrhea

Self-treatment for travelers' diarrhea has become so predictably effective that most physicians no longer recommend drug prophylaxis against diarrhea except in immunocompromised travelers or when the trip is deemed critical. You might consider prophylaxis with either Pepto-Bismol or antibiotics if you will be traveling short-term (less than three weeks) and cannot afford to have your trip interrupted, or travel plans altered, because of illness. You might be, for example, a businessperson, diplomat, musician, or athlete who can't afford to miss even one hour of an important meeting or event.

Or, you might have a medical condition that would be adversely affected by any additional illness. Medical conditions warranting consideration of prophylaxis would include cancer, AIDS, severe inflammatory bowel disease (colitis), and brittle insulin-dependent diabetes. If you also have peptic ulcer disease and take a stomach acid-reducing drug (e.g., Zantac, Tagamet, Pepcid, or Prilosec), your risk of travelers' diarrhea is increased. Consider switching your anti-ulcer drug to Carafate (sucralfate). This may actually reduce your risk of diarrhea because Carafate has antibacterial properties.

Pepto-Bismol—Taking Pepto-Bismol (bismuth subsalicylate) can reduce your chances of getting travelers' diarrhea by about 65% (compared with 90% efficacy for antibiotics). This is a good prophylactic drug for adult travelers and older children because not only is it quite effective, but there is minimal chance of an allergic or toxic reaction, as sometimes caused by antibiotics.

How does it work? Medical studies indicate that Pepto-Bismol actually eliminates harmful bacteria from the stomach. This antibacterial action is due to the bismuth component of the medication. The salicylate in Pepto-Bismol has an antisecretory and anti-inflammatory effect on the bowel wall, reducing the output of diarrheal fluid.

Dosage: 2 tablets (or 2 oz. of the liquid), 4 times daily. Take with meals and at bedtime. The tablet form of Pepto-Bismol is as effective as the liquid preparation, and the tablets are easier to carry.

Children's dosage: Pepto-Bismol can be used by children older than three years. They should use one-half the adult dose. For using Pepto-Bismol in a child under age three, consult with your pediatrician.

NOTE: 2 tablespoons or tablets of Pepto-Bismol has the salicylate content of about one adult aspirin tablet.

Pepto-Bismol is most effective when taken with meals because if the food is contaminated the drug comes into immediate contact with the microorganisms.

Contraindications: Pepto-Bismol should be avoided by people who (1) are allergic to, or intolerant of, aspirin, (2) have any type of bleeding disorder, (3) are taking an anticoagulant (warfarin, [Coumadin]), or (4) have a history of peptic ulcer disease or gastrointestinal bleeding.

Side effects: Pepto-Bismol causes blackening of the tongue and stool, but this is not harmful. Excessive use can cause ringing in the ears (tinnitus), due to salicylate toxicity. Don't take aspirin and Pepto-Bismol simultaneously—the risk of salicylate toxicity (tinnitus, easy bruising) will be increased. If you are on a warfarin anticoagulant (e.g., Coumadin), you should not take Pepto-Bismol because the chance of bleeding will be increased.

Check with your doctor about the safety of Pepto-Bismol if you have any chronic condition for which you are taking medication. Pepto-Bismol should not be taken with doxycycline since it can prevent the absorption of the latter. Pepto-Bismol may also inhibit the absorption of other antibiotics but the extent of this interaction has not been well studied.

Prophylactic antibiotics—Taking an antibiotic (especially one of the quinolones) can significantly reduce your risk of travelers' diarrhea. However, since all antibiotics have potential side effects, physicians are hesitant to prescribe them routinely to healthy travelers. Also, if diarrhea occurs while taking the antibiotic, then what should you do? It can be argued that an antibiotic, such as a quinolone, should not be used for prophylaxis when it is also the treatment of choice, and therefore should be reserved for that purpose.

Prophylactic antibiotics are not generally recommended for children; Pepto-Bismol is safer for them.

Pepto-Bismol combined with standby antibiotics—Before insisting on prophylactic antibiotics, be aware that the quinolone antibiotics (below) are rapidly effective in the treatment of most cases of diarrhea. In fact, a quinolone usually stops diarrhea within 10 hours or less. Therefore, if you take Pepto-Bismol prophylactically, and carry the antibiotic in reserve, you can significantly reduce your chance of travelers' diarrhea and at the same time preserve the therapeutic option of an antibiotic. Pepto-Bismol prophylaxis, combined with quick antibiotic treatment, as needed, is a reasonable choice for most travelers requesting prophylaxis. The main problem with Pepto-Bismol is that you need to take it four times a day, and you might not always remember to take all those doses.

NOTE: Don't take Pepto-Bismol and an antibiotic simultaneously—the absorption of the antibiotic may be impaired. Wait 2 hours after the dose is taken.

Antibiotics Used to Prevent Travelers' Diarrhea

Norfloxacin (Noroxin)	400 mg daily
Ciprofloxacin (Cipro)	500 mg daily
Ofloxacin (Floxin)	400 mg daily
Levofloxacin (Levaquin)	500 mg daily

TREATMENT OF TRAVELERS' DIARRHEA

The treatment of travelers' diarrhea (depending upon the severity) consists of one or more of the following:

- Fluids
- Pepto-Bismol (bismuth subsalicylate)
- Loperamide (Imodium-AD)
- Antibiotics
- Hospitalization should be considered in cases with dehydration and toxicity.

Fluids

If you are having frequent, copious diarrhea, dehydration is a potential threat and you may need treatment with an oral rehydration solution, as described in the special section "Oral Hydration Therapy" starting on page 88. If your diarrhea is not particularly severe, then follow these guidelines:

Mild/moderate diarrhea: Adults—If your diarrhea is of large volume and watery, you have more risk of dehydration. Continue with your regular diet (soup and salted crackers are good additions) and drink at least 3–4 liters of fluid (mostly water) daily, or more if you are in a hot climate. Avoid dairy products (milk and cheese) during the acute phase of diarrhea.

Mild diarrhea: Infants—They should continue to receive their regular formula or food and full amounts of whatever liquids they normally consume. Start oral rehydration solutions if the diarrhea becomes more severe.

Pepto-Bismol (bismuth subsalicylate)

In addition to its role in prophylaxis, Pepto-Bismol (bismuth subsalicylate), in conjunction with oral rehydration therapy, can also be used for the treatment of travelers' diarrhea. Pepto-Bismol reduces the number of unformed stools by 50% through its antimicrobial, antisecretory, and anti-inflammatory actions. Bloody diarrhea (dysentery) is not a contraindication to the use of Pepto-Bismol.

Adult dosage: 2 tablets or 2 tablespoonfuls (1 dose cup, 30 ml), repeated hourly, as needed. Do not exceed a total dose of 16 tablets, or 8 oz. of the liquid, in any 24-hour period. Don't take aspirin at the same time you are taking Pepto-Bismol since salicylate toxicity could occur. Use acetaminophen (Tylenol) if you need medication for pain or fever while taking Pepto-Bismol. If your diarrhea is not adequately controlled with Pepto-Bismol in 6–12 hours, discontinue the medication and start antibiotics.

Pediatric use: A study reported in the *New England Journal of Medicine* June 1993 (reference on page 74) has shown the efficacy of bismuth subsalicylate (BSS) along with oral rehydration for the treatment of infantile diarrhea. Infants given 100–150 mg/kg/day of BSS had significant reductions in their total stool output, total intake of oral rehydration solution, and duration of hospitalization. (Levels of bismuth and salicylate in the blood were well below levels considered toxic.)

Child dosage:

>12 years	2 tbsp. (1 dose cup, 30 ml)
9–12 years	1 tbsp. (1/2 dose cup, 15 ml)
6–9 years	2 tsp. (1/3 dose cup, 10 ml)
3–6 years	1 tsp. (1/6 dose cup, 5 ml)
<3 years	1/2 tsp. every 4 hours for a maximum of 6 doses/24 hours

Over age 3: Repeat dose hourly, as needed, to a maximum of 8 doses in any 24-hour period. Temporary, harmless darkening of the stools may occur. Do not give this medication if the child has chickenpox or the flu because of the slight risk of Reye's syndrome. NOTE: To date, Reye's syndrome has not been associated with the use of nonaspirin salicylates such as found in bismuth subsalicylate.

Loperamide

Loperamide (Imodium-AD) reduces diarrhea (both the frequency of passage of stools and the duration of illness) by up to 80%. Its action is due to its antimotility effect (reducing peristalsis) as well as its antisecretory effect (blocking the bowel's output of salt and water).

Adult dosage: 2 capsules (4 mg) immediately, then 1 capsule after each loose or watery stool. Don't take more than 8 capsules over any 24-hour period. Don't take loperamide if you have bloody diarrhea or a high fever.

Child dosage: Young infants and children appear to be more susceptible to side effects such as paralytic ileus, vomiting, and drowsiness. If loperamide is used in older children, a dose of 0.8 mg/kg/day divided into three equal doses is appropriate. Do not give loperamide to infants and children less than two years old unless you have consulted with your pediatrician.

NOTE: A theoretical concern about antimotility drugs is that they may prolong illness by interfering with the body's natural "flushing" mechanism. In reality, when travelers have used loperamide to treat watery diarrhea, no prolongation of illness has been observed, even when stool cultures have later shown the presence of an invasive microorganism (e.g., shigella). Nevertheless, some medical experts still advise you not to take loperamide if you have bloody diarrhea and/or a fever greater than 101°F. However, the *HealthGuide* believes that when a quinolone antibiotic (below) is administered with loperamide, the benefits of combined treatment outweigh any theoretical risk of adverse effects.

Loperamide Plus Antibiotics

The problem with loperamide, used alone, is that it does not treat the cause of the diarrhea—only the symptoms. Recent studies indicate that combining loperamide with an antibiotic is better therapy for diarrhea because it combines the antimotility action of the former with the curative effects of the latter. Studies in Mexico, for example, showed that when travelers took only loperamide for watery diarrhea, their immediate symptoms did improve but their diarrhea also lasted an average of 50 hours; when they took both loperamide and TMP/SMX, their diarrhea lasted an average of only 4.5 hours.

Antibiotics

The quinolone (fluoroquinolone) antibiotics have revolutionized the treatment of travelers' diarrhea. These antibiotics achieve very high fecal drug concentrations, and just one or two doses are often curative. There is, however, increasing evidence that antimicrobial resistance is on the rise as evidenced by 70% resistance of campylobacter to ciprofloxacin in Thailand.

The quinolones currently remain the first choice of treatment for all travelers, including pregnant women and children (see below). Alternative drugs include azithromycin, furazolidone, cefixime, and trimethoprim/sulfamethoxazole.

Which Quinolone to Use?

Ciprofloxacin and ofloxacin are the most frequently prescribed quinolones for the treatment of travelers' diarrhea. Levofloxacin has the advantage of once-a-day dosing. Nalidixic acid is the only quinolone available in liquid form. Ciprofloxacin, ofloxacin, and levofloxacin can be given intravenously if the patient is vomiting.

1. Ciprofloxacin (Cipro)—Ciprofloxacin has excellent activity against *E. coli* as well as bacteria causing dysentery (shigella, salmonella, campylobacter, and yersinia).
   Dosage: 500 mg twice daily for 1–3 days.
   Alternative dosage: 750 mg–1,000 mg as a single dose.
2. Ofloxacin (Floxin)—Ofloxacin is as effective as Cipro against diarrhea-causing bacteria but has better activity against certain other microorganisms, such as chlamydia and some of the Gram's-positive bacteria.
   Dosage: 400 mg twice daily for 1–3 days for diarrhea.
3. Levofloxacin (Levaquin)—This antibiotic is the active component of ofloxacin and has the advantage of once-daily dosing.
   Dosage: 500 mg once daily for 1–3 days.
4. Nalidixic acid (NegGram)—Available in liquid form and usually considered the best choice for the pediatric age group due to ease of administration.
   Adult dose: 1 gm 4 times daily.
   Child dose: Under age 12, the dosage is 50 mg/kg/day given in 4 equally divided doses. The manufacturer recommends this drug not be given to children under 3 months.

Although just one or two doses of a quinolone will terminate many cases of travelers' diarrhea, sometimes longer treatment is required. When diarrhea is caused by *Shigella dysenteriae* (a more virulent strain of shigella bacteria), a 5- to 7-day course of treatment is usually necessary.

Use in other infections—The quinolones are effective in urinary infections and all are generally effective for the treatment of typhoid fever. Ofloxacin and levofloxacin are more effective than ciprofloxacin against community acquired pneumonia, acute bacterial exacerbations of chronic bronchitis, uncomplicated skin infections, and uncomplicated pelvic inflammatory disease due to gonorrhea and chlamydia.

Alternative Drugs Used to Treat Travelers' Diarrhea

Azithromycin (Zithromax)—This antibiotic is effective against shigella, salmonella, *E. coli*, and campylobacter and it has also shown activity against typhoid fever. In Thailand, azithromycin has shown more effectiveness against campylobacter than ciprofloxacin.

Adult dosage: 2 tablets (500 mg) daily for 3 days.

Child dosage: 10 mg/kg/day for 3 days.

Cefixime (Suprax)—This is a cephalosporin antibiotic that is effective against most bacteria causing infectious diarrhea, but there have been reports of shigella resistance. Cefixime is also a useful drug for treating ear infections (otitis media), pharyngitis and tonsillitis, acute bacterial bronchitis, urinary tract infections, and gonorrhea. It is available in a liquid form.

Adult dosage: 400 mg once daily for 3–5 days.

Child dosage: 8 mg/kg once daily for 3–5 days.

Furazolidone (Furoxone)—Although not as rapidly effective as the quinolones, furazolidone has activity against the majority of gastrointestinal pathogens, including *E. coli*, salmonella, shigella, campylobacter, and the vibrio species (which cause cholera). Furazolidone is also effective against giardia.

Adult dosage: 100 mg (1 tablet) 4 times daily for 3 days. For giardiasis, the drug should be given for 7–10 days.

Child dosage: Children 5 years and older should receive 25 to 50 mg (1/4 to 1/2 tablet) 4 times daily.

Liquid furazolidone contains 50 mg per tablespoonful (15 ml).

5 years and older—1/2 to 1 tbsp. 4 times daily.

1 to 4 years—1 to 1-1/2 tsp. 4 times daily.

1 month to 1 year—1/2 to 1 tsp. 4 times daily.

Not to be given to infants under age 1 month.

Trimethoprim/sulfamethoxazole (TMP/SMX, co-trimoxazole)—TMP/SMX is now considered a last-choice drug, to be used by the traveler who is allergic or intolerant to the other antibiotics mentioned in this section.

Adult dosage: One double-strength tablet every 12 hours for 1–3 days.

Child dosage: 8 mg/kg trimethoprim and 40 mg/kg sulfamethoxazole per 24 hours, given in 2 divided doses every 12 hours.

NOTE: TMP/SMX remains an effective treatment for cyclosporiasis.

Adult dosage (cyclosporiasis): One double-strength tablet every 12 hours for 7 days.

Metronidazole (Flagyl)—If you have diarrhea that persists longer than two weeks, you could be harboring giardia parasites. It is reasonable to start self-treatment for giardiasis if you will be unable to get timely medical consultation.

Adult dosage: 250 mg three times daily for 5 to 7 days. Don't drink alcohol when taking Flagyl—severe nausea and vomiting may occur.

Treatment of Children and Pregnant Women

Children—The quinolones are currently the most effective treatment for travelers' diarrhea. In some experimental animals, these compounds damage cartilaginous end plates of long bones, but there are no data that show a similar process in humans. In addition, children with cystic fibrosis and cancer have been treated with long courses of ciprofloxacin without apparent complications.

Many travel experts now believe that it is unacceptable that a child, who may be more likely to get travelers' diarrhea, become more dehydrated with it, and have a more prolonged illness, receive less effective treatment than an adult. The illness can result in significant suffering for the child and have a major impact on the travel experience for the whole family.

Standby treatment for children should consist of either ciprofloxacin or azithromycin. Ciprofloxacin may be the preferred agent. As it is not licensed for use in children in the United States or Canada, careful discussion with parents is necessary, weighing the very low risks of giving ciprofloxacin for a very short course against the need for an effective, proven therapeutic agent.

When using ciprofloxacin for children, give 20 to 30 mg/kg/day, divided into 2 doses per day, for 3 days. When using azithromycin for children, to prescribe 10 mg/kg po, once daily for 3 days.

Pregnant women—The same reasoning also justifies the use of quinolones during pregnancy. If antibiotic treatment of diarrhea is indicated, then the most effective drug should be used, especially if the women could face a prolonged illness with toxicity and dehydration. According to the Physicians Desk Reference (PDR), "quinolones should be used during pregnancy only if the potential benefit justifies the potential risk to the fetus." In other words, quinolones are *not* contraindicated during pregnancy (as some authorities would have you believe); they should be administered when maternal illness clearly may harm the fetus.

Standby treatment for pregnant women should also consist of either ciprofloxacin or azithromycin.

Always follow this principle: The mother's health takes priority. In the case of infectious diarrhea, if her illness is severe, treatment with a quinolone antibiotic should not be withheld simply because of a theoretical concern about risk to the fetus.

Summary of Treatment of Travelers' Diarrhea

- Treatment options for travelers' diarrhea include Pepto-Bismol (bismuth subsalicylate), Imodium (loperamide), antibiotics, and antibiotics combined with loperamide. If your symptoms are relatively mild, you could start treatment with Imodium and/or Pepto-Bismol. If you are not better after 4 to 6 hours, start antibiotics, preferably a quinolone.
- If you have copious or explosive diarrhea, take an antibiotic *and* loperamide immediately. Start oral rehydration therapy (see below). A 1–3 day course of a quinolone antibiotic combined with loperamide is usually curative. Take the antibiotic, as prescribed, but don't take loperamide more than 24–48 hours.
- Always treat dysentery (bloody diarrhea, high fever) with antibiotics.
- Quinolones are the most effective antibiotics and should not be withheld from pregnant women or children, especially from those who have dysentery or severe diarrhea with dehydration.
- Azithromycin, furazolidone, cefixime, and ceftriaxone are alternative choices, particularly for pregnant women and infants/children, but are generally less effective than a quinolone.
- Furazolidone acts somewhat slower than the quinolones but has the advantage of also being effective against giardia parasites.
- Diarrhea danger signs include bloody diarrhea, high fever, persistent vomiting, severe abdominal pain, prostration, and dehydration. Seek qualified medical care if your symptoms are not improved after 24 hours of antibiotic treatment, or if you are becoming dehydrated.
- Prevent dehydration. The addition of soup or broth, salted crackers, and extra water to your diet will maintain hydration while also providing nutrients. If you have copious diarrhea, follow the instructions in this chapter for preparing and administering oral rehydration solutions.
- If you have mostly vomiting—and minimal diarrhea—sipping plenty of slightly salty fluids and taking Pepto-Bismol is a good treatment.
- About 10% of chronic diarrhea is caused by a parasitic disease such as giardiasis or amebiasis. Treat with metronidazole (Flagyl), furazolidone (Furoxone), or tinidazole. Trimethoprim/sulfamethoxazole is effective against cyclosporiasis.
- Antacids containing magnesium, aluminum, or calcium; sucralfate; iron tablets; or multivitamins containing iron or zinc may interfere with the absorption of the quinolone antibiotics. They should not be given concomitantly or within two hours of the administration of a quinolone.

SPECIAL ORAL REHYDRATION THERAPY SECTION

The initial treatment of moderate to severe travelers' diarrhea begins by replacing the salt and water lost through your intestinal tract. Severe watery diarrhea (as seen with cholera, for example) can cause life-threatening fluid losses from the intestine of one liter or more per hour. Treating dehydration of this magnitude is an urgent priority, especially in infants, young children, and the elderly. Early, vigorous treatment is even more important in hot, tropical climates where fluid requirements are higher. Hospitalization and intravenous fluid therapy is required if oral intake cannot keep up with fluid losses.

The first mistake that most people make when treating copious diarrhea is that they don't drink enough fluids. The second mistake they make is using the wrong fluids. They may drink salt-free, high-sugar beverages or a too-salty beverage without the correct glucose concentration necessary to optimize salt and water absorption. Not drinking enough, or using too much of the wrong fluids to treat severe diarrhea, can make matters worse, especially in infants.

On the other hand, you may be in a location (e.g., a hotel room in Khartoum at 3:00 a.m.) where you can't get the right fluids or the necessary ingredients (sodium and potassium-containing salts, a source of glucose or carbohydrate) to prepare a balanced solution. Under these circumstances, just about any kind of beverage (disinfected tap water, bottled water, tea, coffee, diluted soda pop, etc.) is better than no fluid replacement at all. This will buy enough time to procure the necessary ingredients and prepare a proper solution—or get to a medical treatment facility if you don't improve. First, though, review these basic facts about how the body absorbs salt and water.

Facts About Sugar, Salt, and Water
- Glucose (sugar) promotes water absorption. Your intestine first absorbs glucose by the process of active intestinal transport.
- Sodium absorption is coupled with glucose. One sodium molecule travels with each absorbed glucose molecule in an obligatory, linked fashion. The cotransport of sodium with glucose forms the basis for oral rehydration therapy.
- The absorbed glucose and sodium create an osmotic force that pulls water through the intestinal wall. The movement of water into the body is entirely passive.
- Maximum absorption of water occurs when the glucose concentration in a solution is about 2.5%.
- A high-sugar concentration in the intestine inhibits the absorption of water. Highly sweetened drinks, in fact, can increase intestinal fluid loss by causing osmotic diarrhea. Apple juice, Gatorade, nondiet cola drinks, and Jell-O have high glucose concentrations of 6% or more.
- Starchy foods (e.g., rice cereal, potatoes) also supply glucose, but in a form that

enhances the absorption of water. The lower intestinal osmotic pressure of a starch solution increases salt and water absorption, and decreases diarrheal volume as well as the duration of symptoms.
- Even in the presence of most diarrheal diseases, your intestine is still able to absorb glucose, salt, water, and other nutrients.

Oral Rehydration Solutions (ORS) for Travelers

WHO formula—Packets of World Health Organization (WHO) rehydration formula are widely used for the emergency treatment of dehydration, especially in infants and children. Just add the contents of a packet to a liter (or 4 cups) of potable water. The packets (photo right) contain the right balance of sodium, potassium, bicarbonate, and glucose and are favored by many travelers who want a quick, convenient source of full-strength ORS in an easy-to-carry form.

Quick ORS formula #1—If you don't have packets of ORS, you can prepare a basic emergency oral rehydration solution by adding one teaspoon of salt and 2–3 tablespoons of sugar or honey to a liter of water. Although lacking bicarbonate and potassium, the solution is easy to prepare and will effectively maintain blood volume and tissue hydration.

Quick ORS formula #2—Mix one 8-oz. cup of orange juice (or other fruit juice) with three cups of water and add one teaspoon of salt.

Carbohydrate- and Food-Based Rehydration Solutions

The glucose-based ORS solutions described above can keep you hydrated, but they do not decrease stool volume or shorten the duration of acute diarrhea. Cereal- and food-based ORS do both. They also supply up to four times more calories during a time when appetite may be suppressed. With cereal-based ORS, partially hydrolyzed cooked starches (complex carbohydrates) are broken down into glucose on the intestinal wall. Water and salts are better absorbed with less osmotic penalty.

CeraLyte—CeraLyte (photo right) contains rice carbohydrate, which more effectively promotes water absorption than glucose does. This product is available in lemon and chicken broth flavors and can be served hot or cold.

Food-based oral rehydration—If you don't have CeraLyte, you can prepare an effective homemade solution with these ingredients:

One liter of water

8 oz. mashed-up potato (about 1/2 pound). Cook the potato in the water and allow to cool. Then add:

1/2 tsp. salt

1/4 tsp. baking soda (provides bicarbonate)

1/4 tsp. salt substitute (provides potassium)

If you can't obtain baking soda or salt substitute, use 1 teaspoon of table salt per liter/quart of solution.

Treatment Technique for Older Children and Adults

Step 1. Vigorously treat dehydration. Drink 3–6 liters, or more, of full-strength oral rehydration solution over 2–4 hours. Don't stop ORS as soon as your thirst is quenched—drink enough to restore urine output.

Step 2. Diet and maintenance fluids—After replacement of fluid losses (rehydration), your energy and sense of well-being will improve. If you are not vomiting, start to eat (see below) and continue to drink fluids to maintain hydration. The best fluids are dilute fruit juices and water. If you are not eating, however, use half-strength ORS as a maintenance fluid.

Step 3. If watery diarrhea continues after rehydration, prevent recurrent dehydration by drinking 8–12 oz. of full-strength ORS each time you have a watery stool. Continue to eat and also consume water as thirst dictates.

Step 4. Start antibiotics. If you start treatment, especially with a quinolone antibiotic, chances are you will shorten your illness significantly.

Diet

Your intestine continues to absorb water and nutrients despite diarrhea. Food promotes the absorption of water and also stimulates intestinal enzyme activity. Remember that food, especially easy-to-digest starches, reduces the volume of diarrhea. Food enhances water absorption and is also a source of sodium and energy-providing calories.

Soup or broth, plus toast and/or salted crackers, is an excellent starting diet. (The best soups are lightly salted rice and noodle soups.) Also good are lightly salted oatmeal, cream of wheat, and Gerber Rice Cereal. The **BRAT diet** (bananas, rice, applesauce, toast) is well-tolerated and easy to prepare. With improvement, you can add lean meats and cooked vegetables. A regular diet can be resumed as soon as your appetite allows.

What Not to Eat and Drink

Omit dairy products (lactose may aggravate diarrhea). Also avoid other highly sweetened drinks (see below), coffee, alcoholic drinks, and high-fat foods.

Treatment Technique for Infants and Young Children

You should know when a child has the potential to become dehydrated. The history is critical: How long has the child been having diarrhea, and what is the frequency and volume? Has he or she also been unable to take oral fluids because of vomiting?

Signs of dehydration: Observe the child for increased thirst, lethargy, decreased urine output, and dry mucous membranes. Severe dehydration requires hospitalization and intravenous fluid therapy. Early, vigorous administration of ORS usually keeps a child from reaching this stage.

In general, children with diarrhea should continue to be fed, but you can interrupt these feedings until enough rehydration fluids have been administered. Give a dehydrated infant or child 1 to 1-1/2 oz. (30–45 ml) of ORS per pound of body weight. Administer this amount of fluid over 2–4 hours. A dehydrated 22-lb. infant, for example, might require as much as a quart of ORS during the first 2–4 hours of treatment. If the child is not vomiting, give ORS as rapidly as the infant or child will accept it. Use a spoon, dropper, or a baby bottle for infants. Some parents squirt the solution into the child's mouth with a small syringe (ask your doctor for one before leaving or purchase the EZY DOSE® syringe, or similar product; these are available in most pharmacies). Watch for the return of urine output and improvement in the child's appearance and behavior.

Vomiting—Don't let it deter you from giving ORS! Even if the child has been vomiting, you should be able to give 1 teaspoon (5 ml) of ORS about every minute. If available, use a syringe (see above), an infant bottle, or a medicine cup. Giving just a teaspoon of ORS every minute avoids stomach distention caused from too-rapid fluid administration, but can provide an hourly intake of 10 oz. (300 ml). This process often requires time and patience, and it may take you 4–6 hours to rehydrate a sick child. Seek medical care if vomiting continues to interfere with oral feedings and rehydration. Intravenous fluids may be necessary.

CAUTION: Don't give full-strength soft drinks or fruit juice to dehydrated infants or children as their only source of fluid replacement. The high sugar content of these solutions will draw water out of the intestine, increase diarrhea, worsen dehydration, and possibly lead to a condition called hypernatremia, where the blood sodium concentration is dangerously high. Typical drinks NOT to give for dehydration (although small amounts are OK) include the following:

Apple juice	Grape juice
Cola (Coke, Pepsi, etc.)	Jello
Gatorade	Orange juice
Ginger ale	7-Up

If you do give a dehydrated child a sugar-containing soft drink, be sure to dilute it 3:1 with water.

Refeeding Infants and Children After Rehydration

If your baby is breast-fed, continue breast-feeding. If the diarrhea gets worse, or if the child is vomiting, supplement feedings with the solutions described on the preceding pages.

If your baby is formula-fed, give breast milk or formula (dilute formula 1:1 with water). Cow's milk, if given, should be diluted 1:1 with water. **Early feeding is important**—the intestine continues to absorb water and nutrients despite diarrhea. The World Health Organization, in fact, advises parents *not* to stop giving infants with diarrhea their regular formula or food. Starving an infant (or yourself) to rest the intestine will only make matters worse.

Older infants and children—Restore a child's regular diet as soon as possible. After rehydration and cessation of vomiting, start the BRAT diet, mentioned earlier. Children, like adults, recover more quickly when fed.

Ansdell VE, Ericsson CD. Prevention and Empiric Treatment of Travelers' Diarrhea. Med. Clin. N. Am. 1999; 83:945–973.

Buck ML. Ciprofloxacin Use in Children: A Review of Recent Findings. Pediatric Pharmacotherapy 4(12) 1998.

DuPont HL, Ericsson CD. Prevention and treatment of travelers' diarrhea. N Engl J Med 1993;328:1821–27.

Ericsson CD. Travelers' Diarrhea. Epidemiology, Prevention, and Self-Treatment. Inf. Dis. Clin. N. Am. 1998;12: 285–304.

Figueroa-Quintanilla D, Salazar-Lindo E, Sack RB, et al. A controlled trial of bismuth subsalicylate in infants with acute watery diarrheal disease. N Engl J Med 1993 Jun 10;328(23):1653–8.

Helvaci M, Bektaslar D, Ozkaya B et al. Comparative efficacy of cefixime and ampicillin-sulbactam in shigellosis in children. Acta Paediatr Jpn 1998 Apr; 40(2):13–4.

Khan WA, Seas C, Dhar U, et al. Treatment of shigellosis: Comparison of azithromycin and ciprofloxacin. A double-blind, randomized, controlled trial. Ann Int Med 1997 May 1;**126**(9):697–703.

Kuschner R, Trofa AF, Thomas RJ, et al. Use of azithromycin for the treatment of campylobacter enteritis in travelers in Thailand, an area where ciprofloxacin resistance is prevalent. Clin Inf Dis 1995 Sep;21:536–541.

Leibovitz E, Janco J, Piglansky L, Press J, Yagupsky P, Reinhart H, Yaniv I, Dagan R. Oral ciprofloxacin vs. intramuscular ceftriaxone as empiric treatment of acute invasive diarrhea in children. Pediatr Infect Dis J 2000;19:1060-7.

Salam I, Katelaris P, Leigh-Smith S, et al. Randomized trial of single-dose ciprofloxacin for travelers' diarrhea. Lancet 1994;344:1537–39.

Salam MA, Seas C, Khan WA, Bennish ML. Treatment of shigellosis: IV. Cefixime is ineffective in shigellosis in adults. Ann Intern Med 1995 Oct 1;123(7): 505–8.

Schaad UB. Toxicity of quinolones in pediatric patients. Adv Antimicrob Antineoplast Chemother 1992;11:259–65.

Taylor DN, Connor BA, Shlim DR. Chronic Diarrhea in the Returned Traveler. Med. Clin. N. AM. 1999; 83:1033–1052.

6 Malaria

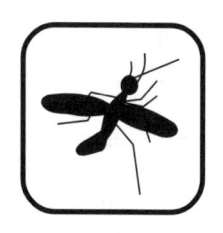

In 2000, more than 100 countries were considered malarious and this disease threatens nearly 40% of the world's population. Over 300 million acute episodes of illness occur every year, and it is estimated that over 270 million people are chronically infected with malaria parasites.

The World Health Organization (WHO) estimates that as many as 2.7 million people die each year of malaria. The vast majority of malaria deaths occur among young children in sub-Saharan Africa, especially in rural areas with inadequate or nonexistent health care services.

Each year over 7 million Americans travel to countries where malaria occurs and 1,000–1,500 cases are reported (though many more go unreported). While sub-Saharan Africa (except South Africa) is visited by only 2% of American travelers who visit countries where malaria exists, this region (especially East Africa) accounts for 83% of the cases.

Malaria is the most important parasitic disease that you will face in most tropical and subtropical countries. A delay in diagnosis and treatment can have fatal consequences. If you travel to a malarious region, there are five things you must do:

1. Become informed about your risk of acquiring malaria in that particular region.
2. Take measures to prevent mosquito bites. This very important malaria-prevention measure is often underutilized.
3. Take a prophylactic drug such as chloroquine (Aralen), mefloquine (Lariam), atovaquone/proguanil (Malarone), or doxycycline, if necessary. Don't skip prescribed doses.
4. Know the symptoms of malaria.
5. Seek immediate medical treatment if symptoms of malaria occur, especially if you are in, or have returned from, a country where falciparum malaria is endemic. Always consider malaria if you develop a fever after returning from a malarious area. Be aware that the symptoms of malaria can be delayed for weeks or months, sometimes years, after exposure and that you can sometimes get malaria even if you took an effective prophylactic drug. Ninety percent of U.S. and Canadian travelers who acquire malaria don't develop symptoms until after they return home.

Your Risk of Getting Malaria

It depends upon where you travel and can vary markedly from country to country. The risk of malaria can also vary within any particular destination because the disease may be transmitted only in certain locations within a country, during certain seasons, or below certain altitudes.

Various categories of travelers are also at different risk. Tourists staying in urban air-conditioned, mosquito-free hotels, for example, will usually be at less risk than travelers venturing into low-lying rural areas during the rainy season.

Table 5.1 shows disease rates worldwide. Travel to Oceania (Papua New Guinea, Solomon Islands, and Vanuatu) and sub-Saharan Africa entails the greatest risk, especially from the potentially-fatal *P. falciparum* malaria.

The risk also varies within these regions. The coast of East Africa carries more risk than the interior. In West Africa, the incidence of malaria is less than 2 cases per 1,000 travelers in Senegal and Gabon, 2 to 4 per 1,000 in Burkina Fasso, Ivory Coast, and Cameroon, and 4 to 7+ per 1,000 in Togo, Mali, Guinea, Benin, Congo, and the Central African Republic.

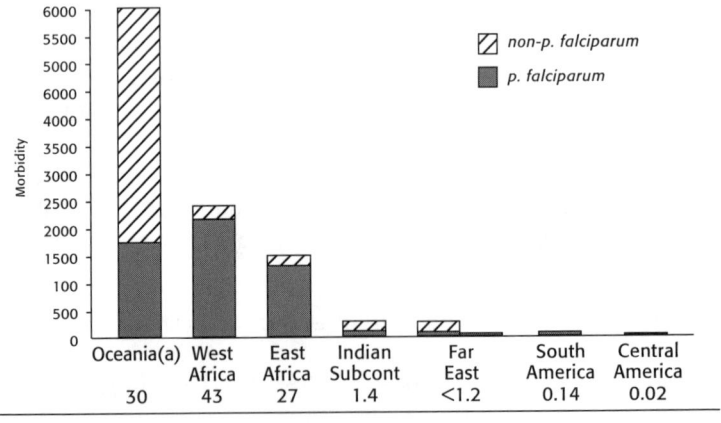

Region	Rate
Oceania(a)	30
West Africa	43
East Africa	27
Indian Subcont	1.4
Far East	<1.2
South America	0.14
Central America	0.02

(a) Solomon Islands, Vanuatu, Papua New Guinea

Table 5.1* Morbidity and Mortality in 100,000 nonimmune travelers exposed for 1 month without chemoprophylaxis.

* Steffen R, DuPont H. *Manual of Travel Medicine and Health.* Hamilton: B.C. Decker Inc. 1999:220.

There is intermediate risk on the Indian subcontinent and low risk in frequently visited tourist sites in Latin America and Southeast Asia. NOTE: some areas of Brazil, India, and Thailand carry increased risk.

Tropical Africa is a much higher-risk destination compared to Latin America and Asia for the following reasons:

- Tourists in Africa spend considerable time in rural areas such as game parks, where mosquito activity is high.

- Tourists in Latin America and Asia, however, spend more time in urban or resort areas, where there is little, if any, risk of exposure, and they usually travel to rural areas only during daytime hours when there is little malaria-transmitting mosquito activity.
- In Latin America and Asia, malaria transmission is more seasonal, or focally distributed in rural areas away from the usual tourist routes. For example, 52% of the 1.1 million malaria cases reported from the Americas in 1989 were from Brazil, but 97% of these cases were reported from three gold-mining areas rarely visited by tourists. In Asia (e.g., Thailand), most malaria occurs in remote forested areas—places where few tourists go.
- Malaria is transmitted in most large cities in sub-Saharan Africa, whereas almost all large cities in Latin America (with the exception of Guayaquil, Ecuador) and Southeast Asia are malaria-free. There is no malaria in Hong Kong, Bangkok, Kuala Lumpur, Jakarta, Singapore, Rangoon, Phnom-Penh, Manila, and most other major urban areas. There are some exceptions, such as urban areas of Papua New Guinea and some urban areas in India and Pakistan.
- Mosquitoes in Africa are more apt to be carrying malaria parasites. For example, the mean rate of infected anopheles mosquitoes in western Kenya may exceed 20%, whereas in Latin America and Asia less than 1% of anopheles mosquitoes are infected.

Malaria Fact

In countries where malaria occurs, the highest rates of transmission occur in low-lying rural areas during, and just after, the rainy season. In parts of Africa and Oceania, however, malaria transmission may be high year-round, even in urban areas.

The Cause of Malaria

Malaria is caused by a single-cell protozoan parasite of the genus Plasmodium. There are four different species of Plasmodium parasites that infect humans:

1. *Plasmodium falciparum*, which accounts for 40%–60% of malaria cases worldwide and >95% of all malaria deaths.
2. *Plasmodium vivax*, which causes 30%–40% of malaria cases worldwide, but is rarely fatal.
3. *Plasmodium ovale*, an uncommon parasite found mostly in West Africa.
4. *Plasmodium malariae*, also uncommon, but distributed worldwide.

Worldwide Distribution of Malaria Species

The occurrence of each plasmodium species varies from region to region.

P. falciparum causes 80%–95% of malaria in sub-Saharan Africa. It is also the most common species in Haiti and the Dominican Republic, the Amazon Basin, and parts of Oceania. In South America, outside the Amazon Basin, *P. falciparum*

Figure 5.1. The Cycle of Malaria Transmission

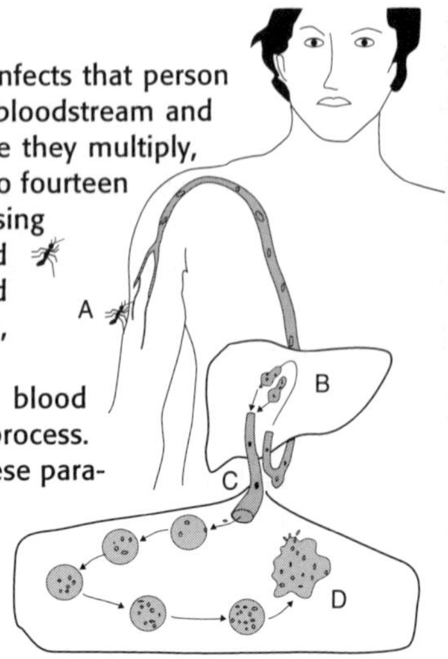

When the anopheles mosquito bites a victim (A) it infects that person with parasites, called sporozoites, which enter the bloodstream and travel rapidly (within 30 minutes) to the liver, where they multiply, producing daughter cells, called merozoites (B). Six to fourteen days later (approximately), the liver cells burst, releasing huge numbers of merozoites which invade red blood cells (C), where they multiply again, rupturing the red cells and releasing even more merozoites (D), triggering an attack of malaria.

The merozoite parasites released from the red blood cells then invade new red blood cells, continuing the process.

Infections with *P. vivax* and *P. ovale*: Some of these parasites (called hypnozoites) remain behind in the liver cells and can cause delayed attacks of malaria, months or years later.

NOTE: The common prophylactic drugs (chloroquine, mefloquine, doxycycline) eliminate malaria parasites only in the blood, at stages C and D. They don't prevent parasites from invading the liver and don't prevent multiplication of parasites within liver cells. They are called *suppressive* prophylactics. Proguanil, atavoquone, and primaquine DO prevent parasite development within the liver. For this reason, these drugs are called *causal* prophylactics.

---

accounts for 10%–50% of cases. *P. falciparum* is also common on the Indian subcontinent and in SE Asia.

P. vivax causes about 95% of malaria in Mexico and Central America and is also found in South America, North Africa, the Middle East, the Indian subcontinent, China, Asia, and Oceania. Except for Somalia and Ethiopia, vivax malaria is very rarely encountered in sub-Saharan Africa.

P. malariae causes up to 10%–15% of malaria in sub-Saharan Africa and 1%-5% of cases elsewhere, worldwide.

P. ovale is rare. It exists primarily in West Africa where it causes up to 5% of malaria, but it also occurs sporadically in Oceania and SE Asia.

Malaria is uncommon at high altitudes because reproduction of the parasites within the mosquito is temperature sensitive. For this reason, falciparum malaria rarely occurs over 1,000 meters (3250 feet) elevation. Vivax parasites, which are hardier, can reproduce at altitudes as high as 2,000 meters (6,500 feet).

How Malaria Is Transmitted

Malaria is only transmitted by female anopheles mosquitoes. They require a blood meal every 3–4 days to promote the fertilization and growth of their eggs. Worldwide, there are over 400 species of anopheles mosquitoes, of which 60 are known to transmit malaria.

Anopheles mosquitoes feed from dusk to dawn, so when evening comes you need to take extra measures to prevent bites. Not every mosquito transmits malaria, but it takes just one bite from an infective insect to give you the disease; therefore, even a brief trip to a malarious area can put you at risk.

How Malaria Causes Illness

After they are injected into the body by a feeding mosquito, malaria parasites first invade the liver, then the red blood cells (Figure 5.1), where they again multiply. When the parasite-filled red cells rupture, an attack of malaria occurs.

Falciparum malaria is the most serious and sometimes fatal form of malaria. The severity of *P. falciparum* infections is due to the high percentage of red blood cells (RBCs) that are infected by this particular plasmodium. In extreme infections, up to 80% of RBCs can be parasitized and destroyed. This massive red cell destruction has two primary effects: (1) severe anemia, and (2) clogging of the circulation to vital organs, particularly the brain and kidneys. This circulatory clogging occurs because the infected RBCs produce sticky projections that bind the cells to the walls of the small blood vessels (capillaries) and to other RBCs, forming obstructing clumps of cells (called rosettes). Also, chemicals (called cytokines) are released, causing fever, malaise, and other signs of inflammation.

In contrast, the three other forms of malaria are usually nonlethal. In malaria caused by *P. vivax, P. ovale,* and *P. malariae,* only about 1%–2% of RBCs become parasitized, and fatalities are rare.

Severe malaria occurs when more than 5% of RBCs are parasitized. Other criteria defining severe malaria include decreased consciousness (indicates cerebral malaria), severe anemia, hypoglycemia (low blood sugar), kidney/liver failure, pulmonary edema (fluid in the lungs), hyperthermia (high fever), and persistent vomiting and diarrhea.

If you are treated appropriately for malaria, you should improve within 48–72 hours. Indications of successful treatment include (1) reduction of fever and (2) at least a 75% reduction in the number of red blood cells that are parasitized.

Malaria Fact

Travelers do not become immune to malaria after having had the disease. There are no vaccines available at present.

Delayed Attacks of Malaria

If you have been bitten by mosquitoes transmitting *P. vivax* or *P. ovale,* you can have a delayed attack of malaria because some of these parasites (called hypnozoites) can remain dormant in your liver for many months, even years.

Prophylactic drugs such as chloroquine, mefloquine, and doxycycline only work in the blood to suppress the multiplication of parasites in RBCs. You're safe from an attack of malaria only as long as you take the suppressive (prophylactic) drug. To get rid of dormant liver parasites (*P. vivax, P. ovale*), you'll need to take another drug, primaquine, discussed later.

Fortunately, *P. falciparum* and *P. malariae* parasites don't have a dormant liver phase, so prophylaxis continued for 1 to 4 weeks after exposure usually gives your body enough time to eliminate them. However, inadequately suppressed *P. falciparum* or *P. malariae* can sometimes result in low-grade blood stream infections, leading to recurrence of symptoms. *P. malariae*, in fact, can cause infections lasting 25 years or more.

Symptoms of Malaria

Getting malaria makes you feel like you have the flu—only worse. Before an attack of malaria begins, you may have one or two days of headache, fatigue, loss of appetite, and a low-grade fever. The acute attack starts abruptly with chills, soon followed by a high fever, lasting 2–6 hours. During this time you may also notice pains in your chest, back, stomach, joints, and muscles. The attack ends with 2–3 hours of heavy sweating. If you are not treated promptly, symptoms will recur and complications may develop, especially if the attack is caused by *P. falciparum*. In some cases, malaria fevers recur periodically, every 48 to 72 hours.

NOTE: Malaria can occur as soon as seven days after an infective bite, and almost all cases of falciparum malaria occur within 60 days after the bite in people not taking a prophylactic drug or people using inadequate prophylaxis.

Other important causes of fever in the returned traveler include typhoid fever, dengue, brucellosis, hepatitis, urinary tract infections, tick typhus, and, rarely, amebic liver abscess.

Although a blood smear is required to make the final diagnosis, the most important aspect of diagnosis is always *to think of malaria as a possible cause of your illness*. This is especially important because not every case of malaria presents with the typical periodic fever pattern. If you are in a malarious area and you develop fever, and medical care is not available within 24–48 hours, it may be advisable for you to start self-treatment before a diagnosis is established. Self-treatment is discussed later, starting on page 115.

The self-test kit employs a 10-minute enzymatic assay to measure plasmodium LDH isoforms in a patient's blood. More details can be found at www.malariatest.com

Diagnosis

Malaria is diagnosed by observing under the microscope plasmodium parasites within red blood cells. This technique can also distinguish the more dangerous *P. falciparum* from the other species. The problem with the blood smear test is its sensitivity. Parasites may not be observed unless prolonged, repeated searches are done, or they may not be appropriately recognized by the technician, especially in facilities where malaria is rarely seen. Malaria should not be excluded as a diagnosis until three blood films, obtained 12–24 hours apart, have been examined.

Advances in technology have now made the rapid diagnosis of malaria potentially much easier and faster. One example, the OptiMAL® assay, is a sensitive, simple to use dipstick assay that permits the detection of all major species of human malaria and can distinguish between *P. falciparum* and *P. vivax*. The test has a reported sensitivity of 88% and a specificity of 99% for *P. falciparum*.

NOTE: Although these rapid diagnostic tests for malaria appear promising, recent studies have shown that travelers, especially when ill, may be unable to perform these test satisfactorily, and thus may fail to diagnose the disease. In addition, the kits must be stored at temperatures not exceeding 20°C—25°C. Storing the kits under adverse environmental conditions could invalidate the test results.

MALARIA PREVENTION

Virtually all cases of malaria can be prevented. Most studies show that a high proportion of travelers who acquire malaria simply did not receive appropriate information on, or did not comply with, malaria prevention measures.

Avoiding malaria requires that you (1) know where it exists, (2) prevent mosquito bites, and (3) take a prophylactic drug (see Table 5.2)

Chapter 6 summarizes the best methods of insect-bite prevention.

Figure 5.2. Distribution of Malaria and Chloroquine-Resistant Falciparum Malaria—1997

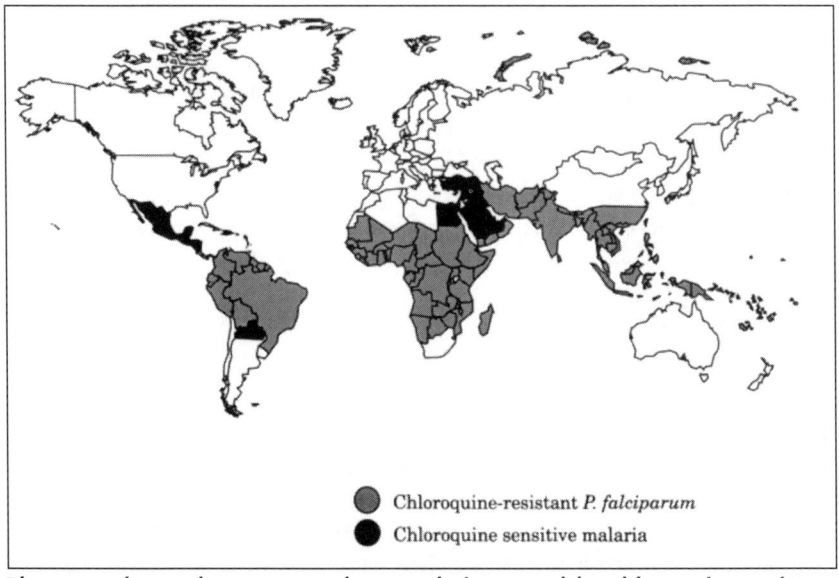

The map shows those areas where malaria caused by chloroquine-resistant *P. falciparum* is reported. NOTE: Chloroquine-resistant *P. vivax* is now reported in Papua New Guinea, Irian Jaya, Colombia, Guyana, Brazil, Myanmar, and Malaysia. Both mefloquine- and chloroquine-resistant falciparum malaria are found along the Thai/Myanmar & Cambodian borders.

Chemoprophylaxis

Before departing for a malarious area, you and your doctor should decide if prophylaxis is indicated and which drug, if any, you should take. Current malaria prophylaxis recommendations are summarized in Table 5.2. In general, if your risk of exposure will be moderate to high, prophylaxis is necessary and the drug you will use, depending on your itinerary and other factors, will be chloroquine (Aralen), mefloquine (Lariam), doxycycline (Vibramycin), or atovaquone/proguanil (Malarone).

If the risk of malaria is low, the benefits of prophylaxis have to be more carefully assessed. In low-risk situations where prompt medical care is available, it may be acceptable not to take a prophylactic drug, but to rely instead on immediate treatment. However, the malaria branch of the CDC recommends prophylaxis in any situation, no matter how low the risk.

Mefloquine and chloroquine should be started 1–2 weeks before departure, continued regularly during travel and taken for 4 weeks after leaving the malarious area. Atovaquone/proguanil and primaquine can be started one day before exposure, continued daily during travel, and discontinued one week after leaving the risk area. Doxycycline can be started one day before entering the malaria risk area, taken daily, and discontinued 4 weeks after leaving the risk area.

Factors determining your need for, and choice of, prophylaxis include (1) your itinerary, (2) the intensity and duration of your exposure to mosquito bites, especially those transmitting *P. falciparum*, (3) your ability to obtain rapid, qualified medical care should symptoms occur, (4) your own knowledge of malaria and its symptoms, (5) your medical history and personal health status, (6) your history of known drug allergies or known ability (or inability) to tolerate certain prophylactic drugs, (7) your use of other medications that may be incompatible with prophylactic drugs, (8) your age, and (9) your pregnancy status, if applicable.

The complexity of the situation is one reason why seeing a travel medicine specialist is advisable when exposure to malaria is likely. Remember, though, that the best prophylaxis is still mosquito-bite prevention. If you don't get bitten, you can't get malaria.

Important Malaria Information

Since no current antimalarial prophylactic drug regimen is 100% protective, travelers must also take measures to prevent mosquito bites (see Chapter 6). Travelers who develop a fever during travel or during the first year of return from a malarious area should seek medical attention promptly, inform their health-care provider of their possible exposure, and request blood films for diagnosis. Serial blood films, repeated daily for 3 days, may be necessary to rule out the infection. Results of these tests should be expected within 24 hours.

Table 5.2

Malaria Prophylaxis According to Geographic Area[1]		
Chloroquine-Sensitive Areas	**First-Line Drug(s)**	**Alternative Drug(s)**
Central America Caribbean Middle East, N. Africa	chloroquine " "	mefloquine doxycycline[1] atovaquone/proguanil
Chloroquine-Resistant Areas		
South America	mefloquine atovaquone/proguanil doxycycline	primaquine[3]
Africa[2] (sub-Saharan)	mefloquine doxycycline atovaquone/proguanil	primaquine[3]
Indian subcontinent	mefloquine atovaquone/proguanil doxycyline	primaquine[3]
Southeast Asia	mefloquine	primaquine[3]
Oceania Papua New Guinea Vanuatu Solomon Islands	atovaquone/proguanil doxycycline	
Thailand (border areas only)	doxycycline	atovaquone/proguanil or, proguanil plus sulfonamide[4]

1. In Central and South America and Southeast Asia, travelers are generally at risk only in rural areas during evening and nighttime hours. In sub-Saharan Africa and Oceania, malaria is often transmitted in both urban and rural areas.
2. Fansidar (page 91) can be carried for use as emergency treatment in remote areas if malaria is suspected in travelers taking chloroquine and/or proguanil.
3. Requires G-6-PD screening test.
4. Combination of proguanil and a sulfa is an alternative for travelers in Thailand unable to take doxycycline or atovaquone/proguanil. Dosage: proguanil, 200 mg daily, plus either sulfisoxazole, 75 mg/kg daily, or sulfamethoxazole, 1,500 mg daily. Mefloquine resistance is common along the Thai/Myanmar and Thai/Cambodian borders.

Chloroquine

Chloroquine phosphate is a synthetic 4-aminoquinolone that is the drug of choice to prevent susceptible strains of *P. vivax*, *P. ovale*, *P. malariae*, and *P. falciparum*. The drug is used when prophylaxis is needed in malarious areas of the Caribbean (parts of the Dominican Republic and Haiti), Mexico and Central America, temperate South America, North Africa, and parts of the Middle East.

Adult dosage—500 mg salt (300 mg base) once weekly, beginning one week before and continuing four weeks after leaving the malarious area. Starting chloroquine before you leave gives you a protective blood level and also lets you know if any unusual side effects will occur.

Child dosage—8.3 mg/kg salt (5 mg/kg base) once weekly, up to maximum adult dose of 500 mg salt/week.

Generic chloroquine tablets are sold in the United States in strengths of 250 mg and 500 mg. Brand name chloroquine (Aralen™) is available only in the 500 mg tablet strength. Only the tablet form of chloroquine is available in the United States, but liquid chloroquine for pediatric use is readily available overseas. The Aralen tablet is difficult to crush for children. The generic tablets are easier to split and crush, but are bitter. Parents can crush tablets into powder, divide it, and then mask flavor with syrup, jam, etc. Another strategy is to have a pharmacist pulverize the tablets and prepare gelatin capsules with the proper weekly dose. Mixing the powder from the capsule with food (e.g., chocolate sauce or ice cream) or drink will make the bitter taste more palatable.

Side effects—Chloroquine is generally well-tolerated and serious side effects rarely occur. Nausea, however, is not uncommon. Gastrointestinal side effects can usually be controlled by taking chloroquine with meals. Dizziness, headache, blurred vision, and itching may also occur, but these symptoms will rarely require you to stop taking the drug. Itching is a frequent occurrence among people of African descent and is not an allergic reaction. Fears about long-term prophylaxis causing degenerative eye (retinal) changes are unfounded. Chloroquine can safely be taken by pregnant women and children, including infants.

CAUTION: An overdose of chloroquine (even *one* tablet in a small child) can be fatal. The drug should be kept in a child-safe container at all times.

NOTE: Chloroquine interferes with the antibody response to rabies vaccine when the vaccine is administered intradermally. If you are taking chloroquine prophylaxis and need rabies vaccination, the vaccine must be given intramuscularly.

Hydroxychloroquine

An alternative to chloroquine phosphate is hydroxychloroquine (Plaquenil). It has the same action as chloroquine, but causes fewer gastrointestinal side effects. (Hydroxychloroquine can also be used to treat chloroquine-sensitive malaria.)

Adult prophylactic dosage—400 mg salt (310 mg base) weekly.

Child dosage—6.5 mg/kg salt (5.0 mg base/kg) weekly, up to the adult dosage.

Chloroquine-Resistant *P. vivax*

Resistance of *P. vivax* to chloroquine has been confirmed in Myanmar (Burma), Papua New Guinea, the island of Nias (Indonesia), Irian Jaya (Indonesian New Guinea) Sabah, Borneo (Malaysia), Colombia, and Guyana. Mefloquine and doxycycline are effective prophylactic agents for these strains of malaria.

Mefloquine

Mefloquine (Lariam) is currently one of the recommended drugs for malaria prophylaxis in almost all countries where there is chloroquine-resistant *P. falciparum*. The drug is also effective against *P. vivax*, *P. ovale*, and *P. malariae*. In western Cambodia and along the border areas of Thailand, however, the incidence of mefloquine-resistant *P. falciparum* is as high as 50%, and prophylaxis with doxycycline is recommended. Recent reports also indicate possible, as yet undocumented, mefloquine resistance in West Africa.

Adult dosage—250 mg (one tablet) once weekly during travel in malarious areas and for 4 weeks after leaving such areas. Mefloquine should be started at least one to two weeks prior to departure to see if bothersome side effects will occur and to ensure adequate blood levels build up. Some travel doctors recommend starting the mefloquine dosing even earlier, at 3–4 weeks prior to departure, to ascertain tolerance to the drug.

Child dosage—Children: 5–14 kg, 1/8 tablet weekly; 15–19 kg 1/4 tablet weekly; 20–30 kg, 1/2 tablet weekly; 31–45 kg, 3/4 tablet weekly; and > 45 kg, 1 tablet weekly. Under 5 kg an proportionately lower dose should be given.

Mefloquine Facts

- The rate of dizziness, anxiety, and insomnia is greater for mefloquine as compared with chloroquine.
- Serious neuropsychiatric adverse events with mefloquine are rare. Severe side effects (seizures and psychotic episodes) occur in 1:10,000–13,000 prophylactic users. Several case reports and recent media publicity suggest that side effects may occur much more frequently than suggested, and two recent studies showed that "disabling" side effects, sufficient to impact on daily activities, occur in 1:250 to 1:500 users. However, fewer than 3% of those taking mefloquine discontinue the drug because of side effects. (about 10% in the U.K.)
- Older travelers and children have fewer side effects than younger adults. Women have more side effects than men.
- A liquid form of mefloquine is not available.
- Contraindications to mefloquine use are epilepsy, neuropsychiatric disorders, and cardiac conduction disorders.
- There is still controversy regarding the true incidence and severity of mefloquine-induced adverse events. A case of fatal toxic epidermal necrolysis has been reported. Cardiac conduction disorders may occur if halofantrine is used in conjunction with mefloquine. By itself, mefloquine has no adverse cardiac effects.

Loading dose of mefloquine—Some travel medicine physicians give a loading dose (250 mg daily for 3 days, then once weekly) to achieve therapeutic levels rapidly—and to "screen" for side effects. A loading dose ensures that if there are any significant side effects, they will occur within one week instead of 3–7 weeks when the drug is initiated on a weekly basis. The loading dose should be taken 2 weeks prior to travel. This approach appears to be safe and well-tolerated, but the CDC states that there is no documentation of cases related to not giving a loading dose. NOTE: If you have been taking quinidine or procainamide for cardiac problems, 12 hours should elapse before you take mefloquine.

Side effects—Mefloquine in prophylactic doses is generally well-tolerated, but about 10% of users report mild-to-moderate side effects—strange dreams, insomnia, nausea, dizziness, and weakness. Serious neuropsychological side effects (anxiety, depression, agitation, nightmares) requiring discontinuation of the drug may occur in 0.5% of users, and severe neuropsychiatric side effects (psychosis, seizures) may affect 0.01% of users. Side effects may be reduced by splitting the weekly dose and taking one-half tablet twice weekly. Taking the drug with food lessens stomach upset.

CAUTIONS: The CDC and the manufacturer recommend that mefloquine not be used by travelers with a history of epilepsy, psychiatric disorders, or cardiac conduction disturbances. Cautions are also listed by the manufacturer for use by drivers of vehicles, pilots, operators of machinery and heavy equipment, scuba divers, and mountain climbers. These latter cautions, however, are based on limited data or theoretical concerns only and are not absolute contraindications.

Mefloquine is now considered safe for prophylaxis during the second and third trimesters of pregnancy (and, by extension, safe for infants). The drug has not been associated with congenital malformations or adverse postnatal outcomes when used for prophylaxis. There may be a slight trend toward miscarriage when mefloquine is taken during the first trimester, but the data are not firm. Travel medicine physicians will prescribe mefloquine during the first trimester when exposure to chloroquine-resistant falciparum malaria is high and unavoidable. Inadvertent use of mefloquine during the first trimester is not an indication for therapeutic abortion. However, a recent study showed that high-dose mefloquine treatment (3–5 times the prophylactic dose) was associated with an increased risk of fetal death.

Doxycycline

Doxycycline is a tetracycline-related drug that is more than 90% effective against multidrug-resistant *P. falciparum*. You can use doxycycline as an equally effective alternative to mefloquine. The drug is also effective against *P. vivax*, *P. ovale*, and *P. malariae*. Doxycycline is the prophylactic of choice in forested border areas in Thailand and some parts of Cambodia where there is a high incidence of malaria due to chloroquine- and mefloquine-resistant *P. falciparum*.

An advantage of doxycycline is its price. Generic doxycycline costs 10 to 20 cents a tablet, versus $7–$10/tablet for mefloquine. Another advantage is that it will also protect against other important infections such as typhus, plague, Lyme disease, and leptospirosis.

A disadvantage of doxycycline is that it must be taken every day. One or two missed doses will put the traveler at risk of malaria.

Doxycycline is contraindicated for pregnant women and children under the age of 8 unless required for the treatment of a serious infection such as falciparum malaria or ehrlichiosis.

Adult dosage—100 mg daily. Doxycycline should be started 1 to 2 days prior to travel. It should be continued daily in malarious areas and for 4 weeks after departure from the area.

Child dosage (for children older than 8 years of age)—2 mg per kg of body weight per day up to the adult dose of 100 mg daily.

Side effects—Most travelers tolerate doxycycline well, but nausea, vomiting, and heartburn can occur. Doxycycline should be taken with sufficient liquid or food to ensure complete passage of the drug into the stomach because if the tablet remains in the esophagus it can cause mucosal erosions or even esophageal perforation. In addition, doxycycline can cause phototoxicity (an exaggerated sunburn reaction to strong sunlight). Risk is reduced by avoiding prolonged, direct exposure to the sun, using a broadspectrum sunscreen (these contain both a UVA and UVB blocker), and taking the drug in the evening. Women taking doxycycline may develop a vaginal yeast infection and therefore should carry a self-treatment dose of an antifungal agent such as fluconazole (Diflucan).

Atovaquone/proguanil (Malarone)

The FDA has just approved the combination of atovaquone (250 mg) and proguanil (100 mg) for the prophylaxis or treatment of malaria caused by *P. falciparum*. This drug is a welcome addition because it not only is very effective, but it provides an alternative for persons intolerant of mefloquine or doxycycline, for children younger than eight, who cannot take doxycycline, and for those going on short trips (it is expensive). Prophylaxis studies conducted in Kenya, Zambia, and Gabon demonstrated that Malarone was 98% to 100% effective in partially-immune subjects. An unpublished trial showed similar efficacy in nonimmune transmigrants in Irian Jaya.

The CDC no longer recommends that Malarone be used only by travelers who cannot take either mefloquine or doxycycline.

Malarone acts against both the blood and liver phases of *P. falciparum*. However, it will not kill the liver parasites (hypnozoites) of *P. vivax* or *P. ovale* so persons at high risk for these infections should receive terminal prophylaxis with primaquine.

Adult prophylactic dose: 1 tablet, started one or two days before travel, taken daily during the stay, and for 7 days after leaving the malarious region.

Child dosage: In the United States a pediatric formulation is available and the dosage is based on weight: 10 kg–20 kg=1 pediatric-strength tablet, 21–30 kg=2 pediatric-strength tablets, 31–40 kg=3 pediatric-strength tablets, and more than 40 kg, 1 adult-strength tablet.

Tablets should be taken with food or a milky drink at the same time each day. If vomiting occurs within one hour after dosing, a repeat dose should be taken. Side effects are minimal; they include stomach upset, cough, and skin rash. Atovaquone/proguanil is contraindicated during pregnancy.

Proguanil

Proguanil (Paludrine) is active against chloroquine-sensitive falciparum malaria as well as *P. vivax*, *P. ovale*, and *P. malariae*. In chloroquine-sensitive areas, proguanil can be used as an alternative to chloroquine. In sub-Saharan Africa, proguanil, combined with weekly chloroquine, is a widely used prophylactic regimen, but is much less efficacious than mefloquine or doxycycline (65% efficacy for proguanil vs. 85–90% for mefloquine or doxycycline).

Adult dosage—200 mg daily, and continue for 4 weeks after leaving the area. Proguanil is not available in the United States but is available over the counter in many countries and by prescription in Canada. It is not available in liquid form.

Child dosage—Less than 2 years, 50 mg daily; 2–6 years, 100 mg daily; 7–10 years, 150 mg daily; over 10 years, 200 mg daily.

Side effects—Toxicity is very low. Nausea, vomiting, and mouth ulcers are common. Serious reactions (such as neuropsychiatric events) are not reported. Proguanil is safe to take during pregnancy.

Chloroquine & Proguanil

Chloroquine, combined with proguanil, is only 65% effective against chloroquine-resistant *P. falciparum* in East Africa and is recommended only when a traveler to sub-Saharan Africa is unable to take either mefloquine or doxycycline. This combination is not recommended for prophylaxis against chloroquine-resistant *P. falciparum* in geographic regions outside of Africa.

Dosage (adults)—chloroquine, 500 mg weekly, plus proguanil, 200 mg daily. Continue prophylaxis for 4 weeks after exposure.

Side effects—Mainly nausea and mouth ulcers. The relatively high incidence (about 30%) of gastrointestinal side effects from the combination is reported to cause a significant number of travelers to discontinue prophylaxis.

Proguanil & sulfonamide—Combining proguanil with a sulfonamide, such as sulfisoxazole or sulfamethoxazole, may dramatically increase prophylactic effectiveness, especially against chloroquine-resistant *P. falciparum*. Studies done in Thailand with this combination in the 1980s have shown over 90% protection. (see Table 5.2)

Other Drugs for Malaria Prevention

Primaquine—When taken by adults in a daily dose of 30 mg (or 0.5 mg/kg), an effectiveness of 85%–95% against *P. falciparum* and *P. vivax* has been demonstrated. This is comparable to the effectiveness of doxycycline and mefloquine. Primaquine, unlike these other two drugs, does not have to be taken for 4—6 weeks after leaving a malarious area. Taking the drug for one week post-exposure is sufficient. This is because primaquine is a "causal prophylactic" and eradicates parasites in the liver. Delayed infections are therefore prevented.

Side effects: Primaquine is better tolerated than chloroquine, but it causes methemoglobinemia and red blood cell destruction (hemolysis) in people with the G-6-PD enzyme deficiency. *A G-6-PD screening test is required before using this drug.* Primaquine is contraindicated in pregnant women. Stomach upsets can be reduced by taking the drug with food.

Note: Primaquine is not routinely recommended at this time, but some physicians are prescribing the drug for the traveler who cannot tolerate mefloquine or doxycycline.

RADICAL CURE

Primaquine

If you have traveled to a region where vivax malaria predominates, and have discontinued prophylaxis after returning, you may be at risk for a delayed malaria attack, caused by dormant *P. vivax* parasites released from your liver. Your risk of malaria is proportional to your degree of exposure to mosquito bites, and primaquine treatment (called "radical cure") may be advised. You have two options:

1. Treat: Take primaquine, as outlined below, to eliminate any possible dormant P. vivax liver parasites. If you were in a malarious area for more than 2 months, then your chance of harboring dormant parasites is probably high enough to justify treatment (except in sub-Saharan Africa where P. vivax malaria is almost nonexistent). Start the 2-week course of primaquine after finishing prophylaxis.

   OR

2. Wait and watch: If your exposure was low to moderate, the chance of infection is less. Defer primaquine and watch for symptoms. Get treated for malaria if it occurs. Another reason for waiting is that primaquine is occasionally toxic and also requires that you get a pretreatment blood test to screen for G-6-PD enzyme deficiency. This enzyme deficiency is most common in blacks, Asians, and people of Mediterranean descent. If primaquine is administered to a person with G-6-PD deficiency, hemolytic anemia will occur.

   Adult dosage—15 mg base (26.3 mg salt) daily for 14 days.
   Child dosage—0.3 mg base per kg (0.5 mg/kg salt) daily for 14 days.

Primaquine is contraindicated during pregnancy. Pregnant women who are at significant risk of *P. vivax* malaria should continue prophylaxis during gestation and receive primaquine after delivery.

Primaquine-Resistant *P. vivax*

Primaquine-resistant strains of *Plasmodium vivax* are reported in scattered areas throughout SE Asia and Oceania, and recently in Somalia. Some travel medicine experts treat individuals returning from these areas who have had heavy exposure to mosquitoes with a higher dose of primaquine (a total of 6 mg base per kg of body weight) for two weeks. For adults, this higher dose of primaquine is usually given as 30 mg per day for 14 days.

MALARIA TREATMENT

Principles of Malaria Treatment

Malaria is a medical emergency, particularly in expatriates who, unlike nationals living in an endemic area, lack immunity to infection. Treatment should be initiated as soon as possible. Individuals who develop malaria, but who have been compliant with their chemoprophylactic regimen, should take an alternative drug for malaria treatment. When in doubt about the diagnosis or the infecting species, presumptive treatment should always be directed against life-threatening chloroquine-resistant falciparum malaria. In addition, malaria that develops in an individual located in an area known to have drug resistance, or in an individual on chemoprophylaxis, should be treated as a drug-resistant infection. When more than one drug is required for the treatment of malaria, quinine or artemisinin should be administered first because of their rapidity of action.

If you suspect that you have malaria, urgently seek medical care. If medical care is not readily available within 48 hours, don't wait—if you are carrying standby antimalarial drugs, start self-treatment (page 93).

Chloroquine

In areas where chloroquine-resistant *P. falciparum* or chloroquine-resistant *P. vivax* is NOT reported, start treatment on the following schedule:

- Day 1. Chloroquine 500 mg (salt) by mouth immediately, then chloroquine, 250 mg (salt), six hours later. (500 mg salt=300 mg base)
- Day 2. Chloroquine 250 mg orally.
- Day 3. Chloroquine 250 mg orally.

Severe chloroquine-sensitive malaria requires an intravenous infusion of chloroquine, 0.83 mg/kg/hr (base), or intramuscular chloroquine, 3.5 mg/kg (base) repeated every 6 hours until parasitemia decreases. Oral chloroquine can then be started: the total dose is 25 mg/kg (base).

Note: Since intravenous chloroquine is not readily available in the U.S. or Canada, intravenous quinidine or quinine may be substituted (see below).

Mefloquine (Lariam)

This drug is highly active against all malaria strains, except in Thailand, where cure rates against *P. falciparum* have fallen to 50%–70%.

Dosage—1,250 mg (15–25 mg/kg) is best given as a divided dose of 750 mg (or 15 mg/kg) followed by 500 mg (or 10 mg/kg) 6 hours later. (25 mg/kg is required to treat falciparum malaria from Thailand and 15 mg/kg elsewhere.)

Side effects—Adverse side effects are much more frequent with treatment dosages of mefloquine than with prophylactic doses (page 82). Reports of severe neuropsychiatric side effects, in fact, have tempered the enthusiasm for using mefloquine in the treatment of malaria. The frequency of severe neuropsychiatric symptoms (hallucinations, seizures, delirium, acute psychosis) with treatment doses of mefloquine is estimated at about 1:250-1:1700 treatment courses.

Other adverse reactions include nausea and vomiting, loss of balance and coordination, dizziness, inability to concentrate, headache, and insomnia. Side effects usually last for only a few days but occasionally persist for several weeks and rarely for many months.

Mefloquine should be administered cautiously when the patient has previously received, or is receiving, chloroquine, quinine, quinidine, or procainamide. If these drugs are being used, mefloquine administration should be delayed at least 12 hours after the last dose. Cardiac side effects may occur when halofantrine is administered following mefloquine treatment. Mefloquine has no adverse cardiac effects when given by itself.

Atovaquone/Proguanil (Malarone)

This combination (atovaquone, 250 mg plus proguanil, 100 mg), is now available in the United States. Malarone has been shown to be effective in regions where high failure rates occur with other antimalarials including chloroquine, halofantrine, and mefloquine. In fact, Malarone now appears to be the most effective treatment for acute uncomplicated falciparum malaria, including multidrug-resistant strains. In Thailand, Malarone cured 100% of cases of *P. falciparum* malaria vs. 86% for mefloquine. Elsewhere, an overall success rate of 98.7% has been reported.

Adult dosage:	4 tablets once daily for 3 days
Child dosage:	11–20 kg: 1 adult tablet daily for 3 days
	21–30 kg: 2 adult tablets once daily for 3 days
	31–40 kg: 3 adult tablets once daily for 3 days
	> 40 kg: 4 adult tablets once daily for 3 days

Side effects—Nausea, vomiting, loss of appetite, abdominal pain, headache, and itching. Dividing the dose and giving it twice daily may reduce the gastrointestinal side effects which occur in 10%–15% of patients.

Treatment of vivax malaria—Malarone has not yet been recommended for the prophylaxis or treatment of *P. vivax* malaria, but efficacy has been high in reported cases. However, even with treatment, primaquine is needed to prevent relapse because Malarone does not eradicate P. vivax liver parasites.

Atovaquone/Doxycycline

If Malarone is not commercially available, the combination of atovaquone with doxycycline (1 gm of atovaquone and 200 mg of doxycycline daily for 3 days) has been shown to be as effective as Malarone.

Pyrimethamine/sulfadoxine (Fansidar)

Fansidar is a combination of pyrimethamine and sulfadoxine, and may be used for self-treatment. Resistance to the drug is widespread in Southeast Asia and South America and is becoming more of a problem in Africa.

Fansidar is slower in action than chloroquine or quinine and should not be used alone for the treatment of a severe infection. Nor should Fansidar be used as sole treatment for chloroquine-resistant falciparum malaria, even though the infection may be uncomplicated. Fansidar can be used to treat vivax malaria, but *P. vivax* infections clear more slowly after treatment with Fansidar than after treatment with other drugs (chloroquine, quinine, or mefloquine).

Adult dosage—3 tablets, taken at once.

Child dosage—Less than 1 year, 1/4 tablet; 1 to 3 years, 1/2 tablet; 4 to 8 years, 1 tablet; 9 to 14 years, 2 tablets.

Side effects—Minor side effects can include headache, nausea, vomiting, and skin rash. The risk of a life-threatening reaction (e.g., exfoliative dermatitis) from a single treatment dose of Fansidar is estimated to be 1: 50,000.

Contraindications include people who are allergic to sulfa drugs and infants less than one month of age. Fansidar has been used to treat malarial infection in large numbers of pregnant women without apparent harmful effects on the fetus.

Halofantrine (Halfan)

Halofantrine is chemically similar to mefloquine, with which it shares cross resistance. It is highly effective against all four plasmodium species, including *P. falciparum*. Outside of Thailand, the cure rate is generally more than 90% with a 1-day course of treatment and 100% effective when two courses of treatment are administered.

In Thailand, there is a high incidence of mefloquine-resistant falciparum malaria, and the standard 1-day treatment course of halofantrine is only about 65% effective. High-dose halofantrine (3-day treatment) is 90% curative but side effects, some of which may be potentially fatal, are also increased.

Halofantrine is currently available in many countries in Africa and Europe but is not approved in the U.S. or Canada.

Standard dose—500 mg (or 8 mg/kg) every 6 hours for 3 doses. A second 3-dose treatment should be administered 7 days later.

Because of its erratic absorption and short half-life, halofantrine is not used for chemoprophylaxis. The drug is available in 250 mg tablets and in a pediatric suspension of 100 mg/5 ml. Halofantrine should be taken on an empty stomach.

Side effects—Minor side effects consist of GI upset (diarrhea, nausea, abdominal pain), pruritus (itching), skin rash, and a slight elevation of liver transaminase enzymes.

Serious cardiac side effects—Halofantrine causes a dose-related prolongation of atrioventricular conduction and QTc interval. This effect is increased by mefloquine. Mobitz type I and II conduction blocks have been observed with high-dose halofantrine. The effects of halofantrine (even in standard doses) on cardiac conduction may increase the risk of ventricular tachyarrhythmias and cardiac arrest in people with a prolonged QTc interval (Romano-Ward syndrome). Contraindications to the use of halofantrine are as follows:

- QTc interval >0.44 msec
- A family history of prolonged QTc interval
- A history of ventricular arrhythmias or syncope
- Recent mefloquine use. Halofantrine not to be used to treat mefloquine failures.

Prior to treatment with halofantrine, an ECG to measure the QTc interval is mandatory, followed by in-hospital cardiac monitoring for 8–12 hours. Even with these precautions, *the CDC does not recommend halofantrine for treatment because of the potential side effects and the availability of safer alternative drugs.*

The drug should not be used for self-treatment unless a pretreatment ECG has been done. This is an unlikely scenario and the drug has basically been eliminated as a choice for self-treatment in the field.

Halofantrine is contraindicated during pregnancy or breast feeding.

Quinine

Quinine is an ancient drug that originated from the cinchona plant. It is active against all four species of plasmodia. Quinine is also one of the most rapidly-acting drugs for treatment of severe falciparum malaria. Oral quinine is available as quinine sulfate in tablet and capsule form. In the United States, intravenous quinine is not available and quinidine (see below) must be used if intravenous treatment is required.

Although quinine rapidly reduces parasite counts, quinine by itself may not be adequate for eliminating all parasites permanently from the blood, and recrudescent infections can occur. Therefore a second drug, such as doxycycline, tetracycline, Fansidar, or clindamycin, must also be used in conjunction with quinine.

Despite its effectiveness, resistance to quinine is increasing. In Thailand, quinine cures only 90% of patients with falciparum malaria, even when the drug is combined with tetracycline. Malarone (see below) appears to be more effective.

Dosage for complicated malaria—Quinine dihydrochloride salt by intravenous infusion, 20 mg/kg loading dose over 4 hours, followed by 10 mg/kg every 8 hours given over 2–4 hours. Oral therapy with quinine sulfate, followed by tetracycline, doxycycline, or clindamycin, should be instituted as soon as possible.

Table 5.3

Summary of Treatment of Malaria (by oral route)

A Chloroquine-sensitive malaria (*P. vivax, P. ovale, P. malariae* and sensitive strains of *P. falciparum*)

	Adult Dose	Pediatric Dose
Chloroquine phosphate (Aralen) (250 mg salt = 150 mg base per tablet)	1 gram of salt (4 tabs) immediately; then 500 mg (2 tabs) in 6 hrs, then 500 mg (2 tabs) once/day for 2 days	10 mg base/kg (max 600 mg) immediately; then 5 mg/kg in 6 hrs, then 5 mg/kg/day for 2 days

B *P. vivax* and *P. ovale* malaria
To prevent relapses after chloroquine therapy, add:

Primaquine (21.5 mg salt = 15 mg base/tablet)	15 mg base (1 tab) daily for 14 days	0.3 mg/kg/day for 14 days

C Chloroquine-resistant malaria

Malarone	4 tablets daily x 3 days	See page 91
Quinine sulphate	600 gm salt q8h* x 5–7 days (7 days required in SE Asia)	10 mg salt/kg q8h x 5–7 days (7 days required in SE Asia)

Plus one of the following:

1. Fansidar** or	3 tablets (75 mg pyrimethamine and 1,500 mg sulfadoxine) once	1.25 mg/kg of pyrimethamine and 25 mg/kg of sulfadoxine once
2. Tetracycline or doxycycline or	250 mg q6h x 7 days 100 mg q12h x 7 days	Contraindicated under 8 years of age
3. Clindamycin	10 mg/kg q8h x 7 days	Same as adult dose

Alternative treatments:

Mefloquine	1–1.5 gm (15–25 mg/kg) in a divided dose over 12 hours	Inadequate studies
Halofantrine	500 mg (2 tabs) q6h x 3 doses; repeat in 1 week	8 mg/kg dose q6h x 3 doses; repeat in 1 week

* q8h = every 8 hours   ** In SE Asia, use tetracycline or doxycycline.

Dosage for uncomplicated malaria—Quinine sulfate, 650 mg (or 10 mg/kg) orally every 8 hours for 3 to 7 days. Follow quinine with one of the following: (1) doxycycline, 100 mg twice daily, (2) tetracycline, 250 mg four times daily, or (3) clindamycin, 450–900 mg three times daily. For malaria acquired in SE Asia, quinine should be administered for 7 days, and for 5 days if acquired elsewhere; doxycycline and clindamycin are administered for 7 days.

Side effects—Headache and tinnitus (ringing in the ears) are the most common side effects of quinine. Cinchonism—nausea, vomiting, abdominal pain, blurred vision, vertigo, and tremors—is common during the first several days of treatment. Serious, occasionally fatal side effects (hypotension, convulsions, heart block, ventricular fibrillation) can occur with too rapid intravenous injection of the drug. Slow IV administration, or oral administration, is usually safe but can cause minor ECG changes (prolongation of the QT interval and T-wave flattening). Quinine can also cause hypoglycemia (low blood sugar) from stimulation of the insulin producing cells of the pancreas; therefore, the parenteral preparation should be administered with glucose, and blood glucose levels must be measured frequently during therapy.

Quinine can be used, if necessary, during pregnancy. On the third day of parenteral therapy, the dose should be reduced by one-half to one-third. Although quinine has been thought to induce abortion, the doses used in malaria treatment are not associated with this side effect.

Quinidine

Quinidine, the d-isomer of quinine, is a commonly used cardiac drug. It can also be used either intravenously or orally to treat chloroquine-resistant falciparum malaria. It is particularly useful in Thailand for the treatment of multidrug-resistant malaria.

Dosage—A loading dose of quinidine gluconate, 10 mg/kg (salt), in normal saline is given intravenously over 1–2 hours, followed by a constant infusion at 0.02 mg/kg/min (1.0–1.5 mg/kg/hour). As soon as the parasite density drops below 1% of red cells infected, intravenous quinidine should be stopped and oral quinine sulfate started and continued for a total of 5 days (7 days in Thailand). Tetracycline, doxycycline, or clindamycin should be given for 7 days.

Side effects—Intravenous quinidine therapy should be administered in an intensive care unit. ECG monitoring is essential. Cardiac effects are similar to those caused by quinine, dose-related QT interval prolongation, and QRS widening.

Artemisinin (Qinghaosu) and Derivatives

Artemisinin (qinghaosu) and its two derivatives, artesunate (water soluble) and artemether (oil soluble), are the most rapidly acting antimalarial drugs. Artemisinin is found in the medicinal herb *Artemeisia annua* (sweet wormwood), a plant used by traditional Chinese practitioners since A.D. 341 for the treatment of fever. Artemisinin was isolated in 1972 and is a sesquiterpene lactone peroxide chemically unrelated to any other currently used antimalarial drug.

Artemisinin is effective against *P. vivax* as well as chloroquine-resistant strains of *P. falciparum*, but recrudescence of infection is common when the drug is used as sole therapy. To prevent recrudescent infections, artemisinin should always be given in conjunction with another antimalarial such as doxycycline or mefloquine. Artemisinin is produced for clinical use in China and Vietnam and is presently available in those countries as well as several others in Asia and Africa. It is now being widely used in Africa, on its own, for the treatment of falciparum malaria.

Oral dosage—3 gm (or 50 mg/kg) given over 3 to 5 days.

Intramuscular dosage—1.0 to 1.2 gm (adult dose) over 3 to 5 days.

Suppositories—2,800 mg total dose given over 3 days.

Side effects—Nausea, vomiting, rash, fever, transient first-degree heart block.

There are several semisynthetic derivatives of artemisinin.

- **Artesunate** is an oral, water-soluble derivative of artemisinin and has been combined with single-dose mefloquine to treat drug-resistant *P. falciparum* in Southeast Asia.

Dosage (Oral, IV, IM, suppository)—100 mg, then 50 mg every 12 hours for three to six days.

- **Artemether** is an oil-soluble compound that is rapidly effective in severe malaria. Oral artemether given over 5 days was found to have a higher cure rate, with fewer side effects, than mefloquine against multidrug-resistant *P. falciparum* in Thailand. In studies done in Malawi, intramuscular artemether acted more rapidly than intravenous quinine in clearing coma and reducing parasite counts in children with cerebral malaria. In Vietnam, intramuscular artemether was as effective as intramuscular quinine in curing severe falciparum malaria. Quinine, however, acted more rapidly in reducing fever and was associated with a shorter hospital stay.

Oral dosage—700 mg given over 5 days.

Intramuscular dosage—3.2–4 mg/kg initially, then 1.6–2 mg/kg every 24 hours for five to seven days. Artemether, dissolved in oil, is supplied in 1.0-ml ampoules containing 80 mg of the drug for intramuscular injection. The average treatment for adults is six ampoules.

Side effects—Oral artesunate and artemether appear to be among the safest and best-tolerated antimalarial drugs, but their side-effect profile has not been fully delineated. These drugs should therefore be used with caution, especially when repeat courses are being administered. Recent studies have shown that brain stem damage may occur from repeated or prolonged artemisinin use in laboratory animals, including primates.

- **Co-artmether (Riamet)** combines the fast-acting artemether with the prolonged action of lumefantrine. The drug is currently available in Switzerland. Unlike halofantrine, lumefantrine is not associated with adverse cardiac effects, such as prolongation of the QT interval. There have been no reports of significant neurological symptoms. A 6-dose regimen over 3 days is reported to cure over 95% of acute uncomplicated multidrug-resistant

Table 5.4

Self-Treatment Options (Adults)	
Drug	**Dose**
chloroquine	1,000 mg initially, followed by 500 mg 6, 24, and 48 hours later
Malarone	4 tablets once daily for 3 days
Fansidar	3 tablets at once
mefloquine	3–5 tablets (750 mg–1,250 mg) in divided doses over 12 hours
Riamet	2 tablets daily for 3 days
quinine	650 mg every 8 hours for 5 to 7 days
quinine plus tetracycline*	650 mg every 8 hours for 5 to 7 days 250 mg 4 times daily for 7 days
quinine plus clindamycin*	650 mg every 8 hours for 5 to 7 days 900 mg 3 times daily for 7 days

* Doxycycline, 100 mg twice daily, can be used in place of tetracycline or clindamycin.

falciparum malaria. Because of its rapid onset of action, co-artmether may prevent progression to cerebral malaria. In countries where it is available, the drug is currently recommended as first-line treatment for acute *P. falciparum* malaria and for standby emergency treatment.

SELF-TREATMENT

Several studies have shown that travelers who carry a self-treatment drug rarely use it appropriately and often do not seek medical attention after use as is recommended in all cases. Self-treatment should be considered a last resort since it may delay treatment of another cause of fever. For this reason, medical attention is recommended ASAP whenever self-treatment is initiated.

To date, sulfadoxine-pyrimethamine (Fansidar) has been the drug recommended by the Centers for Disease Control and Prevention (CDC) for presumptive self-treatment for persons with illness suspected to be malaria who are not on optimal prophylaxis regimens. This might be a traveler taking chloroquine in an area with chloroquine-resistant *P. falciparum* who cannot reach medical care within 24 hours. Other travelers who should consider the self-treatment options include:
- Travelers who will be traveling or living in remote areas with chloroquine resistance where they will not have access to medical care within 24 hours and travelers who are unable to tolerate an optimal chemoprophylactic regimen.

- Travelers whose exposure to malaria is likely to be so low that chemoprophylaxis is not desirable. Some North American experts, however, feel that even a single exposure in a high-risk area such as Africa or Oceania requires preventive medication.

Malarone is a new option for self-treatment and is the drug of choice for presumptive self-treatment for travelers to areas with Fansidar-resistant malaria, including the following areas:

- Amazon Basin of South America
- Southeast Asia
- Some countries in eastern and southern Africa: specifically, Kenya, Malawi, Mozambique, South Africa, Tanzania, and Uganda.

Baird JK, Hoffman SL. Prevention of Malaria in Travelers. Med. Clinics N. Am. 1999; 83:923–944.
Manual of TRAVEL MEDICINE and HEALTH by Herbert L. DuPont, M.D., and Robert Steffen, M.D. (B.C. Decker Inc. 1999. ISBN: 1-55009-078-X).
Hill DR. Travel Medicine Advisor Update Jan/Feb 1998.
Kain KC, Keystone JS. Malaria in Travelers. Inf. Dis. Clinics N. Am. 1998; 12:267–284.
Lobel HO, Kozarsky PE. Update on Prevention of Malaria in Travelers. JAMA 1997; 278:1767–1771.
Vugt MV, Wilairatana P, Gemperli B. Efficacy of six doses of artmether-lumefantrine (benflumetol) in multidrug-resistant Plasmodium faciparum malaria. Am J Trop Med Hyg 1999 Jun;60(6):936–42.
White N. Atovaquone/proguanil Review. J.Travel Med. 1999; 6, Suppl. 1: 1–32.

7 Insect-Bite Prevention

Mosquitoes

Mosquitoes are ubiquitous insects. They are found in every region of the world except Antarctica. Mosquitoes breed in standing water in diverse aquatic habitats, including freshwater (even if heavily polluted), saltwater marshes, brackish water—and even water found in discarded containers and old tires.

Both male and female mosquitoes feed on flower or fruit nectar, but only female mosquitoes bite; they require a blood meal every three to four days for the protein necessary to produce eggs.

Mosquitoes can be divided generally into two types: daytime and nighttime biters. Those mosquitoes that transmit malaria and Japanese encephalitis (anopheles and culex mosquitoes) bite mostly at twilight or during the night, whereas aedes mosquitoes, which transmit dengue and yellow fever, are daytime biters. Mosquitoes also bite indoors, so you need to prevent mosquitoes from gaining entry into living and sleeping quarters and to eliminate those that might already be there.

The most common mosquito-transmitted diseases that you need to protect yourself from in tropical and subtropical climates are the following:

- Malaria
- Dengue fever

Less common mosquito-transmitted diseases include the following:

- Yellow fever
- Filariasis
- Viral encephalitis (e.g., Japanese encephalitis, Venezuelan equine encephalitis)
- Miscellaneous viral illnesses. In addition to Rift Valley fever, West Nile fever, Chikungunya fever, and Sindbis fever, there are about 30 rarely diagnosed viral illnesses, such as epidemic polyarthritis, that are also mosquito transmitted.

NOTE: Mosquitoes cannot transmit HIV. The virus neither survives nor replicates in mosquitoes, and the blood from the last bitten person is not flushed into the next bitten person.

Ticks and Biting Flies

The same personal protection measures that you use against mosquitoes will also protect you against ticks and biting flies—insects that transmit Lyme disease, tick-borne encephalitis, relapsing fever, typhus, leishmaniasis, onchocerciasis, trypanosomiasis, and several other tropical and infectious diseases. Of these diseases, leishmaniasis, transmitted by sand flies, is the most common.

You will want to avoid mosquitoes and biting flies for another reason—insect bites, even without the risk of disease, can make you miserable. Bites usually cause localized swelling and itching, and certain bites, such as from black flies, are very painful. Bites can also become secondarily infected, usually from excessive scratching (excoriation). Rarely, bites can cause systemic reactions, including anaphylaxis, from a person's sensitivity to the insect's salivary antigens.

Protecting yourself from insect bites entails more than just applying an insect repellent to your skin. *A multipronged approach is essential.* The combined use of an insect repellent, permethrin, and protective clothing and/or shelters is the best way to avoid insect bites. By using the personal protection methods described in this chapter, you can achieve over 90% protection against mosquitoes and other biting insects.

Not every mosquito or insect carries disease, but just *one* bite from an infected mosquito or other insect can make you sick.

INSECT REPELLENTS

Insect repellents fall into two categories (1) Chemical, and (2) Botanical.

Chemical Repellents

DEET—Repellents containing DEET (acronym for the chemical N, N-diethyl-3-methylbenzamide—previously called N, N-diethyl-m-toluamide) are the most effective and widely used. DEET was developed in the 1930s by the U.S. Department of Agriculture and registered for use by the general public in 1957. DEET-containing repellents are now used by over 200 million persons worldwide each year. In the past 42 years, people have applied DEET more than 8 billion times.

- DEET is effective against more species of biting insects than any other repellent.
- With careful product choice and application, DEET is effective for up to 12 hours.
- DEET is the best studied and analyzed of all repellents.
- DEET remains the gold standard of chemical insect repellents.
- Forty years of testing >20,000 compounds has not led to a better repellent being brought to market.

How DEET works—DEET works in part by masking the insect-attracting odor of carbon dioxide and lactic acid given off by the human body. At very close range, DEET appears to work primarily by interfering with an electrophysiological homing mechanism in a mosquitoe's antennae.

DEET is effective in relatively small amounts provided it is spread evenly and completely over all exposed areas. DEET, however, has little "spatial activity," meaning that nearby, untreated skin is still likely to be bitten. Factors playing a role in any repellent's effectiveness include its concentration, the frequency and uniformity of application, and the number and species of insects attempting to bite. Evaporation and absorption from the skin surface, wash-off from rain or sweat, higher temperatures, or a windy environment all reduce effectiveness.

Higher concentrations of DEET provide longer-lasting protection, but as the concentration of applied DEET climbs above 50%, each incremental increase provides relatively less additional protection. Extended-release formulations, however, have made it possible to reduce the concentration of DEET without sacrificing duration of action (See Figure 6.2).

DEET is most effective against mosquitoes and ticks, less so against gnats, blackflies, biting flies, fleas, and mites. It has no effect against bees and wasps.

DEET Toxicity/Safety

It is not known exactly how many adverse reactions might be caused by DEET, but millions of people (including about one-third of the U.S. population) have used DEET over the last 40 years without significant problems. To meet newer, more stringent safety requirements, the Environmental Protection Agency (EPA) completed a comprehensive re-evaluation of DEET in 1998 and concluded: "As long as consumers follow label directions and take proper precautions, insect repellents containing DEET do not present a health concern." (See summary on next page).

There have been very few reports in the medical literature of major adverse effects associated with DEET. These adverse effects include:

Dermatological side effects—Skin reactions to DEET are exceedingly rare; they include itching, hives, blisters, or redness. Contact with the mouth can cause transient burning or stinging of the lips, tongue, and oral mucosa. Between 1961 and 1999, there were 12 cases of bullous irritant contact dermatitis, reported solely in military personnel.

Neurological side effects—Concerns over the potential neurological toxicity of DEET are based on a small number of case reports in the medical literature. Between 1961 and 2000, there were only 23 reported cases of possible neurological symptoms associated with DEET use. Of these:

- 6 were deliberate ingestions (3 died).
- 17 cases had behavioral changes (14 resolved, 3 died).
  – Details of these cases were often poorly documented, making causal relationships difficult to establish.
  – Most cases reported "heavy, frequent, or whole-body" application.
  – There was no correlation seen between the severity of side effects and the concentration of DEET.

In some of these cases, symptoms could not be positively attributed to DEET. Seizures, for example, in children could have been coincidental with a viral infection.

The potential of greater DEET toxicity in children has been a concern because their thinner skin and greater body-surface-area-to-weight ratio theoretically could enhance DEET absorption. This concern, however, has not been upheld by scientific study, and neurological toxicity in children has not been substantiated

> **EPA 1998 Analysis of DEET Risks**
> - DEET is "slightly toxic" by eye, skin, oral routes.
> - There is no evidence of oncogenicity or teratogenicity.
> - DEET has no effect on fertility or reproduction.
> - DEET is not a selective neurotoxin.
>   - Seizures could not be positively related to DEET.
>   - There is no apparent correlation between DEET concentration and seizure incidence.
>   - Maximum seizure risk, based on known cases, would be 1 in 100 million users.
> - DEET is not uniquely toxic to children.
> - DEET does not represent a health concern when applied with common sense.

Courtesy of Mark S. Fradin, M.D.

by detailed surveillance. In a 1994 report reviewing 9,086 cases of DEET exposure from 71 poison control centers in the United States, the most severe reactions to DEET were caused by inhalation or eye contact, not skin application. The report also reached the following conclusion: There was no correlation between the severity of symptoms and age, gender, or concentration of applied DEET.

These reports, and others, indicate that side effects from the proper DEET use are rare. Despite years of use and millions of applications, no clear pattern of DEET toxicity has emerged. It should be noted in this respect that the EPA does not require a cautionary statement on the label of repellents warning about the possibility of seizures or other neurological side effects.

Although a direct link between DEET and significant health problems is extremely remote, the EPA recommends you follow these precautions to minimize any possible risks.

- Apply just enough repellent to lightly cover the areas of exposed skin. Do not saturate the skin. DEET may also be applied to clothing.
- Do not get in eyes or mouth and avoid applying repellents to children's hands to prevent contact with these areas.
- Avoid inhaling DEET aerosol or spray.
- Wear long sleeves and long pants, when possible, to reduce the skin surface area that needs to be treated with DEET.
- Don't apply repellents on open cuts, or inflamed or irritated skin.
- Shower or wash repellent-treated skin after coming indoors.

Until recently, manufacturers of 5–10% DEET repellents have made label claims that their products are safer for use in children. However, since there is no evidence that DEET toxicity correlates with DEET concentration, the EPA has ruled that manufacturers can no longer place child safety claims on products. One other potential problem with the low-concentration "for children" formulas is that they usually last for shorter periods of time, requiring more frequent application of the repellent, with potential greater risk of toxicity.

Table 7.1. Repellents That Contain DEET

Product Brand Name	Available Forms	DEET %
Ultrathon	Cream	33.0
Sawyer Gold	Pump spray	17.5
Sawyer Controlled Release	Lotion	20.0
Sawyer Gold Composite	Aerosol	38.0
Sawyer Maxi-DEET	Solution, pump spray	100.0
OFF! Skintastic Unscented	Pump spray	7.0
OFF! Skintastic Fresh Scent	Lotion	7.5
OFF! Skintastic Unscented	Lotion	7.5
OFF! Unscented	Aerosol spray	15.0
Deep Woods OFF! Unscented	Aerosol spray	30.0
Deep Woods OFF! for Sportsmen	Aerosol spray	30.0
Maximum Protection Deep Woods OFF!	Pump spray	100.0
Deep Woods OFF! for Sportsmen	Pump spray	100.0
Ben's Backyard	Lotion, pump spray	24.0
Ben's Wilderness	Aerosol	27.0
Ben's Max 100	Lotion, pump spray	100.0
Cutter Unscented	Aerosol spray	10.0
Cutter Backwoods Unscented	Aerosol spray	23.0
Cutter Outdoorsman Unscented	Aerosol spray, lotion, stick	30.0
Repel! Soft Scented	Gel	7.0
Repel Soft Scented	Pump spray	18.0
Repel Family Formula	Pump spray	18.0
Repel Sportsman Formula	Pump spray	18.0
Repel Sportsman Formula	Lotion	20.0
Repel Soft Scented	Lotion	20.0
Repel Family Formula	Aerosol	23.0
Repel Classic Sportsman Formula	Aerosol	40.0
Repel 100	Pump spray	100.0

Figure 7.2. Repellents often recommended for international travel. DEET PLUS has 38% DEET and is useful in areas of high insect activity. Ultrathon has 33% DEET in a 12-hour controlled-release formulation. Ultrathon is used by the U.S. and U.K. military. Sawyer Controlled Release contains 20% DEET and is a good choice for travelers of all ages.

How Low Should You Go?

Despite the lack of scientific evidence showing that higher DEET concentrations are more toxic, manufacturers have responded to consumer fears of "DEET toxicity" by producing repellents with DEET concentrations in the 5%–10% range. These low-concentration products may be perfectly acceptable for preventing nuisance bites, but may well not provide enough protection in areas of the world where insect-borne diseases are a real threat.

What Should the Traveler Do?

The *HealthGuide* believes that travelers (including children) who are visiting areas where insect-transmitted infectious and tropical diseases are found should use a repellent with a DEET concentration of 20%–35%. Under conditions of high temperatures or humidity, which increases loss of repellent from the skin surface, or when there is intense insect-biting activity, higher concentrations of DEET may be justified. Choosing a controlled-release formulation of DEET (Ultrathon or Sawyer's Controlled Release) is another way to prolong the efficacy of a repellent without requiring the use of DEET concentrations over 35%.

There is no convincing evidence that infants and children are harmed by DEET if the repellent is used according to the label. If parents choose to use a low-concentration DEET repellent on their children, additional measures of protection, like permethrin-treated clothing, mosquito nets, and elimination of indoor insects, should be used.

Botanical Repellents

Long before the advent of synthetic chemicals, people used plant-derived substances to repel mosquitoes. Plants whose essential oils are reported to have repellent activity include citronella, camphor, clove, geranium, soybean, eucalyptus, peppermint, and others. Citronella is the most common botanical oil found in natural repellents. When compared to DEET, however, citronella (the main ingredient in Natrapel, the most popular natural brand in the United States) and most other essential oils give only short-lasting protection, lasting anywhere from minutes to under 2 hours. An exception may be Blocker®, a repellent which contains soybean oil, geranium oil, and coconut oil. One field study conducted in Canada showed that this product gave 97% protection against *Aedes* mosquitoes for 3.5 hours.

One reason natural repellents have become popular is because consumers have been exposed to numerous articles warning them about "DEET toxicity" and also because of the undesirable cosmetic features of DEET (e.g., its odor and its adverse effect on certain synthetic fabrics and plastics). The true safety profile of natural repellents, however, has yet to be determined. Plant-derived repellents are not inherently safe just because they are "natural". Citronella, for example, caused the death of a 21-month-old child after ingestion of only one ounce of the oil. Drinking eucalyptus oil has also caused poisonings and fatalities.

Table 7.3. Plant-Derived Insect Repellents

Product Brand Name	Forms	Active Ingredient
Skin-So-Soft Moisturizing	Lotion	Citronella oil, 0.05%
Skin-So-Soft Bug Guard	Pump spray	Citronella oil, 0.10%
Blocker	Lotion, oil, pump spray	Soybean oil, 2%
Buzz Away	Towelette, pump spray	Citronella oil, 5%
Buzz Away (SPF 15)	Lotion	
Natrapel	Lotion, pump spray	Citronella, 10%
Herbal Armor	Lotion	Citronella oil, 12%, oils of
Herbal Armor (SPF 15)	Lotion	Cedarwood, lavender, lemongrass, and peppermint
Herbal Armor	Pump spray	Citronella oil, oils of clove, cedarwood,
Green Ban for People (Regular)	Oil	Citronella oil, 5%; peppermint oil, 1%
Green Ban (Double Strength)	Oil	Citronella oil, 10%; peppermint oil, 2%

SPF = sun protection factor

Table 7.4. Permethrin Sprays & Solutions

Permethrin Sprays & Solution

Duranon (Coulston)	Aerosol spray, pump spray	Permethrin, 0.5%
Outdoorsman Gear Guard (Cutter)	Aerosol spray	Permethrin, 0.5%
Permanone (WPC Corp.)	Aerosol spray	Permethrin, 0.5%
Permethrin Arthropod Repellent	Aerosol spray, pump spray	Permethrin, 0.5%
Permethrin Spray (Sawyer)	Aerosol spray, pump spray	Permethrin, 0.5%
PermaKill (Coulston Products)	Concentrate solution	Permethrin, 13.3%

The Bottom Line

Using DEET is an essential step in preventing insect bites. If you are traveling in an area where insect-borne disease is a real threat, the most prudent repellent choice is one that contains DEET. These products are effective and necessary to safeguard your health. Because of their relatively poor efficacy, the *HealthGuide* does not recommend that plant-derived repellents be used when either children or adults are traveling to areas where insect-borne diseases may be found.

PROTECTIVE CLOTHING

Clothing provides a physical barrier to biting insects, provided it is sufficiently thick or tightly woven. For increased protection, especially when there is more intense mosquito activity (e.g., in the evening), you should wear long-sleeved shirts and trousers. Tucking your pant leg into your socks or boots can prevent both mosquito bites and tick attachment.

Chemically Treated Clothing

Clothing protection is dramatically increased when the fabric is sprayed or impregnated with a chemical that will either repel or directly kill any insect that alights on the fabric. Both DEET and permethrin are used as clothing treatments, but DEET has been largely replaced for this purpose by the more-effective permethrin.

PERMETHRIN

Unlike DEET, which is used primarily on the skin, permethrin is applied to fabric, such as clothing or mosquito nets. Permethrin, however, is not a repellent—it is a powerful, rapidly acting contact insecticide that knocks down, or kills, insects that come in contact with it. Features of permethrin:

- Permethrin kills or stuns insects touching treated fabric.
- Permethrin adheres tightly to fabric and will last through multiple washings. It will not harm or stain fabric, even silk.
- Unlike DEET, permethrin will not soften plastic or synthetic materials.
- It is effective against mosquitoes, ticks, flies, and chiggers. Permethrin is more effective against ticks than DEET.
- Permethrin is biodegradable and does not accumulate in the environment. However, it should not be disposed of in ways that will harm marine life.

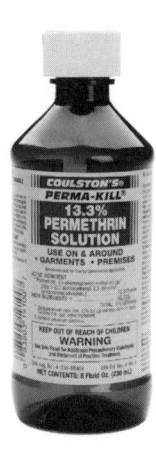

Figure 7.5. Permethrin comes as a solution and in an aerosol or pump spray. Using permethrin and a DEET repellent, in combination, 100% protection against bites can be achieved.

Permethrin is a synthetic chemical analogue of the naturally-occurring insecticide pyrethrum which is found in chrysanthemums. It acts as a neurotoxin. The stunning and direct killing effects of permethrin are due to its blockage of sodium transport in insect nerve fibers.

Although highly toxic to insects, permethrin is not hazardous to mammals; skin absorption of the chemical is extremely low, and any absorbed permethrin is rapidly metabolized. To date, no cases of human toxicity, carcinogenicity, or mutagenicity have been reported. In fact, products such as 5% ELIMITE® antiscabies cream contain permethrin, and are safe enough to be applied overnight directly to scalp and skin for medical purposes.

Permethrin and DEET—The Ideal Combination?

The best way to avoid insect bites—and the diseases that insects transmit—is to apply a DEET repellent to your exposed skin and treat your clothing with permethrin. The effectiveness of this combination is confirmed by many studies. In

Figure 7.6. Technique for Impregnating Clothing or Mosquito Netting with Permethrin Solution

1. Pour 4 to 8 oz. of 13.3% permethrin solution (PermaKill) into the plastic bag or a small basin.

2. Add 2 to 4 quarts of water. Mix. Solution will turn milky white.

3. Place mosquito net or 1 to 2 garments in bag or basin. (Tie bag shut.)

4. Submerge fabric in solution to impregnate. Let rest 10 minutes.

5. Remove items from solution. Wring out excess solution.

6. Hang up clothing or netting for 2 to 3 hours to dry. You can also lay out fabric to dry on a clean surface.

NOTE: Permethrin is toxic to fish and other aquatic life. Don't flush leftover permethrin solution into streams or waterways—bury it or take it to the dump!

Directions for Spraying with Permethrin Aerosol

One 6 oz. aerosol will treat 2 sets of clothing (shirt & trousers = 1 set) or 1 net.

1. Place the clothing or mosquito net on a plastic sheet out-of-doors.
2. Spray, using a slow, circular motion, holding the can 8"–12" above the fabric. Moisten all areas. Fabric will temporarily darken when moistened.
3. Shirts: Spray each side 30–45 seconds. Trousers: Spray each side 30–45 seconds. Jackets: Spray each side 30–45 seconds.
4. Mosquito nets: Partially unroll the net onto the plastic sheet. Spray 30–45 seconds. Turn net and spray another 30–45 seconds. Keep turning and spraying the net until you've moistened all areas.
5. Hang up, or lay out, clothing or net to dry. Allow 2–3 hours for complete drying. Effective for 2–6 weeks. Permethrin, when applied, is odorless and nonstaining.

one study, conducted in Alaska, the use of permethrin-treated clothing and 33% DEET afforded 99.9% protection. In comparison, untreated control subjects sustained over 1000 bites/hour!

How to Use Permethrin
Follow the directions in Figure 7.6.

Preventing Tick Bites
The measures described above are also dramatically effective against ticks. In all studies, 100% protection against tick attachment has been shown when using a combination of DEET-containing repellent on exposed skin and permethrin-treated clothing. If you are not wearing much protective clothing, you need to rely more on an insect repellent and vigilant self-inspection for ticks, especially about the legs, thighs, neck, and waist, the regions where ticks like to migrate. Tip: wear a bandana treated with permethrin. This will deter ticks from attaching about the head and neck.

Treating mosquito bites
Topical corticosteroid creams and ointments can reduce redness, itching, and swelling. Topical antihistamines and topical anesthetics, like benzacaine, should not be used because they can cause allergic contact dermatitis. Oral antihistamines, however, can be effective in reducing the symptoms of mosquito bites. One study showed that the non-sedating oral antihistamine cetirizine (Zyrtec) is effective in reducing localized reactions when used prophylactically in highly sensitized individuals. After Bite©, a 3.6% ammonium solution, can also relieve the itching associated with mosquito bites.

MOSQUITO NETS

Mosquito nets play an important role in preventing malaria and other insect-borne illnesses such as leishmaniasis, filariasis, and encephalitis. Nets are less important in preventing dengue since the aedes mosquitoes that transmit dengue are primarily daytime biters. The use of bed nets and other personal protection measures against bites is increasing as more travelers are being exposed to multidrug-resistant malaria, for which no prophylactic drug regimen is 100% effective. The prevention of mosquito bites, in fact, is the best defense against malaria and other insect-transmitted illnesses.

Bed nets, however, have certain problems. They are often not well-fitted and can be easily torn, and mosquitoes can feed through the mesh if part of the body touches it during the night. These factors provide a rationale for treating nets with permethrin; the insecticide kills or knocks down mosquitoes and other insects that land on the net before they have a chance to find a hole to enter or to feed.

Treatment of nets with insecticidal or repellent compounds started in the 1930s in the USSR, using lysol, and in the American and German armies during World

War II, using DDT. In 1973 photostable insecticidal pyrethroids, developed as molecular analogues of the natural plant insecticide pyrethrum, were synthesized and found to be highly effective against mosquitoes when applied to fabric.

In 1984, field trials of permethrin-impregnated nets were first carried out. These and subsequent trials demonstrated that (1) permethrin binds tightly to nylon, polyester, and cotton; (2) insecticidal fabric levels can be maintained for 6 to 12 months; (3) permethrin-treated nets kill insects that land on it; and (4) treated nets reduce mosquito counts within dwellings. Studies from many countries have also shown that malaria rates are reduced in communities where permethrin-treated nets are used. Many tropical countries now have public health programs that supply permethrin-impregnated nets to villages in malaria-endemic areas.

Figure 7.7. The SleepScreen

Types of Nets

One problem with the use of bed nets in a hot climate is lack of adequate ventilation. Tightly woven nets (used mostly to prevent the entry of tiny sand flies) reduce airflow more than nets with a larger mesh. This problem can be overcome by treating the larger-mesh nets with permethrin. Since insects always stop first on the fabric before going through an opening, a permethrin-treated net, even with a large mesh, will kill or repel any insect that tries to get through it, while also providing better ventilation.

The type of mosquito net you should use depends upon several factors. If you are traveling solo from location to location, you'll want something compact, light, and easy to set up. On the other hand, if one or two of you are residing in a fixed location for an extended period of time, then a roomier model is preferable, even if it may be somewhat larger and heavier to transport.

Figure 7.8. The Spider net. Products shown in this chapter are available from Travel Medicine, Inc. 800-TRAVMED.

The Spider—This conical net (Figure 7.8) has a fairly large mesh to provide good ventilation and is large enough to cover a king-size bed but is also lightweight and compact.

SleepScreen—The double-wide SleepScreen (see Figure 7.7) accommodates one or two people in sleeping bags or in a double (or wider) bed. Comes with 5-piece shock-corded poles and nylon stuff sack. Available also in a single model. Both the single and double models have the advantage of being very lightweight, compact, and easy to set up.

TropicScreen—Similar to the SleepScreen, this lightweight, very portable bed net completely encloses two people on the ground or one sleeper on a cot.

Insect Proofing Your Sleeping Quarters

Even if you are staying in an air-conditioned hotel or a well-screened house, you should use a permethrin-based aerosol to rid your sleeping quarters of mosquitoes and other biting insects that might have gotten into your room. Several brands are effective and widely available in the United States. RAID Flying Insect Spray and Green Thumb Flying Insect Killer (Figure 7.8; available at most hardware stores) contain permethrin-type insecticides. In East Africa, Doom® Insect Spray, which contains permethrin and pyrethrum, is locally available. Spray your sleeping quarters with one of these aerosols one hour before bedtime to help guarantee an insect-free indoor environment. The effect of these aerosol sprays should last several days after a single treatment.

NOTE: When spraying indoors, vacate the sprayed areas until the product "settles." Avoid spraying on food or eating surfaces.

Figure 7.9. Flying Insect Killer

Fradin MS. Mosquitoes and mosquito repellents: A clinician's guide. Ann Int Med 1998;128:931–940.

Goodyer L, Behrens RH. Short Report: The safety and toxicity of insect repellents. Am J Trop Med Hyg 1998;59(2):323–324.

Snodgrass HL. Permethrin transfer from treated cloth to the skin surface: potential for exposure in humans. J Toxic and Envir H 1992;35:91–105.

The Medical Letter 1989;31:45–47.

Traveling Healthy Newsletter, May/June 1997;10:1–4.

8 Insect-Borne Diseases

Overview of Insect-Borne Diseases

This chapter describes a number of important but rather uncommon (at least for the traveler) diseases caused by viruses, parasites, and bacteria. Unlike a common disease like hepatitis A, these insect-borne diseases often require the diagnostic and treatment expertise of a travel/tropical medicine or infectious disease specialist.

YELLOW FEVER

In 1900 Dr. Walter Reed demonstrated that yellow fever is a viral illness transmitted by mosquitoes. The disease is so named because jaundice, the result of liver damage, is a common sign of this illness.

There are two distinct cycles of transmission, but the resulting disease is the same. Urban yellow fever is transmitted by an *Aedes aegypti* mosquito from an infected person to another person. In jungle yellow fever, mosquitoes transmit the infection between nonhuman primates (e.g., monkeys) and humans or vice versa.

Yellow fever occurs in tropical areas of certain countries in Africa and South America. These countries comprise the yellow fever endemic zones. Interestingly, there is no yellow fever in other regions with warm climates and aedes mosquitoes, such as the Middle East, Southeast Asia, and the Pacific. The reason for this has never been clearly understood.

Since the 1980s, yellow fever has reemerged across Africa and South America. In Africa, both jungle and urban transmission cycles occur. The largest number of cases in Africa has been reported from Nigeria. In 1992, yellow fever reappeared in Kenya after an absence of 50 years, and in 1994 and 1995 Gabon reported its first outbreak ever. Outbreaks have also been reported from Cameroon, Ghana, Liberia, Senegal, and Sierra Leone.

In South America in 1995, Peru experienced the largest yellow fever outbreak from any country in South America since 1950. Between 1985 and 1998, yellow fever cases have been reported from Bolivia, Brazil, Colombia, Ecuador, and Peru. In South America, the jungle transmission cycle predominates, and about 80% of yellow fever cases are reported in adult male forest workers. Urban yellow fever has not been reported from South America since 1954, but the *Aedes aegypti* mosquitoes have reinfested many tropical cities of South America, setting the stage for potential urban outbreaks of this disease.

Yellow fever is underreported; epidemiological investigations have found the true number of cases to be 10 to 500 times higher than the number reported.

Symptoms

Most yellow fever infections are mild and go unrecognized, but severe, life-threatening illness occurs in about 15% of people exposed to the disease. Symptoms of severe illness start with fever, headache, muscle aches, nausea, abdominal pain, and vomiting. These acute symptoms last for 3–4 days and are followed by a toxic phase characterized by jaundice, hematemesis (vomiting of blood), melena (bloody stools), coma, and, in 50% of severe cases, death, usually after about two weeks of illness.

The differential diagnosis includes malaria, leptospirosis, viral hepatitis, typhus, dengue fever, and other viral hemorrhagic fevers. The laboratory diagnosis of yellow fever can be made by measuring IgM antibody response.

Treatment

There is no specific drug treatment available. Supportive care is indicated.

Prevention

Vaccination—Being immunized is the best way to prevent yellow fever and a highly effective vaccine is available. All travelers to rural areas of endemic zone countries should be immunized, and to meet international requirements the vaccine must be administered at least 10 days prior to arrival.

Side effects: A recent study has shown that elderly travelers are at risk (albeit slight) of severe effects from the yellow fever vaccine, including death. Therefore, a careful evaluation of the need for the vaccination in this age group should be made by a travel health advisor.

See Table 2.2, Chapter 2 for yellow fever vaccine schedule, indications, precautions and contraindications.

Mosquito protection measures—All travelers should also take measures to prevent mosquito bites during daylight hours (especially early morning and late afternoon) when aedes mosquitoes are most likely to bite. These measures include applying a DEET-containing insect repellent, wearing permethrin-treated clothing, eliminating indoor mosquitoes through screening and spraying, and sleeping under a permethrin-treated bed net.

DENGUE FEVER

This viral illness occurs in many tropical and subtropical countries, with over half the population of the globe at risk for infection. The incidence and geographical distribution of the disease have greatly increased in recent years. Dengue (pronounced DENG-ee) is now prevalent in the Caribbean, Central and South America, Mexico, the Pacific islands, the tropical countries of Asia, and sub-Saharan Africa (see map, page 131). In the United States, the majority of dengue fever cases occur in tourists who have returned from Puerto Rico, the Virgin

Islands, Mexico, and Thailand. Unless there is an epidemic in progress, the risk of acquiring dengue by the average tourist is low, perhaps 1 per 1,000 travelers who are on an average-length itinerary.

Dengue is spread primarily by the *Aedes aegypti* mosquito, but can also be transmitted by *Aedes albopictus* mosquitoes. Aedes mosquitoes feed during the day, with most biting activity in the morning for several hours after daybreak and in the late afternoon for several hours before dark, but the mosquito may feed at any time during the day, especially indoors, in shady areas, or when it is overcast. In urban and periurban areas the mosquitoes usually breed in stagnant water that collects in discarded tires, buckets, bottles, flower vases, barrels, and similar containers; it's therefore not surprising that development has increased the incidence of dengue in many countries.

There are four types (serotypes) of dengue viruses. If you are infected with one type of virus, you will gain lifelong immunity against that particular serotype, but not against the other serotypes. In fact, a subsequent infection with a different serotype may result in more severe disease (due to the presence of cross-reacting, but non-neutralizing antibodies)—dengue hemorrhagic fever or dengue shock syndrome.

Symptoms

Dengue virus infections may be asymptomatic—or lead to a range of symptoms, even death. The vast majority of infections, especially in children under age 15 years, are asymptomatic or minimally symptomatic. More severe illness is seen with increasing age, or with repeat infections with a different serotype, especially in children.

Dengue fever (DF)—Typical symptoms include chills and fever ("breakbone fever"); severe headache, especially behind the eyes; muscle and joint pain; nausea

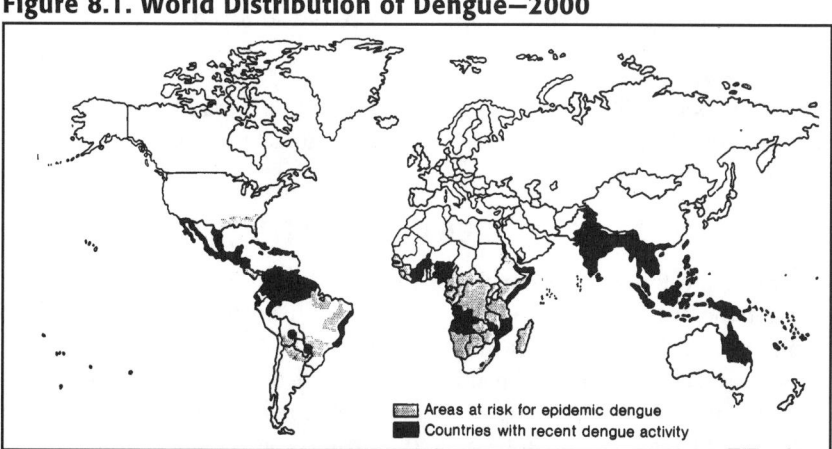

Figure 8.1. World Distribution of Dengue—2000

Source: Division of Vector-Bourne Infectious Diseases, National Center for Infectious Diseases, Centers for Disease Control and Prevention

and vomiting; flushing of the face, neck, and chest; and a maculopapular rash. The rash appears in three to four days and spreads from the torso to the arms, legs, and face (at this stage the disease can be confused with measles). Leukopenia (low white blood cell count) and thrombocytopenia (low platelet count) are frequent. Less frequent, but not rare, are hemorrhagic signs, such as a petechial rash, or bleeding from the nose, gums, or intestinal tract. In uncomplicated cases, acute symptoms resolve in 5–7 days, but fatigue may linger for many weeks.

NOTE: Other illnesses that can mimic dengue include malaria, leptospirosis, typhoid, measles, and chikungunya fever. You should be checked immediately for malaria if you develop fever while in, or after visiting, a malaria-endemic area.

Dengue hemorrhagic fever (DHF)—This is a severe, sometimes fatal form of dengue fever. It rarely strikes Western tourists because they usually have never been previously exposed to the dengue virus, which is a risk factor for DHF. Dengue hemorrhagic fever is diagnosed when there is minor or major bleeding, thrombocytopenia, and evidence of plasma leakage from capillaries into the tissues or body cavities. Plasma leakage, which differentiates DHF from DF, causes edema, pleural effusions (fluid around the lung), and hemoconcentration (increased concentration of red blood cells). A progressively decreasing platelet count and a rising hematocrit from on-going plasma loss herald the impending onset of dengue shock syndrome (DSS).

Treatment

Treatment consists of bed rest, fluid replacement, and analgesics. Aspirin and other nonsteroidal antiinflammatory drugs should be avoided since they interfere with platelet function and may promote further bleeding. Antibiotics and steroids are not beneficial. The prognosis in DHF and DSS depends on the prevention or early recognition and treatment of shock. Early, judicious treatment with intravenous fluids and plasma expanders can keep mortality under 1%. Once dengue shock syndrome is established, mortality can exceed 40%.

Prevention

No vaccine is available. Reduce your risk by preventing mosquito bites. Remember, the aedes mosquito is a day biter. Follow the guidelines in Chapter 7. Eliminate any nearby aedes mosquito breeding sites.

JAPANESE ENCEPHALITIS (JE)

This mosquito-transmitted viral illness is the number one cause of encephalitis in Asia and the Western Pacific. Over 50,000 cases of JE are reported annually from Southeast Asia, India, China, Japan, and Korea.

Japanese encephalitis (encephalitis=inflammation of the brain) occurs in rural-agricultural areas throughout Asia. In temperate regions such as the People's Republic of China, Japan, and Korea, JE transmission is highest from April to September. In northern India and Nepal, peak transmission is from June to

November. In the tropical regions of Asia and Oceania, JE occurs year-round.

Figure 8.2. Distribution of Japanese Encephalitis

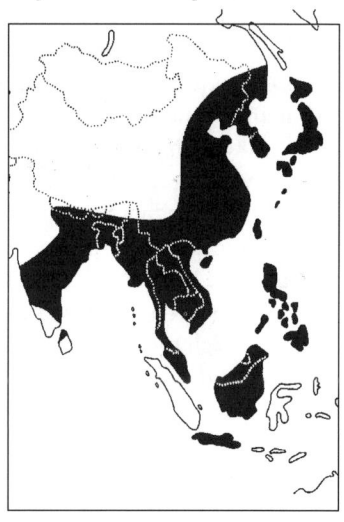

The virus of Japanese encephalitis is transmitted by culex mosquitoes. These mosquitoes breed where there is abundant water, such as in rice paddies, and feed primarily on birds and local domestic animals, usually pigs. Visiting a rural-agricultural rice-growing, pig-farming region, therefore, can put you at risk. About 1%–3% of the culex mosquitoes in endemic areas are infective. Since these mosquitoes are night feeders, there is less risk of JE transmission during the day.

The average tourist is not at risk. If you are a short-term traveler, and if you are visiting only urban areas, your risk of getting JE is very low—approximately one in one million. You will be at greater risk if living in rural agricultural (rice-growing, pig-farming) areas during the season of peak transmission. Your risk then rises to approximately 1 in 5,000 per month of exposure. Of the small number of Americans who have developed this illness in the last two decades, most were military personnel or their dependents.

Symptoms

Watch for nausea, vomiting, headache, and fever. A severe attack will cause lethargy and coma. Fortunately, most JE infections are asymptomatic—only 1 in 250 infected individuals becomes sick. Unfortunately, if you do develop symptoms, the resulting illness can be severe, with a mortality as high as 25%, and the incidence of permanent neurological damage about 30%.

Treatment

There is no drug treatment for JE. Good nursing care is essential in severe cases.

Prevention

Mosquito protection measures—All travelers should take measures to prevent mosquito bites.

Vaccination—See Table 2.2, Chapter 2 for JE vaccine schedule, indications, precautions and contraindications.

AFRICAN TRYPANOSOMIASIS
(SLEEPING SICKNESS)

African trypanosomiasis, or sleeping sickness, is transmitted by the tsetse fly. This disease is endemic in sub-Saharan Africa, and major outbreaks are now occurring in Sudan, Uganda, Congo, and Angola. The numbr of prevalent cases is estimated at 300,000, with about 60 million people at risk. Sleeping sickness, however, almost never occurs in tourists, although occasional cases are reported in travelers, usually those visiting game parks. Long-term travelers or expatriates living in rural endemic areas may be at slightly increased risk.

There are two forms of this disease. Gambian, or West African trypanosomiasis (caused by *T. brucei gambiense*) is a chronic disease that takes several years to reach the advanced stage. It occurs primarily in the forested areas of western and central Africa. Rhodesian, or East African trypanosomiasis (caused by *T. b. rhodesiense*), presents more acutely and progresses more rapidly. It occurs primarily in the savannah and woodlands of eastern and southern Africa and is the form seen (rarely) in travelers.

Symptoms

Symptoms start 5 to 15 days after the bite of an infected fly. (NOTE: Tsetse fly bites may be quite common on safari but only a very small percentage of tsetse flies are infected.) An inflamed nodule (inoculation chancre) develops at the site of the bite and may measure one-half inch or more in diameter. Chancres are typically seen only in *T. rhodesiense* infections. Other symptoms include fever, headache, rash, lymph node swelling, splenomegaly, edema of the face and joints, and, occasionally, carditis (heart muscle inflammation). In East African disease, there is early CNS invasion which, unless treated, progresses to lethargy, coma, and, ultimately, death within 6 weeks to 9 months. The onset of West African trypanosomiasis is more insidious. A localized skin lesion is the first symptom. Fever, rash, and lymph node swelling take weeks to months to appear. CNS symptoms occur later.

The diagnosis of East African sleeping sickness is made by demonstrating trypanosomes in blood, chancre, or spinal fluid.

Treatment

Management of this disease requires the expertise of a specialist. Suramin is the treatment of choice for early-phase East African (Rhodesian) trypanosomiasis. Melarsoprol, an organoarsenic compound, is indicated for the treatment of second-stage disease, when there is central nervous system involvement. Treatment of the second stage, however, is long and complicated, and can be hampered by severe adverse reactions to melarsoprol. A new 10-day course of treatment may have practical advantages over the standard 26-day treatment course.

Prevention

The only prevention is to avoid the day-biting tsetse fly.

AMERICAN TRYPANOSOMIASIS
(CHAGAS' DISEASE)

This is another disease that almost never occurs in travelers, even those living long-term in endemic areas. Chagas' disease is caused by a small single-cell parasite called *Trypanosoma cruzi* (*T. cruzi*), which, when it infects a human, may cause an acute illness, but usually causes an asymptomatic infection. This may be followed in 30% of people infected (usually years later) by damage to the heart or gastrointestinal tract.

T. cruzi is transmitted by species of reduviid or triatomid bugs, commonly called assassin, or kissing bugs because of their predilection for biting the face while the victim is sleeping. Chagas' disease can also be transmitted by unscreened blood transfusions. (Up to 1.9%–6.5% of blood in some blood banks in Latin America is contaminated by *T. cruzi* parasites.)

Chagas' disease occurs in Latin America in rural areas extending north from Chile and Argentina to Mexico. Most risk occurs in Brazil. A few cases have been reported in the southern United States (Texas, Oklahoma, and California). Transmission occurs primarily in areas where there are poorly constructed adobe-style native huts. The assassin bugs (not all are infective) live in the thatch roofs and mud walls of these huts and come out at night to feed on the blood of sleeping humans, usually biting the exposed face near the eye or the corner of the mouth.

People staying in tourist accommodations are rarely infected. If you are traveling only to large cities, or to remote jungle sites, you are not at risk. If, however, you are a traveler staying in villages with adobe-style huts, you should take the precautions listed below.

Symptoms

Only about one-third of infected persons develop symptoms of acute Chagas' disease. The first symptom may be confused with a simple "bedbug bite," usually on the face. One to three weeks after exposure there may be a swollen nodule or pimple at the site of the bite, followed by fever and localized lymph node enlargement. If you were bitten near the eye, you may develop swelling of your face and eyelid, and conjunctivitis (reddening of the eye). These localized symptoms may last 1–2 months, then disappear. Parasites can then spread throughout the body, infecting many tissues, particularly the heart, skeletal muscles, and the nervous system. At this stage you may develop a flu-like illness. In severe cases a condition called myocarditis (inflammation of the heart) can occur and you would notice rapid heart rate, shortness of breath, and other symptoms of cardiac rhythm disturbances and heart failure.

The most serious aspect of Chagas' disease is the delayed damage it can inflict on the heart and intestinal tract. About 10% of infected people go on to develop heart block and congestive heart failure. Chagas' disease, in fact, is the leading cause of congestive heart failure in endemic areas of Latin America and is responsible for one-quarter of all deaths in the 25- to 44-year-old age group in these endemic areas. Chronic enlargement of the esophagus (megaesophagus) and colon (megacolon) can also occur.

Acute Chagas' disease can be confused with malaria, mumps, eye infections, sinusitis, and cellulitis of the skin. To diagnose Chagas' disease, an examination of your blood in the acute phase of illness may demonstrate parasites. Special blood cultures and/or lymph node aspiration can also be diagnostic. Serologic screening tests may be useful. An ELISA assay using purified antigen is available and is specific and more accurate. Consult an expert in tropical medicine.

Treatment

Acute illness can be treated with either benznidazole (Ragonil®, Roche) or nifurtimox (Lampit®, Bayer) and complete clinical, parasitologic, and serologic cures are possible if treatment is administered within the first year or two. There is no drug that currently provides satisfactory treatment for chronic Chagas' disease, although there is an increasing trend to treat silent chronic infections before late illness begins.

Prevention

Preventing Chagas' disease means avoiding the assassin bug. If you are camping in an endemic area, stay some distance away from adobe hut–type structures. If you are living in an endemic area in an adobe hut, take the following precautions:

- Spray an insecticide in your living and sleeping quarters. RAID Formula II Crack and Crevice Spray is a good choice.
- Fumigant canisters can prevent reinfestation.
- Use a residual insecticide on the walls and roofs of houses.

Chagas' disease can also be spread by unscreened blood transfusions, so these should be avoided, if possible.

FILARIASIS

Filariasis is prevalent throughout the tropics and is a group of diseases caused by threadlike roundworms, called filaria, which are transmitted by various mosquitoes, flies, and biting midges. Varieties of filariasis include (1) the more common lymphatic filariasis—bancroftian and malayan filariasis ("elephantiasis"), (2) subcutaneous filariasis—onchocerciasis ("river blindness"), and (3) loiasis.

BANCROFTIAN AND MALAYAN FILARIASIS

These illnesses are transmitted by aedes, culex, Mansonia, or anopheles mosquitoes found in tropical regions of Central and South America, the Caribbean, Africa, China, India, Southeast Asia, and Oceania. Infective larvae (microfilariae) are injected into the skin by the bite of the mosquito. The larvae migrate through the lymphatic channels of the skin and become trapped in lymph nodes, where the adult worms develop. The offspring of these adult worms (microfilariae) then migrate farther in the tissues and also circulate in the blood, leading to a variety of symptoms.

Symptoms

If you have sustained only a few infective insect bites and have only a light infection, you may be completely without symptoms. If you depart the infected area, and thus limit your exposure, no treatment is usually needed. Heavier exposure (many bites over many months) is generally necessary to cause symptomatic disease. Initial symptoms consist of redness of the skin and swelling of lymph nodes of the arms and legs, headache, weakness, muscle pain, coughing, wheezing, and fever. Thousands of mosquito bites may be required, in fact, before microfilariae are evident in the blood. Continued exposure may result in permanent lymphatic inflammation and obstruction. Progression of the disease, usually observed only in the indigenous population of the endemic area, can cause the grotesque swelling of the legs (and scrotum in males) known as elephantiasis.

To check for exposure to filariasis, your doctor can examine your blood for eosinophilia and at midnight for microfilaria, since these larvae enter the bloodstream mostly between 10 p.m. and 2 a.m. ELISA-based serological tests are over 90% sensitive but are rather nonspecific. A negative antibody test virtually rules out any active infection.

Treatment

Treatment of filariasis with diethylcarbamazine (DEC) is effective. The dosage is 6 mg/kg/day for 3 weeks. Repeated single doses of DEC at monthly intervals for 6–12 months appear to increase effectiveness. An effective alternative is albendazole plus ivermectin.

Prevention

See measures described below.

ONCHOCERCIASIS

One type of subcutaneous filariasis that is particularly devastating is onchocerciasis, or river blindness, common in equatorial Africa, the Sahara, Yemen, and parts of Latin America (Mexico, Guatemala, Venezuela, Ecuador, Colombia, and Brazil). The disease is transmitted by black flies that breed in vegetation along fast-flowing rivers in these regions. Onchocerciasis is occasionally acquired by long-term travelers such as expatriates and Peace Corps volunteers.

Symptoms
Symptoms include a skin rash with intense itching (the most common symptom in infected travelers), skin nodules, swollen lymph nodes, inflammation of the eyes, and, in heavy, prolonged infections, blindness.

Symptoms don't occur for several months or more after exposure. By this time, the blood eosinophil count will usually be elevated; therefore, a complete blood count is often a good screening test. Blood tests (antifilarial antibody and antigen assays) can help establish the diagnosis. (The Clinical and Parasitology section of the National Institutes of Health [NIH] can do the serology testing; call 301-496-5398.) To make a definitive diagnosis, skin snips are obtained to identify filarial larvae.

Treatment
Treatment is with ivermectin (Stromectol, Merck), 150–220 µg/kg in a single dose every 6 months until symptoms do not recur. (Two 6-mg tablets is the usual adult dose.) Ivermectin does not kill the adult worm, but only suppresses symptoms by temporarily reducing the number of larvae in the skin. The CDC's Parasitology Hot Line (301-496-5398) can answer further questions.

Prevention
There is no prophylactic drug. Take precautions to prevent insect bites.

LOIASIS

This form of subcutaneous (below the skin surface) filariasis is common to the rain forests of West and Central Africa. Loiasis is also the most frequently diagnosed blood filarial infection in travelers returning to North America and the United Kingdom from Africa, though it is still quite uncommon. The *Loa loa* larvae (microfilariae) are transmitted by the bite of an infective Chrysops fly, also known in Africa as the deer fly. This is a day-biting fly that breeds in wet mud on the edge of shaded streams in the rain forests. After the microfilariae enter the body they develop into adult worms in the subcutaneous tissues (under the skin). The adult worms can survive for up to 17 years.

Symptoms
Symptoms of loiasis are due to migration of the adult *Loa loa* worms just under the skin. Symptoms, which take 12 months or more to develop, include fever, itching, and skin swelling (Calabar swelling), usually involving the hands, wrists, forearms, or face. Adult worms can also be observed migrating on the surface of the eye, beneath the conjunctiva. Expatriates with loiasis may develop an exaggerated immune response leading to a skin rash or heart or kidney disease.

Diagnosis

A blood test for eosinophilia and microfilariae (which peak in the blood during the day), and an ELISA screening test, can be done to check for exposure.

Treatment

Diethylcarbamazine (DEC) is the current treatment of choice for *Loa loa* infections and consists of a total dose of 75 mg/kg of diethylcarbamazine. It is curative in 60% of non-endemic patients with loiasis. Although DEC is usually innocuous to humans, the allergic reactions induced from the destruction of filarial worms can be serious and even life-threatening. In heavy infections, the full dose of medication should be administered over 2–3 weeks. Refractory cases of loiasis have responded to albendazole, 200 mg orally, twice a day, for 21 days.

Prevention of Filariasis and Loiasis

No vaccines are available. You should take measures to prevent insect bites during the day for loiasis and at night for Bancroftian filariasis. These measures include applying a deet-containing skin repellent, wearing permethrin-treated clothing, and sleeping under a mosquito net or in an insect-free room.

Prophylaxis—You can take DEC either weekly or monthly to prevent loiasis or lymphatic (bancroftian or Malayan) filariasis. These regimens are recommended rarely to expatriates living in highly endemic areas.

Dosage—300 mg DEC weekly to prevent loiasis and 500 mg DEC 2 days each month to prevent lymphatic filariasis. CAUTION: If you have previously been infected with filariasis, do not initiate prophylaxis with DEC until you have been treated and your system cleared of parasites.

NOTE: DEC is no longer available in the U.S. or Canada for prophylaxis. The drug may be obtained from the CDC as an investigational drug for treatment of filariasis. It is available in many developing countries.

LEISHMANIASIS

Leishmaniasis is one of the most common parasitic infections in the world, occurring in various forms in 80 countries. The disease is found on all continents except Australia and Antarctica. It is an important public health problem in Mexico, Central and South America, North Africa, sub-Saharan Africa, the Middle East, central Asia, southern Russia, northern China, and India. Scattered areas of disease activity occur in southern Europe, mainly Portugal, southern France, Italy, the Greek Isles, the Costa del Sol, and Majorca. In the United States, cases of the disease have been reported in Texas and Oklahoma.

Leishmania are single-cell organisms (protozoa) just a bit smaller than a red blood cell. Infection occurs when these tiny parasites are injected into the body by the bite of an infective sand fly. Which form of leishmaniasis (visceral, cutaneous, mucocutaneous) that you develop depends upon (1) which species of Leishmania (there are about 20) causes the disease, (2) which organs and cells are predominantly infected, and (3) your state of immunity (many cases of leishmaniasis are self-healing).

Sand flies are usually found in focal areas on the edge of forested areas or in rodent burrows. They feed from dusk to dawn and have a limited flight range.

Visceral Leishmaniasis (kala-azar)

This disease affects primarily the internal organs and bone marrow. Hallmarks of the disease are marked enlargement of the liver and spleen, anemia, and fever.

Kala-azar is found in around the Mediterranean Basin, southern Russia, eastern India, China, East Africa (Kenya, Sudan, Uganda), Central America, Brazil, Venezuela, and Paraguay. In India and China it is widespread throughout rural areas.

Symptoms

Symptoms include fatigue, muscle aches, chills and fever, weight loss, cough, and diarrhea. Warty skin nodules or skin ulcers may also occur. Many kala-azar infections are self-limited and never progress to cause illness; however, the infection may remain dormant and cause severe disease at a later date if the immune system is destroyed as in patients with AIDS.

Diagnosis

To diagnose kala-azar, blood tests and a bone marrow examination and culture may be necessary. An antibody test may be helpful.

Diseases that can be confused with kala-azar include malaria, typhoid fever, brucellosis, Chagas' disease, schistosomiasis, tuberculosis (miliary variety), and amoebic liver abscess. Since massive enlargement of the spleen sometimes occurs, kala-azar can also mimic leukemia or lymphoma.

Treatment

Untreated symptomatic kala-azar is usually fatal. However, prompt treatment with the drug sodium stibogluconate (Pentostam) is often curative. Pentostam is given in an intravenous dose of 20 mg/kg daily for 30–40 days. Pentostam is available from the Parasitic Disease Drug Service Branch of the Centers for Disease Control in Atlanta, Georgia. Amphotericin B is also a first-line drug in countries where resistance to pentostam is common. Second-line treatments include pentamidine and stibogluconate plus interferon-gamma. Their use should be discussed with an expert. For further information about drug treatment and the serological diagnosis of leishmaniasis, physicians should contact the **Parasitic Disease Drug Service of the CDC** at 770-488-7760 or 770-488-7775.

Cutaneous Leishmaniasis (old world variety)

This infection is characterized by ulcerative skin lesions, and occasionally nodules, caused by one of several species of Leishmania. Local names for this disease include Oriental sore and Baghdad boil. Risk areas include the Mediterranean

Basin, the Middle East, Africa (stretching from Senegal to Sudan, Ethiopia, and Kenya), southern Russia, central Asia, and northwestern India.

Symptoms
As the name implies, cutaneous leishmaniasis affects the skin. A variety of lesions can occur: self-healing skin nodules or ulcers, chronic mutilating or nonhealing sores or ulcers, or nonulcerating and warty skin nodules. The skin sites involved are those areas usually not covered by protective clothing, that is, the face, forearms, back of hands, and legs. Symptoms usually occur 2–8 weeks after a bite. The lesions may ulcerate and discharge fluid, or they may remain dry. Spontaneous healing tends to occur over a period of several months to two years.

Cutaneous leishmaniasis (new world variety)
Two species complexes of leishmania (*Leishmania mexicana* and *L. braziliensis*) are responsible for most of the cutaneous leishmaniasis occurring in Mexico and in central and South America.

Symptoms
Skin nodules and/or ulcers are found on exposed skin areas, usually the face and ear. These lesions appear 2–8 weeks after exposure. Spontaneous healing may take 6 to 18 months, or longer.

Mucocutaneous Leishmaniasis (espundia)
This disease is almost exclusively confined to the Western Hemisphere, occurring mostly in the northern half of South America.

Symptoms
This illness occurs when parasites spread from the skin to the mucus membranes of the mouth, nose, and throat. Espundia is usually preceded by a simple skin ulcer, which may heal. Then one month to many years after the initial exposure, destructive ulcerations of the nose and mouth occur. Severe, potentially fatal, disease with disfigurement (espundia) results if treatment is delayed.

Diagnosis
To diagnose cutaneous leishmaniasis, tissue samples are obtained from your skin for examination under the microscope, or for culture. Antibody tests (immuno fluorescent, complement fixation, ELISA, Western blot) are of limited use except in Espundia and the nodular form of the disease. The Parasitic Disease Branch of the Centers for Disease Control can identify parasites from tissue, carry out appropriate antibody tests, and offer advice on treatment.

Treatment
The treatment of choice for large cutaneous lesions is intravenous sodium stibogluconate (Pentostam) in a dose of 20 mg/kg daily for 30 days.

Other drugs are available (dapsone, ketoconazole, pentamidine), but their effectiveness depends upon the species of infecting parasite, the geographic location where the infection was acquired, and the form of the disease.

Prevention
This illness in its various forms is transmitted by sand flies. To protect yourself, you must use a DEET-containing insect repellent, treat your clothing with permethrin, and, if necessary, sleep under a mosquito net. There is no vaccine.

RELAPSING FEVER

This is an acute bacterial infection that can be transmitted to humans by ticks or lice. The cause is a spirochete (*Borrelia recurrentis*). Tick-borne relapsing fever is found in Asia, Africa, Europe, and the Americas, including mountainous areas of the western United States. Louse-borne relapsing fever is found in Asia, Africa, and Europe.

Symptoms include chills, fever, nausea, vomiting, severe headache, and a variety of rashes. The most effective treatment is tetracycline, erythromycin, or penicillin. Without treatment, the attack terminates in 3–10 days but may recur in a milder form 1–2 weeks later. Prevention consists of tick- or louse-bite prevention.

RIFT VALLEY FEVER

This is a viral disease of animals, but it can be transmitted to humans by mosquitoes. Rift Valley fever occurs primarily in sub-Saharan Africa. The initial symptoms (chills, fever, headache, backache, weakness, and vomiting) are similar to malaria and dengue, but reddening of the eyes helps distinguish Rift Valley fever from malaria. The illness lasts 4 to 7 days and complete recovery is the rule, but 2% of infected people develop hemorrhagic complications, jaundice, or meningoencephalitis (inflammation of the brain and/or the membranes covering the spinal cord). No specific treatment is available, but ribavirin and interferon may offer some benefit. Prevention entails avoiding mosquito bites.

SANDFLY FEVER

Sandfly fever is a viral disease transmitted by the bite of an infective sand fly and occurs in parts of Europe, Asia, Africa, and Latin America. It occurs primarily in tropical and subtropical areas with hot, dry weather. The vector of the causative virus is the common sand fly, which bites at night.

Symptoms appear 3 to 6 days after the sand fly bite and consist of fever, headache, nausea, weakness, and myalgia. These symptoms may be severe but are rarely, if ever, fatal, and treatment with fluids and analgesics is usually sufficient. Prevention of sandfly fever consists of nighttime protection against insect bites.

SCRUB TYPHUS

This is a mite-transmitted disease found in Asia, the western Pacific, and Australia. Scrub typhus is endemic in a triangular area between northern Japan and southeast Siberia to the north; Queensland, Australia, to the south; and Pakistan to the west. The cause is a rickettsial organism, *Rickettsia tsutsugamushi*. The disease is transmitted in scrub lands and forest clearings where mites abound on the vegetation.

Symptoms
Humans who come in contact with infected vegetation can be bitten by the larval form of mites, called chiggers. One to three weeks after the mite bite, symptoms occur and consist of chills, fever, rash, lymph node swelling adjacent to the bite, and prostration. A blister, followed by a black scab, or eschar, may occur at the site of the bite. This infection may be fatal.

Treatment
Tetracycline or doxycycline are the treatments of choice.

Prevention
Prevention consists of using personal protection measures against mite bites. In particular, permethrin-impregnated clothing should be worn (long-sleeved shirts suggested) with trousers tucked into boots when walking through grasslands and forests in endemic areas. Prophylaxis with 200 mg of doxycycline weekly is effective.

HEMORRHAGIC FEVER WITH RENAL SYNDROME

Hemorrhagic fever with renal syndrome refers to a viral disease characterized by fever and renal failure, with or without hemorrhagic manifestations. The causative viruses are known as Hantaviruses. These viruses have a worldwide distribution and are harbored primarily by rodents. Human infection results from inhalation or contact with virus-infected rodent urine, saliva, or feces. Severe disease caused by Hantaan virus occurs in Korea, China, eastern Russia, and Eastern Europe, including the Balkan countries. A milder form of the disease occurs in Scandinavia and other European countries.

PLAGUE

Plague is a disease of extreme poverty. The risk of tourists contracting plague is extremely low.

Plague is caused by infection with the bacterium *Yersinia pestis*, which is carried by rats, other rodents, and their fleas. Cats can also acquire plague and transmit the disease directly to humans. Most cases result from the bites of infected fleas, but can also result from handling infected animals or inhaling infectious airborne droplets from persons with plague pneumonia (pneumonic plague), who may spread the disease by coughing.

The disease occurs rarely and sporadically in the southwest United States, and from 1979 to 1994 it was reported from 22 countries in Africa, Asia, Asia Minor, Europe, and South America. Vietnam and Bolivia report the largest number of cases annually.

Symptoms of plague start 2 to 7 days after exposure with rapid onset of fever, chills, headache, generalized aches and pain, and exhaustion. Patients with the bubonic form develop painful swelling of the lymph glands (buboes) in the groin, armpit, or neck; those with the pneumonic form develop a cough and difficulty breathing.

Treatment

Plague is fatal in 50%–60% of untreated cases. Early treatment with antibiotics is effective, especially if started within a few hours of the onset of symptoms. The preferred drugs are streptomycin, chloramphenicol, and tetracycline.

Prevention

The plague vaccine is of unproven effectiveness; moreover, the vaccine is no longer available in the United States. Prophylactic antibiotics can prevent plague; they should be taken by certain individuals (medical personnel, relief workers, etc.) when face-to-face transmission of bacteria has potentially occurred or is anticipated. Adults should take doxycycline, 100 mg daily, or tetracycline, 500 mg twice daily; children 9 years of age, or under, sulfonamides. The most important measure to prevent bubonic plague is to avoid fleas and rodents such as rats, rabbits, squirrels, and chipmunks in endemic areas. Sick or dead animals should also not be handled. Regular use of flea powders on domestic pets having access to both human and rodent habitats is strongly advised in plague-active areas. The application of DEET-containing repellents on exposed skin and permethrin on clothing will reduce the chance of flea bites. People at high risk of exposure to infected fleas should also consider prophylactic antibiotics.

MEDITERRANEAN SPOTTED FEVER

This tick-borne rickettsial disease is also known as boutonneuse fever in North Africa, African or Kenyan tick typhus in sub-Saharan Africa, and Indian tick typhus in southern Asia. The disease is caused by *Rickettsia conorii* in the Mediterranean and *Rickettsia africae* in southern Africa and is transmitted by ixodid ticks. Exposure to the ticks usually results from close contact with tick-carrying dogs, rodents, or cattle. Tick typhus is one of the more frequent causes of fever in returned travelers.

Symptoms include chills, fever, headache, and a rash. An ulcer with a black crust (eschar) may be noted at the site of the tick bite.

Treatment
Tetracycline and doxycycline are both effective.

Prevention
Take the standard measures (DEET and permethrin) to prevent insect bites.

TICK-BORNE ENCEPHALITIS (TBE)
This viral disease occurs in forested areas of the former Soviet Union, eastern and central Europe, and Scandinavia. TBE is transmitted by ixodes ticks (the same ticks that transmit Lyme disease) and presents a small risk primarily to people such as campers and hikers engaging in prolonged outdoor activities in endemic areas. The disease can also be spread by the consumption of unpasteurized dairy products from infected cows, goats, or sheep.

The greatest risk of disease occurs during periods of high tick activity—usually March–September. Infective ticks are found in mixed coniferous-deciduous forests, extending into the shrubby forest edge and meadows as well as along river and stream valleys (including forests bordering large cities).

Treatment
Treatment consists of supportive care only. This is a viral disease and antibiotics are not effective.

Prevention
A vaccine is available in Canada and Europe and is administered in three doses over 6 months. Immunization is only recommended for people who anticipate intense, long-term exposure in endemic areas. It is not recommended for the average tourist. Travelers who expect to have significant exposure should take precautions against tick bites while in endemic areas.

CRIMEAN-CONGO HEMORRHAGIC FEVER
Crimean-Congo hemorrhagic fever (CCHF) is a potentially lethal hemorrhagic fever caused by a tick-borne bunyavirus distributed widely throughout arid regions of Africa, Eastern Europe, the Middle East, and Asia. Humans become infected through the bite of an ixodid tick, by handling infected domestic animals, or by contact with blood from an infected person.

Symptoms include severe headaches, fever, chills, and muscle and joint pain. Bleeding gums and hemorrhagic skin lesions are common. Severe thrombocytopenia (low blood platelet count) occurs and fatal intestinal bleeding may occur, but bleeding is due primarily to leaky blood vessels rather than to low platelets.

Treatment
Treatment with oral or intravenous ribavirin may be dramatically effective. A 2-gm loading dose should be given initially, followed by 4 gm/day in divided doses for four days, then 2 gm/day for six days.

Prevention
Travelers should take measures to avoid tick bites, and all medical personnel caring for people with CCHF should exercise appropriate barrier precautions. Postexposure prophylaxis with ribavirin may be effective.

EHRLICHIOSIS

This disease is caused by rickettsial-like, intracellular coccobacilli bacteria (ehrlichia) transmitted by ticks. Five species infect humans: *Ehrlichia chaffeensis*, *E. sennetsu*, *E. canis*, *E. ewingii*, and the agent of human granulocytic ehrlichiosis.

Two types of human ehrlichial infections are recognized in the United States. The infections have the same symptoms and the same treatment but differ in their geographic distribution due to the fact they are transmitted by different species of ticks.

- Human monocytic ehrlichiosis (HME), caused by *Ehrlichia chaffeensis*, is transmitted by Lone Star ticks (*Amblyomma americanum*). These ticks are found predominantly in the Southeast and Mid-Atlantic states. The first case of HME was reported in Arkansas in 1986.
- Human granulocytic ehrlichiosis (HGE) was first recognized in 1994 in Minnesota and Wisconsin. Two ehrlicia species are now identified as causing HGE. The species currently identified as "the agent of human granulocytic ehrlichiosis" causes most cases of HGE. The other species, *Ehrlichia ewingii*, has just recently been identified as causing illness in humans. Previously, *E. ewingii* had been known to cause HGE only in dogs.

HGE is transmitted primarily by deer ticks (*Ixodes scapularis*) and thus the disease occurs predominantly in the Northeast, upper Midwest, and other areas where deer ticks make their habitat. Cases of HGE caused by *E. ewingii*, but transmitted by the Lone Star tick, have been reported in Missouri.

Overseas, cases of HGE have been documented in many countries in Europe, as well as Argentina. In Japan and Malaysia, ehrlichial disease caused by *E. seenetsu* is reported, and disease caused by *E. canis* has been reported in Venezuela.

Symptoms
Symptoms of the two infections are practically identical. Most patients have a nonspecific flu-like illness with chills, fever, headache, muscle aches, and malaise. In 15% of the cases, however, the disease is more severe and patients can develop kidney failure, pneumonia, and neurological changes such as seizures and coma. The fatality rate is 2% to 5%. The outcome of the disease is usually related to a delay in diagnosis and treatment.

Diagnosis
Typical laboratory findings include a low white blood cell count (leukopenia), a low platelet count (thrombocytopenia), and abnormal liver function tests. The white blood cells of some patients with HME will have characteristic inclusion

bodies (neutrophilic morulae); a much higher percentage of patients with HGE will have these telltale inclusions in their white blood cells. Polymerase chain reaction (PCR) amplification may be used to establish an early diagnosis. Indirect immunofluorescent antibody titers will be increased—but not until convalescence.

Treatment

When a case of ehrlichiosis is suspected, treatment should be started immediately. A typical candidate for treatment is somebody with a flu-like illness who has leukopenia and thrombocytopenia and who has had potential exposure to ticks in an endemic area, especially between April and September.

The best drug is doxycycline, 100 mg twice daily for 10 to 14 days given orally or intravenously. Chloramphenicol, the rifamycins, and some of the newer quinolones may be active against some or all ehrlichial infections, but clinical experience with these agents is limited.

Prevention

This is a tick-borne illness that can be prevented by insect bite prevention measures, as outlined in Chapter 7.

OTHER TICK-BORNE DISEASES IN THE USA

Lyme disease (Chapter 10) and ehrlichiosis are not the only illnesses transmitted by ticks in the United States. Rocky Mountain spotted fever, Colorado tick fever, tick paralysis, tularemia, babesiosis, and relapsing fever are some of the other important diseases. A summary of the tick vectors that spread these diseases and their geographic distribution appears on the following page.

Important Ticks in the USA

The deer tick (*Ixodes scapularis*) is found in great abundance from Virginia to Maine, as well as in Wisconsin and Minnesota, while its first cousin the **western deer tick** (*Ixodes pacificus*, the black-legged tick) is active along the West Coast. The deer tick is a very small tick, much smaller than the dog tick or wood tick. Deer ticks, both adults and nymphs, are dark reddish brown and have black legs and a pear-shaped body. All stages, especially nymphs and adults, feed on people. The deer tick is the most important carrier of Lyme disease and is the only known carrier of babesiosis. It is also the primary transmitter of human granulocytic ehrlichiosis.

The American dog tick (*Dermacentor variabilis*) is widely distributed in the eastern half of the United States and is also found on the West Coast. It resembles the wood tick in appearance. The unfed female has silvery-gray markings on the shield on her back; the rest of the body is reddish brown. It is bigger than other ticks—approximately one-eighth inch to one-quarter inch long—and although it prefers dogs, it does bite people. The dog tick is the most important transmitter of Rocky Mountain spotted fever. It also transmits tularemia and probably transmits human granulocytic ehrlichiosis. The dog tick can cause tick paralysis.

The Rocky Mountain wood tick (*Dermacentor andersoni*) is a hard tick that resembles the American dog tick and the Pacific Coast tick. The female has silvery-gray markings on the shield on her back; the rest is reddish brown. This tick is the prime carrier of Rocky Mountain spotted fever in the West, and it also transmits tularemia and Colorado tick fever (mountain fever). It is the most important cause of tick paralysis in the United States.

The Lone Star tick (*Amblyomma americanum*) is found throughout the southeastern United States, with a high density in the Ozarks. Adults are about one-quarter inch long; nymphs, which are the most aggressive biters, are pinhead size. The ticks are reddish brown, and the female has a white mark on the middle of her back. The smaller male has lacy white markings on the rear edge of his back. Lone Star ticks transmit monocytic ehrlichiosis, tularemia, and probably a variant form of Lyme disease.

Relapsing fever ticks (*Ornithodoros hermsi, O. parkeri, O. talaje, O. turicata*) are soft ticks that transmit relapsing fever, a spirochetal disease. Their bites can be painful. Relapsing fever ticks are widely scattered west of the Mississippi River. Adults are oval-shaped and colored gray to pale blue. Larvae and nymphs are gray.

The brown dog tick (*Rhipiceohalus sanguineus*) is found throughout the United States wherever you find dogs. Although suspected of carrying ehrlichiosis, these ticks are probably not disease transmitters. The male is uniform dark brown. The female is brown but the shield on her back is darker than the rest of her body.

Bakken JS, Krueth J, Wilson-Nordskog MT et al. Clinical and laboratory characteristics of human granulocytic ehrlichiosis. JAMA 1996;275:199–205.

Bill PLA. Schistosomiasis in Tropical Neurology. Shakir RA et al. (eds.) W. B. Saunders London 1996: 295–316.

Breman JD. Human leishmaniasis: Clinical, diagnostic, and chemotherapeutic developments in the last 10 years. Clin Infect Dis 1997;24:684–703.

Burri C, Nkunku S, Merolle E, et al. Efficacy of new, concise schedule for melarsoprol in treatment of sleeping sickness caused by *Trypanosoma brucei gambiense*: A randomised trial. Lancet 2000;355:1419–25.

Dumler JS, Bakken JS. Ehrlichial diseases of humans: Emerging tick-borne infections. Clin Inf Dis 1995;20:1102–10.

Fishbein DB, Dennis DT. Tick-borne disease—A growing risk (editorial). N Engl J Med 1995;333:452–453.

Kautner I, Robinson MJ. Dengue virus infection. J. Pediatr 1997; 131:156–524.

Kirchhoff LV. American trypanosomiasis (Chagas' disease). Gastro Clin N Am 1996;25:517–533.

Lucey DR, Maguire JH. Schistosomiasis. Infect Dis Clin N Am 1993;7:635–53.

Marshall MM, Naumovitz D, Ortega T, et al. Waterborne protozoan pathogens. Clin Micro Rev 1997;10:67–85.

Ottesen EA. Filarial infections in parasitic infections. Maguire JH, Keystone JS (eds). Inf Clin N Am 1993;7:619–633.

Pearson RD, Jeronimo SMB, de Queiroz-Sousa A. Leishmaniasis. Tropical Infectious Diseases (Guerant RL, et al 1999. Churchill Livingstone (Philadelphia): 797–813.

Rigau-Perez JG, Clark GG, Gubler DJ, et al. Dengue and dengue hemorrhagic fever. Lancet 1998;352:971–77.

Rynkiewicz DL, Liu LX. Human ehrlichiosis in New England (letter). N Engl J Med 1994;330:292–293.

Robertson SE, Hull BP, Tomori O, et al. Yellow fever: A decade of reemergence. JAMA 1996;276:1157–1161.

Schaffner W, Standaert SM. Ehrlichiosis: In pursuit of an emerging infection (editorial). N Engl J Med 1996;334:262–263.

Schwartz E, Mendelson E, Sidi. Dengue fever among travelers. Am J Med 1996;101:516–520.

Spach DH, Liles WC, Campbell GL, et al. Tick-borne diseases in the United States. N Engl J Med 1993;329:936–947.

Strickland GT. Gastrointestinal manifestations of schistosomiasis. Gut 1994;35:1334–37.

Walterspiel JH, Pickering LK. Giardia and giardiasis. Progress in Clin Parasitol 1994;4:1–26.

Wilson ME. Breakbone basics: Dengue fever in the 1990s. Infect Dis in Clin Pract 1996;5:376–379.

Zaat JM, Mank TG, Assendeft WJJ. A systematic review on the treatment of giardiasis. Trop Med & Int Health 1997;2:63–82.

9 Other Travel-Related Diseases

Giardia lamblia

GIARDIASIS

The parasite that causes giardiasis *(Giardia lamblia)* is found in contaminated food and water as a result of fecal contamination from humans or animals (mostly dogs, beaver, and cattle). Giardiasis occurs worldwide, but a high incidence has been reported in travelers returning from Russia. Contaminated municipal tap water, especially in St. Petersburg, appears to be the main problem. While travelers to Mexico and Latin America and the countries in Asia and Africa may also acquire infection, fewer than 3% of travelers returning from these areas have been found to harbor giardia parasites.

Giardia cysts can be easily spread person-to-person within households and day care centers. Poor personal hygiene, lack of handwashing, and close physical contact, especially oral-anal sexual contact, promote transmission.

Giardiasis is also known as backpacker's diarrhea because the parasites may be found in ponds, lakes, and streams in rural or mountainous areas, even within the U.S. and Canada, and pose a potential risk to campers and hikers drinking from these sources. NOTE: Published reports of confirmed giardiasis among outdoor recreationists in North America clearly demonstrate a high incidence among this population. However, the evidence for an association between drinking backcountry water and acquiring giardiasis is minimal. Person-to-person spread appears to be a more significant factor in acquiring backpacker's diarrhea, and perhaps more emphasis should be placed on handwashing, personal hygiene, and other behavior modifications during backcountry travel, rather than simply on water purification.

Symptoms can be sudden and severe or occur gradually. Some travelers may have no complaints except one large, loose bowel movement daily. Nausea, fatigue, weight loss, abdominal cramps, nonbloody diarrhea, excessive gas, abdominal rumblings (borborygmi) and bloating can also occur to varying degrees. A taste of "rotten eggs" is common. Fever is very rare in giardiasis. When the illness is chronic, symptoms may last for weeks or months and be passed off as indigestion, or irritable bowel syndrome. Some cases of chronic fatigue syndrome may be due to giardiasis.

If you have diarrhea lasting more than 2–3 weeks, you should be tested for intestinal parasites. Most likely, your doctor will ask you to submit several stool samples for microscopic examination. Detecting giardia parasites can be difficult because organisms are not constantly present in stool; therefore, if the microscopic examination is negative, a more invasive method, such as a small bowel biopsy, may be required. Recently, a very sensitive and specific screening test has been introduced that simplifies diagnosis. (GiardEIA is available from **Antibodies Incorporated**, Davis, California; 916-758-4400.) If the enzyme immunoassay test is negative, then giardiasis is unlikely. Less common intestinal parasites that can also cause chronic diarrhea include *D. fragilis*, *I. belli*, cryptosporidia, *C. cayetensis* (cyclospora), and *E. histolytica* (the cause of amebiasis).

Treatment

Single-dose metronidazole (2 gm in adults) administered with food at bedtime once daily for 3 days is as effective as the standard 5-day course of 250 mg three times daily. The regimen for children under 25 kg is 35 mg/kg (in a single dose daily for 3 days). For children who weigh 25 kg to 40 kg, the daily dose is 50 mg/kg for 3 days. Alternative treatments include tinidazole (2 gm once), furazolidone, albendazole, and bacitracin zinc. Furazolidone (Furoxone), 100 mg 4 times daily for 7 to 10 days, is a good, but very expensive, alternative for several reasons: (1) it is available in a liquid preparation (useful for children), and (2) the drug is also effective against most bacterial causes of travelers' diarrhea, making furazolidone useful as broad spectrum treatment when the cause of the diarrhea is not known. Albendazole, 400 mg twice daily for 7 days, is a safe alternative drug with a variable cure rate.

If you are in a remote area and testing is not available, start treatment with one of the drugs above on the assumption that giardiasis is the probable cause of your diarrhea. If no improvement occurs, get medical consultation as soon as possible. NOTE: Lactose intolerance frequently accompanies giardiasis and may persist for weeks or months following parasite eradication.

Prevention

There is presently no prophylactic drug or vaccine to prevent giardiasis. Follow the food, drink, and water disinfection guidelines as outlined in Chapter 4, but note that chlorine and iodine may not be effective against parasites. Handwashing and good personal hygiene are important measures.

AMEBIASIS

This potentially serious illness is caused by *Entameba histolytica* parasites that invade the wall of the large intestine, causing either acute dysentery or chronic diarrhea of variable severity. The parasites can also infect the liver, causing inflammation and liver abscess. In the carrier state, which is common, parasites live in the intestine without causing symptoms. Recent studies show that 90% of those with "*E. histolytica*" are actually infected with a microscopically identical but nonpathogenic protozoan now called *Entameba dispar*, for which treatment is unnecessary.

Transmission occurs through ingestion of fecally contaminated food or water. Flies can serve as carriers of the amebic cysts. Infected food handlers can spread the disease. Person-to-person contact is important in transmission; household members and sexual partners can easily become infected.

High-risk areas (where up to 50% of the population carry the parasite) are Mexico, South America, India, and West and southern Africa.

Amebic colitis is distinctly rare in travelers and is frequently overdiagnosed in developing countries. Most cases of gastrointestinal infection are not due to *E. histolytica,* but the presence of the harmless *E. dispar* can confuse the diagnosis. An amebic antibody test can differentiate these two identically appearing parasites. If serology for amebiasis is negative, you can presume that you are infected with *E. dispar,* but some other organism is causing the illness. Recent studies show that *E. histolytica* antigen or DNA can be detected by a stool test, differentiating the parasite from *E. dispar.*

The symptoms of amebiasis are variable. Most infected persons carry the parasite and have no symptoms whatsoever. Mild illness causes crampy abdominal pain, little or no fever, and semiformed stools. Mucus may be present but usually without blood. Soft stools or diarrhea may alternate with constipation. You may experience fatigue, loss of appetite, and some weight loss. The symptoms at this stage are similar to those of giardiasis, except that the abdominal discomfort is in the lower abdomen and the diarrhea is of smaller volume.

More severe illness (amebic dysentery) is characterized by fever, bloody diarrhea, generalized abdominal tenderness, vomiting, and much greater toxicity. Illness at this stage requires urgent care.

Travelers who develop an amebic liver abscess usually don't have diarrhea or other intestinal symptoms. Instead, they may note fever, right upper abdominal pain, and have an enlarged, tender liver. Sweating, chills, weight loss, and fatigue are usually present. NOTE: Amebic abscess is rare, even in long-term travelers.

A microscopic stool examination to identify trophozoites or amebic cysts will point toward the diagnosis, especially if red cells are detected in the parasites. Antibody tests are usually diagnostic, especially if an amebic liver abscess or colitis is suspected. Amebic dysentery must be distinguished from other infections causing bloody diarrhea (e.g., enterocolitis caused by shigella, campylobacter, yersinia, or *Clostridium difficile*). Crohn's disease and ulcerative colitis can mimic amebiasis and must be considered in the younger patient. In older persons, diverticulitis or malignancy should be suspected.

Treatment

Standard treatment of invasive amebiasis (colitis or abscess) is metronidazole, 750 mg, 3 times daily for 5 days, followed by iodoquinol, 650 mg, 3 times daily for 20 days. This regimen cures 100% of those with amebic liver abscess and 93% of those with amebic colitis. A single dose of metronidazole (2.5 gm) is usually effective in curing an uncomplicated abscess. Asymptomatic cyst-passers and those without documented invasive disease require iodoquinol alone.

CHOLERA

This disease is caused by *Vibrio cholerae* bacteria, which are commonly transmitted by contaminated food and water. Cholera sometimes causes life-threatening diarrhea, but large numbers of bacteria must be consumed and the severe form of the disease is rarely seen in healthy tourists who follow prudent dietary habits.

Cholera occurs both sporadically and in worldwide epidemics. Sub-Saharan Africa has the highest reported cholera incidence and mortality rates in the world. By the end of 1999 61 countries reported cases, but the disease is much more widespread than officially recognized.

Cholera is basically a disease of poverty, and most illness occurs among people in lesser-developed countries who are exposed to heavily contaminated water or food. Most travelers on a tourist itinerary don't need to worry about this disease. In fact, cholera is officially reported in only 1 in 500,000 returning travelers. The healthy people who do get the disease often work in high-risk environments, such as refugee camps.

Unlike some microbes, cholera bacteria are readily killed by stomach acid. However, if you do ingest a large dose of bacteria from heavily contaminated water—or if you are taking antacids or antiulcer drugs—bacteria can get past the stomach and enter your small intestine. Cholera enterotoxin then acts on the intestinal wall to cause an outpouring of water and salt into the gut.

The clinical picture of cholera varies widely. Seventy-five percent of infections are mild or without any symptoms. Only 2%–5% of infections cause severe symptoms.

Cholera in its most severe form is characterized by massive watery diarrhea, vomiting, and muscle cramps. Vomiting is common and may be severe. The frequent, watery stools soon lose all fecal appearance ("rice water stools") and practically all odor. Loss of fluids and electrolytes can cause shock and death in hours if fluids are not replaced.

Milder cases of cholera can mimic travelers' diarrhea caused by toxigenic *E. coli*, salmonella, intestinal viruses, and parasites. The absence of blood or pus in the stools, and the lack of fever, are distinguishing features of cholera.

Treatment

Cholera kills solely by dehydration. If you develop severe watery diarrhea, you should start immediate rehydration treatment.

Fluids—Drinking an oral rehydration solution (ORS) is essential and its prompt use has saved many lives. ORS prepared from packets of rehydration salts e.g., CeraLyte (see Chapter 5) is the best fluid to use for immediate treatment. After rehydration with ORS, you should drink 8 to 12 ounces, or more, of full-strength rehydration solution after every loose stool. If your diarrhea is very profuse and exceeds the amount of rehydration solution you can drink, or if you are vomiting and can't retain fluids, you will need to be hospitalized and treated with intravenous fluids.

NOTE: Don't underestimate fluid requirements—some patients with severe watery diarrhea require 10–12 liters of fluid replacement daily.

Antibiotics—Antibiotics will shorten the duration of illness and are an important adjunct to fluid therapy. The best antibiotics for treating cholera are the quinolones, such as ciprofloxacin (Cipro), ofloxacin (Floxin), or levofloxacin (Levaquin). These antibiotics are effective when given as single-dose therapy (ciprofloxacin, 1 gm; ofloxacin, 800 mg; or levofloxacin, 500 mg). The greater effectiveness of the quinolones versus other antibiotics is due to their higher concentration in the stool. Alternative antibiotics are doxycycline, tetracycline, trimethoprim/sulfamethoxazole, furazolidone (Furoxone), and azithromycin (Zithromax). NOTE: Globally, resistance of cholera to tetracyclines and trimethoprim/sulfamethoxazole is increasingly common.

Treatment of children: Although the quinolones are generally contraindicated in children, single-dose therapy with these drugs is not harmful. Furazolidone and azithromycin are safe for children of all ages.

Prevention

Food and drink precautions—The best prevention against cholera is to pay careful attention to what you eat and drink (Chapter 4). It is particularly important (1) to avoid raw or undercooked food and seafood (e.g., ceviche), and (2) to drink only bottled, boiled, filtered, or chemically disinfected water, without ice.

Vaccination—The manufacture and availability of the cholera vaccine in the United States ceased in June 2000. Many countries license an oral cholera vaccine, although there is only slight evidence that it is more effective than the injectable formulation. It is effective for 6 months in a single dose but is only effective against the El Tor strain. The oral cholera vaccine is not available in the United States, but is available in Canada. See Chapter 2 "Vaccines for Travel" for additional information on cholera.

TYPHOID FEVER

Typhoid fever (sometimes called enteric fever) is a serious, sometimes life-threatening disease caused by one particular species of salmonella bacteria (*Salmonella typhi*) and is contracted by the consumption of contaminated food or water, or by contact with an infected person. Untreated, typhoid lasts 2–6 weeks with a mortality rate up to 30%.

Although typhoid fever is found in all countries in the developing world, the highest disease rates are reported from Peru, Chile, Haiti, Nigeria, India, Pakistan, SE Asia, and Indonesia. Most cases of typhoid seen in American travelers originate in the Indian subcontinent or Latin Amercia.

The early symptoms of typhoid fever usually consist of chills and fever, headache, weakness, loss of appetite, abdominal pain, body aches (myalgia), cough, and constipation. A rash, with pink spots measuring 2–4 mm, may appear on the chest and abdomen. There is a 50% occurrence of diarrhea, which is sometimes bloody in the second to third week of illness. In fact, if your doctor considers diarrhea a prerequisite for the diagnosis of this disease, the diagnosis may be missed.

The usual method for diagnosing typhoid fever is a blood culture combined with a stool culture (40%–80% positive). Although a bone marrow aspirate is more sensitive (80%–95% positive), it is a more painful and invasive procedure.

Treatment

Strains of *Salmonella typhi*—resistant to ampicillin, trimethoprim/sulfamethoxazole, and chloramphenicol—have become increasingly prevalent, especially outside of Latin America (where these drugs may still be effective). Multidrug-resistant strains retain considerable sensitivity to the quinolones and the third-generation cephalosporins, although in India and Vietnam there are reports of increasing resistance to the quinolones. The quinolones are currently the drugs of choice, with ciprofloxacin and ofloxacin preferred over some of the newer formulations. Oral administration of a quinolone results in (1) very high fecal drug concentrations, (2) rapid control of diarrhea and elimination of salmonella from stool, (3) reduction in rate of relapse and carrier rates, and (4) prevention of bacteremia and other complications. A distinct advantage of the quinolones in uncomplicated typhoid is their efficacy with treatment courses as short as 3 days. Cure rates with ofloxacin given for 3 days (15 mg/kg daily) have been as high as 96%–100%, but most experts recommend a full 10-day course of treatment to reduce relapses. The longer course of treatment is recommended for individuals who acquire the illness in Asia or Southeast Asia. Third-generation cephalosporins (for example, ceftriaxone) are also effective, but patients may remain ill for more than 1 week whereas the average time to fever clearance with the quinolones is about 4 days. Also, the quinolones can be self-administered by a traveler, whereas most cephalosporins must be given by intravenous or intramuscular injection. The quinolones are very effective in children with multidrug-resistant typhoid fever or other systemic salmonelloses. Quinolones, however, should not be used to treat salmonella meningitis; a third-generation cephalosporin is preferred.

Azithromycin (Zithromax) may also be an effective drug. One thousand milligrams (1,000 mg), taken on the first day, followed by 500 mg daily for 6 additional days, was 100% effective in one study. In children, a dose of 10 mg/kg/day for 7 days was over 90% effective with few adverse effects.

Prevention

Salmonella typhi bacteria are transmitted by human carriers of the organisms, and in all countries with substandard sanitation, there is risk of typhoid transmission. Pay close attention to dietary safety. Especially avoid raw vegetables and salads because these items are often grown in contaminated irrigation water. All food should be well cooked. You should drink only bottled, boiled, or treated water, or commercial beverages. Flavored ices sold by street vendors are especially risky.

Vaccination—See Table 2.2, Chapter 2 for typhoid vaccine schedule, indications, precautions and contraindications.

The manufacturer claims approximately 70% vaccine effectiveness. However, travelers can still acquire typhoid, or paratyphoid (a similar illness), if exposed to a heavy dose of bacteria, or if the vaccine had not been properly administered or handled, as can happen with the oral vaccine. In 1994, eight Dutch travelers in a tour group to Indonesia were diagnosed with typhoid fever, despite having received the oral Ty 21a vaccine. Therefore, dietary discretion remains an important factor in disease prevention. Don't rely entirely on the typhoid vaccine for protection.

SALMONELLA ENTERITIS (SALMONELLOSIS)

Other species of salmonella bacteria (*S. enteritidis*, *S. cholerae-suis*) can cause an intestinal illness termed enteritis. Typical symptoms include fever, nausea, vomiting, crampy abdominal pain, and diarrhea. Occasionally, salmonella bacteria enter the bloodstream and cause a severe, life-threatening illness termed salmonella bacteremia, characterized by chills, high fever, and prostration. Fatalities from bacteremia occur most often in infants, the elderly, the chronically ill, and those with immune deficiencies.

Unlike *Salmonella typhi* bacteria, which are harbored only by humans, other salmonella species are found in a variety of animals including poultry (especially chickens), turkeys, ducks, livestock (pigs, horses, sheep), dogs, cats, rodents, and reptiles (snakes, lizards, turtles). Be aware that purchasing a pet anywhere in the world carries the risk of salmonellosis. Up to 60% of turtles, snakes, iguanas, and lizards in pet stores may be infected.

Infection is usually transmitted by direct contact with the flesh of an infected animal (e.g., during butchering or food preparation) or by the consumption of undercooked, contaminated food. Undercooked chicken eggs and unpasteurized dairy products are also common sources of illness. Poultry products account for over half the cases of salmonellosis.

Treatment

Salmonellosis is best treated with a course of a quinolone antibiotic. A third-generation cephalosprin is an alternative drug.

Prevention

There is no vaccine. The typhoid fever vaccine is not effective against the other salmonella bacteria that cause salmonellosis. Prevention is entirely dependent upon eating well-cooked food (especially dairy products) and avoiding disease-carrying pets.

SHIGELLOSIS
(BACILLARY DYSENTERY)

The most common cause of bacterial dysentery is shigellosis. This disease accounts for 10% to 40% of diarrhea worldwide. Since very small numbers of bacteria are needed to transmit this disease, you can easily pick up the infection, either from contaminated food or from person-to-person contact with carriers of the bacteria. Flies can also carry and transmit shigella.

Bacillary dysentery is characterized by an abrupt onset of high fever, abdominal cramps, small-volume bloody diarrhea, and the repeated feeling of incomplete bowel evacuation. Voluminous, watery diarrhea may precede the onset of bloody diarrhea. In contrast, amebic dysentery presents with a gradual onset of diarrhea, associated with low-grade fever. Fulminant colitis with shigellosis is uncommon.

Although a stool culture is needed for exact diagnosis, shigellosis can be suspected on the basis of your symptoms. Other bacteria that can cause similar symptoms include campylobacter, salmonella, *Vibrio parahemolyticus*, yersinia, and enteroinvasive *E. coli*. Since these microorganisms, like shigella, can all be treated with a quinolone antibiotic, it is not necessary to know the exact bacterial diagnosis before starting treatment.

Treatment

Because bacterial resistance to tetracycline, trimethoprim/sulfamethoxazole, and furazolidone has increased worldwide, shigellosis is best treated with a quinolone antibiotic. The oral cephalosporins do not appear to be effective. If your initial symptoms are severe with high fever and dehydration, hospitalization may be necessary. One species of shigella (*S. dysenteriae*) is more resistant to antibiotics and 5–7 days of quinolone treatment is usually required.

Azithromycin (Zithromax) is also an effective drug. Take 500 mg on the first day, then 250 mg for an additional 5 days. Cure rate is approximately 82%, which is similar to a quinolone. (The cure rate with ciprofloxacin is about 89%.)

MENINGOCOCCAL MENINGITIS

This illness is caused by bacteria (*Neisseria meningitidis*) that infect the membranes lining the brain and spinal cord. Untreated, meningococcal meningitis can be rapidly fatal.

Invasive disease is caused by one of five serogroups. Group A, the most common cause of meningitis in lesser-developed countries, accounts for most epidemics in nations such as China and those in the African "meningitis belt." Group B is responsible for most outbreaks in industrialized countries. Group C has lately been responsible for most cluster outbreaks in the United States and has the ability to cause epidemics. Groups W135 and Y are less common.

The neisseria bacteria are normally carried harmlessly in the nasal passages of a small percentage of healthy people. This carriage of bacteria tends to be seasonal and increases during the dry season. Bacteria are spread person-to-person by coughing and sneezing. Crowded living conditions, often present in lesser-developed countries, increases the number of carriers and the transmission of disease. Travelers are usually exposed to infection only through close contact with local population in endemic areas. It is not entirely clear what triggers an acute infection in people who carry the bacteria. In some cases it may be that an upper respiratory infection has damaged the immune defenses of the mucous membranes of their nose and throat; climatic conditions, as well as temperature and humidity, may also play a role.

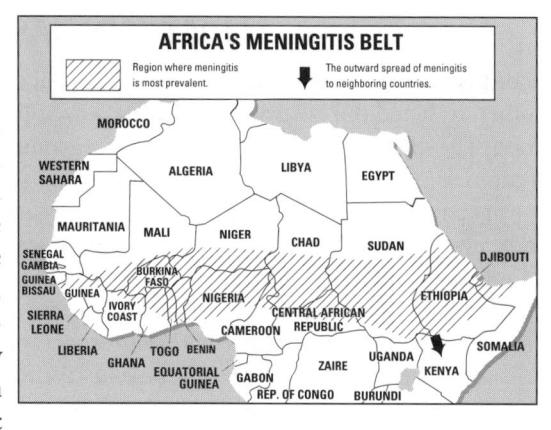

Fever, vomiting, headache, neck pain and stiffness, and confusion or lethargy are the most common symptoms, but early illness can also mimic "the flu."

Treatment

Effective antibiotics for treating meningococcal meningitis include ceftriaxone (Rocephin) and cefotaxime (Claforan). Chloramphenicol can be used in penicillin-allergic patients, although resistant strains have been reported. Quinolones are being studied because they exhibit adequate CNS penetration. Patients treated with penicillin G may take longer to recover due to the occurrence of relatively resistant strains of *Neisseria meningitidis*.

Prevention

Don't smoke—smoking cigarettes and exposure to secondhand smoke has recently been shown to be a risk factor for contracting meningitis.

A tetravalent vaccine (Menomune, Aventis) contains capsular polysaccharides for serogroups A, C, Y, and W135. Meningococcal vaccine is recommended for travelers to sub-Saharan Africa (see map, above) during the dry season, which is from December through June, and especially if close contact with locals is anticipated. Saudi Arabia requires the vaccine for all pilgrims to the Hajj.

See Table 2.2, Chapter 2 for meningococcal vaccine schedule, indications, precautions and contraindications.

The occurrence of meningitis outbreaks worldwide can be checked on the CDC's Web site (*http://home.iatronet.net/epitravel.htm*).

SCHISTOSOMIASIS

Schistosomiasis (called bilharzia in Africa) is a parasitic disease caused by schistosomes, or blood flukes. The disease affects over 200 million people in 75 countries. The disease is endemic in Africa (most countries), South America (Brazil, Venezuela, Suriname), and parts of the Middle East and Asia (see map on the following page). In the Caribbean, schistosomiasis has been reported to occur sporadically in Puerto Rico, Antigua, Dominica, Guadeloupe, Martinique, Montserrat, and Saint Lucia.

The three most common schistosome species are *Schistosoma mansoni* (the cause of intestinal schistosomiasis), *Schistosoma hematobium* (the cause of urinary schistosomiasis), and S*chistosoma japonicum* (Far Eastern schistosomiasis). Other species, such as *S. mekongi*, found in Southeast Asia, and *S. intercalatum*, found in Africa, are less common. Infection takes place when schistosome cercariae (larvae), shed into freshwater by snail intermediate hosts, penetrate within a few minutes the unbroken skin of an individual who is washing, bathing, or swimming in ponds, lakes, rivers, streams, or irrigation ditches in endemic areas. After skin penetration, there follows a four- to six-week incubation period during which time the young schistosome worms migrate to the liver and to the veins draining the intestine or the bladder. The fully grown worms live in the veins of the urinary bladder or the wall of the intestine where they produce large numbers of eggs that cause inflammation and progressive tissue damage. The adult worms can persist for decades, producing various, often puzzling, symptoms.

Light infections are usually asymptomatic. If you are exposed, you should towel off vigorously and wash your skin with rubbing alcohol. This may prevent penetration of the cercariae. When schistosome larvae penetrate the skin, there may be brief tingling and a rash, called swimmer's itch. Corticosteroid creams and antihistamines can help control symptoms.

Acute schistosomiasis (Katayama fever)—Four to six weeks after a heavy exposure, you may develop an acute illness called Katayama fever. Symptoms include fever, headache, cough, a rash (hives), fatigue, abdominal pain, tender enlargement of the liver and spleen, weight loss, and muscle aches. These symptoms are thought to represent an allergic reaction to the egg deposition. Katayama fever can be confused with malaria or typhoid fever but a white blood count will usually show eosinophilia.

NOTE: Most persons will not develop Katayama fever during the acute infection; sometimes just a feeling of fatigue or ill health occurs.

Central nervous system (CNS) schistosomiasis—Rarely, migrating eggs or adult worms can invade the central nervous system. Symptoms of cerebral schistosomiasis include headaches, visual loss, and seizures, if the infection is in the brain. Symptoms of spinal cord schistosomiasis include urinary incontinence, leg pain, and paralysis.

Chronic schistosomiasis—Heavy infections (seen mainly in the indigenous populations) can last for years and can damage the liver, bladder, bowel, and/or nervous system. *S. mansoni*, *S. japonicum*, and *S. mekongi* parasites primarily affect the bowel and liver; chronic infections can lead to enlargement of the liver and spleen, followed by scarring of the liver and gastrointestinal bleeding from dilated esophageal veins. Bowel involvement may lead to chronic diarrhea, suggestive of inflammatory bowel disease. *S. hematobium* primarily affects the genitourinary tract; chronic infections can lead to persistent cystitis, blood in the urine, obstructive kidney disease, and an increased incidence of bladder cancer.

One of the most important elements in diagnosing schistosomiasis is obtaining a history of freshwater exposure in an endemic area. A white blood cell count may show eosinophilia, but this finding is not specific for schistosomiasis. (About 20%–30% of patients will have eosinophilia.) The standard diagnostic test is an examination of stool and urine for schistosome eggs. In some cases, a rectal or bladder biopsy will demonstrate eggs; schistosome eggs, however, do not appear for at least 40 days following the initial exposure. In suspected schistosomiasis, a highly accurate serology test using an enzyme-linked immunosorbent assay (ELISA) will usually be diagnostic 6 weeks or more after exposure. This test is far more sensitive than stool or urine examination. Contact the CDC's **Parasitic Disease Branch (404-488-4050)** for information about the ELISA assay. A positive test indicates present or past infection, but does not distinguish between the two.

Schistosomiasis of the nervous system, which is extremely rare, causes variable neurological symptoms. The blood eosinophil count can be normal, and the stool and urine egg examination can be negative. Diagnosis is made with the ELISA assay combined with an MRI examination of the central nervous system.

Worldwide Distribution of Schistosomiasis

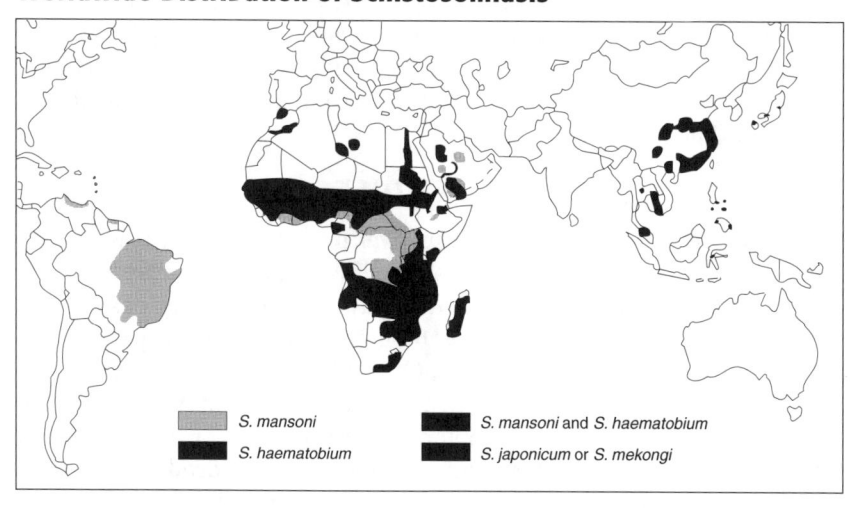

Treatment

For *S. mansoni* and *S. hematobium*, praziquantel is curative in a single dose of 40 mg/kg. For the treatment of *S. japonicum* and *S. mekongi*, praziquantel, 60 mg/kg, is given in three divided doses six hours apart.

Schistosomiasis Facts

- Always assume that bodies of freshwater in endemic areas are infested with schistosomes. Even deep water, far offshore, may be infective, but is usually safer than the shoreline. Salt and brackish water are safe.
- Water sports are risky because of the degree of exposure.
- A history of exposure to infested water is one of the most important elements in the diagnosis of schistosomiasis. A schistosome antibody assay should be done when stool or urine tests are negative for eggs.
- High-risk areas for schistosomiasis include the Nile River, the Omo River in Ethiopia, Lake Victoria, the Tigris and Euphrates rivers, Lake Malawi, Lake Kariba in Zimbabwe, and Lake Volta in Ghana.

CDC Schistosomiasis Information

http://www.cdc.gov/ncidod/dpd/parasites/schistosomiasis/factsht_schistosomiasis.htm

---

Prevention

There is no vaccine; therefore avoiding contact with infested water is the most important preventive measure. Do not swim in slow-moving freshwater unless a reliable source assures you that it is safe. (Chlorinated swimming pools and sea water are safe.) Water for bathing is considered safe if it has been heated to above 50°C (122°F) for more than five minutes, if it has stood more than 48 hours in a tub or container, or if it has been chemically treated (e.g., chlorinated) like drinking water. If you cannot avoid freshwater exposure, swim or bathe in a rapidly flowing river or stream and stay away from the shoreline of a lake. Researchers have suggested that applying controlled-release DEET may prevent cercarial skin penetration, but data are preliminary.

LIVER FLUKE DISEASES

These other flukes, unlike the blood flukes (which cause schistosomiasis), are acquired by eating raw or undercooked fish, shellfish, or raw water vegetables.

Clonorchiasis—Infection with *Clonorchis sinensis* occurs after the consumption of raw, undercooked, pickled, or smoked freshwater fish that contain parasitic larvae. Clonorchiasis is common in Laos, Cambodia, Thailand, southern China, Hong Kong, Korea, Japan, and far eastern Russia. Travelers can avoid this disease by eating only well-cooked fish. Symptoms relate to obstruction of the bile ducts and include abdominal pain and jaundice. Most infected individuals, however, are asymptomatic. It is treated with praziquantel, 75 mg/kg in 3 divided doses in one day. Albendazole has also been shown to be an effective alternative. Untreated clonorchiasis has been associated with bile duct cancer, and gallstones.

Opisthorchiasis—This disease is caused by opisthorchis species of flukes. It is acquired in the same way as clonorchiasis, and the symptoms and treatment are also the same.

Fascioliasis—Human infection is quite widespread, occurring in 66 countries in Africa, China, Latin America, and Europe. *Fasciola hepatica* parasites are acquired by ingesting parasitic larvae attached to aquatic plants, usually watercress. Symptoms include fever, upper abdominal pain, weight loss, and marked eosinophilia. Hypodense lesions are frequently found in the liver. Treatment is with triclabendazole, 11 mg/kg in a single dose.

LUNG FLUKE DISEASE

Paragonimiasis—Humans develop paragonimiasis after consuming raw, salted, or wine-soaked crustacea (freshwater crabs, crayfish, and shrimp). The species *Paragonimus westermani* is prevalent in parts of China, Korea, Japan, the Philippines, and Taiwan. Other paragonimus species infect humans in West Africa and Central and South America. Symptoms include coughing up blood and chest pain. It is treated with praziquantel, 75 mg/kg in 3 divided doses on 2 consecutive days. Triclabendazole has also been shown to be effective. Travelers can avoid lung fluke disease by not eating raw or undercooked freshwater shellfish.

INTESTINAL FLUKE DISEASE

Fasciolopsiasis—Giant intestinal fluke disease is common in the Far East and is acquired through the ingestion of parasitic larvae attached to aquatic plants such as water chestnuts, which have been contaminated by sewage from mammals (pigs, humans). The causative parasite is *Fasciolopsis buski*. Symptoms of heavy infection include abdominal pain, chronic diarrhea, loss of appetite, and weight loss. Treatment is with praziquantel.

INTESTINAL ROUNDWORM DISEASES

Whipworm disease (trichuriasis)—*Trichuris trichuria* is one of the most prevalent helminth infections in the world. The adult worms can live up to 7 years in the intestinal tract, producing thousands of eggs that are passed in the stool. Heavy infections can cause abdominal pain, chronic diarrhea, rectal prolapse, and stunting of growth in children. Most infections are asymptomatic. Treatment with mebendazole, 100 mg twice a day for 3 days, or albendazole, 400 mg daily for 3 days, is recommended. Travelers can prevent infection by eating only cooked food and rinsing vegetables in hot water (65°C or above), an iodine solution, or bleach.

Intestinal capillariasis—This is a serious infection that occurs in the Philippines, in Thailand, and occasionally in other countries in SE Asia. The infection is acquired by the ingestion of raw freshwater fish that harbor infective worm larvae. The parasitic worms, *Capillaria philippinensis*, invade the small intestine and can cause chronic diarrhea, malnutrition, and wasting. The disease may be fatal.

The diagnosis of capillariasis is made by finding characteristic eggs in the stool or by examining tissue obtained from a biopsy of the small intestine. A blood serology (ELISA) test is available in certain research laboratories. Eosinophilia occurs but is a nonspecific finding. Treatment with mebendazole, 200 mg twice daily for 20 days, is curative. Albendazole is also effective. Avoiding raw fish prevents this infection.

Ascariasis—This is the most common helminth infection in the world. The roundworm, *Ascaris lumbricoides*, lives in the intestine and produces eggs that are passed in human feces. When these eggs are ingested through fecally contaminated food or water, they enter the intestinal tract and hatch into larvae that penetrate the gut wall and are carried to the lung, coughed up, and swallowed. Then larvae develop into adult worms and produce eggs, and the life cycle is completed.

Symptoms of ascariasis are produced by migration of larvae through lung tissue during early migration and also by the presence of adult worms in the intestinal tract. Symptoms include cough, wheezing, fever, and chest pain. There may be eosinophilic inflammation of lung tissue. Intestinal symptoms from heavy infection include nausea, loss of appetite, and abdominal pain. Intestinal perforation, bile duct obstruction, appendicitis, and pancreatitis can be caused by migrating worms. In children in the developing world, ascariasis is the most common cause of bowel obstruction. Most infections are asymptomatic. Occasionally, the 8-inch worm (it looks like an adult earthworm) will pass spontaneously in the stool or out the mouth or nose.

Treatment with a single 400 mg dose of albendazole cures 100% of infections. Mebendazole, 100 mg twice daily for 3 days, or pyrantel pamoate, 11 mg/kg in one dose, are also effective.

Hookworm disease (ancylostomiasis)—This disease is acquired by walking barefoot in areas where there is fecally contaminated soil harboring hookworm larvae. The larvae enter the body by penetrating the unbroken skin of the foot, pass through the lungs, and end up in the intestine, where they develop into adult worms. Symptoms of hookworm disease may include coughing and wheezing, peptic ulcer-like pain, and fatigue from anemia. Most infections are asymptomatic. Treatment with mebendazole, 100 mg twice daily for 3 days, albendazole, 400 mg (single dose), or pyrantel pamoate, 11 mg/kg daily for 3 days, are also effective.

Strongyloidiasis—Like hookworm, strongyloides larvae also enter the body through skin penetration, pass through the lungs, and enter the intestine. In travelers, strongyloidiasis is one of the most important intestinal helminths because it is a potentially dangerous disease that can cause death due to hyperinfection in those whose immune system is compromised by conditions such as cancer, AIDS, radiation, and medication (especially corticosteroids). Symptoms include hives and peptic ulcer-like abdominal pain. Diarrhea and a cough are early symptoms in heavily infected individuals. However, most infected individuals are asymptomatic.

Strongyloidiasis and hookworm disease are a common cause of undiagnosed eosjnophilia in travelers. Strongyloides infection is often missed even after multiple stools have been examined. Serology by CDC (95% sensitive and 90% specific) should be carried out when the diagnosis is suspected and stool exams are negative.

Treatment is with ivermectin, 200 µg/kg daily for 2 days, or albendazole, 400 mg daily for 7 days.

Anisakiasis—This is a parasitic disease transmitted by eating raw, undercooked, or lightly pickled saltwater fish, especially salmon, herring, mackerel, whitefish, cod, pollock, bonito, and sole. The parasite is the larval form of a marine roundworm, which may be present in the muscles and organs of the fish mentioned above. Symptoms include nausea and vomiting, or abdominal pain that mimics appendicitis. The treatment is surgical excision of the worm from the intestinal tract.

INTESTINAL TAPEWORM DISEASES

Diphyllobothriasis (fish tapeworm disease)—This is an infection caused by a fish tapeworm called *Diphyllobothrium latum* and occurs among people who eat raw, smoked, pickled, or undercooked freshwater fish. These include Eskimos, fishermen, devotees of sushi bars, and people who taste raw fish (such as whitefish) while cooking. Symptoms are primarily crampy abdominal pain and diarrhea, but fatigue and anemia from vitamin B_{12} deficiency can also occur because fish tapeworms consume this important vitamin. Treatment (adults and children) is with a single dose of praziquantel, 10 mg/kg.

Beef tapeworm disease—This is an infection acquired through eating raw or undercooked beef and is caused by the beef tapeworm *Taenia saginata*. Many infections are asymptomatic. Classically, people with this infection may notice a small worm segment, or longer piece of the worm, passed in their stool during a bowel movement or crawling out of their anus between bowel movements. Symptoms may include nausea and crampy abdominal pain. Treatment (adults and children) is with a single dose of praziquantel, 10 mg/kg.

Pork tapeworm disease—This intestinal infection, similar to beef tapeworm disease, is caused by the pork tapeworm *Taenia solium* and is acquired through eating undercooked pork that contains the encysted larvae of the tapeworm.

Cysticercosis—This is a more serious infection than pork tapeworm disease because it involves organs outside the intestine. Cysticercosis occurs when a person ingests pork tapeworm eggs (not the larvae), usually by eating fecally contaminated food. The eggs hatch within the intestine and develop into larvae that penetrate the intestinal wall and invade various organs and tissues of the body. The most serious illness that results, neurocysticercosis, occurs when tapeworm larvae invade the brain and form cysts, causing seizures and other neurological symptoms.

Cysticercosis is common in Mexico, Central and South America, Africa, India, China, Eastern Europe, and Indonesia.

Both praziquantel and albendazole are effective drugs for treating cysticercosis, but the latter is preferred (15 mg/kg/day for 10–30 days, or up to 400 mg twice daily for 10–30 days). The dose of praziquantel is 50–75 mg/day for 15 days. Corticosteroids are often prescribed as adjunctive treatment to prevent serious allergic reactions to dying larvae.

Trichinosis—This disease (also called trichinellosis) occurs worldwide, except in Australia, and is most often acquired when people eat raw or undercooked pork containing the larval cysts of the parasite *Trichinella spiralis*. Trichinosis, however, can also be acquired by the ingestion of undercooked meat of other carnivorous animals and wild game such as black bear, polar bear, walrus, wild boar, bush pigs, and wart hogs.

During the first week after ingestion, the larvae in the intestine develop into adult worms, causing abdominal pain, diarrhea, nausea, vomiting, and prostration. Next, there is tissue invasion by newly produced larvae, bringing fever, headache, swelling of the eyelids and face, conjunctivitis, muscle pain, weakness, and hives. Symptoms caused by larval invasion of the heart and central nervous system include heart rhythm disturbances and seizures.

Treatment with prednisone (60 mg/day) is used in acute trichinosis to reduce inflammation and alleviate symptoms. Albendazole, 400 mg twice daily for 14 days, is the treatment of choice. An alternative treatment is mebendazole, 400 mg, three times daily for 4 days, then 400–500 mg/day for 10 days.

Adequate cooking will prevent this infection. Freezing, smoking, or pickling is as effective.

BRUCELLOSIS

This is a bacterial disease contracted through (1) the consumption of contaminated dairy products, particularly unpasteurized soft cheeses and milk, or (2) by exposure to the flesh of infected animals, particularly that of cattle, hogs, or goats. In this regard, farmers, herdsmen, veterinarians, and slaughterhouse workers are at particular risk.

The highest incidence of brucellosis occurs in Middle Eastern countries such as Saudi Arabia, Kuwait, and Lebanon, but the incidence is also high in Central and South America, sub-Saharan Africa, India, Greece, France, and Spain. Brucellosis should be suspected in travelers who have visited these areas and then develop a prolonged illness with fever.

The brucella bacteria may incubate in the body for a month or more before causing symptoms, and the diagnosis, initially, may not be suspected. The most common symptoms include fever, chills, sweating, muscle and joint aches, abdominal pain, weakness, weight loss, and headache. Backache and testicular pain are not uncommon. The physical examination often demonstrates enlargement of the spleen and liver and swelling of the lymph nodes. Other diseases that mimic brucellosis include typhoid, mononucleosis, leishmaniasis, and tuberculosis.

Early diagnosis of brucellosis depends upon a high index of suspicion for the illness, and therefore knowing the travel history and exposure is very important. A positive serology test and positive blood or bone marrow cultures will confirm the diagnosis. Blood and bone marrow cultures should be held for three weeks.

Treatment

Brucellosis bacteria often persist inside white blood cells despite antibiotics. Treatment with two antibiotics for at least 6 weeks is therefore required. Doxycycline, 100 mg twice daily, is administered for 6 weeks, while a second agent (rifampicin, streptomycin, gentamicin) is given in conjunction for at least several weeks. The quinolones and co-trimoxazole are also effective.

Prevention

Brucellosis can be prevented by the destruction of infected dairy animals, immunization of susceptible animals, and pasteurization of milk and milk products. Travelers should not consume unpasteurized milk and other dairy products and should avoid contact with animal carcasses in risk countries.

LEPTOSPIROSIS

Leptospirosis is the most common zoonosis in the world. Distribution is worldwide (except in polar regions), but the disease is most prevalent in the tropics. The causative spirochete *Leptospira interrogans* is transmitted by contact with contaminated freshwater or moist soil, including jungle swamps and mud. (Contamination is usually from the urine of infected animals, such as rats, mice, pigs, cattle, and dogs.) Contact with the tissue of infected animals can also spread disease. Leptospires enter through cuts or abrasions on the skin or exposed mucous membranes (nose, mouth, eyes). Traditionally recognized as an occupational disease (e.g., farmers, sewage workers, butchers) leptospirosis is becoming more frequently associated with recreational exposure (e.g., hiking, swimming, rafting) and major outbreaks have recently occurred in Nicaragua, Honduras, and Guatemala following heavy flooding. Recreational and wilderness travelers to the tropics should be aware of the risk for infection.

Many cases are asymptomatic or mild. More severe cases present with high fever, headache, conjunctival suffusion (eye redness and edema without secretions), severe myalgia, and stiff neck (from aseptic meningitis). Weil's disease, the most severe and sometimes fatal form of leptospirosis, is associated with liver dysfunction and jaundice, but death is almost always the result of renal failure, not liver failure. Other findings in severe leptospirosis include bleeding from hemorrhagic coagulopathy and capillary damage, marked leukocytosis, and hemorrhagic pneumonitis. Differential diagnosis includes hepatitis, malaria, typhoid fever, dengue fever, scrub typhus, and hemorrhagic fever with renal syndrome.

Treatment and Prevention

The incubation period is usually 7–14 days (range 2–21 days). You should seek prompt medical advice if symptoms suggestive of leptospirosis develop within the incubation period after freshwater exposure.

Effective antibiotics include penicillin, amoxicillin, erythromycin, doxycycline, and ceftriaxone. Dialysis is indicated for acute renal failure. Prevention consists of avoiding potentially contaminated freshwater (rivers, lakes, streams) and soil. Drinking water should be filtered, boiled, or treated with iodine. Chemoprophylaxis with doxycycline, 200 mg weekly, is effective and safe for short-term, high-risk exposure.

RABIES

Rabies is one of the most ancient and feared diseases. It is estimated that up to 50,000 people worldwide die each year from rabies, mostly in the developing countries of Africa, Asia, and Latin America, and travelers to these countries (especially those visiting small villages and rural areas) need to assess their potential risk of exposure. The highest risk of rabies occurs in El Salvador, Guatemala, Mexico, Colombia, Ecuador, Peru, Nepal, India, Pakistan, Bangladesh, Sri Lanka, Thailand, Vietnam, and the Philippines. More than 50 countries reportedly have no rabies cases. These include Australia, New Zealand, Papua New Guinea, most islands of the Pacific Ocean, most Caribbean islands, the United Kingdom, Cyprus, Finland, Iceland, Norway, Portugal, Spain, Sweden, Japan, Korea, Malaysia, Singapore, and Taiwan.

Dogs transmit most cases of human rabies in lesser-developed countries. In the United States, Canada, and most of Western Europe, where dogs are routinely vaccinated, animals such as skunks, raccoons, foxes, coyotes, bats, and other wild carnivores are the main reservoirs of disease. The mongoose is important in Puerto Rico, the jackal in much of Africa, the wolf in Iran and neighboring countries, and the vampire bat in certain Latin American countries. Therefore, at the very least, travelers should not approach or pet stray dogs, cats, monkeys, or feral animals.

Predeparture vaccination—The risk of rabies is often underestimated by adventure travelers and long-term expatriates. If you plan to stay for more than 30 days in a country where rabies is a constant threat, especially if you travel to remote areas, you should strongly consider predeparture rabies vaccination. This is particularly important for children who are often attracted to animals and who may not report a bite. Advantages to predeparture vaccination include:

- You won't need rabies immune globulin (RIG), which is often not available in developing countries.
- You will need to receive only 2—not 5—doses of rabies vaccine after exposure.
- A delay in treatment will be less critical. If rabies vaccine is not locally available, you will need to travel to where rabies vaccine is available. This could take several days.

There are three equally effective rabies vaccines commercially available in the United States: (1) Imovax (human diploid cell vaccine—HDCV), (2) RabAvert (purified chick embryo cell culture—PCEC), and (3) Rabies Vaccine Adsorbed (RVA from fetal rhesus lung cells).

Predeparture vaccination schedule (see Table 2.2 Chapter 2): Rabies vaccine is given as three doses on days 0, 7, and either 21 or 28. RabAvert and RVA must be given intramuscularly into the deltoid. Imovax can be administered intramuscularly (IM) or intradermally (ID). The ID dose is 0.1 mL. NOTE: Intradermal rabies vaccination must be completed prior to starting chloroquine or mefloquine. If this is not feasible, then the vaccine must be given IM.

Accelerated schedule: 2 doses, one week apart (intramuscular route only) when time does not allow three doses to be administered over 21–28 days.

Post-exposure treatment—Following exposure to an animal known or suspected of being rabid, nonvaccinated individuals should receive rabies immune globulin (RIG) *and* rabies vaccine. People already vaccinated should receive rabies vaccine *only*. NOTE: Exposure consists of a bite or a scratch, or the licking of a minor wound or abrasion, by the animal. Coming into contact with a bat, even without an observed bite, may constitute exposure.* The rabies virus is contained in the saliva and certain body tissues (e.g., the brain and spinal fluid) of the infected animal. Therefore, contact with the blood, urine, or feces of the animal does *not* constitute exposure and does not require vaccination.

If you completed a predeparture rabies vaccination series, you will need two additional doses of intramuscular vaccine (given on days 0 and 3). If not vaccinated, you must receive RIG followed by five doses of rabies vaccine (given on days 0, 3, 7, 14, 28). Treatment is best started within the first 24 hours after exposure. *If anatomically feasible, the entire calculated dose of rabies immune globulin (either human or equine) should be injected directly into the bite(s) and the tissue around the bite(s).* If there are large or multiple bites, RIG can be diluted with normal saline if more volume is needed to infiltrate all wound areas. If it is not anatomically feasible to inject the entire volume of RIG into the wound(s), any remaining volume should be injected intramuscularly at a remote site, usually into the gluteal muscles or anterolateral thigh.

RIG dosage: 20 IU/kg (human RIG) or 40 IU/kg (equine RIG)

NOTE: Theoretically, chloroquine may interfere with the immune response, and this drug should be discontinued during post-exposure rabies prophylaxis.

---

* A bat bite may go unnoticed. Cases of bat-associated rabies have occurred in patients where there was no definite history of a bite, scratch, or mucous membrane exposure. Post-exposure prophylaxis should be considered in situations where there was exposure to bats but unawareness that a bite or direct contact had occurred (e.g., a sleeping person awakens to find a bat in the room or an adult witnesses a bat in the room with a previously unattended child, mentally disabled person, or intoxicated person) and rabies cannot be ruled out by testing the bat.

The patient, of course, should be monitored for malaria symptoms if chloroquine has been discontinued.

Treatment failures can occur, but these failures are usually preventable and due to: (1) bite wounds not having been immediately and thoroughly cleaned with soap and water, (2) delayed (over 24 hours) treatment, (3) RIG not given with the vaccine, or (4) RIG not infiltrated directly into and around the wound(s). The wounds with the highest risk involve bites of the head, neck, and hands.

Vaccines overseas—In lesser-developed countries, the vaccines used in the United States and Canada are often not available, due to their high cost. The same is true for human rabies immune globulin (Imogam, BayRab), also a very expensive product. In the event of rabies exposure abroad, you would likely be given a Vero cell vaccine, a chick cell–derived vaccine, or a purified duck embryo–derived vaccine. These products are effective and safe and have few side effects. Instead of human RIG, you might get purified equine RIG, which has the potential to cause significant side effects unless the newer preparations (from Europe) are used. If you return to the United States or Canada after starting post-exposure treatment abroad, the vaccination schedule can be completed using intramuscular Imovax (HDCV), RabAvert (PCEC), or RVA. In many developing countries, neural-tissue vaccines (Semple, Fermi, suckling mouse) are still in common use. These vaccines are cheap but are less effective and potentially very dangerous. They should be avoided, if possible. In the event of a possible rabies exposure, contact the nearest U.S. Embassy to obtain the location of the nearest reliable medical facility. You should be prepared to evacuate to another country for appropriate medical care (with rabies immune globulin and tissue culture vaccines) if necessary. However, if you begin treatment overseas with a neural-tissue (Semple, Fermi, suckling mouse brain) vaccine, you should try, as soon as possible, to get to a facility (even if it means returning to the United States) that can re-initiate vaccination with one of the newer cell-culture vaccines.

SEAFOOD TOXINS

Poisonous toxins in seafood can be an important and often overlooked cause of illness in travelers. Unfortunately, the toxins are often difficult or impossible to detect because they do not usually affect the appearance, smell, or taste of the fish or shellfish. In addition, they are not usually destroyed by freezing, drying, smoking, or cooking.

Fish Poisoning

Scombroid poisoning occurs after eating fish that has been inadequately chilled after capture. It occurs most commonly in tuna and related species and also mahi-mahi. Affected fish contains histamine and may have a sharp, bitter, or peppery taste. Often, however, the fish looks, smells, and tastes normal. Symptoms of scombroid poisoning resemble an allergic reaction and include flushing, headache, nausea, vomiting, abdominal cramps, and diarrhea. In addition, there may be hives and wheezing. Treatment with antihistamines is very effective.

Ciguatera poisoning occurs after eating coral reef fish containing potent toxins that originate in algae found in coral reefs, especially after storms which may cause an increase in algae. The toxin is passed up the food chain through herbivorous fish to carnivorous fish and eventually to humans. Any part of the fish may contain toxin but the highest concentrations are found in the head, gut, roe, and liver. Almost any reef fish can cause ciguatera poisoning, but it is commonest in barracuda, moray eel, grouper, snapper, jack, and sea bass. Large carnivorous fish weighing more than six pounds are the most dangerous. Symptoms include diarrhea, nausea, vomiting, and abdominal cramps followed by neurologic symptoms such as numbness and tingling involving the arms and legs and the area around the mouth. There may be temperature reversal where cold objects feel hot. For example, ice cream may cause a burning sensation in the mouth. Another bizarre symptom is where the teeth often feel numb or loose. In addition, there may be muscle aches, fatigue, itchiness of the skin, and depression. Some of the symptoms may last weeks or several months. After an episode, travelers should avoid, for several months, alcohol, fish of any kind, and nuts. These substances may exacerbate symptoms. Treatment is directed to relieving the symptoms, but mannitol given intravenously within 72 hours of onset may sometimes produce a dramatic improvement. A commercial test (Cigua-check, Oceanit Test) has recently become available to test fish for ciguatoxin (*http://www.cigua.com*). This test is very sensitive and easy to perform, but it is relatively expensive and probably of limited value for travelers.

Pufferfish or fugu poisoning occurs after eating pufferfish and less commonly porcupine fish or ocean sunfish containing a highly potent toxin known as tetrodotoxin. It is 50 times more potent than strychnine and is usually concentrated in the ovaries, liver, gut, and skin of affected fish. Most cases of pufferfish poisoning occur in Japan where pufferfish or fugu is eaten as a very expensive and prized delicacy. The fugu experience is a feeling of euphoria and exhilaration and is the result of ingesting minute amounts of toxin. Unfortunately, larger quantities of toxins can be rapidly fatal. Symptoms of poisoning include nausea, sweating, dizziness, and neurologic symptoms such as numbness, tingling, and weakness. In severe cases, there is widespread paralysis often involving the respiratory muscles. Mortality rates of up to 60 percent have been reported. Unfortunately, there is no specific antidote, and treatment is directed at relieving the symptoms and providing supportive care

Shellfish Poisoning

There are two important types of shellfish, crustaceans (e.g., crabs, shrimp, and lobster) and bivalve mollusks (e.g. oysters, mussels, clams, and scallops). Most cases of toxic shellfish poisoning occur after eating bivalve mollusks. The toxins originate in algae, and outbreaks of shellfish poisoning are particularly common after algal blooms or "red tides." There is no specific treatment or effective antidote for any of the shellfish poisonings, and treatment is directed at relieving symptoms and providing supportive care.

Paralytic shellfish poisoning is the commonest and most serious form of shellfish poisoning. Typical symptoms include numbness, tingling, and a sensation of floating. In severe cases, there may be paralysis of respiratory muscles. Deaths are commonest in children, and mortality rates of over 40% have been reported.

Neurotoxic shellfish poisoning causes nausea, vomiting, diarrhea, and neurologic symptoms such as numbness, tingling, weakness, and dizziness. When the toxin is aerosolized in rough surf, there may be wheezing, coughing, and eye irritation in exposed individuals.

Diarrheic shellfish poisoning causes gastroenteritis with symptoms such as diarrhea, nausea, vomiting, abdominal cramps, weakness, and chills. No deaths have been reported.

Amnesic shellfish poisoning is rare but can cause a gastroenteritis and neurologic features such as headaches, memory loss, seizures, and long-term dementia. It may be fatal in elderly patients.

GUIDELINES FOR PREVENTION OF SEAFOOD POISONING

- Avoid fish that has not been promptly chilled after capture (scombroid).
- Avoid fish that has an ammonia smell or sharp, peppery taste (scombroid).
- Avoid reef fish, especially large carnivorous fish such as barracuda, moray eel, grouper, snapper, jack, and sea bass (ciguatera).
- Never eat shellfish associated with algal blooms or "red tides."
- Avoid consumption of bivalve mollusks (oysters, clams, scallops, and mussels) in developing countries.
- Some authors suggest that ciguatoxin-laden fish can be detected by rubbing a piece of the fish along the gums (before ingestion) to see if a tingling feeling occurs.

Section on Seafood Toxins courtesy of Vernon Ansdell, M.D.

Cobelens FG, et al. Typhoid fever in group travelers: Opportunity for studying vaccine efficacy. J Trav Med 2000;7:19–24.

Nguyen TC, Solomon T, Mai XT, et al. Short courses of ofloxacin for the treatment of enteric fever. Trans R Soc Trop Med Hyg 1997 May–June91(3):347–9.

Smith MD, Duong NM, Hoa NT. Comparison of ofloxacin and ceftriaxone for short-course treatment of enteric fever. Antimicrob Agents Chemother 1994;38:1716-20.

Vinh H, Wain J, Hanh VTN, et al. Two or three days of ofloxacin for uncomplicated multidrug-resistant typhoid fever in children. Antimicrob Agents Chemother 1996;40:958–61.

Welch TP. Risk of giardiasis from consumption of wilderness water in North America: A systematic review of epidemiologic data. Int J Infect Dis 2000;4: 100–103.

10 Lyme Disease

Lyme disease is a potentially serious illness that occurs worldwide. The disease was first recognized in the United States in 1975, following an investigation of a group of children with arthritis in Lyme, Connecticut. Lyme disease is now the most common tick-transmitted illness in the United States. In 1998, more than 16,000 cases were reported, an increase of nearly 20% over the number of cases reported in 1995.

The most serious aspect of Lyme disease is not knowing you have it. Early signs and symptoms may not be noticed or may be misdiagnosed. Untreated illness can cause serious health problems.

Lyme disease is caused by spirochete-type bacteria belonging to the *Borrelia burgdorferi* complex. The disease is transmitted by various hard bodied ixodid ticks.

Larval ticks feed in the late summer, nymphs feed during spring and early summer, and adults feed predominantly in the fall. The tiny nymphs are your chief threat because they are the most active feeders, and their small size makes casual detection very difficult (see Figure 9.1).

Figure 9.1 Actual Size of Deer Ticks in 5 Stages. From left to right: larva, nymph, adult male, adult female, and engorged (fed) female.

Ticks like to live in grassy or wooded areas, but can also be found in your backyard. They are not found on sand dunes, where there is no grass. Ticks don't fly, jump up from the ground, or drop from trees. Instead, they climb to the tips of vegetation and wait for you to brush by. Since the ticks are so small, and their bite is painless, you will probably be unaware when a tick attaches itself to your clothing or skin. Depending on the geographic location, the percentage of ticks infected with the borrelia bacteria can vary, ranging from a very small percentage to a large percentage of ticks.

People most at risk—People most at risk are those engaged in outdoor activities—campers, hikers, mountain bikers, hunters, fishermen, farmers, gardeners, telephone lineworkers, foresters, and military personnel on training maneuvers.

Where Lyme Disease Commonly Occurs

United States and Canada—Forty-five states and the District of Columbia report Lyme disease, but it mostly occurs in the Northeast, the Mid-Atlantic states, the upper Midwest, and the Pacific Coast. Ninety percent of cases have been reported from eight states: Connecticut, Delaware, Maryland, New Jersey, New York, Pennsylvania, Rhode Island, and Wisconsin. Connecticut has the highest Lyme disease rate in the country: 94.8 cases per 100,000 population. Alaska and Hawaii are low-risk areas. In Canada, the disease is concentrated in Ontario and Manitoba.

Overseas—Most cases are reported from Europe (especially Germany's Black Forest region, southern Sweden, southern and eastern Austria, and the northern Swiss plateau), the former Soviet Union (from the Baltics to the Pacific), China, Japan, and Australia. The incidence of Lyme disease in Latin America appears to be very low. In Africa, cases have been reported from Nigeria, Angola, Kenya, Tanzania, and Zambia. Antarctica is apparently free of the disease.

Symptoms

Because you may not have noticed the tick bite and because the symptoms of Lyme disease are sometimes passed off as "the flu," illness can be overlooked or misdiagnosed. Ten to 20% of infected people may not even develop early symptoms. Up to 40% of victims may not develop or recall having the typical rash.

Stage I (early localized infection)—A spreading, circular, pink or red rash (erythema migrans) is the hallmark of early Lyme disease. This rash, which originates at the site of the tick bite, is caused by the *Borrelia burgdorferi* spirochetes migrating in an expanding fashion from the central point of inoculation. The rash can become quite large—5 to 10 inches, or more, in diameter. The appearance of the rash is somewhat variable. In some cases it is halo-shaped with an almost clear central area surrounded by a pink or red outer ring (bull's-eye rash). Other rashes have a deep red center with secondary rings and a red outer border. The red areas may be slightly raised and warm to the touch. You may also notice localized lymph node swelling and fatigue.

There's a 15% – 40% chance you won't have the characteristic rash. Absence of the typical rash makes early diagnosis more difficult.

Stage II (early disseminated infection)—After Stage I, the spirochetes spread throughout the body, causing flu-like symptoms: fever, headache, muscle and joint aches, swollen glands, increased fatigue, nausea, and loss of appetite. Other symptoms include multiple skin rashes; pains in the muscles, joints, and tendons (fibromyalgia); meningitis; encephalitis; and facial nerve paralysis (Bell's palsy). Cardiac problems include conduction abnormalities with variable degrees of heart block, myopericarditis, and cardiomyopathy.

Stage II symptoms can occur while the primary erythema migrans rash is still visible or can be delayed by weeks or months.

Stage III (late infection)—If untreated, you can develop prolonged arthritis attacks in one or multiple joints (often the knees), chronic fatigue, and disorders of the nervous system (polyneuritis, paralysis, encephalopathy).

Neuritis symptoms include backache with shooting pains and lack of feeling in the hands and feet.

Symptoms of encephalopathy include mental changes such as forgetting names, misplacing objects, or missing appointments. There may be problems speaking and trouble finding words. A variety of rashes with inflammation and thinning of the skin may also occur.

Diagnosis

The diagnosis of early Lyme disease should be based primarily on a history of possible exposure in an endemic area and on the presence of typical symptoms. To be diagnosed with Lyme disease, you need to have either the characteristic erythema migrans rash alone—or symptoms consistent with Lyme disease in combination with either a four-fold rise in anti-*Borrelia burgdorferei* antibody or a positive *B. burgdorferei* polymerase chain reaction (PCR) test. If the ELISA antibody test is negative four weeks or more after exposure, Lyme disease can usually be excluded.

Treatment

If the diagnosis seems clear cut on the basis of your exposure and symptoms (especially the rash), you should receive immediate antibiotic treatment. The treatment of choice for early Lyme disease is doxycycline. Don't let your doctor withhold treatment just to see if your blood test will turn positive.

Treatment recommendations are based on limited data. The duration of treatment is not well established for any stage of the disease and relapses are possible despite a full course of a recommended antibiotic. A second course of antibiotic treatment may therefore be required. Table 9.1 summarizes current treatment recommendations.

Treatment of children and pregnant women—Amoxicillin is the drug of choice for pregnant women and children under eight years of age. Women who are allergic to penicillin should receive erythromycin base, 250 mg–500 mg, four times daily for 4 weeks.

Should You Take Antibiotics After a Tick Bite?

Finding a tick attached to you doesn't automatically mean you will get Lyme disease because (1) the tick may not be infective, or (2) the tick may not have been attached long enough to transmit spirochetes. (Transmission of spirochetes takes 24–36 hours.) Nevertheless, a tick bite signifies potential risk. Your risk is increased if the tick has fed long enough to become engorged with blood.

In geographic areas where a high percentage of ticks are known to be infective, a case can be made for taking prophylactic antibiotics after a bite, rather than waiting for symptoms (e.g., a telltale rash) to develop. You should consider the following factors in making this decision:

Table 9.1
Treatment of Lyme Disease[1]

	Drug	Adult Dosage	Pediatric Dosage[2]
ERYTHEMA MIGRANS	Doxycycline[3] (Vibramycin, and others)	100 mg PO b.i.d. x 14–21 d	
	OR Amoxicillin (Amoxil, and others)	500 mg PO t.i.d. x 14–21 d	25–50 mg/kg/day divided t.i.d.
	OR Cefuroxime axetil (Ceftin)	500 mg PO b.i.d. x 14–21 d	250 mg b.i.d.
NEUROLOGIC DISEASE			
Facial nerve palsy	Doxycycline[3]	100 mg PO b.i.d. x 21–28 d	
	OR Amoxicillin	500 mg PO t.i.d. x 21–28 d	25–50 mg/kg/day divided t.i.d.
More serious CNS disease	Ceftriaxone (Rocephin)	2 g/day IV x 14–28 d	75–100 mg/kg/day IV
	OR Cefotaxime (Claforan)	2 g q8h x 14–28 d	90–180 mg/kg/day in 3 doses
	OR Penicillin G	20–24 million units/day IV x 14–28 d	300,000 units/kg/day IV
CARDIAC DISEASE			
Mild	Doxycycline[3]	100 mg PO b.i.d. x 21 d	
	OR Amoxicillin	250–500 mg PO t.i.d. x 21 d	25–50 mg/kg/day divided t.i.d.
More serious[4]	Ceftriaxone	2 g/day IV x 14–21 d	50–75 mg/kg/day IV
	OR Penicillin G	20–24 million units/day IV x 14–21 d	300,000 units/kg/day IV
ARTHRITIS[5]			
Oral	Doxycycline[3]	100 mg PO b.i.d. x 28 d	
	OR Amoxicillin	500 mg PO q.i.d. x 28 d	50 mg/kg/day divided t.i.d.
Parenteral	Ceftriaxone	2 g/day IV x 14–28 d	50–75 mg/kg/day IV
	OR Penicillin G	20–24 million units/day IV x 14–28 d	300,000 units/kg/day IV

©1997 The Medical Letter, Vol. 39. Reprinted with Permission

1. Recommendations are based on limited data and should be considered tentative. The duration of treatment is not well established for any indication. Relapse has occurred with all of these regimens; patients who relapse may need a second course of treatment. There is no evidence, however, that either repeated or prolonged treatment benefits subjective symptoms attributed to Lyme disease.
2. Should not exceed adult dosage.
3. Neither doxycycline nor any other tetracycline should be used for children under age eight or for pregnant or lactating women.
4. A temporary pacemaker may be necessary.
5. In late disease, the response to treatment may be delayed for several weeks or months.

- Can you identify the tick? Is it a deer tick? • Was the tick engorged with blood?
- How prevalent is Lyme disease in the area? • Do you have a history of drug allergies? • What degree of anxiety do you have about possible illness?

There's no question that it is advantageous to treat Lyme disease at the earliest possible time. Also, your level of anxiety about the disease should not be ignored. If your anxiety level is high, and there is a possibility of disease transmission, then prophylactic antibiotics are reasonable. Finally, if you are a female and are pregnant, and you discover a blood-engorged tick, you certainly should be treated.

Lyme Disease Fact

Tests for Lyme disease may not be diagnostic during Stage I. Therefore, prompt, aggressive antibiotic treatment of early Lyme disease can be started solely on the basis of symptoms, especially a typical rash. The absence of the rash, however, should not eliminate Lyme disease from consideration if the symptoms also suggest other features of the infection.

Prevention

The primary defense against Lyme disease and other tick-borne diseases remains avoidance of tick-infested habitats, use of personal protection measures, and checking for and removing ticks.

Tick bite prevention—The best way to prevent tick bites is to combine protective clothing with "chemical warfare." Cover as much exposed skin areas as weather conditions allow. Tucking long pants into socks is highly effective. Treat outer clothing with the insecticide permethrin (Chapter 7). Apply a DEET-containing insect repellent to exposed skin. Inspect your body daily for attached ticks.

Vaccination—A vaccine (Lymerix) is now available. Another vaccine, ImuLyme, is available in Europe. Lymerix is approved for people ages 15–70 to be administered in 3 doses over a 12-month period. Using the accelerated schedule (equally effective), the vaccine can be given over two months (doses at 0, 1, and 2 months). Booster doses may be needed, but as yet there are no recommended schedules. The vaccine is recommended for travelers who will spend considerable time outdoors in modrate- to high-risk areas. Since Lymerix is about 78% effective after three doses, and since the duration of protection is not known, vaccinated travelers should still take tick bite precautions, as outlined above.

Vaccine side effects include chills, fever, myalgias, and achiness. These symptoms are usually temporary, but the long-term safety profile of the vaccine is still somewhat vague. Vaccination is not recommended during pregnancy.

NOTE: Lymerix is effective only against strains of borrelia spirochetes found in the United States, not strains found in Europe or Asia.

Tick Removal

1. Grasp the head of the tick with tweezers as near to the skin as possible and gently pull upward and backward until the head of the tick is completely removed. Try not to crush or puncture the tick. Don't try to twist or jerk it out.
   If the mouth parts are embedded and tear off, consult a doctor immediately.
2. If the tick won't release with the above technique, apply a small amount of permethrin spray to the tick. Wait 10 minutes and try the removal technique again.
3. Don't try petroleum jelly or a hot object to remove the tick.
4. Never use bare fingers to remove a tick. The infection could be passed to you.
5. After removing the tick with tweezers, wipe off the attachment site with disinfectant (such as alcohol or Betadine). Wash your hands with soap and water.
6. Kill the removed tick by immersing it in 70% alcohol or cremate it with a match. However, if you want the tick examined or tested for the possibility of Lyme infectivity, don't kill it; put it in a bottle for later examination.

After removing the tick, observe the bite area for any sign of a rash. The typical Lyme disease rash, if it's going to occur, appears from 3 to 30 days after the bite. If you get a rash immediately, or within 24 hours after being bitten, it is not a Lyme disease rash—it is an allergic (hypersensitivity) reaction to the bite. (These allergic rashes are usually itchy.)

Is The Tick Infected?

Once you have removed a tick, you can have it tested for Lyme disease by polymerase chain reaction (PCR), a technique that detects the DNA of the Lyme disease spirochetes in the tick. Without knowing if the tick is infected, the medical profession is divided on whether to treat on the basis of a tick bite alone. A positive PCR test is a strong indication that you should take antibiotics after a tick bite.

The PCR test can be done on live or dead ticks sent through the mail. A doctor's order is not necessary to have testing done.

Procedure: Place the tick (dead or alive) in a clean, covered prescription vial that has been thoroughly washed and rinsed with tap water. Refrigerate the vial until it can be sent. Mail the vial with a check or money order for $35 to **Imugen**, 220 Norwood Park South, Norwood, MA 02062. Tel: 617-255-0770.

Specify that you want Lyme disease testing done since other PCR tests are also performed at this laboratory.

Bozler E (ed.) Basic and Clinic Approaches to Lyme Disease: A Lyme Disease Foundation Symposium. Clin Inf Dis 1997;25(suppl 1):S1–S75.

Magid DM, Schwartz B, Craft J, et al. Prevention of Lyme Disease After Tick Bites: A Cost-Effective Analysis. N Engl J Med 1992;**327**:534–541.

Nowak D, Fedorowski JJ. Current Concepts of Lyme Disease. Hospital Physician September 1997:16–35.

11 Hepatitis

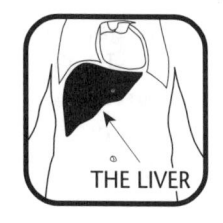

THE LIVER

Four Distinct Types

Hepatitis is a generic term for inflammation of the liver. It is caused by a number of viruses, other infectious agents, and toxins. However, for the traveler, viral hepatitis is the major concern. There are four hepatitis viruses of which all travelers should be particularly aware: A, B, C, and E.* The means of transmission and long-term effects vary, depending upon which virus causes the disease.

Hepatitis A and E are transmitted primarily by contaminated food and water. High-risk areas are lesser-developed countries where poor sanitation results in fecal contamination of groundwater, tap water, and well water. Outbreaks of hepatitis A are also caused by food that has been contaminated by an infected foodhandler.

Hepatitis B and C are spread by sexual contact, exchange of body fluids, injections from contaminated needles and syringes, and unscreened blood transfusions.

Symptoms of Hepatitis

The symptoms can be variable. Most cases of hepatitis, in fact, go completely unnoticed. In a textbook case, however, you would develop fever, fatigue, loss of appetite, jaundice (yellow skin), dark urine, abdominal pain, and aching joints.

Symptoms of acute hepatitis may occur weeks to months after exposure and typically last from two to six weeks. The likelihood of complete recovery depends on the particular viral infection and your underlying health. Complete recovery occurs in most cases of types A and E hepatitis, but 5% to 80% of types B and C may progress, causing chronic, sometimes fatal, liver disease.

HEPATITIS A

This is the most frequently diagnosed form of hepatitis in travelers returning from developing countries. Worldwide, hepatitis A is very widespread and close to 100% of the nationals of most lesser-developed countries are infected with the hepatitis A virus (HAV) by 10 years of age. In some industrialized countries, however, no more than 10% of the population has been previously infected. In the USA, about 33% of the population has serological evidence of previous HAV infection.

---

*A fifth virus, hepatitis D, is an incomplete virus that requires the presence of hepatitis B virus and is of little concern to the average traveler. It can occur in people who are chronically infected with hepatitis B, or occasionally as a combined acute infection with hepatitis B. It is contracted primarily through intravenous drug use or sexual contact with a carrier. Most hepatitis D is found in southern Italy, parts of North Africa adjacent to the Mediterranean, and the upper reaches of the Amazon Basin.

Risk to travelers—The risk to a nonimmune traveler of acquiring hepatitis A is estimated at 1 per 1,000 per week of exposure in resort areas, and 5 per 1,000 per week in remote areas of developing countries. Although the risk of hepatitis A is certainly higher in countries with substandard sanitation and hygiene, travel to developed or industrialized countries still carries some risk.

Symptoms usually appear 2–6 weeks after exposure. HAV infection is often mild or asymptomatic in children, but there is increased morbidity and mortality in adults. About 0.15% to 0.5% of infected adults develop fulminant liver failure, fatal in half of these cases. Above age 50, mortality may reach 3%. In individuals with chronic hepatitis C or other forms of chronic liver disease a superimposed HAV infection may carry an even higher risk of severe disease and death.

Treatment

Treatment consists of supportive care. Eat a nutritious diet and avoid alcohol. Be aware that the combination of alcohol and acetaminophen can cause direct hepatic toxicity, but acetaminophen alone in therapeutic doses is acceptable in the presence of hepatitis. There is no specific treatment that will shorten your illness. Limiting exercise has no effect on your rate of recovery. Hospitalization is unnecessary unless you suffer more severe signs of acute liver failure. Shortly after symptoms appear, the virus is no longer in your stool or blood, and you are no longer infectious, so quarantine or isolation procedures are not necessary. Close contacts such as family members or companion(s) who have not previously been infected or vaccinated should immediately receive immune globulin (if available) or hepatitis A vaccine.

Prevention

Hepatitis A vaccine—Hepatitis A is the most frequent vaccine-preventable disease, and there are several vaccines now available. VAQTA (Merck) and Havrix (SmithKline Beecham) give rise to measurable antibody levels within two weeks after a single injection; a booster dose, recommended at 6–12 months, dramatically boosts antibody levels and provides virtually 100% immunity for at least 10–20 years, and probably for life. Hepatitis A vaccine (see Appendix A, Table I) is now recommended for all nonimmune travelers over age two, especially those going to lesser-developed countries.

Immune globulin (IG)—When nonimmune travelers are departing imminently for hepatitis A endemic areas, it has previously been recommended that the traveler receive either (1) immune globulin alone, for brief visits, or (2) hepatitis A vaccine, plus immune globulin. The rationale for giving IG with the vaccine is to provide immediate protection until vaccine-derived immunity kicks in. Most travel medicine physicians, however, now believe that giving immune globulin is unnecessary. The reason? Because it takes the hepatitis A virus 2–6 weeks to cause clinical infection, vaccine-derived immunity develops in sufficient time to prevent illness—and therefore supplemental IG is really not needed. Already in Switzerland, and in an increasing number of travel clinics in North America, immune globulin (which is often in short supply anyway) is no longer used to protect travelers against hepatitis A.

Vaccination of children—Extensive safety and efficacy studies have not been done on the use of the vaccine in children under two years of age, and therefore it is not FDA-approved for this group. Nevertheless, the vaccine does appear to be effective in infants who have not acquired maternal HAV antibody. In cases where the mother has been previously infected and has transmitted HAV antibody to the child, this passive immunity wears off by about 12 months, so vaccination of such a child in the second year is likely to be effective. Studies are now underway to clear the vaccine for use in the under-age-two group.

Safe food and drink—Even if you have been immunized against hepatitis A, it is important to follow these rules to reduce your risk of other infections transmitted by contaminated food and water:

- Drink only boiled, commercially bottled, carbonated, or chemically treated water, soft drinks, fruit juices, beer, or wine.
- Don't put ice cubes in your drinks unless they have been made from safe water.
- Eat only well-cooked foods. Avoid raw or undercooked meat, fish and shellfish, and raw fruits and vegetables, unless you peel them yourself. Stick to piping hot foods, if possible.
- Avoid salads.

HEPATITIS B

This is the most important type of hepatitis because of its potential severity and widespread occurrence worldwide. Although the hepatitis B virus is not as lethal as the AIDS virus, it is 100 times more infectious and is more easily spread by person-to-person contact.

Acute hepatitis B occurs from 40 to 180 days after exposure, with an average of 75 days. The most common response to the virus is asymptomatic infection, so you may not even be aware of the illness. (Your chance of developing jaundice during the infection is less than 50%.) Whether you are symptomatic or not, your illness may last for several weeks, or even months, but if you are an adult you have a 90% to 95% chance of recovering completely and having lifelong immunity against any further attacks. Hepatitis B, though, differs in an important respect from hepatitis A: there is a 0.1% to 1% risk of death with the acute infection and an overall fatality rate of 1%–3%. Five percent, or less, of infected adults (but up to 90% of infected newborns) become chronic carriers of the virus. Seniors who become infected also are at greater risk—they have a 5- to 6-fold increase in chronic viral carriage.

If you do become a carrier of the virus, you can infect others, and you are also at risk for the development of chronic hepatitis, cirrhosis, and liver cancer. In fact, 10% of chronic carriers develop liver cancer.

High-Risk Countries and Exposure to the Virus

Areas where up to 5% to 20% of the population are carriers of the hepatitis B virus include all of sub-Saharan Africa, the Balkans, the Middle East, China, Southeast Asia, including Korea and Indonesia, the South Pacific Islands (Oceania), the interior Amazon Basin, Haiti, and the Dominican Republic. Travelers to these areas are at increased risk if they are exposed to the blood or body fluids of infected people. Sexual contact appears to be the most frequent mode of disease transmission, especially among expatriates staying long-term in a risk area. The risk of hepatitis B in expatriates is 1:1,000 per month of stay abroad. Virus transmission also occurs from intravenous drug use, medical injections or vaccinations with contaminated needles and/or syringes, receipt of unscreened blood transfusions, or skin-to-skin contact with carriers of the virus who have

Table 10.1

Summary of Serological Tests for Hepatitis B		
Tests	**Results**	**Interpretation**
HBsAg anti-HBc anti-HBs	negative negative negative	susceptible
HBsAg anti-HBc anti-HBs	negative negative or positive positive	immune
HBsAg anti-HBc IgM anti-HBc anti-HBs	positive positive positive negative	acutely infected
HBsAg anti-HBc IgM anti-HBc anti-HBs	positive positive negative negative	chronically infected
HBsAg anti-HBc anti-HBs	negative positive negative	four interpretations possible*

* Possible interpretations:
1. May be recovering from acute HBV infection.
2. May be distantly immune and test not sensitive enough to detect very low level of anti-HBs in serum.
3. May be susceptible with a false positive anti-HBc.
4. May be undetectable level of HBsAg present in the serum and the person is actually a carrier. HBsAg: If positive, obtain IgM anti-HBc to differentiate acute hepatitis B from chronic hepatitis B. Chronic hepatitis B is also defined by two HBsAg-positive tests separated by at least 6 months.

open sores due to tropical ulcers, impetigo, scabies, or infected insect bites. Fluid from these open sores can transmit the virus, and children especially may be at risk from playmates who have these open skin sores.

Diagnosis of Acute and Chronic Hepatitis B Virus (HBV) Infection

Table 10.1 gives a summary of the serological tests used to evaluate the status of a traveler who may be (1) acutely infected with HBV, (2) chronically infected and a carrier of HBV, or (3) nonimmune and susceptible to infection.

Treatment

The treatment of hepatitis B is summarized on the next page.

Prevention

Both hepatitis B immune globulin and vaccination will protect you against hepatitis B. The vaccines available in the United States, Recombivax-HB and Engerix-B, are genetically engineered vaccines derived from yeast. These vaccines are completely safe and virtually 100% effective in those who develop an antibody response after three doses have been administered. About 10% of recipients do not develop measurable antibody levels; some of these recipients will respond to additional high-dose boosters.

If you have not been immunized, your risk of getting hepatitis B can also be reduced or eliminated by practicing safe sex (or practicing abstinence). You should avoid medical injections or surgical procedures in lesser-developed countries, if possible, because the equipment may not be sterile. Consider carrying a sterile needle and syringe kit (see SteriKit™, Chapter 1).

Accelerated immunization—Because most travelers leave within a month after their first travel clinic visit, they may not have enough time to be fully immunized against hepatitis B if it is administered according to the standard schedule (0, 1, and 6 months). Studies have shown, however, that an accelerated vaccination schedule (0, 1 and 2 months or 0, 7, and 21 days) produces measurable antibodies in 80% of recipients by day 28 and over 90% protection at three months. If you are departing to a risk area on short notice, have your doctor administer the hepatitis B vaccine according to this accelerated schedule.

NOTE: Even a single dose of hepatitis B vaccine may possibly "prime" your immune system and afford some protection. If you have time for only one injection of vaccine before departure, it seems worthwhile to receive it.

Immunization should be considered for the following groups: Frequent short-term travelers, including children; persons living for prolonged periods (more than 3 months) in high-risk areas; adventure travelers; travelers with chronic diseases, such as chronic liver disease due to hepatitis C or other causes; older travelers; people who will have close, prolonged contact with the local population, such as health-care workers, missionaries, and relief workers; travelers who might have sexual contact with the local population; any risk-averse traveler desiring maximum pre-travel preparation, especially if they are traveling in a country where the sterility of needles and syringes for medical injections cannot be guaranteed.

Booster doses—Booster doses of vaccine are not recommended if your immune system is healthy. Recent studies suggest that about one-third of people vaccinated against hepatitis B will no longer have measurable antibodies after 5 years, yet they will still be protected against infection. This protection is considered to be lifelong because of the body's "immune memory." (For this reason the measurement of hepatitis B neutralizing antibody is not routinely recommended.)

Prevention after exposure—If you are exposed to hepatitis B and have not been vaccinated, you should receive hepatitis B immune globulin (HBIG), as well as the vaccine. This should be done within 24–48 hours following exposure to blood. If you have sexual exposure, you should receive HBIG plus the vaccine within 14 days of sexual contact.

HEPATITIS C

Hepatitis C typically does not cause acute symptomatic illness when initially acquired. It is usually diagnosed, often by chance years or even decades later. In 80% of cases, the infection is permanent and people become "chronic carriers." The carrier state is a persistent, active viral infection (chronic hepatitis C) and may cause liver scarring, which in 20%–50% of carriers progresses over decades to cirrhosis or, more rarely, liver cancer.

The number of new cases of hepatitis C in developed countries has decreased more than five-fold since the discovery of the hepatitis C virus (HCV). In the 60's and 70's, when there was a lot of experimentation with drugs, HCV got into the population that donated blood. Today, when all blood in developed countries is screened for HCV, the most common means of transmission is the sharing of needles by drug users.

In developed countries, HCV is acquired by:

- Intravenous drug use (50%–60% of cases).
- Sexual contact (10%–15%). NOTE: HCV is not spread by sexual contact as efficiently as is HBV or HIV.
- Miscellaneous or unknown causes: Some people are thought to have been exposed while working in a hospital, while receiving hemodialysis, during birth, or by sharing a toothbrush or razor or being exposed in some other way to infected blood. For 10% of people, there is simply no explanation for the infection. One possibility: intranasal cocaine use has recently been associated with HCV infection in persons without other risk factors.

Comparable information on trends of HCV incidence in lesser-developed countries is unavailable. Some lesser-developed countries don't screen blood for HCV, so transfusions in these countries must be avoided, unless the situation is a dire emergency. Needles and syringes may also be contaminated, and you should avoid unnecessary medical injections or other forms of skin puncturing, e.g., acupuncture, in these areas.

Treatment of Hepatitis B and C

With either hepatitis B or C, supportive treatment is indicated, but bed rest is neither necessary nor helpful. Your diet should be nutritious, but otherwise can be unrestricted. However, alcohol, the most important factor in disease progression, must be eliminated. Even more damaging is the combination of alcohol and acetaminophen. It is not common knowledge, but even healthy persons who drink moderate amounts of alcohol, perhaps as little as three to four beers or mixed drinks per day for at least several weeks, and who take normally recommended doses of acetaminophen (6 to 8 extra-strength tablets) per day, are at risk for acute toxic hepatitis. NOTE: Acetaminophen *alone* is not toxic in therapeutic doses when alcohol is not consumed. It can be administered safely to people with chronic liver disease who do not drink.

Interferon—At this time, interferon α-2b (Intron A, Schering) is the only FDA-approved drug for the treatment of hepatitis B. About 40% of patients who are HBeAg(+) become HBeAg(−) after 6 months of treatment. Recently, the drug lamivudine has been associated with substantial histological improvement in many patients with chronic hepatitis B.

Interferon and ribavirin—Three interferons have been approved for treatment of chronic hepatitis C: interferon α-2b (Intron-A, Schering-Plough); interferon α-2a (Roferon, Roche); alfacon-1 (Infergen, Amgen). The combination of ribavirin and interferon α-2b (Rebetron, Schering-Plough) has been demonstrated to be superior to interferon α-2b alone. The genotype of hepatitis C determines the duration and response rates with combination treatment. Thirty percent of persons with genotype 1, which accounts for 70%–80% of persons with HCV infection, remain virus-free 6 months after completion of a 12-month course of treatment, whereas over two-thirds of persons with genotype 2 or 3 clear HCV after 6 months of therapy. Liver transplantation is the treatment of last resort for either disease.

Prevention of Hepatitis C

You should avoid unscreened blood transfusions in lesser-developed countries. If a blood transfusion is required, locate a family member or colleague who would be a compatible donor. If a donor is not available, consider medical evacuation to a country with more advanced facilities.

Also avoid unsafe sex and the use of potentially contaminated needles and syringes.

Persons with hepatitis C should not share toothbrushes or grooming implements, should cover cuts and open sores, and should not donate blood or tissue.

There is no vaccine to prevent hepatitis C and immune globulin is not recommended after exposure. However, HCV carriers should be vaccinated against hepatitis A and hepatitis B because a superimposed infection with either virus can cause further liver damage.

HEPATITIS E

Hepatitis E has many features in common with hepatitis A. They are transmitted by the same route, and in most cases the infection they cause is acute and self-limiting. The hepatitis E virus can be transmitted from person-to-person, but such secondary transmission is much less common, the incidence being 5% in hepatitis E compared to 50% for hepatitis A. This is probably because larger doses of virus are needed to cause disease. Hepatitis E is endemic in many tropical and subtropical countries, with outbreaks being reported in India, southeast Asia, China, and Russia. No outbreaks have been described in developed countries presumably because water supply and sanitary systems are satisfactory.

Most cases of hepatitis E are reported in young adults, who usually experience mild symptoms, followed by complete recovery. Chronic liver disease does not develop. However, fulminant liver failure, with a mortality of 20%, can occur in pregnant women, especially in the third trimester. Infected mothers can also transmit the hepatitis E virus to the fetus with significant consequences.

The risk to the average tourist is quite low, but the data are scarce. The risk to long-term expatriates appears to be higher. A recent study found an overall seroprevalence of 5.2% in development aid workers who lived in various underdeveloped countries for nine years. The Indian subcontinent showed the highest incidence (10%) of infection. Infection rates for Latin America, East Africa, West and Central Africa, and Asia ranged between 6% and 9%. The Middle East had a prevalence of 2.1%. Individual countries with the highest risk of acquiring hepatitis E include Burma, Nepal, Pakistan, Sudan, China, and India.

Diagnosis

Hepatitis E should be considered in returned travelers with fever and hepatitis. If tests for other forms of hepatitis are negative, serological testing for HEV should be done. Information regarding serological testing can be obtained from the CDC's Hepatitis Branch in Decatur, Georgia (404-371-5910).

Treatment

No specific treatment is available. Follow the same advice as given on page 162 for hepatitis A.

Prevention

A vaccine is not available. If you are in an endemic area, especially a rural area, strictly adhere to food and water precautions, especially if you are pregnant. Avoid untreated tap water, well water, or surface water. If you are treating potentially contaminated water, remember to use a method that eliminates viruses, such as boiling, chemical disinfection, or purification with a water purifier, not a filter. Purifiers, unlike filters, eliminate viruses.

Immune globulin is not protective against hepatitis E since the product in this country is not made from donors carrying sufficient antibodies to this virus.

Lai CL, Chien RN, Leung, N. A One-Year Trial of Lamivudine for Chronic Hepatitis B. N Eng J Med 1998;**339**;61–68.

Janisch TH. Emerging viral pathogens in long-term expatriates (1): Hepatitis E Virus. Trop Med Internatl Health 1997;**2**:885–891.

Chen LH. The Emergence of New Hepatitis Viruses. Travel Medicine Advisor Update March/April 1998;**8**:9–10.

Bader TF. Hepatitis A Vaccine. Am. J. Gastro 1996;**91**:217–222.

Lee WM. Hepatitis B Virus Infection. N Engl J Med 1997;**337**:1733–45.

Mast EE, Krawczynski K. Hepatitis E: An Overview. Ann. Rev. Med. 1996;**47**:257–266.

McHutichison JG, Gordon SC, Schiff ER, et al. Interferon alpha-2b alone or in combination with ribavirin as initial treatment of chronic hepatitis C. N Engl J Med 1998;339:1485–92.

Reichard O, Norkrans G, Braconier JH, et al. Randomized, double-blind, placebo-controlled trial of interferon alfa-2b with and without ribavirin for chronic hepatitis C. Lancet 1998;**351**:83-87.

Vento S, Garofano T, Renzini C. Fulminant hepatitis associated with hepatitis A virus superinfection in patients with chronic hepatitis C. N Engl J Med 1998;**338**:286–90.

Koff RS. Hepatitis A. The Lancet 1998;351:1643–1647.

Wiens BL, Bohidar NR, Pigeon JG, et al. Duration of protection from clinical hepatitis A disease after vaccination with VAQTA. J. Med. Virol. 1996;**49**:235–241.

12 Diabetes

The thought of traveling with diabetes can discourage the most confident of travelers. Diabetes may not be the ideal travel companion, but with adequate preparation and common sense, the two are very compatible. Anticipating and avoiding common health problems in both tropical and temperate climates, and being able to manage them on your own, will ensure a more pleasurable, healthier journey. Being cavalier and leaving home without the necessary preparation can be fraught with danger, whereas excess caution might lead you to avoid adventurous travel altogether; the appropriate balance is somewhere inbetween.

Preparing for departure

Visit your diabetes physician at least 4–6 weeks before the trip. Ask for a signed and dated letter on official letterhead outlining your diabetes care, any other medical conditions, and the need for you to carry medications and equipment such as syringes/needles. This letter will reduce hassles from overly suspicious customs officials either looking for a bribe, or thinking that your equipment is being used for the administration of recreational drugs.

Obtain a summary of your medical history, including allergies and prescriptions. You should carry double the amount of needed medication and monitoring supplies for your planned length of stay (the latter to allow for increased testing). Carrying rapid- or short-acting insulin (e.g., Humalog—see below) to deal with emergencies is advisable even if it isn't part of your usual routine. Those with type I diabetes should carry glucagon, and every traveler should pack glucose gels or tablets since they travel so well. It is always nice to have a travel companion for a variety of nonmedical reasons but also for helping administer an injectable medication, such as glucagon, should the need arise.

Finding a travel clinic—The other obvious reason to see your physician is to obtain an assessment of your fitness to travel. Remember, you want an opinion, not permission; the decision to travel is yours, after carefully weighing the risks and benefits. Unless your personal physician has experience in travel medicine, it is wise to visit a travel medicine specialist 6–8 weeks before departure. You can find one on the Web sites of Travel Medicine, Inc. (www.travmed.com), the International Society of Travel Medicine (www.istm.org/disclinics.html), and the American Society of Tropical Medicine and Hygiene (www.astmh.org/clinics/clinindex.html).

Travel medicine advisors usually focus on five main areas: (1) pretravel immunization; (2) prevention of malaria; (3) prevention and self-treatment of travelers' diarrhea; (4) prevention of injuries, accidents, and infections (including sexually transmitted diseases, which are almost always accidental); and (5) the first aid travel kit.

Immunizations—Travel immunizations are classified as "routine" (those childhood or adulthood vaccinations that may require updating, such as tetanus/diphtheria and polio), "required" (such as yellow fever, which is needed to cross certain international borders), and "recommended" (those recommended according to risk of infection, such as hepatitis A & B, typhoid, meningococcal, Japanese encephalitis, etc.).

For the most part, having diabetes will not worsen vaccine-preventable infections, but it may predispose you to some (e.g., pneumococcal disease). Almost all travelers should be protected against hepatitis A. Since you may require an injection in an emergency situation with a potentially unsterile needle, you should be protected against hepatitis B as well. A new combined hepatitis A/B vaccine (TwinRix) is now available. For full protection, travel vaccines may need to be administered several months in advance—the most important reason to seek advice early.

Medications—Depending on your itinerary, the travel medicine clinic advisor may wish to prescribe antimalarial medication, antifungals (to treat yeast infections, which worsen in the heat and humidity of the tropics), antiemetics (for nausea and vomiting), and an all-purpose broad-spectrum antibiotic such as levofloxacin (Lēvaquin) or azithromycin (Zithromax), which are useful for the self-treatment of travelers' diarrhea and other infections. No traveler with diabetes should leave home without an antibiotic for self-treatment of travelers' diarrhea since its consequences may lead to loss of blood sugar control and/or salt and water imbalance. A first aid kit is another travel necessity, especially when traveling to an exotic destination.

Packing: All medications and glucose-monitoring equipment should be placed only in your carry-on luggage. Checked bags may be exposed to extremes of temperature, and, most importantly and likely, your bags may end up elsewhere, without you. Insulin, however, travels well except above 86°F and below 32°F. Where temperatures might be an issue, consider carrying a designated insulin travel case or widemouthed thermos.

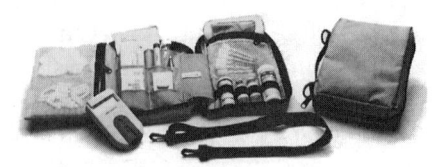

Consider carrying all of your diabetic supplies in a specially designed case, such as the DIA-PAK®.

Never keep insulin in direct sunlight or on ice. Although insulin can be stored for 30 days at room temperature, in warm climates you may wish to request a room with a refrigerator or air conditioning. Before using insulin, check vials for signs of damage (crystals, clumps, discoloration, etc.) and discard frozen or damaged vials.

In the event of unanticipated delays or a sudden change in plans, your carry-on luggage should contain food (ample amounts of carbohydrates) and water (to prevent dehydration on long flights).

Medical care abroad—Other pretravel "to-dos" include the issue of travel insurance for overseas medical care and emergency medical evacuation coverage, and diabetes identification. Identification cards and useful phrases in foreign languages (such as "sugar, please") are available from the American Diabetes Association (www.diabetes.com). Information on health-care providers abroad can be obtained from the International Diabetes Federation (www.idf.org) and from the following commercial organizations, which charge a fee or request a donation: The International Association for the Medical Assistance of Travelers (IAMAT) (www.sentex.net/~iamat/), International SOS/AEA (www.intsos.com/), The Travel Emergency Network (www.tenweb.com), and Medex (www.medexassist.com).

It is advisable to have some knowledge of your destination before leaving home so that you can identify potential risks and customs. The Internet is a useful source of information.

Enroute

For security reasons, keep your carry-on bags within sight and easy reach. Show your travel companion, or tour group leader, where your glucose meter and medications for the treatment of hypoglycemia are located. When traveling at altitude (>8,000 ft.), or by plane, pressure in insulin vials needs to be equalized; be sure to re-equalize the pressures once you are back at sea level. Insert the syringe without the plunger into the vial. Then, withdraw the syringe, replace the plunger, and withdraw insulin as usual. Also, it isn't necessary to inject air into the vial at high altitude.

Rapid-acting insulin—Since you as a passenger can't predict air turbulence or other reasons for delays in meal delivery, administer premeal insulin only when food is in sight and reach. This is where Humalog (insulin lispro) can play a role (see below).

Since airline diabetic meals are often low in carbohydrates, fats, and flavor, most travelers with diabetes find it easier (and more palatable) to request a "regular" meal and eat the foods that best match their usual meal plan.

Adjusting insulin dose across time zones—One of the most confusing and worrisome aspects of diabetes management is the problem of travel across several time zones. No matter whether you adjust your insulin dose or snack times, *the key to success is frequent monitoring of blood glucose.* It is best to consult with your diabetes caregiver to work out a plan before departure. As a general rule, traveling east shortens the day and thus decreases insulin need. Traveling west, on the other hand, lengthens the day and the need for more insulin and the snacks with it. If the time difference is three or fewer hours, no insulin adjustment is necessary. It is best to keep your watch on home time during travel to determine when your meal/insulin doses should be taken. Set your watch on local time the morning after arrival to get in step with meal activities of the destination country. North-south travel does not require insulin dosing adjustment.

If you take pills to manage your diabetes, use your usual dosing and meal schedules. Some oral medications (e.g., sulfonylureas) can cause hypoglycemia, so extra snacks may be necessary.

Tables (such as Table 1) that summarize insulin dose adjustments across time zones can be helpful, but there is no magic formula for insulin dosing; *common sense and more frequent monitoring are the mainstays in maintaining adequate blood glucose control.* The goal of control during travel is to avoid extremes—tight control is not the objective. Better to let your glucose level run a bit higher than usual than to suffer a bout of hypoglycemia in a strange land with strange people speak-

---

Insulin lispro—Most travelers receiving regular insulin do not follow instructions to inject their insulin 30–45 minutes before eating a meal. Because insulin lispro (Humalog®) has a much faster onset of action, it can be injected immediately before a meal, increasing compliance and more closely matching insulin action to postprandial glucose levels. Traveling diabetics benefit from both the convenience and the short action profile of insulin lispro.

Regular human insulin is absorbed slowly since it consists of hexamers of insulin that are crystallized around zinc molecules. To be absorbed from its subcutaneous injection site, it must first dissociate into monomers and dimers. Insulin lispro derives its name from the switching of two amino acids, proline and lysine, within the beta chain of insulin. After subcutaneous injection, this insulin dissociates more rapidly into dimers and monomers. The peak serum concentrations of insulin lispro occur 30–90 minutes following administration, and regardless of the site of administration, there is a better match between carbohydrate absorption and insulin availability with less chance for late-peaking regular insulin to cause postprandial hypoglycemia.

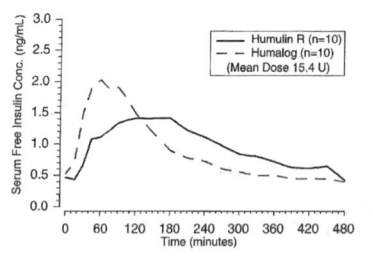

Humalog can be mixed, if required, immediately prior to injection, with Humulin NPH, Lente, or Ultralente.

The Humulin® Pen

Table 1

Insulin Adjustment During Jet Travel Across Multiple Time Zones*

East Bound

Daily insulin regimen	Day of departure	First morning at destination	10 hours after morning dose	Second day at destination
Single dose schedule	Usual dose	2/3 usual dose	If blood sugar over 240, take remaining 1/3 of morning dose.	Usual dose
Two dose schedule	Usual morning and evening doses	2/3 usual dose	Usual evening dose. If blood sugar over 240, take remaining 1/3 of morning dose.	Usual two doses

West Bound

Daily insulin regimen	Day of departure	18 hours after morning dose	First day at destination
Single dose schedule	Usual dose	If blood sugar over 240, take 1/3 usual morning dose, followed by snack.	Usual dose
Two dose schedule	Usual morning and evening doses	If blood sugar over 240, take 1/3 usual morning dose, followed by snack.	Usual two doses

*Reprinted with permission from Edward A. Benson, MD (Virginia Mason Clinic, Seattle, WA)

ing a strange language. At the risk of being redundant, "monitor, monitor, monitor!" This is the only way to determine how travel is affecting you and what adjustments you need to make in diet or insulin dosing. Be aware that glucose meters may be affected by high altitude. Check the manual or contact the customer service toll-free hot line before departure, and be sure to carry an extra battery.

Two additional health tips to consider during flight: Prevent dehydration by drinking fluids liberally, and exercise regularly to improve lower limb circulation and glucose control. Take a walk for at least 10 minutes every two hours, and do isometric exercises such as pressing your toes against the seat in front of you to tighten calf muscles.

After Arrival

Your blood glucose meter is your best travel guide to continued good health, and it is a must because your eating pattern and activity level are likely to be different during travel. *You must test your blood glucose level more often in order to make appropriate adjustments and give you peace of mind.*

Insulin abroad—Insulin produced in other countries may have reduced purity, and hence reduced activity. Outside of North America, insulin is often dispensed as U80 or U40 concentration, instead of the standard U100. Syringes corresponding to these concentrations may be the only ones available. Read labels carefully to avoid dosing disasters. It is not recommended using a u100 syringe to draw up u40 or u80 insulin, since a very serious dosing error could occur. Also, cartridges and/or pen needles may not be available worldwide. The best safeguard is to bring extra medication and supplies from home.

When going on an outing, always take vital supplies with you regardless of the proposed duration and type of outing. Don't forget bottled water. Try to eat as close to your usual meal plan as possible. Counting carbohydrates and the plate method of meal planning can be especially useful.

Travelers' diarrhea—Although the standard food rules for the prevention of travelers' diarrhea are often impractical, for the record, here they are: avoid raw, undercooked foods (e.g., salads); roadside stands; unpurified water and ice cubes; buffets; and unpasteurized milk products. This is why every traveler with diabetes should carry an antibiotic (preferably a quinolone) for self-treatment of travelers' diarrhea.

Sun exposure—Travel to hot climates brings the risk of sunburn, a particular concern for those with diabetes, because healing is slower and secondary infection is more likely to occur. Wear light colored, cotton clothing and a hat, and use sunscreen (minimum 15 SPF). All travelers need time to acclimatize to tropical heat; postpone strenuous activity soon after arrival and drink enough sugar-free fluids to promote urination, whether or not you are thirsty. Moderate intake of alcohol and caffeine is acceptable.

Altitude sickness—At high altitudes, hypothermia may be mistaken for hypoglycemia, and vice versa. At about 16,000 feet, retinal hemorrhages may occur, a particular concern for those with preexisting diabetic retinopathy. Altitude sickness, characterized by headache and fatigue, can usually be prevented by slow ascent and acetazolamide (Diamox).

Foot care—Foot problems can ruin your trip. Never travel with a new pair of shoes that has not been broken in. Take one or more pairs of worn-in walking shoes, slippers for your hotel room, and beach shoes. Avoid pressure points by changing socks and shoes frequently. Inspect feet daily for blisters, redness, and skin breakdown. Never delay treatment of injuries. Never walk barefoot, even on a beach.

Don't forget to review potential risks of travel medications with your pharmacist or health-care provider: glyburide and doxycycline increase sun sensitivity; chloroquine, quinine, and Pepto-Bismol may increase hypoglycemia; acetazolamide (Diamox) may aggravate hyperglycemia; and antibiotics predispose to vaginal yeast infections. Keep in mind that not taking medication, such as antimalarial medication, may increase your risk of illness, which in turn can cause loss of blood sugar control. In this regard, protection with DEET repellents (e.g., Ultrathon), permethrin fabric spray, and protective clothing (and often a mosquito net) is crucial to the prevention of malaria (transmitted by night-biting mosquitoes) and dengue fever, (transmitted by day-biting mosquitoes).

Accidents—Finally, it is worthwhile to keep in mind that the major cause of preventable death during travel is not an infectious disease such as malaria, cholera, or Ebola virus. A motor vehicle accident is much more likely cause. Your risk of an accident is increased overseas (especially in lesser-developed countries) because of poor road conditions, badly maintained vehicles (often without seat belts), inexperienced and/or reckless drivers, and a general disregard for "rules of the road." Here are three important safety tips to remember: don't ride on motorcycles, don't travel in overcrowded public vehicles, and *never* travel by road at night in rural areas.

The vast majority of diabetic travelers return safe and sound from their trip. Remember that healthy, comfortable travel is enhanced by adherence to common sense precautions with respect to food, water, insect bites, safe sex, and road travel, as well as close attention to diabetic control.

13 AIDS, HIV & Sexually Transmitted Diseases

Travelers' Concerns About AIDS
Travel has contributed in a general way to the global spread of HIV, but fear of traveling because of AIDS is not justified. Following the guidelines in this chapter will make the chance of contracting the virus extremely remote. You may have heard stories of travelers getting HIV from emergency transfusions of unsafe blood, but these situations are rare; "emergency injections" that might lead to HIV infections are almost never required.

Knowing the causes and prevention of AIDS is no different than knowing about any other infectious disease; there are guidelines to protect you. This chapter will give you those specific guidelines. Don't let exaggerated or distorted information keep you at home.

AN OVERVIEW OF AIDS WORLDWIDE

AIDS in the USA, Canada, Europe, Australia, N. Zealand
In these countries, AIDS is still largely a disease of men who have sex with men (MSM) and urban drug users. However, in spite of greater awareness of HIV, the incidence among young MSM, injecting drug users (IDU), and women is increasing. (In 1992, women accounted for 13% of persons living with AIDS; by 1998, the number increased to 24%.) About 75% of people who are infected with HIV through heterosexual transmission are women, and the majority are women who had sex with men who were infected by injecting illicit drugs. Many women contracted HIV during sex with these men during "crack" cocaine binges, or while they were abusing drugs and/or alcohol, when they disregarded safe sex precautions.

The addicts who are becoming infected are mostly young minority men and women who live in the inner cities. Many have other sexually transmitted diseases, such as syphilis and gonorrhea, that facilitate HIV transmission.

Sharing syringes and other equipment for drug injection is a well known source of HIV transmission, yet this mode of transmission contributes to the epidemic's spread well beyond the circle of those who inject. People who have sex with an IDU and children born to mothers who contract HIV through sharing needles or who have sex with an IDU may become infected as well.

Since the epidemic began, injecting drug use directly or indirectly accounts for more than one-third (36%) of AIDS cases in the United States. This disturbing trend appears to be continuing. Of the 48,269 new cases of AIDS reported in 1998, 31% were IDU associated.

AIDS in the Middle East, E. Europe, and Former Soviet Union

Only small numbers of cases are reported in the Middle East, usually among persons who have brought the disease back from infected areas. In North Africa little is known, and the generally conservative social and political attitudes tend to make it difficult to address risk behavior directly. Recently, many more cases of AIDS have been reported from the former Soviet Union and Romania. Belarus, Moldova, the Russian Federation, and Ukraine have all registered astronomical growth in HIV infection rates over the past three years. Now there may be nearly four times as many infections in Ukraine as there were in the whole of the Eastern European region just three years ago. Transmission of HIV in these countries is primarily through contaminated blood and the use of unclean needles and syringes, though commercial sex is on the rise, and heterosexual transmission is increasing.

AIDS in Africa

In sub-Saharan Africa, AIDS has become a devastating problem. In the "AIDS-belt" countries of central and east Africa (see map on the next page), the infection is spread primarily by heterosexual intercourse, not homosexuality or IV drug use. Men and women are infected almost equally. Over 5% of the general population in most of these countries is infected with HIV. In the urban areas of AIDS-belt countries, however, up to 30% or more of sexually active people carry HIV; up to 90% of prostitutes in some cities are infected. Four out of 5 HIV-positive women in the world live in Africa. In West Africa, another strain of the AIDS virus, HIV-2, is prevalent and causes a disease similar to AIDS.

Factors Causing the Epidemic

- Multiple sexual partners—There is widespread, culturally tolerated promiscuity in many countries.
- Commercial sex—Up to 90% of commercial sex workers in the larger cities in sub-Saharan Africa are HIV-infected.
- Widespread sexually transmitted diseases—These diseases greatly enhance the spread of the virus. Diseases such as syphilis and chancroid cause open sores on the genitals, and these sores allow easier transmission of the virus between partners. Gonorrhea also facilitates HIV transmission.
- Public health factors—Social resistance to the use of condoms, lack of education, and rudimentary public health programs against AIDS and venereal disease also stymie efforts to control the epidemic.
- Unclean needles and syringes—These are widely used for medical injections, and they help spread the disease. Few countries can afford sterile, disposable supplies for safe injections and this equipment is often recycled over and over.
- Blood transfusions—The transmission of HIV from contaminated blood and blood products is a serious problem in sub-Saharan Africa, as well as elsewhere. Some countries do not have the means to screen blood for HIV. Except in life-threatening situations, transfusions should be avoided unless reliable HIV-antibody screening has been done.

AFRICA'S AIDS BELT

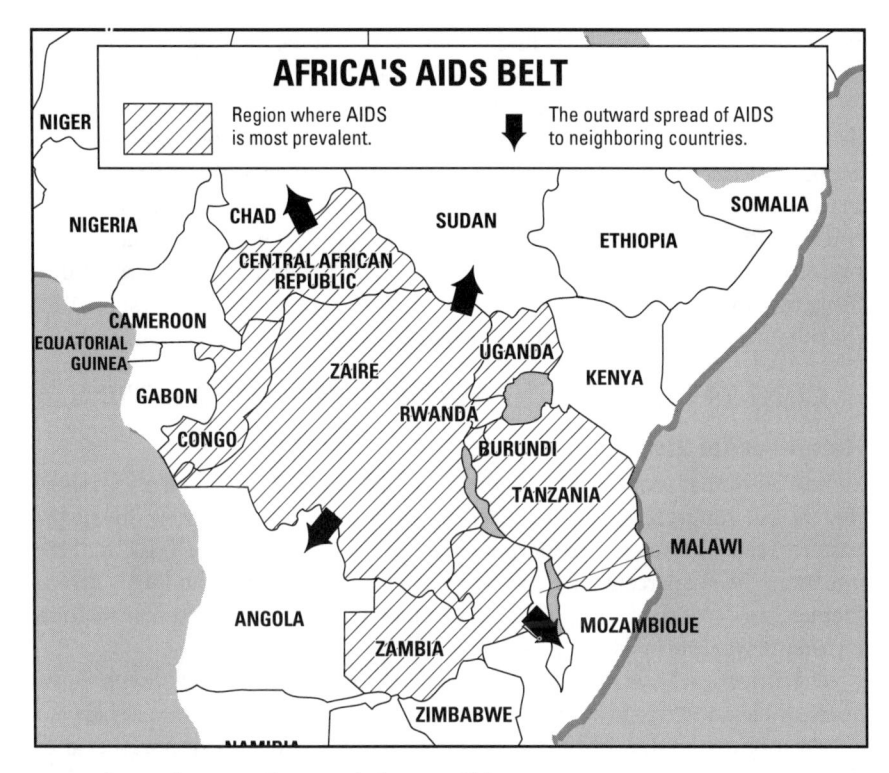

Region where AIDS is most prevalent.
The outward spread of AIDS to neighboring countries.

AIDS in Latin America and the Caribbean

HIV is now spreading rapidly in Latin America, the Bahamas, and the Caribbean, with roughly 1.3 million people believed living with HIV in these regions. The reason: HIV is spilling over to women from infected bisexuals, intravenous drug abusers, and through drug-related commercial sex. The average ratio of infected men to women is 2.4:1—approaching the 1:1 ratio found in Africa, though this is very country-dependent.

AIDS in India, China, SE Asia, Japan, and the Pacific

The AIDS epidemic in India is rapidly expanding. Though surveillance is patchy, it is estimated that more than 4 million people in India are living with HIV, which makes India the country with the largest number of HIV-infected in the world. Thirty percent, or more, of commercial sex workers are infected. Lack of public education, prostitution, sexually transmitted diseases (which help transmit HIV), and the absence of circumcision in the Hindu population are responsible for the increased epidemic in India.

No AIDS cases were reported in China until 1988, when an outbreak was reported among the tribesmen of the Yunnan Province in the western part of the country, bordering the "Golden Triangle." The government of China estimated that at the end of 91996 up to 200,000 people were living with HIV/AIDS. It is estimated that this figure had doubled by the beginning of 1998. The increase in injection drug use, particularly in the Southwest, and the increase in commercial sex at the eastern seaboard are primarily responsible.

In Thailand infection rates among drug users has increased from 1% to 43% between 1987 and 1998. Up to 70% of rural commercial sex workers in Thailand are now infected, and spillover into the heterosexual population is occurring, causing a serious public health problem. Control efforts are being made, however.

In the Philippines, Indonesia, Malaysia, Sri Lanka, Taiwan, and Korea, the HIV rate among commercial sex workers still remains very low, although spread into the heterosexual population is a threat wherever commercial sex is widespread. At the present, the incidence of AIDS in Japan and Oceania also is still low.

CONTRACTING AND PREVENTING HIV INFECTION

Heterosexual Risk of Contracting HIV

Surveys show that people continue to practice unsafe sex. Gallup poll results show that 20% of young, single women have had three or more sex partners during the past five years without using condoms, possibly placing them at "high risk" for HIV infection. Twelve percent have had two partners without using condoms, placing them at "medium risk." The poll also concludes that "smart, rich women are fooling themselves into believing that AIDS is not an issue for them."

The *Travel Medicine Advisor* reports that sex tours remain popular with European travelers and that long-term travelers and overseas workers are very likely to engage in sexual contact involving some degree of risk. They also report that after six months abroad, 70% of men and 45% of women that were interviewed had had high-risk sexual contact. Studies also revealed very low condom use among men over age 40 (only 27% used condoms) and noncaucasian women of all ages who were sexually active (zero percent used condoms).

High-risk behavior appears to be continuing. The *Archives of Internal Medicine* (1998) reports that of 203 consecutive HIV-positive patients at two U.S. hospitals, 40% had not told their partners, and nearly two-thirds of them had not always used a condom. People with multiple partners were three times less likely to reveal their HIV status than those with one partner.

Can You Quantify Your Risk?

Drs. Norman Hearst and Stephen Hulley, writing in the *Journal of the American Medical Association* (*JAMA*, April 22, 1988), have attempted to define the statistical chances of becoming HIV positive after sex with various partners. Your risk of getting HIV, they say, depends primarily upon your partner's probability of being infected—and also whether you use a condom.

Their *JAMA* article confirms that your chance of contracting AIDS from a single act of intercourse can vary enormously. Their conclusion: *Choosing a "low-risk partner" is the most important strategy.*

If your partner is HIV positive, they estimate your chance of picking up the AIDS virus from one-time intercourse at 1 in 500. Receptive anal intercourse and the presence of genital ulcers and venereal warts will increase your risk *tenfold*, or more.

If your partner is known to be HIV negative, the risk of contracting AIDS from such an HIV-negative partner (using a condom) is estimated at 1 in 5 billion. There's still a slight risk since people can be infectious before their test turns positive—and condoms can fail.

If your partner is not in a high-risk group (see above), but his/her HIV test status is unknown, your risk is 1 in 5 million for one-time sex (without a condom) with such a low-risk partner.

Can You Really Be Sure?

In theory, choosing a low-risk partner will protect you. But these statistics can also mislead you. It can be a potentially fatal mistake to assume or hope that your partner is in a low-risk category.

Unfortunately, there are people who continue to have sex and don't tell the truth about their condition or background. Your intuitive sense about the safety of the relationship may be misleading. Asking your new-found acquaintance about his or her past sexual habits or drug use may not be enough.

Abstinence

A good case can be made for avoiding sexual contact with casual acquaintances. Indeed, abstinence probably is your safest course of action.

Condoms

You've decided you are going to be sexually active, but you're not sure about your partner's risk category; you think it's low. Then bear this in mind: *AIDS is possible after a single act of unprotected intercourse with an infected partner.* That's why it's imperative to take added precautions.

Use of condoms is the best preventive measure short of abstinence. If you are a man, always use a condom; if you are a woman, insist on male condom use. For added protection with a male condom, use a diaphragm and spermicidal jelly (the jelly may inactivate the AIDS virus). Condoms and diaphragms also help prevent other sexually transmitted diseases, hepatitis, and pregnancy.

NOTE: Women taking oral contraceptives have a lower risk of HIV transmission. Women using IUDs have a higher risk of HIV transmission. Men who are circumcised have a lower risk of acquiring HIV.

Summary
Aids Is Not Spread Through:
- Casual contact at work or school
- Touching or hugging
- Handshaking
- Coughing or sneezing
- Insect or mosquito bites
- Food or water

- Eating utensils, cups, plates
- Toilets
- Swimming pools or baths

You Can Avoid Contracting AIDS If You:
- Abstain from sex
- Have sex only with your spouse or a monogamous, noninfected partner
- Avoid blood products, syringes, and needles unless assured of their sterility

- Do not share razor blades, tooth brushes, or other personal items that may come in contact with blood

If You Are Sexually Active, You Should:
- Avoid sex with high-risk partners
- Always use a condom
- Avoid anal intercourse

HIV TESTING AND FOREIGN TRAVEL

In most countries, tourists staying less than one month don't need to show evidence of an HIV test. But dozens of countries—including the United States—do require an HIV test for those coming to study, work, stay for long periods, or apply for immigrant status. Under those rules, those who test HIV-positive usually are denied entry, although sometimes a waiver may be issued. Countries that screen immigrants for HIV include Argentina, China, Colombia, Costa Rica, Cuba, Hungary, Iraq, Israel, Mongolia, Myanmar (Burma), the Philippines, Russia, South Africa, South Korea, Syria, Thailand, and the United States. Furthermore, several countries have policies of rejecting or expelling all foreigners with AIDS. Among those countries are Indonesia, Malaysia, Sri Lanka, and Thailand.

Sometimes visa forms ask whether a visitor has any infectious or communicable diseases, so if you are HIV positive, be prepared to face this question—and rejection if you answer truthfully. The World Health Organization regards HIV screening as discriminatory and unnecessary from a public health perspective.

For the most current HIV testing requirements for foreign travel, contact the **Bureau of Consular Affairs Web site** *(www.travel.state.gov/HIVtestingreqs.html)*. To confirm requirements, telephone that country's consulate in the United States. These requirements may change frequently. Some of the countries requiring testing will accept a test done in the United States. If you need a test, contact the country's nearest consulate to find out which laboratories in the United States can run the test and how the results are authenticated and certified. You want to avoid, if possible, having your blood drawn overseas. Consider carrying sterile, disposable needles and syringes with you if you anticipate overseas testing. If you will be tested overseas, call the U.S. Embassy in the country of your destination to inquire about the safety of a test done locally and if sterile needles are used.

Be aware that a country's announced policy and what actually happens may differ. If you are an African American, you might be singled out for random testing. Also, travelers found carrying an anti-HIV drug, such as AZT, may be turned away.

SEXUALLY TRANSMITTED DISEASES

In addition to AIDS, you can acquire other sexually transmitted diseases (STDs), especially by having sex with a high-risk partner. STD risk factors also include the number of your sexual exposures, number of different partners, number of anonymous partners (including prostitutes), and use (or nonuse) of condoms.

Causes of STDs

Unlike AIDS, some STDs can be spread by kissing and mouth-to-genital contact. Sexually transmitted diseases include those caused by viruses, bacteria, and protozoa.

Virus-caused STDs
- AIDS • hepatitis B • hepatitis C
- Hepatitis A (oral-anal contact)
- Genital herpes • genital warts

Bacteria-caused STDs
- Gonorrhea • syphilis • chancroid • chlamydia infections
- Shigella, salmonella, or other bacteria in MSM

Protozoa-caused STDs
- Giardia, isospora, cryptosporidia, *E. histolytica*, or other parasites in MSM
- Vaginal or urethral infections due to trichomonas

Symptoms of STDs

The most common STDs are infections caused by gonococcus and chlamydia bacteria. In men, a penile discharge, burning on urination, or rectal pain or discharge may indicate infection. If you have any of these symptoms, receive treatment and notify your partner.

Pelvic inflammatory disease—Women who develop lower abdominal pain, vaginal discharge, and fever should be examined for the possibility of pelvic inflammatory disease (PID), which is an infection of the uterus and/or fallopian tubes. This is often a mixed infection, usually caused by gonococci and/or chlamydia. Bear in mind that appendicitis, an ovarian cyst, and even an ectopic pregnancy can mimic pelvic inflammatory disease, so a precise diagnosis is important.

If you notice any ulcers or sores on your genitals, herpes, syphilis, or chancroid may be the cause. A *painless* ulcer may indicate syphilis, while herpetic ulcers are usually shallow and quite painful. These lesions require exact diagnosis and appropriate treatment. Be sure to seek qualified medical care.

Treatment

Uncomplicated PID can be caused by a mixed infection with gonorrhea and chlamydia bacteria. PID can be treated with a 250-mg injection of **ceftriaxone** (Rocephin) plus a 7-day course of **doxycycline,** 100 mg twice daily, or **tetracycline,** 500 mg four times daily. Monotherapy with a 7-day course of **ofloxacin** (Floxin), 400 mg twice daily, will eradicate both microorganisms. A single 1-gm dose of **azithromycin** (Zithromax) will also cure uncomplicated PID.

For the treatment of gonorrhea in men, a co-infection with chlamydia must also be considered in which case the same drugs administered for PID are effective.

Since a single 1-gm oral dose of azithromycin is effective against both gonorrhea and chlamydia, it is probably the ideal treatment because it's easy to administer and there's no problem with compliance.

If ceftriaxone, ofloxacin, or azithromycin is not available, a single dose of one of the following drugs can be used:

- Ciprofloxacin (Cipro), 500 mg   • Cefixime (Suprax), 400 mg

A 7-day course of doxycycline or tetracycline should also be administered.

Drug-resistant gonorrhea—Decreased quinolone susceptibility has been identified in Asia, Canada, Europe, and Australia.

Treatment during pregnancy—If you are pregnant and have PID, you can safely be treated with ceftriaxone, cefixime, or procaine penicillin plus Benemid. Combine treatment with erythromycin, 500 mg, 4 times daily for seven days, to eliminate chlamydia. Azithromycin is a Class B pregnancy drug and would be effective monotherapy. Avoid the quinolones (e.g., ciprofloxacin and ofloxacin), which are contraindicated during pregnancy.

Post-treatment follow-up—If you were treated for gonorrhea or PID while traveling, you should contact your physician when you return home. Women should have follow-up cultures of the cervix to see if they are still carrying gonorrhea and/or chlamydia. Both men and women should have a blood test to check for syphilis and should be screened for HIV infection. HIV screening tests may not be positive for 12 weeks or longer after exposure. Early diagnosis of HIV infection is important since early, aggressive anti-HIV therapy with antiretroviral drugs may preserve crucial components of the immune system.

Prevention of STDs

Practice abstinence or have sex only in a monogamous relationship. If you are, however, sexually adventuresome, follow the same prevention guidelines as for HIV (page 164).

Lalvani A, Shastri JS. HIV epidemic in India: Opportunity to learn from the past. Lancet 1996;347:1349–50.

Stephenson J. Studies reveal early impact of HIV infection, effects of treatment. JAMA 1998;279:641–42.

Weisfuse IB. Gonorrhea control and antimicrobial resistance. Lancet 1998;351:928.

Wilson ME. Infections in HIV-infected travelers: Risks and prevention. Ann Intern Med 1991;114:582.

14 Altitude Sickness

Even if you are in perfect health, you can develop altitude sickness if you ascend to elevations over 8,000 feet. The most common ascent-related illness is acute mountain sickness (AMS), and it is essentially a neurologic disorder, the symptoms caused primarily by the effects of low oxygen (hypoxia) on the brain. AMS may be defined as the presence, after a recent ascent, of headache together with one or more of the following symptoms: nausea, vomiting, loss of appetite, fatigue, dizziness, and insomnia. The headache is dull and throbbing, worse during the night and in the morning, and increased by straining or bending over.

Symptoms of AMS usually start 6–12 hours after arrival at high altitude, attain maximum severity within 1–2 days, and begin to decrease about the third day, providing additional ascent does not occur.

You should remember that AMS represents the mild end of the spectrum of altitude sickness. The major concern is that it may progress to a life-threatening form of altitude sickness, namely high altitude cerebral edema (HACE).

High altitude pulmonary edema (HAPE) is another form of altitude sickness that is also potentially life threatening. Therefore, if you ignore the symptoms of AMS and/or HAPE—and some people do if they are determined climbers—you could be courting disaster.

Incidence of AMS and HAPE

The incidence of AMS is primarily dependent upon the elevation, the rate of ascent, and individual susceptibility. AMS occurs in about one-fourth of adults ascending to 8,500 feet, and approximately three-fourths going to 15,000 feet. One study in Nepal showed an attack rate of 58% among trekkers who were ascending to 16,000 feet and also sleeping at high altitudes. A special cohort of potential victims are climbers ascending to, and often staying at, very high (12,000–18,000 feet) and extremely high (18,000+ feet) altitudes. About 8% of the climbers who develop AMS at over 15,000 feet go on to develop cerebral and/or pulmonary edema.

Factors That Increase Your Chance of Getting AMS

Susceptibility to AMS can vary over time. Previous ability to ascend to high altitudes without getting AMS is no guarantee you won't become afflicted in the future, but if you have been to a certain altitude before with no problems, you probably can return to that altitude without developing symptoms as long as you acclimatize properly. Factors that are associated with an increased incidence of AMS include the following:

- Fast ascent (more than 3,000 feet/day)
- Altitude attained, especially a sleeping altitude over 10,000 feet
- Strenuous exertion at high altitudes
- Time spent at altitude
- Previous history of AMS (the most important risk factor)
- Not being sufficiently acclimatized

Factors NOT Associated with, or Protective Against, AMS

- Previous high-altitude experience • Smoking • Age • Gender
- Pre-ascent training • Good physical condition

It may seem surprising that good physical condition does not prevent AMS, but young, fit climbers often climb higher and faster than others and they also engage in more strenuous activity at high altitudes. Although smoking is not a risk factor for AMS, smokers may have less physical endurance than nonsmokers.

Normal Symptoms at Altitude

Shortness of breath on exertion—Shortness of breath on exertion (dyspnea on exertion) is normal for anyone exercising at high altitudes. If dyspnea also occurs at rest, however, high altitude pulmonary edema should be considered.

Frequent nocturnal awakening—This often occurs because of periodic breathing or the need to urinate.

Edema of altitude—Edema of the extremities and face due to fluid retention can occur as an isolated finding without symptoms of AMS. It responds to diuretics, dexamethasone, and descent.

Periodic breathing—Periodic breathing occurs normally at altitude during sleep. It is characterized by periods of rapid, deep breathing followed by slowing of respiration, then complete cessation of respiration (apnea). The period of apnea may last 10–15 seconds before breathing begins and the cycle starts over. This can be quite startling to observe since the person really does (briefly) stop breathing. It occurs in everyone above their personal altitude "threshold."

Acetazolamide (see page 167) is a respiratory stimulant that reduces or eliminates periodic breathing, improving oxygenation as well as sleep quality.

Hypoxic Ventilatory Response (HVR)

A person with a lower hypoxic ventilatory response is more likely to suffer AMS and HAPE than are those with a high HVR. What is HVR? Simply put, it is the increase in breathing rate that occurs when you're not getting enough oxygen. The HVR is controlled by a receptor in the carotid artery (the carotid body), and it signals the respiratory center in the brain to increase ventilation when hypoxia occurs. The increased rate and depth of respiration blows off carbon dioxide, allowing for a corresponding increase in arterial oxygen. Persons who have a sluggish HVR and who underventilate remain more hypoxic, especially during sleep. Adverse effects of hypoxia include increased cerebral blood flow and vasogenic cerebral edema, pulmonary vasoconstriction and increased pulmonary artery pressure, and increased fluid retention by the kidney.

The Causes of AMS

The physiological changes that occur during ascent to high altitudes are complex, and there is considerable variation in how each individual responds. Perhaps the most important change that occurs is the increase in cerebral blood flow. The resulting rise in cerebral artery capillary pressure, in association with hypoxia, results in fluid leakage across the blood-brain barrier. The resulting increase in brain water can lead to vasogenic cerebral edema. This process appears to be the critical step in the genesis of AMS and the syndrome of high altitude cerebral edema (HACE).

Facts About AMS

- Of all the organs, the brain seems to be most vulnerable to the hypoxia of high altitudes, particularly extreme altitudes.
- The arterial vasodilatation caused by hypoxia is mitigated by cerebral vasoconstriction caused by hypocapnia (low arterial carbon dioxide). Overall oxygen delivery to the brain is a result of the balance between vasodilatation and vasoconstriction. In general, vasodilatation overrides vasoconstriction.
- The combination of increased cerebral blood flow and hypoxia can lead to vasogenic cerebral edema (as described above).
- Increased cerebral blood flow can also cause brain swelling from engorgement of the brain itself with blood.
- All brains swell on ascent to high altitudes, either as a result of cerebral edema and/or engorgement with blood, but not all climbers develop AMS.
- According to the "tight fit" hypothesis, cranial anatomy determines who develops AMS. In climbers who remain relatively asymptomatic, the brain volume increase and corresponding rise in intracranial pressure is "buffered" by decreased intracranial blood flow (from vasoconstriction) as well as increased displacement of cerebral spinal fluid out of the skull.
- If buffering is unsuccessful, cerebral edema and intracranial pressure continue to rise, resulting in the symptoms of AMS.
- AMS can evolve into high altitude cerebral edema (HACE). HACE, though, strikes only a minority of climbers, usually those at extreme altitudes.
- Cases of mild AMS are probably due to early cerebral edema, but this has not been definitely proven; for example, the headache of mild AMS may be from another source, e.g., migraine.
- There is a hazy line between moderate to severe AMS and HACE. Symptoms of more severe AMS include unrelieved headache, decreased urine output, vomiting, and lethargy, but not the loss of balance (ataxia) or the mental confusion or coma which define HACE.

High Altitude Cerebral Edema (HACE)

This is the most severe form of AMS. At this stage, significant brain edema and increased intracerebral pressure have developed. HACE can be preceded by symptoms of AMS or occur suddenly. Symptoms include confusion, disorientation, irrational behavior, lethargy, and ataxia. Nausea and vomiting may be severe. The progression from initial symptoms to coma may take as little as 12 hours. Death follows if early treatment is not administered.

High Altitude Pulmonary Edema (HAPE)

The second organ of the body most affected by hypoxia is the lung, but the pathophysiology of high altitude pulmonary edema is completely different from AMS/HACE. Basically, in HAPE, a high-pressure fluid leak occurs in the lung. Here's the mechanism: Hypoxia causes pulmonary artery vasoconstriction and an elevation of pulmonary artery pressure. The vasoconstriction, however, is unevenly distributed throughout the lung, and those regions of lung tissue less constricted become overperfused with blood, resulting in regional elevations of pulmonary capillary pressure. The increased capillary pressure forces water and proteins through the capillary walls into the pulmonary air spaces, resulting in pulmonary edema (high-pressure overperfusion edema). The flooding of these patchy areas of lung tissue further reduces oxygen delivery to the blood, further increasing hypoxia.

Persons who have a low hypoxic ventilatory response (HVR) have more pulmonary hypertension and are thus more susceptible to HAPE. More importantly, a low HVR may permit extreme hypoxemia during sleep, explaining why HAPE often strikes in the middle of the night.

HAPE usually occurs after a rapid, strenuous ascent to high or very high altitudes and staying there. The early symptoms of HAPE are breathlessness on exertion and reduced exercise tolerance, greater than expected for the altitude. Untreated, there is progression to breathlessness at rest, especially at night, and persistent cough. The cough can either be dry or progress to produce white, watery, or frothy fluid. Severe fatigue or exercise intolerance is nearly universal and may be the most reliable hallmark of HAPE. The most reliable combination of diagnostic signs and symptoms is dry cough and fatigue plus lung crackles and oxygen desaturation (measured with a pulse oximeter and more pronounced than calculated for the altitude) or tachycardia and increased oxygen desaturation.

HAPE strikes 1% to 2% of those who climb above 12,000 feet. It kills more people each year than any other altitude-related condition but is reversible if recognized early and treated properly. (Fatal cases, however, have occurred as low as 8,000 feet.) At increased risk are climbers who have previously experienced HAPE; they have a 60% chance of recurrence during another exposure to high altitudes.

REDUCING THE RISK OF AMS & HAPE

Eat a high carbohydrate diet—Eat a diet that is 70% to 80% carbohydrates. This provides the greatest build-up in muscle glycogen. Avoid high-protein diets.

Reduce activity—If you travel rapidly to an elevation over 8,000 feet (2,500 meters), you can reduce your chance of illness by not engaging in strenuous activity for several days.

Acclimatize—The major cause of altitude sickness is going too high too fast. You can avoid or lessen AMS by making a slow, gradual ascent. Slow ascent means not increasing your sleeping altitude by over 2,000–3,000 feet (600–900 meters) on successive nights, especially when climbing above 10,000 feet. An alternate strategy, called staging, is to spend two to three days at an intermediate altitude (e.g., 8,000 to 10,000 feet) before resuming ascent. Every 3,000–4,000 feet thereafter, you should stop for a day to acclimatize further.

In addition, no matter how high you are climbing during the day, try to sleep at a lower altitude, if this is an option.

Unfortunately, cautious guidelines on the rate of ascent are impractical for most climbers. For example, if you were to climb Mt. Kilimanjaro on a guided tour, you would find yourself ascending on a schedule that forces you to sleep at much higher altitudes each successive night. You begin the climb at 5,000 feet. The huts where you sleep are at 9,000, 12,000, and 14,500 feet. Only a single rest day is spent (sometimes) at the highest hut before the final ascent to the 19,000-foot summit the following morning. Needless to say, AMS is a frequent occurrence among those climbing Mt. Kilimanjaro.

Take a prophylactic drug—In situations where you are climbing rapidly to altitudes above 8,000 feet, or arriving by airplane at a high destination (see Table 12.1), there are two drugs that can help: (1) Acetazolamide, which accelerates acclimatization, and (2) dexamethasone, which reduces symptoms, but which has no effect on acclimatization itself. Prophylaxis is especially important if you have previously experienced altitude sickness, but drug prophylaxis isn't uniformly recommended by some experts for climbers who plan a reasonably slow ascent schedule to moderate altitudes. The problem here is, How many climbers actually practice "slow ascent"?

1. Acetazolamide (Diamox)—Acetazolamide has been shown to reduce susceptibility to AMS and the incidence of HAPE and HACE. This is the drug of choice for preventing AMS. Acetazolamide works through several mechanisms: (1) It forces the kidneys to excrete bicarbonate, acidifying the blood. The resulting metabolic acidosis acts as a respiratory stimulant, increasing ventilation and improving arterial oxygenation. The drug is especially effective in preventing extreme hypoxia during sleep—a situation that can also trigger HAPE, especially in persons with a history of this disorder. (2) It reduces cerebrospinal fluid (CSF) formation and possibly CSF pressure. And (3) it causes a diuresis, counteracting the fluid retention which occurs in AMS.

Standard dosage: 250 mg every 12 hours, or 500 mg daily of the slow release preparation (Diamox-SR). Start acetazolamide 24 hours before starting your ascent and continue it for three days at the higher altitude. A recent study in the British Medical Journal, however, found that for altitudes over 4,000 meters (13,123 feet), a total daily dose of 750 mg was effective, whereas 500 mg was not.

Side effects include frequent urination (polyuria) and a tingling sensation of the face and lips (paresthesia). Use acetazolamide with caution if you have an allergy to sulfa drugs because acetazolamide is a sulfa derivative. A trial course of the drug *before* going to a remote location is advisable.

2. Dexamethasone (Decadron)—Although effective in treating cerebral symptoms of AMS, dexamethasone is not routinely recommended as a prophylactic agent for AMS. It may be a useful drug, however, for those who need to ascend abruptly to very high altitudes—for example, those going on a mountain rescue mission—or for those climbers allergic to acetazolamide. The drug is usually used for the treatment of AMS (see the Treatment Section on the following page).

Prophylaxis dosage: 2 to 4 mg every 6 hours, begun the day of ascent, continued for three days at the higher altitude, then tapered over five days. Side effects: weaning from dexamethasone may increase risk of depression.

3. Nifedipine—In someone who has a history of HAPE, use either the 20 mg slow-release capsule (available in Europe and Asia under various brand names) every 8 hours, or the 30 mg slow-release (available as Adalat-CC or Procardia-XL in North America) every 12 hours. All climbers above 10,000 feet should also carry standby treatment doses of the rapid-acting 10 mg capsules.

4. Aspirin—Pretreatment with aspirin before travel to high altitudes appears to decrease the incidence and severity of headaches, the main symptom of mild AMS. Take one aspirin tablet every four hours for three doses before arrival. After arrival, take two tablets three times daily for three days.

DIAGNOSING AMS

Before treating AMS, HACE, or HAPE, you need to be sure the correct diagnosis has been made. The following is a list of other medical conditions that can mimic AMS, HACE, and HAPE:

- Dehydration (can cause nausea, weakness, headache)
- Hypothermia (can cause loss of balance, staggering gait)
- Exhaustion (can cause lethargy, loss of balance, staggering gait)
- Respiratory infection (causes coughing, shortness of breath)
- Carbon monoxide poisoning (causes rapid breathing, headache, mental changes)
- Hyperventilation (rapid breathing) may simulate pulmonary edema)
- Psychiatric problems (can cause hyperventilation or irrational behavior)
- Trauma (can cause any of the symptoms above)
- Pulmonary embolus (causes shortness of breath; may mimic HAPE; has been reported in female climbers taking birth control pills)

TREATMENT

Mild AMS by itself is a benign illness but you must watch for progression to more severe AMS, HACE, or HAPE. In general, management depends on the acuity and severity of symptoms. The principles of treatment are as follows:
- Stop further ascent and rest. Administer adjunctive treatment, as indicated.
- Descend if there is no improvement or if symptoms worsen.
- Descend immediately if there are symptoms or signs of cerebral or pulmonary edema.

Mild AMS

The first rule applies: Stop your ascent and rest. Symptoms may clear in 12 hours but can persist for three to four days. To help the headache, take aspirin, acetaminophen, or ibuprofen. Acetazolamide (Diamox), 250 mg every 12 hours for 3–4 days, relieves symptoms, improves arterial oxygenation, and prevents further impairment of pulmonary gas exchange. Also effective is dexamethasone (Decadron), 4 mg orally or intramuscularly every 6 hours for 2–3 doses. No further ascent should be attempted until you are well and at least 18 hours after the last dose of dexamethasone. Contrary to popular belief, drinking extra fluids doesn't help AMS—in fact, extra fluids theoretically could aggravate symptoms by increasing edema. Non-AMS headaches, however, often improve with fluids and analgesics.

More Severe AMS

Treatment of more severe AMS (which is essentially a pre-HACE condition) is directed at reducing brain volume and intracranial pressure and to stop the formation of vasogenic cerebral edema. A descent of at 1,500–3,000 feet is the best initial treatment. Adjunctive measures include oxygen, steroids, acetazolamide, rest, and keeping the patient warm. Start oxygen, if available (flow rate of 2 to 4 liters/minute), plus dexamethasone (8 mg immediately, then 4 mg every 6 hours), and acetazolamide (250 mg every 12 hours).

High Altitude Cerebral Edema (HACE)

The hallmarks of HACE are confusion and ataxia. To test for ataxia, have the ill climber walk a straight line, one foot in front of the other, heel to toe. A climber who struggles to stay on the line, falls off to one side, or falls down should be considered to have HACE. At the first sign of ataxia, if not before, descent should be started. Adjunctive treatment measures include steroids and oxygen. Dexamethasone, 8 mg, should be administered immediately (intramuscular or intravenous route preferred), then 4 mg every six hours. Give oxygen, 2 to 4 liters/minute, if available. A portable hyperbaric chamber, such as the Gamow bag (see below), will improve oxygenation and give temporary relief and will facilitate descent, but use of the Gamow bag should not unduly delay descent.

NOTE: HACE and high altitude pulmonary edema (HAPE) often occur simultaneously, but HACE can also occur as a single entity without pulmonary symptoms.

High Altitude Pulmonary Edema (HAPE)

Treatment depends on the severity of the illness and the environment. If oxygen and medical expertise are not available, immediate descent is indicated. If diagnosed early, a descent of 1,500–3,000 feet usually gives rapid improvement with two or three days of rest at the lower elevation usually adequate for complete recovery. Once the symptoms have resolved, cautious reascent may be attempted. NOTE: Some authorities state, however, that once a diagnosis of HAPE is made the individual should be evacuated to a medical facility for proper follow-up treatment. This is probably indicated only in more severe cases. If reascent is attempted, prophylactic acetazolamide and nifedipine should be considered.

Adjunctive treatment measures include the following:

- Give oxygen, if it's available, at a flow rate of 4 liters/minute. When descent is delayed, oxygen can be lifesaving.
- Administer nifedipine. Although oxygen and descent are the best treatments for HAPE, nifedipine is an effective adjunct. If conscious, have the patient chew one 10-mg capsule and also swallow an additional 10-mg capsule for the first dose. If comatose, pierce the capsule and squirt it into the mouth. Continue to give 10 mg every 4–6 hours until improvement occurs and then switch over to the slower-release form. Nifedipine rapidly reduces pulmonary vasoconstriction, thus reducing pulmonary hypertension and overperfusion edema. The reduction in vasoconstriction also makes pulmonary blood flow more homogeneous, which improves oxygenation. According to Thomas E. Dietz, M.D., author of *The High Altitude Medicine Guide*, sublingual administration of nifedipine results in a 10% rise in arterial oxygen saturation within 10–15 minutes. Dr. Dietz also states that nifedipine can sometimes be used alone with strict bedrest in a person with only very mild HAPE—otherwise it is used only in combination with the other treatments—descent, oxygen, hyperbaric therapy.
- Administer hyperbaric treatment in the Gamow bag (see below) for a total of 2–4 hours usually results in dramatic improvement, facilitating descent.
- Keep the patient warm. Hypothermia increases pulmonary artery pressure.

The Portable Hyperbaric Chamber (Gamow Bag)

This device is an airtight, 7-foot cylindrical bag made of coated nylon weighing about 18 lb. with pump and/or rebreathing unit. It is used for the immediate treatment of more severe AMS or HACE, especially to facilitate descent when a climber is incapacitated. It is not a substitute for descending to a lower altitude.

The stricken climber is placed inside the bag, which is then pressurized with a foot or hand pump. This pressurization simulates a decrease of 1,500 to 2,500 meters in altitude and, depending upon the starting altitude, is usually sufficient to raise arterial oxygen saturation to over 90%. A one-hour treatment provides rapid relief from most symptoms of AMS, but the effect is temporary, lasting only 10–11 hours. This may buy enough time to walk the stricken climber to a lower

Table 12.1 AMS Treatment Options

Descent
Pro Rapid recovery; patients generally improve during descent, recover totally within several hours.

Con Loss of "progress" towards summit or trek goal; descent may be difficult in bad weather or at night; personnel need to accompany patient.

Rest at same elevation
Pro Acclimatization to current altitude; no loss of forward progress.

Con It may take 24–48 hours to become symptom-free; condition of climber may deteriorate.

Rest plus acetazolamide
Pro Benefits of rest alone, plus acclimatization is accelerated; recovery likely within 12–24 hours.

Con Recovery may take 12–24 hours.

Rest plus dexamethasone
Pro Benefits of rest alone, plus recovery of moderate AMS in 2–6 hours. Essentially as rapid as descent, without the walk.

Con Potential for steroid side effects (unlikely).

Rest plus acetazolamide plus dexamethasone
Pro Benefits of rest alone, plus acceleration of acclimatization and resolution of pathology.

Con Probably treatment of choice for most cases of AMS if immediate descent not indicated.

Oxygen and/or hyperbaric treatment
Pro Oxygen at 4 L/m, or simulated descent in a hyperbaric bag works as well as descent in the short term, without the walk.

Con Not generally used as oxygen tanks are heavy, and hyperbaric bags are very expensive and labor intensive; these are usually reserved for more serious illness and are usually found only on more elaborately-equipped, very high-altitude expeditions. Treatment for 2 hours with either will resolve symptoms in most patients, but rebound symptoms can occur.

Copyright© Thomas E. Dietz, M.D. Used with permission.

---

altitude. By contrast, climbers receiving dexamethasone will improve more slowly but with sustained, longer-lasting effects. While the administration of dexamethasone is simple, the same can't be said for the mobile hyperbaric chamber. Maintaining therapeutic pressure and air flow in often-extreme weather can be a daunting task. In addition, access to the stricken climber is restricted.

The main advantages of the Gamow-type bag are its rapid action and independence from consumable oxygen. The device is best suited for alpine expeditions and search and rescue teams that don't carry bottled oxygen. For further information contact Portable Hyperbarics, Inc., P.O. Box 510, Ilion, NY 13357; 315-895-7485.

Oxygen
This is usually supplied by "E" type cyclinders that weigh about 18 lbs. One full tank will last 2.5 hours at a flow rate of 4 liters/minute. Supplemental oxygen is slightly more effective than the Gamow bag in raising arterial oxygen saturation and its use does not restrict access to the victim.

Sleeping Pills
It is usually recommended that climbers not take sleeping pills because they might depress respiration, increase oxygen desaturation and hypoxia, and increase the incidence or severity of AMS. However, a recent study (conducted at 5,300 meters elevation) among members of the British Mount Everest Expedition found that small doses (10 mg) of the short-acting benzodiazepine, temazepam (Restoril), improved the subjective quality of sleep without adversely affecting respiration. Better sleep, defined as longer periods without arousal, resulted in less daytime drowsiness and improved endurance. In 1996 French researchers found that a 10-mg dose of zolpidem (Ambien) taken at a simulated altitude of 4,000 meters was associated with fewer sleep arousals and no increase in period breathing. From these studies, it appears that the short-acting hypnotics may actually be safe adjuncts for improving comfort and rest as well as high altitude performance.

Acute Altitude Sickness in Children
The incidence of AMS in children is about the same as in adults, but diagnosing the condition can be problematic because the symptoms—cough, headache, irritability, loss of appetite—are often mistaken for a viral illness. Parents are advised not to take their children to high altitudes, but if they do become sick, assume that AMS is a good possibility, descend, and seek prompt medical consultation.

Drug prophylaxis/treatment for AMS could be considered as for adults, but with appropriate pediatric doses. However, these medications have not been specifically studied for treating children with AMS.

Before You Travel to High Altitudes
If you have a history of heart disease or other chronic disease, your "exercise prescription" has to be carefully individualized. Your physician should review your medications, if any, and present you with the possible risks and hazards based on your past history, symptoms, and test results. You should make your decision to travel based on this advice, plus your own desire to go. Bear in mind that if problems occur, you will be far away from a hospital. See a cardiologist, or other specialist, when the issue is not clear cut, or you want a second opinion. However, many intelligent, well-informed people who understand the risks, as well as their own capabilities and limitations, want to live life to the fullest. This is a human desire that should not unnecessarily be restricted.

THE HEART AT HIGH ALTITUDES

Travel to High Altitudes

What about your heart? What are the risks at high altitudes? This issue is discussed below, but suffice it to say that there seems to be little risk, even for those with known cardiac conditions. For example, it takes only 3–5 hours to travel from Lima, Peru, near sea level, to La Oroya, elevation 12,400 feet, yet there are few, if any, reports of sudden cardiac death occurring in travelers shortly after they arrive. And in a survey of medical evacuations among 148,000 persons trekking in Nepal, medical researchers reported no cardiac causes of death.

If you have a history of heart disease that is symptomatically stable, there is good news: Altitude appears to have less effect on climbers with heart disease than previously believed. In fact, it appears that exercise after acclimatization at a high altitude is of no greater risk to your heart than similar exercise performed at sea level. Some physicians, however, discourage any heart patient from going to altitude out of fear that the patient will have increased symptoms, or even a heart attack. Therefore, what tests, if any, should you have to help assess your risk? And what precautions should you take to avoid problems? And who shouldn't engage in high altitude activity? The following checklist will help you plan your high altitude activities.

Facts About Heart Disease and Altitude

- High altitude increases cardiac work during the first few days. However, there is no evidence that cardiac work at altitude puts a greater stress on your heart than does similar cardiac work at sea level.
- If you have few or no symptoms at sea level while doing moderate to heavy exercise, you are probably at no greater risk of a heart attack at altitudes even as high as 19,000 feet.

Table 12.2

Some Cities at Elevations > 7,500 Feet Above Sea Level	
Addis Ababa, Ethiopia	7,900 feet
Thimphu, Bhutan	7,700 feet
Bogota, Colombia	8,653 feet
Cuzco, Peru	11,152 feet
Arequipa, Peru	7,559 feet
La Paz, Bolivia	12,001 feet
Darjeeling, India	7,431 feet
Toluca, Mexico	8,793 feet
Sucre, Bolivia	8530 feet
Lhasa, Tibet	11,830 feet
Quito, Ecuador	9,300 feet
Mexico City	7,546 feet

- If you have heart disease with symptoms, you may notice an increase in your symptoms (e.g., angina, shortness of breath) while you are acclimatizing.
- While acclimatizing, reduce physical activity and be sure to take your medications. Discuss medication dosages with your doctor.
- If you have moderate to severe symptoms at sea level, you can expect a marked increase in your symptoms after arriving at altitude. You should not travel to high altitudes.
- When angina drugs are required, nitrates and calcium channel blockers are preferable to beta blockers. Beta blockers slow down the heart and may impede acclimatization.
- Your maximal physical exertion at high altitudes is determined more by your lung function than by your cardiac work capacity.
- If you have congestive heart failure, you probably should not travel above 8,000 feet. Altitude-induced fluid retention may cause problems.
- If you have a history of unstable arrhythmia or cardiac arrest, mountain travel is not advisable. If you do travel to altitude, a pacemaker or implantable defibrillator may be advisable.

Climbers without known heart disease—If you are age 40 or older and going on a trek or alpine climb where medical facilities are not available, consider having a stress test if you have one or more of the following cardiac risk factors: systolic blood pressure persistently over 160, high cholesterol, diabetes, cigarette smoking, or a family history of early heart attack. A history of unexplained fainting with exertion warrants stress testing. Note, however, that stress tests in asymptomatic people are controversial. The rationale for screening asymptomatic persons before climbing is to deter those who may have silent coronary artery disease from starting an imprudent exercise program.

Climbers with a normal stress test—Although a normal test does not necessarily exclude coronary artery disease, your chance of having a heart attack is very low with a negative stress test and no symptoms.

NOTE: Recent studies have shown that the risk of an unexpected exercise-related heart attack is much less in people who exercise regularly. Sedentary people with silent coronary heart disease are at higher risk of a heart attack triggered by sudden physical exertion.

Climbers with an abnormal stress test—If you have a stress test where the results are borderline or abnormal, a thallium scan may be the next step to help decide if you have significant coronary artery disease.

Climbers with known heart disease—If you have a history of angina or a previous heart attack, you should have a stress test before commencing vigorous exercise. This will help determine your exercise capacity as well as any tendency to develop dangerous heart rhythms during exertion. If you have sustained a previous heart attack, there are several tests (none of which are infallible) that will help predict your chance of cardiac problems.

There is a lower risk of heart attack if you have the following:

- Well-preserved left ventricular function (ejection fraction >40%)
- No significant ventricular arrhythmias or ST depression on exercise testing
- Normal signal-averaged ECG
- Well-maintained exercise capacity; no systolic BP drop during exercise testing

Climbing after coronary artery bypass grafting (CABG) surgery—Routine screening by exercise testing is generally not recommended for people who are symptom-free after CABG surgery. Recently, however, exercise-thallium-201 SPECT testing has been shown to be a strong independent predictor of subsequent death or nonfatal heart attack when there are thallium-perfusion defects and impaired exercise capacity. An abnormal thallium-201 SPECT test might weigh against you going to a medically underserved area.

How Two Physicians Advise Their Patients Who Climb

Dr. Drummond Rennie, a cardiologist in San Francisco, writing in the *Journal of the American Medical Association*, advises, "My own practice is to take a careful history from people who ask if they can go trekking at high altitudes. I explain that if they are able to carry out strenuous, long, continued exercise at sea level, they can probably expect to do so at high altitude. I suggest also that, if possible, they should give themselves a trial at moderate altitude, say 8,000 feet. If they have any symptoms, say angina, they should ascend even more slowly than usual so that they can acclimatize." And Dr. Charles Houston, who is a world-renowned expert on altitude sickness, says, "Coronary artery disease, per se, is not an absolute contraindication to trekking at higher altitudes. If reserve circulation is sufficient, if the patient is wise in recognizing symptoms and accepting limits, if the anticipated stress of hiking and climbing does not produce signs and symptoms at sea level, then a person may go ahead, properly warned and prepared, because the emotional and psychological benefits are large."

Beaumont M, Goldenburg F, Lejeune D, et al. Effect of zolpidem on sleep and ventilatory patterns at simulated altitude of 4,000 meters. Am J Respir Crit Care Med 1996 Jun;153:1864–9.

Dietz TE. Altitude Illness Clinical Guide for Physicians 1999. http://www.gorge.net/hamg/AMS_medical.html

Dubowitz G. Effect of temazepam on oxygen saturation and sleep quality at high altitude: Randomized placebo controlled crossover trial. British Medical Journal 1998;316:587–589.

Dumont L, Madirosoff C, Tramer MR. Efficacy and harm of pharmacological prevention of acute mountain sickness: quantitative systematic review.BMJ 2000;321:267272.

Hackett PH. The cerebral etiology of high-altitude cerebral edema and acute mountain sickness. Wilderness Environ Med. 1999 Summer; 10(2):97-109.

Keller HR et al. Simulated descent v dexamethasone in treatment of acute mountain sickness: A randomized trial. British Medical Journal, 1995; 310: 1232-5.

Murdoch DR, Pollard AJ. Acute Mountain Sickness. J Travel Med. 1997 Jun 1; 4(2):90-93.

15 Medical Care Abroad

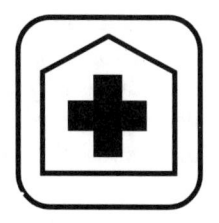

What do you do if you are suddenly taken ill or have a serious accident in a foreign country? How do you find an English-speaking physician? Or a reputable hospital? Where do you turn for help and advice?

The first step in avoiding disaster is prevention. This means careful pretrip planning as outlined in this *HealthGuide*. But what if an unexpected illness or accident occurs?

Statistics show that 25% of travelers develop some type of medical problem over a two-week period. Most accidents and cases of medical illness are relatively minor. The problem may be self-evident. Most conditions resolve by themselves or can be treated with simple first-aid measures or with the medication you have on hand.

But what if you need a physician's treatment or hospitalization? When an emergency happens far from home, even a seasoned traveler may have trouble coping—especially if medical care is urgently needed. What starts out as a routine vacation or business trip could end up as a real nightmare.

How to Cope When Illness or Injury Suddenly Strikes

Stay calm—You may be able to solve the problem yourself. You may already have medicine with you to treat a minor infection, a rash, a cut, a bruise, or a sprain. If diarrhea should occur, follow the treatment guidelines for travelers' diarrhea in Chapter 4. Check to see what's in your medical kit. Home health care guides and first-aid manuals are a source of useful advice, so you may wish to bring one of these with you.

Serious accidents or illness demand immediate attention—If you sustain a deep laceration, a fracture, a possible heart attack, or a stroke, or if you have bleeding, unremitting chest or abdominal pain, or trouble breathing, don't waste your time trying to find a local physician. Go immediately to the nearest hospital. If you are in a large city, go to a hospital associated with a medical school, if possible (these hospitals usually have English-speaking doctors as well as qualified specialists on their staff). You can ask for directions or assistance from your hotel, your tour guide, a taxi driver, or the police. A taxi or private car taken directly from your location may be faster than an ambulance, but call an ambulance if necessary and if one is available. Remember, in an emergency, minutes count. Don't delay!

NOTE: If you're having a possible heart attack, early diagnosis and treatment is critical. If the hospital can administer a clot-dissolving drug during the first four hours, your chance of recovery is greatly improved.

Less urgent illness—This can usually be treated during a daytime visit to a doctor's office, but some doctors will make an after hours hotel "house call." Your hotel can usually provide the names of one or more English-speaking physicians. Better yet, if you have friends, relatives, or business associates who are residents of the area, ask them for a referral to a doctor they know is qualified.

Colds, sore throats, earaches, bronchitis, diarrhea, most urinary infections, and the flu are some of the conditions that usually don't require emergency attention. You may have your own medication to relieve discomfort and tide you over until you can see a physician. However, if you have a fever and think you might have malaria, be sure you are examined and treated within 6 to 12 hours.

NOTE: Foreign brand names of drugs will vary. Insist that all medications that you receive from the doctor be identified or labeled with the generic or trade name. This is important if you have drug allergies and must avoid certain medications or develop a drug-related reaction or have to see another doctor for ongoing care. He or she will need to know what you are taking.

Carry a phrase book—A phrase book that provides medical words and phrases in various foreign languages can be invaluable. Try to find an interpreter as soon as possible.

Call your doctor in the States—If you are hospitalized, a consultation with your own physician can be invaluable. Hopefully your doctor, or an associate, will be available at the time you call. Leave your number if necessary. Describe the history of your illness, your symptoms, what the diagnosis is, and what treatment you are receiving. Let your doctor know if you are in a country where there are tropical diseases. Have your own doctor discuss your case with the local doctor caring for you. Obviously, for certain conditions, treatment is standard and straightforward—surgery for appendicitis, casting for fractures, etc.—and your treatment may have already been rendered. However, for more serious or life-threatening problems, this consultation is important. Your diagnosis may be in doubt, and the hospital and physician possibly may not have the expertise to provide adequate care. Your physician can help assess the situation and reassure you that you are receiving proper care and that there's no need to worry, or your physician may feel that a second opinion is warranted or even that transfer to another facility is advisable.

Locating Physicians Abroad

You have many options when it comes to finding a physician to care for you. The **American and Canadian embassies and consulates** maintain referral lists from which you can choose. The embassy or consulate, however, won't recommend individual doctors on the list. Other options to consider include the following:

Hotel doctors—Most large hotels will refer you to a local doctor or to a doctor who will come to your room to render treatment. Be warned, however, that the main qualification some of these doctors have is a kickback arrangement with the hotel management.

The World Medical Guide section of the *International Travel HealthGuide*—This year's edition has an expanded listing of hospitals, clinics, and individual physicians, including specialists.

IAMAT—The International Association for Assistance to Travelers (IAMAT) is a Canadian foundation that publishes a booklet listing hospitals and English-speaking physicians who have agreed to adhere to a standard schedule of fees. Physicians are not listed by specialty. Contact IAMAT, 417 Center Street, Lewiston, NY 14092; 716-754-4883. Or in Canada, 40 Regal Road, Guelph, Ontario, N1K 1B5; 519-836-0102. No charge, but a donation is encouraged.

Personal Physicians Worldwide—Geared to the sophisticated business, government, or pleasure traveler, this company takes the guesswork out of finding a doctor abroad. Before your departure, Personal Physicians Worldwide reviews your medical history and your itinerary, and then identifies and calls the English-speaking physician(s) in their network to advise them of your arrival. Qualified physicians and specialists are always available 24 hours a day in case you have a medical problem or an emergency. Travelers receive a wallet card listing all of the contact physicians' names and numbers, as well as the preferred hospitals with which these physicians are associated. Personal Physicians Worldwide, 815 Connecticut Avenue NW, Washington, DC 20006; 888-657-8114 or 301-657-8114. Fax 301-718-7725. Internet: *http://www.personalphysicians.com*

Cardholder assistance—Credit-card companies provide 24-hour emergency medical hotlines available to many of their cardholders, usually those in the "Gold card" or "platinum card" category. Typically, the hotlines can refer you to English-speaking doctors and dentists and to hospitals with English-speaking staff members, arrange for replacement of prescription medicines, and help you rent an air ambulance. If you are an American Express cardholder, call the Global Assist hotline at 800-554-AMEX (301-214-8228 collect from overseas). If you are an American Express Platinum cardholder, call your special assistance number, 800-345-2639 (202-331-1688 collect from overseas). Visa Gold and Classic cardholders can call 800-332-2484 (410-581-9994 collect from overseas). MasterCard cardholders can call 303-278-8000 (collect from overseas).

Travel insurance with assistance—If you have purchased a travel health policy with assistance, call the 24-hour hotline number and you'll be connected with an assistance center that can give a physician referral. See Chapter 14 for a listing of companies.

Personal recommendation—Probably the best method of locating a qualified English-speaking physician (assuming time allows it) is to find a satisfied English-speaking patient who lives in the area. Try contacting employees of American or Canadian multinational corporations, or any other expatriate (schoolteacher, relief worker, missionary, etc.). If you have no luck with these sources, you can call an embassy or consulate (American, Canadian, British, Australian, or New Zealand). Try to find a sympathetic staff member, or talk to the embassy nurse, for his or her personal recommendation.

Foreign Physicians

Because of cultural differences, the attitude of physicians toward their patients in foreign countries is often different than in the United States. Physicians abroad are often perceived as being more autocratic and authoritarian. This can make patient-doctor communication difficult. The doctor caring for you may not want you to question his or her care and may not be available to answer your questions (to be fair, this can sometimes be said of American physicians also). This does not mean that your care is substandard. In fact, the doctor caring for you may have more knowledge of local diseases than your own physician and be perfectly well qualified to diagnose and treat your illness.

Foreign Hospitals

Keep in mind that foreign hospitals can range from the very primitive to the most modern, but the quality of your medical care shouldn't necessarily be judged by your surroundings. If you're hospitalized in a lesser-developed country, you might wonder if you should be moved to a "more modern" facility. This question faces hospitalized patients everywhere, not just travelers overseas. An analogy to being hospitalized in the United States might be appropriate. In the United States, the smaller community hospitals are adequate for almost all medical care. Occasionally, however, a patient requires transport to a specialty center for advanced, sometimes lifesaving treatment. The same is true overseas. You may be in a small, seemingly inadequate facility that may, in fact, be perfectly adequate for your medical needs. Having someone available, in serious situations, to assess your diagnosis and treatment will help you or your family know when transfer or medevac is indicated.

Assessing Foreign Hospitals

If you need emergency care and minutes count, go to the closest facility. However, if the situation is not immediately critical—and there's more than one hospital nearby—use the following checklist to get a basic idea of what level of care is available to you. The checklist will also help you tell your doctor at home what services can be provided.

- Does the hospital have a coronary care unit, ICU, recovery room, and advanced resuscitation and diagnostic equipment?
- What medical and surgical procedures can be performed locally? Is a neurosurgeon on staff? If not, where is the closest referral facility?
- Can they treat heart attacks with clot-dissolving drugs (e.g., t-PA or streptokinase)?
- Can the hospital render qualified obstetrical care?
- Is CT and MRI scanning available? Ultrasound?
- Does the hospital or clinic stock disposable supplies, especially needles and syringes?

- Does the blood bank test for the HIV antibody, hepatitis B surface antigen, and hepatitis C antibody?
- What vaccines are available (e.g., tetanus, immune globulin, rabies, rabies immune globulin, hepatitis B, hepatitis B immune globulin)?
- How clean is the hospital? Is it air-conditioned? Are there private rooms? What is the food like?
- Are special nurses available?
- Does the hospital have 24-hour receiving and admitting capability?
- Does the hospital receive ambulances and treat major trauma?
- Is there a list of on-call physicians? What specialists are available and what are their qualifications?
- Do most of the doctors speak English?
- What are the room rates and the charges for various medical and surgical procedures?
- How does the hospital want to be paid? Will they accept direct payments from your travel insurance company? Will they accept a major credit card?

Paying for Medical Care Abroad

Usually, foreign doctors, hospitals, and clinics like to be paid in cash when their services are rendered. Only a few accept Blue Cross/Blue Shield (The American Hospital in Paris, for example). Unless you have a direct-payment travel policy (see Chapter 14), expect to pay in full when leaving the hospital or doctor's office. Most foreign physicians and hospitals are familiar with health insurance forms and should be willing to complete these so you can be reimbursed later.

Have all your bills itemized in legible English, detailing all diagnostic and therapeutic procedures performed as well as the discharge diagnosis. When you return home, file your claim with your insurance company for reimbursement. Normally, there is no problem if you were treated for an emergency, but certain elective procedures, such as cosmetic surgery, won't be covered.

Be sure to keep copies of all bills and receipts, and have the physician prepare a complete summary of your treatment in case there is a dispute over your reimbursement.

If you are a member of an HMO, your coverage extends worldwide and all emergency care will be reimbursed. All other care will have to be authorized for payment by your HMO since you are "out of area." If you are hospitalized overseas, the HMO may find it medically advisable and sometimes cost-effective to evacuate you back home so that ongoing care will be provided by the HMO staff physicians. *It is best to check with your HMO prior to departure about what procedures to follow in event of illness or accident overseas.* Ask if they will make direct payments for hospitalization and under what circumstances they will pay for medical evacuation or repatriation.

How One Traveler Coped with Sudden Illness

In a letter published in the Travel section of *The New York Times* in October 1987, Mr. Carlton Zucker describes the problems of getting sick in a foreign country.[1]

No one, I thought at the time, could prepare adequately for the kind of terror that grabbed me when I awoke abruptly at 5 a.m. in the Tel Aviv Sheraton to find that I was hemorrhaging internally.

Today I realize that with careful planning for a possible medical emergency, I might have avoided the panic.

If, before leaving home, I had asked my doctor for the names of doctors and hospitals in Israel, my wife Joan and I would have saved precious hours. And if we had remembered to call a toll-free number in Geneva set up by the insurance company whose medical policy I carried we might not have fumbled about. Instead, my wife's first action was to call the hotel operator for a doctor (he was to come an hour later) and mine was to call my doctor in Chicago (it was 10 p.m. there) to ask for help. My doctor gave me the name of a physician who, fortuitously, had just returned to Israel from Chicago. If I couldn't reach him, my doctor advised, I should get over to Hadassah Hospital.

We enlisted the operator's assistance. She could not find the physician, and there was no Hadassah Hospital in Tel Aviv. It was in Jerusalem, 40 miles away. My doctor phoned back from Chicago a moment later to confirm what the operator had just told us, and he ordered me to go to the nearest Tel Aviv hospital.

At that moment the hotel doctor arrived, examined me, said I had bleeding diverticulitis (the hemorrhaging in my intestines had stopped) and directed that I go immediately to Ichilov Hospital, a public hospital affiliated with Tel Aviv University. He also warned that I might not find the bedside manner expected in the United States because, he said, Israel has socialized medicine and there wasn't time for manners. He asked for 70,000 shekels, about $47 at that time, and packed his bag.

The hotel operator had called a cab, which whisked us to the emergency room of a sprawling hospital compound. The emergency room had about two dozen empty beds and three nurses who struggled to understand English. I know that I should have been prepared with a phrase book to describe my symptoms quickly and precisely.

The doctor arrived, examined me, and ordered me up to Surgery No. 1, complete with intravenous and stomach tubes. I was wheeled to the fourth floor where I found myself in an ugly, dirty, crowded nine-bed ward.

My experiences over the next three days were a curious mixture of revulsion at the hospital's physical condition and awesome respect for an overworked medical staff. My condition and treatment were, fortunately, simple—no food, just intravenous fluids and bed rest for at least two days, to be followed by tests to determine whether the bleeding had really stopped. Only then would I be discharged. Certainly I would not board the plane for home, as planned, the following morning.

My greatest fear, as I look back, was not that I couldn't leave for Chicago the following day—it was that I might never leave because I would contract some horrible disease from the hospital conditions. The dining alcove outside my ward, I learned when I could get up to eat the third day, included two picnic benches to seat about twenty, hundreds of ants and one visible cockroach. And, in all fairness, a vat of very good chicken soup. The corridors were filled with cigarette smoke—from the doctors, nurses, patients, visitors, orderlies. Israelis, I was told, have more to worry about than cigarettes.

And yet the medical care was superb. From the professor who headed the surgery to the Arab aides who worked on Shabbat (Saturday, the day of rest for Israel's Jews), everyone on the staff displayed the kind of professionalism one could hope to get in the finest hospital in the States. The deputy director, the resident, the intern and the medical students, whom I saw at least twice daily, spent more time meticulously monitoring my condition than I ever expected.

Behind the dirty corridors lay some surprisingly modern equipment, like the elaborate sigmoidoscope machine with which I became intimately acquainted. It had been donated by a Hadassah chapter in an upstate New York hospital. And where else in the world would one find the nurses offering their patients a choice of sleeping tablets?

With few exceptions, these patients accepted without complaint the hospital conditions. After all, this was a paradise compared to what most of them had been through in their battles for survival both before and after the formation of Israel in 1948.

My wife, struggling with her own problems, was aided by some good planning. One thing we had done right before leaving home was to invest in a comprehensive travel insurance policy offered through American Express. For thirty days we were to be protected against losses due to changes in flight plans, medical emergency and missing baggage. I had become ill on the 29th day. Joan called a toll-free number in Geneva to report this emergency (after I entered the hospital) and was told to call New York. It was by then 2 a.m. New York time, and no one was standing by the phone.

Later, though, we learned that the insurance company would honor the medical expenses, to the tune of $860. Medicare would pay no part of medical costs outside the United States. The policy would also cover the cost of arranging another flight home. Joan cancelled our original airline tickets. We were in Israel on a TWA senior pass plan, almost as rigid as for charter flights. She wouldn't know for at least three more days when we would leave.

Another thing we had done right beforehand was to book into hotels where English is easily understood and where hotel employees can take care of emergencies in the appropriate language.

The day I entered Ichilov Joan had met with the chief cashier to discuss payments. Be ready, he told her, to pay 325,600 shekels ($220) a day. Only shekels, he warned. Joan cashed all our remaining traveler's checks. The Sheraton's Bank Leumi office gave her a fistful of shekels.

Medical Care Abroad

On the morning of my discharge, Joan and I hustled down to the cashier to seek my release. The bill produced two immediate reactions. The first: how could the hospital afford to provide medical services at such low prices—electrocardiogram, $10; urinalysis, $6; endoscopy, $34? The second: we were short $71.

Joan counted out the shekels, then offered to pay the balance in dollars, in cash, by check or by credit card. The cashier refused. After 15 minutes of argument, Joan broke into tears. The cashier responded with "Have a cup of tea." Twenty minutes later he agreed to accept dollars for the missing shekels, provided we would accept a receipt that read shekels, not dollars.

We left Ichilov in a taxi, went to a travel agency, booked two seats on a Swissair flight to Chicago the next morning, then strolled back to the hotel. Free at last. Of course, it wasn't until the plane landed at O'Hare, the next evening, that we really felt free.

It's apparent that these travelers did several things right. They had trip interruption insurance. They had the telephone number of their private physician. They had medical insurance; however, it did not provide telephone access to a physician-directed assistance center, nor did it pay their medical bills directly. Luckily, they raised enough currency to pay the hospital bill.

This account also illustrates a little-known fact: medical costs overseas are sometimes far lower than in the United States. A daily rate of $220 is very inexpensive compared to this country. Even so, be aware that in some countries, especially in Europe, hospital and physician's fees may be just as high as in the United States.

1. Copyright 1988 by *The New York Times*. Reprinted by permission.

16 Travel Insurance

Health insurance in the United States, unlike many countries, is characterized by its diversity. There are dozens of Blue Cross/Blue Shield plans, hundreds of commercial insurers, and a multiplicity of managed care plans involving HMOs, IPAs, and PPGs. For some, there is Medicaid, and for those over 65, there is Medicare. All these various types of plans have different benefits, costs, deductibles, exclusions, and restrictions.

Before you travel, check your existing health policy to see what it pays for. It will probably reimburse you for 80% to 100% of the cost of emergency medical care abroad, excluding any deductible or co-payment. For nonemergency care overseas, you may be covered, but you will probably have to call your insurance company or HMO in the United States for authorization of treatment. Check with your health plan about this before you leave home. Failure to get authorization may mean denial of reimbursement if you later file a claim.

If your current health insurance policy doesn't cover medical care abroad, or you are without any coverage whatsoever, you should consider purchasing a travel health-specific insurance policy (see below). And even if your present insurance will pay doctor and hospital bills abroad, you may want to purchase a travel policy to get some important additional benefits, such as coverage for air ambulance transport and on-site payment of medical expenses.

Medicare and Travel

If you're over 65, be aware that Medicare does not cover health care costs outside the United States. Fortunately, there are Medigap policies that offer protection against illness or accident abroad. Eight of the 10 Medigap plans (Plans C through J) cover foreign travel. There is no exclusion for pre-existing conditions if you sign up within six months of eligibility. Commercial insurance agents sell Medigap policies, but not all plans are available in every state. The policies offered through the **American Association of Retired Persons** (800-523-5800), which are underwritten by the Prudential Insurance Company, are an excellent value. These plans may vary state-by-state according to insurance regulations. In Massachusetts, the AARP Medicare Supplement I Plan and Medicare Supplement II Plan cover foreign travel and pay 100% of the Medicare-approved amounts. Unlike some Medigap carriers, AARP will always take applicants over 65, regardless of their health histories.

Another sponsor of Medigap insurance that covers foreign travel is the **National Council of Senior Citizens** (800-596-6272).

An excellent way to get overseas coverage is to join a Medicare HMO. A preexisting medical condition will not disqualify you from joining a Medicare HMO.

Before shopping around for a Medigap policy, find out if you are already covered for foreign travel through an existing policy.

Medical Care Abroad

Foreign doctors and hospitals won't bill your insurance company. They usually want you to pay them with cash or a credit card (not always possible) at the time of treatment or admission to a hospital. You must then submit your claim (with all necessary bills in English and any necessary documentation) to your insurance company when you return home. You'll be reimbursed only after the claim has been processed and the trip long over.

Paying for the Emergency

While most HMOs and insurance companies pay for emergency care when a member is away from home, the rub is the definition of an emergency. A prudent layman's idea of an emergency may differ from the judgment of an HMO or insurance company, and they may reserve the right to deny payment if they conclude, after a full evaluation, that you did not have a life-threatening condition. Expensive diagnostic tests may be needed to determine the severity of your problem—whether chest pains, for example, were caused by a heart attack or by indigestion, ulcers, or some other condition.

You should read your contract very carefully to see how an emergency is defined and see what services will be covered when they are delivered outside your local area. HMOs and insurance companies often relent and agree to pay for emergency care if you appeal. Remember: Most health plans will reimburse you for the costs of emergency care, but you may need to pay the bills with cash, check, or credit card. Get copies of the bills and receipts, preferably in English, to support claims for reimbursement. Take some blank claim forms with you.

Another factor complicating reimbursement for overseas medical care is that most insurance companies, HMOs, and managed care plans now require you to notify their review panel that you have been, or plan to be, admitted to a hospital for treatment. Most private insurers also require a second opinion before they will pay for certain types of treatment. In an emergency, the requirements are relaxed, but nevertheless, getting reimbursed will be more complicated if your medical care was rendered abroad. You may not be able to notify your carrier within the 24-hour time limit for emergency admissions, and if the medical record and copies of your bill are in a foreign language, there may be a delay in payment. Incomplete records, or bills that are not itemized, may not be acceptable. For these, and other reasons, travelers often decide to purchase a separate travel health insurance policy that will make on-site payments, or payment guarantees, to the overseas provider.

In addition to guaranteeing payment to the doctor and hospital, travel health insurance policies provide another very important benefit—they usually pay for medical evacuation, by air ambulance if necessary, to the nearest adequate medical facility. Most policies will also pay to transport you home if further treatment is required after your condition has stabilized—a benefit known as repatriation.

There are two major types of travel insurance policies: (1) policies that can make direct payments for medical care and that also provide "assistance," and (2) reimbursement policies that cover medical expenses, but not up front—you must pay these yourself and then file a claim when you return home.

Travel Insurance with Assistance

Imagine the following scenario: You find yourself hospitalized with a serious illness in a foreign country and the doctor caring for you speaks hardly any English. He's treating you with an unfamiliar drug, and you are worried about an allergic reaction or a serious side effect. The doctor then says you may need surgery, but you're not sure of the diagnosis. The situation is becoming more and more like a nightmare. Where do you turn for help and advice?

If you find yourself in this situation, then having travel insurance with assistance can be a godsend. Here are some of the reasons:

Medical monitoring—Travel insurance with assistance gives you the 24-hour telephone number of an assistance center where multilingual personnel, backed up by physician specialists, are available round-the-clock to evaluate your treatment and to monitor your medical care.

Emergency medical transport/repatriation—If it is determined that you need to be transported immediately by air ambulance, or another form of emergency medical transportation, to a better-qualified medical facility, the assistance center will arrange for it and pay the costs, up to the policy limit. And if you're unable to return home unassisted after your condition has stabilized, the insurer, working through the assistance center, will arrange and pay for transport with a qualified medical attendant so that you can recover closer to home and family.

Emergency medical payments—The assistance center can also guarantee payment to those providing your medical care or, when necessary, can advance money for on-site payment. This means that, aside from possibly paying a small deductible, you will not have to make cash payments yourself, providing the policy covers the illness and the doctor and/or hospital will accept the insurance (which they often will).

Traveler's assistance—Assistance centers can also help with a variety of other problems, including replacement of lost prescriptions, physician referral, or finding you a local dentist. Nonmedical assistance includes travel document and ticket replacement, emergency cash transfer, emergency message center, legal assistance (e.g., lending you bail money, locating a lawyer), and assistance in replacing a lost prescription or lost passport or other document.

What Else Do These Policies Cover?

Accidental death and disability—For an additional fee, most policies will also cover accidental death and disability (AD&D), lost luggage, and trip interruption or cancellation insurance. You may not need extra coverage for AD&D if you already have enough of your own life insurance, and your lost luggage may be covered by your homeowner's policy.

Trip interruption insurance—This can be an important money saver if illness or other problems force you to miss your scheduled flight. Some medical emergency policies offer this benefit in the basic package or as an optional benefit available for an additional fee. A trip interruption policy should cover the following:

- Interruption due to sickness, injury, or death to you, members of your immediate family, your traveling companion, or your business partner.
- An accident or emergency that causes you to miss a scheduled departure (or connection) when you're traveling to the departure point.
- Travel delays due to an unannounced strike, bad weather, or a hijacking.
- Destination-area terrorism that causes trip cancellation.

How Much Travel Insurance Do You Need?

Some travel insurance policies pay medical benefits as low as $2,500 while others pay up to $100,000. How should you choose? The answer depends on (1) whether your existing health insurance covers foreign travel, and how high the benefits, deductibles, and co-payments are, and (2) how much evacuation insurance you might need.

If you don't have a health insurance policy that covers overseas travel, then buy a travel policy with a high dollar benefit, such as **TravMed** or **Health Care Abroad** ($100,000 coverage). If you do have major medical or Medigap coverage, then a $2,500 to $5,000 medical reimbursement benefit is probably sufficient since this amount should be enough to cover any deductible or co-payments.

Be sure, however, that the policy's evacuation benefit is adequate for your needs. A long-range chartered air ambulance flight can cost $75,000, or more. For trips to Europe an evacuation benefit of $20,000 to $25,000 is probably sufficient, but if you are going on a trip to a remote area half way around the world, you want a policy that will pay unlimited evacuation costs, or a high dollar amount, for example, $100,000.

Exclusions—Read Carefully

Read the policy carefully to see what is *not* covered. Exclusions and restrictions vary among the policies. For example, some policies won't pay for complications of pregnancy while other policies do provide this coverage. Sports activities such as scuba diving, sky diving, and mountain climbing are usually not covered, but some policies will cover scuba diving for a supplemental fee.

Probably the exclusion of greatest significance to many travelers—particularly the elderly—is the exclusion for pre-existing medical conditions. This exclusion could prove disastrous if a condition becomes active during travel and requires emergency treatment or medical evacuation. A typical exclusion states that coverage is excluded for "any injury or sickness (or complications arising therefrom) which manifests itself, or for which treatment or medication was prescribed or taken in the 180 days immediately prior to the period of insurance." However, other policies (e.g., Travel Guard International) are much less restrictive, excluding only "any condition that has required treatment in the past 60 days, unless the condition is controlled through the taking of prescription drugs or medication and remains controlled throughout the 60-day period."

One company, **International SOS Assistance**, provides members with an unlimited medical evacuation benefit without any exclusion for pre-existing conditions. **Access America** has eliminated the pre-existing condition proviso as long as you purchase their insurance within seven days of making a deposit on your trip. If you do have an active medical condition, consider one of these policies.

Travel Insurance with Assistance

Worldwide Assistance Services, Inc.
1133 15th Street, N.W., Suite 400
Washington, DC 20005
800-821-2828 or 202-331-1609
This company is a member of the French-owned Europe Assistance Group, the world's largest travelers' support system. Their Travel Assistance International Plan provides up to $60,000 in medical benefits plus unlimited expenses for emergency medical evacuation. Policy covers medical complications of pregnancy through the third trimester. $100 deductible. Pre-existing conditions: 60 days.

TravMed-MEDEX
Box 10623, Baltimore, MD 21285-0623
800-732-5309 or 410-453-6300
$100,000 medical and air ambulance coverage for $3.50 a day. Age 71 and older, $5 a day. $25 deductible. SCUBA coverage, $1.00 a day extra. $25,000 student-abroad coverage available at $2.50 per day. Pre-existing conditions: 90 days.

International Medical Group (IMG)
407 N. Fulton Street
Indianapolis, IN 46202
800-628-4664
IMG offers two plans: (1) Patriot Travel Medical Insurance for the short-term traveler, and (2) Global Medical Insurance that provides major medical coverage for periods greater than one year. Coverage up to $5 million is available. Maternity coverage after one year. Both plans include emergency evacuation, in-patient and out-patient coverage, and choice of deductibles.

AEAInternational /SOS
Box 11568
Philadelphia, PA 31685
800-523-8930 or 215-244-1500
Membership provides assistance (e.g., medical monitoring) as well as worldwide emergency medical transport. There is no cost limit on the evacuation benefit and no pre-existing condition exclusion. AEA also offers an optional insurance policy to cover hospital and doctor costs.

Access America International
Richmond, VA 23286-4991
800-284-8300
$10,000 emergency medical and $50,000 evacuation benefits. Covers complications of pregnancy and scuba diving. No pre-existing condition proviso if purchased within seven days of making trip deposit.

***Assist* Emergency Travel Assistance**
Thomas W. Snyder & Company
1-888-396-8888
Two *Assist* programs are available which are underwritten by American International Group (AIG). Domestic and international travel is covered when the enrollee is more than 100 miles from home (Assist 100), or Worldwide Traveler—when the enrollee is traveling outside the U.S. Kidnap and Ransom and Political Evacuation and Repatriation benefits are also available. The plans offer coverage for a single trip or annual enrollment. The Emergency Medevac benefit is unlimited.

Wright & Co.
1400 Eye Street, NW, Suite 1100
Washington, DC 20005-2285
800-4249801 or 202-289-0200
Global Care® coverage, underwritten by an American International Group company, is available for individuals (and their dependents) who are traveling on foreign business assignments. Included are medical expense and emergency medical evacuation benefits as well as kidnap & ransom, political evacuation & repatriation, and war risk benefits—coverages not usually found on other policies. Medical expense benefit is $1,000,000; medical evacuation benefit is $100,000.
Pre-existing conditions: 2 years.

Travelers Insurance Company
800-243-3174 or 203-277-2318
The Travel Pak Policy pays up to $25,000 for emergency medical evacuation, depending upon how much trip cancellation insurance you purchase. Medical policy covers complications of pregnancy.

Credit-Card Assistance
The American Express Platinum Card will pay for emergency medical transport. Cardholders should contact Travel Emergency Assistance at 800-345-2639 or 202-331-1688 collect from overseas.

Scuba Diving Insurance
Divers Alert Network
800-446-2671 or 919-684-2948
DAN's scuba diving insurance is secondary coverage, available to DAN members. The scuba diving insurance policies listed below are in addition to DAN members' automatic $100,000 DAN TravelAssist medical air evacuation benefits.

1. **DAN Standard Plan**
   - $45,000 (maximum lifetime benefit) coverage for decompression illness incurred within the 130-foot depth limit.
2. **DAN Plus Plan**
   - $50,000 (maximum lifetime benefit) coverage for decompression illness plus up to $10,000 in accidental death/dismemberment benefits resulting from a covered diving illness or injury, plus up to $10,000 in total disability benefits.
3. **DAN Master Plan**
   - $125,000 (maximum lifetime benefit) coverage for decompression illness and ALL covered in-water injuries, plus up to $15,000 in accidental death and dismemberment benefits resulting from a covered diving illness or injury, plus up to $15,000 in permanent total disability, plus the policy pays up to $1,500 for accommodations, $1,000 for airline ticket, and $2,500 for lost dive equipment.

17 Emergency Medical Transport

Arranging Medical Transport
Should air evacuation be necessary, it's much easier to have an insurance company make these arrangements through an assistance company than for you to make them yourself. Suppose, though, you have purchased a policy that only reimburses you for these expenses, or perhaps you didn't purchase emergency medical insurance at all but are counting on your regular health insurance or HMO to reimburse you when you return home.

Without an assistance policy, you'll have to make all the transport arrangements yourself, pay up front, and hope your insurance policy or medical plan will reimburse you for costs up to the policy limit. Before paying you, the insurance company or your HMO will insist on knowing if the transport was "medically necessary," and for this you will need a letter or other documentation from your physician or treatment facility.

Unless it's an urgent situation, it's better to contact the insurance company or HMO before medical transport occurs, tell them why the medevac is necessary and what the cost is, and get the insurance company to preauthorize the cost of the transport. This way you will avoid problems when submitting the bills afterward.

Medical Transport by Commercial Airliner
Stretcher transport with a medical attendant is possible worldwide on many scheduled airlines. Your first step is to call the airline and ask for their medical department, special services department, or "stretcher desk." Explain the problem. (If you're sick abroad, somebody back home will probably do this for you.) Most major airlines are experienced in transporting stretcher patients, and they will explain what the procedures are. In most cases, a section of seats is curtained off and a stretcher unit and oxygen are installed. Extra seats are allotted for a medical attendant and sometimes a family member. The airline's medical director must authorize the transport, and a medical attendant, either a nurse or a doctor, is contracted with to accompany the patient (sometimes a family member can be the attendant when medical treatment will not be needed enroute). Ground ambulance pickup must be arranged at either end and coordinated with departure and arrival. All these arrangements must flow smoothly, especially when the patient is

seriously ill. Making these arrangements can be quite a feat, especially when you may be dealing with non-English-speaking people halfway around the world and many time zones away.

The cost of stretcher transport on a commercial airliner is usually nine to ten times the cost of a one-way economy seat (or four times the cost of a first-class seat). Oxygen, nurse's or doctor's fees, and ground transport will be extra. Scheduling normally takes 48 to 72 hours, or more, and is dependent upon seat availability as well as the airline's acceptance of the transport. Some airlines will not transport stretcher patients. In general, only patients with stable, noncritical medical conditions will be accepted by airlines that do provide stretcher transport.

Let's say you have arranged for stretcher transport of an injured relative back home. The airline probably serves only a limited number of major U.S. cities, which means that you will have to arrange ongoing transport within the United States, either by ground or air ambulance. This is another reason why you may need some type of assistance to coordinate what is sometimes a very complex undertaking. An air ambulance company may be your best bet.

Transport by Air Ambulance

If your medical condition requires immediate air ambulance evacuation, you must contact an air ambulance company that can provide a medically equipped and staffed air ambulance—often a Learjet or turboprop. Most of these companies provide an excellent response, but at a high cost (usually three times the cost of a comparable stretcher-equipped commercial flight). They will also require prepayment of the total fee or pretravel guarantee of payment by your insurance company.

Some air ambulance companies will also make stretcher arrangements for you on a commercial airliner, and this can be very helpful, especially in complex cases where there is considerable legwork involved. They will provide medical attendants, obtain medical clearances and consultations, handle language problems, arrange for ground ambulance pickup, and arrange, as necessary, for ongoing air ambulance transport in the United States after arrival from overseas. The fees charged will vary from company to company, so it's best to get several price quotations.

Because of their geographic proximity, U.S. companies are best suited for air ambulance evacuation from Mexico, the Caribbean, Canada, and South America. They can usually arrange transport from Europe or the Pacific Basin to the United States.

When dealing with medical evacuation in other parts of the world, it is advisable, and in some cases necessary, to deal with a European-based company. This is true when charter aircraft must be flown to Africa, Asia, the Middle East, the former Soviet Union, or Eastern Europe. American companies are too remote to provide this service, and they do not have the necessary flight clearances to enter many third world countries.

In certain situations, an air ambulance can be used to provide immediate evacuation from a remote area to a more advanced medical facility. For example, a patient might be flown from Egypt to Geneva, Switzerland, on a Learjet ambulance to receive lifesaving care. After initial treatment and stabilization, the patient might be flown on a stretcher-equipped commercial airliner to the United States for ongoing treatment and convalescence, if required. This last leg of the trip, since it is being done on a scheduled airliner, would be much less expensive than if done by Learjet.

Companies Providing Air Ambulance Services

If you look in the Yellow Pages of any big-city telephone book, you'll find numerous private air ambulance companies listed. What you can't be sure of is their quality. The following companies are well-established in the air ambulance-medevac field. They provide aircraft, flight doctors and nurses, trip coordinators, and worldwide communication capabilities. They can also arrange stretcher transport on commercial airliners. If a particular transport is outside a company's normal service area, they can make arrangements with another company or airline to provide the service for you directly.

A more extensive listing of air ambulance companies and assistance companies worldwide is found on the State Department's Web site **Medical Information for Americans Traveling Abroad** (http://travel.state.gov/medical.html).

U.S. and Canada-Based Companies

National Air Ambulance
Fort Lauderdale, FL
800-327-3710, 954-359-9900

Air Ambulance Professionals
Ft. Lauderdale, FL
800-752-4195

Care Flight International
Clearwater, FL
800-282-6878, 813-530-7972
(Also provides worldwide medical escorts and repatriation services)

Life Flight
Hermann Hospital
Houston, TX
800-231-4357

AAA Air Ambulance America
Austin, TX
512-479-800

Skyservice Lifeguard
Montreal and Ft. Lauderdale
800-463-3482

Aeromedical Services International
Las Vegas, NV
800-222-9993, 702-798-4600

Air Ambulance Incorporated
San Carlos, CA
800-982-5806, 702-798-4600

Critical Air Medicine
San Diego, CA
800-247-8326, 619-571-0482

Schaefer's Air Service
Van Nuys, CA
800-247-3355, 818-786-8713

AEA International/SOS
Seattle, WA and Singapore
800-468-5232, 206-340-6000
AEA International/SOS
Philadelphia, PA 31685
800-523-8930
Note: AEA International acquired SOS International in 1998

Caribbean/Mexico/Latin America
Bohlke Aviation International
Alexander Hamilton Airport
St. Croix, U.S. Virgin Islands
809-778-9177

Emergencia Aera Nacional
Mexico City
[52] (5)-655-3644 or (5)-573-2100

Vuelo de Vida (Life Flight)
Caracas, Venezuela
[58] (2) 919-054 or (2) 351-143

United Kingdom/Europe
Trans Care International
London, England
[44] (181)-993-6151

Heathrow Air Ambulance Services
London, England
[44] (181)-897-6185
Connecting Europe, the Middle East, North Africa, West Africa

Swiss Air Ambulance
Zurich, Switzerland
[41] (1)-383-1111
Extensive operations in Europe, Russia, Africa, the Middle East

Austrian Air Ambulance
Vienna, Austria
[43] (1)-401-44

German Air Rescue
Stuttgart, West Germany
[49] (711)-701-070

MEDIC'AIR International
Paris, France
[33] (0) 1-4172-1414
Advanced capability. Bilingual aeromedical personnel.

Compagnie Generale de Secours
Paris, France
[33] (0) 1-4747-6666

Euro-Flite Ltd.
Helsinki Int'l. Airport
Vantaa, Finland
[358] (0)-174-655

Jet Flite
Helsinki Int'l. Airport
Vantaa, Finland
[358] (0)-822-766

Turkey
M.A.R.M.
Izmir (Smyrna)
[90] (51)-633-322 or (51)-219-556

Israel
Herzliya Medical Center
Tel Aviv
[972] (9)-592-555
Provides air ambulance evacuation for the Middle East, the former Soviet Union, Africa, and the Eastern Mediterranean. Highly trained medical staff

East Africa
Flying Doctors Society
Nairobi, Kenya
Offers evacuation services from East Africa. Tourists can call about their insurance coverage.
[254] (2)-501-280 or (2)-336-886

Botswana/Zimbabwe/Zambia/ Mozambique
Medical Air Rescue Service, Ltd.
Belgravia, Harare, Zimbabwe
[263] (0)-73-45-13/14/15

South Africa
Medical Rescue International
Johannesburg, SA
[27] (11)-403-7080
Extensive assistance network in sub-Saharan Africa. Has mobile decompression chamber for diver emergencies

EuropAssistance
Johannesburg, SA
[27] (11)-315-3999

Medical Rescue International
Aukland Park, South Africa
[27] (11)-403-7080

India
East West Rescue
New Delhi, India
[91] (11)-698-865/623-738/698-554
Specializes in all of the Indian subcontinent & surrounding islands

SE Asia
AEA International
(Asia Emergency Assistance)
Singapore
[65] 338-2311 or 338-7800
Specializes in evacuations from Hong Kong, China, Far-East Asia, Pacific Rim, and westernmost Pacific islands

Heng-Gref Medical Services
Singapore
[65] 272-6028
Covers SE Asia and Indonesia.
Has assistance office in Bali

Medical Transport of the Overseas Employee
If you are an overseas employee and are sick or injured, your company can help arrange medical transportation to a local hospital. If the local hospital is not adequate, you may need to be flown to another hospital, perhaps in the United States. The following checklist will help your company arrange this type of transportation. They can do the following:

- Assess availability of local ground ambulance and rescue services.
- Establish ground ambulance access protocols. Determine if you will need a language interpreter in emergency situations. Suggestion: Contact the consular section of the U.S. Embassy, a United States consulate, or a corporate neighbor. Since they have already arranged emergency protocols for their own personnel, they can identify reliable English-speaking doctors and also relate their experience with local hospitals, pharmacies, and ambulance services.
- Formulate medical evacuation protocols for emergencies that can't be handled locally, including planning for disasters as well as individual medevac cases.
- Check availability of stretcher transport on commercial airlines for nonemergency cases.
- Establish access and credit arrangements with an international air ambulance company such as Swiss Air Rescue, EuropAssistance, International SOS

Assistance, or one of the other companies listed in this chapter. Commercial airliners will not transport emergency cases.
- Determine if exit visas or other formalities are required.
- Provide on-site employees with 24-hour telephone or telex number(s) of an assistance company, and/or the home office, in case of a medical emergency.

18 Business Travel & Health

Business travel is increasingly international in scope, and more companies are taking steps to protect the health and safety of their employees who are traveling or living abroad. The reason? Business travelers may be at significant risk for travel-related health problems.

Business travel is different from tourism. In addition to the multitude of tropical and infectious diseases that the business or corporate traveler may be exposed to, these travelers are often under higher stress due to job performance requirements, tight schedules, sudden departures, separation from home and family—plus the increased fear of kidnapping and terrorism. If you are on a long-term assignment overseas, not only you but also your spouse must also deal with culture shock and must need to adapt to living abroad.

TRIP PREPARATION

As a corporate or business traveler, you need to maintain a high degree of personal health at home, know your medical history, and have access to your medical records. You should maintain a close relationship with your corporate medical department. If your company does not have a medical department, contact a travelers' clinic for advice. Prior to departure, you should be updated on all routine immunizations and receive, as necessary, any trip-specific immunizations.

- **Routine immunizations**—These immunizations should be kept up-to-date and include the following:
  - Tetanus/diphtheria (Td)
  - Polio
  - Measles/mumps/rubella (MMR)
  - Varicella (chickenpox)
  - Pneumococcal
  - Influenza (for Southern Hemisphere travel between May and September, additional influenza vaccination may be necessary)

- **Trip-specific immunizations**—Because departures to an overseas assignment can be on short notice, corporate travelers may not have enough time to receive certain immunizations (such as hepatitis B) that must be given over 2–3 visits. Therefore, your medical department or a travel clinic should administer ahead of time those immunizations that may be necessary for future travel. Consideration should be given to the administration of the following specialized vaccines: hepatitis A, hepatitis B, meningococcal, rabies, typhoid, and yellow fever. A baseline PPD skin test for tuberculosis should also be administered.

Keep your *International Certificate of Vaccination* for yellow fever current if your job requires a possible departure on short notice to a country requiring this vaccination for entry. This certificate isn't valid until ten days after receiving the yellow fever vaccination. If time is short, have the certificate backdated, but some health-care providers may hesitate to do this. Not having a valid vaccination certificate could mean being quarantined, being denied entry to a country, or, even worse, being given an injection with an unsterile needle or syringe.

Hepatitis A—Especially review your immunization status with regard to hepatitis A, which is highly prevalent in all lesser-developed countries. Hepatitis A is the most common vaccine-preventable disease in the world and vaccination will give long-lasting protection, even if administered just prior to departure. Hepatitis A vaccination is now considered practically routine for foreign travel. NOTE: Immune globulin is now rarely given, even when travelers depart on short notice.

Hepatitis B—Immunization is recommended for health-care workers; expected exposure to blood and/or body fluids; stays of over 3 months, or frequent short-stays in moderate- to high-risk countries; when there is the possibility of receiving medical or dental injections abroad; and the possibility of new sexual partner(s) during stay. Counseling on body fluid/blood precautions and safe sex is strongly recommended prior to departure.

Sexually acquired hepatitis B may be a significant threat to the health of corporate travelers. A study in the *British Medical Journal* reported a 50% exposure to the hepatitis B virus over a five-year period in expatriate male company employees in Southeast Asia. Sexual contact with the local populace was the apparent mode of transmission. Males, especially those traveling to either Asia or sub-Saharan Africa, where there is a high incidence of hepatitis B, and who want maximum protection against hepatitis B, should (1) practice safe sex, (2) practice abstinence, and/or (3) get immunized against hepatitis B.

- **Medication**—Have with you medication, if necessary, for the prevention or treatment of travel-related diseases such as motion sickness, mountain sickness, travelers' diarrhea, jet lag (short-acting sleeping pill?), and malaria.
- **Start medication**—If you're going to a malarious area and your doctor has prescribed the prophylactic drug mefloquine, start this medication two weeks prior to departure. This time period will ensure protective blood levels of the drug and reveal if you'll have side effects.

Under special circumstances, your health-care provider might start you on short-term course (two weeks maximum) of prophylactic antibiotics to prevent travelers' diarrhea. This might be justified if your project demands your complete availability and physical well-being and you will be at high risk of illness.

- **Other medication**—Carry enough of any medication that you might regularly use for the treatment of any chronic medical condition, such as high blood pressure or diabetes.

  Medical kit/travel supplies—Obtain a travel kit that contains basic first-aid supplies, plus analgesics, antacids, a quinolone antibiotic for treating travelers' diarrhea, loperamide (Imodium), antimalarial drugs (if needed), and perhaps a short-acting sleeping pill for jet lag. Mosquito repellents and permethrin clothing spray are very important when traveling to a country where there is the risk of malaria or other insect-transmitted diseases. A permethrin-treated mosquito net is often useful. (See checklist "Medical and personal care items" in Chapter 1.)
- **Avoid unsafe injections**—It's virtually impossible to get infected with HIV or the hepatitis B virus if you avoid unsafe injections and unscreened blood transfusions—and don't have sexual contact with high-risk persons. Although getting an unsafe injection overseas is unlikely, such instances can occur when travelers receive emergency medical or dental treatment in hospitals or clinics in lesser-developed countries. Many health-care facilities abroad can't afford disposable needles and syringes, so these items are often recycled, usually without sterilization. Because of this situation, some travelers now carry kits stocked with sterile needles and syringes, suture supplies, and, in some cases, intravenous fluids, in case they need injections, wound repair, or IV fluids.
- **HIV testing**—See if this applies to you. Test results are required by about 50 countries for long-stay travelers as a condition for granting certain types of visas. Country-specific testing requirements are available on the Internet (*http://travel.state.gov/HIVtestingreqs.html*).
- **Medical care abroad**— Know how to find, or arrange for, medical care (and medications) abroad. (Chapter 15)
- **Travel insurance**—Have sufficient medical insurance that will cover illness abroad, and will provide for emergency medical evacuation, if necessary. You should purchase travel health insurance if your company does not have a program to (1) pay your hospital bills on the spot or (2) evacuate you in event of serious illness or injury. The best travel policies also provide telephone access to an emergency assistance center through a 24-hour hotline. At the assistance center, medically trained multilingual personnel can monitor your condition and, if necessary, arrange emergency transportation if your treatment in a local hospital is inadequate. In Chapter 16, you'll find a list of other companies that underwrite travel health insurance.
- **Medical assistance**—An alternative method of protecting a traveling employee is for a company to purchase travel assistance directly. Your firm sets up a credit account with an assistance company. They monitor your medical care, provide direct payments to overseas doctors and hospitals from your account, and arrange air ambulance evacuation, if necessary. Contact **Medex Assistance Corporation** (410-453-6300), **International SOS** (800-523-8930), **USAssist** (800-756-5900), or **MedLink** (602-417-3385).

KIDNAPPING AND TERRORISM

You may be concerned not only about your health but also about your physical safety. What are the risks of being kidnapped, hijacked, or taken hostage? What's the best way to reduce these risks? How should you react in a terrorist incident? When traveling to a hostile or unstable country, what rules should you follow to maintain a low profile? These and many other questions increasingly concern today's business traveler, and rightly so. Multinational corporations and their employees are often the target of dissident groups who are trying to make a political statement or to extort money.

Preparing for a Safe Trip

If your company has a corporate security division, contact that office for a briefing. You also need to start some essential background reading. Suggested titles include *The Safe Travel Book—A Guide for the International Traveler* by Peter Savage (Lexington Books; 800-462-6420; $13), *The Security Connection for Family Protection* by Issy Boim (Air Security International; 800-502-5814; $30), and *The Safety Minute: 01* by Robert L. Siciliano (Safety Zone Press: 800-438-6223; $15).

Safe Travel Tips

Don't
- Dress like a high-profile businessperson.
- Carry expensive luggage.
- Display tickets from U.S. airlines.
- Wear shirts or hats with logos of U.S. corporations.
- Carry English-language publications in plain view.

Do
- Take a nonstop flight.
- Send sensitive documents separately.
- Leave detailed itinerary at the office.
- Carry medical evacuation insurance.
- Check Department of State travel warnings and advisories (see Introduction).

Risk Management

Risk management firms, usually run by former employees of the State Department or CIA, have sprung up to meet the security needs of multinational corporations and certain high-risk travelers. These firms do more than just arrange kidnap insurance. They can do the following:

- Train employees to reduce their risk of being taken hostage.
- Conduct counterterrorism-training seminars.
- Provide personal security training.
- Prepare a crisis management plan.
- Negotiate hostage release.

- Provide antikidnapping equipment (for example, armored cars).
- Alert you to which airlines are under increased terrorist threat (and advise appropriate travel alternatives).
- Provide detailed security advisory prior to travel to a high-risk country.

A well-known firm is listed below. Kidnap insurance is arranged through their affiliated underwriter.

➤ **The Ackerman Group, Inc.**
1666 Kennedy Causeway
Miami Beach, FL 33141
(305-865-0072)

➤ **Air Security International**
2925 Briarpark Drive, 7th floor
Houston, TX 77042
713-430-7300
www.airsecurity.com

Control Risk Group
17499 Old Meadow Road, suite 120
McLean , VA 22102
703-893-0083
www.control-risk.com

Parvus International/Armor Group
1401 K Street, NW, 10th floor
Washington, DC 20005
202-289-5600
www.armorgroup.com

BUSINESS TRAVEL AND STRESS

Your Health May Be at Risk

Business travel can be stimulating and rewarding, but it also can be stressful to the point of jeopardizing your health. In fact, a study by the Hyatt Hotels Corporation found that business travel lasting more than 5.2 days interfered significantly with a traveler's personal life.

The problem is more than just chronic jet lag. Frequent departures on short notice, high-pressure work schedules, job-performance anxiety, living in hotels and motels, traveling alone and feeling isolated, eating calorie-dense restaurant and airline food, and not exercising all take their toll. Add to this being separated from your home, your family, and your usual routines. No wonder you feel depressed and lonely—even disoriented at times. You may start to smoke and drink too much—or overeat. You need a sleeping pill at night and then a tranquilizer in the morning. Fatigue mounts and performance suffers. Things spiral downward. The possible outcome? Burnout—or worse. You need a plan.

- Start with physical fitness. A regular exercise program promotes physical and mental health. Exercising also helps control your weight and combats insomnia. Not being fit can lower your self-esteem. What's the best exercise? It's the one you like doing, but experts often recommend either walking or jogging. You can do them almost anywhere, without charge, and they build aerobic stamina.
- Plan the exercise activities you want to pursue during your trip and pack the necessary equipment: footwear, gym gear, bathing suit, tennis racquet, etc. Take into account the climate (how hot?) and the geography (seashore? mountains?) at your destination.
- Stay in hotels that cater to travelers interested in fitness. Ask about the facilities when you make your reservation. Most major hotels and resorts now have workout rooms and health clubs. Is there a also swimming pool? Tennis courts? The Hyatt, Hilton, and Marriott even provide guests with information on dealing with all types of stress.
- Use a guidebook to plan walking tours of local tourist attractions, museums, scenic areas, etc. If possible, walk to your business appointments. Wear walking shoes made by companies such as Rockport—many models are also formal enough for business dress.

Emotional needs of travelers—In addition to exercise and diet, you need to care for your emotional and psychological needs.

- Keep in close touch with your office and family. Carry some photos of your spouse and children, or close friend. Write postcards and letters. Keep a diary. Take pictures. Buy gifts and souvenirs to bring home.
- Carry playing cards, a board game, a walkman with your favorite cassettes (or foreign language tapes), and a shortwave radio to listen to music and news on the Voice of America or the BBC. The Grundig 7-band short wave radio ($99 from **Magellan's**; 800-962-4943) is a good choice.
- If you are a recovering alcoholic, find out if there is a local AA chapter or other self-help group in the area. For a directory of AA chapters overseas, contact: **AA World Services**, P.O. Box 459, Grand Central Station, New York, NY 10163; or call 212-686-1100. Price: 75 cents.
- Research your destination. Find out as much as possible about the country you're in, its history, and its culture. Make it a project to learn something specific about some aspect of the culture. If you can speak some of the language, do this as much as possible.
- Turn your trip into a psychic adventure. Stripped of your ordinary surroundings, your friends and family, and your usual routine, you may be forced into a

more direct experience with your new surroundings and yourself. This can be painful, but don't retreat. View your new surroundings not only in terms of work but as an opportunity to learn and grow.

Long-Term Assignments and Stress

If you are being assigned to an overseas post, and will be living abroad for many months, or even years, you and your family will encounter additional stresses. If your spouse and children are traveling with you, how will they adjust? Studies show that spouses (usually the wife of a busy executive) bear the greatest burden adapting to overseas living. Today, most companies anticipate these stresses and provide appropriate counseling. Predeparture orientation and counseling can have a dramatic effect on your psychological well-being and the success of your trip.

To better prepare for your trip also consider the following:

- Survival Kit for Overseas Living—Widely used guide for adapting to living abroad. $7.95 plus $2 shipping: Item #306.
- *Going International*—Videotape on cross-cultural orientation and training. $12.95 plus $2 shipping: Item #535.
- Culture Shock—Explores the psychological consequences of exposure to unfamiliar environments. Includes a section on adjustment experiences of business executives. $15.95 plus $2 shipping: Item #578.

Contact the **Intercultural Press, Inc.**, P.O. Box 700, Yarmouth, ME 04096, 207-846-5168, for their catalog or to order directly.

Stages of adjustment—What happens when you are uprooted and sent overseas to live and work? Research has delved into the lives of people stationed abroad in order to analyze their psychological reactions to their new environment. These studies show that adaptation will typically occur in three phases.

- Phase 1. You experience an initial period of excitement and well-being, usually lasting about a month. You then start to "come down" as the reality of life in a foreign country sets in.
- Phase 2. This is a period of disillusionment, usually lasting several months. The disillusionment may be with your host country, your work, or both. Instead of acknowledging your feelings, you may instead experience physical symptoms such as fatigue, headaches, and stomach problems and pass these off as simple stress. You, or your spouse, may even become overtly depressed. In this case, you should seek psychological counseling. (Some employees, or their spouses, don't get over this phase. They can't adapt to their new environment and consequently reconsider their decision to remain abroad.)
- Phase 3. After about six months, you will have adjusted to your new life in a foreign country. You will also have picked up some of the language, your children will have adjusted to school, your home will be established, and social connections made.

From *Traveling Healthy* newsletter—August 2000

International business travel is big business. The employees of some large corporations log tens of thousands of international missions per year— "mission" is corporate parlance for business trip—making travel stress an important economic and human resource problem. The World Bank, for example, based in Washington, D.C., sends about 5,000 employees and consultants on more than 18,000 overseas missions a year for 250,000 person-days away from home, the largest number of business travelers from one organization. Their annual travel budget is a staggering $120,000,000.

The number of international business travelers continues to increase rapidly, perhaps doubling every decade or so, an increase that is likely to continue. To date, the predicted large-scale replacement of business travel with ever more sophisticated telecommunications, including teleconferencing, has not materialized and may never do so.

The impetus for the World Bank to organize a symposium on stress and business travel in May 2000 was several findings by its own employees, reported in two published studies. One study reports that the bank's employees who travel frequently see physicians and other health-care professionals about three times as often as a matched group of employees who do not travel (**Occup Environ Med 1997;54:499-503.**). Traveling males are 80% more likely to see a health-care professional than matched nontraveling males; while for women, those who travel are 18% more likely to see a health-care professional than matched females who don't travel. Although many of the complaints deal with known travel-related health hazards (e.g., infectious diseases), there is a striking number of psychological complaints. The number of psychological complaints increases as the number of missions per year increase, and the increase is steeper for female travelers than for male travelers.

The other report found that employees on missions tend to feel a strong sense of social and emotional concern for their families and a sense of isolation (**Occup Environ Med 1999;56:245-252**). These traveling employees believe that there is a strong association between such stresses and their physical and emotional health, making frequent international business travel an important, previously overlooked occupational medicine concern. While these findings are those of World Bank employees, the panel of experts at the symposia who were from other corporations readily agreed with the conclusions. Moreover, it is reasonable to assume that the countless business travelers who work for small companies, or who are self-employed, experience similar stress-related problems. Previous studies, performed among both travelers and nontravelers, have shown that an accumulation of work-related psychological stress is associated with physical illness, including a general perception of poor health, cardiovascular disease, and mental health problems. The World Bank studies also found, somewhat surprisingly, that many factors are *not* important determinants of stress, including geographic areas of the world visited, number of time zones crossed, having children at home under the age of 18, satisfaction with work, days off overseas, and length of the mission.

Yet in spite of the frequent complaints raised by business travelers, few missions end in total failure, meaning that it is very rare for a business traveler to return home prematurely because of stress-related problems. But stress does seem to cause many hard-to-quantify, less-than-optimum work performances. Failures are far more common among employees posted overseas (i.e., away for more than six months), and in most cases such failures are due to coping problems experienced overseas by accompanying dependents, rather than employees. In financial terms, each such failure costs employers tens of thousands of dollars in actual costs (less employee training and relocation expenses), and additional lost revenue from disruption of business.

Causes of Stress •

International business travelers experience stressors:

➢ the routine discomforts and annoyances that all long-distance travelers encounter, such as planning the trip, hassles of getting to and through airports, altered eating and sleeping patterns, changes in climate, safety concerns; and
➢ challenges unique to frequent, long-distance business travelers. These fall into three general categories (two already touched upon):
  • concerns about the effects of frequent and extended travel on one's physical and psychological well-being, the effects of jetlag, loneliness, and fear of dangerous ground transportation in many developing countries;
  • the effects on one's family of repeatedly being away from home which is by far the most frequently cited cause of travel-related stress in self-assessment questionnaires, with the number of missions per year an important determinant;
  • the workload that business travelers are expected to accomplish on each mission and the amount of work awaiting them upon their return to the office, workloads frequently perceived as "unreasonable." During the mission, stressful activities may include having to make decisions away from the office without the usual office support system, communicating in foreign languages, operating in an unfamiliar business culture, and spending long hours in negotiations.

The spouse at home often feels abandoned, worries about the traveler's safety, and is sometimes concerned about infidelity. Spouses without children tend to experience stress either before or after the mission; spouses with children primarily experience stress during the mission.

Strategies for Dealing with Stress

Here are some realistic strategies recommended by symposium participants for alleviating stresses when traveling overseas on business.

- **Better selection of employees for travel**—Since about a third of business travelers do not complain of travel-related stress, there are clearly differences in people regarding this issue, but little is known about these differences. Perhaps psychological tests could be developed to better screen job applicants for positions that involve extensive travel.

Employers should be more candid with job applicants about how much travel a position requires, which is not always the case today. Job descriptions sometimes change and non-travel positions can suddenly become travel intensive. Promotions within an organization can also change travel requirements. Job applicants should be apprised of the fact that in many organizations experience gained in missions is an important consideration in promotion. Moreover, overseas travel is often appealing to young (perhaps, unmarried) job seekers, but it becomes tedious and stressful after time.

- **Flexible scheduling of travel to allow more time at home**—Corporate travel budgets are often "penny wise and pound foolish." Cost considerations sometimes force travelers to be away on a Saturday night or to use an airline with limited scheduling flexibility. Ideally, business travelers should be able to return home before weekends and leave home after weekends. When possible, employees should be consulted about the timing of their missions. There should also be realistic limits to the amount of time an employee can spend away from home per year. In fact, many organizations have such limits, but they are rarely followed. Moreover, in many organizations, the official policy of reduced travel assignments is looked down upon by immediate superiors.

- **Travel schedules and work assignments reviewed by senior staff members who have "been there, done that."**—Realistic scheduling from a human resource point of view may require days off from work before a mission and again on return in order to take care of both family chores and office matters. Family chores may involve seemingly mundane tasks such as paying bills, servicing the car, and other tasks that, ideally, should not be left for the stay-at-home spouse. Female business travelers seem to have a tougher time preparing for their absences than do males, perhaps because females are generally more involved with arranging for baby sitters and carpools, for example.

Office workload tends to increase just before a mission—doing routine work plus preparing for the mission—and immediately upon return. Optimum office scheduling may dictate that several days be devoted exclusively to the mission before departure, with no other work assignments, a day or two of "debriefing" upon return, and another day or so to be spent handling desk work and computer work that has piled up.

- **Minimize trip cancellations and date changing**—It is extremely disruptive to frequent business travelers' personal lives to experience repeated changes in travel schedules, which happens quite frequently, albeit often unavoidably. Having to reschedule missions often requires rescheduling family obligations that have already been changed. Employees should be given the option to decline missions if this happens frequently.
- **Counselors to help with the "nuts and bolts" of overseas travel**—Experts can help travelers cope with many of the basic travel issues (e.g., health and safety concerns). In fact, many corporations already have in-house medical departments, sometimes even travel clinics, and some organizations even maintain extensive Web sites to help business travelers better plan trips; however, many travelers do not utilize such available facilities.

Preparing to Leave

The effects of a parent's frequent absence from home on children are not well understood, but presumably they have a negative impact on children; sometimes children show anger, especially when a parent is away for an important event. (However, according to one boy who was interviewed, "My father being away on a trip makes little difference. When he is home he spends so much time at the office that he is never home anyway.") The impact can, perhaps, be minimized by scheduling special family events prior to departure (e.g., a day in the park, a day trip, or a visit to a favorite restaurant). It may also be beneficial to have young children accompany the departing parent to the airport, discuss the itinerary and look at maps, and be provided with books and videotapes about the countries the parent will be visiting.

Coping Overseas and Staying in Touch with Home

Travelers should stay in close touch with spouses and children back home, using regular mail, the telephone, and e-mail, even if the traveler has to bear the costs, which are high. Some organizations cover the cost of daily e-mail and telephone; those organizations that do not cover such costs should be encouraged to do so. Children like to receive regular mail, even though the parents may call or e-mail daily. E-mail appears to be a very effective way for a parent to stay in touch with a child old enough to use a computer. Sending audiocassettes and videos from overseas may help smaller children. According to some experts, adolescents are the most difficult age group with which to maintain a long distance relationship. Some can be interested in the purpose of the mission and kept informed of day-to-day developments, but most adolescents don't care about that either.

Children and spouses at home—Children appear to require more personal attention while one parent is away traveling. They appear more comfortable with familiar routines rather than additional changes (e.g., staying at home rather than being shifted off to a grandparent). Some children seem to find comfort in marking off the days on a calendar until the parent returns home.

Support groups consisting of other families of business travelers working for the same organization and living in one neighborhood appear to be very helpful for spouses at home.

Returning home.
Close to 100% of spouses describe their returning mates as being irritable and withdrawn when they return home, probably the effects of fatigue and stress. Awareness of such behavior helps families deal with it. It's best to postpone any coming-home celebrations for a few days. Travelers should try to return home before a weekend, if possible.

Taking children on work trips is no longer the sole prerogative of Hollywood stars with a legion of nannies, or the last recourse of desperate single parents, says the **International Herald Tribune** (May 12, 2000). Surprisingly, it is a commonplace choice around the world and is often encouraged or at least tolerated by the employer; some of them are even willing to foot the bill. In the United States last year, more than 23 million trips were made with one or more children in tow, about 11% of all business trips. Parents who take children along say it is educational and entertaining and helps build family togetherness. Most parents interviewed believe travel is worth missing a few days of school. Frequent flyer miles often help pay the bill if the boss won't.

There are no figures for how frequently children accompany parents on international business trips, but the percentage is probably far smaller than it is for domestic travel. The obvious reason is the cost. Trips are generally longer and may interfere excessively with children's school and spouses' work schedules, and most destinations are not exactly London, Hawaii, or Hong Kong, but rather dull, uncomfortable, and, occasionally, dangerous locations.

19 Travel & Pregnancy

If you are a healthy woman with an uncomplicated pregnancy, you do not necessarily need to curtail reasonable travel. According to the American College of Obstetricians and Gynecologists, the best time for travel is during the second trimester when your body has adjusted to the pregnancy but is not so bulky that moving about is difficult. The second trimester is also safer because the probability of miscarriage is less. After the sixth month, the risk of premature labor and other complications increase.

When to Limit Travel

A brief trip to major European cities during the second trimester represents a far safer scenario than an extended trip to a developing country where you might have potential exposure to exotic illnesses, as well limited access to medical care. *If you will be far away from expert medical and obstetrical care, and/or have increased exposure to travel-related diseases, such as malaria, then you should consider deferring travel until after delivery.*

After the 28th week—Most obstetricians advise their patients not to travel beyond a 100-mile radius after the 28th week. Problems after this time include increased risk of premature labor, preterm rupture of membranes, development of hypertension, phlebitis, and increased risk of uterine and placental injury should you be involved in a motor vehicle accident.

Pretravel Checklist

A careful assessment of your medical and obstetrical history, and your current state of health, is mandatory prior to departure. It should include the following:

- Obstetrical history—Have you had any of the following conditions?
  (1) spontaneous abortion (miscarriage) (2) ectopic pregnancy (3) toxemia
  (4) premature labor (5) incompetent cervix (6) prolonged labor
  (7) caesarean section (8) premature rupture of membranes
  (9) uterine or placental abnormalities (10) hypertension
  (11) pelvic inflammatory disease (12) phlebitis or pulmonary embolism
  (13) D (Rho) negative blood group (14) severe morning sickness

- Medical history—Do you:

(1) Have diabetes? Take insulin? (2) Take medication for any other illness? (3) Have symptomatic congenital or acquired heart disease? (4) Have anemia, asthma, epilepsy, phlebitis, or any other significant medical illnesses? (5) Get severe motion sickness? (6) Have significant allergies?
- The current pregnancy—Do you have any immediate obstetrical complications (e.g., preeclampsia)?
- Personal comfort—Will it be manageable and acceptable during your trip?
- The duration of your trip—Will it be more than a few days? Will travel require prolonged sitting?
- The destination—Is it more than 100 miles from home?
- The quality and availability of medical and obstetrical care in the countries on your itinerary—Is it available and adequate?

Medical clearance for travel—After reviewing the foregoing checklists, your doctor will be able to discuss with you the relative safety of your travel plans and offer appropriate advice.

Prenatal Checkups

You should have your first prenatal appointment at 10 weeks. The fetal heart tones are usually heard by this time, and their presence is reassuring that your pregnancy is probably proceeding normally. Once fetal heart tones are heard, the chance of spontaneous miscarriage is small. You then should have checkups every four weeks until week 30, then every two weeks until week 36, then weekly until delivery. Travel plans should not interfere with these important checkups.

Pelvic ultrasound—Before leaving, discuss with your obstetrician the advisability of having a pelvic ultrasound examination to check for tubal pregnancy, multifetal pregnancy, or placental abnormalities.

Medical Care Abroad

All travelers should ask "What will I do if an emergency arises?" Before leaving home, learn as much as possible about the availability and quality of obstetrical and medical care in the countries on your itinerary. Unfortunately, most doctors won't be of much help because few physicians or obstetricians are familiar with foreign doctors and hospitals. A travelers' clinic is better able to assist you. U.S. Embassies and Consulates overseas usually have lists of local English-speaking physicians and can give a referral. (Ask which physicians the embassy staff personally would use.)

IAMAT—Travelers can obtain a listing of English-speaking doctors overseas by contacting IAMAT (the International Association for Medical Assistance to Travelers) at 519-836-0102. The list is free but a membership donation to this tax-free foundation is encouraged. **Personal Physicians Worldwide** in Washington, DC, will identify and personally call physicians overseas to ensure their availability during your trip. Travelers get a wallet card with the names and numbers of selected physicians who are on the staff of the preferred hospitals at your destination. Tel: 888-657-8114.

Travel insurance—Travelers going to a lesser-developed country should purchase a supplemental travel health insurance policy that provides a worldwide 24-hour medical assistance hotline number. This type of policy puts you in telephone contact with medical personnel who can help arrange emergency medical consultation and treatment, monitor care, and provide emergency evacuation to a more advanced medical facility, if necessary.

NOTE: Travel insurance policies won't cover medical expenses associated with a normal pregnancy (e.g., delivery). Some policies don't cover complications in the third trimester. Other policies don't cover miscarriage, which is usually a first trimester problem. Check if the policy covers the neonate. You should compare the various policies and read their exclusions before buying one. The following companies' policies cover complications of pregnancy through the third trimester:

Worldwide Assistance Services, Inc.
1133 15th St., Suite 400
Washington, DC 20005
800-821-2828

AEA International/ SOS
Box 11568
Philadelphia, PA 31685
800-523-8930

Calling home—Travelers should always carry their doctor's telephone number or e-mail address with them. It's usually possible to call the United States or Canada when problems arise and the traveler wants direct advice from the physician who knows her best. In addition, providing the personal physician's phone number to overseas physicians may be extremely helpful during an emergency.

Obstetrical Emergencies

Review with your doctor those signs and symptoms that indicate a possible obstetrical emergency and seek immediate, *qualified* obstetrical care if you have any of the following:

- Vaginal bleeding
- Passing of tissue or blood clots
- Lower abdominal pain, cramps, or contractions
- Gush of watery fluid from vagina
- Headaches, blurred vision, ankle swelling, high blood pressure, or seizures

Other causes of illness should not be overlooked. Abdominal pain, for example, does not necessarily indicate that you have an obstetrical emergency. You could have appendicitis, a urinary tract infection, or merely simple indigestion. Diagnosing the cause of abdominal pain is usually more difficult during pregnancy. *Readily available, high-quality medical care is essential if you develop worrisome symptoms.*

Symptoms that may be no cause for concern (but if persistent should be evaluated) include the following:

- Increased urination • fatigue • insomnia • heartburn • indigestion
- Constipation • slight increase in vaginal discharge
- Sore, bleeding gums • leg cramps • occasional mild dizziness
- Mild swelling around ankles • hemorrhoids

TRAUMA DURING PREGNANCY

Motor vehicle accidents—Accidents are the leading cause of death in travelers under the age of 55, and motor vehicle accidents are responsible for most cases of blunt trauma to pregnant women. Maternal mortality is increased sixfold and fetal mortality fivefold when the woman is ejected from the vehicle. Consequently, the use of seatbelts is recommended to decrease maternal and fetal trauma. Use of a lap belt alone, however, has been implicated in placental injury and fetal injury. The best protection is provided by the diagonal shoulder strap with a lap belt. The straps should be above and below the abdominal bulge, thus distributing the energy of impact over the anterior chest and pelvis, as shown in Figure 17.1

Figure 17.1 Proper position of seat belt when pregnant. Place the lap belt well below the abdomen and as low as possible over the pelvic bones. A thin blanket between the belt and your body may increase comfort.

Falls—Women in their third trimester tend to have more falls. Eighty percent of these falls occur after the 32nd week and are mostly due to fatigue, a fainting spell, a protruberant abdomen, a loss of balance and coordination, and increased joint mobility, especially looseness of the pelvic joints. Most of these third trimester falls are usually minor but some might require you to undergo a brief period of observation or fetal monitoring.

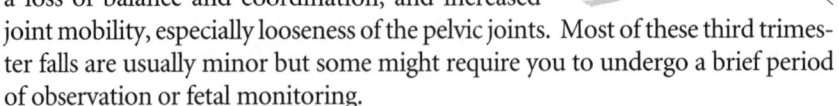

Abruptio placentae (placental separation)—A direct blow to your abdomen is more apt to injure the placenta than the fetus. Mild abdominal trauma may cause placental separation in 1% to 5% of cases. Major blunt abdominal trauma causes separation in 20% to 50% of cases. Symptoms of abruptio placentae are typically abdominal pain and vaginal bleeding.

Fetal monitoring—Early detection and treatment of abruptio placentae is critical in order to prevent fetal death and preserve the mother's health. Fetal monitoring as early as the 20th week of pregnancy can predict abruptio placentae. Studies show that there is frequent uterine activity—more than eight uterine contractions per hour—during the first few hours of monitoring after trauma in virtually all patients in whom abruptio placentae eventually occurs. Monitoring is advised, however, only after the stage of fetal viability (approximately 24 weeks) since no therapy exists for the treatment of fetal distress prior to this developmental stage. Concern for maternal health is the only indication for hospitalization prior to the stage of fetal viability.

Ultrasound—Ultrasonography has been advocated to expedite the diagnosis of abruption but may be unreliable. Fetal monitoring (cardiotocographic monitoring) is superior. Ultrasound is useful to (1) determine fetal well-being if monitoring is equivocal, (2) measure fetal heart rate and verify fetal cardiac activity if fetal death is suspected, or (3) estimate the volume of amniotic fluid if there is a question of ruptured membranes.

When to monitor—If you sustain a direct abdominal blow or a motor vehicle accident (with or without direct abdominal trauma), then you should have continuous monitoring for at least 4 hours, provided the monitoring is begun promptly after the injury.

If you sustain minor trauma, a short period of monitoring or observation is usually indicated.

If fetal monitoring is not immediately possible, you should contact a physician immediately if you have any of the following warning symptoms: vaginal bleeding, leak of fluid from the vagina, decrease in or lack of fetal motion, severe abdominal pain around the uterus, rhythmic contractions, dizziness, or fainting.

VACCINATIONS DURING PREGNANCY

If you are pregnant (or think you might be pregnant or anticipate you may become pregnant while traveling), an immunization strategy for international travel may present special problems. The problem is weighing the peril and benefit of the vaccine against the risk of contracting a serious, possibly life-threatening infection. For many vaccines there are simply no studies documenting their safety in pregnancy, but they are considered safe, on a theoretical basis if indicated by the perceived risk. If possible, your immunizations should be given after the first trimester.

Immunizations Routinely Given During Pregnancy

- **Influenza:** CDC recommends that all women who will be beyond the first trimester of pregnancy (≥ 14 weeks gestation) during the influenza season should be immunized. If you are pregnant and have a medical condition that increases your risk for complications from influenza, you should be vaccinated before the influenza season, regardless of the stage of pregnancy. Be aware that the flu season in the Southern Hemisphere is in our summer.
- **Tetanus-Diphtheria (Td):** This vaccine is routinely indicated for susceptible pregnant women. It is even more important that your Td immunization be current if there is the possibility that your delivery may occur under unhygienic conditions.

Immunizations That May Be Administered during Pregnancy, But Only If Indicated By a Definite Increased Risk of Exposure

- **Cholera:** This vaccine is no longer available in the United States and is not recommended for travel. There is no data regarding its safety in pregnancy.
- **Hepatitis A:** The safety of hepatitis A vaccine during pregnancy has not been determined, but the theoretical risk to the fetus is expected to be very low. Recommended if you are not immune and plan to travel to a developing country.
- **Hepatitis B:** Hepatitis B vaccine is considered safe and may be administered in pregnancy if indicated by the risk of exposure.
- **Japanese Encephalitis:** Significant side effects are possible, including fever, angioedema, and hypotension. There is no data regarding safety in pregnancy. You should receive this vaccine only if travel to an endemic area is unavoidable and your risk of exposure will be significant.
- **Lyme Disease:** Vaccination of women who are known to be pregnant is not recommended.
- **Meningococcal:** This vaccine may be given during pregnancy if you have a substantial risk of exposure.
- **Pneumococcal (polysaccharide):** If you are a candidate for this vaccine, usually because of a chronic infectious or metabolic state, every attempt should be made to administer it before you become pregnant. The vaccine may be given during pregnancy if you have a substantial risk of exposure.
- **Polio:** A one-time booster with IPV (inactivated polio vaccine) is indicated prior to international travel.
- **Rabies:** This vaccine, by either the intramuscular or intradermal route, may be given if there is potential risk of exposure.
- **Typhoid:** The Typhim Vi injectable vaccine is indicated for travelers at risk. It is safe and requires only a single dose. The oral Ty21a vaccine (Vivotif-Berna) is not routinely recommended since it is a live-bacterial vaccine.
- **Yellow Fever:** Although this is a live-virus vaccine, you should receive it if you will be at significant risk in a yellow fever endemic area. Ideally, travel to areas requiring yellow fever vaccination should be delayed until after delivery.

Per WHO, yellow fever vaccine may be given after the sixth month of pregnancy if there is substantial risk of exposure. Get a waiver letter from your physician if vaccine is required solely to comply with international travel requirements.

Immunizations Contraindicated During Pregnancy

- **Measles, Mumps, Rubella (MMR):** These are live-virus vaccines and should never be given alone, or in combination, in pregnancy. If you are not sure about your immunization status, you can be tested for immunity to these diseases. Do not become pregnant for at least 3 months after receiving this vaccine.
- **Varicella (Chickenpox):** This is a live-virus vaccine and should never be given in pregnancy. If you are not sure about your immunization status, you can be

tested for immunity. Chickenpox is a particularly serious disease in pregnancy and every attempt should be made to give this vaccine before any pregnancy. Avoid becoming pregnant for at least 1 month after receiving this vaccine.

MALARIA

Malaria is the most important insect-transmitted disease you need to avoid, especially the falciparum variety. The disease is more severe in pregnancy, due in part to a decrease in immunity that allows a higher percentage of red blood cells to be infected by parasites, as well as the fact that the placenta is a preferential site of sequestration of parasitized red blood cells.

Maternal complications of falciparum malaria include profound hypoglycemia (low blood sugar), increased anemia, kidney failure, adult respiratory distress syndrome, shock, and coma. Maternal mortality rates up to 10% can occur. Obstetrical complications of malaria include spontaneous miscarriage, premature delivery, stillbirth, and neonatal deaths. Vivax malaria is associated with greater anemia and lower birthweight, but not miscarriage or stillbirth.

You are best advised to avoid elective travel to malarious areas, especially areas where chloroquine-resistant malaria is endemic (e.g., sub-Saharan Africa, Oceania). If you must travel to a malarious area, it is imperative to (1) prevent mosquito bites and (2) take an effective prophylactic drug.

Prevention

Mosquito bites—Protection against insect bites is important in the tropics. Malaria, dengue fever, Lyme disease, and other insect-transmitted diseases can seriously affect both you and the fetus. The first line of defense against malaria—and the best—is to prevent bites by mosquitoes. You should apply an insect repellent containing 30%–35% of DEET to exposed skin and treat your clothing with permethrin. This combination is 99%–100% effective in preventing mosquito bites. You should spray residential living areas and sleeping quarters with an insecticide (e.g., RAID™ Flying Insect Spray). Mosquito nets, especially if sprayed or impregnated with permethrin, have been shown to reduce markedly the incidence of malaria in endemic areas. Vigorous insect-bite prevention measures will not only help prevent malaria but also reduce your risk of other insect-transmitted diseases such as dengue and leishmaniasis.

Don't rely on Avon's Skin-So-Soft to prevent disease-causing mosquito bites. It is relatively ineffective and lasts only one-half hour.

Drug prophylaxis—Chloroquine is the drug of choice when traveling to areas endemic for vivax malaria and chloroquine-sensitive falciparum malaria. Chloroquine and proguanil are probably safe to take during pregnancy but the combination is only about 70% (or less) effective against chloroquine-resistant falciparum malaria in Africa.   Atovaquone/proguanil (Malarone) is contraindicated for prophylaxis.

Mefloquine (Lariam), when used for prophylaxis, is the drug of choice for travel to areas with chloroquine-resistant falciparum malaria. Mefloquine has not been associated with an increase in spontaneous miscarriage, congenital malformations, or adverse postnatal outcomes. It is considered safe for use during the second and third trimesters by the Centers for Disease Control and Prevention (CDC) as well as the World Health Organization. As inadvertent use of mefloquine during the first trimester has not been documented to cause an excess of maternal or fetal problems, many travel medicine physicians will prescribe mefloquine during the first trimester when exposure to chloroquine-resistant falciparum malaria is unavoidable. Delay in travel until the second trimester, however, is recommended.

Mefloquine is only 50% effective against *P. falciparum* along the borders of Thailand with Cambodia and Myanmar, and travel to these border areas should be avoided.

You should not take doxycycline for prophylaxis because this drug can stain the teeth of the developing fetus and cause retardation of bone growth. However, doxycycline or tetracycline may be needed for adjunct treatment (with quinine or quinidine) of life-threatening chloroquine-resistant falciparum malaria, although there may be alternatives (see Chapter 6).

Treatment of Malaria

Uncomplicated chloroquine-sensitive *P. vivax* and chloroquine-sensitive *P. falciparum* should be treated with a 3-day course of chloroquine. Uncomplicated chloroquine-resistant *P. falciparum* can be treated with mefloquine or oral quinine plus pyrimethamine/sulfadoxine (P/S) or clindamycin. (A recent study has suggested that high-dose mefloquine treatment is associated with increased risk of fetal death.) In the Amazon Basin and Southeast Asia, P/S may not be effective. Falciparum malaria contracted in Thailand can be treated with quinine and clindamycin, but quinine-resistant malaria is increasing in this region.

Atovaquone/proguanil (Malarone) is rated Cataegory C for use in pregnancy, and should be used only if the potential benefits outweigh the possible risks.

Complicated falciparum malaria requires parenteral therapy with quinidine plus doxycycline or clindamycin. Appropriate treatment to save the mother takes precedence over concerns about drug-related fetal toxicity, and individual circumstances will dictate what regimen is best in a given situation. When possible, malaria in pregnancy is best treated by an expert in this area.

Radical Cure

Primaquine should not be used during pregnancy because it may precipitate glucose-6-PD-induced hemolytic anemia in the fetus. If you have been treated for *P. vivax* or *P. ovale* malaria, you should continue chloroquine prophylaxis until after delivery when you can be treated with primaquine.

DRUG USE GUIDELINES

In general, drugs should be taken only if the severity of the symptoms, or the threat to the mother's health, outweighs the possible risk of fetal damage. As with management of illnesses at home, you should employ nondrug remedies when possible. For example, you can use warm compresses for muscle aches instead of an analgesic. However, if you develop a serious or life-threatening illness, such as an infection, appropriate drugs should not be withheld because of concerns about fetal toxicity.

Drugs for Pain

Acetaminophen (Tylenol)—Safe, in moderation. Analgesic of choice for mild to moderate pain. Kidney disease in the neonate can occur with daily high doses.
Acetaminophen with codeine—Safe.
Aspirin—Avoid, especially in the last trimester. May increase incidence of bleeding, especially maternal and neonatal blood loss following delivery. Data from a study of 58,000 pregnancies also suggest that taking aspirin in the last trimester is likely to increase the duration of labor. Aspirin is a potent prostaglandin synthetase inhibitor, and it has been associated with premature closure of the ductus arteriosus.
Low-dose aspirin—60–100 mg daily reduces incidence of pregnancy-induced hypertension; may be indicated for women at risk of developing preeclampsia. Should be used only as recommended by your obstetrician.
Nonsteroidal anti-inflammatories (NSAIDs, e.g., ibuprofen)—Avoid, due to increased bleeding potential. Theoretically, any NSAID can cause premature ductal closure. Nonsteroidal drugs, however, are not considered to be teratogenic.
Opioids—Considered safe.

Drugs for Diarrhea and Vomiting

Azithromycin (Zithromax)—Considered safe, although studies are lacking. In Thailand, azithromycin was superior to ciprofloxacin in the treatment of campylobacter enteritis. Other studies have demonstrated some effectiveness against shigella as well as salmonella and *E. coli*.
Bismuth subsalicylate (Pepto Bismol)—Avoid (contains salicylate).
Furazolidone—Furazolidone is a broad-spectrum antibiotic effective against many diarrhea-causing pathogens (*E. coli*, salmonella, shigella, *V. cholerae*). Furazolidone is 80% effective against *Giardia lamblia*. No reports of teratogenicity, carcinogenicity, or other adverse fetal effects.
Lomotil—Avoid. Contains atropine. More potential side effects than loperamide.
Loperamide (Imodium)—Acceptable for watery diarrhea. Avoid with diarrhea associated with a high fever and/or bloody stools.
Metronidazole (Flagyl)—Acceptable for the treatment of giardiasis or invasive amebiasis. Although there is some concern about the use of metronidazole because it is carcinogenic in rodents and mutagenic in certain bacteria, a recent analy-

sis of seven studies suggested that there is no increase in birth defects among infants exposed to metronidazole during the first trimester.

Paromomycin—This is an oral aminoglycoside that is nonabsorbed from the intestinal tract and considered to be safe during pregnancy for the treatment of intraluminal, noninvasive amebiasis. As an alternative to metronidazole, it is 60% to 70% effective. Paromomycin can also be used for the treatment of giardiasis.

Piperazines and phenothiazines (Antivert, Compazine)—Acceptable. No reported increased risk of congenital anomalies.

Quinolones—Quinolones are not contraindicated during pregnancy, but they are Category C drugs. According to the Physicians Desk Reference (PDR) "There are no adequate or well-controlled studies in pregnant women. Quinolone antibiotics should be used during pregnancy only if the potential benefit justifies the potential risk to the fetus." Quinolone antibiotics should not be withheld arbitrarily, especially in the presence of serious illness.

Trimethoprim/sulfamethoxazole (e.g., Bactrim, Septra)—In studies of infants exposed to trimethoprim/sulfamethoxazole during early pregnancy, the frequency of congenital abnormalities was not increased. Sulfonamides, however, should be avoided at term due to the risk of hyperbilirubinemia.

Drugs for Altitude Sickness

Acetazolamide (Diamox)—Avoid in first trimester. Acetazolamide is associated with limb abnormalities in animals. A sulfa analog.

Calcium channel blockers (e.g., nifedipine)—No increased risk of fetal anomalies, but decrease in fetal blood flow is possible.

Dexamethasone (Decadron)—Considered to be safe. No association with congenital anomalies has been reported.

Sleeping Pills & Tranquilizers

Alcohol—Teratogenic; avoid, even in small amounts.

Benzodiazepines—Avoid. One study associated diazepam with cleft lip.

Drugs for Motion Sickness, Coughs & Colds

Dramamine, meclizine—Considered safe. Use if motion sickness is a significant problem.

Antihistamines—Probably safe, but Benadryl is in Category C.

Cough medicines with iodine—Avoid. Excess iodine may affect fetal thyroid development. Cough preparations with guaifensin and dextromethorphan are acceptable.

Decongestants—Pseudoephedrine (Sudafed) and oxymetazoline (Afrin) are considered safe.

Drugs for Malaria and Other Infections

Atovaquone/proguanil (Malarone)—Safety in pregnancy has not been established; may be suitable for treatment in select circumstances.
Cephalosporins—Safe.
Chloroquine—Considered to be safe.
Clindamycin—No studies of adverse embryofetal effects. This drug is a good alternative to doxycycline for the treatment of falciparum malaria when used in combination with quinine or quinidine.
Diloxanide—Avoid.
Erythromycin—Considered safe. If used to treat maternal syphilis, however, adequate fetal blood levels may not be achieved since little drug passes the placenta.
Halofantrine—Avoid. Halofantrine is embryotoxic.
Iodoquinol—Avoid.
Mefloquine—Considered safe during second and third trimesters. The use of mefloquine during the first trimester should be reserved for women with unavoidable travel to areas at high risk for chloroquine-resistant falciparum malaria.
Nitrofurantoin—Selected by many obstetricians as the initial choice for most urinary tract infections. Congenital anomalies not reported.
Penicillin, ampicillin, amoxicillin—Considered safe. This includes the newer penicillins such as piperacillin, as well as those combined with b-lactamase inhibitors, clavulanic acid, and sulbactam.
Praziquantel—Probably safe. Use only if clearly indicated.
Primaquine—Avoid until after delivery. May cause hemolytic anemia in G-6-PD-deficient fetus.
Proguanil—Probably safe.
Pyrimethamine/sulfadoxine (Fansidar)—Safe as single-dose (3-tablet) presumptive treatment of malaria. This drug is no longer recommended for prophylaxis.
Quinine and quinidine—Indicated for treatment of chloroquine-resistant falciparum malaria. A study in Thailand found no deleterious effect of quinine on the fetus or increased incidence of drug-induced abortion. Quinine may increase incidence of hypoglycemia in the pregnant patient with malaria.
Sulfisoxazole (Gantrisin)—Acceptable. Avoid at term.
Tetracycline, doxycycline—Avoid unless needed for adjunctive treatment of chloroquine-resistant falciparum malaria or other life-threatening infectious diseases (e.g., ehrlichiosis).

Other Drugs

Iodine tablets and iodine-resin water purifiers—Do not use for more than three weeks in any 6-month period as sole source of purified water. Excess iodine can theoretically cause fetal goiter, but little or no data are available in pregnant travelers using iodine for water purification. Boiling water remains the mechanism of choice for longer-term water purification.

NOTE: Prolonged use (>2 years) of demand-release iodine-resin filters by Peace Corps workers in Africa resulted in a four-fold increased risk of goiter and thyroid dysfunction (*Lancet* 1998). Attaching a carbon cartridge to an iodine-resin filter device will reduce iodine concentration in the treated water.

DEET—Considered safe when used according to the directions on label. There are no reports of teratogenicity nor are there any EPA warnings about the use of DEET during pregnancy.

EXERCISE AND PREGNANCY

Labor is aptly named. Childbearing takes a lot of stamina, and it's no surprise that exercise is appropriate for a healthy pregnant woman. Today, when more and more women are active and sports-minded, many obstetricians say that strenuous exercise, even running or jogging, is not harmful to the fetus and may even help build stamina for labor and recovery afterward. But how much exercise is too much? And who should avoid exercise? Guidelines set forth by the American College of Obstetricians and Gynecologists (ACOG) recommend the following:

- Maternal heart rates during exercise should not exceed 150 beats per minute.
- Strenuous activities should not exceed 15 minutes in duration.
- Avoid hyperthermia. Body temperature should not exceed 38°C (101.4°F).
- No exercise should be performed in the supine position after the fourth month.

Some authorities believe, however, that the 15-minute limitation may be too restrictive for a woman used to vigorous exercise and advocate the following:

- Pregnant women should tailor exercise to their needs and abilities. For a sedentary person who has never exercised vigorously, low intensity workouts that involve walking, stationary cycling, and swimming are best.
- Exercise should be done within a comfort zone. Special caution should be taken when exercising in a hot, humid climate. (It usually takes about two weeks for the body to become heat-acclimated.) Hyperthermia should be avoided, especially during the first trimester when the nervous system is developing.
- If the woman is healthy and accustomed to very vigorous exercise, there's probably no reason she can't exceed the ACOG guidelines as long as she does not become hyperthermic, hypoglycemic, or significantly dehydrated.
- The possible effect of low caloric intake of high endurance athletes also warrants caution—this may represent more of a risk than the actual exercise itself.
- Water skiing is not advised because of the possibility of hydrostatic injury to the vagina, cervix, or uterus. Downhill skiing and horseback rising after the first trimester should be avoided. Cross-country skiing or hiking on uneven terrain should be avoided in the third trimester because of the increased risk of falls.
- Pregnant women should not scuba dive. The fetus is at risk for decompression sickness. No safe depth/time profiles have been established for pregnancy. Snorkeling is safe.

- Relative contraindications to vigorous exercise (or stressful travel for that matter) include hypertension, anemia, thyroid disease, diabetes, cardiac arrhythmia, history of precipitous labor, history of intrauterine growth retardation, any bleeding during present pregnancy, breech presentation during the last trimester, excessive obesity, or leading an extremely sedentary lifestyle.
- Absolute contraindications against exercising include a history of the following conditions: three or more spontaneous miscarriages, ruptured membranes, premature labor, multifetal pregnancy, incompetent cervix, bleeding or a diagnosis of placenta previa, or a diagnosis of heart disease.

HIGH ALTITUDES, TREKKING, AND PREGNANCY

There is no known fetal risk if you go to high altitudes for a few days. Some authorities, however, advise against trekking in remote areas above 8,000 feet. Not only might you develop acute altitude sickness, but emergency medical and obstetrical care will be far away.

Women who remain at high altitudes during their pregnancies have an altitude-associated increase in fetal growth retardation, high blood pressure, and premature delivery. You should consult with your doctor if you will be traveling to, or plan to live at, altitudes greater than 6,000 feet.

COMMERCIAL FLYING

Domestic airlines ordinarily won't allow travel after the 36th week of gestation; the cutoff for foreign airlines is 35 weeks.

After 24 weeks—You should get a letter from your doctor specifying details of your pregnancy and giving you permission to travel. *This letter is mandatory for travel after week 35.* You should call the particular airline you will be using to verify specific requirements.

Unless you have severe anemia (hemoglobin less than 8.5 gm%) or sickle cell disease/trait, the reduced cabin oxygen pressure will not cause harm to you or your fetus. If your blood count is reduced more than 25% to 30%, however, you may require pretravel treatment of the anemia and/or supplemental oxygen en route.

Cosmic radiation is increased at the flight altitudes of commercial jets. Studies suggest that an exposure of 50 millirems of radiation per month (about 80 hours of flight time) will not harm a fetus. This is the permissible monthly exposure allowed pregnant flight attendants.

NOTE: Airport metal detectors will not harm the fetus.

Varicose veins and leg edema can be a problem, especially during the third trimester. You should request an aisle seat so that you can get up and walk around every 20 to 30 minutes. If you are in the third trimester, request a bulkhead seat so that you can extend and elevate your legs. These measures will increase comfort, help relieve swelling, and reduce the risk of deep vein thrombosis.

FOOD AND WATER

You should drink only water that has been boiled, bottled (especially carbonated), or chemically treated to remove bacteria, parasites, and viruses. This is especially important if you are traveling in geographic areas where sanitation is poor, hepatitis E is most prevalent (southern and western China, Nepal, northern India, Indonesia, Myanmar, Pakistan, Algeria, Kenya, Sudan, Ethiopia, and Mexico). The hepatitis E fatality rate can be as high as 25% during the second and third trimesters of pregnancy. If necessary, you can use iodine tablets on a short term basis (2–3 weeks) to treat water of questionable purity. Don't use a water filter alone—it won't remove viruses. Use a water purifier instead. Water purifiers contain an iodine-resin matrix that will eliminate hepatitis E and other viruses. NOTE: It is also recommended that an iodine-resin purifier should not be used as the sole source of drinking water for longer than 3 weeks in any 6-month period due to high levels of residual iodine in the treated water (see Chapter 3).

All foods should be well cooked and served hot to avoid a variety of infectious illnesses.

TRAVELERS' DIARRHEA

The treatment of travelers' diarrhea can be problematic. On the one hand, you don't want to risk causing a drug-related fetal injury (even though this may be highly unlikely)—while on the other hand, not treating diarrhea may result in symptoms ranging from extreme personal discomfort and inconvenience to (rarely) life-threatening illness. Some authorities, worried primarily about the safety of the fetus, focus on fluid replacement and shy away from recommending practically any drug treatment. Others take a different view: they believe that the severity of the symptoms and the circumstances of the particular illness should dictate treatment—not arbitrary guidelines.

Basic treatment—Drink extra fluids to prevent dehydration. If you have mild/moderate watery diarrhea, you can safely take loperamide (Imodium). This drug is especially useful if toilet facilities are not close by and uncontrolled symptoms would cause undue inconvenience, discomfort, or embarrassment.

Antibiotic treatment—Refer to Chapter 5 for antibiotic dosage recommendations. The use of an antibiotic depends upon severity of symptoms: volume and frequency of stools, abdominal pain, general feelings of illness, and degree of inconvenience. The *HealthGuide* believes that if you do use an antibiotic, the first choice should be a quinolone, such as ciprofloxacin or levofloxacin. Quinolones are the best drugs for treating infectious diarrhea, and if antibiotic treatment is indicated, then the most effective agent should be used.

Alternative drugs, in order of preference, are azithromycin, cefixime, and furazolidone.

- Azithromycin (Zithromax) is emerging as an important drug for treating travelers' diarrhea. It is presumed safe in pregnancy. In one study performed in Thai-

land, azithromycin was superior to ciprofloxacin in the treatment of campylobacter enteritis. Other studies have demonstrated effectiveness against multidrug-resistant shigella as well as salmonella, *E. coli*, and *V. cholerae*.
• Cefixime (Suprax), a cephalosporin, is effective against most pathogens causing infectious diarrhea and is considered safe in pregnancy. There are reports, however, of its lack of effectiveness in the treatment of shigellosis.
• Furazolidone (Furoxone) has activity against a wide range of gastrointestinal pathogens, including *E. coli*, salmonella, shigella, campylobacter, and the vibrio species (which cause cholera). It is also effective against giardia.

Treating more severe diarrhea/dysentery—If you have severe or incapacitating diarrhea, diarrhea causing dehydration, or diarrhea with dysentery, start treatment with a quinolone antibiotic. Institute aggressive fluid replacement therapy. Seek medical consultation if you are not better in 24 hours. Although fluids are very important, antibiotics are also essential in order to treat the cause of the illness, not just the symptoms. Often, only a few days of antibiotic treatment are needed, and it is highly unlikely that there will be adverse fetal effects from the medication. NOTE: Quinolones are Category C pregnancy drugs: Adverse effects have been shown in some test animals but have not been demonstrated in humans.) The benefits of treatment with a quinolone will most likely far outweigh any potential harm to the fetus. Remember, the nature and severity of your illness should determine the choice treatment, not fetal risk. Effective treatment of your infection is the first priority, and keeping you healthy is also the best way to ensure a healthy baby.

Khan LK, Li R, Gootnick D, et al. Thyroid abnormalities related to iodine excess from water purification units. Lancet 1998; 352:1519.
Khan WA, Seas C, Dhar U, et al. Treatment of shigellosis: Comparison of azithromycin and ciprofloxacin. A double-blind, randomized, controlled trial. Ann Int Med 1997 May 1; **126(9)**:697–703.
Koren G, Pastuszak A. Drugs in Pregnancy. N Engl J Med 1998; 338:1128–1137.
Nosten F, McReady R, Simpson JA, et al. Effects of plasmodium vivax malaria in pregnancy. Lancet 1999; 354:546–549.
Rose, SR. Pregnancy and Travel. Emerg Med Clinics N America 1997;15:93–111.
Samuel BU, Barry M. The Pregnant Traveler. Infect Dis Clinics N Am 1998;12:325–354.

20 Traveling with Children

Children make great travelers. They are inquisitive, fun, and, when they choose, inexhaustible. Taking them on trips exposes them to new experiences, sows family togetherness, and builds memories for when they are older.

But traveling with children is never all fun and games. Parents must be aware of health and safety concerns, especially when traveling overseas, and even more so when visiting developing countries. Children may need immunizations even when adults do not. Children are susceptible to travelers' diarrhea, malaria, and other travel-related conditions. Children also acquire numerous "routine" illnesses whether or not they travel—for example, fevers, upper respiratory infections, and ear infections. If possible, parents should be familiar with the caliber of medical care in the area that they are visiting.

There are other issues to consider when traveling overseas. Infant car seats and seat belts are often not readily available. Toys bought overseas may not meet the same safety standards of those at home. Hiring local people to watch children may expose the children to infectious diseases (tuberculosis is a serious consideration). Children are vulnerable to severe sunburns during vacations in the tropics, and blistering sunburns are associated with an increased risk of skin cancer, such as melanoma, in later life. Swimming pools rarely have lifeguards. Teenagers often want to participate in potentially dangerous activities not available at home (e.g., parasailing and scuba diving).

Having alerted you to some of the health risks, the bottomline is that the benefits of traveling with children generally far outweigh the risks, provided that pretravel preparation, extra precautions with respect to food, water, and insects, and common sense during travel are utilized.

VACCINATIONS FOR OVERSEAS TRAVEL

Vaccinating children for overseas travel involves two considerations: routine childhood vaccines and travel-related vaccines. For overseas travel, school-age children are generally up-to-date with their routine vaccines and need no further injections. However, infants and preschool-aged children may need additional doses of such vaccines. "Childhood" diseases that no longer exist, or occur rarely, in this country are still prevalent in many developing countries and, sometimes, in developed countries. These diseases include diphtheria, pertussis, measles, mumps, and rubella, to mention the more common ones. While children in the United States are routinely vaccinated against these diseases, the vaccines are administered at the age at which children respond with optimal, long-term protection. This is not necessarily the age at which children first become susceptible. Therefore, for travel, infants and children may need to be vaccinated at an earlier age than if they did not travel. However, when routine vaccinations are given at an earlier than usual age, or the intervals between doses of vaccines are shortened, the vaccines may give only partial immunity—which is better than no immunity at all—and the doses should be repeated at a later date. These additional doses cause no known untoward effects.

Table 18.1.
Changes in Schedule for Routine Immunizations Due to Travel

Vaccine	Age Routinely Given	Accelerated Schedule for Travel
DTaP	2, 4, and 6 mo	6 wk, 10 wk, and 14 wk
Hepatitis B	birth, 1 mo, 6–12 mo	0, 1 mo, 2 mo (booster 12 mo)
Hib	2, 4, and 6 mo	6 wk, 10 wk, and 14 wk
MMR	12–15 mo	6 mo (measles)
Polio	2, 4, and 6 mo	6 wk, 9 wk, and 12 wk

NOTE: When vaccinations are given at younger than recommended ages, and when the intervals between doses are shortened, vaccinations may need to be repeated at a later date.

Up-to-date vaccination schedules are especially important for children who will have close contact with local children overseas. Moreover, parents should check their own immune status for childhood diseases. Traveling with children may increase parents' exposure to local children. Some childhood illnesses are more serious when contracted by an adult; for example, rubella and varicella (chickenpox) are especially serious for pregnant women.

Travel-related Vaccines for Children

- **Cholera:** The cholera vaccine is no longer available in the United States. The risk of cholera to U.S. travelers of any age is extremely low. Breast-feeding is protective against cholera; careful preparation of formula and food from safe water and foodstuffs should protect non–breast-fed infants.
- **Hepatitis A:** Hepatitis A is ubiquitous in countries with poor sanitation; children traveling to such countries should be protected. The disease in childhood rarely causes symptoms and, in fact, results in lifelong immunity. Infected children, especially ones in diapers, can spread the disease to their caretakers. In the United States the hepatitis A vaccine is approved for children 2 years of age and older (in Europe, 1 year and older). Children too young for this vaccine should receive immune globulin (IG), the dose determined by the weight of the child and the

length of exposure to hepatitis A; IG protects no longer than 6 months. Note that IG interferes with replication of live attenuated viruses such as measles, mumps, rubella, and varicella but not oral polio vaccine and yellow fever vaccine.

- **Japanese Encephalitis:** Japanese encephalitis is common throughout eastern Asia and is the leading cause of viral encephalitis worldwide. China, Japan, and other countries in the Far East vaccinate their children against this disease. However, this does not reduce the risk for travelers. Farm animals are the main reservoir for the virus, and mosquitoes spread the virus. Immunization is recommended for all children who will stay for several weeks or more in rural endemic areas, especially on or near farms, during transmission season. Reactions to vaccination are common, possibly more so in children than in adults. Japanese encephalitis vaccine is approved for children 1 year of age and older.
- **Meningococcal:** Meningococcal meningitis is rare among travelers. However, young children (and the elderly) may be more susceptible than other age groups. The effectiveness of the meningococcal vaccine in children is dependent upon the child's age when the vaccine is administered. Protection may not be completely effective in children vaccinated between 3 months and 2 years, especially for vaccination before 3 months of age. The vaccine may be safely given to infants, but it may be less effective than in adults.
- **Rabies:** Pre-exposure rabies vaccine is indicated for prolonged stays in rural areas in developing countries where rabies is transmitted by domestic animals such as dogs and cats. The vaccine may be more important for children than adults. In many areas, 40% of all cases of human rabies in local people occur in children less than 14 years of age. Children tend to be fascinated by animals, use poor judgment around them, do not report minor bites, and, because of their height, may be more likely to suffer bites around the head and neck. Such wounds may be more likely to cause rabies. Pre-exposure rabies vaccination does not preclude proper wound care or postexposure vaccination after an encounter with a possible rabid animal. But pre-exposure vaccination does eliminate the need for rabies immune globulin after an exposure, and it reduces the number of postexposure injections from five to two. NOTE: The newer preparations of rabies vaccine and rabies immune globulin may be difficult or impossible to find in the developing world.
- **Typhoid:** For typhoid fever, breast-feeding is likely to protect infants. Careful preparation of formula and food from boiled or chlorinated water can help protect non–breast-fed infants and children up to 2 years of age. The parenteral heat-phenol-inactivated vaccine licensed for use in children as young as 6 months of age (manufactured by Wyeth-Ayerst) has been discontinued. Because there is no vaccine currently available for use in children under 2 years of age, even more stringent preparation of formula, food, and water is necessary for those under 2 years of age to minimize their risk. The new injectable ViCPS typhoid vaccine is recommended for children between 2 and 6 years of age traveling to areas where there is questionable sanitation.

- **Yellow Fever:** Yellow fever vaccine should not be administered to any infant under 4 months of age, and children 4–6 months old should be considered only under very unusual circumstances. Infants 6–9 months old can receive the vaccine if they cannot avoid traveling to areas of risk and when a high level of protection against mosquito bites is not possible. Infants 9 months or older should be vaccinated as required or recommended for travel to South America or Africa. Unvaccinated children are at risk of acquiring the disease and should travel to infected areas only when travel is essential.
- **Tuberculosis:** Children should be tested for tuberculosis with the PPD skin test before and after travel to developing countries, especially when such travel is prolonged and closely exposes children to the local people. TB vaccine (Bacille Calmette-Guerin, BCG) is almost never used in the United States However, a recent review of the literature strongly suggests that BCG reduces, in children, both the incidence of serious TB infection and its spread to the central nervous system (brain and spinal cord coverings) and overwhelming infection. These latter complications are particularly common in young children who are newly infected. Most developing countries vaccinate all children at birth, and many European countries vaccinate children at risk, including those traveling to developing countries.

Health-care professionals who advise parents about overseas travel with children must thoroughly familiarize themselves with the contraindications, side effects, and interactions of the various vaccines, other injectables, and medications that they administer or prescribe.

TRAVELERS' DIARRHEA

Studies of diarrhea among travelers to developing countries show that children, especially children under the age of 3, have a higher incidence of travelers' diarrhea than adults, have more severe symptoms, and have symptoms that last longer. Children place their fingers and other objects in their mouths, swallow water while bathing and swimming, wash their hands much less frequently than adults, make improper food and beverage selections, and may be cared for by local caretakers. Better parental supervision can reduce the incidence of travelers' diarrhea, but lack of immunity to diarrhea-causing organisms may also be a factor. Moreover, treatment of diarrhea in children can be problematic: small children often refuse fluids when they need them the most; some effective medications given to adults may not be appropriate; and reliable medical facilities may not be at hand. Also, infants in diapers can spread the disease to the people who change those diapers—parents.

Treating Dehydration

Correct treatment of diarrhea is imperative, starting after the first loose stool or bout of vomiting. Fluid replacement and the prevention of dehydration is considered to be the cornerstone of treating diarrhea in the pediatric traveler. Treatment consists of giving oral rehydration solution (ORS) and continuing feedings (see specific instructions in Chapter 5). Young children can dehydrate rapidly, sometimes in a matter of hours. Commonly used treatments—giving clear fluids and withholding food—worsen diarrhea. Clear fluids do not replace salts lost in the vomitus or stool, further worsening electrolyte imbalance and hastening dehydration. In virtually all cases of infectious diarrhea, regardless of severity or causative organism, the impaired intestinal wall continues to function sufficiently well to absorb needed electrolytes and calories. Food increases absorption of nutrients, decreases the volume and frequency of stools, and speeds recovery.

Commercial ORS contains glucose, sodium, potassium, and base (citrate or bicarbonate) in amounts that approximate fluids being lost and in ratios that promote absorption from an impaired intestine. Glucose and sodium promote the absorption of water.

Many traditional treatments of diarrhea are counterproductive. Nondiet soda drinks contain too much sugar and little or no sodium and potassium. Most juices and nondiet juicelike drinks are merely flavored sugar water. Gatorade and other sport drinks are intended to replace fluids lost by sweating and therefore contain too low a concentration of salts. Chicken broth contains much sodium but no glucose.

ORS is available premixed in liquid form or in packets to which measured amounts of water (purified) must be added. Ideally, small children should take about 100 cc (about 3 ounces) of ORS with every loose stool or bout of vomiting. Food should be avoided as long as vomiting continues, which is rarely for more than 12 hours. If small children refuse to drink, they can be given smaller amounts every few minutes, by teaspoon or dropper. Amounts larger than 100 cc (3 ounces) should be avoided when children are vomiting; large amounts may induce vomiting. Unless vomiting occurs more frequently than every 45 minutes, some fluid reaches the intestine and is absorbed. Infants should continue to breast feed or drink formula and regular milk.

ORS does not stop diarrhea, but it prevents and treats dehydration. Children are not dehydrated if they take fluids well and are reasonably active and content, even if the diarrhea continues for a week. Symptoms of impending dehydration include continual vomiting and diarrhea, refusal to take or inability to retain fluids, listlessness, blood or much mucus in the stool, and high fever. In such cases, intravenous fluids or larger amounts of oral replacement fluids may become necessary, and hospitalization may even be required. Parents traveling with small children should keep such eventualities in mind when choosing travel destinations.

Cereal-based ORS (CB-ORS) is more effective than plain ORS in stopping diarrhea. CB-ORS contains cooked starches (usually rice) in place of glucose. Starch cause more calories and water to be absorbed by the intestine. CB-ORS is available in the United States in liquid form (e.g., Ricelye, available in most stores and pharmacies) and in packets (CeraLyte, available from Travel Medicine, Inc. at *www.travmed.com*). If commercial ORS is not available, children can be given plain water with one or more of the following: pretzels, salted crackers, mashed potatoes, or banana flakes. Drinks made with precooked infant rice cereal, unsweetened yogurt, or vegetable juices can also be used. Older children can be offered carbohydrates in the form of rice, potatoes, cereal, pasta, and bread while transitioning back to their regular diet.

Antimotility Drugs

Antimotility drugs (e.g., Imodium-AD, Lomotil) are not considered first-line treatment for diarrhea in infants and children. Loperamide (Imodium-AD) can cause drowsiness, abdominal distention, and ileus (stoppage of intestinal motility). If loperamide is used in older children, a dose of 0.8 mg/kg/day divided in three equal doses seems to be appropriate, but monitoring for side effects is important. Diphenoxylate (Lomotil) gives unpredictable results in children, especially in dehydrated ones, and may result in serious, delayed opiate-related toxicity. This drug is not recommended. In moderate and severe diarrhea, antidiarrheal drugs such as kaolin-pectate (Kaopectate) may reduce the number of stools but may do so by retaining fluids in the intestine, worsening electrolyte imbalance.

Pepto-Bismol (bismuth subsalicylate)

Studies reported in the *New England Journal of Medicine* have shown the efficacy of bismuth subsalicylate (BSS-Pepto-Bismol) along with oral rehydration for the treatment of infantile diarrhea. Infants given 100–150 mg/kg/day of BSS had significant reductions in their total stool output, total intake of oral rehydration solution, and duration of hospitalization. (Measurements of bismuth and salicylate concentrations in blood were well below levels considered toxic.)

Child dosage:

>12 years	2 tbsp (1 dose cup, 30 ml)
9–12 years	1 tbsp (1/2 dose cup, 15 ml)
6–9 years	2 tsp (1/3 dose cup, 10 ml)
3–6 years	1 tsp (1/6 dose cup, 5 ml)
<3 years	1/2 tsp every 4 hours for a maximum of 6 doses/24 hours

Over age 3: Repeat dose hourly, as needed, to a maximum of 8 doses in any 24-hour period. Temporary, harmless darkening of the stools may occur. Do not give this medication to a child who has chickenpox or the flu because of the slight risk of Reye's syndrome. NOTE: Reye's syndrome has never been reported in association with the use of nonaspirin salicylates such as found in bismuth subsalicylate.

Antibiotics

Historically, oral rehydration therapy has been considered the cornerstone of treatment of diarrhea in children, with antibiotics relegated to a secondary role. This secondary status was due to questions of efficacy (because of antibiotic resistance) and/or safety (possibility of harmful side effects). Now, because of their remarkable effectiveness against almost all strains of bacteria that cause travelers' diarrhea—and because of a rethinking of the safety issue—the quinolone antibiotics have become accepted by many authorities as *first-line therapy*, especially in children with severe diarrhea or dysentery. Azithromycin (Zithromax), an antibiotic commonly used in pediatric infections such as otitis media and pneumonia, has also shown good activity against most diarrhea-causing pathogens. This is not to downplay the importance of fluid replacement, but antibiotics, unlike fluids, treat the cause of the illness, and this leads to much faster recovery.

Regarding quinolone safety, the injuries observed in some experimental animals have not been seen in infants and children, even those who have received multiple or prolonged courses of a quinolone antibiotic. It is now felt that the theoretical risk of injury does not justify arbitrarily withholding treatment with a quinolone, especially in more severe diarrhea, since the risk/benefit ratio seems so much in favor of treatment, which is usually of short duration anyway.

Recommended antibiotics, in order of effectiveness, are as follows:
1. Quinolones
2. Azithromycin
3. Furazolidone or cefixime
4. Trimethoprim/sulfamethoxazole (co-trimoxazole)

Quinolones—Ciprofloxacin, ofloxacin, and levofloxacin are not available in a liquid formulation, and the lower-dose adult tablet is recommended. Nalidixic acid is available in both liquid and tablet form. In severe cases with vomiting, ciprofloxacin, ofloxacin, or levofloxacin can be given intravenously.

1. Nalidixic acid (NegGram)—The recommended dose over 12 years of age is 1 gm 4 times daily. Under age 12, the dosage is 50 mg/kg/day given in 4 equally divided doses. The manufacturer recommends that nalidixic acid not be given to children under 3 months.
2. Ciprofloxacin (Cipro)—Ciprofloxacin has excellent activity against *E. coli*, shigella, salmonella, and campylobacter, the bacteria which cause most cases of travelers' diarrhea.
Dosage: 250 mg twice daily for 1–3 days.
3. Ofloxacin (Floxin)—Ofloxacin is as effective as ciprofloxacin but has better activity against chlamydia and some of the gram-positive bacteria.
Dosage: 200 mg twice daily for 1–3 days for diarrhea.
4. Levofloxacin (Lēvaquin)—This antibiotic is the active component of ofloxacin. It is also a useful antibiotic to have for the treatment of other infections such as sinusitis, some pneumonias, bacterial bronchitis, urinary tract infections, typhoid fever, uncomplicated skin infections, and chlamydia.
Dosage: 250 mg once daily for 1–3 days for diarrhea.

Azithromycin (Zithromax)—This antibiotic, which is usually prescribed for ear and respiratory infections, is also active against salmonella, shigella, as well as enteroinvasive, enteropathogenic, enterohemorrhagic, and enterotoxigenic *E. coli*, the most common cause of travelers' diarrhea. In Thailand, azithromycin has been shown to be more effective against campylobacter than ciprofloxacin.

Child dosage: 10 mg/kg/day for 3 days.

Cefixime (Suprax)—This is a broad spectrum cephalosporin with activity against the usual organisms causing travelers' diarrhea. There are reports of shigella resistance. Cefixime is also a useful drug for treating ear infections.

Child dosage: 8 mg/kg once daily for 3–5 days for diarrhea.

Furazolidone (Furoxone)—Although not as rapidly effective as the quinolones, furazolidone has excellent activity against the majority of gastrointestinal pathogens, including *E. coli*, salmonella, shigella, campylobacter, and the vibrio species (which cause cholera). Furazolidone is also effective against giardia.

Child dosage: Children 5 years and older should receive 25 to 50 mg (1/4 to 1/2 tablet) 4 times daily.

Liquid furazolidone contains 50 mg per tbsp (15 ml).

5 years and older—1/2 to 1 tbsp 4 times daily.

1 to 4 years—1 to 1-1/2 tsp 4 times daily.

1 month to 1 year—1/2 to 1 tsp 4 times daily.

Side effects: Occasional nausea and vomiting. Not to be given to infants under age 1 month.

Trimethoprim/sulfamethoxazole (Co-trimoxazole, TMP/SMX)—Most strains of *E. coli*, shigella, salmonella, and cholera bacteria are now resistant to TMP/SMX, and this antibiotic is now considered a last-choice drug.

NOTE: TMP/SMX remains an effective treatment for cyclosporosis.

Child dosage: Depending upon the weight of the child, 1–4 tsp of pediatric suspension every 12 hours for 1–3 days. Above 88 lb, 1 double-strength (DS) tablet every 12 hours for 1–3 days.

Side effects: GI upset, rash.

TMP/SMX is safe for children over age 2 months and can be considered for use by pregnant women.

CHILDREN, INSECTS, AND THE TROPICS

In the tropics, protecting children from insect bites is the first line of defense against malaria, dengue fever, and numerous other vector-borne diseases. Protection includes the following:

- Placing nets over baby carriages and cribs
- Eliminating standing water around living quarters
- Staying indoors at dusk and after dark
- Dressing children, between dusk and dawn, in long-sleeved clothing that fits over neck, wrists, and ankles
- Not allowing children to go barefooted
- Covering exposed skin with an insect repellent containing DEET
- Spraying nets with a permethrin-containing insecticide

- Using a pyrethroid-containing flying-insect spray in living and sleeping areas during evening and nighttime hours
- Sleeping in quarters that are air-conditioned, when possible

Use insect repellents containing 20%–35% DEET. This is especially important in malarious areas. Products with higher concentrations are not much more effective and are more likely to produce skin rashes; neurologic symptoms are extremely rare and appear to be associated only with ingestion or extremely inappropriate overuse. DEET, when used correctly, is a safe product. Skin reactions to DEET can be minimized by applying it only to exposed skin, not using it on irritated skin, and washing it off when protection is no longer required. Permethrin insecticides may cause minor skin rashes but have no known serious side effects.

MALARIA CHEMOPROPHYLAXIS

The effectiveness of preventive medication against malaria depends on the region of the world visited and the risk of acquiring malaria, especially chloroquine-resistant falciparum malaria (CRFM).

Chloroquine—Chloroquine is the drug of choice for chloroquine-sensitive malaria. In the United States, chloroquine is available only in bitter-tasting tablets. Dosage is calculated by body weight. Overseas, it is also available as a syrup. The concentration of chloroquine in syrup varies across countries. Chloroquine is generally well tolerated by children. Side effects are infrequent and tend to be mild. Reactions can be reduced by taking it with meals, or in divided, twice-weekly doses. Store chloroquine in a childproof container out of the reach of children. The ingestion of only a few tablets can be fatal to a small child. NOTE: When calculating a child's dose of chloroquine, tables state the dosage in either "salt" or "base."

Mefloquine—Mefloquine is effective against most CRFM; however, mefloquine-resistant malaria is well documented in rural areas along the borders of Thailand. Doses of mefloquine for children are generally given as fractions of a tablet. No liquid preparation is available. Accurate dosing can be achieved by crushing tablets first and then dividing the powder. The powder can be given with applesauce or a similar substance. Mefloquine was recently approved for children weighing as little as 5 kg, and most advisers would prescribe the drug even to a newborn who is travelling to a high-risk area of CRFM. Many small children vomit mefloquine. The neuropsychological adverse effects of mefloquine that appear to be common among adults appear to be very rare among young children, or have not been reported.

Atovaquone/proguanil (Malarone)—The FDA has just approved the combination of atovaquone (250 mg) and proguanil (100 mg) for the prophylaxis or treatment of malaria caused by *P. falciparum*. This drug is a welcome addition because it not only is very effective but provides an alternative for persons intolerant of mefloquine or doxycycline, for children younger than 8, who cannot take doxycycline, and for those going on short trips (it is expensive). Prophylaxis studies conducted in Kenya, Zambia, and Gabon demonstrated that Malarone was 98% to 100% effective in partially immune subjects.

Child dosage: In the United States a pediatric formulation is available and the prophylactic dosage is based on weight:

10 kg–20 kg	1 pediatric-strength tablet
21–30 kg	2 pediatric-strength tablets
31–40 kg	3 pediatric-strength tablets
>40 kg	1 adult-strength tablet

Tablets should be taken with food or a milky drink at the same time each day. If vomiting occurs within one hour after dosing, a repeat dose should be taken. Side effects are minimal; they include stomach upset, cough, and skin rash.

Primaquine—Primaquine, an old antimalarial used to treat certain types of malaria, has recently been shown to be a very effective and safe preventive medication in a dose of 0.5 mg/kg daily (given with food) to a maximum of 30 mg per day for one week after exposure. Because primaquine can cause anemia in certain ethnic groups, a special blood test, glucose-6-phosphate dehydrogenase (G-6-PD) must be performed before the drug can be safely prescribed. Use of primaquine for prophylaxis must be discussed with a travel medicine expert.

The combination of daily doses of proguanil with weekly doses of chloroquine is an alternative to mefloquine in areas with CRFM, especially in Africa. The chloroquine/proguanil combination, however, is only 70% effective. Proguanil is not available in the United States but is available in Canada and overseas. Side reactions to prophylactic dosages are rare and consist of nausea, vomiting, mouth ulcers, and hair loss.

Doxycycline—Doxycycline is an alternative to mefloquine for the prophylaxis of CRFM. Doxycycline is contraindicated in children less than 9 years of age because it inhibits bone growth and stains teeth. The drug can also exaggerate sunburn reactions; persons taking doxycycline should be instructed to avoid prolonged sun exposure and to use effective sunscreens that protect against UVA as well as UVB rays. Other side effects include monilial vaginitis (rare in children) and upset stomachs. The latter can be minimized by taking doxycycline with meals.

Lactating mothers taking antimalarials secrete small amounts of the drug in their breast milk. The amount is insufficient to harm infants and insufficient to protect infants against malaria.

Treatment

Parents should be made aware that any unexplained fever should be considered a symptom of malaria in areas where malaria exists and must be evaluated immediately, ideally by experts in the disease. The problem is that children frequently have fevers due to viral diseases, medical experts are often not at hand, and antimalarial medication can mask other important infections. Emergency treatment with Atovaquone/proguanil (Malarone), mefloquine (Lariam) pyrimethamine/sulfadoxine (Fansidar), or quinine should be administered when medical help is unavailable. Clear instructions for such eventualities must be provided for parents. See Chapter 6 for pediatric treatment doses of antimalarial drugs.

ACUTE MOUNTAIN SICKNESS

The incidence of acute mountain sickness (AMS) in infants and young children is about the same as in adults, and, as in adults, the higher the altitude, the faster the ascent, the greater the incidence of AMS. Problems seem to develop more often in children who have had recent upper respiratory infections. Identifying AMS in young children can be problematic; children frequently become ill with vague viral illnesses that give symptoms similar to AMS—headaches (irritability), loss of appetite, inability to sleep, and fatigue, for example—and children cannot verbalize what is bothering them. Parents are advised to avoid taking their children to very high altitude destinations and, if they do go and children become ill, to assume that they are ill due to altitude sickness and descend immediately. Acetazolamide (Diamox) may be helpful in reducing AMS when taken just prior to ascent.

AIR TRAVEL

Air travel appears to be safe for children with upper respiratory infections (URIs) and nasal allergies. Children do occasionally experience ear pain during flight, generally during descent, but less commonly than adults. Moreover, such pain does not cause permanent damage to the ear. The use of oral decongestants and nasal sprays for URIs and nasal allergies may help minimize pain, though some studies indicate that decongestants are not helpful in children. Nasal sprays may give some relief. Use sprays as directed and also at the onset of descent and then repeat five minutes later. Older children should blow their noses before using sprays.

Children experiencing ear infections may have less risk of ear pain in flight than children without such infections. Ear infections often produce fluid in the middle ear. The fluid obliterates the middle ear space, and pressure differentials do not occur. Aerating tubes also prevent pressure differentials and prevent pain.

Conventional wisdom recommends giving bottles or nursing infants who cry during flights. The rationale is that infants cry because they are experiencing barotrauma or are dehydrated due to the low humidity aboard the aircraft, but barotrauma is rare and dehydration does not occur. Low cabin humidity dries out the mucus membranes of the mouth and throat, creating a sensation of thirst. Giving frequent feedings may be counterproductive because at the cruising altitude of jet aircraft, the air in the intestine is already expanded 20%. Sucking and feeding adds more air. Therefore, parents should not feed infants more often than at home.

CAR SAFETY

Heavy toys, sharp objects, or unused car seats should not be left loose on the back seat or on the ledge of the back window. These may become missiles in the event of sudden stops or accidents. Some experts recommend seat restraints for large pets. Older children should use seat belts in the back seat, too. Seat belts also minimize roughhousing. However, in many developing countries, seat belts are difficult to find or are not available. Unruly children distract drivers. Worse, sometimes children accidentally poke drivers or end up in the driver's lap. Parents should keep extra car keys in their pockets. Small children lock doors better than they open them, and sometimes parents accidentally lock small children in cars. Parents should remind children not to dart out of the car when they stop.

Car sickness—Motion sickness during automobile travel is more common in children than adults. For susceptible children, parents should not give them large meals just prior to and during trips but should give frequent drinks of fruit juice or soda. When necessary, antimotion sickness medication such as Dramamine (dimenhydrinate) may be effective.

Reading or coloring in moving vehicles may bring on motion sickness. For small children, car seats should be placed at a level where children can see out the window. Cars should be kept cool and well ventilated and no one should smoke. If a child complains of feeling ill, it's best to distract the child with an activity such as singing and not to talk about motion sickness.

LODGINGS

Parents should childproof rooms immediately by checking balconies and bathrooms, covering electrical outlets with furniture or tape, securing lamps and other objects that can be pulled off tables, and rearranging furniture with sharp edges. At night, a small light should be left on to help prevent injuries to children who get out of bed in unfamiliar surroundings. Keeping suitcases and clothes off the floor also helps prevent falls. Because poisonings often occur away from home, check that no medications or caustic substances are reachable and be sure to carry syrup of ipecac in case of accidental ingestion of harmful substances. Since hotel plumbing may be tricky, especially when the usual location for hot and cold taps is reversed, children should be assisted with baths and showers. Even adults occasionally scald themselves by turning the wrong knob.

OUTDOORS AND WILDERNESS

Parents should stop at tourist offices and visitor centers for suggestions about safe and enjoyable activities and to obtain material about local health and safety issues —undertows at beaches, animals and plants to stay away from, for example. Frequently, the most common sources of mishaps in the national parks are knives and axes and campfires.

Teach children to sit down and stay put if they are separated from you. This facilitates your finding them. Have them carry a whistle for such emergencies; whistles are more effective for signaling than shouting.

Have children wear loosely fitting long-sleeved shirts, long pants, and shoes and socks to minimize insect bites, sunburn (use a sunscreen with SPF 30 or greater), scratches from bushes, and exposure to poison ivy. When possible, bathe or shower children after outings. Look daily for insects embedded in the skin. Using soap helps prevent poison ivy, cleans cuts and bruises, and removes insect repellents and sunscreens.

With the heat and humidity of the tropics, children need extra fluids and rest to avoid dehydration. The pace of travel should be slowed to accommodate the children's needs.

Many children who drown or nearly drown do so not while swimming. They sometimes trip, slip, or otherwise fall off boats, docks, and piers, while adults are distracted or picture taking. When possible, children should wear an age- and size-appropriate personal floatation device when playing near water.

Shoes and socks protect feet against cuts, fungi, crawling insects, and the many insects that fly just above the ground. Clothing should be kept off the ground, but if it has been laid on the ground, it should be shaken vigorously to release insects. Insect bites can also occur when children strip leaves from trees and plants, shake bushes, kick logs, and turn over rocks. Use insect repellents when necessary, especially in wetlands in the spring.

Children should be instructed not to drink natural water. Even crystal clear water in streams and lakes far from civilization may contain diarrhea-causing organisms. Ask knowledgeable local people before using well water. Illness may occur weeks later. In case of illness, physicians should always be informed where children have traveled.

Animals often misinterpret the intentions of children who offer them food with outstretched hands, and especially when children make sudden moves as the animal nears. All animal bites and scratches should be reported to local wardens and physicians.

If small children eat unknown berries and plants, samples should be taken to show experts.

ILLNESS ABROAD

Medical kits—A small medical kit is very helpful should children become ill when traveling. The kit should contain medications for illnesses that children experience at home and for potential travel-related illnesses, and it should contain the telephone numbers of all the children's health-care providers. Choosing a destination where there is no ready way of communicating with competent medical professionals adds an element of risk to the trip.

A typical medical kit should include the following:
- Medications that the child has used in the past year
- Antiseptic wipes, thermometer, gauze bandages
- Insect repellents and sunscreens
- Packets of oral rehydrating solutions
- Antibacterial soap
- An antibiotic for general use or travelers' diarrhea (azithromycin, cefixime)
- An antihistamine (Benadryl)
- Antibiotic and antifungal ointment
- Acetaminophen
- Ibuprofen
- Hydrocortisone ointment
- Syrup of ipecac
- Malaria prophylaxis and standby treatment, as required by itinerary

Figueroa-Quintanilla D, Salazar-Lindo E, Sack RB, et al. A controlled trial of bismuthsubsalicylate in infants with acute watery diarrheal disease. N Engl J Med 1993 Jun 10;328(23):1653-8.

World Medical Guide

© *Copyright 2000 Travel Medicine, Inc.*

DISEASE RISK SUMMARYS

Mexico, Central America, and the Caribbean

Malaria: There is low risk of malaria in Mexico. Most cases are confined to rural areas of the West Coast. *P. vivax* accounts for 98.7% of malaria infections; the remainder are attributed to *P. falciparum*. Chloroquine prophylaxis is recommended when visiting malarious areas. Chloroquine-resistant falciparum malaria has not been reported. Drug prophylaxis is not necessary when visiting resort areas in Mexico, but personal protective measures against mosquito bites are recommended.

In other areas of Central America, there is risk of vivax malaria in rural areas. Belize has the highest incidence of malaria in the Americas, followed by Nicaragua and Guatemala. There is no malaria in the major cities of Central America. Chloroquine prophylaxis is recommended for travelers visiting rural areas. Travelers should consider mefloquine prophylaxis in certain malarious areas of Panama, where chloroquine-resistant *P. falciparum* may be present.

There is no risk of malaria in the Caribbean, except in Haiti, the Dominican Republic (low levels), and in southwestern Trinidad where an outbreak of vivax malaria has been recently reported in the town of Icacos.

All travelers to Mexico, Central America, and the Caribbean should take measures to prevent mosquito bites.

These precautions include applying a deet-containing skin repellent, wearing permethrin-treated clothing, and, when appropriate, sleeping under a mosquito bed net.

Yellow fever: Yellow fever is reported active only in the remote jungle areas of Trinidad. Several countries in Central America are in the Yellow Fever Endemic Zone, where yellow fever is potentially active. Vaccination is recommended for persons who plan to travel to rural areas of these Endemic Zone countries.

Cholera: Mexico and the other countries in Central America are currently reporting cases of cholera. Although cholera vaccination is not required for entry to any country if arriving directly from the U.S. or Canada, one may be required if arriving from a cholera-infected area, or required for on-going travel to other countries in Latin America, Africa, the Middle East, or Asia. Travelers should consider vaccination or a doctor's letter of exemption from vaccination. The risk to travelers of acquiring cholera is considered low. Cholera occurs primarily in areas with inadequate sanitation and unsafe water supplies such as urban slums and rural areas. Prevention consists primarily in adhering to safe food and drink guidelines.

Travelers' diarrhea: High risk in Mexico and Central America, except for first-class hotels and major resort areas. Lower risk in Belize and Costa Rica, where sanitation is generally better. Medium risk in most Caribbean islands, except for Haiti, where the risk is high. Travelers should observe all food and drink safety precautions. A quinolone antibiotic is recommended for the treatment of acute diarrhea. Diarrhea not responding to treatment with an antibiotic, or chronic diarrhea, may be due to a parasitic disease such as giardiasis or amebiasis.

Hepatitis: All nonimmune travelers should receive hepatitis A vaccine prior to travel to these regions. The hepatitis B carrier rate in the general population of these regions is generally less than 1%–2% and vaccination is not routinely recommended for tourist travel. Vaccination against hepatitis B is recommended for healthcare workers to this region.

Amebiasis: There is a high incidence of amebiasis in Mexico and Central America, where up to 50% of the high-risk population may be infected with *E. histolytica* parasites. To avoid amebiasis, travelers should drink only safe water and eat only well-cooked food. All fruit should be peeled before eating.

Typhoid fever: Typhoid vaccination is recommended for persons traveling for periods longer than 3–4 weeks in rural areas, and who will be staying in areas where there is substandard sanitation.

Dengue fever: Dengue is widespread throughout Central America and the islands of the Caribbean, including Puerto Rico and the U.S. Virgin Islands. In Mexico, dengue occurs

World Medical Guide

primarily during July, August, and September. There is no dengue in Bermuda, the Cayman Islands, or Costa Rica. The Aedes mosquitoes, which transmit dengue, bite primarily during the daytime and are present in populous urban areas as well as resort and rural areas. Prevention of dengue consists of taking protective measures against mosquito bites.

Schistosomiasis: Risk, albeit low, is present in Antigua, the Dominican Republic, Guadeloupe, Martinique, Montserrat, Puerto Rico, and Saint Lucia. Travelers should avoid swimming or bathing in freshwater ponds or streams that may be snail infested.

Leishmaniasis: Cutaneous leishmaniasis (chicleros ulcer), mucocutaneous leishmaniasis (espundia), and visceral leishmaniasis (kala azar) occur in scattered areas of Mexico and Central America. These diseases are transmitted by sandflies (which bite from dusk to dawn). All travelers should take measures to prevent bites by these insects.

Filariasis (Bancroftian variety): This mosquito-transmitted disease occurs (rarely) in the Lesser Antilles from Trinidad north to Guadeloupe. Puerto Rico and the eastern coastal areas of Central America are also potential risk areas. Highest risk is presently in Haiti and the Dominican Republic. Travelers to these regions should take measures to prevent mosquito bites.

Onchocerciasis: This is a form of filariasis prevalent in southern Mexico and Guatemala. Travelers should take measures to prevent insect (blackfly) bites.

Chagas' disease: Occurs in many areas of rural Central America. Risk occurs primarily in those rural-agricultural areas where there are adobe-style huts and houses that potentially harbor the night-biting triatomid (assassin) bugs. Travelers sleeping in such structures should take precautions against nighttime bites. Unscreened blood transfusions are also a source of infection and should be avoided.

Rabies: This disease is present in all Central American countries, but the risk is highest in Mexico, El Salvador, Guatemala, and Honduras. There is a lower risk of rabies in Costa Rica. Mongoose-borne rabies has been reported in Puerto Rico. There is no risk of rabies in the Caribbean, except for Haiti, the Dominican Republic, and Grenada. Travelers should avoid stray animals, especially dogs, and seek emergency treatment of any animal bite. Pre-exposure rabies vaccination is recommended for all persons planning a long stay (4 weeks or more), or extensive travel in rural areas of Mexico and Central America.

AIDS: In Mexico and Central America, homosexual and bisexual activity is the prevailing mode of transmission, but the heterosexual spread of AIDS is increasing. In the Caribbean, there are high rates of heterosexually transmitted AIDS, especially in the Bahamas, Haiti, and the Dominican Republic.

Helminthic diseases: Hookworm is common, especially in rural areas. Travelers should wear shoes to prevent transmission of this disease. Ascariasis and trichuriasis (roundworm and whipworm diseases), caused by the ingestion of food contaminated with the eggs of these worms, can be prevented by washing vegetables and adequately cooking all food. In Mexico and Central America, pork tapeworm disease (caused by the parasite *Taenia solium*) is common and can be prevented by thoroughly cooking food. Cysticercosis and neurocysticercosis, caused by the ingestion of pork tapeworm eggs, is prevalent. (Pork tapeworm eggs are transmitted by fecally contaminated food and/or water.)

Other illnesses: Anthrax, brucellosis (from consumption of raw dairy products or occupational contact with animals), coccidiomycosis, histoplasmosis, gnathostomiasis (outbreaks in Mexico and Ecuador), toxocariasis, toxoplasmosis, sexually transmitted diseases, and tuberculosis. Leptospirosis with pulmonary hemorrhages (symptoms initially confused with dengue hemorrhagic fever) has been recently reported in Nicaragua.

Animal hazards: Scorpions, black widow spiders, brown recluse spiders, and several species of tarantulas are common in many areas of Mexico and Central America. The beaded lizard, gila monster, and vampire bat occur in Mexico and elsewhere.

Marine hazards: The Portuguese man-o'-war, stingrays, several species of poisonous fish, stinging anemones, coral and hydroids, and jellyfish are present in coastal waters and are a potential hazard to unprotected swimmers.

Accidents: Drownings and motor vehicle accidents are the primary threats. There is a high risk of injury from motor vehicle, motorcycle, and moped accidents in all countries of Central America and the Caribbean.

The Caribbean

Yellow fever: Yellow fever activity is reported only in the remote forested areas of Trinidad. No human cases reported since 1980. Vaccination is recommended for persons who plan to travel to rural areas of this country.

Malaria: Malaria occurs in Haiti and the Dominican Republic, where falciparum malaria accounts for approximately 99% of all cases. CDC (12/99) recommends malaria prophylaxis for travelers to rural areas in the Dominican Republic but not for travel to resorts. There has been a recent observed increase in malaria cases in the Dominican Republic, including a localized outbreak in the Altagracia Province (principally in the Bavaro Beach area) in the southeastern part of the country, which has included some cases in tourists who have stayed in resorts in this area. The risk to tourists appears to be quite low, but as a precautionary measure we are expanding our recommendations to include chloroquine prophylaxis for travelers to resorts in the Altagracia Province, particularly those that travel to the Bavaro Beach area. Chloroquine-resistant *P. falciparum* is not reported. An outbreak of vivax malaria was reported in 1991, 1992, and 1995 in southwestern Trinidad, in the town of Icacos. All other islands in the Caribbean are currently malaria-free. Chloroquine prophylaxis should be considered for travel to islands with malaria risk.

Diarrheal disease: Highly endemic in much of the region. Common pathogens include enterotoxigenic *E. coli*, shigella, and salmonella species. Rotavirus is the most common causative agent of nonspecific diarrhea in children in this region. Amebiasis and giardiasis presumably are moderately endemic in most Caribbean countries. Data for cryptosporidiosis are sparse.

Hepatitis: Hepatitis A is endemic at moderate to high levels in most countries. Vaccine is recommended for all nonimmune travelers. Hepatitis E levels are unclear. The hepatitis B carrier rate in the Caribbean varies from 0.8% to 4.1%. Vaccination against hepatitis B is recommended for healthcare workers and should be considered by long-term visitors to this region.

Dengue fever: This mosquito-transmitted viral disease is widespread throughout the Caribbean, including Puerto Rico and the Virgin Islands. Transmission is year-round in coastal and lowland urban areas. Outbreaks reported on Guadeloupe and Trinidad. Only Bermuda and the Cayman Islands are reported dengue-free.

Arboviral fevers: Low risk. Mosquito-transmitted viral encephalitis is reported in the Caribbean. Venezuelan equine encephalitis is reported from Barbados, St. Vincent, and Trinidad and Tobago.

Leishmaniasis: Low to negligible risk. Currently, cutaneous and mucocutaneous leishmaniasis occur only on the island of Hispaniola (Haiti and the Dominican Republic). Travelers to Hispaniola should take measures to prevent insect (sandfly) bites. Elsewhere, risk of leishmaniasis is low or absent. Members of the *Leishmania mexicana* complex have been historically identified in Trinidad and Tobago, Martinique, and Guadeloupe, as have parasites (presumably *L. chagasi*) of visceral leishmaniasis in Martinique and Guadeloupe.

Filariasis: Bancroftian variety; mosquito-transmitted. Highest risk is in Haiti and the Dominican Republic. Filariasis occurs (rarely) in the Lesser Antilles from Trinidad north to Guadeloupe. Puerto Rico is also a potential risk area. Travelers to these countries should take measures to prevent mosquito bites.

Schistosomiasis: Limited or potential risk is present on Antigua, Guadeloupe, Martinique, Montserrat, Puerto Rico, and Saint Lucia. The disease may occur sporadically in the other islands. Travelers should avoid swimming, bathing, or wading in freshwater ponds or streams that may be snail infested.

Leptospirosis: A disease of considerable public health concern in the Caribbean. Transmission of disease is through skin contact with water or moist soil contaminated with the urine of infected animals. Highest risk occurs in Barbados, Dominica, Jamaica, Saint Lucia, Saint Vincent, and Trinidad and Tobago.

Chagas' disease: This disease has been detected in Trinidad and Tobago. Potential vectors (triatomid bugs) occur on several other islands, including Antigua, Aruba, Curacao, Guadeloupe, Jamaica, and Martinique. Risk occurs in rural-agricultural areas where

World Medical Guide

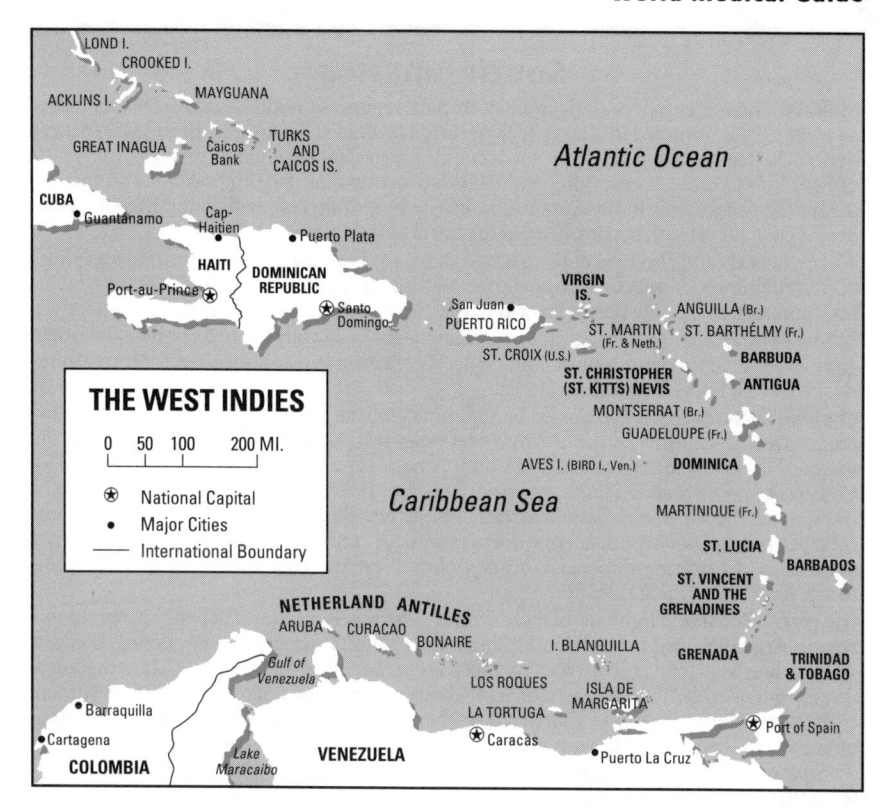

there are adobe-style huts and houses that potentially harbor the night-biting triatomid (assassin) bugs. Travelers sleeping in such structures should take precautions against nighttime bites.

Rabies: Low risk. Mongoose-borne rabies has been reported in Grenada. There is no risk of rabies in the Caribbean, except for Haiti, the Dominican Republic, and Grenada. Travelers should avoid stray animals, especially dogs, and seek emergency treatment of any animal bite.

AIDS: Reported from all Caribbean countries. HIV prevalence throughout the region, based on blood donor screening, is estimated at 0.5%. Most cases of AIDS in this region are transmitted through sexual contact. Highest HIV rates, as well as the highest rates of heterosexually transmitted AIDS, are found in Haiti, the Dominican Republic, and the Bahamas.

Other diseases/health threats: Brucellosis, histoplasmosis, leishmaniasis (not currently endemic, except possibly for the Dominican Republic), fascioliasis (confirmed on Guadeloupe), helminthic infections (ancylostomiasis, ascariasis, strongyloidiasis, and trichuriasis), syphilis (the Turks and Caicos, the Bahamas, the Cayman Islands, and the British Virgin Islands have the highest official rates), toxocariasis (reported from several islands; higher infection rates in children), tuberculosis (endemic throughout the Caribbean), typhoid fever, ciguatera fish toxin poisoning (outbreaks have occurred), and swimming-related hazards (jellyfish, spiny sea urchins, and coral).

South America

Malaria: There is risk of malaria in most tropical regions of South America. Nearly half of all cases (47%) occurred in Brazil; 32% occurred in Bolivia, Colombia, Ecuador, Peru, and Venezuela. The highest incidence rates occur in Guyana, French Guiana, the Amazon Region of Brazil, and Peru. Chloroquine- and Fansidar-resistant falciparum malaria is an increasing problem, especially in the Amazon Basin. Chemoprophylaxis with either mefloquine or doxycycline is currently recommended for travel to these areas.

All travelers should also take anti-insect precautions. These precautions include applying a deet-containing skin repellent, wearing permethrin-treated clothing, and sleeping under a mosquito net, preferably permethrin-treated.

Yellow fever: Risk is present in rural and jungle areas in all countries except Paraguay, Uruguay, Argentina, Falkland Islands, and Chile. Vaccination is recommended for travel to rural areas of all Endemic Zone countries.

Cholera: Disease activity is reported in Argentina, Bolivia, Brazil, Chile, Colombia, Ecuador, French Guiana, Guyana, Peru, Suriname, and Venezuela. Although cholera vaccination is not required for entry to any country in South America if arriving directly from the U.S. or Canada, it may be required if arriving from a cholera-infected area, or required for on-going travel to other countries in Latin America, Africa, the Middle East, or Asia. Travelers should consider vaccination (one dose) or a doctor's letter of exemption from vaccination. The risk to travelers of acquiring cholera is considered low. Prevention consists primarily in adhering to safe food and drink guidelines.

Travelers' diarrhea: High risk outside of first-class hotels and resort areas. Lower risk occurs in Argentina and the Falkland Islands, where sanitation is generally better. Travelers should observe all food and drink safety precautions. A quinolone antibiotic (Cipro or Floxin) is recommended for the treatment of acute diarrhea. Diarrhea not responding to treatment with an antibiotic, or chronic diarrhea, may be due to a parasitic disease such as giardiasis or amebiasis, and treatment with metronidazole (Flagyl) or tinidazole (Fasigyn) should be considered. All cases of diarrhea should be treated with adequate fluid replacement.

Hepatitis A: All susceptible (nonimmune) travelers should receive hepatitis A vaccine prior to travel to South America.

Hepatitis E: Reported from the Brazilian Amazon, the Atlantic coast (Bahia, Brazil), and most likely occurs in other countries as well, although data are scarce.

Hepatitis B: The hepatitis B carrier rate in the Amazon Basin of Brazil is as high as 20%. High rates also reported among aboriginal tribes in Venezuela and French Guiana. Most other countries have hepatitis B carrier rates in the general population of 1%–3%. Hepatitis B vaccination recommended for healthcare workers and those travelers expecting to have close, prolonged contact with the indigenous population of these countries, especially in Brazil.

Typhoid fever: The highest rates of typhoid fever in South America occur in Peru and Chile. Typhoid vaccination is recommended for persons traveling longer than 2–4 weeks in areas with substandard sanitation. The typhoid vaccine is about 70% effective. The best prevention against typhoid fever is avoiding unsafe food and drink.

Amebiasis: There is a high incidence of amebiasis in South America, where up to 50% of the high-risk population may be infected with *E. histolytica* parasites. To avoid amebiasis, travelers should drink only safe water and eat only well-cooked food. All fruit should be peeled before eating.

Dengue fever: There have been dramatic increases in dengue fever and dengue hemorrhagic fever during the past decade in South America. Outbreaks and epidemics are reported from Brazil, Ecuador, Colombia, Peru, Venezuela, and other countries. *Aedes aegypti* mosquitoes, which transmit dengue, bite during daytime and are present in populous urban areas as well as resort and rural areas. Prevention of dengue consists of taking protective measures against mosquito bites, especially during the daytime when the *Aedes* mosquitoes are most active.

Schistosomiasis: Risk is present in Brazil, Suriname, and north-central Venezuela. Travelers should avoid swimming, wading, or bathing in freshwater lakes, ponds, or streams that are possibly infested with schistosome-carrying snail larvae.

World Medical Guide

SOUTH AMERICA

0 200 400 600 MI.

- ✪ National Capital
- • Major Cities
- — International Boundary
- — Major Rivers
- ▲ Mountain Peaks

World Medical Guide

Leishmaniasis: Risk is present in most countries of tropical South America. Cutaneous, mucocutaneous, and visceral leishmaniasis (kala azar) occur in many countries. Travelers to rural areas should take measures to prevent insect (sandfly) bites. Sandflies bite most actively between dusk and dawn and are found in greatest number on the periphery of rural forested areas.

Filariasis: Mosquito-borne; risk is present in parts of Brazil, French Guiana, Guyana, Suriname, and Venezuela. Travelers to risk areas should take measures to prevent insect (mosquito) bites.

Onchocerciasis: This form of filariasis is transmitted by blackflies of the Simulian species. These flies are found near rivers, where they breed in surrounding vegetation. Disease is prevalent in Venezuela, Colombia, Ecuador, and northern Brazil. Travelers to these regions should take personal protective measures against insect (blackfly) bites.

Chagas' disease: Occurs in all tropical areas of South America. Chagas' disease is transmitted primarily in rural areas where there are adobe-style huts and houses that often harbor the night-biting triatomid (assassin) bugs. Travelers sleeping in such structures should take precautions against nighttime bites. These precautions include spraying sleeping quarters with an insecticide (such as Raid), sleeping away from walls, or sleeping under a mosquito net. Unscreened blood transfusions are also a source of infection and should be avoided.

Lyme disease: The incidence of Lyme disease appears to be very low. Five cases of erythema migrans were reported from Brazil in 1991. In Peru, although no cases have been reported, 2% of agricultural workers were found to be seropositive for Lyme disease.

Bartonellosis (Oroya fever): This is a sandfly-transmitted illness found in arid river valleys on the northern slopes of the Andes (Peru, Ecuador, and Colombia) up to 3,000 meters elevation. Prevention consists of preventing insect bites.

Rabies: Animal rabies has been reported from many countries, especially Argentina, Brazil, Colombia, and Ecuador. Human rabies in South America is usually transmitted by dogs, but an outbreak of vampire bat-transmitted rabies has been reported in the Amazon jungle of Peru. Rabies vaccination is indicated following the unprovoked bite of a dog, cat, bat, or monkey. Bites by other animals should be evaluated on an individual basis. Immunization against rabies is recommended for extended travel to remote rural areas.

AIDS: Homosexuality and bisexuality remain the prevailing mode of HIV transmission in South America, but there is a trend toward greater heterosexual transmission, especially in major cities in Brazil and Chile. HIV-1 prevalence estimated at less than 1% of the general population of the countries of Latin America, but in some urban areas (e.g., Rio de Janeiro), up to 28% of female prostitutes and 80% of IV drug users are HIV positive. HIV-2, HTLV-1, and HTLV-2 are reported in South America.

Helminthic infections: Hookworm and whipworm are common, especially in rural areas. Travelers should wear shoes to prevent transmission of these diseases. Ascariasis, caused by the ingestion of food contaminated with the eggs of roundworms, can be prevented by adequate cooking. Pork and beef tapeworm disease is prevalent and can be avoided by thorough cooking of meat.

Other diseases/health threats: Brucellosis, echinococcosis (occurs in sheep-raising regions), coccidiomycosis, cysticercosis and neurocysticercosis (very high incidence in Colombia), histoplasmosis, human hantavirus infection (occurs throughout much of South America), leptospirosis, plague (4 cases in Brazil, 420 cases in Peru in 1994), toxocariasis, trichinosis, tuberculosis (often a serious public health problem), typhoid fever, louse- and flea-borne typhus, and viral encephalitis. Portuguese man-of-war, sea wasps, jellyfish, spiny sea urchins, stinging anemones, and sharp corals may occur in the coastal waters of these countries and pose a potential threat to swimmers. Carnivorous fish (including the piranha) may be found in freshwater bodies of some countries. Animal hazards include snakes (coral snakes, vipers), scorpions, black widow spiders, and large animals of the cat family, especially jaguars.

Accidents: There is a high risk of injury from motor vehicle, motorcycle, and moped accidents in the developing countries due to poor road conditions, chaotic traffic, lack of driver training, and poor vehicle maintenance. Rental vehicles and taxis may not be equipped with seat belts. All travelers should drive with extreme caution.

Europe, Eastern Europe, and Russia

Malaria: There is no risk of malaria in western or eastern Europe.

Travelers' diarrhea: Low risk in most western European countries. Higher risk occurs in Spain, Greece, the Balkans, and eastern Europe, especially Bulgaria, Hungary, and Romania. Travelers to higher risk areas should drink only bottled, boiled, or treated water and avoid undercooked food. A quinolone antibiotic is recommended for the treatment of diarrhea.

Hepatitis: All nonimmune travelers should receive hepatitis A vaccine prior to visiting Spain, Greece, Yugoslavia and the Balkan States, and the eastern European countries, especially Bulgaria, Hungary, and Romania. The hepatitis B carrier rate in the general population of Europe is variable, but is less than 1% in most western European countries. The hepatitis B carrier rate increases to 1%–4% in Spain, Greece, and Eastern Europe. Hepatitis B vaccination should be considered by anyone planning an extended visit to Spain, Greece, the Balkan States, and the eastern European countries, especially Bulgaria, Hungary, and Romania.

Typhoid fever: Persons traveling extensively in Spain, Greece, Yugoslavia and the Balkan States, or the eastern European countries, especially Bulgaria, Hungary, and Romania, should consider typhoid vaccination.

Lyme disease: Risk of transmission occurs throughout Europe in rural brushy, wooded, and forested areas up to 1,500 meters elevation, especially in Scandinavia, Austria, Switzerland, southern Germany, and northern Italy. The ticks that transmit Lyme disease are most

World Medical Guide

abundant and active April through September. The Lyme disease vaccine made in America is not effective against European strains of borrelia.

Ehrlichiosis: Cases of human granulocytic ehrlichiosis have been reported from Slovenia and the Netherlands.

Diphtheria: The diphtheria epidemic that started in Moscow in the 1990s and then spread to the Newly Independent States is still a threat. Cases have declined in Russia but are increasing elsewhere. Vaccine control programs, however, are starting to take effect. All travelers to these countries, especially adults, should be fully immunized against diphtheria.

Pertussis (whooping cough): Reported in the Netherlands. The new strain of Bordetela pertussis bacterium is resistant to a leading vaccine and attacks adults as well as children.

Leishmaniasis: Cutaneous and visceral leishmaniasis is present in the countries bordering the Mediterranean. Risk areas include Portugal, Spain, southern France, the Naples area, Majorca, the suburbs of Athens, and the Greek Isles. Travelers to these areas should take measures to prevent sandfly bites.

Sandfly fever and West Nile fever: Cases reported from Albania and Adriatic area.

Mediterranean spotted fever (boutonneuse fever): Occurs in southern France and in the coastal regions of other Mediterranean countries, and also along the Black Sea coast, in brushy and/or forested areas below 1,000 meters elevation. Peak transmission period is July through September. Disease may be acquired in and around tick-infested houses and terrain, but more than 95% of cases are associated with contact with tick-carrying dogs.

European tick-borne encephalitis (TBE): The tick vector for this disease, *Ixodes ricinus* (the same tick that transmits Lyme disease), is widely distributed in brushy and forested areas at elevations up to 1,500 meters. TBE occurs in all European countries (especially Austria, Germany, Switzerland, the Czech Republic, Hungary, The Balkans, and Eastern Europe) except the Benelux countries and the Iberian Peninsula.

Crimean-Congo hemorrhagic fever: This is a viral encephalitis transmitted by *Hyalomma marginatum* ticks. These ticks are most active from April until August, reaching peak feeding activity April through May.

Hemorrhagic fever with renal syndrome (HFRS): Cases of Hantavirus illness are reported in The Balkans and in eastern Europe. A milder form of HFRS (caused by Puumala virus) occurs in Scandinavia, other European countries, and European Russia. Travelers should avoid contact with rodent urine or rodent feces, which transmit the virus.

Swimmer's itch: Widespread increase in cercarial dermatitis has occurred in Central Europe (primarily Germany, Austria, Czech Republic), especially during the hot summer months. The causative cercariae (which penetrate the skin) are found in ponds and lakes that are snail-infested and where ducks are found.

Rabies: Occurs primarily in wild animals, especially foxes, in many rural areas of Europe. Human cases are infrequent. There is no risk of rabies in Finland, Iceland, Ireland, Sweden, the United Kingdom, Gibraltar, Malta, Monaco, Portugal, and Spain.

AIDS: Increased cases reported especially from eastern Europe (mainly Romania and Bulgaria) and Russia. Infected blood and contaminated needles and syringes are important sources of infection in these countries. Travelers should consider carrying sterile needles and syringes and should avoid, if possible, blood transfusions and medical injections in these countries. Blood supplies are reportedly screened in Czechoslovakia, Hungary, and Poland, but lack of public health funding may hamper complete screening for AIDS and hepatitis B and C viruses. Travelers should consider evacuation to a European medical facility when surgical care, or blood transfusions, are needed.

Road safety: Pedestrians should use extra caution when crossing the street in countries where there is left-sided traffic. There is a higher incidence of motor vehicle fatalities in Spain, Portugal, Yugoslavia, Greece, and eastern Europe. Seat belts should be worn at all times.

Other illnesses/hazards: Brucellosis, echinococcosis (southern Europe), Legionnaire's disease (legionellosis outbreaks have been reported in tourists on package tours to Spain and Naples, Italy; contaminated water probable source), leptospirosis, listeriosis (from contaminated soft cheeses and meat), tick-borne relapsing fever (risk in rocky, rural livestock areas), and soil-transmitted helminthic infections (roundworm, hookworm, and whipworm infections; reported occasionally in southern Europe). There is a high incidence of yersinia infections in Scandinavia from tainted beef. Raw cod ("lutefish") in Scandinavia may contain the fish tapeworm, *Diphyllobothrium latum*, a cause of pernicious anemia.

The Caucasus, Central Asia, Siberia, & Far East regions of former USSR

Health Advisory

Malaria: Limited foci of vivax malaria exist in Kazakhstan and Uzbekistan. Tajikistan has reported an increase in malaria following the civil war (1992–1996), with *P. vivax* identified in 84% of cases, *P. falciparum* in 16%. Most cases of malaria in Tajikistan are reported from the region of Khatlon Oblast. Information on chloroquine resistance is not available.

Travelers' diarrhea: All water supplies are suspect, including municipal tap water, which may be untreated and grossly contaminated.

Hepatitis: All nonimmune travelers should receive hepatitis A vaccine prior to visiting these regions. The hepatitis B carrier rate in the general population of the countries in these regions is estimated as high as 8%.

Lyme disease: Occurs focally in rural forested areas below 1,500 meters elevation.

Tick-borne encephalitis (TBE): Peak transmission period is April through June. Risk is present primarily in rural brushy and forested areas below 1,500 meters elevation. TBE is usually known as "Central European tick-borne encephalitis" or "Russian spring-summer encephalitis" west of the Urals.

Leishmaniasis: Risk for cutaneous leishmaniasis primarily limited to the Uzbekistan, Kazakhstan, and Turkmenistan. Travelers to these regions should take measures to prevent sandfly bites.

Crimean-Congo hemorrhagic fever: Also known as Central Asian hemorrhagic fever. Risk areas are rural steppe, savannah, semi-desert, and foothill/low mountain habitats below 2,000 meters elevation. Outbreaks occurred in southcentral Kazakhstan during 1989.

Arboviral diseases: Tahjna virus fever (mosquito-borne; virus circulates through much of the former USSR), sandfly fever (sandfly-borne; limited to regions of southern central Asia, April–October), dengue fever (mosquito-borne; no recent cases reported), West Nile fever (mosquito-borne; cases have occurred in the Tajikistan), North Asian tick fever (occurs wherever tick vectors are found).

Other illnesses/hazards: Boutonneuse fever (tick-borne; reported most commonly along the shores of the Black and Caspian Seas), brucellosis, echinococcosis (dog feces are infective), legionellosis, leptospirosis, rabies, rickettsialpox, tick-borne relapsing fever (reported from Kirghizstan, Turkmenistan, and Uzbekistan), trichinosis, typhoid fever, tularemia, tuberculosis, and soil-transmitted and helminthic infections (roundworm, hookworm, and whipworm infections and strongyloidiasis).

North Africa

Yellow fever: There is no risk of yellow fever in North Africa.

Malaria: This disease is not a major public health problem in North Africa. Malarious areas are found only in parts of Algeria and Egypt. *P. vivax* is the dominant species, but *P. falciparum* and *P. malariae* are also reported. There are no reports to date of chloroquine-resistant falciparum malaria. Chloroquine prophylaxis is recommended when traveling to malarious areas. All travelers to malarious areas should take personal protection measures against mosquito bites.

Travelers' diarrhea: High risk outside of resort areas and first-class hotels. Piped water supplies in this region are frequently untreated and may be grossly contaminated. Travelers should observe all food and drink safety precautions. A quinolone antibiotic (Cipro or Floxin) is recommended for the treatment of acute diarrhea. Diarrhea not responding to treatment with an antibiotic, or chronic diarrhea, may be due to a parasitic disease such as giardiasis or amebiasis—or an intestinal virus. Treatment with metronidazole (Flagyl) or tinidazole (Fasigyn) should be considered in cases of suspected parasitic disease.

Hepatitis: All nonimmune travelers to North Africa should receive hepatitis A vaccine. The hepatitis B carrier rate in the general population of these countries is estimated at 4%–10%. Vaccination against hepatitis B is advised for healthcare workers and should be considered by all long-term travelers to this region.

Typhoid fever: Vaccination is recommended for extended travel outside the usual tourist routes of these countries.

Arboviral fevers: Few if any cases of dengue are reported from North Africa. Sandfly fever is widely distributed, especially in Egypt, Libya, and Tunisia. Rift Valley fever and West Nile fever are significant risks in Egypt. Crimean-Congo hemorrhagic fever and chikungunya fever: insufficient data are available to indicate whether or not these arboviral fevers have significant transmission in this region.

Mediterranean spotted fever (boutonneuse fever): Scattered cases are reported. Travelers are advised to avoid touching or petting dogs, which harbor dog ticks that transmit most cases of Mediterranean spotted fever.

Leishmaniasis: Both cutaneous and visceral leishmaniasis (kala azar) occur in North Africa. Most cases are reported from the central and/or northern areas of Morocco, Algeria, Libya, and Tunisia. In Egypt, risk areas include the eastern Nile Delta, the Suez Canal zone, and northern Sinai. Travelers to these areas should take measures to prevent insect (sandfly) bites.

Filariasis: Occurs focally in the Nile Delta. Travelers to this region should take measures to prevent mosquito bites.

Schistosomiasis: High risk occurs along the entire Nile River and in the Nile Delta region. Risk is present focally in Algeria (low risk), Libya, Tunisia, Morocco, and Western Sahara. Travelers to these countries should avoid swimming or wading in freshwater lakes, ponds, streams, or irrigation ditches.

Rabies: Animal rabies occurs in all countries. Human cases are also reported, usually from urban areas. Travelers should especially avoid contact with stray dogs and seek immediate treatment for any animal bite. Pre-exposure vaccination against rabies (3 doses) should be considered by anyone planning long-term travel to this region.

AIDS: There is a low prevalence of AIDS in North Africa.

Other illnesses: Brucellosis (usually transmitted by raw goat or sheep milk), echinococcosis (a major health problem in central Tunisia, and occurs elsewhere), meningitis (significant outbreaks have occurred in Egypt, involving Group A and C meningococci; vaccination is recommended for travelers who will have close contact with the indigenous population), relapsing fever (louse-borne and tick-borne; reported in northern Sahara and coastal areas), tuberculosis (common), helminthic infections (roundworm, hookworm, and whipworm) are common in rural areas; incidence is estimated at 5%.

sub-Saharan Africa

Yellow fever: This disease is currently reported active in nine countries—Angola, Cameroon, Gambia, Guinea, Kenya, Mali, Nigeria, Sudan, and Zaire. A vaccination certificate is absolutely required for entry to Benin, Burkina Fasso, Cameroon, Cote d'Ivoire (Ivory Coast), Gabon, Ghana, Liberia, Mali, Mauritania, Niger, Senegal, Sao Tome & Principe, and Togo, even if arriving directly from the United States or Canada. Travelers to Cape Verde Islands, Equatorial Guinea, Gambia, Guinea-Bissau, Nigeria, and Sierra Leone will need a vaccination certificate if arriving from any "infected" or yellow fever endemic countries in Africa or Latin America.

Cholera: This disease is reported active in many countries. Although cholera vaccination is not required for entry if arriving directly from the U.S. or Canada, it may be required for ongoing travel to other countries in Africa, the Middle East, Asia, or Oceania. Travelers who plan to visit several countries should consider vaccination (one dose) or a doctor's letter of exemption from vaccination. Cholera occurs in areas with inadequate sanitation, such as urban slums and rural areas. The risk to tourists of acquiring cholera is considered low, but may be increased in travelers who are using anti-ulcer medication or antacids, or who will be living in less than sanitary conditions in areas of high cholera activity. These travelers should also consider vaccination. Prevention consists primarily in adhering to safe food and drink guidelines.

Malaria: High risk in most countries, including urban areas. Transmission of disease is greater during and just after the rainy seasons when the mosquito population increases. Highest malaria attack rates for tourists are reported from East Africa, Ghana, Nigeria, and Malawi. Most malaria in sub-Saharan Africa is caused by *P. falciparum*, but *P. vivax* occurs in Ethiopia, Somalia, and Sudan. There is widespread occurrence of chloroquine-resistant *P. falciparum* throughout sub-Saharan Africa. Chemoprophylaxis with mefloquine (Lariam) or doxycycline is currently advised for people who travel to malarious areas, but travelers should be aware that cases of mefloquine-resistant *P. falciparum* have been reported (mostly in French travelers who returned from West Africa) and that no prophylactic drug is guaranteed to provide 100% protection against all species of malaria. For this reason, travelers should also take careful measures to prevent mosquito bites. These measures include the frequent application of a deet-containing insect repellent, the wearing of permethrin-treated clothing, and, if necessary, the use of permethrin-treated mosquito bed nets. Travelers should seek immediate medical consultation for a suspected attack of malaria, even if they have been taking prophylactic drugs.

NOTE: Risk of malaria is low or absent in Nairobi, the Ethiopian highlands, or on the islands of Cape Verde, Mauritius, Reunion, and the Seychelles.

Travelers' diarrhea: High risk outside first-class hotels and resorts. Most water sources should be considered potentially contaminated. Travelers should strictly observe safe food and drink precautions. A quinolone antibiotic is recommended for the treatment of adults with diarrhea. Trimethoprim/sulfamethoxazole or furazolidone is recommended for treating children. Diarrhea not responding to treatment with an antibiotic, or chronic diarrhea, may be due to a parasitic disease such as giardiasis or amebiasis, and treatment with metronidazole (Flagyl) or tinidazole (Fasigyn) should be considered.

Typhoid fever: Vaccination is recommended for persons traveling off the usual tourist routes and/or on working assignments whose duration of travel exceeds 3–4 weeks.

Hepatitis: All nonimmune travelers should receive hepatitis A vaccine prior to visiting this region. The hepatitis B virus carrier rate in the countries of sub-Saharan Africa is estimated to exceed 10%. Vaccination against hepatitis B is recommended for all healthcare workers and should be considered by anyone planning an extended visit to this region.

Amebiasis: There is a high incidence of amebiasis in West and South Africa, where up to 50% of the high-risk population may be infected with *E. histolytica* parasites. To avoid amebiasis, travelers should drink only safe water and eat only well-cooked food. All fruit should be peeled before eating.

World Medical Guide

Dengue fever: Low risk. Although the *Aedes aegypti* mosquito that transmits dengue is found in most countries of Africa, cases of dengue appear to be rare. Sporadic outbreaks have been reported most recently in Burkina Fasso, Cote d'Ivoire, Guinea, Nigeria, and Senegal. All travelers should take personal protection measures against mosquito bites to prevent this disease.

Leishmaniasis: Epidemics of visceral leishmaniasis (kala azar) have occurred in East Africa, Ethiopia, and Sudan, but sporadic cases also have been reported in Chad, Burkina Fasso, Central African Republic, Uganda, Zaire, and Zambia. Cutaneous leishmaniasis (Oriental sore) is widespread in Mali, Mauritania, Chad, the Central African Republic and is present, but less active, elsewhere, especially in the drier areas. To prevent leishmaniasis, travelers should take measures to prevent insect (sandfly) bites.

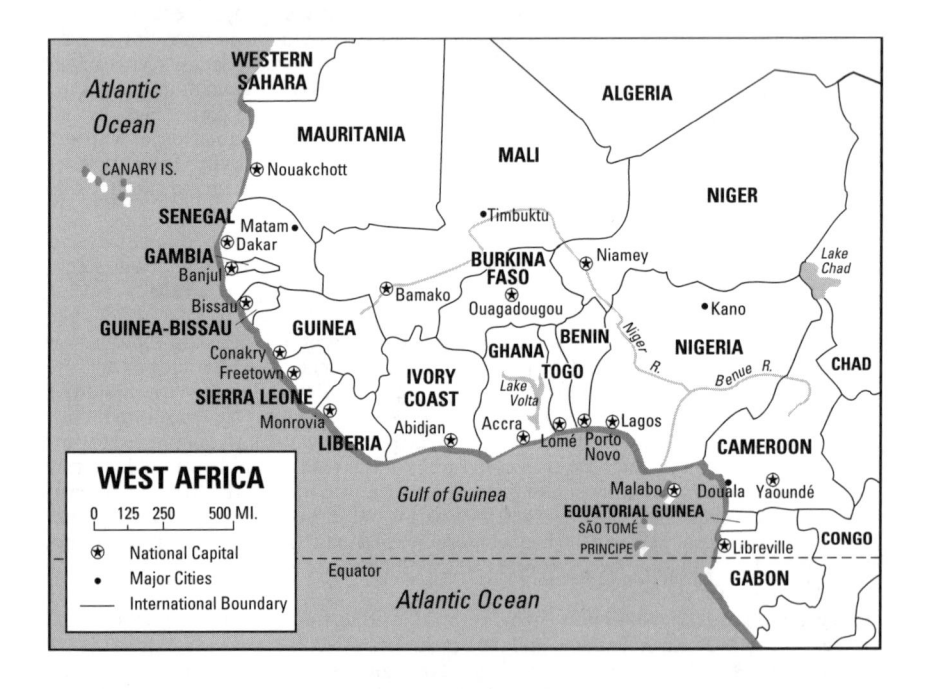

Schistosomiasis: Risk is present in all countries except for Cape Verde, Reunion, and the Seychelles. Travelers should avoid swimming, bathing, or wading in freshwater lakes, ponds, or streams.

Onchocerciasis: Widespread incidence in West and Central Africa, extending into Uganda, Sudan, and the Ethiopian highlands. Western Kenya is risk free. Travelers to risk areas should take measures to prevent blackfly bites. The blackfly is a daytime biter and is rarely found indoors.

Filariasis: Mosquito-borne Bancroftian filariasis is widespread in all countries, except southern Africa. To prevent filariasis, travelers should take measures to prevent mosquito bites.

Loiasis: This form of filariasis is common in equatorial Africa, especially West and Central Africa. It is transmitted by the biting fly (Chrysops). Travelers should take protective measures against insect (fly) bites.

Meningitis: Travelers (especially teachers, relief workers, missionaries, etc.) planning an extended visit to sub-Saharan Africa should be vaccinated against meningococcal meningitis. There is an increased incidence of type A serogroup meningitis in Burundi, Kenya, and Tanzania, and vaccination is recommended for travel to these countries, although the risk to tourists is deemed to be low.

World Medical Guide

African sleeping sickness (trypanosomiasis): This disease occurs in several countries of central and East Africa. Most risk to tourists occurs when visiting game parks. Travelers to rural areas should take measures to prevent insect (tsetse fly) bites.

West Nile fever, Chickungunya fever, Rift Valley fever: These mosquito-transmitted diseases are avoided by taking personal protection measures against insect bites.

Lassa fever: Low risk to tourists. Lassa fever occurs primarily in West Africa (from Nigeria to Guinea). The virus of Lassa fever is thought to be spread by infective rat and rodent urine. Travelers can reduce exposure by avoiding bush areas and the interiors of thatch huts.

Rabies: Animal rabies has been reported from all countries. Most human cases are transmitted by dog bites, with risk occurring in both urban and rural areas. Jackals and mongooses should also be considered potentially rabid. Travelers should seek emergency treatment of any animal bite, especially if the bite was unprovoked. Pre-exposure rabies vaccination is recommended for all travelers (especially children) planning an extended visit or extensive travel in sub-Saharan Africa.

AIDS: Widespread incidence of HIV infection in the countries of central and eastern Africa, where up to 30% of the urban population is HIV-1 positive. In West Africa, HIV-2 is endemic and up to 10% of the urban population is serologically positive. Travelers should avoid unsafe sexual contact, injections with unsterile needles and syringes, and unscreened blood transfusions. Travelers should consider carrying sterile needles and syringes in case an emergency medical injection is required.

Helminthic infections: There is widespread occurrence of hookworm, roundworm, and whipworm infections. Strongyloides infection is also prevalent. Travelers can prevent these infections by wearing shoes to prevent skin penetration by infectious worm larvae and cook food thoroughly to destroy infectious roundworm and whipworm eggs. Paragonimiasis (lung fluke disease) occurs in West Africa and is transmitted by the consumption of raw crustaceans.

Other diseases: African tick typhus (transmitted primarily by dog ticks), anthrax, brucellosis, Crimean-Congo hemorrhagic fever (a tick-borne viral disease; occurs throughout Africa), cysticercosis and pork tapeworm disease, echinococcosis, leprosy, plague (human plague is reported from Madagascar, Malawi, Mozambique, Tanzania, Zaire, and Zimbabwe), syphilis, trachoma (widespread; treatment with azithromycin, 1 gm weekly for three weeks markedly reduces infection rate), tuberculosis (a major health problem in many countries), typhus (louse-borne), and acute hemorrhagic conjunctivitis are reported.

Snake bite: The puff adder, carpet viper, and spitting cobra are the most important species. The average tourist is at low risk; the overland traveler is at much higher potential risk of snake bite. Overland travelers should have prior knowledge of prevailing species and consider the need for access to cool-stored antivenom. Sterile needles, syringes, and cannulas are essential.

The Middle East

Malaria: The risk of malaria is low in this region. There is no malaria in Kuwait, Bahrain, Cyprus, Israel, Jordan, Lebanon, or Qatar. Vivax malaria is found in the northern third of Iraq below 1,500 meters elevation. In Saudi Arabia, malaria is confined to the extreme southwest, about 500 km south of Jeddah. The highest risk of malaria in the Middle East occurs during the rainy season, from December through March. Falciparum malaria accounts for 50%–70% of cases, vivax the remainder. Chloroquine-resistant falciparum is reported in Yemen and Iran, and may occur in Oman and Saudi Arabia; mefloquine prophylaxis should be considered for travel to malarious areas of these countries. In other malarious regions, chloroquine prophylaxis is recommended. Personal protection measures against mosquito bites, including permethrin-impregnated bed nets, should be used by all travelers.

Travelers' diarrhea: Medium to high risk throughout this region. Travelers should drink only commercially bottled, boiled, or chemically treated water, especially in rural areas. All food should be well cooked. Fruit should be peeled. Increased resistance (up to 93% of bacteria tested) of Shigella and *E. coli* to trimethoprim/sulfamethoxazole (Bactrim, Septra) has been reported. A quinolone antibiotic (Cipro or Floxin) is recommended for the treatment of acute diarrhea. Diarrhea not responding to treatment with an antibiotic, or chronic diarrhea, may be due to a parasitic disease such as giardiasis or amebiasis, and treatment with metronidazole (Flagyl) or tinidazole (Fasigyn) should be considered. Diarrhea due to cryptosporidiosis usually does not require antibiotic treatment. All cases of diarrhea should be treated with adequate fluid replacement.

Hepatitis: High risk. All nonimmune travelers should receive hepatitis A vaccine. The hepatitis B carrier rate in the general population of this region is estimated at 2%–10%. Vaccination against hepatitis B is recommended for healthcare workers and all long-term visitors to this region. Hepatitis E is prevalent among guest workers in these countries and may possibly be a threat to travelers. Prevention of hepatitis E requires avoiding the consumption of contaminated water since immune globulin is not protective against this illness.

Cutaneous leishmaniasis: Risk is low, but this sandfly-transmitted disease is reported throughout the Middle East. Travelers should take protective measures to prevent insect (sandfly) bites.

Visceral leishmaniasis (kala azar): Cases are reported throughout the region, especially from rural areas. Twenty cases of kala azar occurred in U.S. Desert Storm troops stationed in Saudi Arabia. All travelers to the Middle East are advised to take protective measures against insect (sandfly) bites.

Schistosomiasis: Risk is present in Yemen, Oman, Jordan, Iraq, Saudi Arabia, and Syria. Travelers should avoid swimming, bathing, or wading in freshwater lakes, ponds, streams, or irrigated areas in these regions.

Rabies: Animal rabies, mainly in dogs and foxes, is a problem in most countries, but human cases occur infrequently. Travelers should consider rabies vaccination if they will be in remote or rural areas for extended periods and unable to obtain prompt medical care after being bitten by a dog or wild animal.

Other diseases: Epidemic typhus, murine typhus, Q fever, sandfly fever (a viral illness transmitted by sandflies), Congo-Crimean hemorrhagic fever (a viral illness transmitted by ticks), brucellosis (transmitted by unpasteurized dairy products), echinococcosis, typhoid fever (most cases occur in the summer and early fall; multidrug-resistant strains of salmonella bacteria are reported; treatment drugs of choice are the quinolones and third generation cephalosporins), tapeworm and hookworm disease, and tuberculosis are reported from many areas. Meningitis occurs in sporadic epidemics in Saudi Arabia, especially among travelers to Mecca. Plague has not been reported in the Middle East for 15 years. A case of human dirofilariasis has recently been reported from Kuwait.

China and the Indian Subcontinent
(Afghanistan, Bangladesh, Bhutan, India, Nepal, Pakistan, Sri Lanka, Tadjikistan, Uzbekistan, Kyrgystan, Kazakhstan, and Turkmenistan)

Malaria: Epidemic vivax malaria has been reported in Tadjikistan, especially near the Afghanistan border. There is risk of vivax malaria as well as chloroquine-resistant falciparum malaria in southern China, India, and in other parts of the Indian subcontinent. Mefloquine prophylaxis is recommended in most malarious areas. Alternatively, some travelers may wish to consult with their physician about taking chloroquine weekly and carrying a treatment dose of Fansidar. All travelers should take measures to prevent mosquito bites.

Yellow fever: This disease does not occur in Asia, but many countries require a vaccination certificate from travelers arriving from infected or endemic areas. Travelers should carefully check their itineraries to determine the necessity for this vaccination.

Cholera: This disease is reported active in India, Bhutan, and Nepal. India and Pakistan may require a certificate from travelers arriving from cholera-infected countries. Other countries in Africa, the Middle East, Asia, and Latin America may also require a certificate from travelers arriving from cholera-infected areas. Travelers who transit between cholera-infected countries should consider vaccination (one dose needed to validate certificate) or a doctor's letter of exemption from vaccination. The risk to tourists of acquiring cholera is considered low. Prevention consists primarily in adhering to safe food and drink guidelines. Travelers to countries where cholera is active should eat only well-cooked food and drink only bottled, boiled, or treated water. An antibiotic (tetracycline or doxycycline preferred) and oral fluids are recommended for the immediate treatment of severe cholera. Travelers who develop watery diarrhea causing dehydration need hospital treatment.

Travelers' diarrhea: High risk outside of resort areas and first-class hotels. Travelers should follow safe food and drink guidelines. All food should be well cooked. Raw fish, crayfish, and crabs should be strictly avoided. Travelers should drink only bottled, boiled, or treated water. A quinolone antibiotic is recommended for the treatment of acute diarrhea. Diarrhea not responding to antibiotics may be due to parasitic diseases such as giardiasis, amebiasis, or cryptosporidiosis—or an intestinal virus.

Typhoid fever: Vaccination is recommended for travel outside the usual tourist routes.

Amebiasis: There is a high incidence of amebiasis in India, where up to 50% of the high-risk population may be infected with *E. histolytica* parasites. Variable risk elsewhere. To avoid amebiasis, travelers should drink only safe water and eat only well-cooked food. All fruit should be peeled before eating.

Hepatitis A: High risk. Nonimmune travelers to this region should receive hepatitis A vaccine.

Hepatitis E: High risk, especially in India, Nepal and Pakistan. This viral illness is similar to hepatitis A and is transmitted primarily by sewage-contaminated water. Travelers should drink only water that is bottled, boiled, or treated to eliminate viruses.

Hepatitis B: A high percentage (10%–20%) of the general population of these countries are chronic carriers of the hepatitis B virus. Vaccination is recommended for healthcare workers, relief workers, corporate employees, and others who will have prolonged contact (more than 4 weeks) with the indigenous population of these countries.

Dengue fever: Epidemics, as well as sporadic cases, occur in India, Pakistan, Bangladesh, and Sri Lanka. In China, dengue occurs in frequent, often widespread outbreaks. There is no risk of dengue in Afghanistan and Nepal. The *Aedes aegypti* mosquitoes, which transmit dengue, bite during the daytime and are present in populous urban areas as well as resort and rural areas. Prevention consists of taking protective measures against mosquito bites.

Japanese encephalitis: This mosquito-transmitted viral disease is widespread in China, southern Nepal, India, Bhutan, Burma, Bangladesh, and Sri Lanka. Vaccination against Japanese encephalitis is recommended for travelers who will be staying in rural-agricultural endemic areas for long periods (more than 4 weeks) during the transmission season. In addition, all travelers should take personal protection measures against mosquito bites, especially in the evening.

World Medical Guide

Leishmaniasis: Visceral leishmaniasis (kala azar) is found in China and India. Cutaneous leishmaniasis is present in northwestern India, Afghanistan, and Pakistan. Travelers to these areas should take protective measures against sandfly bites.

Filariasis: Bancroftian filariasis, transmitted by mosquitoes, is widespread in India, China, Bhutan, Bangladesh, and southern Nepal. Travelers to these areas should take measures to prevent mosquito bites.

Schistosomiasis: Risk is present throughout southern China, as well as eastern China, along the entire Yangtze River and its tributaries. There is no schistosomiasis in the other countries of this region. Travelers to risk areas in China should avoid swimming or wading in freshwater ponds, streams, or irrigated areas.

Lyme disease: Low risk. Cases of Lyme disease have been reported only from the northeastern coastal provinces of China.

Rabies: A high prevalence of animal rabies exists throughout Asia with many human cases reported, especially in India. Travelers should seek emergency treatment of any animal bite, especially from a dog, or a wolf. Bites from other animals should be evaluated on an individual basis. Individual need for pre-exposure rabies vaccination should be evaluated on the duration of travel, especially to rural areas, and availability of rabies vaccine and rabies immune globulin in the areas to be visited. Vaccination is recommended for all travelers who will spend extended periods of time in rural areas, away from medical care. Pre-exposure vaccination does not eliminate the need for additional inoculations should potential rabies exposure occur.

Meningitis: Outbreaks reported in New Delhi, India, and Nepal. Vaccination is recommended for travelers and trekkers to these countries who expect to have close contact with the indigenous population.

Plague: An epidemic of primarily pneumonic plague broke out in western India in August 1994. There are no reports of tourists being infected, and this disease, which is primarily a disease of poverty, is not considered to be a significant threat to travelers.

Helminthic infections: Hookworm and whipworm are common, especially in rural areas. Travelers should wear shoes to prevent transmission of these diseases. Ascariasis, caused by the ingestion of food contaminated with the eggs of roundworms, can be prevented by adequate cooking. Other helminthic diseases (paragonimiasis, clonorchiasis, fasciolopsiasis) are moderately endemic in China. Pork tapeworm disease is prevalent and can be avoided by thorough cooking of meat.

AIDS: The AIDS virus appears to be spreading most rapidly in India, where 20%–30% of the prostitutes in the major cities are now HIV positive, up from 1% in the 1980s. A lower incidence of AIDS is found in the other countries of this region. Travelers should avoid unsafe sex and consider carrying a supply of sterile needles and syringes.

Animal hazards: Snakes common to this region include the Indian krait, king cobra, king snake, Russell's viper, and beaked sea snake. Spiders common to this region include the black and brown widow spiders, black scorpion, and spotted house scorpion. Large leeches, which are not poisonous but inflict slow-healing and easily infected bites, are abundant in the streams, marshes, and jungles of these countries. Crocodiles; pythons; poisonous frogs and toads; large, aggressive lizards; tigers; leopards; and bears may also present a hazard in certain areas. Stingrays, jellyfish, sea wasps, and several species of invertebrates (cones, nettles, cucumbers, urchins, anemones, and starfish) may be found in the estuarial and coastal waters of these countries.

Plant hazards: Bamboo, rattan, and large palm- or fernlike trees, which can cause serious puncture wounds and slow-healing lacerations, are widespread in the forested areas of these countries. Regas are large forest trees whose black resinous sap can cause a potent poison ivy-type skin reaction. Stinging nettles, small thorny trees, and many species of euphorbia can also cause skin eruptions.

Southeast Asia

Yellow fever: This disease does not occur in Asia, but many countries require a certificate of vaccination from travelers arriving from yellow fever-infected countries or from countries in the Yellow Fever Endemic Zones.

Cholera: Sporadic disease activity is reported in many SE Asian countries. Although cholera vaccination is not required for entry to any country if arriving directly from the U.S. or Canada, it may be required if arriving from a cholera-infected country, or required for on-going travel to other countries in Asia, Africa, the Middle East, or Latin America. (Indonesia and Malaysia, e.g., may require a valid cholera vaccination certificate if a traveler is departing for a cholera-endemic area.) To avoid possible entry problems, travelers should consider cholera vaccination (one dose) or a doctor's letter of exemption from vaccination. Cholera vaccine gives only brief, incomplete protection and is not routinely recommended for travelers in good health. Cholera occurs primarily in areas with inadequate sewage disposal and unsafe water supplies such as urban slums and rural areas. The risk to travelers of acquiring cholera is considered low. Prevention consists in strict adherence to safe food and drink guidelines.

Malaria: Both vivax and falciparum malaria occur in SE Asia. The falciparum-vivax ratio is usually about 2:1 in most areas, but may vary. Malaria caused by *P. malariae* accounts for 2%–5% of cases. Chloroquine- and multidrug-resistant *P. falciparum* is reported. In Borneo Kalamantan(Borneo), Papua New Guinea, Irian Jaya, Myanmar, Sumatra, and Sulewesa (Celebes), chloroquine-resistant *P. vivax* has been reported. Mefloquine or doxycycline prophylaxis is recommended when traveling to rural risk areas. Alternative malaria regimes should be discussed with a travel medicine or infectious disease specialist. All travelers to malarious areas should take measures to prevent insect bites. These measures include applying a DEET-containing skin repellent, wearing permethrin-treated clothing, and utilizing, as needed, a mosquito bed net, also treated with permethrin.

Travelers' diarrhea: High risk in many areas, but some major cities (e.g., Singapore, Bangkok) in SE Asia are much safer than others. It is recommended that travelers to SE Asia drink only bottled, boiled, or treated water and consume only well-cooked food. Raw fish, crayfish, and crabs, as well as uncooked aquatic plants (e.g., watercress), should be strictly avoided. Travelers should carry a quinolone antibiotic (Cipro or Floxin) with which to treat acute diarrhea. Diarrhea not responding to antibiotic treatment, or diarrhea that becomes chronic, may be due to a parasitic disease such as giardiasis or amebiasis, and treatment with metronidazole (Flagyl) or tinidazole (Fasigyn) should be considered. All cases of diarrhea should be treated with adequate fluid replacement.

Hepatitis: All nonimmune travelers should receive hepatitis A vaccine prior to visiting SE Asia. The hepatitis B carrier rate in the general population of SE Asia is estimated at 10% to 20%. Vaccination against hepatitis B is recommended for all healthcare workers, overseas corporate employees, expatriates, relief workers, teachers, and others who will have extended (more than 4 weeks) contact with the indigenous populations of the countries in this region.

Typhoid fever: Vaccination is recommended for extended travel outside tourist areas.

Japanese encephalitis (JE): This disease is widespread throughout SE Asia. Japanese encephalitis may be transmitted seasonally, or year-round (in tropical regions). Vaccination against JE (3 doses) is recommended for travelers who will be staying in, or visiting (longer than 30 days), rural-agricultural rice-growing endemic areas during the peak transmission season. Depending upon the epidemic circumstances, vaccine should be considered for persons spending less than 30 days whose activities, such as extensive outdoor activities in rural areas, place them at particularly high risk for exposure. Travelers can inquire from the nearest U.S. consulate about the local availability of JE vaccine. This vaccine is now again available in the United States. All travelers to risk areas should also take measures to prevent mosquito bites.

Dengue fever: This disease is widespread throughout SE Asia in both sporadic and epidemic form and in both urban and rural areas. There is a high incidence of dengue hemorrhagic fever in Bangkok. The *Aedes* mosquitoes, which transmit dengue, are most active during the daytime. Travelers should also take measures to prevent mosquito bites.

Leishmaniasis: Low risk. Leishmaniasis is reported in only Burma (Myanmar). Travelers there should take measures to avoid insect (sandfly) bites.

World Medical Guide

Filariasis: The Bancroftian and Malayan forms are widespread in SE Asia. Filariasis is transmitted by four different species of mosquitoes. Insect precautions are recommended for rural travel. Travelers should apply a DEET-containing skin repellent and a permethrin clothing spray, and a mosquito bed net (permethrin treated) should be used to prevent bites while sleeping.

Schistosomiasis: There is low risk of schistosomiasis in most countries of SE Asia. Risk is present in the Philippines and in central Sulawesi (Indonesia) and also occurs in small foci in the Mekong Delta of Vietnam. There are several small foci among the aboriginal Malays in Perak and Pahang States in Malaysia. Travelers should avoid swimming or wading in freshwater lakes, ponds, or streams in these areas.

Scrub typhus: This chigger mite–transmitted disease is reported from many SE Asian countries. Chigger mites commonly inhabit second-growth forest, fruit, oil palm, or rubber plantations where there is tall grass. People who walk through tropical brush should inspect their skin for the presence of mites or ticks. Repellents and permethrin clothing spray should also be used in these areas.

Helminthic infections: Hookworm, roundworm, whipworm, and strongyloides are highly prevalent in most rural areas of SE Asia. Travelers should wear shoes to prevent the hookworm and strongyloides larvae from penetrating the skin of the foot, and food should be thoroughly washed and/or cooked to destroy roundworm and whipworm eggs.

Helminthic infections (flukes): Oriental lung fluke disease (paragonimiasis) and liver fluke diseases (clonorchiasis, fascioliasis) are prevalent in the Indochina peninsula and the Philippines. Travelers should avoid eating raw, salted, or wine-soaked crustacea such as freshwater crabs or crayfish (which can transmit clonorchiasis and paragonimiasis) and also avoid uncooked aquatic vegetables, such as watercress, which can transmit fascioliasis. Fasciolopsiasis (large intestinal fluke disease) can also be acquired through eating undercooked aquatic plants such as water chestnuts, bamboo shoots, and caltrops. These, too, should be avoided, if uncooked. Anisakiasis and capillariasis are other intestinal infections acquired through eating raw or undercooked fish (including fresh catch, crab, or squid). Cases have been reported from the Philippines, Thailand, Taiwan, and, recently, Indonesia.

Rabies: Animal rabies has been reported from all countries in SE Asia. The highest risk occurs in Thailand. All travelers, especially children, should avoid touching or petting stray dogs. Travelers should seek immediate treatment of any animal bite. Rabies vaccination is indicated following the unprovoked bite of a dog, cat, bat, or monkey. Bites by other animals, including livestock, should be individually assessed. Pre-exposure vaccination against rabies should be considered prior to long-term travel to this region. This is especially true for travelers going to remote rural areas.

AIDS: Although the AIDS virus was only recently introduced to SE Asia, it is spreading with alarming speed. Thailand has the highest incidence. The virus initially affected mostly homosexuals, but then spread quickly to IV drug users (IVDU). By 1992, almost 50% of IVDU in Bangkok were HIV positive. The third wave of the epidemic now involves prostitutes and their heterosexual partners. Up to 70% of prostitutes in some rural areas of Thailand are now seropositive, and contact with infected prostitutes is spreading AIDS into the general population. In the Philippines, Malaysia, Singapore, Taiwan, Korea, and Indonesia, the HIV infection rate among prostitutes and the indigenous population is still relatively low. The potential for the eventual spread of AIDS in these areas, however, is considered high.

Other diseases/hazards: Other illnesses reported with varying frequency include anthrax, brucellosis, leprosy, leptospirosis, melioidosis, meningococcal meningitis, plague, toxoplasmosis, yaws, and tuberculosis. There is low risk to the average traveler of acquiring these illnesses. Stingrays, poisonous fish, sea anemones, the Indo-China man-o'-war, and the very dangerous sea wasp are found along the coral reefs that fringe the countries of SE Asia. Swimmers should take sensible precautions to avoid these hazards.

Plant hazards: Bamboo, rattan, and large palm- or fern-like trees, which can cause serious puncture wounds and slow-healing lacerations, are widespread in the forested areas of these countries. Also common are Regas, which are large forest trees whose black resinous sap can cause a potent poison ivy–type skin reaction. Stinging nettles, small thorny trees, and many species of euphorbs can also cause skin reactions.

Japan, Korea, and Taiwan

Malaria: There is no risk of malaria in these countries.

Travelers' diarrhea: Low risk in Japan. Medium to high risk in Korea and Taiwan, especially in rural areas. In urban and resort areas, the first-class hotels and restaurants generally serve reliable food and potable water. Elsewhere, travelers should observe all food and drink safety precautions. A quinolone antibiotic is recommended for the treatment of acute diarrhea. Diarrhea not responding to antibiotic treatment may be due to a parasitic disease such as giardiasis or amebiasis—or an intestinal virus.

Hepatitis: All nonimmune travelers to these countries should receive hepatitis A vaccine. The hepatitis B carrier rate in the population of Japan is estimated at 2%. In Korea and Taiwan the hepatitis B carrier rate is much higher, 9%–20%. Vaccination against hepatitis B is recommended for all healthcare workers and is recommended for anyone planning an extended visit to these countries, especially Taiwan or Korea.

Dengue fever: A large outbreak of dengue occurred in Taiwan in 1987 after a 40-year absence. Ten thousand more cases were reported in 1988. There is minimal risk of dengue in Japan and Korea. The *Aedes* mosquitoes, which transmit dengue, bite primarily during the daytime and are present in populous urban areas as well as resort and rural areas. All travelers are advised to take precautions against mosquito bites. These precautions include applying a deet-containing skin repellent, wearing permethrin-treated clothing and, if necessary, sleeping under a mosquito bed net, also treated with permethrin.

Japanese encephalitis (JE): Low level of disease activity occurs in rural and peri-urban areas of Taiwan. Unvaccinated travelers to rural rice-growing areas of Japan and Korea may also be at slight risk. No cases of JE have been reported from Seoul, Korea. Vaccination against Japanese encephalitis is recommended for travelers who will be staying in rural-agricultural endemic areas longer than 2–3 weeks during the peak JE transmission season. In addition, all travelers to risk areas should take measures to prevent mosquito bites.

Filariasis: There is a low risk of filariasis in Korea. Travelers to the southern provinces should take measures to prevent mosquito bites.

Helminths: Paragonimiasis (oriental lung fluke disease), clonorchiasis and fascioliasis (liver fluke diseases), and fasciolopsiasis (giant intestinal fluke disease) occur in these countries. Capillariasis is reported from Taiwan. To prevent these diseases, travelers should avoid eating uncooked aquatic plants, such as watercress and water chestnuts, and avoid raw or undercooked fish, crabs, crayfish or other shellfish. (Ke Jang, raw crab in soy sauce, is a common source of paragonimiasis in Korea.) Other helminthic infections (ascariasis, trichuriasis, hookworm disease) may occur in rural areas.

Other illnesses/hazards: Angiostrongyliasis, anisakiasis (transmitted by raw fish; widely distributed in Japan), hemorrhagic fever with renal syndrome (low risk; transmission of hantavirus through airborne dust particles contaminated with rodent excreta is presumed; farmers and outdoor workers at higher risk), viral influenza ("flu" shot recommended), Kawasaki disease (Japan, Korea), Lyme disease (cases reported from Japan), leptospirosis, echinococcosis, rabies (occasional cases reported from Korea), murine typhus (flea-borne; reported rarely in Korea), scrub typhus (mite-borne; risk present in grassy rural areas), tuberculosis (higher rates in Korea), typhoid fever, and trachoma (highly endemic). Portuguese man-of-war, octopuses, stingrays, jellyfish, sea cones, and sea wasps occur in the coastal waters of Japan and, to some extent, Taiwan. Many species of poisonous fish (rabbit fish, peacock sole, scorpion fish, zebrafish, Japanese stingfish, spiny dogfish, sturgeonfish, and puffer fish) can inflict painful stings and even fatalities and pose a potential threat to careless or unprotected swimmers. Sea nettles, cucumbers, bristleworms, and urchins are also potential hazards.

Australia, New Zealand, Papua N. Guinea & Oceania

(Oceania = The Islands of Polynesia, Micronesia, and Melanesia)

Malaria: This disease occurs only in Papua New Guinea, the Solomon Islands, and Vanuatu. Falciparum malaria predominates over vivax approximately 2:1. Chloroquine- and multi-drug-resistant *P. falciparum* malaria occurs. The recommended antimalarial prophylaxis for adult travelers is mefloquine, 250 mg weekly, except in Papua New Guinea where doxycycline, 100 mg daily, is recommended. Chloroquine-resistant *P. vivax* has been reported from Papua New Guinea. There is no risk of malaria in Australia, New Zealand, or the other islands of Polynesia, Micronesia, or Melanesia.

Cholera: Sporadic cases regionwide. The risk to travelers of acquiring cholera is considered low. Prevention consists primarily in following safe food and drink guidelines.

Travelers' diarrhea: Low risk in Australia and New Zealand. Moderate risk in French Polynesia. Higher risk in the Solomon Islands, Vanuatu, and Micronesia. Most risk occurs outside of first-class hotels and resorts. Travelers are best advised to drink only bottled, boiled, filtered, or treated water and consume only well-cooked food. A quinolone antibiotic is recommended for the treatment of acute diarrhea. Diarrhea not responding to antibiotic treatment may be due to a parasitic disease such as giardiasis, amebiasis, or cryptospridiosis. Amebiasis and giardiasis are more common to the Solomon Islands, Kiribati, Vanuatu, and Micronesia, and less common in Fiji and the French Territories.

Hepatitis: Hepatitis A is endemic at moderate to high levels, except for Australia and New Zealand, where the risk is low. The hepatitis B carrier rate in Oceania is estimated as high as 15%. Vaccination against hepatitis B is recommended for people planning an extended visit to Papua New Guinea or Oceania. There is a low risk of hepatitis B in Australia and New Zealand and vaccination is not routinely recommended.

Typhoid fever: Typhoid outbreaks occurred in Vanuatu in 1987 and in Fiji in 1985. Travelers should consider typhoid vaccination prior to travel to Oceania. Typhoid is best prevented by strict adherence to safe food and drink guidelines.

Dengue fever: Sporadic cases and epidemics occur in nearly all of the island groups of the South Pacific. Dengue is also reported in Northern Queensland (Australia). Peak infection rates occur during the rainy season months, December–January and May–June. Prevention of dengue consists of taking protective measures against mosquito bites.

Filariasis: Malayan filariasis is widespread in the rest of Oceania, including the Solomon Islands and Vanuatu. Up to 16% prevalence has been reported in French Polynesia. Hyperendemic foci reported in the Cook Islands. Travelers should take personal protection measures against mosquito bites.

Leptospirosis: Likely occurs regionwide. Most frequently reported from New Caledonia and French Polynesia. Also reported from Fiji, Micronesia, Solomon Islands, and Vanuatu.

Rabies: There is no indigenous rabies in Australlia and Papua New Guinea. Low levels of risk in other countries.

AIDS/HIV: A small number of AIDS cases and HIV infections have been reported from various areas. At the present, AIDS is not considered a major public health problem in Australia, New Zealand, or Oceania.

Other illnesses/hazards: Angiostrongyliasis (human cases reported from Cook Islands, Fiji, French Polynesia, New Calendonia, Western Samoa, and Vanuatu), anisikiasis (endemic regionwide; associated with consumptionm of raw saltwater fish; cases have been reported from Kiribati, brucellosis, echinococcosis, paragonimiasis (enzootic on the Solomon Islands; likely more widespread), scrub typhus (reported in rurals areas of the Solomon Islands and Vanuatu). Ross River fever (viral epidemic polyarthritis; mosquito-borne; endemic in northern and eastern Australia; now reported in Central and South Pacific). Hookworm disease, roundworm disease, strongyloidiasis, and other helminthic infections are reported throughout Oceania. Tuberculosis (moderately endemic), trachoma, and yaws are reported (Oceania). Corals, jelly fish, poisonous fish, sharks, and sea snakes are a potential hazard to bathers.

World Medical Guide

AFGHANISTAN

Embassy: 202-234-3770　　　*Kabul*　　　*GMT +4½ hrs*

Entry Requirements
- Passport/Visa: Passport and visa are required.
- HIV Test: Not required.
- Vaccinations: A yellow fever vaccination certificate is required of travelers arriving from infected areas.

Embassies/Consulates: There is no American representation at this time. U.S. citizens who travel to Afghanistan should register with the U.S. Embassy in India, Pakistan, Tajikistan, Turkmenistan, or Uzbekistan. The nearest U.S. Embassies are in Islamabad, Pakistan ([92]-51-826-161) and in Dushanbe, Tajikistan ([7-3772]-21-0356).

Hospitals/Doctors: Local medical facilities are below Western standards and should be considered for use only in an extreme emergency.

Health Advisory

Cholera: This disease is active in this country.

Malaria: Transmission generally occurs during the warmer months, May through October, with peak transmission during August and September. There is most risk of malaria in the provinces in the east (Konarha, Laghan, and Nangarhar), in the north-northeast (Kunduz, Takhar, and Badakhshan), and in the south (Helmand, Qandahar). Malaria transmission occurs in rural areas of these provinces below 2,000 meters elevation. There is no malaria risk in Kabul. There may be malaria risk, however, in the urban areas in the south. *Plasmodium vivax* accounts for 95%–98% of cases, the remainder being caused by *P. falciparum*. Most cases of falciparum malaria have occurred in the eastern area along the border with Pakistan. Chloroquine-resistant falciparum malaria is reported, and apparently occurs, at this time, only along the border area with Pakistan. Mefloquine, doxycycline, or atovaquone/proguanil (Malarone) is recommended for those travelers visiting rural areas near the border with Pakistan. In other areas, travelers should take weekly chloroquine and carry a treatment dose of atovaquone/proguanil (Malarone)

Travelers' diarrhea: High risk. Shigellosis is a major problem in this country. Only bottled, boiled, or treated water should be consumed. All food should be well cooked. A quinolone antibiotic is recommended for the treatment of diarrhea. Diarrhea not improving with antibiotic treatment may be due to a parasitic infection such as giardiasis.

Hepatitis: All nonimmune travelers should receive hepatitis A vaccine. The hepatitis B carrier rate in the general population is estimated as high as 5%. Vaccination against hepatitis B is recommended for anyone planning an extended visit to this country. Hepatitis E is presumably widespread, especially in rural areas. Prevention consists of treating all drinking water to eliminate viruses. A vaccine against hepatitis E is not available.

Japanese encephalitis: Low risk; historically, this disease has occurred along the eastern borders. Travelers to rural areas should prevent mosquito bites.

Leishmaniasis: Cutaneous leishmaniasis is a major public health problem and occurs in rural and periurban areas, especially in the northern parts of the country at elevations between 400 and 800 meters. Risk areas include the northern Afghan plains and the outskirts of Kabul. Other risk areas include Qandahar in the south and Herat in the west. There are sporadic cases of visceral leishmaniasis reported from Badakhshtan, Badghis, Ghazni, Kabul, and Kandahar Provinces. All travelers to risk areas should take measures to prevent sand fly bites. Sand fly activity is greatest between April and October.

Rabies: Human cases occur sporadically in rural villages. Travelers who will stay for extended periods in rural areas should consider rabies vaccination.

Other illnesses: AIDS (no data available), brucellosis, cholera, echinococcosis, leptospirosis (endemic in the northern and eastern plains), louse-borne typhus, measles (currently epidemic, especially in the northwestern areas), sandfly fever (focally endemic; virus isolated from Soviet troops serving in Parvan Province in central-eastern Afghanistan during the Afghan War), Siberian tick typhus, scrub typhus, tick-borne relapsing fever, typhoid fever (highly endemic), tuberculosis, and intestinal helminthic infections.

World Medical Guide

ALBANIA

Embassy: 202-223-4942 *Tirane* *GMT +1 hr*

Entry Requirements
- Passport/Visa: Passport, visa, and birth certificate are required.
- HIV Test: Not required.
- Vaccinations: A yellow fever vaccination certificate is required from travelers older than 1 year of age arriving from infected areas.

Telephone Country Code: 355

Embassies/Consulates: The United States does not maintain diplomatic or consular relations with Albania. Canadian Embassy: Travelers should contact the Canadian Embassy in Yugoslavia for assistance.

Doctors/Hospitals: Tirane Clinical Hospital #2 (900 beds); general medical/surgical facility; best treatment facility in Albania.

Health Advisory

Cholera: Outbreak of cholera occurred in 1990; sporadic cases are reported.

Travelers' diarrhea: Tirane has a fairly well-developed municipal water system for offices; urban homes, however, are not connected. There is a high risk of travelers' diarrhea outside of first-class hotels and resorts. A quinolone antibiotic is recommended for the treatment of acute diarrhea.

Hepatitis: All nonimmune travelers should receive hepatitis A vaccine. The hepatitis B carrier rate in the general population is estimated at 3%–4%. Vaccination against hepatitis B is recommended for longer-term visitors to this country.

Tick-borne encephalitis (TBE): Also called boutonneuse fever. Increased risk March through September during periods of peak tick activity in bushy or forested area. Greatest risk of TBE in southern districts of Gjirokaster and Permet, the central district of Tirane, and the eastern district of Librazhd.

Leishmaniasis: Cases of cutaneous and visceral leishmaniasis are reported sporadically. Travelers should take measures to prevent sand fly bites, especially May through October, when most transmission occurs.

Hemorrhagic fever with renal syndrome: Most cases reported in rural mountainous regions. Most recent outbreak in Kosovo and Montenegro.

Crimean-Congo hemorrhagic fever (CCHF): Viral illness transmitted by ticks. Sporadic cases occur throughout the summer. Travelers should take measures to prevent tick bites.

Other illnesses/hazards: Anthrax, brucellosis, echinococcosis, leptospirosis, rabies (cases most common in stray dogs and cats, jackals, foxes, and wolves; rare in humans), sandfly fever, tick-borne relapsing fever (risk in rocky, rural livestock areas), murine typhus (probably occurs), and helminthic infections (roundworm, hookworm, and whipworm).

ALGERIA

Embassy: 202-265-2800 *Algiers* *GMT 0 hrs*

Entry Requirements
- Passport/Visa: Valid passport and visa are required.
- HIV Test: Not required.
- Vaccinations: A yellow fever vaccination certificate is required from all travelers older than 1 year arriving from infected areas.

Telephone Country Code: 213

Embassies/Consulates: U.S. Embassy, Algiers. 4 Chemin Cheich Bachir Brahimi; Tel. (2) 601-425/-255/-186. U.S. Consulate, Oran; Tel: (6) 334-509. Canadian High Commission, Hydra. 27 Bis Rue Ali Massoudi; Tel. 606-611.

Hospitals/Doctors: University Hospital, Algiers (2,900 beds); all specialties. Institute Pasteur d'Algerie. University Hospital, Oran (2,200 beds); general medical/surgical facility; all specialties.

World Medical Guide
Health Advisory

Malaria: Risk is primarily limited to the oases in the southern provinces of Adrar, Illizi, Tamanghasset, and Tindouf from July through November. *P. vivax* accounts for over 90% of cases. Occasional cases are caused by *P. malariae*. Less than 1% of malaria is due to *P. falciparum* and these cases are most likely imported. Chloroquine prophylaxis is recommended in risk areas.

Travelers' diarrhea: All water sources in Algeria should be considered potentially contaminated. A quinolone antibiotic is recommended for the treatment of acute diarrhea. Diarrhea not responding to antibiotic treatment may be due to a parasitic disease such as giardiasis or cryptosporidiosis.

Hepatitis: All nonimmune travelers should receive hepatitis A vaccine. The hepatitis B carrier rate in the general population is estimated at 3%. Hepatitis E presumably occurs based on reports of non-A, non-B hepatitis in Algeria and reports of hepatitis E in Morocco.

Mediterranean spotted fever (boutonneuse fever, African tick typhus): Presumed risk occurs primarily in suburban coastal areas.

Schistosomiasis: Risk is present year-round. Urinary schistosomiasis occurs in two areas. One area occurs in the north, primarily in the Mitidja Plain near Alger, and also at Khemis El Khechna commune. The other area occurs in the southeast, in the Tassili N'Ajjer region. Travelers should avoid swimming or wading in freshwater lakes, ponds, or streams.

Leishmaniasis: Transmission occurs primarily from April to October. Cutaneous leishmaniasis is endemic in the semiarid steppe region of the northern part of the Algerian Sahara. Major risk areas include Biskra (especially near Sidi Okba), Bechar (especially near Abadla), and M'sila Provinces. Visceral leishmaniasis (kala azar) occurs primarily in the less humid central and eastern parts of the northern coastal mountainous area; major foci are in the Grande Kabylie Region (Tizi Ouzou and Bejaia Provinces) and in the vicinities of Alger, Boumerdes, and Constantine.

Rabies: About 20 to 30 rabies cases are reported yearly. Dogs are the primary source of human exposure. Stray dogs, jackals, foxes, and cats constitute the primary reservoirs.

Other diseases: AIDS/HIV (low reported incidence), brucellosis, echinococcosis (a major health problem countrywide, particularly in rural and highland areas), fascioliasis (sheep liver fluke disease; acquired by eating contaminated watercress), relapsing fever (tick- and louse-borne), sandfly fever (elevated risk, primarily April through November, in the coastal region and the steppe region of the northern part of the Algerian Sahara), trachoma, typhoid fever, tuberculosis, and intestinal helminthic infections (roundworm, hookworm, and whipworm diseases, as well as strongyloidiasis, are common in rural areas and among lower socioeconomic groups).

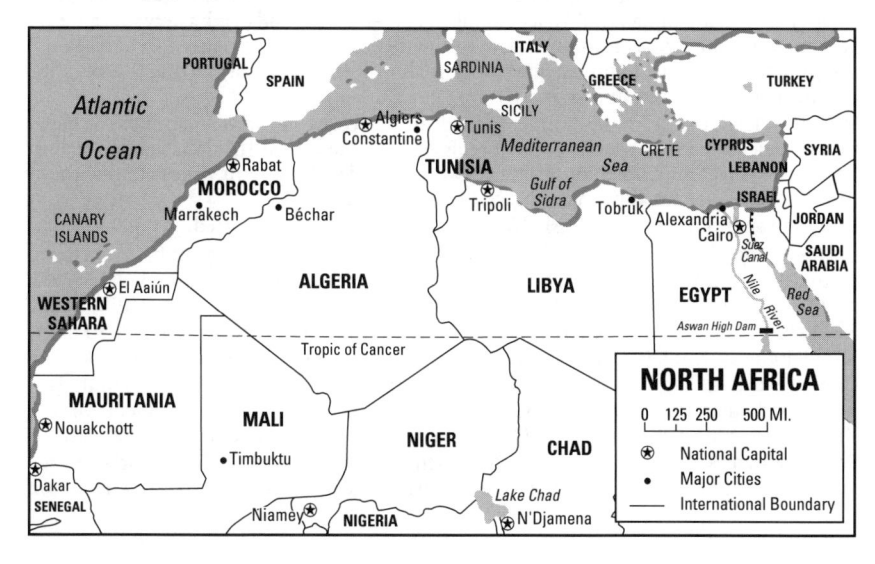

World Medical Guide

ANGOLA

Embassy: 202-785-1156 *Luanda* *GMT +1 hr*

Entry Requirements
- A valid passport and visa are required.
- HIV Test: Not required.
- Vaccinations: A yellow fever vaccination certificate is required from all travelers older than 1 year arriving from infected areas.

Telephone Country Code: 263
Embassies & Consulates: U.S. Embassy, Luanda. Rue Houari Boumedienne; Tel. (2) 345-481. The Consular Section is located at Casa Inglesa, Rua Major Kahangulo No. 132/136; Tel. (2) 396-927.
Hospitals/Doctors: University Hospital, Luanda (500+ beds). Americo Boavioa (600 beds); general medical/surgical facility.

Health Advisory

Yellow fever: This disease is active in this country. Risk is confined to the northeastern forested areas (Luanda and Bengo Provinces). Cases were also reported in the capital city of Luanda in 1988. Yellow fever vaccination is recommended. This country is in the Yellow Fever Endemic Zone. A valid yellow fever vaccination certificate may be required for on-going travel to other countries in South America, Africa, the Middle East, or Asia.

Cholera: This disease is active in this country and occurs year-round. As of 1994 the World Health Organization considered all provinces except Bie, Cabinda, Lunda Norte, Lunda Sol, and Moxico to be cholera "infected." Outbreaks reported in Luanda in 1993. Although cholera vaccination is not required for entry if arriving directly from the U.S. or Canada, it may be required if arriving from a cholera-infected area, or required for on-going travel to other countries in Latin America, Africa, the Middle East, or Asia. Travelers should consider vaccination (one dose) or a doctor's letter of exemption from vaccination. The risk to travelers of acquiring cholera is considered low. Prevention consists primarily in adhering to safe food and drink guidelines.

Malaria: Risk is present year-round throughout this country, including urban areas and the enclave of Cabinda. Falciparum malaria accounts for 90% of cases, followed by *P. malariae*. Chloroquine-resistant falciparum malaria is reported. Prophylaxis with mefloquine or doxycycline is currently recommended when traveling to malarious areas of this country.

Travelers' diarrhea: High risk. Only major urban areas have access to public water systems, which serve primarily the former European sections. Water distribution systems may be damaged and contaminated. Travelers should all observe food and drink safety precautions. A quinolone antibiotic is recommended for the treatment of acute diarrhea. Diarrhea not responding to treatment with an antibiotic, or chronic diarrhea, may be due to a parasitic disease such as giardiasis or amebiasis.

Hepatitis: High risk. All nonimmune travelers should receive hepatitis A vaccine. The hepatitis B carrier rate in the general population is estimated to exceed 10%. Vaccination against hepatitis B is recommended for healthcare workers and all long-term visitors to this country. Hepatitis E presumably occurs, based on regional data.

Dengue fever: Low apparent risk. No recent cases have been reported.

Chikungunya fever: Mosquito-borne; human outbreaks in the region have occurred primarily in rural populations, but explosive urban outbreaks spread by *Aedes aegypti* mosquitoes can also occur. Human outbreaks have been reported in the Luanda area.

Rift Valley fever: Transmitted by culicine mosquitoes and also by contact with flesh of infected domestic animals. Low risk. Human outbreaks have occurred in this region.

Onchocerciasis: Blackfly-borne near fast-flowing rivers. Risk north of 14 degrees south latitude—particularly in the northern provinces of Cuanza Norte, Lunda, Malanje, Uige, and Zaire—and in the plateau region of the central province of Bie, and the Cabinda exclave.

Schistosomiasis: Distribution is very focal and infection rates have been highly variable, even within geographic regions. Infection rates for urinary schistosomiasis have been highest in the coastal provinces of Luanda, Bengo, and Benguela, decreasing in an eastward direction. Intestinal schistosomiasis, presumably distributed countrywide, is most prevalent in the southeastern province of Cuando Cubango. Travelers should avoid swimming, bathing, or wading in freshwater ponds, lakes, or streams.

Trypanosomiasis (African sleeping sickness): Sporadic cases of the Rhodesian form of trypanosomiasis have been reported in the southeast. The Gambian form of trypanosomiasis occurs primarily in the northwestern provinces of Zaire, Uige, Luanda, and Cuanza Norte, and as far south as Bengo Province. Travelers should take measures to prevent insect (tsetse fly) bites.

Rabies: Considered a public health problem in many rural and urban areas; stray dogs are the primary cause of human infection. Travelers should seek immediate treatment of any animal bite. Pre-exposure vaccination against rabies should be considered prior to long-term travel (more than 4 weeks) to this country.

AIDS: Heterosexual transmission is the predominate means of transmission. HIV-1 and HIV-2 prevalences estimated at up to 14% of the urban population. Current infection rates of high-risk groups is presently not available. All travelers are cautioned against unsafe sex, unsterile medical or dental injections, and unnecessary blood transfusions.

Other illnesses/hazards: African tick typhus (contracted from dog ticks, often in urban areas, and bush ticks), brucellosis (from consumption of raw dairy products), Bancroftian filariasis (mosquito-borne; reported in the north, primarily Cabinda enclave and Zaire Province), leishmaniasis (low apparent risk; sporadic cases may have previously occurred), plague (flea-borne; human cases last reported from Benguela Province), polio (this disease is currently active; cases reported 1999; all travelers should be fully immunized), relapsing fever (tick-borne and louse-borne), toxoplasmosis, syphilis, tuberculosis (a major health problem), typhoid fever, typhus (louse-borne and flea-borne), and intestinal worms (very common). Animal hazards include snakes (vipers, cobras, mambas), centipedes, scorpions, and black widow spiders. Sea wasps, Portuguese man-of-war, black sea urchins, weever fish, spiny dogfish are found in the coastal waters of Angola and could be a hazard to swimmers.

ANTIGUA & BARBUDA

Embassy: 202-362-5122   *St. John's*   *GMT -4 hrs*

Entry Requirements
- Passport/Visa: Visa not required.
- HIV Test: HIV testing required of foreign university students and travelers suspected of being HIV infected.
- Vaccinations: A yellow fever vaccination certificate is required from travelers over 1 year of age coming from infected areas.

Telephone Area Code: 809

Embassies/Consulates: U.S. Embassy, St. John's. Tel. 462-3505/06. Independent since 1981, these islands remain within the British Commonwealth.

Hospitals/Doctors: Holberton Hospital, St. John's (215 beds). Travelers should contact the U.S. Embassy for physician referrals.

Health Advisory
See Disease Risk Summary for the Caribbean.

Travelers' diarrhea: Low to moderate risk. In urban and resort areas, the hotels and restaurants serve reliable food and potable water. Elsewhere, travelers should observe safety precautions. A quinolone antibiotic is recommended for the treatment of acute diarrhea.

Hepatitis: Low risk to tourists. Nonimmune travelers should receive hepatitis A vaccine.

Dengue fever: This mosquito-transmitted viral disease is prevalent in the Caribbean. All travelers should take measures to prevent insect bites.

World Medical Guide

Schistosomiasis: Foci of potential infection are present on Antigua. Travelers should avoid swimming, bathing, or wading in freshwater ponds, lakes, or streams unless advised they are safe. Snail-infested water areas are fairly well defined and usually can be avoided.
Other diseases/health threats: Leptospirosis, intestinal worms (helminths), rabies, syphilis, AIDS, tuberculosis, typhoid fever, ciguatera fish poisoning, and swimming related hazards (jellyfish, spiny sea urchins, and coral).

ARMENIA

Armenian Embassy: 202-319-1976. U.S. Embassy, Yerevan: (7)-3742-151-551
For Health Advisory information, see the Health Advisory for Russia on page 404.

ARGENTINA

Embassy: 202-939-6400   *Buenos Aires*   *GMT -3 hrs*

Entry Requirements
- U.S. citizens do not need a visa for a tourist stay.
- HIV Test: Not required.
- Vaccinations: None required.

Telephone Country Code: 54   **AT&T:** 001-800-200-1111   **MCI:** 001-800-333-1111
Embassies/Consulates: U.S. Embassy, Consular Section, Buenos Aires. 4300 Columbia, 1425; Tel. (1) 777-4533.
Doctors/Hospitals: The British Hospital, Buenos Aires (400 beds); general medical/surgical facility; used by the American community. Mater Dei Hospital, Buenos Aires (100 beds); most specialty services; used by the American community. Goodman Mercer, M.D.
San Lorenzo, Santa Fe: Rogelio Beltramone, M.D.
Tucuman: Juan Carlos Farhat, M.D.
San Miguel: Bessone Clinic. Used by American expatriates.

Health Advisory

Yellow fever: Risk in northeastern forested areas only. No activity recently reported. Vaccination is recommended for all travelers more than 9 months of age who visit rural forested areas in the northeastern part of the country.
Cholera: This disease is active in this country. Although cholera vaccination is not required for entry if arriving directly from the U.S. or Canada, it may be required if arriving from a cholera-infected area, or required for on-going travel to other countries in Latin America, Africa, the Middle East, or Asia. Travelers should consider vaccination (one dose) or a doctor's letter of exemption from vaccination. The risk to travelers of acquiring cholera is considered low. Prevention of cholera consists primarily in adhering to safe food and drink guidelines.
Malaria: Risk is year-round in rural areas below 1,200 meters elevation in Jujuy (Ledesma, San Pedro, and Santa Barbara Departments) and Salta (Iruya, Oran, San Martin, and Santa Victoria Departments) Provinces. Occasional cases have been reported in Corrientes and Misiones Provinces. Risk is elevated from October through May. *P. vivax* accounts for virtually 100% of cases. Chloroquine prophylaxis is recommended for travel in these rural malarious areas which are near the Bolivian border.
Travelers' diarrhea: Water supplies in Buenos Aires are considered potable. Higher risk occurs countrywide outside of Buenos Aires. In urban and resort areas, the hotels and restaurants generally serve reliable food and potable water. Elsewhere, travelers should observe all food and drink safety precautions. A quinolone antibiotic is recommended for the treatment of acute diarrhea. Diarrhea not responding to antibiotic treatment may be due to a parasitic disease such as giardiasis, amebiasis, or cryptosporidiosis.
Hepatitis: All nonimmune travelers should receive hepatitis A vaccine. The hepatitis B carrier rate in the general population is estimated at 1.1% but varies among various risk groups. Vaccination against hepatitis B is recommended for all long-term visitors to this country. Hepatitis E is endemic regionally. Hepatitis C occurs but the levels are unclear.

Dengue fever: Low overall risk. Dengue may occur in the northeastern lowlands adjacent to Paraguay. Travelers to the northeast regions should take precautions against insect bites.

Leishmaniasis: Risk of cutaneous and mucocutaneous leishmaniasis is limited to the northern one-third of the country, with the majority of cases reported from Salta, Jujuy, Catamarca, and Santiago del Estero Provinces. Occasional cases of visceral leishmaniasis have been reported from Salta and Chaco Provinces. Travelers to these areas should take measures to prevent sandfly bites.

Chagas' disease: High occurrence in rural areas, particularly in the north-central Chaco region. About 60% of the country's area is endemic for Chagas' disease. Risk of transmission occurs primarily in those rural-agricultural areas where there are adobe-style huts and houses that potentially harbor the night-biting triatomid (assassin) bugs. Travelers sleeping in such structures should take precautions against nighttime bites. Unscreened blood transfusions are also a potential source of infection and should be avoided.

Echinococcosis: High incidence reported in southern cattle/sheep rearing regions. Human prevalence is among the highest reported worldwide. Travelers to these regions should avoid contact with dogs in order to prevent accidental ingestion of infective eggs which are passed in dog feces. Strict personal hygiene, especially handwashing, is important and all travelers should pay close attention to food and drink guidelines in order to avoid ingestion of potentially contaminated food.

Rabies: Low risk; 18 to 20 human cases may occur annually from both urban and rural areas. Travelers, especially children, should avoid stray dogs and seek immediate treatment and evaluation of any animal bite. Rabies vaccination is indicated following the unprovoked bite of a dog. Bites by other animals should be evaluated individually.

Other diseases: Argentine hemorrhagic fever (viral disease transmitted by contact with infected rodent excreta; more common in agricultural areas of the moist pampas region of east-central Argentina), anthrax, arboviral fevers (mosquito-transmitted; eastern equine encephalitis, St. Louis encephalitis, Venezuelan encephalitis are reported), brucellosis (high incidence), fascioliasis (from consumption of contaminated wild watercress), hantaviral disease (hemorrhagic fever with renal syndrome and hantaviral pulmonary syndrome; transmitted by infective rodent urine or feces), leptospirosis, plague, schistosomiasis (endemic status unclear; officially not reported), AIDS, trachoma (occurs in NE areas), trichinellosis, tuberculosis, typhoid fever, strongyloidiasis, and other intestinal helminthic infections are reported.

ARUBA

Embassy: 202-244-5300 *Oranjestad* *GMT -4 hrs*

Entry Requirements
- Passport/Visa: Visa not required.
- HIV Test: Not required.
- Vaccinations: None required.

Telephone Country Code: 297

Hospitals/Doctors: Oduber Hospital, Oranjestad: (279 beds). This hospital is regarded as one of the better medical facilities in the West Indies.

Health Advisory
See Disease Risk Summary for the Caribbean.

Travelers' diarrhea: Low to moderate risk. Food and water are generally safe on this island. Outside of resort and urban areas, travelers are advised to follow safety precautions.

Hepatitis: Low risk to tourists, but nonimmune travelers should consider hepatitis A vaccination.

Dengue fever: Low risk. Travelers should take protective measures against mosquito bites.

Other diseases/health threats: Typhoid fever, dengue hemorrhagic fever, Chagas' disease (potential threat), filariasis, leptospirosis, ciguatera fish poisoning, and swimming related hazards (jellyfish, spiny sea urchins, and coral).

World Medical Guide

AUSTRALIA

Embassy: 202-797-3000 *Canberra* *GMT +10 hrs*

Entry Requirements
- A visitor visa, valid for 1 year, available for multiple entries up to 3 months.
- HIV Test: Required of all applicants for permanent residence age 15 or over. All other applicants who require medical examinations are tested if it is indicated on clinical grounds.
- Vaccinations: A yellow fever vaccination certificate is required of travelers older than 1 year if arriving within 6 days of having stayed overnight or longer in a country any part of which is infected.

Telephone Country Code: 61

Embassies/Consulates: U.S. Embassy, Canberra. Moonah Place; Tel. (6) 270-5000. U.S. Consulate, Sydney; Tel. (2)373-9200. U.S. Consulate, Melbourne; Tel. (3) 9526-5900. U.S. Consulate, Perth; Tel. (9) 231-9400.

Doctors/Hospitals: Royal Melbourne Hospital (702 beds); Tel. (03) 347-7111. Traveller's Medical and Vaccination Centre, Melbourne; Tel. (3) 9602-5788. Royal Prince Alfred Hospital, Sydney (1,532 beds); most specialties and diagnostic capabilities; emergency services; ICU; Tel. (02) 516-6111. Traveller's Medical and Vaccination Centre, Sydney; Tel. (2) 221-7133. Royal Darwin Hospital (648 beds); most specialties and diagnostic capabilities; emergency services. Royal Perth Hospital (1,072 beds); Tel. (09) 325-0101. Traveller's Medical and Vaccination Centre, Perth; Tel. (9) 321-1977. Queen Elizabeth Hospital, Adelaide (Travel Clinic); Tel. 347-0296. Princess Alexandra Hospital, Brisbane (1,104 beds); Tel. (07) 240-2111.

Health Advisory

Malaria: No risk.

Travelers' diarrhea: Low risk. Water in major cities and urban areas is potable, but in rural areas and settlements the water may not meet strict standards of purification. A quinolone antibiotic is recommended for the treatment of acute diarrhea.

Hepatitis: Hepatitis A is endemic at low levels. Nonimmune travelers should consider hepatitis A vaccine. Hepatitis E may occur but has not been reported. The carrier rate of the hepatitis B virus in the general population is only 0.05%–0.1%. Vaccination against hepatitis B is not routinely recommended.

Dengue fever: Reported in parts of Northern Queensland and Torres Strait Islands. Areas of greatest risk are along the coast from Cornavon to Port Darwin to Townsville. Peak infection rates occur during October to March–April. The *Aedes* mosquitoes, which transmit dengue fever, bite during the daytime and are present in populous urban areas as well as resort and rural areas. Prevention of dengue consists of taking protective measures against mosquito bites.

Tick typhus: Queensland tick typhus has been reported in travelers to the northern beaches of Sydney Harbour; cases of scrub typhus are reported from the tropical rainforests of Litchfield Park. A new tick-borne rickettsial disease, Flinders Island spotted fever, is reported to extend down the southeastern coastal areas of mainland Australia to Flinders Island and northern Tasmania.

Viral encephalitis: Outbreaks of Australian encephalitis (caused by the Murray Valley encephalitis virus) occur annually. Highest attack rates occur in the summer and fall (November–May), especially after periods of heavy rainfall. Most cases reported from Western Australia (tropical Kimberly region in the north of Western Australia), Victoria, and South Australia. A small number of cases occur in the Northern Territory. Viral encephalitis is transmitted by mosquitoes. Note: A small outbreak of Japanese encephalitis was recently reported from islands in the Torres Strait off the Australian mainland. All travelers should take precautions to prevent mosquito bites.

Rabies: There are no reported cases of indigenous rabies in Australia.

Legionnaires' disease: The Human Services Department, Public Health Division of the Government of Victoria has confirmed sixty-six cases, including 2 deaths. All the patients, with one exception, had visited the Melbourne Aquarium after April 11, 2000. Laboratory

World Medical Guide

test results confirmed the presence of legionnella bacteriain the cooling towers of the Melbourne Aquarium, which have since been disinfected.

Other illnesses/hazards: Brucellosis (canned goat's milk in Australia need not be pasteurized and is a potential source of illness), Barmah forest disease (mosquito-borne viral disease), HIV (low risk of transmission), leptospirosis, Ross River fever (viral epidemic polyarthritis; mosquito-borne; occurs throughout coastal Australia and in inland mosquito areas), melioidosis, and helminthic infections (endemic at low levels; hookworm disease, strongyloidiasis). Animal hazards include snakes (death adder, Australian copperhead, Australian coral, and others), centipedes and scorpions, and spiders (red back, northern funnel-web, mouse, and brown recluse). Fresh- and saltwater crocodiles occur in Australia, but only the saltwater variety has been known to attack humans. Male platypuses can inflict painful puncture wounds and should be avoided. Rogue scrub cattle (domestic animals gone wild) are particularly dangerous terrestrial animals and have been known to attack humans and vehicles without provocation. The box jellyfish, the most dangerous jellyfish in the world, and also the sea wasp are found in northern coastal waters. Four other varieties of jellyfish (jimble, irukandji, mauve stinger, and hairy stinger) should also be avoided. Other hazards, including sharks, stingrays, and poisonous cone shells, are potential hazards in the coastal waters surrounding Australia. Swimmers should take sensible precautions to avoid these hazards.

AUSTRIA

Embassy: 202-895-6767   *Vienna*   *GMT +1 hr*

Entry Requirements
- Visa: A visa is not required for tourist/business stays up to three months.
- HIV Test: Testing is required of foreign workers applying for residence permits.
- Vaccinations: None required.

Telephone Country Code: 43   **AT&T:** 022-903-011   **MCI:** 022-903-012

American Express: American Express Travel Service. Kaerntnerstrasse 21/23, Vienna; Tel. (1) 51-540.

Embassies/Consulates: U.S. Embassy, Vienna. Boltzmanngasse 16; Tel. (1)-31-339.

Hospitals/Doctors: Vienna Municipal General Hospital (2,460 beds); major teaching facility; all specialties. For a physician referral in Vienna, contact the American Medical Society of Vienna, Tel: (1) 424-568, or the Doctor's Board of Vienna-Service Department for Foreign Patients, Weihburggasse 10–12, Vienna, Tel. (1) 40-144. The Doctor's Board also provides 24-hour physician referral throughout Austria. English spoken.

Air Ambulance: Tyrolean Air Ambulance (Innsbruck). Tel: (0) 512-22422.

Health Advisory

Travelers' diarrhea: Low risk. Tap water supplied by municipal water systems is potable.

Hepatitis: All nonimmune travelers should receive hepatitis A vaccine. The hepatitis B carrier rate in the general population is less than 1%. Hepatitis B vaccination is not recommended for tourist travelers. A single case of hepatitis E was reported in 1998.

Lyme disease: The tick vector (*Ixodes ricinus*) is found in broad-leaf forests (usually oak forests) at elevations below 1,000 meters, especially in the Danube River basin of eastern Austria. Tick activity peaks in April and May, but is high from March through September.

Tick-borne encephalitis (TBE): This viral disease is transmitted by ixodid ticks. Risk is present in the lowland forests of eastern and southeastern Austria, particularly in the areas around Klagenfurt, Graz, Wiener Neustadt, and Linz, as well in the Danube River valley west of Vienna. There is no apparent risk in Tyrol and Voralberg Provinces. Travelers to risk areas should take measures to prevent tick bites. Vaccination against TBE should be considered by people who anticipate significant long-term potential exposure to ticks in rural areas. Vaccination is not recommended for the average traveler.

Swimmer's itch: Cercarial dermatitis ("swimmer's itch") occurs during hot, dry summer months. The cercaria that penetrate swimmer's skin may be found in warm-water lakes harboring snails.

World Medical Guide

Rabies: No human cases have been reported recently, but rabies is enzootic in foxes.
Other illnesses: Echinococcosis, leptospirosis (associated to exposure to livestock or swimming in lakes/streams), Tahyna virus fever, trichinosis (from wild swine), and tularemia (reported sporadically in outdoorsmen after contact with the meat of killed game).

AZERBAIJAN

Embassy of Azerbaijan: 202-842-0001. *U.S. Embassy, Baku:* (9)-9412-980-335
For Health Advisory information, see the Health Advisory for Russia on page 404.

AZORES (PORTUGAL)

Embassy: 202-328-8610   *Lisbon*   *GMT -1 hr*

Entry Requirements
- HIV Test: Not required.
- Vaccinations: A yellow fever vaccination certificate is required of all travelers arriving from infected areas. Transit passengers at Funchal, Porto, Santo, and Santa Maria do not need a certificate.

Telephone Country Code: 351
Embassies/Consulates: U.S. Consulate, Ponta Delgada, Avenida D. Henrique; Tel. 22216. Canadian Embassy (Portugal); Tel. [351] (1) 56-3821.

Health Advisory
Malaria: No risk.
Travelers' diarrhea: Low to moderate risk. Travelers should observe careful food and drink precautions.
Hepatitis: Nonimmune travelers should consider immunization against hepatitis A.

BAHAMAS

Embassy: 202-944-3390   *Freeport*   *GMT -5 hrs*

Entry Requirements
- Passport/Visa: Visa not required.
- HIV Test: Not required.
- Vaccinations: A yellow fever vaccination certificate is required from travelers over 1 year of age coming from infected or endemic areas.

Telephone Area Code: 242   **AT&T:** 1-800-872-2881   **MCI:** 1-800-624-1000
Embassies/Consulates: U.S. Embassy, Nassau. Mosmar Building, Queen Street. Tel. (809) 322-1181 or 328-2206. Canadian Consulate. Tel. 323-2124.
Hospitals/Doctors: Princess Margaret Hospital, New Providence (478 beds); general medical/surgical facility; emergency room. Lucayan Medical Center, Freeport. Rand Memorial Hospital, Freeport (74 beds); general medical/surgical services; emergency room.

Health Advisory
See Disease Risk Summary for the Caribbean.
Travelers' diarrhea: Low to moderate risk. A quinolone antibiotic is recommended for the treatment of acute diarrhea.
Hepatitis: Low/medium risk to tourists. Travelers should consider hepatitis A vaccination.
Dengue fever: Low degree of risk. All travelers, however, should take protective measures against mosquito bites.
Other diseases/health threats: Typhoid fever (low risk), syphilis, AIDS (among the highest incidence in the Caribbean), ciguatera fish poisoning, moped and motorcycle accidents, and swimming related hazards (jellyfish, spiny sea urchins, and coral).

World Medical Guide

BAHRAIN

Embassy: 202-342-0741   *Manama*   *GMT +3 hrs*

Entry Requirements
- Visa: Tourists can obtain a visa on arrival but obtaining a visa before arrival is recommended.
- HIV Test: Not required.
- Vaccinations: A yellow fever vaccination certificate required of travelers arriving from infected areas.

Telephone Country Code: 973   **AT&T:** 800-001   **MCI:** 800-002

Embassies/Consulates: American Embassy, Manama. Bldg. 979, Road No. 3119, Zinj District (next to Al Ahli Sports Club); Tel. 273-300.

Hospitals/Doctors: International Hospital, Bahrain (300 beds); new civilian facility; most specialty services; emergency and surgical capabilities. Al-Salmaniyah Medical Center, Manama (620 beds); government teaching facility; all specialty services except neurosurgery.

Health Advisory

Malaria: There is no risk of malaria in this country.

Travelers' diarrhea: A quinolone antibiotic is recommended for acute diarrhea. Amebiasis and giardiasis are reported.

Hepatitis: Nonimmune travelers should receive hepatitis A vaccine before arrival. Hepatitis E has not been reported. The hepatitis B carrier rate in the general population is 2%. Vaccination is not recommended for routine travel.

Leishmaniasis: May be present in endemic areas. Levels are unclear.

BANGLADESH

Embassy: 202-342-8373   *Dhaka*   *GMT +6 hrs*

Entry Requirements
- A visa is not required for a tourist visit up to 15 days.
- HIV Test: Not required.
- Vaccinations: A yellow fever vaccination certificate is required from all travelers arriving from, or transiting through, any country any part of which is infected. A certificate is required if arriving from any country in the Yellow Fever Endemic Zones or from Malawi, Mauritania, Belize, Costa Rica, Guatemala, Honduras, or Nicaragua.

Telephone Country Code: 880

Embassies/Consulates: U.S. Embassy, Dhaka. Diplomatic Enclave, Madani Avenue, Baridhara; Tel. (2) 884700-22.

Hospitals/Doctors: Holy Family Hospital, Dhaka (286 beds); minimally equipped facility; should be used only for emergency stabilization.

Health Advisory

Malaria: Risk is present year-round throughout this country. There is risk of malaria in all urban areas except Dhaka. Elevated risk occurs in the forested areas and foothills of the southeast and east bordering India and Burma. Falciparum malaria accounts for 50%–75% of malaria cases in this country, vivax the remainder. Chloroquine-resistant falciparum malaria is confirmed in the eastern and northeastern regions. Mefloquine or doxycycline prophylaxis is advised for travel to malarious regions.

Cholera: Occurs year-round, although not reported "active" by the World Health Organization. The risk to tourists of acquiring cholera is low. To prevent cholera, travelers should follow safe food and drink guidelines.

Travelers' diarrhea: High risk. Water supplies in Bangladesh are obtained from ditches, ponds, and streams in rural areas and from canals and ponds in urban areas of the country. Generally, water sources are contaminated with human and animal waste. In addition, the mineral content of the water is high. Travelers should observe strict food and

World Medical Guide

drink guidelines. A quinolone antibiotic is recommended for the treatment of acute diarrhea. Diarrhea not responding to treatment with an antibiotic, or chronic diarrhea, may be due to a parasitic disease such as giardiasis, amebiasis, or cryptosporidiosis.

Hepatitis: All nonimmune travelers should receive hepatitis A vaccine prior to visiting this country. Hepatitis E is endemic, with intermittent outbreaks. The hepatitis B carrier rate in the general population is estimated at 10%. Hepatitis B vaccination is recommended for all healthcare workers or anyone planning an extended visit to this country.

Japanese encephalitis: Risk of transmission is greatest from June through October countrywide in rural agricultural areas. Sporadic cases occur year-round. Last report of disease was in 1977 during an outbreak in the central district of Tangail. Vaccination against Japanese encephalitis is recommended for travelers who will be staying in rural-agricultural endemic areas for long periods (more than several weeks). In addition, all travelers should take measures to prevent mosquito bites, especially in the evening.

Dengue fever: Year-round risk, countrywide. Increased incidence during the monsoon season, June through September. All travelers should take measures to prevent mosquito bites.

Leishmaniasis: Transmission occurs year-round under 600 meters elevation. Visceral leishmaniasis (kala azar) is transmitted countrywide, including urban areas, with an increased incidence in the central delta districts of Mymensingh and Pabna. Travelers should take measures to prevent insect (sandfly) bites, especially in rural areas.

Filariasis: Bancroftian filariasis is reported, with 10% of the population infected. The prevalence is highest in the northern and central districts. Travelers should take measures to prevent mosquito bites.

Rabies: Over 2,000 deaths occur annually. Most rabies in Bangladesh is transmitted by stray dogs. Pre-exposure rabies vaccination should be considered by travelers to this country.

Other illnesses/hazards: Echinococcosis, leprosy (affects a small percentage of the population), sandfly fever (endemic countrywide at low levels), scrub typhus, tuberculosis (a major health problem), typhoid fever, and intestinal worms (whipworms, roundworms, hookworms) are reported. Animal hazards include snakes (kraits, cobras, vipers), centipedes, scorpions, black widow spiders, brown recluse spiders, and large leeches (not poisonous, but can cause slow-healing ulcers). Other possible hazards include crocodiles, pythons, poisonous frogs and toads, lizards, tigers, leopards, and bears (sloth, Himalayan black, and Malayan sun).

BARBADOS

Embassy: 202-939-9200 *Bridgetown* *GMT -4 hrs*

Entry Requirements
- Passport/Visa: Visa not required.
- HIV Test: Not required.
- Vaccinations: A yellow fever vaccination certificate is required from travelers over 1 year of age coming from infected or endemic areas.

Telephone Area Code: 246

Embassies/Consulates: U.S. Embassy, Bridgetown, Broad Street.

Hospitals/Doctors: Diagnostic Clinic & Hospital, St. Michael. Queen Elizabeth's Hospital, Bridgetown. Westgate Clinic, Bridgetown.

Health Advisory
See Disease Risk Summary for the Caribbean.

Travelers' diarrhea: Low to moderate risk. In urban and resort areas, the hotels and restaurants serve reliable food and potable water. A quinolone antibiotic is recommended for the treatment of acute diarrhea.

Hepatitis: Low risk to tourists. Travelers should consider immune globulin prophylaxis or vaccination against hepatitis A.

Other diseases/health threats: Typhoid fever, dengue, leptospirosis, filariasis, ciguatera fish poisoning, and swimming related hazards (jellyfish, spiny sea urchins, and coral).

World Medical Guide

BELARUS
Belarus Embassy: 202-986-1606. *U.S. Embassy, Minsk:* (375)-172-31-5000
For Health Advisory information, see the Health Advisory for Russia on page 404.

BELGIUM
Embassy: 202-333-6900   *Brussels*   *GMT +1 hr*
Entry Requirements
- Passport/Visa: A valid passport is required.
- HIV Test: Not required.
- Vaccinations: None required.

Telephone Country Code: 32   **AT&T:** 0800-100-10   **MCI:** 0800-100-12
Embassies/Consulates: U.S. Embassy, Brussels. 27 Boulevard du Regent; Tel. (2) 508-2111.
Hospitals/Doctors: Hospital Universitaire St. Pierre, Brussels (567 beds); all specialties; emergency room; burn unit; considered one of Belgium's best hospitals.

BELIZE
Embassy: 202-332-9636   *Belmopan*   *GMT -6 hrs*
Entry Requirements
- No visa required for stays less than 30 days. Passports must be valid for at least 6 months
- HIV Test: Testing required of travelers seeking permits for employment or immigration, or staying longer than 3 months.
- Vaccinations: A yellow fever vaccination certificate is required of all travelers arriving from infected areas.

Telephone Country Code: 501   **AT&T:** 555
U.S. Embassy: Belize City. Gabourel Lane and Hutson Street. Tel. (2) 77161.
Doctors/Hospitals: British Forces Belize Hospital (11 beds); the best hospital in Belize but will treat nonmilitary patients only in emergencies. Tel. (2)52-191. Belize City Hospital (75 beds); general medical/surgical; rudimentary x-ray/laboratory services.
Scuba diving emergencies: A decompression chamber is located in San Pedro.

Health Advisory
See Disease Risk Summary for the Caribbean.
Cholera: This disease is active in this country. Although cholera vaccination is not required for entry if arriving directly from the U.S. or Canada, it may be required if arriving from a cholera-infected area, or required for on-going travel to other countries in Latin America, Africa, the Middle East, or Asia. Travelers should consider vaccination (one dose) or a doctor's letter of exemption from vaccination. The risk to travelers of acquiring cholera is low.
Malaria: Belize has the highest incidence of malaria in the Americas. Risk is present year-round in all rural areas of the country under 400 meters elevation. Overall officially reported incidence is highest in the southern districts, but most falciparum cases are reported from northern districts. There is no risk of malaria in Belize City. *P. vivax* causes 96% of cases, *P. falciparum* 4%, but falciparum has been reported as high as 16%. Occasional cases are due to *P. malariae*. Chloroquine-resistant falciparum malaria has not been reported. Chloroquine prophylaxis is currently recommended for overnight visits to rural areas, rain forests, or the offshore islands. All travelers should take measures to prevent mosquito bites.
Travelers' diarrhea: Moderate risk except for tourist resorts, where the risk is low. Raw sewage emptied into the ocean is a cause of beach contamination. Travelers should follow safe food and drink precautions. A quinolone antibiotic is recommended for the treatment of acute diarrhea.

World Medical Guide

Hepatitis: Hepatitis A is endemic. Vaccination is recommended for all nonimmune travelers. Hepatitis E has been reported, but levels are unclear. The hepatitis B carrier rate is estimated at 4%–11%%. Hepatitis B vaccination should be considered by long-term visitors.
Dengue fever: Year-round risk, countrywide, especially in both urban areas. All travelers are advised to take measures to prevent mosquito bites.
Leishmaniasis: Year-round risk, especially in rural forested areas. Prevalence is highest in the central part of the country, lowest in the south. Increased transmission May through December, Cases of cutaneous leishmaniasis have been reported among tourists and field study participants. All travelers are advised to take measures to prevent insect (sandfly) bites.
Rabies: Low risk. One or two cases of human rabies are reported each year. Dogs are main vectors, but vampire bats may also transmit disease. Travelers should avoid contact with dogs and seek immediate treatment of any unprovoked animal bite.
Other diseases: Amebiasis and giardiasis (low incidence), brucellosis, Chagas' disease (endemic at low levels in Cayo District), cutaneous myiasis (caused by larvae of the human bot fly), cysticercosis, histoplasmosis (outbreaks associated with guano in bat caves), leptospirosis, tuberculosis (low incidence), typhoid fever (few officially reported cases), and intestinal helminthic infections.

BENIN

Embassy: 202-232-6656   *Porto-Novo*   *GMT +1 hr*

Entry Requirements
- A visa is required. Travelers should obtain details from the Embassy of Benin.
- HIV Test: Not required.
- Vaccinations: A yellow fever vaccination certificate is required from all travelers arriving from ALL COUNTRIES, including the United States and Canada.

Telephone Country Code: 229
Embassies/Consulates: U.S. Embassy, Contonou. Rue Caporal Anani Bernard; Tel. 300-650, 300-513, or 301-792
Hospitals/Doctors: General Hospital, Porto-Novo; general medical/surgical facility; ENT, pediatrics. General Hospital, Cotonou (350 beds); general medical/surgical facility; teaching hospital. Clinique "Les Graces". Centre Hospitalier Universitaire.

Health Advisory
Yellow fever: This disease is active at this time. An outbreak of yellow fever has been reported in the Department of Atakora in the northeast region of the country. A valid yellow fever vaccination certificate is required to enter this country and may be required for travel to other countries in South America, Africa, the Middle East, or Asia.
Cholera: This disease is reported active at this time. Although cholera vaccination is not required for entry if arriving directly from the U.S. or Canada, it may be required if arriving from a cholera-infected area, or required for on-going travel to other countries in Latin America, Africa, the Middle East, or Asia. Travelers should consider vaccination (one dose) or a doctor's letter of exemption from vaccination. The risk to travelers of acquiring cholera is low. Prevention consists primarily in adhering to safe food and drink guidelines.
Malaria: Risk is present throughout this country, including urban areas. Increased transmission occurs during and after the rainy seasons, April through October. Falciparum malaria accounts for 85% of cases. Chloroquine-resistant falciparum malaria is common. Mefloquine resistance has been reported from the southern provinces of Zou and the Cotonou region. Prophylaxis with mefloquine or doxycycline is currently recommended.
Travelers' diarrhea: High risk in most areas. Although larger cities have piped water systems, all water supplies should be considered contaminated. Travelers should observe all food and drink safety precautions. A quinolone antibiotic is recommended for the treatment of acute diarrhea. Diarrhea not responding to treatment with an antibiotic, or chronic diarrhea, may be due to a parasitic disease such as giardiasis, amebiasis, or cryptosporidiosis.

World Medical Guide

Hepatitis: All nonimmune travelers should receive hepatitis A vaccine. Hepatitis E is likely endemic, but the incidence is unclear. The hepatitis B carrier rate in the general population is estimated at 16%. Vaccination against hepatitis B is recommended for healthcare workers and all long-term visitors to this country.

Schistosomiasis: Urinary schistosomiasis is focally distributed. Highest rate of disease is found in Mono Province, followed by Atakora and Borgou Provinces. Lowest rate in Oueme Province. Intestinal schistosomiasis reported in Borgou, Zou, and Atlantique Provinces. Travelers should avoid wading or swimming in freshwater streams, lakes, or ponds.

Trypanosomiasis: Sporadic cases reported in the 1980s. Tsetse fly vectors are found in the northern areas, particularly in Atakora Province and Pendjari National Park. Travelers should take personal protective measures against insect (tsetse fly) bites.

Meningitis: Benin lies within the sub-Saharan meningitis belt, and there is a high incidence of Group A meningococcal meningitis. Vaccination is recommended for travelers staying in this country longer than 4 weeks.

AIDS: HIV-1 virus prevalence estimated at 25.3% of the high-risk urban population. HIV-2 prevalence is estimated at 13.3% of high-risk individuals. All travelers are cautioned against unsafe sex, unsterile medical or dental injections, and unnecessary blood transfusions.

Other illnesses/hazards: African tick typhus, brucellosis (from consumption of raw dairy products), Bancroftian filariasis (mosquito-borne), dengue (low risk; cases not officially reported from Benin but virus may occur in neighboring Nigeria), dracunculiasis (highest rate in Zou Province), Lassa fever (may occur), leishmaniasis (low apparent risk; sporadic cases have previously been reported), leprosy, loiasis (deer fly-borne; most risk in southern rain forests and swamps), mansonellosis, onchocerciasis (black-fly-borne; transmitted near fast-flowing rivers; high incidence in coastal areas), paragonimiasis (low risk), rabies (transmitted primarily by stray dogs), toxoplasmosis, tuberculosis (a major health problem), typhoid fever, and intestinal worms (very common). Animal hazards include snakes (boomslangs, cobras, vipers), centipedes, scorpions, and brown and black widow spiders.

BHUTAN

U.N. Mission: 212-826-1919   *Thimphu*   *GMT +5½ hrs*

Entry Requirements
- Visa: Tourists admitted only in groups by prearrangement with Bhutan's Ministry of Tourism. A visa is required. Contact the Bhutan Travel Service in New York City at 212-838-6382.
- HIV Test: Not required.
- Vaccinations: A yellow fever vaccination certificate is required from all travelers arriving from infected areas.

Telephone Country Code: 975

Embassies/Consulates: No formal diplomatic relations exist between the United States and Bhutan. The U.S. Embassy in New Delhi (Tel: [91] (11) 688-9033) handles informal diplomatic contact.

Health Advisory

Cholera: This disease is active in this country.

Malaria: Endemic at moderate to high levels. Risk is present year-round in the south and southeastern districts bordering India, including urban areas. Risk generally limited to the Duars Plain and the mountain valleys of the Lesser Himalayas up to 1,700 meters elevation in the Chirang, Gaylegphug, Samchi, Samdrup Jongkhar, and Shemgang Districts. Risk may be elevated during the rainy season, May through mid-October. Thimbu is risk free. *P. falciparum* causes 45% of cases countrywide, *P. vivax* the remainder. Chloroquine- and Fansidar-resistant *P. falciparum* reported from southern border areas. Mefloquine or doxycycline prophylaxis is advised in risk areas.

Travelers' diarrhea: Water supplies in Bhutan are frequently contaminated as a result of substandard sanitary conditions. Prevention of diarrhea consists primarily in following

World Medical Guide

strict adherence to safe food and drink guidelines. A quinolone antibiotic is recommended for treating acute diarrhea. Diarrhea not responding to antibiotic treatment may be due to a parasitic disease such as giardiasis or cryptosporidiosis.
Hepatitis: All nonimmune travelers should receive hepatitis A vaccine. The hepatitis B carrier rate is estimated at 6%. Vaccination against hepatitis B is recommended for anyone planning an extended visit to this country. Hepatitis E is the predominant cause of acute adult hepatitis in Bhutan. Sporadic outbreaks as well as large epidemics occur. Transmission is primarily through sewage-contaminated water.
Dengue fever: Likely endemic in southern plains region, year-round, with risk elevated during the rainy season, May through mid-October.
Sandfly fever: Endemic countrywide at low levels.
Japanese encephalitis: Low-level risk in rural southern (terai) foothill districts, with transmission increased during the rainy season, from May through mid-October.
Leishmaniasis: Visceral leishmaniasis is reported countrywide, with higher risk in the Bramaputra and Ganges River Valleys.
Rabies: Highly prevalent. Stray dogs are the main source of infection. Rabies vaccination should be considered if extended travel is anticipated.
Other illnesses/hazards: Brucellosis (reported in low numbers), filariasis (currently not reported), leprosy (highly prevalent; an estimated 5–10 cases/1,000 population), scabies, murine and scrub typhus, trachoma, tuberculosis (a major health problem), typhoid fever, and intestinal worms (whipworms, roundworms, hookworms) are reported.

BOLIVIA

Embassy: 202-483-4410   *La Paz*   *GMT -4 hrs*

Entry Requirements
- Visa: U.S. citizens do not need a visa for a one-month stay.
- HIV Test: Not required.
- Vaccinations: A yellow fever vaccination certificate is required from all travelers arriving from infected areas.

Telephone Country Code: 591   **AT&T:** 0-800-1112   **MCI:** 0-800-2222
Embassies/Consulates: U.S. Embassy—Consular Section, La Paz. Edificio Tobia, Calle Potosi, corner with Calle Colon; Tel. (2) 356-685.
Hospitals/Doctors: Methodist Hospital, La Paz (113 beds); private hospital; limited emergency services. In Cochabamba: Centro de Salud; In Santa Cruz: Clinica Angel Foianini; comparable to many U.S. hospitals; expensive.

Health Advisory

Yellow fever: This disease is active in jungle areas east of the Andean highlands. A yellow fever vaccination is recommended for all travelers who are destined for high-risk areas (the Departments of Beni, Cochabamba, La Paz, and Santa Cruz). This country is in the Yellow Fever Endemic Zone. A yellow fever vaccination is required from travelers arriving from infected areas and may be required for on-going travel to other countries in Latin America, Africa, the Middle East, and Asia.
Cholera: This disease is active in this country, especially in Cochabamba and Santa Cruz Departments. Although cholera vaccination is not required for entry if arriving directly from the U.S. or Canada, it may be required if arriving from infected areas, or for on-going travel to other countries in Latin America, Africa, the Middle East, or Asia. Travelers should consider vaccination (one dose) or a doctor's letter of exemption from vaccination. The risk to travelers of acquiring cholera is considered low.
Malaria: There is no risk of malaria in the highlands of La Paz, the provinces of Oruro and Potosi (southwestern portions of the country), and the cities of Cochabamba and Sucre. All other rural areas of the country below 1,000 meters elevation should be considered risk areas, especially the lowlands east of the Andean Cordillera and Pando Department. Limited risk may extend up to 2,500 meters elevation in some rural areas. Vivax malaria accounts for nearly

95% of all cases, while falciparum malaria accounts for the remainder. Falciparum malaria, however, may predominate in northern areas. Chloroquine-resistant falciparum malaria is becoming more prevalent in the north and along the Brazilian border. Prophylaxis with mefloquine or doxycycline is recommended when traveling to northern risk areas near the Brazilian border; elsewhere, antimalarial prophylaxis with chloroquine is recommended.

Travelers' diarrhea: High risk outside of first-class hotels and tourist resorts. Travelers should follow all food and drink precautions. A quinolone antibiotic is recommended for the treatment of acute diarrhea. Diarrhea not responding to antibiotic treatment may be due to a parasitic disease such as giardiasis or amebiasis. Cryptosporidiosis has been reported in the Bolivian Altiplano where the infection rate in children is over 30% in some communities. Cyclosporiasis may also be present in this country.

Hepatitis: Hepatitis A vaccine is recommended for all nonimmune travelers. The hepatitis B carrier rate in the general population is estimated at 1.6%. Vaccination against hepatitis B is recommended for healthcare workers. Hepatitis E may occur but has not been reported.

Dengue fever: Risk occurs primarily in urban areas below 1,200 meters elevation. The most recent large outbreak of dengue occurred in southeastern Bolivia in 1993. To prevent dengue, travelers to all regions should take measures to prevent mosquito bites.

Leishmaniasis: Cutaneous and mucocutaneous leishmaniasis occurs year-round below 2,000 meters elevation. Risk is elevated in the Yungas region, the forested foothill valleys at 1,000 to 2,000 meters elevation east of the Andean Cordillera. A few cases of visceral leishmaniasis have been reported from the Yungas region, which is northeast of La Paz. All travelers to rural areas should take measures to prevent insect (sandfly) bites.

Plague: Very low risk. Plague occurs only in very limited areas. Recent outbreaks of flea-borne plague occurred in Santa Cruz Department near the Cochabamba-Chuquisaca border and north of Lake Titicaca, along the border with Peru.

Chagas' disease: Widely distributed in rural areas at elevations up to 3,600 meters, including portions of the Altiplano. In southcentral Cochabamba, up to 100% of villagers are seropositive. Risk occurs especially in those rural-agricultural areas where there are the adobe-style huts and houses that can harbor the night-biting triatomid (assassin) bugs. Travelers sleeping in such structures should take precautions against nighttime bites.

Altitude sickness (AMS): Risk is present for those arriving in La Paz (altitude 3,500 meters) and/or traveling to the Altiplano zone in southwestern Bolivia where the altitude lies between 3,350 and 4,265 meters elevation. Travelers should consider starting acetazolamide (Diamox) prophylaxis before traveling to high altitudes and should also follow standard medical advice meant to reduce symptoms of AMS. Descent to lower altitude is the best treatment for moderate to severe AMS.

Rabies: Dogs are the primary source of human infection. Rabies vaccination is indicated following the unprovoked bite of a dog, cat, vampire bat, monkey, or other animal. Pre-exposure vaccination against rabies is recommended for long-term travelers to this country and for travelers going to remote rural areas.

Other diseases: Bolivian hemorrhagic fever (low risk, but potentially fatal; outbreak occurred in 1994 in El Beni Department in northeastern Bolivia. The virus is transmitted by aerosolized rodent urine. Risk may be increased by sleeping in primitive shelters near rodent habitats. Person-to-person transmission can also occur), brucellosis, coccidiomycosis (endemic near border with Paraguay), echinococcosis (occurs primarily in sheep-raising regions of the Altiplano), fascioliasis (liver fluke disease; high incidence in northwestern Altiplano), Lyme disease (may occur), AIDS (low incidence), tuberculosis (a serious public health problem; highest incidence in South America), strongyloidiasis and other helminthic infections, toxoplasmosis, typhoid fever, and typhus (louse-borne).

World Medical Guide

BONAIRE (NETH. ANTILLES)

Embassy: 202-244-5300 *GMT -4 hrs*

Entry Requirements
- Passport/Visa: Visa not required.
- HIV Test: Not required.
- Vaccinations: None required.

Telephone Country Code: 599 (7)

Health Advisory
See Disease Risk Summary for the Caribbean.

BOSNIA & HERZEGOVINA

U.S. Embassy, Sarajevo: (387)-71-659-992. Entry to Bosnia/Herzegovina is granted at the border on a case-by-case basis

For Health Advisory information, see the Disease Risk Summary for Europe on page 259.

BOTSWANA

Embassy: 202-244-4990/4991 *Gaborone* *GMT +2 hrs*

Entry Requirements
- Travelers should contact the Embassy of Botswana for entry requirements.
- HIV Test: Not required.
- Vaccinations: None required.

Telephone Country Code: 267
Embassies/Consulates: U.S. Embassy, Gaborone. Embassy Drive, Government Enclave; Tel. 353-982. After hours tel: 357-111.
Hospitals/Doctors: Princess Marina Hospital, Gaborone (237 beds); general medical and surgical services. A. E. Bhoola, M.D., Gaborone; Tel. 352-221/312-610.

Health Advisory

Malaria: Moderate seasonal risk in northern areas and sporadic risk in southeastern border areas. Increased transmission during and just after the rainy season (October to mid-April). Malaria is moderately endemic in northern areas, including the Boteti, Chobe, Ngamiland, Okavango, and Tutume districts/subdivisions. Limited transmission occurs in the southeastern border with South Africa, extending along the Molopo River bordering South Africa. Gaborone is essentially risk free, except in years with very heavy rainfall. *P. falciparum* accounts for 95% of malaria cases. Occasional cases due to *P. malariae* have been reported. Chloroquine-resistant falciparum malaria has been confirmed. Prophylaxis with mefloquine or doxycycline is currently advised.

Travelers' diarrhea: High risk. Water from deep boreholes may be unpalatable due to high salinity. Indiscriminate disposal of human waste causes serious contamination of ground water in many villages, and in some towns. Piped water is available to 90% of the urban population but many water treatment and distribution systems are poorly maintained and may be contaminated. Travelers should observe all food and drink safety precautions. A quinolone antibiotic is recommended for the treatment of acute diarrhea. Diarrhea not responding to treatment with an antibiotic, or chronic diarrhea, may be due to a parasitic disease such as giardiasis, amebiasis, or cryptosporidiosis.

Hepatitis: Hepatitis A is highly endemic. All nonimmune travelers should receive hepatitis A vaccine. Hepatitis E is endemic, with outbreaks reported in north-central areas. The hepatitis B carrier rate in the general population is estimated at 12%. Vaccination against hepatitis B is recommended for healthcare workers and all long-term visitors to this country.

Leishmaniasis: Low risk. Sporadic cases have been reported in the medical literature.

Schistosomiasis: Risk areas of urinary schistosomiasis are widely distributed along the eastern border from Francistown to Lobatse, with scattered foci in the north. Risk areas for intestinal schistosomiasis are confined to the Okavango Delta marshlands in the northwest district of Ngamiland and the northeastern Chobe drainage system, including the Kasane vicinity. Travelers to these areas should avoid swimming, bathing, or wading in freshwater ponds, lakes, or streams.

Plague: An outbreak in Central District, near Lake Xau, was reported in 1989–1990, with 164 human cases and 12 fatalities. Doxycycline prophylaxis is recommended only if travelers expect to have on-going, close contact with rodents (e.g., field biologists, military personnel).

African sleeping sickness: Incidence data not available. Sporadic cases were reported in the 1980s from the northern areas, including cases among foreign visitors to the Okavango swamps in the northwest district of Ngamiland. All travelers should take measures to prevent insect (tsetse fly) bites.

Rabies: Dogs are the primary source of human infection. Rabid jackals are also a potential threat, especially in the rural eastern areas, where an outbreak of wild animal rabies was reported in 1987. Travelers should seek immediate treatment of any animal bite. Rabies vaccination should be considered prior to long-term travel (more than 4 weeks) to this country. Vaccinated travelers who are bitten require an additional two doses of rabies vaccine.

AIDS: Heterosexual contact is the predominate mode of transmission. HIV prevalence among adults of sexually active age was estimated to be 17% in Gabarone and 24% in urban Francistown as of mid-1996. All travelers are cautioned against unsafe sex, unsterile medical or dental injections, and unnecessary blood transfusions.

Other illnesses/hazards: African tick typhus (contracted from dog ticks, often in urban areas; disease also transmitted by bush ticks), arboviral fevers (mosquito-transmitted; West Nile and Rift Valley fever may occur; explosive urban outbreaks of chikungunya fever have occurred, but human cases are primarily reported from rural areas), brucellosis, dengue (not reported recently), leptospirosis, tick-bornerelapsing fever, flea- and louse-borne typhus, tuberculosis (a major health problem), trachoma, typhoid fever, and intestinal helminthic infections (very common). Animal hazards include snakes (vipers, cobras), centipedes, scorpions, and black widow spiders.

BRAZIL

Embassy: 202-745-2700 *Brasilia* *GMT -3 hrs*

Entry Requirements
- Passport/Visa: A valid passport and visa are required.
- HIV Test: Not required.
- Vaccinations: A yellow fever vaccination certificate is required from travelers arriving from infected areas. A certificate is also required if arriving from Africa from Angola, Cameroon, Gabon, Gambia, Ghana, Guinea, Kenya, Mali, Nigeria, Sudan, and Zaire.
Americas: Certificate required if arriving from Bolivia, Colombia, Ecuador, Peru.

Telephone Country Code: 55 **AT&T:** 000-8010 **MCI:** 000-8012

Embassies/Consulates: U.S. Embassy, Brasilia. Avenida das Nocoes, Lote 3; Tel. (61) 321-7272. U.S. Consulate, Rio de Janeiro. Avenida Presidente Wilson, No. 147; Tel. (21) 292-7117. U.S. Consulate, Sao Paulo. Rue Padre Joao Manoel, No. 933; Tel. (11) 881-6511.

Hospitals/Doctors: Brasilia: Hospital de Base (600 beds); most specialty services including trauma; 24-hour emergency room. Casa de Saude Santa Lucia; some specialty and emergency services. **Sao Paulo:** Hospital Samaritano; 24-hour emergency services. Clinica Hamermesz; highly recommended by expats. Albert Einstein Hospital. Excellent facility, but nurses may be undertrained. Dr. Maria Cecilia; OB/GYN; recommended. **Rio de Janeiro:** Hospital Miguel Couto (117 beds); some specialty services including trauma and emergency. Hospital Souza Aguiar (480 beds); most specialty services including orthopedics, trauma, and emergency. **Anapolis (Goias):** Hospital Evengelico; mission hospital staffed by British expats. **Cuiaba (Mato Grosso State):** Dr. Joaquim Spadoni; U.S.-trained surgeon. **Salvador (Bahias):** Sao Rafael Hospital; advanced facility with CT, MRI. ultrasound, but nursing care may not be adequate. **Manaus:** Adventist Hospital. **Mineiros (Goias):** The Evangelical Hospital; efficient, capable facility.

World Medical Guide

Health Advisory

Yellow fever: This disease is active in widely scattered foci, primarily in the Amazon Basin. Yellow fever vaccination is recommended for travel to rural areas in Acre, Amazonas, Maranhao, Mato Grosso, Mato Grosso do Sol, Para, Rondonia, and Tocantins States, and the Territories of Amapa and Roraima. Recently, two fatal cases of yellow fever occurred in tourists traveling to the Amazon Basin.

Cholera: This disease is active in this country. Although cholera vaccination is not required for entry if arriving directly from the U.S. or Canada, it may be required if arriving from a cholera-infected area, or required for on-going travel to other countries.

Malaria: Risk is present year-round below 900 meters elevation in all areas of Acre, Amapa, Rondonia, and Roraima States, and in most rural areas of Amazonas (including outskirts of urban areas), Goias, Maranhao, Mato Grosso, Para, and Tocantins States; limited risk also may exist in some rural areas of coastal states from Piaui in the north to Santa Catarina in the south. Risk may be elevated from December through May in more temperate southern areas. In the Amazon Basin risk is usually associated with the transition from rainy to dry and from dry to rainy seasons. Risk is high in the areas of mining and agricultural colonization: the north of Mato Grosso; the south of Para, the northern part of Rondonia, the west of Amapa; the settlement areas in the valley of the Accre River and along the road Tarauca-Cruzeiro do Sol, the areas of the Yanomani and Macuxis in Roraima and those bordering Maranhao and Para; the scattered regions in the State of Amazonas and along the Javari, Madeira, Purus, Solimoes, and Negro Rivers.

At least 80% of malaria cases are reported from Mato Grosso, Para, and Rondonia States. Countrywide, *P. falciparum* accounts for 40% of officially-reported malaria cases. Nearly all other cases are caused by *P. vivax*. About 2% of malaria is caused by *P. malariae*. Multidrug-resistant falciparum malaria is a major problem, particularly in the Amazon region where chloroquine- and Fansidar-resistant *P. falciparum* occurs. Chemoprophylaxis with mefloquine or doxycycline is recommended when traveling to risk areas. All travelers planning an Amazon River cruise should take chemoprophylaxis and measures to prevent mosquito bites.

Travelers' diarrhea: High risk outside of resorts and first-class hotels. Travelers should follow all food and drink precautions. A quinolone antibiotic is recommended for the treatment of diarrhea. Diarrhea not responding to antibiotic treatment may be due to a parasitic disease such as giardiasis, amebiasis, or cryptosporidiosis.

Hepatitis: Hepatitis A vaccine is recommended for all nonimmune travelers. The overall hepatitis B carrier rate is between 1%–2%, but may approach 20% in some areas of the Amazon Basin. Hepatitis E is endemic but levels are unclear.

Dengue fever: Mosquito-transmitted. Most recent outbreaks have occurred from December through June in southern areas. Risk may be elevated from April through August in more northern areas. Risk is present year-round in Rio de Janeiro State and Sao Paulo and Ceara States.

Insect-transmitted viral diseases: Oropouche fever (vectored by biting midges; explosive outbreaks occur), Mayaro virus disease (dengue-like illness, mosquito-vectored; attack rates up to 20% in the Amazon Basin, including Paro State), eastern equine encephalitis, St. Louis encephalitis, Western equine encephalitis, and Venezuelan equine encephalitis are reported. At least 30 other insect-borne viral illnesses are associated with illness in humans.

Leishmaniasis: Cutaneous, mucocutaneous and visceral leishmaniasis occur in rural and periurban areas. Cutaneous leishmaniasis and mucocutaneous leishmaniasis occur nearly countrywide in rural and periurban areas with risk elevated in the more humid areas of northern, north-central, and central states; most visceral leishmaniasis occurs in the semi-arid northeastern states (with sharp increases in Maranhao, Piaui, and Rio Grande do Norte States), but has also been reported as far west and south as extreme western Mato Grosso do Sul State and Rio de Janiero State, respectively. All travelers to these regions should take protective measures to prevent insect (sandfly) bites.

Onchocerciasis: Risk is present near swift-flowing streams in densely forested highlands in northern Amazonas and Poraima States. Travelers to these areas should take measures to prevent insect (blackfly) bites.

Filariasis: Focally endemic in northeastern urban coastal areas, including Belem, Maceio, and Recife. Travelers to these regions should take measures to prevent insect (mosquito) bites.

Schistosomiasis: Intestinal schistosomiasis is a major public health problem. Risk appears elevated in the northeast. Most cases are reported from Minas Gerais and Bahia States. Risk is present in northern and eastern states from Maranhao south to Parana, including both urban and rural areas. There is no apparent risk in the Amazon Basin. Travelers to these areas should avoid swimming, wading, or bathing in freshwater ponds, lakes, or streams.

Chagas' disease: Risk is present in most rural areas of eastern and southern Brazil. Risk occurs primarily in well-populated rural-agricultural areas where there are adobe-style huts and houses that often harbor the night-biting triatomid (assassin) bugs. Travelers sleeping in such structures should take measures to prevent nighttime bites.

Plague: Most cases are reported from the drier northern and eastern states from Bahia and Ceara south to Minas Gerais. Thirty-five to 150 cases are reported annually. Travelers to these regions should avoid close contact with rodents (which may be carrying infective fleas). Prophylaxis with tetracycline is protective.

Rabies: High risk, relative to other South American countries. Forty to 120 human cases are reported annually, usually transmitted by stray dogs. Vampire bats have also been implicated. Most cases occur in the northeastern states, but cases are also reported countrywide from both urban and rural areas.

Lyme disease: The incidence of Lyme disease is unclear; it appears to be very low. Five cases with "Lyme disease" were reported from Brazil in 1991.

AIDS: The highest AIDS rate in South America occurs in Brazil. Most cases are reported from Rio de Janeiro and Sao Paulo. Causative factors are heterosexual promiscuity, prostitution, bisexuality, and IV drug use. Both HIV-1 and HIV-2 occur.

Other diseases: Angiostrongyliasis, brucellosis, cutaneous larva migrans, cryptococcosis, cysticercosis (an important health problem in northeastern Brazil, and probably elsewhere), echinococcosis, leprosy (highly endemic in Recife area), leptospirosis (mostly in rat-infested urban slums), mansonellosis, measles, meningitis (epidemics reported from Sao Paulo; most cases due to serogroup B meningococci), trachoma, toxocariasis, tuberculosis (a serious public health problem; 25% of children in some areas may be infected), strongyloidiasis, and other helminthic infections.

BRITISH VIRGIN ISLANDS
(TORTOLA, VIRGIN GORDA, ANEGADA, JOST VAN DYKE)

Embassy: 202-462-1340   Tortola   GMT -4 hrs

Entry Requirements
- Passport/Visa: Visa not required for stay less than 90 days.
- HIV Test: All immigrants and work permit applicants are required to have HIV testing.
- Vaccinations: None required.

Telephone Area Code: 809
Embassies/Consulates: Contact U.S. Embassy, Bridgetown, Barbados; 809-436-4950.
Doctors/Hospitals: Peebles Hospital, Tortola (50 beds); limited medical/surgical services.

Health Advisory
See Disease Risk Summary for the Caribbean.

Travelers' diarrhea: Low to moderate risk. In resort areas, the hotels and restaurants serve reliable food and potable water. Elsewhere, travelers should observe safety precautions. A quinolone antibiotic (Floxin or Cipro) is recommended for the treatment of acute diarrhea.

Hepatitis: Low risk to tourists. Susceptible travelers should consider hepatitis A vaccination.

Dengue fever: This mosquito-transmitted viral disease is prevalent in the Caribbean. Travelers should take measures to prevent insect bites.

Other diseases/health threats: Typhoid fever, sexually transmitted diseases, ciguatera fish poisoning, and swimming related hazards (jellyfish, spiny sea urchins, and coral).

World Medical Guide

BRUNEI DARUSSALAM

Embassy: 202-342-0159   *Bandar Seri Begawan*   *GMT +8 hrs*

Entry Requirements
- Passport/Visa: A valid passport, visa, and tourist card are required.
- HIV Test: Not required.
- Vaccinations: A valid yellow fever vaccination certificate is required of all travelers older than one year coming from infected areas or coming from or transiting through any country in the Yellow Fever Endemic Zones within the previous 6 days.

Telephone Country Code: 673
Embassies/Consulates: U.S. Embassy, Bandar Seri Begawan; Tel. (2) 29670. Canadian Embassy (Malaysia); Tel. [60] (3) 261-2000.

Health Advisory

Malaria: There is no risk of malaria within this country.
Cholera: Not reported active, but sporadic cases occur.
Travelers' diarrhea: The food and drink in first-class restaurants and hotels are considered generally safe. Elsewhere, travelers should observe food and drink safety precautions. A quinolone antibiotic (Cipro or Floxin) is recommended for the treatment of acute diarrhea. Diarrhea not responding to treatment with an antibiotic, or chronic diarrhea, may be due to a parasitic disease such as giardiasis or amebiasis, and treatment with metronidazole (Flagyl) or tinidazole (Fasigyn) should be considered. All cases of diarrhea should be treated with adequate fluid replacement.
Hepatitis: All nonimmune travelers should receive hepatitis A vaccine. The hepatitis B carrier rate in the general population is estimated at 10%–12%. Vaccination against hepatitis B is recommended for all healthcare workers and should be considered by anyone planning an extended visit to this country.
Dengue fever: There is risk of both dengue and dengue hemorrhagic fever. The *Aedes* mosquitoes, which transmit dengue, bite primarily during the daytime and are present in populous urban areas as well as resort and rural areas. To prevent dengue, all travelers are advised to take precautions against mosquito bites.
Japanese encephalitis: Vaccination against Japanese encephalitis is recommended for travelers who will be staying in rural-agricultural areas for extended periods (more than 4 weeks). In addition, all travelers should take precautions against mosquito bites, especially in the evening.
Other disease/risks: Fasciolopsiasis (giant intestinal fluke), helminthic infections (e.g., hookworm, roundworm), filariasis (transmitted by mosquitoes), mite-borne typhus, melioidosis, rabies, and typhoid fever are reported. Other possible hazards include snake bites and leeches.

BULGARIA

Embassy: 202-387-7969   *Sofia*   *GMT +1 hr*

Entry Requirements
- Passport/Visa: Passport required. A visa is required only if travel exceeds 30 days.
- HIV Test: Testing required for all foreigners staying longer than one month for purpose of study or work.
- Vaccinations: None required.

Telephone Country Code: 359
Embassies/Consulates: U.S. Embassy, Sofia. 1 Alex. Stambolinsky Blvd; Tel. 88-48-01.
Hospitals/Doctors: Institute of Traumatology and Orthopedics, Sofia (400 beds); specialized treatment center for entire country.

Health Advisory

Malaria: Although Bulgaria has been officially "malaria free" since the 1970s, cases have been rising (over 2,500 reported in 1990). Many of these cases may be imported, but indigenous malaria cannot be excluded. Risk appears to be limited to the southern regions (bordering Greece and Turkey) and the southeastern coastal areas. Indigenous malaria most likely is vivax, but 50% of imported malaria may be due to *P. falciparum*. Travelers to the southern regions are advised to take precautions against mosquito bites and seek medical attention of any sudden illness with fever.

Travelers' diarrhea: High risk outside of first-class hotels and resorts. Piped water is potable in most cities but travelers are advised to drink only bottled, boiled, filtered, or treated water and consume only well-cooked food. A quinolone antibiotic (Floxin or Cipro) is recommended for the treatment of acute diarrhea. Diarrhea not responding to antibiotic treatment may be due to a parasitic disease such as giardiasis—or an intestinal virus.

Hepatitis: Bulgaria has among the highest rates of hepatitis A in Europe (200 cases/100,000). All nonimmune travelers should receive hepatitis A vaccine. The hepatitis B carrier rate in the general population is estimated at 3.5%. Vaccination against hepatitis B is recommended for healthcare workers and should be considered by long-term visitors to this country.

Lyme disease: Occurs focally in rural forested areas up to 1,500 meters elevation. Vector ticks (*Ixodes ricinus* or *I. persulcatus*) are most abundant and active from April through September.

Mediterranean spotted fever (boutonneuse fever): Endemic in eastern regions and along the Black Sea coast in brushy and/or forested areas.

European tick-borne encephalitis (TBE): Low apparent risk. The tick vector for this disease, *Ixodes ricinus* (the same tick that transmits Lyme disease), is widely distributed in brushy and forested areas at elevations up to 1,000 meters.

Crimean-Congo hemorrhagic fever: This is a viral encephalitis transmitted by ticks (*Hyalomma marginatum*). Ticks are most active from April until August, reaching peak feeding activity in April and May. Main risk areas are the southern provinces of Kurdzhali and Khaskovo and the southeastern provinces of Yambol and Burgas.

Other illnesses/hazards: Anthrax (sporadic human cases; exposure to livestock in rural areas), brucellosis (risk associated with consumption of raw dairy products), echinococcosis, leptospirosis, rabies (cases may occur in stray dogs and cats, jackals, foxes, and wolves; rare in humans; country officially "rabies free"), tick-borne relapsing fever (risk in rocky, rural livestock areas), murine typhus (probably occurs), and soil-transmitted helminthic infections (roundworm, hookworm, and whipworm infections reported occasionally).

BURKINA FASO

Embassy: 202-332-5577   *Ouagadougou*   *GMT 0 hrs*

Entry Requirements
- Passport/Visa: Valid passport and visa are required.
- HIV Test: Not required.
- Vaccinations: A yellow fever vaccination certificate is required from all travelers arriving from ALL COUNTRIES, including the United States and Canada.

Telephone Country Code: 226
Embassies/Consulates: U.S. Embassy, Ouagadougou. Tel. 306-723 or 306-724.

Health Advisory

Yellow fever: Two cases of yellow fever were reported in 1998. Each occurred in a village in Batie district (Gaoua region) near the border with Cote d'Ivoire. Vaccination is required for all travelers entering this country. This country is in the Yellow Fever Endemic Zone. A valid yellow fever vaccination certificate may also be required for on-going travel to other countries in South America, Africa, the Middle East, Asia, or Oceania.

Cholera: This disease is reported active in this country. Although cholera vaccination is not required for entry if arriving directly from the U.S. or Canada, it may be required if arriving

World Medical Guide

from a cholera-infected area, or required for on-going travel to other countries in Latin America, Africa, the Middle East, or Asia. Travelers should consider vaccination (one dose) or a doctor's letter of exemption from vaccination. The risk to travelers of acquiring cholera is low. Prevention consists primarily in adhering to safe food and drink guidelines.

Malaria: Risk is present throughout this country year-round, including urban areas. Risk is elevated during and immediately following the rainy season (June through October). *P. falciparum* malaria accounts for 85%–95% of cases, followed by *P. ovale*. Multidrug-resistant falciparum malaria is reported. Chemoprophylaxis with mefloquine or doxycycline is currently recommended.

Travelers' diarrhea: High risk. All surface water sources should be considered potentially contaminated. Water from deep wells is usually free of bacterial contamination, but may contain high levels of minerals and sediment. Travelers should observe all food and drink precautions. A quinolone antibiotic is recommended for the treatment of acute diarrhea. Diarrhea not responding to treatment with an antibiotic may be due to a parasitic disease such as giardiasis, amebiasis, or cryptosporidiosis.

Hepatitis: All susceptible travelers should receive hepatitis A vaccine. Hepatitis E is probably endemic, but the incidence is not clear. The hepatitis B carrier rate in the general population exceeds 10%. Vaccination against hepatitis B is recommended for all healthcare workers and long-term visitors to this country.

Schistosomiasis: Urinary schistosomiasis is widely distributed, especially in the eastern one-third of this country, with focal areas of risk in all major river basins. Intestinal schistosomiasis is widely distributed in the southwest, with scattered foci in other areas. Travelers should avoid swimming, wading, or bathing in freshwater lakes, ponds, or streams.

Leishmaniasis: Low apparent risk. Cutaneous leishmaniasis has been reported in the western and eastern areas, and a focus was identified near Arabinda (northeastern province of Soum) in 1986. Travelers should take precautions against insect (sandfly) bites.

Trypanosomiasis (African sleeping sickness): Undetermined risk. Disease activity apparently has been reported in the vicinities of Banfora and Bobo Diolasso in the southwest, and the Koudougou vicinity west of Ouagadougou. Travelers to these regions should take protective measures against insect (tsetse fly) bites.

Onchocerciasis: May be transmitted near fast-flowing rivers. Incidence is declining, due to control programs. Travelers should take measures to prevent blackfly insect bites.

Filariasis: Bancroftian filariasis is reported. Travelers should take measures to prevent mosquito bites.

Meningitis: Outbreaks of meningococcal meningitis were reported in February 1996 in Yatenga and Bam Provinces. Vaccination is recommended for all travelers staying in this country longer than 4 weeks, especially those who anticipate close contact with the indigenous population.

Rabies: Vaccination is recommended for long-term travel (more than 4 weeks) to this country, especially for travelers going to remote rural areas who will be unable to receive antirabies treatment within 24 hours of exposure to a potentially rabid animal.

AIDS: Heterosexual contact is the predominate mode of transmission. HIV-1 prevalence estimated at 17% of the high-risk urban population. All travelers are cautioned against unsafe sex, unsterile medical or dental injections, and unnecessary blood transfusions.

Other diseases: African tick typhus (transmitted by dog ticks and bush ticks), anthrax, brucellosis, dengue (low apparent risk; last cases reported in 1982), dracunculiasis (risk is countrywide), leprosy (overall prevalence 2 cases/1,000 population), leptospirosis, loiasis, louse-borne (epidemic) typhus and relapsing fever, Lyme disease (one case report in 1991), tuberculosis (a major health problem), intestinal worms (common), and typhoid fever are reported. Lassa fever probably occurs but the incidence is not known.

World Medical Guide

BURMA (MYANMAR)

Embassy: 202-332-9044   *Rangoon*   *GMT +6 hrs*

Entry Requirements
- Passport/Visa: A valid passport and visa required. Rangoon only port of entry. Overland travel in and out of Burma not permitted. Group travel only is permitted.
- HIV Test: Not required.
- Vaccinations: A yellow fever vaccination certificate is required of all travelers arriving from infected areas. A certificate is also required of nationals and residents of Myanmar departing for an infected area.

Telephone Country Code: 95
Embassies/Consulates: U.S. Embassy, Rangoon. 581 Merchant Street; Tel. (1) 282-055 and 282-182.
Hospitals/Doctors: JICA Hospital, Rangoon (220 beds); general medical/surgical facility; ICU. Travelers should be aware that the U.S. Embassy evacuates its personnel to Bangkok, Thailand, in lieu of using local Burmese hospitals.

Health Advisory

Malaria: Occurs countrywide with the greatest risk of transmission during the wetter months, May through December. Malaria is most prevalent in forested foothill areas below 1,000 meters elevation. There is less malaria in the plains and urban areas. Malaria risk is present in all cities except Rangoon and the urban centers of Mandalay, Magwe, Pegu, and Sagaing. Falciparum malaria accounts for 86% of cases. There is widespread occurrence of chloroquine-resistant falciparum malaria in this country. Mefloquine or doxycycline prophylaxis is recommended for travel to rural areas. Multidrug-resistant malaria is reported along the Thai-Burmese border. Doxycycline prophylaxis is recommended for those traveling to border areas adjacent to Thailand.

Travelers' diarrhea: Potable water is almost nonexistent in Burma. Rural water supplies usually are grossly contaminated and urban water supplies invariably are subject to contamination. Local dairy products are considered unsafe. Local fruits and vegetables should be scrubbed and soaked in a chlorine or iodine solution before consumption. Travelers should observe all food and drink safety precautions. A quinolone antibiotic is recommended for the treatment of acute diarrhea. Diarrhea not responding to treatment with an antibiotic, or chronic diarrhea, may be due to a parasitic disease such as giardiasis or amebiasis.

Hepatitis: Hepatitis A is highly endemic. All nonimmune travelers should receive the hepatitis A vaccine. The hepatitis B carrier rate in the general population is estimated at 10%. Vaccination against hepatitis B is recommended for all expatriates, relief workers, teachers, and others (including family members) who will have prolonged contact with the indigenous population of this country. There is a high incidence of hepatitis E in this country. Explosive outbreaks occur, most commonly due to the consumption of sewage-contaminated water. All travelers, especially pregnant women, should follow safe drinking water guidelines. Hepatitis C is endemic.

Typhoid fever: Vaccination is recommended for all travelers.

Dengue fever: Highly endemic. The peak infection rate usually occurs during the wetter months, May through October. Dengue occurs countrywide, but predominates in urban areas. Dengue hemorrhagic fever (a severe form of the disease) often occurs in persons who have had one or more previous dengue infections. The *Aedes* mosquitoes transmitting dengue bite during the daytime. A vaccine is not available. Prevention consists of taking personal protection measures against mosquito bites.

Japanese encephalitis: Both rural and urban areas may experience epidemics of Japanese encephalitis. Sporadic cases occur year-round, countrywide. Peak transmission occurs during the monsoon season, May through December. Vaccination against Japanese encephalitis is recommended for travelers who will be staying in rural-agricultural areas longer than 3-4 weeks. In addition, all travelers to endemic areas should take personal protection measures against mosquito bites, especially in the evening.

World Medical Guide

Filariasis: Bancroftian and Malayan filariasis (mosquito-borne) are highly endemic in rural and urban areas. All travelers should take measures to prevent insect (mosquito) bites.

Other illnesses/hazards: Anthrax, brucellosis (low incidence), helminthic infections (ascariasis and hookworm disease are highly endemic in urban and rural areas), paragonimiasis (lung fluke disease; presumed endemic in small foci in rural areas), echinococcosis, leishmaniasis (low risk; sand-fly-borne, probably visceral type, reported historically), leprosy (highly endemic), rabies (dogs are the primary source of infection), epidemic typhus (louse-borne; may occur in northern upland provinces), murine typhus (flea-borne), scrub typhus (mite-borne; risk elevated in grassy rural areas), tuberculosis (highly endemic), and trachoma (highly endemic). Animal hazards include snakes (vipers, cobras), centipedes, scorpions, and black widow spiders. Other possible hazards include crocodiles, pythons, and large, aggressive lizards, all abundant in and near Burma's swamps and rivers, and leopards, wildcats, and bears, all found in the hilly regions of the country. Stingrays, sea wasps, cones, jellyfish, spiny sea urchins, and anemones are common in the country's coastal waters and are potentially hazardous to unprotected or careless swimmers.

BURUNDI

Embassy: 202-342-2574 *Bujumbura* *GMT +2 hrs*

Entry Requirements
- Visa: A visa is required. Travelers should contact the Embassy of Burundi for information.
- HIV Test: Not required.
- Vaccinations: A yellow fever vaccination certificate is required for all travelers older than 1 year of age arriving from infected areas. Vaccination against meningococcal meningitis is required.

Telephone Country Code: 257
Embassies/Consulates: U.S. Embassy, Bujumbura. Avenue des Etas Unis; Tel. 223-454.
Hospitals/Doctors: Hospital Prince Regent Charles; general medical/surgical facility; ICU. Clinique Prince Louis Rwagasore (13 beds). Travelers should contact the U.S. Embassy for physician referrals.

Health Advisory

Yellow fever: Vaccination is recommended and is required for entry. This country is in the Yellow Fever Endemic Zone. A valid vaccination certificate may be required for on-going travel to other countries.

Cholera: This disease is reported active in this country. Although cholera vaccination is not required for entry if arriving directly from the U.S. or Canada, it may be required for on-going travel to other countries in Africa, the Middle East, or Asia. Travelers should consider vaccination (one dose) or getting a doctor's letter of exemption from vaccination. The risk to travelers of acquiring cholera is considered low. Prevention consists primarily in adhering to safe food and drink guidelines.

Malaria: Risk is present year-round throughout this country, including urban areas. Transmission is highest during and immediately after the rainy seasons, September through December and March through May. Peak transmission in the Rusizi Valley occurs during the drier months of May through September. Risk may be lower in locations above 1,800 meters elevation. Falciparum malaria accounts for approximately 80% of cases, followed by *P. malariae* in up to 20% of cases. Chloroquine-resistant falciparum malaria is reported. Prophylaxis with mefloquine or doxycycline is currently recommended.

Travelers' diarrhea: High risk. Travelers should observe all food and drink safety precautions. A quinolone antibiotic is recommended for the treatment of acute diarrhea. Diarrhea not responding to treatment with an antibiotic, or chronic diarrhea, may be due to a parasitic disease such as giardiasis, amebiasis, or cryptosporidiosis.

Hepatitis: High risk. All nonimmune travelers should receive hepatitis A vaccine. The hepatitis B carrier rate in the general population is estimated at 4.7% or higher. Vaccination against hepatitis B is recommended for healthcare workers and all long-term visitors to this country. Hepatitis E occurs with seroprevalence of 14% reported in the general population.

World Medical Guide

Schistosomiasis: Risk is present mainly in three areas: the western Imbo lowlands extending across the Rusizi River and Plain and along the shores of Lake Tanganyika, including Bujumbura, the northeast around Lake Cohoha, and the eastern Moso lowlands.
Meningitis: Outbreaks of Group A meningococcal meningitis are occurring in this country. Over 2,500 cases of meningitis were reported in 1992, but none apparently occurred in tourists. Vaccination is recommended for all travelers to this country, especially if they will be staying longer than 4 weeks, or will be having close contact with the indigenous population.
AIDS: HIV-1 prevalence estimated at 20% of the high-risk urban population. All travelers are cautioned against unsafe sex, unsterile medical or dental injections, and unnecessary blood transfusions.
Other illnesses/hazards: African tick typhus, brucellosis, Ebola-Marburg disease (virus widespread in region but no cases reported in Burundi), echinococcosis, filariasis, leishmaniasis (probably endemic; data not available), rabies (transmitted primarily by dogs), trypanosomiasis (undetermined incidence; may be present in Bururi and Ngozi Provinces), tuberculosis (a major health problem), trachoma, typhoid fever, typhus (louse-borne; reported from the highlands), and intestinal worms (very common). Animal hazards include snakes (vipers, cobras), centipedes, scorpions, and black widow spiders.

CAMBODIA (KAMPUCHEA)

Embassy: 202-726-7742   **Phnom Penh**   **GMT +7 hrs**

Entry Requirements
- A visa, valid for 30 days, is required.
- HIV Test: Visa applicants must present a medical certificate. Enforcement of this requirement is inconsistent.
- A yellow fever vaccination certificate is required of travelers arriving from infected areas.

Telephone Country Code: 855
Embassies/Consulates: The U.S. Embassy, Phnom Penh. 27, Street Anghanouvong 240; Tel. 2342-6436 or 2342-6438.
Hospitals/Doctors: 7 Jan 1979 Hospital, Phnom Penh (500 beds); some specialties; emergency services; may be best hospital in country. Battambang Provincial Hospital (325 beds).

Health Advisory
Cholera: This disease is active in this country. Although cholera vaccination is not required for entry if arriving directly from the U.S. or Canada, it may be required if arriving from a cholera-infected area, or required for on-going travel to other countries in Latin America, Africa, the Middle East, or Asia. Travelers should consider vaccination (one dose) or a doctor's letter of exemption from vaccination.
Malaria: Risk is present year-round throughout this country. Malaria is endemic at high levels in forested areas along the borders, moderate levels in central areas, and low levels from Tonle Sap Lake through Phnom Penh and down the Mekong River to the Vietnamese border. There is increased risk in mountainous and rural areas. Falciparum malaria accounts for an estimated 90% of cases, vivax the remainder. Multidrug-resistant falciparum malaria is common, especially near the Thai-Cambodian border. Doxycycline prophylaxis is recommended for travel to malarious areas.
Travelers' diarrhea: Travelers should observe strict food and drink safety precautions. A quinolone antibiotic is recommended for the treatment of acute diarrhea. Diarrhea not responding to treatment with an antibiotic may be due to a parasitic disease such as giardiasis or amebiasis—or an intestinal virus. Infection rates for cryptosprididosis are not available.
Hepatitis: There is a high risk of hepatitis A in this country. All nonimmune travelers should receive hepatitis A vaccine. Hepatitis E is reported, but data not available. The hepatitis B carrier rate in the general population is estimated to exceed 10%. Vaccination against hepatitis B is recommended for all long-term visitors. Hepatitis C is endemic.
Dengue fever: Endemic at high levels year-round. Increased risk may occur in urban areas. The *Aedes* mosquitoes, which transmit dengue, bite primarily during the daytime and are

329

World Medical Guide

present in populous urban areas as well as resort and rural areas. All travelers are advised to take precautions against mosquito bites.

Japanese encephalitis: Sporadic cases occur throughout the year, primarily in rural areas, but occasionally near or within urban areas. Vaccination is recommended for travelers planning an extended stay (more than 3–4 weeks) in rural-agricultural areas during the peak transmission season, June through October.

Schistosomiasis: Risk is present year-round, especially along the Mekong and Mun Rivers and in Battambang Province. Travelers should avoid swimming, bathing, or wading in freshwater lakes, ponds, or streams.

Other diseases/health threats: AIDS (14% HIV seropositivity among prostitutes), anthrax (associated with eating buffalo meat), chikungunya fever (regionally endemic, with outbreaks), echinococcosis, filariasis (endemic; current levels unclear), leprosy (highly endemic), leptospirosis, plague, rabies, scrub typhus, tuberculosis (highly endemic), typhoid fever, soil-transmitted helminthic diseases (ascariasis, hookworm disease, strongyloidiasis), and other helminthic infections (fasciolopsiasis, gnathostomiasis, opisthorchiasis, and clonorchiasis) are reported. Animal hazards include snakes (cobras, vipers), spiders (black and brown widow), crocodiles, and leeches. Stingrays, jellyfish, and several species of poisonous fish are common in the country's coastal waters and are potential hazards to unprotected swimmers.

CAMEROON

Embassy: 202-265-8790   *Yaounde*   *GMT +1 hr*

Entry Requirements
- Passport/Visa: Valid passport and visa are required.
- HIV Test: Not required.
- Vaccinations: A yellow fever vaccination certificate is required from all travelers older than 1 year of age arriving from ALL COUNTRIES.

Telephone Country Code: 237

Embassies/Consulates: U.S. Embassy, Yaounde. Rue Nachtigal; Tel. 234-014. U.S. Consulate, Douala; 21 Avenue du General De Gaulle; Tel. 425-331. Canadian Embassy, Yaounde. Edifice Stamatiades, Place de l'Hotel; Tel. 221-090.

Hospitals/Doctors: University of Yaounde Medical Center; general medical services; radiology. Central Hospital, Yaounde (554 beds); general medical services; blood bank. Polyclinique Sende; Yaounde; general medical services. LaQuintinie Hospital, Douala (930 beds); general medical services; ICU; X-ray. Polyclinique de Douala.

Health Advisory

Yellow fever: This disease is active in this country. Yellow fever is transmitted by aedes mosquitoes. This disease is highly endemic, with peak transmission occurring from September through November. As of 1993, the World Health Organization considered Extreme-Nord Province to be "infected," but risk exists countrywide. Yellow fever vaccination is recommended and is also required to enter this country. This country is in the Yellow Fever Endemic Zone. A valid yellow fever vaccination certificate may be required for on-going travel to other countries in Africa, Asia, and South America.

Cholera: This disease is active in this country. The World Health Organization considers Extreme-Nord, Littoral, Nord, Ouest, Sud, and Sud-Ouest Provinces to be "infected." Although cholera vaccination is not required for entry if arriving directly from the U.S. or Canada, it may be required if arriving from a cholera-infected area, or required for on-going travel to other countries in Latin America, Africa, the Middle East, or Asia. Travelers should consider vaccination (one dose) or a doctor's letter of exemption from vaccination. The risk to travelers of acquiring cholera is considered low. Prevention consists primarily in adhering to safe food and drink guidelines.

Malaria: Risk is present year-round throughout this country, including urban areas. Risk is elevated during and immediately following the rainy seasons (March through June and September through November in the south; June through September in the north), particularly in the more arid north. Falciparum malaria (due to *P. falciparum*) accounts for approximately 90% of cases, followed by malaria due to *P. ovale* and *P. malariae*. Chloroquine-resistant falciparum malaria is prevalent throughout the country. Mefloquine- and quinine-resistant falciparum malaria have been reported in the northern regions. Prophylaxis with mefloquine or doxycycline is currently recommended. All travelers should take precautions to prevent mosquito bites.

Travelers' diarrhea: High risk. Several urban areas in the south, including Douala, Yaounde, and Mbalmayo, have treatment plants and piped water systems, but improper operation and poor maintenance of the plants allow bacterial recontamination. All water sources should be considered potentially contaminated. A quinolone antibiotic is recommended for the treatment of acute diarrhea. Diarrhea not responding to treatment with an antibiotic, or chronic diarrhea, may be due to a parasitic disease such as giardiasis, amebiasis, or cryptosporidiosis. Rotavirus is an important cause of diarrhea in children.

Hepatitis: High risk. All susceptible travelers should receive immune globulin or hepatitis A vaccine. The hepatitis E virus is endemic, but the incidence is not known. The hepatitis B carrier rate in the general population is estimated at 10%–12%. Vaccination against hepatitis B is recommended for healthcare workers and all long-term visitors to this country.

Leishmaniasis: Cutaneous leishmaniasis is endemic in northern Cameroon, but risk may exist focally countrywide. Foci of cutaneous leishmaniasis occur in the north in the vicinity of Mokolo (50 kilometers west of Maroua) and also may occur in areas bordering Chad (including the N'Djamena vicinity); other foci historically have been reported from the eastern areas. A recently identified focus of visceral leishmaniasis has been reported from Kousseri in Extreme-Nord Province.

Onchocerciasis: Highly endemic foci presumably persist along fast-flowing rivers in the south and the southwest, and in the savanna area of northern Cameroon. All travelers should take measures to prevent insect (blackfly) bites, especially in the vicinity of rivers.

Loiasis: Highly endemic foci presumably persist in southern rain forest and swamp forest areas. All travelers should take measures to prevent insect (deer fly) bites.

Schistosomiasis: Urinary and intestinal schistosomiasis are highly endemic in the north and in the southwest. Intestinal schistosomiasis, caused by *S. Mansoni*, is endemic in Nord Province and in Center-Sud Province. Areas also infested include Yaounde, Edea, and Douala. Travelers should avoid swimming, bathing, or wading in freshwater ponds, lakes, or streams.

Trypanosomiasis (African sleeping sickness): Most risk is found in the vicinities of Bafia (Mbam Division, Centre Province) and Fontem/Mamfe (Manyu/Fontem Division, Sud-Ouest Province). Mbam Division reports the most cases of sleeping sickness. Potential areas for recurrence include Extreme-Nord Province bordering Chad, and Est Province, bordering the Nola vicinity of the Central African Republic. Travelers to risk areas should take measures to prevent insect (tsetse fly) bites.

Paragonimiasis (lung fluke disease): This disease is endemic; travelers should avoid eating uncooked freshwater crabs.

Meningitis: Northern Cameroon lies within the sub-Saharan meningitis belt. Outbreaks occurred in 1988 in the northern districts of Nord Province and in 1989 from Nord-Ouest Province. Vaccination is recommended for travelers who expect close, prolonged (more than 2–4 weeks) contact with the indigenous population.

Rabies: Last officially reported outbreak involving human cases occurred in the northwest in 1988. Pre-exposure vaccination (3 doses) is recommended for long-term travel (more than 4 weeks) to this country, especially for travelers going to remote rural areas who will be unable to receive antirabies treatment within 24 hours of exposure to a potentially rabid animal. Pre-exposure vaccination does not preclude the need for post-exposure treatment (2 additional doses of vaccine; rabies immune globulin not needed). Rabies post-exposure vaccination in previously unvaccinated travelers: 5 doses of vaccine, plus rabies immune globulin.

AIDS: Heterosexual transmission is the predominate means of transmission. HIV-1 prevalence estimated at 9% of the high-risk urban population and 45% among prostitutes in Douala. All travelers are cautioned against unsafe sex, unsterile medical or dental injections, and unnecessary blood transfusions.

World Medical Guide

Other illnesses/hazards: Brucellosis (from consumption of raw dairy products or occupational exposure), Bancroftian filariasis (mosquito-borne; over 7,000 cases reported in 1985), cutaneous larva migrans, dengue (serologic evidence has been reported in Cameroon), Lassa fever (current endemic status unclear), leprosy (up to 1.9 cases/1,000 population), mansonellosis, toxoplasmosis, tuberculosis (a major health problem), typhus (murine- and louse-borne), relapsing fever (louse-borne), Rift Valley fever, typhoid fever, and intestinal worms (very common). Animal hazards include snakes (vipers, mambas, cobras), centipedes, scorpions, and black widow spiders.

CANADA

Embassy: 202-682-1740   *Ottawa*   *GMT -5 hrs, -4 hrs (Apr–Oct)*

Entry Requirements
- Passport/Visa: Americans visiting Canada are required to carry proof of citizenship. Acceptable documents are (1) a passport; (2) an original birth certificate, or a notarized copy; (3) a voter's registration card; (4) a Selective Service card; (5) a naturalization certificate; or (6) a baptismal certificate, for infants. A driver's license is not accepted as proof of citizenship, but may be used to verify the other documents. Children under 16 must have written travel permission if not accompanied by parent or guardian. For further information, contact the Canadian Embassy in Washington at (202) 682-1770.
- HIV Test: Not required.
- Vaccinations: None required.

Telephone Country Code: 1
Embassies/Consulates: U.S. Embassy, Ottawa, 100 Wellington Street; Tel. (613) 238-5335. Canadian Embassy, 501 Pennsylvania Ave., N.W., Washington, D.C. 20001; Tel. (202) 682-1740.

Health Advisory for Canada

No unusual health risks are present. Degree of sanitation is comparable to the United States.
Health insurance: U.S. citizens visiting Canada should carry adequate health insurance coverage. Travelers over 65 are not covered by medicare in Canada, and supplemental travel insurance is recommended. See Ch.14 for listing of companies underwriting travel insurance.
Giardiasis: Occurs sporadically in wilderness areas. Rural streams, lakes, and ponds may be contaminated with the parasite. Campers and hikers should follow safe food and water guidelines in risk areas. Water filtration is usually adequate to prevent transmission of disease. To help prevent the spread of giardiasis, all campers should dispose of fecal material in a safe fashion.
Insects: Blackflies and mosquitoes are a significant problem during the spring and summer months. Travelers to outdoor rural areas (especially campers, hikers, fishermen) are urged to have adequate protection against insects. Adequate protection consists of head nets, mosquito bed nets, a skin repellent containing deet, and permethrin-treated clothing.
Hepatitis B: There is a high carrier rate of the hepatitis B virus in the Inuit population in northern Canada. Hepatitis B vaccination is recommended for healthcare workers and others who will have close contact with this population.
Rabies: Very low risk to humans. Less than 5% of cases are transmitted by dogs. Most rabies in Canada is confined to animals, particularly arctic and red foxes. Travelers should seek immediate treatment for any unprovoked animal bite, particularly if from a fox, raccoon, skunk, or bat. Other wild animals in Canada that can potentially transmit rabies include groundhogs, wolves, bobcats, and black bears.
Liver fluke disease: An outbreak of acute liver fluke disease caused by the consumption of parasite-contaminated raw fish (white sucker) caught in the Pembina River north of Montreal occurred in 1993. Symptomless human infection has been reported from Quebec to Saskatchewan, and on the eastern coast of Greenland. Fish that potentially carry the North American liver fluke parasite (*Metorchis conjunctus*) include the longnose sucker, yellow perch, brooktrout, and fallfish.

World Medical Guide

CAYMAN ISLANDS (BRITISH WEST INDIES)
Embassy: 202-462-1340   *Grand Cayman*   *GMT -5 hrs*
Entry Requirements
- Passport/Visa: Visa not required.
- HIV Test: Not required.
- Vaccinations: None required.

Telephone Area Code: 345   **AT&T:** 1-800-872-2881   **MCI:** 1-800-624-1000
Electricity/Plugs: AC 50 Hz, 115/230 volts; plug types A, B.
American Express: Cayman Travel Services, Ltd., Grand Cayman. Tel. 949-8755.
Hospitals/Doctors: General Hospital, Georgetown (52 beds); general medical services; emergency room.
Scuba diving: A decompression chamber is located on Grand Cayman.

Health Advisory
See Disease Risk Summary for the Caribbean.
Travelers' diarrhea: Low to medium risk. Hotel food and water is considered generally safe in this country.
Dengue fever: Low risk, but dengue fever is again being reported. (Until 1989, the Cayman Islands were disease free.) All travelers are advised to take measures to prevent mosquito bites.

CENTRAL AFRICAN REPUBLIC
Embassy: 202-483-7800   *Bangui*   *GMT +1 hr*
Entry Requirements
- Visa: A visa is required.
- HIV Test: Not required.
- Vaccinations: A yellow fever vaccination certificate is required from all travelers older than 1 year of age arriving from ALL COUNTRIES.

Telephone Country Code: 236
Embassies/Consulates: U.S. Embassy, Bangui. Avenue David Dacko; Tel. 610-200, 612-578, or 614-333.
Hospitals/Doctors: National University Hospital Center, Bangui; general medical/surgical facility; some French military medical officers on staff. American Lutheran Church Missionary Hospital. Bouar; general medical services. Clinicas las Condes, Bangui.

Health Advisory
Yellow fever: Vaccination is required of all travelers. This country is in the Yellow Fever Endemic Zone.
Malaria: Risk is present year-round throughout this country, including urban areas. Falciparum malaria accounts for 85% of cases. Chloroquine-resistant falciparum malaria is reported. Mefloquine prophylaxis is currently advised.
Travelers' diarrhea: All water, including piped water from municipal treatment facilities, is considered contaminated. Travelers should observe all food and drink safety precautions. A quinolone antibiotic is recommended for the treatment of acute diarrhea. Diarrhea not responding to treatment with an antibiotic, or chronic diarrhea, may be due to a parasitic disease such as giardiasis, amebiasis, or cryptosporidiosis.
Hepatitis: High risk. All nonimmune travelers should receive immune globulin or hepatitis A vaccine. Up to 20% of cases of acute infectious hepatitis are antibody positive for hepatitis E. The hepatitis B carrier rate in the general population is estimated at 15%. Vaccination against hepatitis B is recommended for healthcare workers and all long-term visitors to this country.
Schistosomiasis: Widespread throughout most of the country. Highest infection rates are reported in the northwest.

World Medical Guide

Leishmaniasis: Sporadic cases of cutaneous leishmaniasis reported in the northwest and southwest. Visceral leishmaniasis may occur in the southwest.
Loiasis: Highly endemic focus in southwestern rain forest and swamp forest areas. Travelers should take measures to prevent insect (deer fly) bites.
Trypanosomiasis (African sleeping sickness): About 150 cases reported annually. Risk areas include the Ouham Valley in the northwest, the Nola vicinity (extreme southwest near the Cameroon border), and the southeast. Travelers should take measures to prevent insect (tsetse fly) bites.
Meningitis: North Central African Republic lies within the sub-Saharan meningitis belt. Extensive outbreaks of Group A disease occurred in 1987 and 1992. Vaccination is recommended for long-term travelers anticipating close contact with the indigenous population.
AIDS: Heterosexual transmission is the predominate means of transmission. HIV-1 prevalence estimated at 21% of the high-risk urban population. All travelers are cautioned against unsafe sex, unsterile medical or dental injections, and unnecessary blood transfusions.
Other illnesses/hazards: African tick typhus (contracted from dog ticks, often in urban areas, and bush ticks), brucellosis, filariasis (mosquito-borne; 1,000 cases reported during the 1980s), chikungunya fever (documented outbreak occurred in 1978), dengue (not reported), Crimean-Congo hemorrhagic fever, Lassa fever (low risk; current endemic status unclear), leprosy (up to 2.7 cases/1,000 population), rabies (transmitted primarily by dogs in urban and rural areas), syphilis, toxoplasmosis, tuberculosis (a major health problem), typhoid fever, and intestinal worms (very common). Animal hazards include snakes (boomslang, viper, cobra), centipedes, scorpions, and spiders (black widow, brown recluse).

CHAD

Embassy: 202-462-4009   *N'Djamena*   *GMT +1 hr*

Entry Requirements
- Passport/Visa: Valid passport and visa are required.
- HIV Test: Not required.
- Vaccinations: None required.

Telephone Country Code: 235
Embassies/Consulates: U.S. Embassy, N'Djamena. Avenue Felix Eboue; Tel. (51) 62-18/32-69. Canadian Embassy (Cameroon); Tel. [237] 221-090.
Hospitals/Doctors: N'Djamena Central Hospital (620 beds); general medical services; some specialties. Sahr Hospital (325 beds); general medical facility. Travelers should contact the U.S. Embassy for physician referrals.

Health Advisory

Yellow fever: Vaccination is recommended for all travelers over 1 year of age. No cases reported recently, but the southern part of this country is within the Yellow Fever Endemic Zone. A valid vaccination certificate may be required for travel to other countries.
Cholera: This disease is active in this country. Although cholera vaccination is not required for entry if arriving directly from the U.S. or Canada, it may be required if arriving from a cholera-infected area, or required for on-going travel to other countries in Latin America, Africa, the Middle East, or Asia. Travelers should consider vaccination (one dose) or a doctor's letter of exemption from vaccination. The risk to travelers of acquiring cholera is considered low. Prevention consists primarily in adhering to safe food and drink guidelines.
Malaria: Risk is present year-round throughout this country, including urban areas. Malaria is moderately to highly endemic in southern and southwestern Chad during and immediately following the rainy season, June through November. There is lower risk of malaria in the drier northern Sahara Desert. *P. falciparum* accounts for approximately 85% to 90% of cases, followed by *P. malariae* and *P. ovale*. Chloroquine-resistant falciparum malaria is reported. Prophylaxis with mefloquine or doxycycline is currently recommended.

World Medical Guide

Travelers' diarrhea: The capital city and some other major urban areas are supplied with well water which, although treated, is consistently contaminated. Travelers should observe all food and drink safety precautions. A quinolone antibiotic is recommended for the treatment of acute diarrhea. Diarrhea not responding to treatment with an antibiotic, or chronic diarrhea, may be due to a parasitic disease such as giardiasis, amebiasis, or cryptosporidiosis.

Hepatitis: All susceptible travelers should receive hepatitis A vaccine. Hepatitis E is strongly suspected as the causative agent in an outbreak of hepatitis non-A, non-B that occurred in 1984 among French troops. The hepatitis B carrier rate in the general population is estimated at 15%, or higher. Vaccination against hepatitis B is recommended for healthcare workers and all long-term visitors to this country.

Leishmaniasis: Sporadic cases are reported and foci of infection probably occur throughout most of Chad. Visceral leishmaniasis occurs in the N'Djamena and Lake Chad areas, with foci extending eastward throughout southern Chad. Cutaneous leishmaniasis occurs in Chari-Baguirmi Prefecture (which also includes N'Djamena), along the Chari River in southcentral Chad, and in the northern and northeastern subdesert and desert areas. Transmission occurs primarily from April through November. Travelers to these areas should take precautions against insect (sandfly) bites.

Filariasis: Mosquito-borne; sporadic cases are reported in rural areas of southern Chad.

Onchocerciasis: Black-fly borne; moderate to highly endemic along most rivers.

Loiasis: Deer fly-borne: Risk of transmission may occur in southwestern swamp forest areas.

Schistosomiasis: Transmission of urinary schistosomiasis occurs year-round along Lake Chad and is endemic throughout the southern half of Chad, particularly in prefectures bordering Cameroon and Central African Republic. Intestinal schistosomiasis is transmitted primarily along the Logone and Chari River Basins. Travelers should avoid swimming or wading in freshwater lakes, ponds, or streams.

Trypanosomiasis (sleeping sickness): Low risk. Sporadic cases reported in the Logone and Chari River valleys of the southwest, primarily in the prefectures of Logone Oriental (Gore Sub-Prefecture), Logone Occidental (Moundou Sub-Prefecture), and Moyen-Chari (Moissala Sub-Prefecture). Travelers to these areas should take measures to prevent insect (tsetse fly) bites.

Meningitis: Outbreaks of meningococcal meningitis were reported in March 1996 from three prefectures—Moyen-Chare, Logone oriental, and Ouaddai. Vaccination is recommended for all travelers who anticipate close or prolonged contact with the indigenous population.

AIDS: HIV prevalence is estimated to be low, but incidence data are generally lacking. HIV rate in pregnant women was 3.3% in 1993. All travelers are cautioned against unsafe sex, unsterile medical or dental injections, and unnecessary blood transfusions.

Other illnesses/hazards: Anthrax, brucellosis, dracunculiasis (low levels in southern areas), leprosy, rabies, relapsing fever (louse-borne and tick-borne), syphilis, tuberculosis (a major health problem), typhoid fever, typhus (flea-borne and louse-borne), and intestinal helminths (very common). Animal hazards include snakes (adders, vipers, cobras), scorpions, and black widow spiders. Crocodiles and hippos inhabit Lake Chad.

World Medical Guide

CHILE
Embassy: 202-785-1746   *Santiago*   *GMT -4 hrs*

Entry Requirements
- U.S. citizens do not need a visa for a 3-month stay. Travel to frontier areas for scientific, technical, or mountaineering activities requires 90-day prior authorization.
- HIV Test: Not required.
- Vaccinations: No vaccinations are required to enter this country.

Telephone Country Code: 56   **AT&T:** 00-0312   **MCI:** 00-0316
Embassies/Consulates: U.S. Embassy, Santiago. 2800 Andres Bello, Vitacura. Tel. (2) 232-2600.
Hospitals/Doctors: Jose Joaquin Aguirre Hospital (1,700 beds); general medical/surgical facility; Clinica las Condes, Santiago. La Clinica Francesca, Concepcion. La Clinica Sanitorio Aleman, Concepcion.

Health Advisory
Malaria: There is no risk of malaria in Chile.
Yellow fever: There is no risk of yellow fever in Chile. Although a vaccination is not required to enter Chile, yellow fever vaccination may be required or recommended for travel to other countries in South America. Travelers should carefully review their itinerary.
Cholera: This disease is active in this country. Although cholera vaccination is not required for entry if arriving directly from the U.S. or Canada, it may be required if arriving from a cholera-infected area, or required for on-going travel to other countries in Latin America, Africa, the Middle East, or Asia. Travelers should consider vaccination (one dose) or a doctor's letter of exemption from vaccination. The risk to travelers of acquiring cholera is considered low. Prevention consists primarily in adhering to safe food and drink guidelines.
Travelers' diarrhea: High risk in most areas, especially outside resort areas and first-class hotels. Water supplies in Santiago are considered potable but breakdowns in the system can occur and travelers are advised to drink only boiled, bottled, or treated water. All water outside Santiago should be considered contaminated. Food and drink in first-class hotels in Santiago, Valparaiso, Valdiva, and Antofagasta are generally considered safe, but travelers should use caution. A quinolone antibiotic is recommended for the treatment of acute diarrhea. Diarrhea not responding to antibiotic treatment may be due to a parasitic disease such as giardiasis, amebiasis, or cryptosporidiosis.
Typhoid fever: There is a high incidence of typhoid fever in this country. Vaccination is recommended for travelers staying longer than 2 weeks in-country. All travelers should adhere to safe food and drink guidelines.
Hepatitis: All nonimmune travelers should receive hepatitis A vaccine prior to visiting this country. Hepatitis E has not been reported but could occur. The hepatitis B carrier rate in the general population is estimated at 0.5%. Vaccination against hepatitis B is recommended for all long-term travelers to this country. Hepatitis C is endemic.
Chagas' disease: Reported in the rural and suburban areas in the northern half of this country. Transmission of Chagas' disease occurs primarily in rural areas where there are adobe-style huts and houses that often harbor the night-biting triatomid (assassin) bugs. Travelers sleeping in such structures should take precautions against nighttime bites. Precautions include sleeping under a mosquito net (well tucked in), sleeping away from walls, and spraying sleeping quarters with an insecticide (such as RAID Flying Insect Spray) prior to retiring. Unscreened blood transfusions are also a potential source of infection. The rate of contaminated blood reported by Chilean blood banks is in the 1.9%–6.5% range.
Rabies: Low risk. No human cases have been reported in this country since 1972. All travelers, nevertheless, should avoid contact with stray dogs. Any unprovoked attack by an animal should be considered a medical emergency and immediate medical care sought to evaluate the possible risk of rabies.
AIDS: Relatively low rates of HIV infection are reported, but the incidence is increasing, especially in urban areas. Seventy-two percent of cases of AIDS are currently due to homo- and bisexual transmission. Cases due to heterosexual transmission are increasing.

World Medical Guide

Climate-related illness: Severe air pollution exists in Santiago and to a lesser extent in the Chilean countryside. Travelers with emphysema, asthma, and bronchitis may experience an increase in respiratory symptoms.

Other diseases/hazards: Brucellosis (rare cases are associated with contact with cattle), echinococcosis (risk is highest in rural southern areas), hantavirus pulmonary syndrome (21 cases have been identified), meningitis (outbreaks of Group B meningococcal meningitis are reported; the meningococcal polysaccharide vaccine [A/C/Y/W-135] is not protective against this strain), taeniasis (pork and beef tapeworm disease), tuberculosis (a serious public health problem), fascioliasis (reported from Curico, Talca, and Linares Provinces), strongyloidiasis and other helminthic infections. Insect-borne diseases are relatively unimportant in Chile. Animal hazards include black widow and brown widow spiders. There are no venomous land snakes on the mainland of Chile. Portuguese man-of-war, sea wasps, and several species of stingrays are found in the country's coastal waters and are potential hazards to swimmers.

CHINA, PEOPLE'S REPUBLIC OF

Embassy: 202-328-2500   *Beijing*   *GMT +8 hrs*

Entry Requirements
- Passport/Visa: Valid passport and visa are required. For visa information, contact the Chinese consulate visa section at 202-328-2517.
- HIV Test: Test required for those staying 6 months or more.
- Vaccinations: A valid yellow fever vaccination certificate is required from all travelers arriving from infected areas.

Telephone Country Code: 86   **AT&T:** 10811

Embassies/Consulates: U.S. Embassy Consular Section, Beijing. 2 Xiu Shui Dong Jie; Tel. (10) 6532-3431/3831. After hours: (10) 6532-1910. U.S. Consulate, Shanghai; Tel. (21) 6433-6880. U.S. Consulate, Guanghou. Tel: (20) 8188-8911. U.S. Consulate, Shenyang. Tel: (24) 2322-2374.

Hospitals/Doctors: Beijing Airport Health Quarantine Bureau, 20 Hepinglibeijie, Beijing 100013; Tel: (10) 456-2801. Beijing Union Medical College Hospital (1,200 beds); emergency services; Tel. 6512-7733, ext. 372. The Sino-German Clinic, Beijing (located in the Landmark Building); staffed by Chinese, German, and U.S. physicians; open 24 hours a day. In Shanghai: Shanghai Medical University, Zhong Shan Hospital; Tel. 6310-400.

The following two emergency medical assistance firms have offices and clinics in Beijing:

Asia Emergency Assistance Ltd. (AEA International)
No. 1 North Road, Xing Fu San Cun
Chaoyang District
Tel: (10) 6462-9112
U.S. office: Tel: 206-621-9911

MEDEX
Beijing Lufthansa Center
No. 50, Liangmaqiao Rd.
Tel: (10) 6465-1264
U.S. office: Tel: 410-453-6300

Health Advisory

Cholera: This disease is active. Although cholera vaccination is not required for entry to this country if arriving directly from the United States or Canada, it may be required if arriving from cholera-infected areas—or required for on-going travel from China to other countries in Latin America, Africa, the Middle East, or Asia. Travelers should carefully check their itinerary and consider cholera vaccination (one dose) or a doctor's letter of exemption from vaccination.

Malaria: Risk occurs in certain rural areas below 1,500 meters elevation. No significant risk of malaria occurs in the northern and western provinces of Nei Mongol, Gansu, Beijing, Heilongjiang, Jilin, Kirin, Ningxia, Qinghai, Shanxi, Xianjiang (except along the valley of the Yili River), and Xizang (Tibet—except along the valley of the Zangbo River in the southeast). The highest risk of malaria in China occurs in southern and eastern areas including Guangdong, Guizhou, Yunnan, Hainan, Sichuan, and Fujian Provinces and the Guangxi Autonomous Region. Most cases of malaria are reported from Hainan and Andhui Provinces, Hainan Island, and the areas bordering Laos, Vietnam, and Burma (Myanmar). Year-round

World Medical Guide

risk of malaria is present in the tropical provinces (Guangdang, Guangxi, Yunnan) and Hainan Island. Lower risk occurs in Anhui, Hubei, Hunan, Jiangsu, Jiangxi Shandong, Shanghai, and Zhejiang Provinces.

In northern and central malarious areas, *P. vivax* predominates, while in southern China *P. falciparum* predominates and mixed infections are common. Ninety seven percent of *P. falciparum* cases occur in Hainan and Yunnan Provinces. Sporadic cases of *P. malariae* are reported. Although malaria is transmitted in rural lowland areas during the warmer months, the risk to most travelers appears to be very low. Travelers visiting only cities and popular rural tourist sites (including Yangtze River cruises), or taking only daytime trips to the countryside (especially in northern and central areas), are not deemed to be at significant risk and malaria prophylaxis is not routinely recommended. Travelers to central areas within China who venture into the countryside on overnight trips should consider chloroquine prophylaxis, and insect-bite prevention measures should also be taken. Travelers on special scientific, educational, or recreational visits should check whether their itineraries include evening or nighttime exposure in areas of risk, and if travel includes southern China. In southern and southeastern China (especially Yunnan and Guangxi Provinces), multidrug-resistant falciparum malaria is reported. In areas bordering Burma, Laos, Vietnam, the Gulf of Tonkin, and the areas southwest of Canton, including Hainan Island, mefloquine or doxycycline prophylaxis is recommended.

Travelers' diarrhea: Moderate to high risk. In urban and resort areas, most hotels have generally safe restaurants and potable water. Travelers should observe safety precautions and drink only boiled, bottled, or chemically treated water and consume only well-cooked food.

World Medical Guide

Raw fish and shellfish, and undercooked aquatic plants (e.g., watercress salad), should specifically be avoided. A quinolone antibiotic is recommended for the treatment of acute diarrhea. Diarrhea not responding to antibiotic treatment may be due to a parasitic disease such as giardiasis, amebiasis, or cryptosporidiosis. The giardiasis infection rate in the adult population is about 1%. Amebiasis infection rate is about 0.4%. About 5% of diarrhea in children is caused by cryptosporidiosis.

Hepatitis A & E: There is a high risk of hepatitis A in this country. All nonimmune travelers should receive hepatitis A vaccine. Hepatitis E is a leading cause of sporadic acute viral hepatitis in China. A high incidence is reported in rural areas. Transmission is primarily by water from contaminated pools and canals. To avoid hepatitis E, all travelers, especially to rural areas, should drink only boiled, bottled, or chemically treated water.

Hepatitis B & C: The hepatitis B carrier rate in the general population is estimated at 10% (rates up to 26% among some population groups). Vaccination is recommended for all susceptible long-term visitors. Hepatitis C virus is endemic. Travelers should avoid acupuncture treatments or medical injections unless assured that all needles have been heat sterilized or are of the disposable variety.

Typhoid fever: Moderate risk. Vaccination is recommended for extended travel outside of tourist areas.

Dengue fever: Occurs as frequent, often widespread outbreaks. Incidence is highest in southeastern China south of 42 degrees north latitude. Elevated risk occurs in coastal urban areas below 1,500 meters elevation. Most disease transmission occurs during the summer months; in the tropical provinces, however, the transmission period extends from March through November. The *Aedes* mosquitoes, which transmit dengue, bite during the daytime. Prevention of dengue fever consists of taking protective measures against mosquito bites.

Japanese encephalitis: Disease is present in all regions, except in Qinghai Province and Xinjiang and Xizang Autonomous Regions. Risk of JE is greatest in rural pig-breeding agricultural areas of the central and eastern provinces, especially during the warm, rainy months from May to September. Risk of JE is year-round in the tropical southern provinces. There is low risk of transmission in urban areas due to the relative absence of mosquitoes. Vaccination against Japanese encephalitis is recommended for travelers who will be staying in rural-agricultural endemic areas for extended periods (more than 3–4 weeks).

Schistosomiasis: Year-round risk in southern tropical areas and seasonally (June–August in temperate areas. Widespread south of 35 degrees north latitude, including the provinces of Anhui, Hubei, Jiangsu, Hunan, Jiangxi, Sichuan, Yunnan, and Zhejiang. Major endemic areas include the Yangtze River Valley, including tributaries and adjacent lakes. All travelers should avoid swimming, wading, or bathing in freshwater lakes, ponds, or streams.

Leishmaniasis: Visceral leishmaniasis (kala azar) occurs in the temperate central and northeastern provinces, mainly Gansu, Shaanxi, Shanxi, Shandong and Sichuan provinces, and Xinjiang and Nei Mongol Autonomous Regions. Most cases reported from Gansu Province. Risk of disease transmission is elevated from May through October, when sandflies are more active. Cutaneous leishmaniasis has been reported from the Xinjiang Autonomous Region. All travelers to these areas should avoid sandfly bites when visiting these areas.

Filariasis: Both the Bancroftian and Malayan forms are reported in the southwestern provinces. Travelers to these areas should take measures to prevent mosquito bites.

Scrub typhus: Year-round incidence in warmer southern areas.

Rabies: Higher than average incidence reported in urban and rural areas, with stray dogs the main threat. Travelers should seek immediate treatment of any unprovoked animal bite. Rabies vaccination is indicated following the unprovoked bite of a dog, cat, bat, or monkey. Bites by other animals should be considered on an individual basis. Pre-exposure vaccination against rabies should be considered for long-term travel to this country.

Helminthic diseases: Moderately to highly endemic in rural and urban areas. Diseases caused by soil-transmitted helminths (hookworm disease, strongyloidiasis) can be prevented by wearing shoes and not walking barefoot outside. Food-transmitted roundworm infections (ascariasis, trichuriasis) can be prevented by washing salads and/or vegetables or thoroughly cooking food to destroy infective eggs. Lung fluke and liver fluke disease (paragonimiasis, clonorchiasis) can be prevented by not eating raw freshwater

World Medical Guide

crabs, crayfish, or fish. Fasciolopsiasis (large intestinal fluke disease) and fascioliasis (sheep liver fluke disease) can be prevented by not eating undercooked or raw water plants, such as watercress and other aquatic vegetables. Anisakiasis can be avoided by not eating raw saltwater fish, including raw octopus and squid; capillariasis can be prevented by avoiding raw or undercooked freshwater fish.

Echinococcosis: Human alveolar echinococcosis, a potentially fatal disease caused by *E. multilocularis*, occurs in northern Xinjiang Autonomous Region and central China. This disease, caused by the larval stage of the fox tapeworm, is spread to humans by close contact with infected domesticated dogs or by contact with fox/canine feces. Cystic hydatid disease, caused by *E. granulosus*, is common throughout western and northwestern China.

Air pollution: Harsh conditions exist in Beijing, where the air is severely polluted. Pollutants include windblown dust and dirt, soot from coal burning stoves, and exhaust from vehicles.

Influenza: Vaccination is recommended for travelers visiting China from October to May.

Other diseases/health threats: Anthrax, AIDS/HIV (Yunnan Province has highest incidence, especially among injecting drug users), brucellosis, Crimean-Congo hemorrhagic fever (low endemicity; in Xinjiang Province only), Chikungunya fever, leptospirosis (periodic outbreaks countrywide; highest incidence in Yunnan Province), Lyme disease (human cases reported from Henan, Jiangsu, Fujian, Anhui, and Heilomgiang Provinces, and Xinjiang Autonomous Region), melioidosis (endemic in Guangdong and Hainan Provinces, and Guangxi Autonomous Region; risk elevated June through August), plague (reported in Gansu, Qinghai, and Yunnan Provinces and Nei Mongol and Xinjiang, and Xizang Autonomous Regions), Russian spring-summer encephalitis (presumably occurs in northern China, especially Inner Mongolia), Siberian tick typhus, tuberculosis (highly endemic), trachoma (widespread), and murine and epidemic (louse-borne) typhus (low risk).

COLOMBIA

Embassy: 202-387-8338   *Bogota*   *GMT -5 hrs*

Entry Requirements
- Visa: A visa is required for stays exceeding 30 days. All travelers should read the most recent State Department Travel Warning for this country.
- HIV Test: Not required.
- Vaccinations: No vaccinations are required for entry.

Telephone Country Code: 57   **AT&T:** 980-11-0010   **MCI:** 980-16-0001

Embassies/Consulates: U.S. Embassy (Consular Section), Bogota; Calle 22-D Bis, No. 47-51; Tel. (1) 315-0811.

Hospitals/Doctors: Hospital Militar Central, Bogota (800 beds); all specialties; ambulance service. Clinic Marly (100 beds). Clinica de la Mujer, Bogota; obstetrical hospital with good reputation. Fundacion Santa Fe de Bogota; general hospital with good reputation.

Health Advisory

Yellow fever: This disease is active in this country in the Departments of Antioquia, Boyaca, Cesar, Choco, Cundinamarca, Norte de Santander, Santander, and Vichada and in the Intendencias of Arauca, Caqueta, Casanare, Cucuta, Guaviare, Meta, and Putumayo. Vaccination is strongly recommended, especially for travel to rural infected areas in the middle valley of the Magdalena River, eastern and western foothills of the Cordillera Oriental from the frontier with Ecuador to that with Venezuela, Uraba, foothills of the Sierra Nevada, eastern plains (Orinoquia), and Amazonia. This country is in the Yellow Fever Endemic Zone. Although yellow fever vaccination is not required for entry into this country, it may be required for on-going travel to other countries in Latin America, Africa, the Middle East, or Asia. Travelers should carefully check their itinerary.

Cholera: This disease is active in this country. Although cholera vaccination is not required for entry if arriving directly from the U.S. or Canada, it may be required if arriving from a cholera-infected area, or required for on-going travel to other countries in Latin America, Africa, the Middle East, or Asia. Travelers should consider vaccination (one dose) or a

World Medical Guide

doctor's letter of exemption from vaccination. The risk to travelers of acquiring cholera is considered low.

Malaria: There is no risk of malaria in Bogota Department, the major urban areas, and the islands of San Andres and Providencia. Elsewhere, this disease is highly endemic countrywide year-round in rural areas below 800 meters elevation. Malaria activity varies markedly among regions and from year-to-year within specific areas. Risk may be elevated during and immediately following local rainy seasons. Vivax malaria accounts for 60% of cases overall; the remainder are falciparum. (In some Pacific coastal areas, however, falciparum accounts for 98% of cases in some foci.) Chloroquine-resistant malaria is reported in all malarious areas. Widespread Fansidar resistance is reported in Amazonia, Orinoquia, and the Caribbean regions and the Cauca River Valley. Unconfirmed mefloquine resistance has been reported in the Amazonian region. Mefloquine or doxycycline prophylaxis is recommended when traveling to risk areas.

Travelers' diarrhea: Tap water is generally considered safe in large Colombian cities (Bogota, Medellin, and Cali), but all other water sources should be considered contaminated. Travelers should follow food and drink precautions. A quinolone antibiotic is recommended for the treatment of diarrhea.

Hepatitis: All nonimmune travelers should receive hepatitis A vaccine prior to visiting this country. The hepatitis B carrier rate in the general population is estimated to be 1.3% and as high as 20% in high-risk groups (e.g., prostitutes, drug addicts). Vaccination against hepatitis B should be considered by anyone planning an extended visit to this country.

Dengue fever: Year-round risk (elevated during local rainy seasons) in widely scattered urban and periurban areas below 1,800 meters elevation. Risk may be elevated in the northern, north-central (Magdalena River Valley), and western areas. All travelers are advised to take measures to prevent mosquito bites.

Leishmaniasis: Risk of cutaneous leishmaniasis (the cause of 95% of cases) is widely distributed in many jungle and forested highland areas up to 1,500 meters elevation. Many cases are reported in the Pacific coastal region. Visceral leishmaniasis risk occurs below 900 meters elevation in the valleys of the Magdalena River and its tributaries in southern Cundinamarca County. All travelers should take measures to prevent insect (sandfly) bites.

Chagas' disease: Widely distributed below 2,700 meters elevation in northern and western areas (primarily west of the eastern Andean foothills). Elevated risk in Norte de Santander Department. Risk of transmission occurs primarily in those rural-agricultural areas where there are adobe-style huts and houses that often harbor the night-biting triatomid (assassin) bugs. Travelers sleeping in such structures should take precautions against nighttime bites.

Bartonellosis (Oroya fever): This severe bacterial disease is transmitted by sandflies between 800 and 3,000 meters elevation in the southwestern areas. Treatment of the first phase of the disease (fever and anemia phase) is effective with chloramphenicol, penicillin, or tetracycline. The second phase (skin lesion phase) is best treated with rifampin or streptomycin. Prevention consists of avoiding insect (sandfly) bites.

Rocky Mountain spotted fever: Three cases of this rickettsial disease were reported in 1994. In 1985 the disease killed 62 persons. All travelers should take precautions against tick bites.

Typhoid fever: Increased risk from contaminated food and water. Vaccination is recommended.

Rabies: A relatively minor health threat in this country. Incidence appears to be decreasing. Travelers should seek immediate treatment of any animal bite, especially from a dog.

AIDS: HIV prevalence estimated at up to 41% of homosexual males and 30% of prostitutes. Heterosexual contacts now responsible for spreading more cases than homosexual contacts.

Acute mountain sickness (AMS): Risk is present for those arriving in Bogota (altitude 2,600 meters) or traveling to the Central Highlands where the elevation exceeds 3,000 meters in many areas. Travelers should consider acetazolamide prophylaxis and gradual acclimatization. The best treatment of moderate to severe AMS is immediate descent to a lower altitude.

Other diseases/hazards: Brucellosis (increased incidence in Uraba region of Antioquia Department), coccidiomycosis, cysticercosis, echinococcosis, filariasis (mosquito-borne; a small focus is reported near Cartegena), leptospirosis, mansonellosis (black-fly-borne; endemic areas limited to riverine valleys in extreme eastern and southern Colombia), onchocerciasis

World Medical Guide

(black-fly-borne; endemic in the south-central Pacific coastal area), paragonimiasis (transmitted by infected raw freshwater shrimp or crayfish), tuberculosis (a serious public health problem), viral encephalitis (mosquito-transmitted), and strongyloidiasis and other helminthic infections are reported. Animal hazards include snakes (vipers, coral snakes), centipedes, scorpions, and spiders (black widow, brown recluse, banana, wolf). Caimans and crocodiles are abundant and electric eels and poisonous frogs are found in the country's freshwaters. Pumas, jaguars, wild boar, and large tropical rodents also occur in Colombia. Sea wasps, Portuguese man-of-war, sea wasps, and stingrays are found in the coastal waters of Colombia and could be a hazard to swimmers.

COMOROS ISLANDS

Embassy: 212-972-8010   *Moroni*   *GMT +3 hrs*

Entry Requirements
- Passport/Visa: Valid passport and visa are required.
- HIV Test: Not required.
- Vaccinations: None required.

Health Advisory

Cholera: Reported active.

Malaria: Risk is present throughout this country, including urban areas. Prophylaxis with mefloquine or doxycycline is currently recommended. All travelers should take precautions against mosquito bites.

Travelers' diarrhea: High risk. Travelers should observe all food and drink safety precautions. A quinolone antibiotic (Cipro or Floxin) is recommended for the treatment of acute diarrhea. Diarrhea not responding to treatment with an antibiotic, or chronic diarrhea, may be due to a parasitic disease such as giardiasis or amebiasis and treatment with metronidazole (Flagyl) or tinidazole (Fasigyn) should be considered. All cases of diarrhea should be treated with adequate fluid replacement.

Hepatitis: High risk. All nonimmune travelers should receive hepatitis A vaccine. The hepatitis B carrier rate in the population is estimated to exceed 10%. Vaccination against hepatitis B is recommended for healthcare workers and all long-term visitors to this country.

CONGO

Embassy: 202-726-5500   *Brazzaville*   *GMT +1 hr*

Entry Requirements
- Passport/Visa: Valid passport and visa are required. Return or onward ticket required.
- HIV Test: Not required.
- Vaccinations: A yellow fever vaccination certificate is required from all travelers older than 1 year of age arriving from ALL COUNTRIES.

Telephone Country Code: 242

Embassies/Consulates: U.S. Embassy, Brazzaville. Avenue Amilcar Cabral; Tel. 832-070/832-624. Canadian Embassy (Zaire); Tel. [243] (12) 27551.

Hospitals/Doctors: Brazzaville General Hospital (900 beds); general medical services. Travelers should contact the U.S. Embassy for physician referral.

Health Advisory

Yellow fever: No cases recently reported. This country is in the Yellow Fever Endemic Zone.

Malaria: Risk is present year-round countrywide, including urban areas. Risk is elevated during and just after the rainy season—April through October north of the equator, October through May south of the equator. Transmission decreases in the south during the coolest and driest season (June–September.) Falciparum malaria accounts for 91% of cases, followed by *P. malariae* (6% of cases) and *P. ovale* (3% of cases). Chloroquine-resistant *P. falciparum* is reported. Prophylaxis with mefloquine or doxycycline is recommended when traveling to risk areas.

Travelers' diarrhea: High risk. Rural villages and towns obtain water from untreated sources. Brazzaville, Point Noire, and some other major cities have modern filtration and purification plants, but the water is subject to recontamination. Travelers should observe all food and drink safety precautions. A quinolone antibiotic is recommended for the treatment of acute diarrhea. Diarrhea not responding to treatment with an antibiotic, or chronic diarrhea, may be due to a parasitic disease such as giardiasis, amebiasis, or cryptosporidiosis.

Hepatitis: All susceptible travelers should hepatitis A vaccine. The hepatitis B carrier rate in the general population is estimated as high as 17.5%. Vaccination against hepatitis B is recommended for healthcare workers and all long-term visitors to this country.

Dengue fever: Not reported, although the mosquito vector, *Aedes aegypti*, is present in this country.

Leishmaniasis: Sporadic cases have been reported. Travelers should take personal protection measures against insect (sandfly) bites.

Onchocerciasis: High prevalence in two southwestern areas: the Djoue River basin and the bank region of the Congo River. Travelers should take personal protection measures against insect (blackfly) bites.

Loiasis: Areas in the rain forest and villages in the Chaillu mountains are highly endemic. Travelers should take personal protection measures against biting deer flies.

Schistosomiasis: Risk of urinary schistosomiasis is present in the southwestern regions of Bouenza, Niari, and Kouilou, as well as the Brazzaville vicinity. Less risk occurs in the northern areas of the country, where the acidic soil is less conducive to the establishment of the freshwater snail intermediate hosts. Travelers should avoid swimming, bathing, or wading in freshwater lakes, ponds, or streams.

Hemorrhagic fever: Outbreaks of Marburg virus hemorrhagic fever reported, starting in April 1999, in Durba, Watsa Zone in the northe-eastern part of Congo.

Trypanosomiasis: Major risk areas include the southern savanna of Niari and Bouenza Regions, along the Congo River north of Brazzaville to north of Betou, and in the northwest (Etoumbi vicinity) and the extreme southwest of Cuvette Region (Okoyo vicinity); risk also occurs along the Lefini River. All travelers to these regions should take measures to prevent insect (tsetse fly) bites.

AIDS: Heterosexual contact is the predominate mode of transmission. Prevalence of HIV estimated at 17.5% of the high-risk urban population. Rate in prostitutes estimated as high as 64%. All travelers are cautioned against unsafe sex, unsterile medical or dental injections, and blood transfusions.

Other illnesses/hazards: Brucellosis (from consumption of raw dairy products or occupational exposure), chikungunya fever (cyclic outbreaks occur regionally), mansonellosis (mosquito-borne form of filariasis), leprosy (up to 4 cases/1,000 population), leptospirosis, paragonimiasis (from eating raw crabs), human monkeypox (most cases in Akungula and Ekanga), rabies, toxoplasmosis, tuberculosis (a major health problem), typhoid fever, and intestinal helminths (very common). Animal hazards include snakes (mambas, adders, vipers, cobras), centipedes, scorpions, and black widow spiders.

CHRISTMAS ISLAND (AUSTRALIA)

GMT +7 hrs

Entry Requirements
- Passport/Visa: A passport is required.
- Vaccinations: Same requirements as Australia.
- HIV Test: Same requirements as Australia.

Health Advisory

Malaria: No risk.

Travelers' diarrhea: Low risk. A quinolone antibiotic (Cipro or Floxin) is recommended for the treatment of diarrhea.

Dengue fever: Endemic. Travelers should take protective measures against mosquito bites.

World Medical Guide

COOK ISLANDS (NEW ZEALAND)

Avarua, Rorotonga　　　　　　　　　　*GMT -10½ hrs*

Entry Requirements
- Passport/Visa: Passport required.
- HIV Test: Not required.
- Vaccinations: None required.

Telephone Country Code: 682
Embassies/Consulates: There are no local embassies. The U.S. Embassy in Wellington, New Zealand, has jurisdiction.
Hospitals/Doctors: General Hospital (89 beds); general medical facility; x-ray, laboratory, pharmacy. Tupapa Outpatient Clinic, Avarua.

Health Advisory

Malaria: No risk.
Travelers' diarrhea: Low to medium risk. Tap water on Rarotonga is generally safe to drink. (Most hotels have filtration systems.) Tap water on Aitutaki is not considered safe and travelers are advised to consume only bottled, boiled, or treated water. All fruit should be peeled prior to consumption. A quinolone antibiotic (Floxin or Cipro) is recommended for the treatment of acute diarrhea. Diarrhea not responding to antibiotic treatment may be due to a parasitic disease such as giardiasis or amebiasis—or an intestinal virus.
Hepatitis: Hepatitis A vaccine is recommended for all nonimmune travelers. The hepatitis B carrier rate in the general population is estimated at 10%. Vaccination against hepatitis B is recommended for healthcare workers and should be considered by long-term visitors to this country.
Dengue fever: This disease is active. The number of dengue fever cases has increased steadily on the island of Rarotonga since the beginning of January 1997. Only dengue virus type 2 has been isolated in this outbreak. The mosquitoes that transmit dengue (*Aedes aegypti*) bite primarily during the daytime. All travelers should take measures to prevent insect bites.
Ross River fever: This mosquito-transmitted viral illness occurs in periodic epidemics. Travelers should take protective measures against insect bites.
Filariasis: The Malayan variety of filariasis is reported. Travelers should take protective measures against mosquito bites.
Japanese encephalitis: Vaccination against Japanese encephalitis is recommended for travelers who will be staying in rural-agricultural endemic areas for long periods (more than several weeks). All travelers should take protective measures against mosquito bites, especially in the evening.

COSTA RICA

Embassy (consular sec.): 202-328-6628　　*San Jose*　　　*GMT -6 hrs*

Entry Requirements
- A visa is not required for travelers holding U.S. or Canadian passports.
- HIV Test: Testing required of travelers staying more than 90 days. Travelers can contact the Costa Rican embassy in Washington (202-234-2945) for further information.
- Vaccinations: No vaccinations are required to enter this country.

Telephone Country Code: 506　　　　**AT&T:** 114　　　　**MCI:** 162
Embassies/Consulates: U.S. Embassy, Pavas, San Jose. Tel. 220-3050. After hours: Tel. 220-3127 and ask for duty officer.
Hospitals/Doctors: Hospital Clinica Biblica; private hospital with extensive medical/surgical capabilities, including cardiac surgery, 24-hour emergency room, and ambulance service. CT and MRI are now available. Hospital-based physician group is 90% English-speaking; many staff physicians have received advanced training in the United States. Hospital Clinica Biblica is used by embassy personnel, tourists, and expatriates. Address: Calle Central and Ave. 14.

World Medical Guide

Health Advisory

Yellow fever: No recent cases have been reported. Because this country is in the Yellow Fever Endemic Zone, a valid certificate may be required for on-going travel to other countries that require a certificate of vaccination.

Cholera: This disease is reported active in this country but the risk to travelers of acquiring cholera is extremely low. Although cholera vaccination is not required for entry if arriving directly from the U.S. or Canada, a certificate of vaccination may be required for on-going travel to other countries in Latin America, Africa, the Middle East, or Asia that require a certificate.

Malaria: Risk occurs year-round in rural areas below 500 meters elevation. Risk is increased during, and just after, the rainy season, May through November, peaking during September–October. Risk may be levated in the Atlantic coastal lowlands and along the northern border with Nicaraguan. Seventy percent of malaria cases are reported from Limon Province on the Atlantic coast. Vivax malaria accounts for over 97% of cases. No cases of drug-resistant falciparum malaria have been reported. Chloroquine prophylaxis is not routinely recommended for tourists going to Costa Rica but should be considered by anyone staying overnight near the border with Nicaragua.

Travelers' diarrhea: Low risk in most areas. Tap water in San Jose is potable. A quinolone antibiotic is recommended for the treatment of acute diarrhea. Amebiasis, giardiasis, cryptosporidiosis, and viral diseases are other reported causes of diarrhea.

Hepatitis: Hepatitis A is endemic. Hepatitis A vaccine is recommended for all nonimmune travelers. Hepatitis E has not been reported, but could occur. The hepatitis B carrier rate in the population is less than 1%. Vaccination against hepatitis B should be considered by long-term visitors to this country. Hepatitis C is endemic but levels are unclear.

Dengue fever: Year-round risk, countrywide, below 1,300 meters elevation in urbanized areas. Risk is elevated in coastal provinces. To prevent dengue, travelers should take measures to prevent mosquito bites.

Leishmaniasis: Focally endemic. Potential for transmission of cutaneous leishmaniasis occurs in most rural forested areas below 800 meters elevation. Increased transmission from May through July. Officially reported incidence has been highest in areas bordering Panama. Travelers take precautions against insect (sandfly) bites.

Other diseases: Abdominal angiostrongyliasis, brucellosis, Chagas' disease (occurs sporadically in rural areas of Alajuela, Guanacaste, Heredia, and San Jose Provinces at elevations below 1,300 meters, but is not considered a major public health problem), cysticercosis, filariasis (transmitted by blackflies; endemic near Puerto Limon), fascioliasis (liver fluke disease; from contaminated water plants), filariasis (3% infection rate reported in Puerto Limon), leptospirosis (nine white-water rafters developed leptospirosis in 1996 after floating down flooded rivers), paragonimiasis (lung fluke disease; from ingestion of raw freshwater crabs or crayfish), rabies (very low risk), tick-borne rickettsioses (Rocky Mountain spotted fever reported from Limon Province; tick-borne relapsing fever), and strongyloidiasis and other helminthic infections are reported.

CROATIA

Embassy of Croatia: 202-588-5899. U.S. Embassy, Zagreb: (385)-1-455-5500
For Health Advisory information, see the Disease Risk Summary for Europe on page 259.

World Medical Guide

CUBA

Embassy: 202-797-8518   *Havana*   *GMT -5 hrs*

Entry Requirements
- U.S. travelers should contact the State Department (202-376-0922) regarding travel restrictions applying to U.S. citizens.
- HIV Test: Testing required for all travelers except tourists upon arrival in Cuba.
- Vaccinations: None required.

Embassies/Consulates: U.S. Interest Section, Havana. Calzado, between Calles L and M, Vedado. Tel. 32-0551-59. The United States does not maintain formal diplomatic relations with Cuba.

Hospitals/Doctors: Hermanos Almajeiras Hospital, Havana (950 beds); full range of specialty services; nuclear medicine, CT scanner; burn unit. U.S. Navy Hospital, Guantanamo Bay; Te¹. (5) 399-7230. Dr. Ernesto Guevara Hospital de la Serna General Hospital, Las Tunas (630 beds); emergency and intensive care services; burn unit.

Health Advisory

Malaria, yellow fever: No risk.

Travelers' diarrhea: Moderate to high risk. In large urban areas tap water frequently is contaminated due to the poor condition of the water distribution system. In resort areas, the hotels generally serve reliable food and potable water. Elsewhere, travelers should observe all safety precautions. Shigella infections outnumber salmonella 2:1. A quinolone antibiotic is recommended for the treatment of acute diarrhea. Diarrhea not responding to antibiotic treatment may be due to a parasitic disease such as giardiasis or amebiasis. (Nearly 50% of schoolchildren in a Havana suburb were found infected with giardia organisms. Recent data on amebiasis not available.)

Hepatitis: Low to moderate risk. All nonimmune travelers should receive hepatitis A vaccine. The hepatitis B carrier rate in the general population is estimated at 0.8%. Vaccination against hepatitis B is recommended for healthcare workers and all long-term visitors to this country.

Dengue fever: The first dengue epidemic since 1981 occurred in 1997 with over 3,000 cases of dengue serotype 2 confirmed. Over 200 cases of dengue hemorrhagic fever (DHF) with 12 fatalities occurred. The epidemic demonstrates that adults with a primary dengue infection are at risk of developing DHF if they become infected with a different serotype. The *Aedes* mosquitoes, which transmit dengue, bite primarily during the daytime and are present in populous urban areas as well as resort and rural areas. All travelers are advised to take measures to prevent mosquito bites.

Typhoid fever: High incidence reported. Vaccination is recommended for those traveling extensively outside of tourist areas.

Leptospirosis: More than 300 cases are reported annually. Transmission of disease occurs primarily in low-lying, poorly drained areas where animal urine-infected water accumulates. Holguin Province is reportedly a high-risk area, especially September–October, during the rainy season.

Rabies: Low risk, but several human cases are reported annually. Travelers should seek immediate treatment of any animal bite. Rabies post-exposure vaccination is indicated following the unprovoked bite of a dog, cat, mongoose, bat, or monkey. Bites by other animals should be considered on an individual basis. Pre-exposure vaccination against rabies (3 doses) should be considered for long-term travel to this country. This is especially true for travelers going to remote rural areas if they will be unable to receive antirabies treatment within 24 hours of exposure to a potentially rabid animal.

Other diseases/health threats: Abdominal angiostrongyliasis, brucellosis, dengue hemorrhagic fever, eastern equine encephalitis, fascioliasis (more commonly reported than in any other Latin American country) toxocariasis, toxoplasmosis, tick-borne rickettsioses (may occur), ciguatera fish poisoning, and swimming related hazards (jellyfish, spiny sea urchins, and coral).

World Medical Guide

CYPRUS

Embassy: 202-462-5772 *Nicosia* *GMT +2 hrs*

Entry Requirements
- Passport/Visa: A valid passport is required.
- HIV Test: Foreign entertainers may be required to have test. Contact the Cyprus Embassy in Washington (202-462-5772) for further details.
- Vaccinations: None required.

Telephone Country Code: 357 **AT&T:** 080-90010 **MCI:** 080-90000

Embassies/Consulates: American Embassy. Therissos St. and Dositheos St., Nicosia; Tel. (2) 465-151. Canadian Embassy. 3 Thermistocles St., Tel. (2) 451-630.

Hospitals/Doctors: Nicosia General Hospital (485 beds); ICU; emergency room; neurosurgery. Lanarca General Hospital (225 beds); government-operated civilian facility; five surgical suites. George Partelides, M.D., 28 Sofoules St., Nicosia.

Health Advisory

Malaria: There is no malaria on Cyprus.

Travelers' diarrhea: Low to moderate risk. In urban and resort areas, the hotels and restaurants generally serve reliable food and potable water. Major cities have piped, potable water. Elsewhere, travelers should observe all food and drink safety precautions. A quinolone antibiotic (Floxin or Cipro) is recommended for the treatment of acute diarrhea. Diarrhea not responding to antibiotic treatment may be due to a parasitic disease such as giardiasis or amebiasis.

Hepatitis: Hepatitis A vaccine is recommended for all nonimmune travelers. The hepatitis B carrier rate in the general population is estimated at 1%. Vaccination against hepatitis B is recommended for healthcare workers and should be considered by long-term visitors to this country.

Leishmaniasis: Cutaneous leishmaniasis is not reported on Cyprus. There have been a few reports of visceral leishmaniasis in tourists, but the risk is deemed to be low.

CZECH REPUBLIC

Embassy: 202-363-6315 *Prague* *GMT +1 hr*

Entry Requirements
- A visa is not required for stays up to 30 days.
- HIV Test: Not required.
- Vaccinations: None required.

Telephone Country Code: 42 **AT&T:** 00-420-00101 **MCI:** 00-42-000112

Embassies/Consulates: U.S. Embassy, Prague. Trziste 15; Tel. (2) 2451-0847. After hours: Tel. (2) 531-200.

Hospitals/Doctors: Health Care Unlimited, Revolucni 19, Prague. Canadian Medical Centres, 1/30 Veleslavinska; Outpatient care in a modern, private medical clinic. English-speaking Czech physicians provide primary care on a drop-in basis, or as part of a membership package.

Health Advisory (includes the Slovak Republic)

Travelers' diarrhea: Medium risk. Water supplies in urban areas are potable. Amebiasis and cryptosporidiosis are endemic, but levels are unclear. Giardiasis rates of 13% reported in daycare centers.

Hepatitis: Low to medium risk; hepatitis A vaccine recommended for nonimmune travelers.

Tick-borne diseases: Both Central European tick-borne encephalitis (TBE) and Lyme disease occur in the lowland forested areas. Higher risk areas for TBE are south of Prague in the Vlatva (Moldau) River basin, north of Brno, the vicinity of Plzen, and in the Danube River basin near Bratislava. In the Slovak Republic there are widely distributed foci of tick-borne encephalitis in western Slovakia, in central Slovakia (including the Krupin Hills), and in east-

ern Slovakia (including the Slovak karst and Slanske hills). Risk of Lyme disease occurs primarily April through October in forests throughout these countries.
Other illnesses: Brucellosis, echinococcosis, leptospirosis, cysticercosis, rabies (moderately enzootic, with foxes serving as primary zoonotic reservoir; approximately 60% of domestic animal rabies occurs in stray cats), tularemia, and intestinal helminthic infections. Listeriosis, transmitted through the consumption of contaminated meat and milk products, has been reported in South Bohemia and North Moravia.

DENMARK

Embassy: 202-234-4300   *Copenhagen*   *GMT +1 hr*
Entry Requirements
- No visa required for visits up to 3 months (including Greenland & the Faroe Islands).
- HIV Test: Not required.
- Vaccinations: None required.

Telephone Country Code: 45   **AT&T:** 8001-0010   **MCI:** 8001-0022
Embassies: U.S. Embassy, Copenhagen. Dag Hammarskjolds Alle 24; Tel.(31) 423-144. **After hours:** (31) 429-270.
Hospitals/Doctors: Bispebjerb Hospital, Copenhagen (1,150 beds); emergency room and trauma unit.

Health Advisory
Travelers' diarrhea: Low risk; potable water is available throughout the country.
Hepatitis: Low risk; incidence of hepatitis A in this country is among the lowest in Europe. Carrier rate of the hepatitis B virus in the general population is less than 1%.
Lyme disease: Up to 20% of ticks in forested areas throughout the country are infected. Peak tick density occurs in April and May. Most cases of Lyme disease occur in the summer months and peak in July and August. Travelers to brushy or forested areas should take measures to prevent tick bites.
Other illnesses: An epidemic of mycoplasma pneumonia reported in 1998, primarily in school children and young adults.

DJIBOUTI

Embassy: 202-331-0270   *Djibouti*   *GMT +3 hrs*
Entry Requirements
- Passport/Visa: Valid passport and visa are required.
- HIV Test: Not required.
- Vaccinations: A yellow fever vaccination certificate is required for all travelers older than 1 year of age arriving from infected areas.

Telephone Country Code: 253
Embassies/Consulates: U.S. Embassy, Djibouti. Villa Plateau du Serpent Boulevard; Tel. 353-849, 353-995, 352-916. Canadian Embassy (Ethiopia); Tel. [251] (1) 151-100.
Hospitals/Doctors: Peltier Hospital, Djibouti City (700 beds); limited emergency and surgical facilities; old and poorly maintained buildings.

Health Advisory
Cholera: This disease is reported active in this country.
Malaria: Present year-round, countrywide, including urban areas. Higher malaria risk occurs from November through March, which is a relatively cool period with some rainfall. There is only minimal risk of malaria in Djibouti City. Major outbreaks, however, have occurred in the Ambouli suburb of Djibouti City, as well as in the Dikhil and Ali Sabih Districts and villages south of Djibouti City. Falciparum malaria causes 80% of cases, with vivax

malaria accounting for the remainder. Chloroquine-resistant falciparum malaria has been reported. Prophylaxis with mefloquine or doxycycline is currently recommended when traveling to malarious areas.

Travelers' diarrhea: Djibouti has limited urban, and no rural, water treatment and distribution systems. Rural inhabitants obtain water from untreated sources. All water is potentially contaminated. A quinolone antibiotic is recommended for the treatment of acute diarrhea. Diarrhea not responding to treatment with an antibiotic, or chronic diarrhea, may be due to a parasitic disease such as giardiasis, amebiasis, or cryptosporidiosis.

Hepatitis: All susceptible travelers should receive hepatitis A vaccine. Hepatitis E presumably occurs. The hepatitis B carrier rate in the general population is estimated as high as 12%. Vaccination against hepatitis B is recommended for healthcare workers and all long-term visitors to this country.

Leishmaniasis: Presumably occurs, but recognized foci of disease have not been reported.

Rabies: Presumed to occur, but levels unclear. Stray dogs, jackals, foxes, and hyenas are most likely carriers of the virus.

AIDS: HIV prevalence is increasing. Street prostitute seropositivity now 43%, up from 3% in 1987. All travelers are cautioned against unsafe sex, unsterile medical or dental injections, and unnecessary blood transfusions.

Other illnesses/hazards: African tick typhus, anthrax, brucellosis, Crimean-Congo hemorrhagic fever; tick-borne; presumably enzootic), dengue fever (probably active), meningitis (cyclic outbreaks of meningococcal disease occur), sandfly fever, schistosomiasis (considered a low to negligible risk), West Nile fever, tuberculosis, typhoid fever, and intestinal worms.

DOMINICA

Consolate 212-599-8478 **Roseau** **GMT -4 hrs**

Entry Requirements
- Passport/Visa: Visa not required.
- HIV Test: Not required.
- Vaccinations: A yellow fever vaccination certificate is required from travelers over 1 year of age coming from infected or endemic areas.

Telephone Area Code: 809

Embassies/Consulates: Canadian High Commission (Barbados); Tel. (809) 429-3550.

Hospitals/Doctors: General Hospital, Portsmouth (50 beds); limited medical services. Princess Margaret Hospital, Roseau (247 beds); general medical/surgical facility.

Health Advisory
See Disease Risk Summary for the Caribbean.

Malaria: No risk.

Travelers' diarrhea: Low-medium risk. In urban and resort areas, the hotels and restaurants serve reliable food and potable water. Elsewhere, travelers should observe safety precautions. A quinolone antibiotic is recommended for the treatment of acute diarrhea. Diarrhea not responding to antibiotic treatment may be due to a parasitic disease such as giardiasis.

Hepatitis: Low risk to tourists. All nonimmune travelers should receive hepatitis A vaccine.

Schistosomiasis: Foci of infection are possibly present on this island. Travelers should avoid swimming, bathing, or wading in freshwater ponds, lakes, or streams unless advised they are safe. Schistosomiasis is of limited risk to nonindigenous personnel because the foci of snail-infested water are fairly well defined and can be avoided.

Dengue fever: Risk is present. All travelers are advised to take measures to prevent mosquito bites.

Other diseases/health threats: Brucellosis, strongyloidiasis, toxoplasmosis, tuberculosis, typhoid fever, viral encephalitis, ciguatera fish poisoning (outbreaks have occurred), and swimming related hazards (jellyfish, spiny sea urchins, and coral).

World Medical Guide

DOMINICAN REPUBLIC

Embassy: 202-332-6280 *Santo Domingo* *GMT -4 hrs*

Entry Requirements
- Tourist card or visa required. Travelers should contact the Embassy of the Dominican Republic for further information.
- HIV Test: Not required.
- Vaccinations: None required.

Telephone Area Code: 809 **MCI:** 1-800-751-6624
Embassies/Consulates: U.S. Embassy, Santo Domingo. Corner of Calle Cesar Nicolas Penson & Calle Leopoldo Navarro; Tel. 541-2171. Consular Section: Tel. 221-5036. U. S. Consular Agency, Puerta Plata; Tel. 586-4204.
Hospitals/Doctors: Clinica Abreu (76 beds); general medical/surgical facility; emergency room; frequently used by embassy personnel. Centro Medico Universidad Hospital (200 beds); general medical/surgical facility; In Santiago: Clinica Corominas;

Health Advisory
See Disease Risk Summary for the Caribbean.

Malaria: CDC (12/99) recommends malaria prophylaxis for travelers to rural areas in the Dominican Republic but not for travel to resorts. There has been a recent observed increase in malaria cases in the Dominican Republic, including a localized outbreak in the Altagracia Province (principally in the Bavaro Beach area) in the southeastern part of the country, which has included some cases in tourists who have stayed in resorts in this area. The risk to tourists appears to be quite low, but as a precautionary measure we are expanding our recommendations to include chloroquine prophylaxis for travelers to resorts in the Altagracia Province, particularly those that travel to the Bavaro Beach area.

ECUADOR

Embassy: 202-234-7200 *Quito* *GMT -5 hrs*

Entry Requirements
- A passport and return/onward ticket are required to obtain an entry permit valid for 90 days.
- HIV Test: Testing may be required for students or long-term visitors. Travelers should contact the Ecuadorian Embassy in Washington, D.C., for information; Tel: 202-234-7200.
- Vaccinations: A yellow fever vaccination certificate is required from travelers older than 1 year of age arriving from a yellow fever infected area.

Telephone Country Code: 593 **AT&T:** 119 **MCI:** 170
Embassies/Consulates: U.S. Embassy, Quito; corner Avenida 12 de Octubre and Avenida Patria; Tel. (2) 562-890. After hours: Tel. 561-749. U.S. Consulate, Guayaquil; 9 de Octobre and Garcia Moreno; Tel. (4) 323-570.
Hospitals/Doctors: Hospital Militar (450 beds), Quito; military hospital; most specialty services; helipad. Clinica Adventista. Quito Hospital Villalengue (278 beds); private hospital; emergency services.

Health Advisory

Yellow fever: This disease is currently active in this country. Provinces reporting yellow fever activity include Morona-Santiago, Napo, Pastaza, Sucumbios, and Zamora-Chinchipe. Vaccination is recommended for travel outside urban areas. This country is in the Yellow Fever Endemic Zone. Although yellow fever vaccination is not required for entry into this country if arriving from the United States or Canada, it may be required for on-going travel to other countries in Latin America, Africa, the Middle East, or Asia.

Cholera: This disease is active and sporadic cases occur throughout the country. Although cholera vaccination is not required for entry if arriving directly from the U.S. or

World Medical Guide

Canada, it may be required if arriving from a cholera-infected area, or required for ongoing travel to other countries in Latin America, Africa, the Middle East, or Asia. Travelers should consider vaccination (one dose) or a doctor's letter of exemption from vaccination. The risk to tourists of acquiring cholera is considered low. Prevention of cholera consists primarily in adhering to safe food and drink guidelines. Raw seafood, ceviche in particular, should be avoided.

Malaria: This disease occurs countrywide in coastal and rural areas below 2,000 meters elevation; overall risk may be elevated in the northern lowlands on both sides of the Andes. There is no risk of malaria in Quito and vicinity, Cuenca, the central highland tourist areas, and the Galapagos Islands. In malarious areas, risk may be increased February through August. The coastal provinces of Esmeraldas, Guayas (including Guayaquil), and Manabi account for two-thirds of all officially reported malaria, followed by Los Rios, Pinchincha, and Napo Provinces. Other provinces with malaria include El Oro, Morona-Santiago, Pastaza, Sucumbios, and Zamora-Chinchipe. Countrywide, 65%–70% of malaria is vivax, 30% to 35% is falciparum, but falciparum causes 70% of malaria in Manabi Province. Chloroquine-resistant *P. falciparum* likely occurs in all malarious areas. Mefloquine or doxycycline prophylaxis is advised for prophylaxis in endemic areas.

Travelers' diarrhea: High risk. Contaminated water is a major problem throughout Ecuador. Even the two largest cities, Quito and Guayaquil, do not have reliable sources of safe, potable water. Travelers should follow food and drink precautions. A quinolone antibiotic is recommended for the treatment of diarrhea. Diarrhea not responding to antibiotic treatment may be due to a parasitic disease such as giardiasis, amebiasis, or cryptosporidiosis—or an intestinal virus. Diarrhea due to *Balantidium coli*, an intestinal parasite, is also reported.

Hepatitis: All nonimmune travelers should receive hepatitis A vaccine prior to visiting this country. Hepatitis E is regionally endemic. The overall hepatitis B carrier rate in the general population is estimated at 2%. Vaccination against hepatitis B is recommended for anyone planning an extended visit to this country.

Dengue fever: The greatest risk of infection occurs in the coastal urban areas, especially in Guayas, Loja, and Esmeraldas Provinces, but dengue is also endemic in urban and rural areas throughout this country. The *Aedes aegypti* mosquitoes, which transmit dengue, bite primarily during the daytime.

Typhoid fever: Vaccination is recommended. Focal outbreaks occur throughout the country. Large outbreaks have occurred in Quito. Prevention also consists in following safe food and drink guidelines.

Leishmaniasis: This disease is considered a public health problem in rural areas under 2,000 meters elevation on the Pacific coast, the Andean plains, and the eastern Amazonian lowlands (particularly in Imbabura and Pichincha Provinces, as well as Zamora, Esmeraldas, and Manabi Provinces). Over 90% of cases are cutaneous, the rest mucocutaneous. "Uta," a form of cutaneous leishmaniasis, may occur at elevations up to 3,000 meters. Visceral leishmaniasis has not been confirmed.

Onchocerciasis: This disease occurs along river systems in Esmeraldas Province (northwestern Ecuador). Infection rates up to 95% are reported among some Amerindian communities in the Santiago River basin. Outbreaks are reported spreading from Esmeraldas Province to other parts of the country. All travelers to rural areas with fast-flowing rivers should take measures to prevent insect (blackfly) bites.

Chagas' disease: Widely distributed in rural areas, but more common in the Pacific coastal provinces of Manabi and Guayas. Risk of transmission occurs in rural-agricultural areas where there are adobe-style huts and houses that potentially harbor the night-biting triatomid (assassin) bugs. Travelers sleeping in such structures should take measures to prevent nighttime bites. Unscreened blood transfusions are also a potential source of infection.

Bartonellosis: The severe febrile form of this disease with hemolysis (Oroyo fever) has been reported for decades in the highland provinces and cities bordering Peru, including the villages of Zumba, Ibarra, and Zaruma. Transmission of this disease by sandflies occurs primarily between 500 and 3,000 meters elevation. In the coastal lowland province of Manabi, however, there are a growing number of cases of cutaneous bartonellosis, characterized only by chronic verrucous skin lesions.

World Medical Guide

Fascioliasis (liver fluke disease): This disease is not uncommon in the highlands of western Ecuador, especially in Chimborazo, Cotopaxi, and Azuay. Domestic livestock are the primary host. Travelers should avoid uncooked foods.

Paragonimiasis (lung fluke disease): This may be one of the most prevalent and least recognizable public health problems in Ecuador. Nearly one-half of Ecuador's rural population is estimated to be infected. Risk may be elevated in the northern and western coastal areas including Esmeraldas and Manabi Provinces. All travelers should avoid eating uncooked crustacea, especially raw freshwater crabs and crayfish, which harbor the infective cercariae.

Rabies: Human rabies occurs countrywide in both urban and rural areas, with risk increasing. Most cases are reported from the western provinces of Guayas, especially in and around Guayaquil. Rabid dogs are the primary threat. Rabid bats are reported in the Province of Napo. Rabies vaccination is recommended for long-term travelers to this country.

Altitude sickness: Extreme variations in altitude occur in this country. Risk of altitude sickness is present for tourists arriving in Quito (altitude 3,000 meters) and other high-altitude destinations. Travelers to high altitudes should consider Diamox prophylaxis as well as gradual acclimatization prior to further ascent to higher altitudes.

AIDS: Incidence of HIV infection appears relatively low at the present time. Highest incidence reported in the port city of Guayaquil.

Yaws: This sexually transmitted disease is prevalent in the northern province of Esmerladas.

Other diseases/hazards: Cysticercosis (risk elevated in El Oro and Loja Provinces; 9% incidence in Quito), gnathostomiasis (transmitted primarily by raw freshwater fish; occurs in coastal provinces), leprosy (endemic, particularly in Bolivar, El Oro, Loja, and Los Rios Provinces), taeniasis, tuberculosis (a serious public health problem, especially in the Amazon region), and strongyloidiasis and other intestinal helminthic infections. Animal hazards include snakes (vipers, coral snakes), centipedes, scorpions, black widow spiders, brown recluse spiders, banana spiders, and wolf spiders. Electric eels and piranha may be found in the country's fresh waters. Vampire bats are also present in this country. Portuguese man-of war, sea wasps, and stingrays are found in the coastal waters of Ecuador and could be a hazard to swimmers.

EGYPT

Embassy: 202-895-5400　　　*Cairo*　　　*GMT +2 hrs*

Entry Requirements
- Visa: A visa is required. For travelers arriving by air, a renewable 30-day tourist visa can be obtained at airport points of entry.
- HIV Test: Testing is required for foreign contractors.
- Vaccinations: A yellow fever vaccination certificate is required from all travelers older than 1 year arriving from yellow fever–infected areas. Infected areas are considered to be any country in the Yellow Fever Endemic Zones in Africa, and Central and South America, plus Botswana, Malawi, Belize, Costa Rica, Guatemala, Honduras, Nicaragua, and Trinidad & Tobago. In addition, all travelers from Sudan must possess a certificate stating that they have not been in any part of Sudan south of 15 degrees N latitude within the previous six days.

NOTE: Travelers arriving from any cholera-infected areas may be required to show proof of vaccination against cholera or have a letter of medical contraindication. A cholera vaccination certificate is recommended.

Telephone Country Code: 20

Embassies/Consulates: U.S. Embassy, Cairo. 8 Kamal El-Din Salah Street; Tel. (2) 355-7371. Consular Section: Tel. (2) 357-2201.

Hospitals/Doctors: Al-Salam Hospital, Cairo (300 beds); civilian; private hospital; quality of care probably Egypt's best; most major specialties; ambulance service. El Nasr City Medical Center, Cairo (600 beds); government hospital; sophisticated diagnostics and most medical specialties; ambulance service.

World Medical Guide

Health Advisory

Malaria: Transmission occurs primarily during the summer and fall (June–October). Risk exists in focal rural areas of Al Fayyum Governorate, particularly Sennoris District. Possible risk exists in the Nile River Delta, along the Suez Canal, the northern Red Sea coast, part of southern Egypt (likely the rural areas near Aswan), and scattered oases (including Siwa Oasis and El Gara, a small oasis near Siwa) Urban centers, including Cairo and Alexandria, are risk-free. Vivax malaria accounts for the majority of cases. Falciparum malaria is endemic only in the El Faiyum Governorate, where it predominates. Chloroquine resistance has not been reported. Chloroquine prophylaxis is recommended for travel to risk areas.

Travelers' diarrhea: High risk outside of first-class hotels. A quinolone antibiotic is recommended for the treatment of acute diarrhea. Amebiasis is common (a high incidence is reported from the Nile River Delta and along the Nile River). Cryptosporidiosis is a common cause of diarrhea in children. Giardiasis is endemic.

Hepatitis: All nonimmune travelers should receive the hepatitis A vaccine. Hepatitis E is endemic, with 28% of cases of acute viral hepatitis caused by this virus. The hepatitis B carrier rate is estimated 4% of the population. The hepatitis C virus is hyperendemic in Egypt, with seroprevalence rates up to 67% in older villagers, 12%–15% in others. Travelers should be advised not to receive transfusions of blood unscreened for hepatitis B and C virus.

Arboviral fevers: West Nile fever, Rift Valley fever, and sandfly fever are regularly reported. Highest transmission rates are June–October with more risk in the Nile River Delta and Nile Valley, with risk increasing from north to the south. There appears to be negligible risk of dengue fever in Egypt. All travelers to this country, particularly to the Nile Valley and Nile Delta, should take measures to prevent insect (mosquito and sandfly) bites.

Crimean-Congo hemorrhagic fever: No human cases have been reported.

Leishmaniasis: Cutaneous leishmaniasis is focally distributed countrywide in rural and periurban areas, including Cairo. Primary risk areas include the Nile River Delta, the Suez Canal Zone, and the Sinai Peninsula (primarily northeastern Sinai). Visceral leishmaniasis possibly occurs near Alexandria. Travelers should take measures to prevent insect (sandfly) bites. Sandflies bite predominantly between dusk and dawn.

Filariasis: Reported primarily from the eastern Nile Delta, including Ad Daqahliyah, Al Qalyubiyah, and Ash Sharqiyah Governorates, and possibly Asyu't Governorate.

Schistosomiasis: This disease is widespread in Egypt. Urinary and intestinal schistosomiasis are found in the Nile River Delta, throughout the Nile Valley (particularly in the canals and irrigation ditches in rural farming areas), and along the Suez Canal. Areas above the Aswan Dam are heavily infected. Travelers should avoid swimming or wading in freshwater lakes, streams, or irrigated areas. Chlorinated swimming pools, however, are safe.

Intestinal helminthic infections: Fascioliasis (liver fluke disease) is common in Cairo and the Nile Delta. Aquatic plants (e.g., wild watercress) are a source of infection, but the disease can also be transmitted by undercooked sheep and goat livers. Fascioliasis is suspected in travelers suffering from fever, an enlarged liver, and eosinophilia. Travelers should avoid eating watercress salad and undercooked sheep and goat livers. Eating Fessikh (salted raw fish) puts the traveler at risk for acquiring heterophyiasis, an intestinal infection of tiny flukes. Ascariasis (roundworm infection), ancylostomiasis (hookworm disease), trichuriasis (whipworm infection), and taeniasis (pork tapeworm disease) are common in rural areas of the Nile River Delta and Nile River Valley.

Meningitis: Significant outbreaks of meningococcal meningitis have occurred in Egypt, involving primarily Group A disease, but serogroups B and C also reported. Up to 2,000 cases officially are reported annually with most risk in the Al-Jizah and Al-Sharqiyah Governorates. Vaccination is recommended for travelers expecting to have extended contact with the indigenous population.

Rabies: Primarily a risk in urban areas, including Cairo. Stray dogs are the primary source of human exposure, but jackals are also a reservoir of infection. Long-term visitors should consider rabies vaccination.

Other diseases/hazards: Anthrax, AIDS (HIV prevalence of less than 1% reported), Mediterranean spotted fever (low prevalence; also known as boutonneuse fever and African tick typhus; reported from Ghiza and the Sharqiya and Aswan Governorates), brucellosis (risk

World Medical Guide

from raw goat/sheep milk and cheese), cholera (sporadic outbreaks occur), echinococcosis, filariasis (endemic in eastern Nile Delta and possibly in Asyut Governorate), flea-borne typhus, leprosy, leptospirosis, toxoplasmosis, trachoma, tuberculosis, **typhoid fever** (reported countrywide; elevated risk in populated areas with poor sanitation; vaccination is advised), murine typhus (flea-borne). Animal hazards include snakes (cobras, vipers), scorpions, and black widow spiders.

EL SALVADOR

Embassy: 202-331-4032   *San Salvador*   *GMT -6 hrs*

Entry Requirements
- A multiple-entry visa can be obtained by travelers staying more than 30 days.
- HIV Test: Not required.
- Vaccinations: A yellow fever vaccination certificate is required from travelers over 6 months of age coming from infected or endemic areas.

Telephone Country Code: 503   **AT&T:** 190   **MCI:** 195 **Embassies/Consulates:** U.S. Embassy, San Salvador. Final Boulevard Santa Elena, Urbanizacion Santa Elena, Antiguo Cuscatlan; Tel. 278-4444.

Hospitals/Doctors: Policlinica Salvadorena Hospital (103 beds); some specialties; emergency services; ICU; CCU.

Health Advisory

Yellow fever: Yellow fever vaccination is recommended for travel outside urban areas. A yellow fever vaccination certificate may be required for on-going travel to other countries.

Cholera: This disease is active in this country. Although cholera vaccination is not required for entry if arriving directly from the U.S. or Canada, it may be required if arriving from a cholera-infected area, or required for on-going travel to other countries in Latin America, Africa, the Middle East, or Asia.

Malaria: Risk is present rear-round in rural areas below 1,000 meters elevation. Greatest risk is in coastal areas below 600 meters elevation and is minimal in northern and central zones. There is no risk of malaria in urban areas. This disease is highly active. Vivax malaria accounts for 98% of cases. Chloroquine prophylaxis is recommended for travel in rural areas.

Travelers' diarrhea: Piped water supplies may be contaminated. Travelers should observe all food and drink safety precautions. A quinolone antibiotic is recommended for the treatment of acute diarrhea. Diarrhea not responding to treatment with an antibiotic, or chronic diarrhea, may be due to a parasitic disease such as giardiasis, amebiasis, or cryptosporidiosis.

Hepatitis: Hepatitis A vaccine is advised for all nonimmune travelers. Hepatitis E may occur, but data are lacking. The carrier rate of the hepatitis B virus is estimated at 1.2% in the general population. Hepatitis C presumably occurs, but data are lacking.

Dengue fever: Year-round risk, elevated June through December. Most cases occur in urban areas at lower elevations in the vicinity of San Salvador and in the eastern regions bordering Honduras. Travelers should take measures to prevent mosquito bites.

Leishmaniasis: Cutaneous leishmaniasis is reported from the Rio Lempa valley. Most risk occurs in forested rural areas. There is risk of visceral leishmaniasis in the warm, dry valleys near the Honduran border. Travelers should avoid insect (sandfly) bites.

Chagas' disease: Occurs in all rural areas under 1,500 meters elevation where there are adobe-style dwellings that potentially harbor the night-biting triatomid (assassin) bugs. Travelers sleeping in such structures should take precautions against nighttime bites.

Rabies: About 10–12 human deaths annually are reported. Rabid vampire bats are common, but dogs are the primary source of human infection. Rabies vaccination is indicated following the unprovoked bite of a dog, cat, bat, monkey, or other animal. Vaccination against rabies is recommended for long-term travel to this country.

Other diseases: Anthrax, brucellosis, coccidiomycosis, cysticercosis, leptospirosis, measles, relapsing fever (tick-borne), syphilis, AIDS (low number of cases reported), tuberculosis (highly endemic), typhoid fever, strongyloidiasis and other helminthic infections, and typhus are reported. Hazardous animals include venomous snakes, scorpions, spiders, and biting bats.

World Medical Guide

ESTONIA
Estonian Embassy: 202-588-0101. U.S. Embassy, Tallinn: (372)-6-312-021
For Health Advisory information, see the Disease Risk Summary for Europe on page 259.

ERITREA
Embassy of Eritrea: 202-319-1991. U.S. Embassy, Asmara: (291)-1-120-004
For Health Advisory information, see the Disease Risk Summary for Ethiopia.

ETHIOPIA
Embassy: 202-234-2281   *Addis Ababa*   *GMT +3 hrs*

Entry Requirements
- Passport/Visa: A valid passport and visa are required.
- HIV Test: Not required.
- Vaccinations: A yellow fever vaccination certificate is required from all travelers older than 1 year of age arriving from yellow fever infected areas.

Telephone Country Code: 251
Embassies/Consulates: U.S. Embassy, Addis Ababa. Entoto Avenus; Tel. (1)550-666, extension 316/336. After hours: Tel. (1) 552-558.
Hospitals/Doctors: Empress Zauditu Memorial Hospital, Addis Ababa (207 beds); basic diagnostic and treatment services. Tikur Anbessa Hospital. Mekan Hiwet Hospital, Addis Ababa (750 beds); basic treatment and emergency services; surgical capabilities.

Health Advisory
Yellow fever: Yellow fever not reported in this country, but epidemics occurred in the southwest in the 1960s. Yellow fever vaccination should be considered by all travelers. This country is in the Yellow Fever Endemic Zone. A valid vaccination certificate may be required for on-going travel to other countries.

Cholera: Outbreaks occur, but this disease is not officially reported. Although cholera vaccination is not required for entry if arriving directly from the U.S. or Canada, it may be required if arriving from a cholera-infected area, or required for on-going travel to other countries in Latin America, Africa, the Middle East, or Asia. Travelers to this country should consider vaccination (one dose) or a doctor's letter of exemption from vaccination.

Malaria: Transmission occurs year-round in most lowlands and urban areas below 1,500 to 2,000 meters elevation, especially in areas near or around lakes, swamps, streams, and irrigation ditches. Recent outbreaks reported from the Harerge Administrative Division, including the Ogaden Region. Risk is elevated during and immediately following the rainy season (from June through September). There is no malaria in Addis Ababa (elevation 2,450 meters) or the Ethiopian highlands. *P. falciparum* causes 80%–90% of human infections, followed by *P. vivax* and *P. malariae*. Chloroquine-resistant *P. falciparum* is reported, primarily along the southern and western borders. Rafters on the Omo River have reported *P. vivax* infections. Prophylaxis with mefloquine, Malarone, or doxycycline is currently recommended when traveling to malarious areas. Travelers should consider primaquine prophylaxis when there is the threat of vivax malaria.

Travelers' diarrhea: High risk. Most rural water supplies consist of unprotected wells, streams, or natural springs. Large-scale international aid has improved rural wells and reservoirs. In urban areas, piped water is commonly available at public distribution points. Piped water supplies may be contaminated. Travelers should observe all food and drink safety precautions. A quinolone antibiotic is recommended for the treatment of acute diarrhea. Diarrhea not responding to treatment with an antibiotic, or chronic diarrhea, may be due to a parasitic disease such as giardiasis, amebiasis, or cryptosporidiosis. Rotavirus is a common cause of diarrhea in children.

World Medical Guide

Hepatitis: All susceptible (nonimmune) travelers should receive the hepatitis A vaccine prior to departure. Hepatitis E is endemic, but the levels are unclear. The hepatitis B carrier rate in the general population is estimated at 11%. Vaccination against hepatitis B is recommended for healthcare workers and all long-term visitors to this country. Hepatitis C is endemic.

Dengue and other arboviral fevers: Dengue most likely occurs in the coastal regions. Sandfly fever, West Nile fever, Chikungunya fever, Sindbis fever, and Rift Valley fever may occur.

Leishmaniasis: Widespread incidence, with focal distribution countrywide. Cutaneous leishmaniasis occurs in most areas of the Ethiopian highland plateau (elevation 1,500–2,700 meters), including Addis Ababa. Areas of risk for visceral leishmaniasis (kala azar) include the northwestern, southwestern, and southern lowlands, and the northeastern low-lying arid areas along the Red Sea coast. Travelers to these areas should take measures to prevent insect (sandfly) bites.

Schistosomiasis: Peak transmission occurs during the dry season. Intestinal schistosomiasis is widely distributed in highland areas, primarily occurring in agricultural communities along streams between 1,300 and 2,000 meters elevation. Limited areas of urinary schistosomiasis are confined to warmer lowland areas (below 800 meters elevation), including the middle and lower Awash Valley, the lower Wabi Shebele Valley near the Somali border, and near Kurmuk, Welega Administrative Division, near the Sudan border. Travelers to these areas should avoid swimming or wading in freshwater lakes, ponds, or streams.

Onchocerciasis: Blackfly-borne; occurs primarily along rivers in the Angered Valley and Humera area in Gonder, western Gojam, and most of Kefa, Ilubabor, and Welega Administrative Divisions; additional foci may occur in lowland areas of Gonder, Gama, Gofa, and Western Shewa and Sidamo Administrative Divisions.

Trypanosomiasis (African sleeping sickness): Areas of transmission of the Rhodesian form of sleeping sickness occur in southwestern Ethiopia in Gamo, Gofa, Ilubabor, Kefa, and Welega Administrative Divisions. Gambien sleeping sickness may occur in areas adjacent to southern Sudan. Travelers to these areas should take measures to prevent insect (tsetse fly) bites.

Meningitis: Risk is elevated in central and northern areas. Major meningococcal meningitis outbreaks (due predominantly to Group A disease) were reported in 1988–1989. Vaccination is advised for those travelers anticipating close, extended contact with the indigenous population.

Rabies: Higher than average risk. There is a large stray dog population, especially in Addis Ababa and other urban areas, that is primarily responsible for disease transmission. Travelers should seek immediate treatment of any animal bite. Vaccination against rabies should be considered by longer-term travelers to this country.

Other illnesses/hazards: African tick typhus, anthrax (in Gonder region), brucellosis, cholera, echinococcosis (high prevalence among nomadic pastoralists in the southwest), filariasis (endemic focus of Bancroftian filariasis at Gambela), leptospirosis, relapsing fever (tick-borne and louse-borne; epidemics of louse-borne disease reported in prisoner-of-war transit camps in Bahr Dar and Mekele), toxoplasmosis, syphilis, tuberculosis (a major health problem), trachoma (up to one-half of the population infected), typhoid fever, typhus (louse-borne and flea-borne; endemic in highlands), and intestinal helminthic infections (very common). Animal hazards include snakes (vipers, cobras, mambas), centipedes, scorpions, and black widow spiders.

World Medical Guide

FIJI
Embassy: 202-337-8320 *Suva* *GMT +12 hrs*

Entry Requirements
- Visa: Travelers can obtain a 4-month tourist visa. Travelers should contact the Embassy of Fiji in Washington for additional information.
- HIV Test: Not required.
- Vaccinations: A yellow fever vaccination certificate is required of travelers arriving from infected or endemic areas.

Telephone Country Code: 679
Embassies/Consulates: U.S. Embassy, Suva. 31 Loftus St; Tel. 314-466. Canadian Consulate, Suva. 50 Thompson Street; Tel. 311-844.
Hospitals/Doctors: Gordon Street Medical Center, Suva; Tel. 313-131 or 313-355. Colonial War Memorial Hospital, Suva (376 beds); emergency room, x-ray, pharmacy.

Health Advisory
Travelers' diarrhea: Moderate to high risk. Urban areas of Fiji have some water treatment facilities, but most water should be considered potentially contaminated. Travelers are advised to drink only bottled or treated water. Food and milk are considered safe. A quinolone antibiotic (Cipro or Floxin) is recommended for the treatment of acute diarrhea.
Hepatitis: Hepatitis A vaccine is recommended for all nonimmune travelers. The hepatitis B carrier rate in the general population is estimated at 10%. Vaccination against hepatitis B is recommended for healthcare workers and should be considered by long-term visitors to this country.
Typhoid fever: An outbreak occurred in 1985. Typhoid vaccination is recommended for those travelers on extended visit (more than 4 weeks) to this country.
Dengue fever: Increased risk during the rainy season months, December–January and May–June. Travelers should take precautions to avoid mosquito bites.
Ross River fever: Mosquito-transmitted viral illness occurs in periodic epidemics.
Filariasis: Malayan filariasis occurs year-round. Travelers should take precautions against mosquito bites.

FINLAND
Embassy: 202-298-5800 *Helsinki* *GMT +2 hrs*

Entry Requirements
- Passport/Visa: A valid passport is required.
- HIV Test: Not required.
- Vaccinations: None required.

Telephone Country Code: 358   **AT&T:** 9800-100-10   **MCI:** 9800-102-80
Embassies/Consulates: U.S. Embassy, Helsinki; Itainen Puistotie 14A; Tel. (0) 171-931. After hours: Tel. (0) 605-414.
Doctors/Hospitals: Helsinki Health Center (1,350 beds); most specialties, including critical care. Eira Hospital, Helsinki; Tel. (0) 659-944.

Health Advisory
Travelers' diarrhea: Low risk. Giardiasis is reported.
Lyme disease: Travelers should take tick bite precautions in brushy and broad-leaf forest (usually oak forest) areas in the southern coastal areas at elevations below 1,500 meters.
Tick-borne encephalitis: Rare cases are transmitted by *Ixodes ricinus* ticks found in brush and wooded areas. Most cases reported in forested areas along the coast of the Gulf of Finland from Kotka to the border with Russia, and all the islands south of Turku including the Aland islands.
Pagosta disease: Viral illness with encephalitis transmitted by culex mosquitoes, especially in the mid-eastern region of Finland. Travelers should avoid mosquito bites.

World Medical Guide

FRANCE

Embassy: 202-944-6000 Paris *GMT +1 hr*

Entry Requirements
- Visas not required for tourist/business stays up to 3 months (1 month in Polynesia).
- HIV Test: Not required for tourists.
- Vaccinations: None required.

Telephone Country Code: 33 **AT&T:** 0-800-99-00-11 **MCI:** 0-800-99-00-19
U.S. Embassy: Paris. 2 Avenue Gabriel; Tel. (1) 43-12-22-22.
Hospitals/Doctors (Paris): The American Hospital, Paris; 63 Blvd. Victor Hugo, Neuilly-sur-Seine; all specialties; bilingual staff; 85% have had additional training in the United States; large corporate and international clientel; the hospital has angioplasty and coronary artery bypass grafting surgery (CABG) capability; emergency room with English-speaking doctors open 24 hours. Tel. (01) 47-47-70-15 for emergency advice as well physician or outpatient clinic referrals. S.O.S. Doctors on Duty; will go to hotels or residences; Tel. (01) 47-07-77-77. SOS 92: 24-hour house/hotel calls; serves primarily western Paris area (7th, 8th, 9th, 14th, 15th, 16th, 17th, arrondissements); Tel. (01)-46-03-77-44. Urgence Medicale de Paris (Medical Emergencies in Paris): Tel. (01) 48-28-40-04. Serves primarily the central Paris area. S.O.S. Dentists on Duty: Tel. (01) 43-37-51-00.
Hospitals/Doctors (France): If you have a medical problem, dial 15 on any telephone in France (including Paris) and this countrywide assistance service (similar to the 911 service in the USA, but more comprehensive) will evaluate your problem; if necessary, they will dispatch a physician, or doctor-staffed ambulance, to your hotel or residence.

Health Advisory

Travelers' diarrhea: Low risk. The domestic water supplies in urban areas are generally safe for drinking. Giardiasis is reported.
Hepatitis: Low risk. Hepatitis A vaccination is not considered necessary for routine travel to France but nonimmune travelers may wish to be immunized. The carrier rate of the hepatitis B virus in the general population is less than 1%. Hepatitis E may occur, but endemic levels are unclear.
Lyme disease: Risk of transmission occurs throughout the country in wooded, brushy areas or in broad-leaf (oak) forests. Risk is elevated in eastern France. Travelers to rural areas countrywide should take measures to avoid tick bites.
Boutonneuse fever (Mediterranean spotted fever): Occurs in southern France in regions below 1,000 meters elevation. Peak transmission occurs July through September. The primary endemic areas are the southern Mediterranean coast (especially the vicinity of Marseille) and the island of Corsica. Disease may be acquired in and around tick-infested houses and terrain, but more than 95% of cases are associated with contact with tick-carrying dogs.
Leishmaniasis: Low risk, but visceral and cutaneous leishmaniasis do occur in rural areas of southern France, primarily in the departments of Bouche-de-Rhone, Provence, and Alpes-Maritimes, and on Corsica. Transmission occurs between May and November, peaking in July and August. Travelers should take measures to prevent insect (sandfly) bites.
Listeriosis: Outbreaks of listeriosis, caused by consumption of unpasteurized dairy products, especially soft cheeses, such as Brie, are reported. Some cases fatal. Young children, pregnant women, and travelers with compromised immunity should avoid soft cheese products.
Rabies: No human cases reported, but rabies is reported enzootic in the fox population.
Other diseases: Brucellosis, echinococcosis, fascioliasis (cases reported from Orne and Manche Departments in Normandy), leptospirosis, legionellosis, giardiasis, hemorrhagic fever with renal syndrome, tick-borne meningoencephalitis (due to *Rickettsia slovaca*; reported in central France/Pyrennes mountains), toxoplasmosis (from ingesting undercooked beef), trichinellosis (outbreaks associated with consumption of poorly cooked imported horsemeat are reported), pork and beef tapeworm disease, and typhoid fever (uncommon). Tick-borne encephalitis occurs; risk is elevated in the Alsace Region.

FRENCH GUIANA

Embassy: 202-944-6000 *Cayenne* *GMT -3 hrs*

Entry Requirements
- No visa required for stays up to 3 months.
- HIV Test: Not required.
- Vaccinations: A yellow fever vaccination certificate is required from all travelers over 1 year of age arriving from ALL countries.

Telephone Country Code: 594

Embassies/Consulates: The United States maintains no diplomatic representation in French Guiana, which is an overseas department of France. For assistance in French Guiana, U.S. citizens may contact the U.S. Embassy in Paramaribo, Suriname, which has consular jurisdiction in this area. Tel. (country code 597) 477-881.

Doctors/Hospitals: Clinique Saint Paul, Cayenne (81 beds); general medical/surgical facility; ob/gyn; cardiology; pediatrics. Clinic Veronique (230 beds); medical/surgical facility; ob/gyn.

Health Advisory

Yellow fever: The first case of yellow fever in French Guiana since 1902 was reported in March 1998 in an Amerindian woman living in a forest area on the Maroni River. A yellow fever vaccination certificate is required for entry to this country. This country is in the Yellow Fever Endemic Zone.

Cholera: This disease is active in this country. Although cholera vaccination is not required for entry if arriving directly from the U.S. or Canada, it may be required if arriving from a cholera-infected area, or required for travel to other countries in Latin America, Africa, the Middle East, or Asia. Travelers should consider vaccination (one dose) or a doctor's letter of exemption from vaccination. The risk to travelers of acquiring cholera is considered low. Prevention consists primarily in adhering to safe food and drink guidelines.

Malaria: Risk is present in all areas of this country year-round. The highest risk of malaria occurs near the borders with Brazil and Suriname. The risk of malaria is low in major urban areas. Falciparum malaria accounts for 70% of cases and chloroquine-resistant falciparum malaria is reported. Quinine-resistant falciparum malaria may also occur. The risk of falciparum malaria is greatest in the western areas bordering Suriname. The risk of vivax malaria is greatest in the east and along the coast. Chemoprophylaxis with mefloquine (Lariam) or doxycycline is currently recommended.

Travelers' diarrhea: Water in Cayenne is considered generally safe for consumption. Travelers should follow food and drink precautions, especially outside first-class hotels and resorts. A quinolone antibiotic is recommended for the treatment of diarrhea. Diarrhea not responding to antibiotic treatment may be due to a parasitic disease such as giardiasis or amebiasis— or an intestinal virus.

Hepatitis: Hepatitis A vaccination is recommended for all nonimmune travelers. Hepatitis E has not been reported but could occur. The hepatitis B carrier rate in the population is 2%–13% with the higher rates in some rural areas. Vaccination against hepatitis B is recommended for all long-term visitors to this country. Hepatitis C is endemic.

Leishmaniasis: Cutaneous leishmaniasis has become a public health problem, primarily among people living in forested areas. Mucocutaneous leishmaniasis is occasionally reported. Visceral leishmaniasis has not been reported, but occurs in neighboring Brazil. Transmission occurs primarily from November through May with the highest risk of transmission during periods of lowest rainfall, October–December. Most cases of leishmaniasis occur in the eastern one-half of the country. U.S. military units undergoing jungle training have experienced attack rates exceeding 50% during a 3- to 4-week exposure. Travelers to forested areas should take protective measures against sandflies, which bite from dusk to dawn.

Schistosomiasis: Currently not reported, but may occur just across the border near Albina, in Suriname.

Dengue fever: Risk is present; with intermittent epidemics. All travelers should take measures to prevent mosquito bites.

World Medical Guide

Rabies: An outbreak of rabies occurred in 1984. Dogs are the primary source of infection although rabid vampire bats have also transmitted the disease. Travelers should especially avoid stray dogs and seek immediate treatment of any wild animal bite. Rabies vaccination is usually indicated following the unprovoked bite of a dog, cat, vampire bat, monkey, or other animal. Pre-exposure vaccination is recommended for long-term travelers to this country and for travelers going to remote rural areas if they will be unable to receive antirabies treatment within 24 hours of exposure to a potentially rabid animal.
AIDS: Endemic at moderate levels. The primary risk factor for HIV infection is multiple heterosexual contacts, with HIV seropositivity highest among Haitian immigrants.
Other diseases: Filariasis (Bancroftian variety; endemic in coastal urban areas), Chagas' disease (occurs in rural areas, but few cases are actually reported), leptospirosis, leprosy (highly endemic, with countrywide prevalence), syphilis, tuberculosis (a serious public health problem), tungiasis, typhoid fever, strongyloidiasis and other helminthic infections are reported. Animal hazards include snakes (vipers), centipedes, scorpions, black widow spiders, brown recluse spiders, banana spiders, pruning spiders, and wolf spiders. Electric eels and various carnivorous fish (including piranha) may be found in the country's fresh waters. Vampire bats are also present in this country. Portuguese man-of-war, sea wasps, and stingrays are found in the coastal waters and could be a hazard to swimmers.

FRENCH POLYNESIA

Embassy: 202- 944-6200   *Papeete*   *GMT -10 hrs*

Entry Requirements
- Passport/Visa: No visa required for stay of less than 30 days. French Polynesia is a French overseas territory.
- HIV Test: Not required.
- Vaccinations: A yellow fever vaccination certificate is required of travelers arriving from infected areas.

Telephone Country Code: 689
Embassies/Consulates: There is no U.S. Embassy nor diplomatic post on the island of Tahiti, nor any of the other islands. For assistance, travelers should contact the U.S. Embassy in Suva, Fiji; Tel. (679) 314-466.
Hospitals/Doctors: Mamao Territory Hospital (400 beds); emergency room; x-ray. Jean Prince Hospital (140 beds); emergency room; burn unit; ambulance service. Clinique Cardella, Rue Anne Marie Javouhey. Clinique Paofai, Blvd. Pomare.

Health Advisory

Malaria: No risk.
Travelers' diarrhea: Low to medium risk. The tap water on most of the main islands is generally safe, but travelers are advised to drink bottled, boiled, or treated water. Food and milk are considered safe, but food should be eaten well cooked. All fruit should be peeled prior to consumption. A quinolone antibiotic is recommended for the treatment of acute diarrhea. Diarrhea not responding to antibiotic treatment may be due to a parasitic disease such as giardiasis or amebiasis—or an intestinal virus.
Hepatitis: Hepatitis A vaccine is recommended for all nonimmune travelers. The hepatitis B carrier rate in the general population of Oceania is estimated at 5.5%–15%. Vaccination against hepatitis B is recommended for healthcare workers and should be considered by long-term visitors to this country.
Typhoid fever: Outbreak of typhoid fever was reported in 1983, but the incidence of this illness is low. Travelers should follow safe food and drink guidelines. Vaccination is recommended for long-term travelers to this country.
Dengue fever: This disease occurs sporadically. Highest risk is during the rainy season months. Travelers should take protective measures against mosquito bites.
Filariasis: Moderately high rates (up to 19%) of Malayan filariasis reported in the general population. Travelers should take protective measures against mosquito bites.
AIDS: A small number of AIDS cases and HIV infections have been reported. The hospital blood supply is screened for HIV and is considered safe.

World Medical Guide

GABON

Embassy: 202-797-1000 *Libreville* *GMT +1 hr*

Entry Requirements
- Passport/Visa: Valid passport and visa are required.
- HIV Test: Not required.
- Vaccinations: A yellow fever vaccination certificate is required from all travelers older than 1 year of age arriving from ALL COUNTRIES.

Telephone Country Code: 241
Embassies/Consulates: U.S. Embassy, Libreville. Boulevard de la Mer; Tel. 762-003, 743-492. Canadian Embassy, Libreville; Tel. 743-464.
Hospitals/Doctors: Libreville General Hospital (630 beds); general medical/surgical facility; maternity wing. The Albert Schweitzer Hospital, Lambarene. Bongolo Evangelical Hospital, La Bomba (80 beds); missionary hospital; emergency care available.

Health Advisory

Yellow fever: This disease is reported active in Ogooue-Invindo Province. A yellow fever vaccination certificate is required to enter this country.
Malaria: Risk is present year-round, countrywide, including urban areas. Risk is elevated during and immediately after the rainy seasons (October through December and February through April). Falciparum malaria accounts for 95% of cases. Chloroquine-resistant falciparum malaria is reported. Prophylaxis with mefloquine or doxycycline is recommended.
Travelers' diarrhea: High risk. Piped water supplies in Libreville, Port-Gentil, and Bata may be grossly contaminated. Travelers should observe all food and drink safety precautions. A quinolone antibiotic is recommended for the treatment of acute diarrhea. Diarrhea not responding to treatment with an antibiotic, or chronic diarrhea, may be due to a parasitic disease such as giardiasis, amebiasis, or cryptosporidiosis.
Hepatitis: All susceptible travelers should receive immune globulin or hepatitis A vaccine. Hepatitis E is likely endemic. The hepatitis B carrier rate in the general population is estimated at 7%–12%. Vaccination against hepatitis B is recommended for healthcare workers and all long-term visitors to this country. The hepatitis C virus is endemic.
Onchocerciasis: Widely distributed, especially in Ndjole, Fougamou, Mimongo, Lebamba, Latoursville, and Makokou. Travelers should take measures to prevent insect (blackfly) bites.
Loiasis: High risk present in the southeastern rain forest and swamp forest. Infection rate of 25% reported in the Franceville vicinity. Travelers should take measures to prevent insect (deer fly) bites.
Schistosomiasis: Foci of disease are scattered throughout all provinces, with a major focus in the Libreville area. Travelers should avoid swimming, bathing, or wading in freshwater lakes, ponds, or streams.
Sleeping sickness: Risk areas persist along the coast, primarily the Komo estuary around Libreville, and the mouth of the Ogooue River near Port Gentil.
Other illnesses/hazards: African tick typhus, brucellosis (from consumption of raw dairy products), cholera, Chikungunya fever, Crimean-Congo hemorrhagic fever, dracunculiasis, Ebola hemorrhagic fever (19 fatalities from eating contaminated chimpanzee meat occurred in Makokou in northern Gabon in 1995), echinococcosis, filariasis, Lassa fever (endemic status unclear), leprosy (up to 3 cases/1,000 population), rabies, paragonimiasis, toxoplasmosis, tuberculosis (a major health problem), typhoid fever, and intestinal helminths, particularly ancylostomiasis. Animal hazards include snakes (vipers, cobras), centipedes, scorpions, and black widow spiders.

GEORGIA

Embassy of Georgia: 202-393-6060. *U.S. Embassy, Tbilisi:* (995)-8832-989-967
For Health Advisory information, see the Health Advisory for Russia on page 259 and 404.

World Medical Guide

GERMANY

Embassy: 202-298-4360 *Berlin* *GMT +1 hr*

Entry Requirements
- A valid passport is required.
- HIV Test: Testing is required for those applying for residence permits (Bavaria only).
- Vaccinations: None required.

Telephone Country Code: 49 **AT&T:** 0130-0010 **MCI:** 0130-0012
Embassies/Consulates: U.S. Embassy, Bonn. Deichmanns Aue 29; Tel. 228-3391. U.S. Embassy Office, Berlin. Neustaedtische Kirchstrasse 4-5; Tel. (30) 238-5174. U.S. Consulate, Munich; Tel. (89) 288-8722. U.S. Consulate, Frankfurt; Tel. (69) 75-350.
Hospitals/Doctors: Universitatklinik, Bonn (1,774 beds); private hospital, all specialties. Universitatklinik, Cologne; all specialties. Klinikum Berlin-Buch; Wiltbergstrasse 50, Berlin-Buch. Dr. Manfred Peters (internal medicine, tropical medicine); Wandsbeker Markstr. 73, Hamburg; Tel. (40) 652-6000.

Health Advisory

Travelers' diarrhea: In western Germany, drinking water in urban areas is safe, but well water in rural areas may be contaminated. In the new states of the former East Germany, advanced water treatment systems that reduce contamination from industrial solvents, pesticides, heavy metals, and other pollutants may be lacking. Water is safe to drink only in major cities and at the better hotels and restaurants. Travelers to eastern Germany should drink only commercially bottled water or other safe beverages. A quinolone antibiotic is recommended for the treatment of acute diarrhea. Giardiasis and cryptosporidiosis are reported.
Hepatitis: The incidence of hepatitis A in western Germany is among the lowest in Europe. Nonimmune travelers to the eastern regions, however, should consider hepatitis A vaccine. The hepatitis B carrier rate in the general population is estimated at less than 1%. Vaccination against hepatitis B is recommended for healthcare workers and should be considered by long-term visitors to this country. Hepatitis E possibly occurs.
Lyme disease: This disease is reported countrywide, but most cases are reported in the south, primarily in Bavaria. Up to 34% of ticks in some endemic areas are infected. The ticks that transmit Lyme disease (*Ixodes ricinus*) are found in brushy, wooded areas and broad-leaf (mostly oak) forests under 1,000 meters elevation.
Tick-borne encephalitis (TBE): Most cases reported from the southern lowland forested and wooded areas of Bayern and Baden-Wurttemburg. Cases are reported from Baden-Wurttemburg (Black forest, upper Rhine valley) region. The valleys of Kinzig, Elz, and Dreisam as well as the regions around Freiburg and Pforzheim are endemic areas. Travelers to these areas should take extra measures to prevent tick bites. A vaccine is available for people at high risk of exposure to ticks (e.g., forestry workers). Vaccination against TBE is not recommended routinely for travelers to Germany.
Rabies: No human cases have been officially reported for several years. Wild foxes are the primary reservoir of the disease. Animal rabies has been declining in the west, but there is potential risk of transmission to humans, especially in the eastern regions. Travelers should seek immediate medical evaluation and treatment of any wild animal bite.
AIDS: Most cases are reported from the western regions. Primary risk groups include homosexual males and intravenous drug users.
Other diseases: Brucellosis, boutonneuse fever (reported from a region SE of Frankfurt in the 1980s), hemorrhagic fever with renal syndrome (transmitted by infective rodent excreta; 14 cases reported in an outbreak in soldiers in 1989), echinococcosis (risk greatest in Swabbian uplands of central Wurttemberg State), legionellosis, leptospirosis (risk may be elevated in the south) and Q fever (outbreak reported in 1996 in Rollshausen and vicinity; some cases had breathed infectious aerosols when walking near sheep farms that had infected animals).

World Medical Guide

GHANA
Embassy: 202-686-4520   *Accra*   *GMT 0 hrs*

Entry Requirements
- Travelers should contact the Embassy of Ghana for entry information.
- HIV Test: Not required.
- Vaccinations: A yellow fever vaccination certificate is required from all travelers arriving from ALL COUNTRIES, including the United States and Canada.

Telephone Country Code: 233
Embassies/Consulates: U.S. Embassy, Accra. Ring Road East. Tel. (21) 775-347. U. S. Consulate. Tel. (21) 776-601 (to obtain updated information on travel and security in Ghana).
Hospitals/Doctors: Police Hospital, Accra; used by U.S. Embassy personnel. Nyaho Hospital, Accra; used by U.S. Embassy personnel. Korle Bu Central Hospital, Accra (1,500 beds); general medical/surgical facility and cardiothoracic center. Tudu Clinic, Accra.

Health Advisory

Yellow fever: This disease is currently active in the Upper West Region. An outbreak of yellow fever previously occurred along Lake Volta in the Eastern Region during late 1987. A vaccination certificate is required for entry to this country. Ghana is in the Yellow Fever Endemic Zone. A valid yellow fever vaccination certificate may be required for travel to other countries in South America, Africa, the Middle East, or Asia.

Cholera: This disease is reported active in this country. Most cases are occurring in the Accra, Ashanti, Central, Upper East, and Volta Regions. Although cholera vaccination is not required for entry if arriving directly from the U.S. or Canada, it may be required for on-going travel to other countries in Africa, the Middle East, or Asia. Travelers should consider vaccination (one dose) or getting a doctor's letter of exemption from vaccination. Cholera occurs in areas with inadequate sewage disposal and unsafe water supplies such as urban slums and rural areas. The risk to travelers of acquiring cholera is considered low. Prevention consists primarily in adhering to safe food and drink guidelines.

Malaria: Risk is present throughout this country year-round, including urban areas. Risk may be elevated during and immediately following the rainy seasons (March through June and October through November in the south; March through October in the north). *P. falciparum* accounts for 85% of cases, followed by *P. malariae* and *P. ovale*. Multidrug-resistant falciparum malaria is reported. Mefloquine or doxycycline chemoprophylaxis is recommended.

Travelers' diarrhea: Large urban areas have treated, piped water which is subject to recontamination during distribution. All water sources should be considered potentially contaminated. Travelers should observe safe food and drink precautions. A quinolone antibiotic is recommended for the treatment of acute diarrhea. Diarrhea not responding to treatment with an antibiotic may be due to a parasitic disease such as giardiasis, amebiasis, or cryptosporidiosis.

Hepatitis: All nonimmune travelers should receive hepatitis A vaccine. Hepatitis E is likely endemic, but the levels are unclear. The hepatitis B carrier rate in the general population is estimated to exceed 10%. Vaccination against hepatitis B is recommended for all long-term visitors to this country.

Schistosomiasis: Swimming or bathing is unsafe in any of Ghana's bodies of freshwater. Urinary schistosomiasis is widely distributed. Many cases occur in the southeast (southern shore of Lake Volta, the area below the Akosombo Dam along the lower Volta River, and the Accra vicinity) and in the northeast. Limited foci of intestinal schistosomiasis are distributed sporadically, occurring predominantly in the extreme north, the southwest (Tarkwa), and the southeast (along the lower Volta River). Acute infection (Katayama fever) has resulted from swimming in the estuary of the Volta.

Leishmaniasis: Low risk. Cases of cutaneous and visceral leishmaniasis have been reported from neighboring countries. Travelers should take precautions against insect (sandfly) bites.

World Medical Guide

Onchocerciasis: Widely distributed along fast-flowing rivers, but incidence has declined due to blackfly control programs. Moderate risk remains in central mountainous areas along the Pru River. Travelers should take precautions against insect (blackfly) bites.

Filariasis: Bancroftian filariasis is reported in northeastern areas. Infection rates of 20% have been reported from the Vea and Tono rice irrigation project areas. Travelers should take measures to prevent mosquito bites.

African sleeping sickness (trypanosomiasis): Low apparent risk, but cases were reported in Ghana in the early 1980s. Sleeping sickness is reported in Ivory Coast, a neighboring country. All travelers should take measures to prevent insect (tsetse fly) bites.

Meningitis: Northern Ghana lies in the sub-Saharan meningitis belt, but cases have also been reported from the central regions of this country. Vaccination is recommended for travelers who will have close, prolonged contact with the indigenous population.

Rabies: High incidence of dog rabies with frequent human cases reported. Rabies vaccination should be considered prior to travel to this country, especially for travelers going to remote rural areas.

AIDS: HIV prevalence is estimated at 2% of the low-risk urban population and 38% of the high-risk urban population, including prostitutes.

Other diseases: Brucellosis (from consumption of raw dairy products), African tick typhus (transmitted by dog ticks, often in urban areas, and bush ticks), anthrax, leprosy, leptospirosis (39% of agricultural workers have been exposed), tuberculosis (a major health problem), and intestinal worms (very common) are reported.

GREECE

Embassy: 202-939-5800 *Athens* *GMT +1.5 hrs*

Entry Requirements
- No visa is required for tourist/business stays up to 3 months.
- HIV Test: Testing required for students on scholarship, and performing artists. Travelers should contact the Greek Embassy in Washington for details.
- Vaccinations: A yellow fever vaccination certificate is required from all travelers older than 6 months arriving from infected or endemic areas.

Telephone Country Code: 30 **AT&T:** 00-800-1311 **MCI:** 00-800-1211

Embassies/Consulates: U.S. Embassy, Athens. 91 Vasilissis Sophias Boulevard; Tel. (1) 721-2951. U.S. Consulate, Thessaloniki; (31) 242-905.

Hospitals/Doctors: The Diagnostic and Therapeutic Center of Athens, "HYGEIA" (350 beds); well-equipped modern facility. Apostolos Accident Hospital, Athens (1,000 beds); orthopedics; trauma care.

Health Advisory

Malaria: No risk. Greece declared malaria-free in 1986.

Travelers' diarrhea: Low- to medium-risk for acute diarrheal disease due to bacteria (mainly *E. Coli*, salmonella, shigella, campylobacter), parasites, and viruses. Multi-drug resistance common among salmonella and shigella bacteria. Amebiasis, usually seen in adults, is more common in Greece than in most other parts of Europe. Tap water in small urban areas and rural areas is not considered safe. Travelers are advised to drink only bottled, boiled, filtered, or chemically treated water and consume only well-cooked food. A quinolone antibiotic is recommended for the treatment of acute diarrhea. Diarrhea not responding to antibiotic treatment may be due to a parasitic disease such as giardiasis, amebiasis, or cryptosporidiosis.

Hepatitis: Higher risk than in other western European countries. Hepatitis A vaccine is recommended for nonimmune travelers. The hepatitis B carrier rate in the general population of Greece is estimated at 1%–4%. Vaccination against hepatitis B should be considered by long-term visitors. Hepatitis E has not been reported, but could occur.

World Medical Guide

Leishmaniasis: Risk of transmission is highest between May and October. Cutaneous leishmaniasis occurs sporadically, with the highest prevalence in the Ionian Islands. Visceral leishmaniasis occurs focally on the mainland, including the Athens area, and on the islands, especially Crete. Travelers to these regions should take measures to avoid sandfly bites.

Tick-borne encephalitis (TBE): Low apparent risk; some cases of TBE occur in northern Greece where the tick vector *Ixodes ricinus* is present.

Hemorrhagic fever with renal syndrome: Most cases are reported in the rural mountain regions in northern and northwestern Greece. Also reported on Crete and the Ionian Islands, including Corfu. Transmission is apparently via aerosolized dried rodent excreta.

Other illnesses/hazards: Boutonneuse fever (tick-borne; likely limited to brushy or forested coastal areas), brucellosis, echinococcosis, legionellosis (reported sporadically, usually in summer tourists), rabies (country now officially "rabies-free." Rabies occurs primarily in jackals, foxes, and wolves, with some dog and cat rabies. Rare in humans; most cases in the northeast and Peloponnese), sandfly fever (endemic), tick-borne relapsing fever (risk in rocky, rural livestock areas), murine typhus (probably occurs), helminthic infections (roundworm, hookworm, and whipworm infections reported occasionally from rural areas), and trichinosis.

Air pollution: Severe air-quality problems occur in Athens and other urban areas.

GRENADA

Embassy: 202-265-2561   *St. George's*   *GMT -4 hrs*

Entry Requirements
- Passport/Visa: Visa not required. Grenada has been independent from Britain since 1974.
- HIV Test: Not required.
- Vaccinations: A yellow fever vaccination certificate is required from all travelers coming from infected areas.

Telephone Area Code: 809   **AT&T:** 1-800-872-2881   **MCI:** 1-800-624-8721

Embassies/Consulates: U.S. Embassy, St. George's; Tel. (809) 440-1731.

Doctors/Hospitals: St. George's General Hospital (240 beds); general medical/surgical facility; Tel. 440-2051.

Health Advisory
See Disease Risk Summary for the Caribbean.

Malaria: No risk.

Travelers' diarrhea: Low to moderate risk. In urban and resort areas, the hotels and restaurants generally serve reliable food and potable water. Elsewhere, travelers should observe all food and drink safety precautions. A quinolone antibiotic (Floxin or Cipro) is recommended for the treatment of acute diarrhea. Diarrhea not responding to antibiotic treatment may be due to a parasitic disease such as giardiasis or amebiasis.

Hepatitis: Low overall risk to tourists. All nonimmune travelers should receive hepatitis A vaccine.

Dengue fever: This mosquito-transmitted viral disease is prevalent in the Caribbean. Travelers should take measures to prevent insect bites.

Schistosomiasis: This disease is present, but is of limited risk. Most snail-infested freshwater foci have been identified and can be avoided.

Other diseases/health threats: Brucellosis, Bancroftian filariasis (mosquito-borne; may be a threat), histoplasmosis, intestinal helminthic infections (ancylostomiasis, ascariasis, strongyloidiasis, and trichuriasis), syphilis, AIDS, toxocariasis, toxoplasmosis, tuberculosis, typhoid fever, viral encephalitis, ciguatera fish toxin poisoning (outbreaks have occurred), and swimming related hazards (jellyfish, spiny sea urchins, and coral).

World Medical Guide

GUADELOUPE (FRENCH WEST INDIES)
Embassy (France): 202-944-6000   Gosier   GMT -4 hrs

Entry Requirements
- Passport/Visa: Visa not required. Guadeloupe is a French possession (French Overseas Department).
- HIV Test: Not required.
- Vaccinations: A vaccination certificate is required of all travelers older than 1 year arriving from infected areas.

Telephone Country Code: 590
Embassies/Consulates: U.S. Embassy, French Caribbean Dept., 14 Rue Blenac, Martinique; Tel. (596) 631-303. Canadian High Commission (Trinidad); Tel. (809) 623-4787.
Hospitals/Doctors: Regional Hospital, Pointe-a-Pitre; general medical/surgical facility; numerous specialties; Tel. (8) 910-10. In Gosier: Nicole Duhamel, M.D. Tel. (84) 3562.

Health Advisory
See Disease Risk Summary for the Caribbean.
Malaria: No risk.
Travelers' diarrhea: Low to moderate risk. In urban and resort areas, the hotels and restaurants generally serve reliable food and potable water. Elsewhere, travelers should observe all food and drink safety precautions.
Hepatitis: Low risk to tourists. All nonimmune travelers should receive hepatitis A vaccine.
Dengue fever: This mosquito-transmitted viral disease is prevalent in the Caribbean. Travelers should take measures to prevent insect bites.
Leishmaniasis: Limited risk (historically) of cutaneous and visceral leishmaniasis. Travelers should take measures to prevent insect (sandfly) bites.
Schistosomiasis: This disease is present, but risk of transmission is deemed low. Most snail-infested freshwater foci have been identified and can be avoided.
Other diseases/health threats: Brucellosis, fascioliasis, filariasis (Bancroftian variety; mosquito-borne; may occur in the Lesser Antilles from Trinidad north to Guadeloupe), histoplasmosis, intestinal helminthic infections (ancylostomiasis, ascariasis, strongyloidiasis, and trichuriasis), leptospirosis, mansonellosis (vectored by *Culicoides* midges; may occur), sexually transmitted diseases, AIDS, tuberculosis, typhoid fever, viral encephalitis, ciguatera fish toxin poisoning, and swimming related hazards (jellyfish, spiny sea urchins, and coral).

GUAM (U.S. TERRITORY)
Agana   GMT +10 hrs

Entry Requirements
- Passport/Visa: Not required for U.S. citizens.
- HIV Test: Not required.
- Vaccinations: None required.

Telephone Country Code: 671
Hospitals/Doctors: Adult Care & Pediatric Clinic. Calvo's Center, Dededo. The Women's Clinic and The Good Samaritan Clinic. 416 Chalan San Antonio, Tamuning.

Health Advisory
Travelers' diarrhea: Food and water are safe in the major hotels. A quinolone antibiotic (Floxin or Cipro) is recommended for the treatment of acute diarrhea. Diarrhea not responding to antibiotic treatment may be due to a parasitic disease such as giardiasis or amebiasis—or an intestinal virus.
Hepatitis: Hepatitis A vaccine is recommended for all nonimmune travelers. The hepatitis B carrier rate in the general population of Oceania is estimated at 5.5%–15%. Vaccination against hepatitis B is recommended for long-term visitors to this country.
Tropical diseases: Filariasis, dengue fever, and Japanese encephalitis are reported. To avoid these illnesses, all travelers should take measures to prevent mosquito bites.

World Medical Guide

GUATEMALA

Embassy: 202-745-4952 **Guatemala City** **GMT -6 hrs**

Entry Requirements
- Travelers must have either a visa or a tourist card, and carry identification at all times.
- HIV Test: Not required.
- Vaccinations: A yellow fever vaccination certificate is required from travelers over 1 year of age coming from infected or endemic areas.

Telephone Country Code: 502 **AT&T:** 190 **MCI: 189**

Embassies/Consulates: U.S. Embassy, Guatemala City. Avenida de la Reforma 7-01 in Zone 10; Tel. 311-1541.

Hospitals/Doctors: Hospital Herrera Llerandi (68 beds); most specialties. Tel. (2) 36-771 or 66-775. Hospital Centro Medico (76 beds); Tel. 365061.

Health Advisory

Yellow fever: A yellow fever vaccination is recommended for travel outside urban areas.

Cholera: This disease is active in this country. Although cholera vaccination is not required for entry if arriving directly from the U.S. or Canada, it may be required if arriving from a cholera-infected area, or required for on-going travel to other countries in Latin America, Africa, the Middle East, or Asia. Travelers should consider vaccination (one dose) or a doctor's letter of exemption from vaccination.

Travelers' diarrhea: High risk. Travelers should drink only bottled, boiled, or treated water. All food should be thoroughly cooked. A quinolone antibiotic is recommended for the treatment of diarrhea. Diarrhea not responding to antibiotic treatment may be due to a parasitic disease such as giardiasis or amebiasis, which are highly endemic. Cryptosporidiosis is reported.

Malaria: Risk exists year-round countrywide below 1,500 meters elevation, except for Guatemala City and the central highland areas, which are risk-free. Incidence of malaria is highest in the Pacific lowlands, along the border with El Salvador, and in the north (Peten Department). *P. vivax* accounts for 97% of all cases. Chloroquine prophylaxis is recommended for travel to malarious areas.

Hepatitis: Hepatitis A vaccine is recommended for all nonimmune travelers. Hepatitis E has not been reported, but could occur. The hepatitis B carrier rate in the general population is estimated at 1.4% to 3.0%. Hepatitis B vaccination is recommended for long-term travelers to this country.

Dengue fever: Risk occurs year-round countrywide in urban areas at lower elevations; extensive outbreaks were reported in 1991 and 1992 in central Guatemala.

Onchocerciasis: Risk occurs near fast-flowing rivers between 300 and 1,600 meters elevation in the Pacific coast foothills and along the border with Mexico in the south. Travelers to these areas should take measures to prevent insect (blackfly) bites.

Leishmaniasis: Cutaneous leishmaniasis is reported occurring in northern departments, especially in the forested areas in Peten Department. Limited risk of visceral leishmaniasis occurs in the semiarid valleys and the foothills of east-central Guatemala in the Department of El Progresso. Travelers to these areas should take measures to prevent sandfly bites.

Schistosomiasis: No cases have been reported since 1980. Risk appears negligible.

Rabies: Travelers should avoid stray animals, especially dogs, and seek emergency treatment of any animal bite. Pre-exposure rabies vaccination (3 doses) is recommended for all persons planning a long stay (4 weeks or more) or extensive travel in rural areas.

Other diseases: Abdominal angiostrongyliasis ("eosinophilic enteritis" - cases reported from the ingestion of raw mint), anthrax, brucellosis, Chagas' disease (endemic in many rural areas), coccidiomycosis, measles, paralytic shellfish poisoning, relapsing fever (tick-borne), syphilis, typhoid fever, tuberculosis, strongyloidiasis and other helminthic infections, and typhus are reported.

World Medical Guide

GUINEA

Embassy: 202-483-9420   *Conakry*   *GMT 0 hrs*

Entry Requirements
- Passport/Visa: Valid passport and visa are required.
- HIV Test: Not required.
- Vaccinations: A yellow fever vaccination certificate is required from all travelers older than 1 year arriving from infected areas.

Telephone Country Code: 224
Embassies/Consulates: U.S. Embassy, Conakry. 2nd Boulevard & 9th Avenue. Tel. (4) 441-520/21/23/24.
Hospitals/Doctors: Donka Hospital Center, Conakry (400 beds); general medical/surgical facility. Centre Hospitalier Universitaire. Tel. 442-018/461-326.

Health Advisory

Yellow fever: This disease is active in this country, with cases reported in the northeastern region of Siguiri. Vaccination is recommended for travel to this country. This country is in the Yellow Fever Endemic Zone.

Cholera: This disease is active in this country. Although cholera vaccination is not required for entry if arriving directly from the U.S. or Canada, it may be required if arriving from a cholera-infected area, or required for on-going travel to other countries in Latin America, Africa, the Middle East, or Asia. The risk to travelers of acquiring cholera is considered low. Prevention consists primarily in adhering to safe food and drink guidelines.

Malaria: Risk is present throughout this country year-round, including urban areas. Risk is increased during and immediately after the rainy season (usually May through October). Falciparum malaria accounts for 90% of malaria cases; the rest are due to *P. malariae* or *P. ovale*. Multidrug-resistant falciparum malaria is reported. Prophylaxis with mefloquine or doxycycline is currently recommended.

Travelers' diarrhea: High risk outside of first-class hotels and resorts. All water sources should be considered potentially contaminated. Travelers should observe food and drink precautions. A quinolone antibiotic is recommended for the treatment of acute diarrhea.

Hepatitis: All susceptible travelers should receive immune globulin or hepatitis A vaccine. Hepatitis E is endemic but the level is unclear. The hepatitis B carrier rate in the general population is reported as high as 18%. Hepatitis B vaccination is recommended for all healthcare workers and long-term residents, and their families.

Onchocerciasis: Widely distributed along fast-flowing rivers in northern and central areas, particularly Faranah and Dinguiraye, and also in the southeast and the southwest. Travelers should take measures to prevent blackfly bites.

Schistosomiasis: Risk is present year-round throughout Guinea except for the coastal plain, where only Forecariah Region near the Sierra Leone border is infected. Highest infection rates occur in the regions of Gueckedou, Macenta, Faranah, and Nzerekore. Travelers should avoid swimming, bathing, or wading in freshwater lakes, ponds, or streams.

Meningitis: Sporadic outbreaks of meningococcal disease have been reported, the most recent in the Kerouane and Kissidougou Regions in early 1993 and in the Mali region in 1987. Vaccination is recommended for long-term travelers who anticipate close contact with the indigenous population of this country or surrounding regions.

Trypanosomiasis (African sleeping sickness): Limited foci reportedly exist along the coast, in northern Guinea, and in the forests of central Guinea.

AIDS: Heterosexual transmission is the predominate means of transmission. Both HIV-1 and HIV-2 occur. Current infection rates of high-risk groups is presently not available.

Other illnesses/hazards: African tick typhus, anthrax, brucellosis, dengue (low apparent risk), Bancroftian filariasis, Lassa fever (cases have been reported "in significant numbers" in Conakry), leishmaniasis (low risk; sporadic cases of cutaneous leishmaniasis were reported in the mid 1970s from the western areas), leprosy (up to 2 cases/1,000 population), rabies, toxoplasmosis, syphilis, tuberculosis (a major health problem), typhoid fever, and intestinal worms (very common).

World Medical Guide

GUINEA-BISSAU

Embassy: 202-872-4222 **Bissau** **GMT 0 hrs**

Entry Requirements
- Passport/Visa: Valid passport and visa are required.
- HIV Test: Not required.
- Vaccinations: A yellow fever vaccination certificate is required from all travelers arriving from infected areas and from all countries in the Yellow Fever Endemic Zones, including Cape Verde, Djibouti, Madagascar, and Mozambique.

Embassies/Consulates: U.S. Embassy, Bissau. Avenida Domingos Ramos. Tel. 21-2816, 21-3674. Canadian Embassy (Senegal). Tel. [221] 21-0290.

Doctors/Hospitals: Simao Mendes National Hospital, Bissau (100 beds); general medical/surgical facility; orthopedics, emergency services.

Health Advisory

Yellow fever: Vaccination is recommended. No cases are recently reported, but yellow fever is active in neighboring Guinea. Guinea-Bissau is in the Yellow Fever Endemic Zone. Although a vaccination certificate may not be required for entry to this country, one may be required for on-going travel to other countries in Africa, the Middle East, and Asia.

Cholera: This disease is active. An extensive outbreak occurred in 1987. Although cholera vaccination is not required for entry if arriving directly from the U.S. or Canada, it may be required if arriving from a cholera-infected area, or required for on-going travel to other countries in Africa, the Middle East, or Asia. The risk to travelers of acquiring cholera is considered low.

Malaria: Risk is present year-round throughout this country, including urban areas. Increased risk occurs during and immediately after the rainy season, June through October. *P. falciparum* accounts for 90% of cases, the remainder being due to *P. malariae* and *P. ovale*. Chloroquine-resistant falciparum malaria is reported. Prophylaxis with mefloquine or doxycycline is currently recommended when traveling to malarious areas.

Travelers' diarrhea: High risk. All water sources should be considered potentially contaminated. Potable water is accessible to only 30%–40% of the population. Travelers should observe all food and drink precautions. A quinolone antibiotic is recommended for the treatment of acute diarrhea.

Hepatitis: High risk. All susceptible travelers should receive immune globulin or hepatitis A vaccine. The hepatitis B carrier rate in the general population exceeds 10%. Vaccination against hepatitis B is recommended for all long-term residents and their families.

Onchocerciasis: Reported to occur in the eastern Corubal and Geba River basins. Travelers should take precautions against insect (blackfly) bites.

Schistosomiasis: Urinary schistosomiasis occurs in the northern half of Guinea Bissau, extending from the coastal region of Cacheau to the border with Guinea, including the valleys of the Cacheau and Geba River basins. Travelers should avoid swimming, bathing, or wading in freshwater streams, lakes, or ponds.

Trypanosomiasis (African sleeping sickness): Sporadic cases were reported in the 1980s. Low-level transmission probably occurs in the coastal and northcentral areas. Travelers should take measures to avoid insect (tsetse) fly bites.

Rabies: Human cases have been reported countrywide from both urban and rural areas, but exact incidence is not known. Pre-exposure vaccination (3 doses) is recommended for long-term travel (more than 4 weeks) to this country, especially for travelers going to remote rural areas.

AIDS: Heterosexual contact is the predominate mode of transmission. HIV-2 is currently the predominate infection with up to 10% of the urban population being seropositive. Highest seroprevalence rates are found in high-risk groups, such as female prostitutes. All travelers are cautioned against unsafe sex, or receiving unsterile medical or dental injections.

Other diseases: African tick typhus (transmitted by dog ticks, often in urban areas, and bush ticks), brucellosis (from consumption of raw dairy products), lassa fever (risk undetermined), leprosy, tuberculosis (a major health problem), typhoid fever, and intestinal worms (very common).

World Medical Guide

GUYANA

Embassy: 202-265-6900   *Georgetown*   *GMT -3 hrs*

Entry Requirements
- No visa or tourist card required for stays up to 30 days.
- HIV Test: Not required.
- Vaccinations: A yellow fever vaccination certificate is required from travelers arriving from infected areas or from any country in the Yellow Fever Endemic Zones of Central and South America and sub-Saharan Africa. Travelers arriving from Belize, Bolivia, Brazil, Colombia, Costa Rica, Ecuador, French Guiana, Guatemala, Honduras, Nicaragua, Panama, Peru, Suriname, and Venezuela are required to have a valid certificate. The *HealthGuide* recommends that any traveler arriving from any country in sub-Saharan Africa be in possession of a valid yellow fever certificate.

Telephone Country Code: 592   **AT&T:** 165

Embassies/Consulates: U.S. Embassy (Consular Section). 99-100 Young and Duke Streets, Kingston, Georgetown; Tel. (2) 54-900. After hours: Tel. (2) 57-963.

Hospitals/Doctors: St. Joseph Mercy Hospital, Georgetown; hospital used by embassy personnel. Davis Memorial Georgetown; used by embassy personnel. Georgetown Hospital (991 beds); government hospital; used for paramedical training.

Health Advisory

Yellow fever: No recent cases have been reported. There were unconfirmed reports of cases occurring in 1983 in the extreme south near the Brazil border. Vaccination is recommended for travel to this area. This country is in the Yellow Fever Endemic Zone. Although yellow fever vaccination may not be required for entry into this country, it may be required for on-going travel to other countries in Latin America, Africa, the Middle East, or Asia.

Cholera: This disease is active in this country. Although cholera vaccination is not required for entry if arriving directly from the U.S. or Canada, it may be required if arriving from a cholera-infected area, or required for on-going travel to other countries in Latin America, Africa, the Middle East, or Asia. Travelers should consider vaccination (one dose) or a doctor's letter of exemption from vaccination.

Malaria: Occurs year-round countrywide below 900 meters elevation. The highest risk is in the northwestern areas bordering Venezuela and in rural areas of the southern interior. In the coastal plain, including the outskirts of Georgetown, increased transmission occurs during and just after the rainy seasons (May–mid-August and November–January). There is little if any malaria in a narrow strip of coastal plain in the northeast. Falciparum malaria accounts for 60% of cases, vivax 40%. Chloroquine-resistant *P. vivax* has been reported. Prophylaxis with mefloquine or doxycycline is currently recommended in malarious areas.

Traveler's diarrhea: High risk outside of first-class hotels and resorts. Travelers are advised to drink only bottled, boiled, filtered, or treated water, and consume only well-cooked food. A quinolone antibiotic is recommended for the treatment of acute diarrhea. Diarrhea not responding to antibiotic treatment may be due to a parasitic disease such as giardiasis or amebiasis—or an intestinal virus. Cryptosporidiosis likely occurs.

Hepatitis: All nonimmune travelers should receive hepatitis A vaccine. Hepatitis E has not been reported but could occur. The hepatitis B carrier rate in the general population is less than 5%. Vaccination against hepatitis B is recommended for all healthcare workers and should be considered by anyone planning an extended visit to this country.

Leishmaniasis: Outbreaks of cutaneous leishmaniasis have occurred in military personnel. Most cases are acquired in the interior forests and savanna areas in the northeast. Visceral leishmaniasis not reported. Travelers to these areas should take measures to prevent insect (sandfly) bites.

Filariasis: Bancroftian filariasis is endemic in Georgetown and other cities in the coastal plain, with up to 10% of the population infected. Travelers should take standard precautions to prevent mosquito bites.

Other diseases/hazards: Chagas' disease (very low prevalence in the northwest district), mansonellosis (blackfly borne), onchocerciasis (regionally endemic), AIDS (HIV infects 25%

World Medical Guide

of prostitutes), paracoccidiomycosis, rabies, schistosomiasis (not reported, but occurs in neighboring Suriname), tuberculosis (incidence increased in the 1980s), typhoid fever, strongyloidiasis and other helminthic infections are reported. Animal hazards include snakes (vipers), centipedes, scorpions, black widow spiders, brown recluse spiders, banana spiders, pruning spiders, and wolf spiders. Electric eels and various carnivorous fish (including piranha) may be found in this country's fresh waters. Portuguese man-of-war, sea wasps, and stingrays are found in the coastal waters and could be a hazard to swimmers.

HAITI

Embassy: 202-322-4090   *Port-au-Prince*   *GMT -5 hrs*

Entry Requirements
- Passport/Visa: Travelers should possess valid passport. A visa is not required.
- HIV Test: Not required.
- Vaccinations: A yellow fever vaccination certificate is required from all travelers arriving from infected areas.

Telephone Country Code: 509   **AT&T:** 001-800-972-2883   **MCI:** 001-800-444-1234
Embassies/Consulates: U.S. Embassy, Port-au-Prince. Harry Truman Blvd; Tel. 22-0200. After hours: 22-0368. U.S. Consulate (Rue Oswald Durand): Tel. 23-7011 or 23-8971. Canadian Embassy, Port-au-Prince. Edifice Banque Nova Scotia. Tel: 22-2358.
Hospitals/Doctors: Rene Charles, M.D., Port-au-Prince. Bois Zerne, #15; Hospital du Canape Vert (46 beds); some specialty services; no physician on duty in emergency department; care must be pre-arranged; commonly used by U.S. Embassy personnel. Tel. 45-10-52. Hospital Adventiste de DiQuini (42 beds); private hospital; modern equipment; 24-hour emergency room physicians on duty; ambulance service.

Health Advisory

Malaria: Malaria is a major public health problem in Haiti. Risk is present countrywide year-round at elevations under 500 meters. Peak transmission occurs from September through January, with a secondary peak from April through June. There is increased risk of malaria in the northern coastal areas. Falciparum malaria accounts for 99%–100% of cases. Chloroquine-resistant falciparum malaria has not been reported. Prophylaxis with chloroquine is currently recommended.

Travelers' diarrhea: Sanitary conditions in Haiti are the poorest in the Western Hemisphere. All travelers should observe strict food and drink precautions, especially outside of resort areas. Tap water should be avoided. A quinolone antibiotic is recommended for the treatment of acute diarrhea. Diarrhea not responding to antibiotic treatment may be due to a parasitic disease such as giardiasis, amebiasis, or cryptosporidiosis.

Hepatitis: All nonimmune travelers should receive hepatitis A vaccine. The hepatitis B carrier rate in the general population is estimated at 5.5%–13%. Vaccination against hepatitis B is recommended for healthcare workers and long-term visitors to this country. Hepatitis E has not been reported but could occur.

Dengue fever: Year-round risk, increasing April through September. Dengue occurs primarily in the coastal-urban areas and is probably under-reported. To prevent dengue, travelers should take protective measures against mosquito bites.

Filariasis: Bancroftian filariasis occurs in coastal areas, primarily in the north and around the Gulf of La Gonave. Another focus is reported near Leogane. To prevent filariasis, travelers to risk areas should take protective measures against mosquito bites.

Rabies: Low apparent risk, since only occasional human cases are reported. Any unprovoked animal bite, however, should be considered a medical emergency. Rabies vaccination is recommended for anyone planning an extended stay in this country.

AIDS: High incidence of HIV infection in the general population with heterosexual and bisexual contact the predominate mode of transmission. There is also a high incidence of maternally transmitted HIV infections. HIV prevalence is estimated at 5.8% of the general population. High-risk groups have a much higher prevalence of HIV infection, with HIV prevalence of female prostitutes estimated at 69%. Tropical spastic paresis, due to the human

World Medical Guide

T-lymphotropic virus, type 1 (HTLV-1), is endemic. All travelers are cautioned against unsafe sex, unsterile medical injections, IV drug use, and blood transfusions.
Tuberculosis: A major public health problem; all medical personnel, relief workers, and others having close contact with the Haitian population should be skin tested with PPD and consider BCG vaccination.
Other diseases/health threats: Brucellosis, helminthic infections (ancylostomiasis, ascariasis, strongyloidiasis, and trichuriasis), leptospirosis, mansonellosis, relapsing fever (louse-borne), toxoplasmosis, typhoid fever (highly prevalent; vaccination recommended), viral encephalitis, and ciguatera fish toxin poisoning.

HONDURAS

Embassy: 202-223-0185   *San Pedro Sula*   *GMT -6 hrs*

Entry Requirements
- A valid passport is required.
- HIV Test: Not required.
- Vaccinations: A yellow fever vaccination certificate is required from travelers coming from infected or endemic areas.

Telephone Country Code: 504   **AT&T:** 123   **MCI:** 001-800-674-7000
Embassies/Consulates: U.S. Embassy, Tegucigalpa. Avenida La Paz; Tel. 369-320.
Hospitals/Doctors: Hospital Escuela, Tegucigalpa (400 beds); government hospital; some specialties; Tel. 322-322. JTF-Bravo Medical Element (USA Field Hospital); Tel. 31-5300/72-0454, ext. 153. Hospital Leonardo Martinez (286 beds); general medical/surgical facility; some specialties; Tel. 32-2322.

Health Advisory

Yellow fever: Yellow fever is currently not reported but vaccination is recommended for travel outside urban areas.
Cholera: This disease is active in this country. Multidrug resistant *Vibrio cholerae* has been reported. Although cholera vaccination is not required for entry if arriving directly from the U.S. or Canada, it may be required if arriving from a cholera-infected area, or required for on-going travel to other countries in Latin America. Travelers should consider vaccination (one dose) or a doctor's letter of exemption from vaccination.
Malaria: Risk occurs year-round in rural areas below 1,000 meters elevation. Most cases occur in the coastal lowlands along the border with Nicaragua. In 1993, an outbreak of malaria occurred in the vicinity of El Progresso in the extreme westcentral Yoro Province. *P. vivax* accounts for 98% of reported cases. Falciparum malaria is reported along the Nicaraguan border and in the Caribbean coastal region. In Gracias a Dios Dept. on the Caribbean coast, *P. falciparum* malaria accounts for 10% of cases. Chloroquine-resistant *P. falciparum* has not been reported. Chloroquine prophylaxis is recommended in malarious areas. Chloroquine is also recommended for travelers who will visit Ceiba, Tela, or the Bay Islands.
Travelers' diarrhea: High risk. Honduras is the least-developed country in Central America and has inadequate treatment and distribution systems for piped water. Tap water is commonly contaminated. A quinolone antibiotic is recommended for the treatment of diarrhea. Amebiasis, giardiasis, and cryptosporidiosis are reported.
Hepatitis: Hepatitis A vaccine is recommended for all nonimmune travelers. Hepatitis E has not been reported but could occur. The hepatitis B carrier rate in the population is estimated at 3%. Vaccination against hepatitis B should be considered by long-term visitors.
Dengue fever: Most outbreaks have occurred in southern Honduras, but risk of disease also occurs along the northern coast, particularly in the San Pedro Sula area. All travelers, especially to these higher risk areas, should take measures to prevent mosquito bites.
Leishmaniasis: Cutaneous and mucocutaneous leishmaniasis is widespread in rural areas, with elevated risk in the northern one-half and western one-third of the country. Visceral leishmaniasis has been reported on Tigre Island and in southern rural areas. Travelers should take measures to prevent insect (sandfly) bites.

World Medical Guide

Chagas' disease: Risk is present predominately in the southern half of the country, especially in the Tegucigalpa area. In endemic areas, up to 24% of the population is seropositive. Blood transfusions are a significant means of transmission of Chagas' disease in Honduras.

Rabies: Higher risk of dog rabies than in all other countries of Latin America, except Mexico. Travelers should seek immediate medical evaluation/treatment of any animal bite.

Other diseases: Brucellosis (limited risk in cattle raising areas), coccidiomycosis, cysticercosis, leptospirosis, measles, myiasis (caused by human bot fly), syphilis, AIDS (Honduras has the highest incidence of AIDS cases in Central America), typhoid fever, tuberculosis, strongyloidiasis and other helminthic infections, and typhus are reported.

HONG KONG (CHINA)

Embassy: 202-328-2500 *Beijing* *GMT +8 hrs*

Entry Requirements
- Passport/Visa: Travelers should possess valid passport. A visa is not required.
- HIV Test: Not required.
- Vaccinations: None required.

Telephone Country Code: 852

Embassies/Consulates: U.S. Embassy, Hong Kong. 26 Garden Road; Tel. (5) 239-011.

Hospitals/Doctors: Dr. Hans Schrader, Matilda Hospital Family Practice, The Peak; Tel. 2848-1500. Dr. John W. Simon, M.R.C.P., D.T M.&H.; The Central Medical Practice, 1501 Prince's Building; Tel. 2521-2567 or 2526-7719. George T.F. Tong, M.D., Manning House, 38 Queen's Road Central; Tel. (5) 238-295 or 813-0375 (H). Hong Kong Adventist Hospital; 24-hr. emergency service; Tel. (5) 574-6211. TST Medical Clinic, Kowloon; Tel. (3) 723-1199.

Health Advisory

Malaria: The urban area of Hong Kong is risk free. Malaria has been reported in rural northern border areas. Travelers to the northern border areas should take weekly doses of chloroquine. Chloroquine-resistant falciparum malaria has not been reported.

Travelers' diarrhea: All drinking water in Hong Kong is purified and chlorinated. In urban and resort areas, the hotels and restaurants serve reliable food and potable water. Elsewhere, travelers should observe food and drink safety precautions. Raw shellfish should be avoided. A quinolone antibiotic (Floxin or Cipro) is recommended for the treatment of acute diarrhea. Diarrhea not responding to antibiotic treatment may be due to a parasitic disease such as giardiasis or amebiasis.

Hepatitis: Outbreaks of hepatitis A usually have occurred every 2–3 years, but the incidence of hepatitis A has declined during the past decade due to improvements in sanitation. The commonest source of hepatitis A in Hong Kong is improperly cooked or raw shellfish, oysters in particular. (These are often bred in sewage-contaminated sea-beds.) To prevent hepatitis A, all nonimmune travelers should receive hepatitis A vaccine. The hepatitis B carrier rate in the general population is estimated at 10%. Vaccination against hepatitis B is recommended for healthcare workers, corporate employees, expatriates, teachers, and others (including family members) who will have close, prolonged contact with the indigenous population. Hepatitis C is endemic but only 0.5% of the population are carriers of the antibody. Hepatitis E is present in Hong Kong, but no major outbreaks have been reported.

Typhoid fever: Vaccination is recommended for those traveling more than four weeks outside of tourist or resort areas.

Dengue fever: Risk is currently negligible but outbreaks have previously occurred. The *Aedes* mosquitoes, which potentially transmit dengue, bite primarily during the daytime and are present in periurban areas as well as resort and rural areas. All travelers are advised to take measures to prevent mosquito bites.

Japanese encephalitis: Sporadic cases are reported year-round; nine cases have been reported in Hong Kong over the past 10 years. Vaccination (now available again in the United States, as well as Canada) is recommended for extended travel in this region. Travelers to Hong Kong should also take measures to prevent mosquito bites.

World Medical Guide

Scrub typhus: Risk currently exists in rural and forested areas. All travelers having contact with vegetation (e.g., along roads or forest paths) should take measures to prevent bites of larval mites (chiggers). Measures include wearing protective clothing (preferably treated with permethrin) and applying a deet repellent to exposed skin.
Other hazards/risks: Travelers should avoid swimming in local waters due to contamination by raw sewage. Hotel swimming pools are safe.

HUNGARY

Embassy: 202-362-6730 *Budapest* *GMT +1 hr*

Entry Requirements
- A visa is not required for stays up to 90 days.
- HIV Test: Not required.
- Vaccinations: None required.

Telephone Country Code: 36 **AT&T:** 00-800-01111 **MCI:** 00-800-01411
Embassies/Consulates: U.S. Embassy, Budapest. V. Szabadsag Ter 12; Tel. (1) 267-4400. After hours: Tel. (1) 269-9331.
Hospitals/Doctors: Trauma Hospital (Orszagos Traumatologiai Intezet); handles all major accidents. May Korhaz Central Railroad Hospital, Budapest (1,200 beds); general medical services available. Institute for Advanced Medical Training, Budapest (2,500 beds); most specialties, including cardiology; pediatrics.

Health Advisory

Travelers' diarrhea: Low to moderate risk. Ninety percent of the population has access to piped, treated water supplies. In urban and resort areas, the hotels and restaurants generally serve reliable food and potable water. Elsewhere, especially in rural areas, travelers should observe food and drink safety precautions. A quinolone antibiotic is recommended for the treatment of acute diarrhea. Giardiasis and amebiasis have been reported.
Hepatitis: There is a lower risk of hepatitis A in Hungary than in other eastern European countries. Hepatitis A vaccine, however, is recommended for all nonimmune travelers. Hepatitis E has not been reported, but presumably occurs. The hepatitis B carrier rate in the general population is estimated at 1%. Vaccination against hepatitis B is recommended for long-term visitors to this country. Hepatitis C is endemic.
Tick-borne diseases: Both European tick-borne encephalitis (TBE) and Lyme disease are reported, especially in the lowland forests where the tick vector, *Ixodes ricinus*, is most abundant. The highest incidence of TBE in Hungary occurs in forested areas of the three western counties neighboring Austria and Slovenia and in the northern Komarom County bordering Czechoslovakia. Most adult cases occur among male forestry workers. A vaccine is available to prevent TBE but is not routinely recommended for tourists.
Lyme disease: Fifty-eight confirmed cases were reported in 1986. To prevent Lyme disease (as well as TBE), all travelers should take measures to prevent tick bites, especially during the peak transmission period, March through September.
Rabies: Risk is present, but human cases have not been reported recently. Foxes are the main reservoir of the virus. Travelers should avoid wild animals, especially foxes and raccoons, in rural areas.
Other diseases: Anthrax (from exposure to livestock), brucellosis (from consuming unpasteurized dairy products), echinococcosis, Crimean-Congo hemorrhagic fever, cysticercosis, hemorrhagic fever with renal syndrome (sporadic cases and outbreaks), leptospirosis (from swimming or bathing in water contaminated by animal urine), tularemia, and intestinal helminthic infections (hookworm disease, strongyloidiasis, ascariasis, and trichuriasis).

ICELAND

Embassy of Iceland: 202-265-6653. U.S. Embassy, Reykjavik: (354)-562-9100

World Medical Guide

INDIA

Embassy: 202-939-9839   *New Delhi*   *GMT +5½ hrs*

Entry Requirements
- Passport/Visa: A valid passport and visa are required.
- HIV Test: Required for foreign students over 18 years of age and those staying beyond 1 year. Travelers should contact the Indian Embassy for further information.
- Vaccinations: India requires a yellow fever vaccination certificate from all travelers arriving from any country any part of which is infected, as well as from many countries in the Yellow Fever Endemic Zones, including Trinidad & Tobago. The *HealthGuide* recommends that all travelers arriving from any country in sub-Saharan Africa, or from Central or South America, have a valid yellow fever vaccination certificate in their possession.

Cholera: A valid certificate of vaccination against cholera (or a letter of exemption from vaccination) is recommended for all travelers to India who will be proceeding to other countries in Asia, Africa, or the Middle East.

Telephone Country Code: 91   **AT&T:** 000-117
Embassies/Consulates: U.S. Embassy, New Delhi. Shanti Path, Chanakyapuri; Tel. (11) 688-9033. American Consulates: Bombay; Tel. (22) 363-3611. Calcutta; Tel. (033) 22-3611. Madras; Tel. (44) 827-3040.
Hospitals/Doctors: Irwin Hospital, New Delhi (1,173 beds); most specialties; Tel. 275-071. East-West Medical Center, New Delhi; Tel. 623-738. J.J. Hospital, Bombay (1,272 beds); most specialties, including orthopedics. The Bombay Hospital Centre; Tel. 297-100. Woodlands Hospital & Medical Center, Calcutta (preferred for private patients); Tel. 479-1951. Dr. Santanu Chatterjee, Wellesley Medicentre, Calcutta; Tel. 29-9920.

Health Advisory

Yellow fever: No risk.
Cholera: This disease is active in this country. Although cholera vaccination is not required for entry to India if arriving directly from the U.S. or Canada, it may be required if arriving from infected countries, or required for on-going travel to other countries in Latin America, Africa, the Middle East, or Asia. Depending upon their itinerary, travelers should consider vaccination or a doctor's letter of exemption from vaccination. The risk to travelers of acquiring cholera is low. Prevention consists in adhering to safe food and drink guidelines.
NOTE: A new strain of epidemic cholera has appeared in the Bay of Bengal. It is not prevented by the cholera vaccine in current use.
Malaria: Risk of malaria is present countrywide year-round, excluding high altitude areas (above 2,000 meters elevation) of the states of Himachal Pradesh, Jammu and Kashmir, and Sikkim. Malaria risk occurs year-round in the tropical cities of Bombay, Calcutta, and Madras. Malaria risk in the more temperate New Delhi is seasonal, with the major risk being from July to November, peaking in September. The incidence of malaria has increased recently in Delhi, Tamil Nadu State, and Haryana State. The most intense malaria transmission in India occurs in the eastern and northeastern states. Large outbreaks of falciparum malaria occurred during 1994 in Rajasthan State and during 1995 and 1996 in Assam State and had high fatality rates due to chloroquine-resistant falciparum malaria. Chloroquine-resistant vivax malaria has also been reported in this country. *P. vivax* malaria accounts for 60%–65% of cases countrywide; *P. falciparum* accounts for the remainder.
Travelers' diarrhea: High risk year-round, countrywide. Risk is higher in rural villages. Water supplies are frequently obtained from wells which commonly are contaminated. Untreated sewage, industrial wastes, and agricultural runoffs contaminate most of India's rivers. Piped water supplies throughout India are quite limited and all water should be considered nonpotable. Travelers should observe food and drink safety precautions, especially outside major hotels and resorts. A water filter with an iodine resin attachment is recommended when traveling outside of resort/hotel areas. A quinolone antibiotic is recommended for the treatment of acute diarrhea. Diarrhea not responding to antibiotic treatment may be due to a parasitic disease such as giardiasis, amebiasis, or cryptosporidiosis. The incidence of cryptosporidiosis is reported to be 14% among patients with chronic diarrhea. Amebiasis in-

fection rates up to 84% have been reported in northern India and amebic liver abscess is a serious problem in many areas. Giardiasis infection rates of 21%–62% are reported.

Hepatitis: All nonimmune travelers should receive hepatitis A vaccine. The hepatitis B carrier rate in the general population is estimated at 5%. Vaccination against hepatitis B should be considered by anyone planning an extended visit to this country. Hepatitis E is the most common form of hepatitis in adults in India and accounts for 70% of sporadic acute viral hepatitis and 95% of "epidemic" hepatitis. Most cases are transmitted by sewage-contaminated water in rural areas. A vaccine against hepatitis E is not available. Travelers can reduce their risk of illness by drinking only boiled, bottled, or chemically treated water. Hepatitis C is endemic and the hepatitis C carrier rate is estimated at 1%.

Typhoid fever: Highly endemic. Vaccination is recommended.

Dengue fever: Periodic epidemics of dengue and dengue hemorrhagic fever occur in urban and semi-rural areas countrywide below 1,000 meters elevation, with most outbreaks occurring in the north-central states. New Delhi reported a severe epidemic in 1996 with 400 deaths from dengue hemorrhagic fever and dengue shock syndrome. Relatively few cases are reported from the western states. In southern areas, the of risk of dengue is year-round. In the northern states, the risk is elevated from April through November. To prevent dengue, travelers should take measures to prevent mosquito bites.

Japanese encephalitis: This disease occurs year-round, except in northern India, where the risk is primarily April–November. The risk is low in the western states. Only sporadic cases occur in the southern states. Most Japanese encephalitis occurs along the eastern coastal states, the northern states bordering Nepal, the northeastern states, and the southwestern state of Kerala. The disease has spread into Uttar Pradesh, with yearly epidemics reported. The culex mosquito transmits this disease, mostly in rural areas below 1,000 meters elevation. Vaccination against Japanese encephalitis is recommended for travelers who will be staying more than 2–4 weeks in rural-agricultural endemic areas during the peak transmission period. In addition, all travelers should take personal protection measures against mosquito bites, especially in the evening.

Leishmaniasis: Cases of visceral leishmaniasis occur in large numbers in rural areas of the eastern states, but this disease is also reported from northern Bihar State. Sporadic cases of cutaneous leishmaniasis have been reported in the western states along the Pakistani-Indian border. Most cases of cutaneous leishmaniasis occur in adults in urban or periurban hutment areas (slums). Travelers should take measures to prevent insect (sandfly) bites.

Filariasis: Mosquito-borne. Bancroftian filariasis is widespread in southern, central, and northern India, especially in Uttar Pradesh and Bihar States. Malayan filariasis occurs in southern India, especially Kerala State. The risk to tourists is low. All travelers, however, should take standard measures to prevent mosquito bites.

Schistosomiasis: There is a negligible risk of schistosomiasis in India. A focus may occur in Gimvi village along the western coast in Maharashtra State.

Meningitis: Increased risk of meningococcal meningitis (types A and C) is reported in the New Delhi region and adjacent southern areas (Madhya Pradesh State). There is increased risk in rural areas and urban slums. Risk may be elevated during the cooler months, November–April. Because sporadic meningitis outbreaks occur countrywide, vaccination is recommended for all travelers planning extended travel in India.

Plague: Outbreaks of plague occurred in western India in 1994. This epidemic was declared over as of 1996.

AIDS/HIV: With a population nearing one billion and an estimated four million HIV-infected people, India is now considered the country that has the largest number of people infected with HIV in the world. HIV has spread beyound high-risk groups and is now firmly embedded in the Indian population and is fast spreading into rural areas. Commercial sex workers continue play a critical part in the heterosexual spread of HIV, which is the dominant mode of transmission in India. In Bombay, over 60% of commercial sex workers are HIV-positive. The second most important mode of transmission is through infected blood and blood products. All travelers are cautioned against unsafe sex, receiving medical or dental injections with equipment of questionable sterility, and unnecessary blood transfusions.

Rabies: This country has the highest reported incidence of dog rabies in the world. More than 25,000 human cases occur annually. Travelers should seek immediate treatment of any animal bite. Rabies vaccination is indicated following the unprovoked bite of a dog, cat, bat, or monkey. Bites by other animals should be considered on an individual basis. Rabies vaccination is recommended for anyone planning long-term travel to this country. Rabies vaccine (Verorab) is widely available in India.

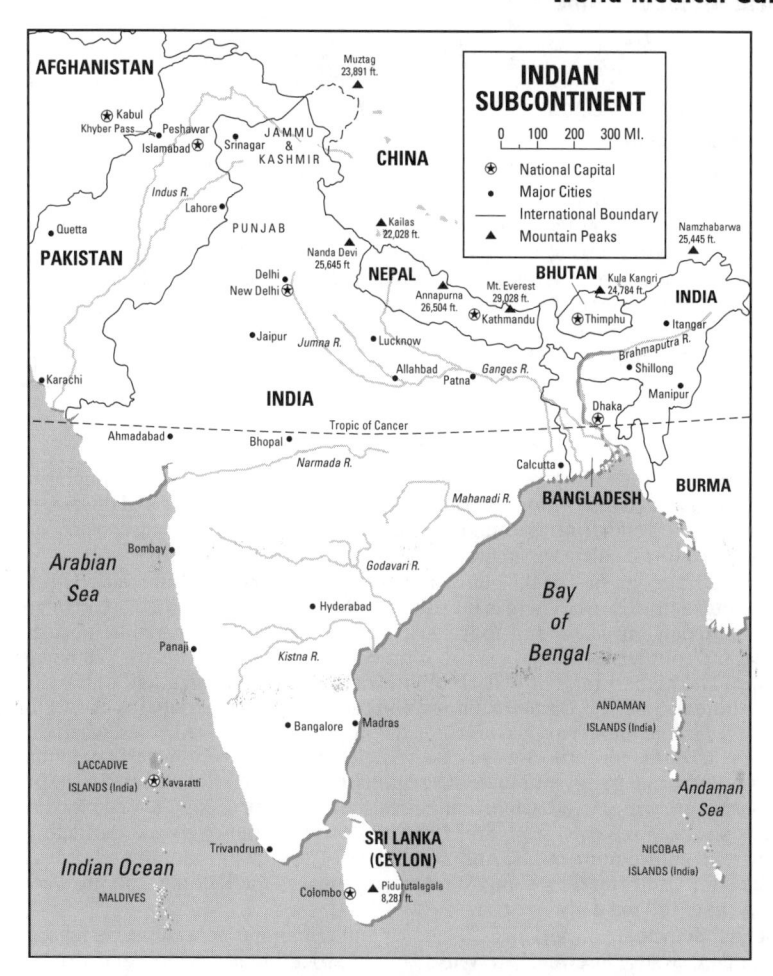

Other diseases/health threats: Anthrax, angiostrongyliasis (human cases from ingesting raw snails, slugs, prawns, fish, land crabs, and vegetables), brucellosis, Crimean-Congo hemorrhagic fever, cysticercosis (neurocysticercosis causes 2% of epileptic seizures in this country), dracunculiasis (reported only from Rajasthan State), echinococcosis, Kyasanur Forest disease (tick-borne arboviral fever; risk elevated during the dry season), leprosy, leptospirosis, Indian tick typhus (reported in southern India), helminthic infections (ascariasis, ancylostomiasis, trichuriasis, and strongyloidiasis are prevalent), leptospirosis, melioidosis, paragonimiasis (human cases from ingesting raw crabs), scabies, polio (all travelers should be fully immunized), trachoma (widespread in rural areas), tuberculosis (highly endemic; 2% of population infected), typhus (both murine and scrub typhus occur), and West Nile fever. Animal hazards include snakes (kraits, cobras, coral snakes, vipers), scorpions, spiders, and leeches (abundant in the streams, marshes, and jungles). Stingrays, sea wasps, cones, jellyfish, urchins, and anemones are common in India's coastal waters and are potential hazards to unprotected swimmers.

World Medical Guide

INDONESIA

Embassy: 202-775-5200　　　*Jakarta*　　　*GMT +7 to +9 hrs*

Entry Requirements
- No visa is required for tourist/business trips of less than two months.
- HIV Test: Not required.
- Vaccinations: A yellow fever vaccination certificate is required of all travelers arriving from infected areas or from any country in the Yellow Fever Endemic Zones.
Cholera: A vaccination certificate may be required of a traveler who is departing Indonesia for a country where cholera is reported active.

Telephone Country Code: 62
Embassies/Consulates: U.S. Embassy, Jakarta. Medan Merdeka Selatan 5; Tel. (21) 344-2211. U.S. Consulate, Surabaya; Tel. (31) 568-2287. U.S. Consul, Bali: Tel. (361)-233-605.

Health Advisory

Cholera: This disease is not reported officially active by the WHO and CDC, but historically cholera has plagued this country. All travelers should assume there is risk of disease and take appropriate food and drink precautions. The risk to travelers of acquiring cholera, however, is considered low. Cholera vaccination is not routinely recommended.

Malaria: About one-half of the population is at risk of exposure, but relatively few travelers acquire the disease. There is no risk of malaria in the major metropolitan areas of Jakarta, Medan, Surabaya, and Yogyakarta and the main resort and tourist beach areas of Java and southern Bali. Malaria risk is primarily in rural areas below 1,200 meters elevation. The highest rates of malaria are in Irian Jaya (the western half of the island of New Guinea), Sulawesi, Sumatra, Flores, and the Kokap Subdistrict area of Java. In Java and Bali, *Plasmodium vivax* accounts for the majority of reported cases, whereas *P. falciparum* accounts for 30%–50% of cases. Elsewhere, falciparum malaria predominates 2:1 over vivax malaria in mountainous regions. Chloroquine- and Fansidar-resistant *P. falciparum* are widespread. Chloroquine-resistant *P. vivax* occurs in a patchy distribution. It has been reported from Sumatra and Irian Jaya, but *P. vivax* appears to be still sensitive to chloroquine in Java and Lombok as of 1997. The recommended drug prophylaxis for adult travelers going to malarious areas is mefloquine, 250 mg weekly, or doxycycline, 100 mg daily.

Travelers' diarrhea: In resort areas, the hotels and restaurants generally serve reliable food and potable water. Elsewhere, travelers should strictly observe food and drink safety precautions. A quinolone antibiotic is recommended for the treatment of acute diarrhea. Diarrhea not responding to treatment with an antibiotic, or chronic diarrhea, may be due to a parasitic disease such as giardiasis or amebiasis. Cryptosporidiosis is reported, occurring mostly in children, with the highest incidence during the rainy season. Cryptosporidiosis is associated with contact with animals (mostly cats), contaminated water, and crowded living conditions.

Hepatitis: There is a high risk of hepatitis A in this country. All nonimmune travelers should receive hepatitis A vaccine. Outbreaks of hepatitis E have been reported in West Kalimantan and the virus is assumed to be widespread. The hepatitis B carrier rate in the general population is estimated at 8%–10%. Vaccination against hepatitis B is recommended for healthcare workers, corporate employees, expatriates, relief workers, teachers, and others who will have close, prolonged contact with the indigenous population.

Typhoid fever: There is a relatively high risk of typhoid fever in Indonesia. Vaccination is recommended for all travelers staying in this country longer than 2–3 weeks, or traveling outside the usual tourist sites or resorts. All travelers should meticulously follow safe food and drink guidelines.

Dengue fever: Year-round risk, elevated during the rainy season from November through April. Risk is higher in densely populated urban areas where mosquitoes breed in stagnant pools of water. The highest incidence of dengue is in East Java. Dengue hemorrhagic fever is common.

World Medical Guide

Japanese encephalitis: Cases of Japanese encephalitis occur throughout the Indonesian archipelago, but the risk of illness is generally low. Most cases are reported from East Java, followed by Lombok, Kalimantan, and Sumatra. The peak transmission period is from October through April (the rainy season). Vaccination against Japanese encephalitis is recommended for travelers who will be staying in rural-agricultural endemic areas for 2–4 weeks or more during the peak transmission season. In addition, all travelers should take personal protection measures against mosquito bites, especially in the evening when culex mosquitoes are most active.

Filariasis: Highly endemic. The Bancroftian and Malayan varieties of this disease are transmitted by mosquitoes in both urban and rural environments. Travelers should take measures to prevent mosquito bites.

Schistosomiasis: Risk is present year-round in the Lindu and Napu Valleys of central Sulawesi. Travelers to these areas should avoid swimming, bathing, or wading in freshwater lakes, ponds, or streams.

Rabies: Significant risk occurs in rural as well as urban areas of this country. About 75 human cases are officially reported annually. All animal bites, but especially dog bites, should be considered a medical emergency. Pre-exposure vaccination against rabies is recommended for long-term travel to this country. This is especially true for travelers going to remote rural areas if they will be unable to receive antirabies treatment within 24 hours of exposure to a potentially rabid animal.

World Medical Guide

AIDS: Cases have been reported, but HIV testing is erratic, and HIV seroprevalence data are generally lacking. Travelers should assume that the incidence of HIV is increasing in this region, as it is in many other parts of Asia.

Other diseases/health threats: Angiostrongyliasis (from ingesting raw seafood, snails, or vegetables), anthrax (low risk; seen mostly in farm workers), brucellosis, capillariasis (from eating raw fish, especially fresh catch, crab, squid), paragonimiasis (associated with eating raw freshwater crabs and crayfish), clonorchiasis (isolated cases reported; associated with eating raw freshwater fish or crayfish), cysticercosis (outbreaks may have occurred on Irian Jaya), echinococcosis, influenza (vaccination advised, especially for travelers over age 65), leprosy (highly endemic), leptospirosis, polio (only 12 cases reported in 1995), relapsing fever (tickborne), scrub typhus (year-round in grassy, rural areas), tuberculosis (highly endemic, although not a major risk for travelers. Long-term visitors should get a PPD skin test;) TB is the leading cause of death of people between the ages of 15 and 45), helminthic infections (ascariasis, trichuriasis, hookworm disease, strongyloidiasis; up to 90% of population infected in some areas), and yaws (decreasing, but still significant in Sumatra, Kalimantan, and Irian Jaya). Animal hazards include snakes (kraits, cobras, pit vipers), spiders, scorpions, tarantulas, crocodiles, panthers, bears, wild pigs, and wild cattle. Stingrays, jellyfish, sea wasps, poisonous fish (multiple species), and the Indo-Pacific man-of-war are common in the country's coastal waters and are potential hazards to careless or unprotected swimmers.

IRAN

Interests Section: 202-965-4990   *Tehran*   *GMT +3½ hrs*

Entry Requirements
- Passport/Visa: A valid passport and visa required.
- HIV Test: Not required.
- Vaccinations: No vaccinations required, but cholera recommended to avoid entry delays.

Telephone Country Code: 98

Embassies/Consulates: The U.S. government does not maintain diplomatic relations with Iran. American interests are represented by the Swedish Embassy; Tel. 675-011 or 675-020.

Hospitals/Doctors: Local medical facilities are substantially below Western standards and should be used by U.S. citizens only in the case of emergency.

Health Advisory

Cholera: This disease is reported active. Vaccination is recommended.

Malaria: Risk is present in various areas. Transmission occurs year-round in the southwest, south, and southeast, but only during the summer in the north and northeast. Malaria is endemic in approximately one-third of the land area of Iran, in the southwest and south (along the Persian Gulf, south of the Zagros mountains), in the southeast (Sistan-Baluchistan), and in the north and northeast (along the Caspian Sea and south of the border with the former USSR). Malaria transmission occurs in rural areas at elevations up to 1,500 meters. Transmission may occur in urban areas in the south and southwest. Other urban areas (including Tehran) are risk free. The majority of malaria cases occur in the southwest, south, and southeast (Sistan-Baluchestan, Kerman, and Hormozgan Provinces). Falciparum malaria accounts for 25% of the cases in the southeast and 5% to 10% of the cases in the southwest and south. Vivax malaria accounts for the rest of the cases. Chloroquine-resistant falciparum malaria is reported. Prophylaxis with mefloquine or doxycycline is currently recommended when traveling to malarious areas.

Hepatitis: All nonimmune travelers should receive hepatitis A vaccine prior to visiting this country. The hepatitis B carrier rate in the general population is estimated at 4%. Vaccination against hepatitis B is recommended for all healthcare workers and should be considered by anyone planning an extended visit to this country.

Leishmaniasis: Cutaneous leishmaniasis occurs throughout Iran in the rural and semirural areas at the margins of deserts throughout the country. Visceral leishmaniasis (kala azar) is widespread (except for the arid zones in the southeast and deserts), particularly in Fars,

World Medical Guide

Azarbbayjan-e Khavari, and the northeastern Khorasan provinces. Travelers to these areas should take protective measures against sandfly bites.

Filariasis: Reported in the southeastern province of Baluchistan-Sistan where the mosquito vector is present. Travelers to these areas should take measures to prevent mosquito bites.

Schistosomiasis: Transmission occurs year-round and increases in the spring rainy seasons, March to May. Distribution is focal along a branch of the Rud-e Karun River, between Ahvaz and Dezful, in the western province of Khuzestan. Travelers to these areas should avoid swimming or wading in freshwater ponds, lakes, or streams.

Rabies: Animal rabies is common in the wolf and stray dog population. Twenty to 50 human rabies cases occur annually, usually in rural villages.

Other illnesses: Brucellosis, Crimean-Congo hemorrhagic fever (tick-transmitted; most cases reported from East Azerbaijan and areas near the Caspian Sea), echinococcosis, north Asian tick typhus, flea-borne typhus, tick-borne relapsing fever, tuberculosis, and helminthic infections.

IRAQ
Baghdad   *GMT +3 hrs*

Entry Requirements
- Passport/Visa: Valid passport and visa required. Tourist visas not issued.
- HIV Test: Testing required for visits lasting 5 days or more. Contact the Iraqi Embassy in Washington (202-483-7500) for details.
- Vaccinations: A yellow fever vaccination certificate is required of travelers arriving from infected areas.

Telephone Country Code: 964
Operator-assisted calls only

Embassies/Consulates: American Embassy, Baghdad. Opposite Foreign Ministry Club (Masbah Quarter); Tel. (1) 719-6138/9. Canadian Embassy; Tel. (1) 542-1459.

Health Advisory

Malaria: Occurs in northern Iraq. Risk areas include rural and urban areas in the northern provinces of Dahuk, Ninawa, Irbil, Tamin, and As Sulaymaniyah below 1,500 meters elevation. Small, scattered, sporadic outbreaks probably occur in the southern and central areas from the Tigris-Euphrates River basin to the border with Iran. Nearly all cases of malaria in Iraq are currently of the vivax variety. Chloroquine-resistant falciparum malaria has not been reported. There is no malaria in Baghdad. Travelers to risk areas are advised to take weekly chloroquine and avoid mosquito bites.

Travelers' diarrhea: High risk. There is a high incidence of shigellosis and salmonellosis in this country. Travelers should drink only bottled, boiled, or treated water. All food should be well cooked. A quinolone antibiotic is recommended for the treatment of acute diarrhea. Diarrhea not improving with antibiotic treatment may be due to a parasitic disease such as amebiasis or giardiasis.

Hepatitis: All nonimmune travelers should receive hepatitis A vaccine prior to visiting this country. The hepatitis B carrier rate in the general population is estimated at 4%. Vaccination against hepatitis B is recommended for anyone planning an extended visit to this country.

Leishmaniasis: Cutaneous leishmaniasis occurs commonly in the central regions, sporadically in the north, and is rare in the south. Visceral leishmaniasis (kala azar) occurs in the central region, with most cases reported from December through March. Travelers to these areas should take measures to prevent insect (sandfly) bites.

Schistosomiasis: Risk occurs near the Tigris and Euphrates Rivers, especially in the central regions. No transmission occurs south of Basra. Travelers should avoid swimming or wading in freshwater ponds, lakes, or streams in risk areas.

Other illnesses: Boutonneuse fever (infrequently reported), brucellosis (usually transmitted by raw goat or camel milk), Crimean-Congo hemorrhagic fever (tick-borne; the virus is also transmitted through exposure to livestock), dengue fever (may occur in

World Medical Guide

southern regions), echinococcosis (carried by stray dogs; reported sporadically from rural and urban areas), rabies (transmitted by jackals, foxes, and dogs), relapsing fever (louse-borne; endemic in northern Iraq), sandfly fever (risk may be limited to the southwestern border with Saudi Arabia), trachoma, tuberculosis, typhus (flea-borne; sporadic cases in southern areas), typhoid fever, and helminthic infections (roundworm, hookworm, and whipworm infections are common).

IRELAND

Embassy: 202-462-3939 *Dublin* GMT 0 hrs

Entry Requirements
- Passport/Visa: Passport required.
- HIV Test: Not required.
- Vaccinations: None required.

Telephone Country Code: 353 **AT&T:** 1-800-550-000 **MCI:** 1-800-55-1001

Embassies/Consulates: U.S. Embassy, Dublin. 42 Elgin Road, Ballsbridge; Tel. (1) 688-777. Canadian Embassy; Tel. (1) 781-988.

Hospitals/Doctors: Our Lady's Hospital for Sick Children, Dublin (pediatrics); Tel. 558-511 or 800-365. Consultant's Clinic, Dublin (OB/GYN); Tel. 544-506. St. Jane's Hospital, Dublin (595 beds); all specialties; 4-bed ICU unit. Tel. 532-867/8. W.A. Ryan M.D., Dublin; Tel. (1) 2691-581. Blackrock Clinic, Rock Road, Blackrock Co. Dublin; Tel. 883-364. Charlemont Clinic, Dublin (Professor Risteard Mulcahy, cardiology); Tel. 784-277.

Health Advisory

Travelers' diarrhea: Low risk. Water throughout Ireland is potable. Cryptosporidiosis and giardiasis are endemic at low levels. Incidence of amebiasis is not known but presumed low.

Hepatitis: Low risk. Hepatitis A vaccine is not routinely recommended. The carrier rate of the hepatitis B virus in the general population is less than 0.5 percent. Hepatitis E has not been reported.

Lyme disease: Endemic level undetermined but clinical cases reportedly occur among all age groups, usually during the summer months. *Ixodes ricinus* tick population peaks in May and September. Travelers to rural areas should take measures to prevent tick bites, especially in brushy, wooded, and forested areas.

Other diseases: Hemorrhagic fever with renal syndrome (no cases currently reported although virus appears to be circulating in the rodent population of Ireland), leptospirosis (acquired through contact with infective animal urine, often when swimming in polluted water), leptospirosis (human infection from exposure to livestock), and Q fever (rare cases in humans).

ISRAEL

Embassy: 202-364-5500 *Jerusalem* GMT +2 hrs

Entry Requirements
- Entry requirements: An onward or return ticket, and proof of sufficient funds, is required for entry to Israel. A 3-month visa may be issued for no charge on arrival. No visa is required for travel to the Gaza Strip.
- Vaccinations: None required.

Telephone Country Code: 972 **AT&T:** 177-100-2727 **MCI:** 177-150-2727

Embassies/Consulates: The U.S. Embassy, Tel Aviv. 71 Hayarkon St., Tel. (3) 517-4338. United States Consulate in Jerusalem: Tel. (2) 253-288.

Hospitals/Doctors: Herzliya Medical Centers, Haifa and Tel Aviv. Official referral hospitals for the Multinational Forces in Sinai; the Haifa facility can do open heart procedures; both of these prestigious private hospitals also accept Blue Cross/Blue Shield payments; in Haifa, Tel. (4) 305-222; in Tel Aviv, Tel. (9) 592-554/5; Chaim Sheba Medical Center, Tel Aviv (1,500 beds); all specialties; emergency room; Tel. (3) 530-530. Ichilov Municipal Hospital, Tel Aviv

World Medical Guide

ISRAEL

0 — 25 — 50 MI.

- ✪ National Capital
- • Major Cities
- — International Boundary
- ▨ Areas Occupied by Israel Since 1967
- ▲ Mountain Peaks

Mediterranean Sea

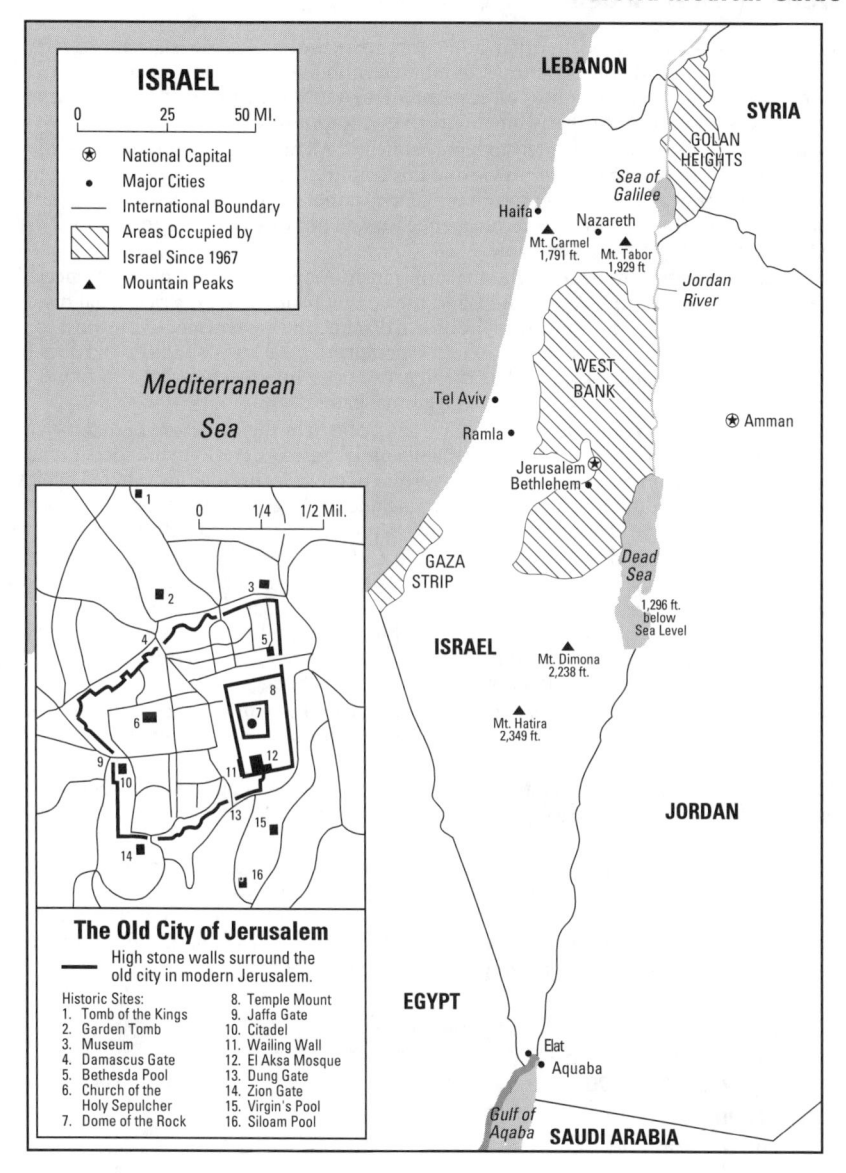

LEBANON
SYRIA
GOLAN HEIGHTS
Sea of Galilee
Haifa
Nazareth
Mt. Carmel 1,791 ft.
Mt. Tabor 1,929 ft.
Jordan River
Tel Aviv
WEST BANK
Ramla
✪ Amman
Jerusalem ✪
Bethlehem
GAZA STRIP
Dead Sea
1,296 ft. below Sea Level
ISRAEL
Mt. Dimona 2,238 ft.
Mt. Hatira 2,349 ft.
JORDAN
EGYPT
Elat
Aquaba
Gulf of Aqaba
SAUDI ARABIA

The Old City of Jerusalem

High stone walls surround the old city in modern Jerusalem.

Historic Sites:
1. Tomb of the Kings
2. Garden Tomb
3. Museum
4. Damascus Gate
5. Bethesda Pool
6. Church of the Holy Sepulcher
7. Dome of the Rock
8. Temple Mount
9. Jaffa Gate
10. Citadel
11. Wailing Wall
12. El Aksa Mosque
13. Dung Gate
14. Zion Gate
15. Virgin's Pool
16. Siloam Pool

(public hospital; 500 beds); all specialties; emergency room; Tel. (3) 697-4444. Hadassah-Hebrew Medical Center, Jerusalem (680 beds); Tel. (2)427-427. Rothschild Hadassah University Hospital, Jerusalem (680 beds); all specialties. Rambam Medical Center, Haifa (850 beds); all specialties; Soroka University Hospital, Beer-Sheva (700 beds); Tel. 660-485.

Health Advisory

Malaria: No risk.

Cholera: Cases reported in the Gaza Strip.

Travelers' diarrhea: Medium risk. Although the risk of bacterial gastroenteritis is lower than in the neighboring Arab countries, it is markedly higher than in Europe. Tap water may be contaminated. Shigellosis both occurs sporadically and in large outbreaks. Amebiasis occurs infrequently. Travelers are advised to drink only bottled, filtered, or treated water and con-

World Medical Guide

sume only well-cooked food. In urban and resort areas, the hotels and restaurants generally serve reliable food and potable water. A quinolone antibiotic is recommended for the treatment of acute diarrhea. Diarrhea not responding to antibiotic treatment may be due to a parasitic disease such as giardiasis, amebiasis, or cryptosporidiosis.

Hepatitis: Hepatitis A is moderately to highly endemic. All nonimmune travelers should receive the hepatitis A vaccine prior to visiting this country. Hepatitis E may occur, but levels are unclear. The hepatitis B carrier rate in the general population is estimated at less than 1%. Vaccination against hepatitis B is recommended for all persons planning an extended visit to this country. Hepatitis C is endemic.

Mediterranean spotted fever: Highest risk of transmission is in southern Israel, especially the northwest part of the Negev desert and the coastal plain area. This rickettsial disease (caused by R. conorii) is transmitted by the brown dog tick and has emerged as the most common insect-borne disease in Israel. Travelers, especially to rural areas, should avoid dogs (as well as sheep and goats), which harbor the infective ticks. Infective ticks are also found on grass and around hay stacks, and along wild animal paths.

Tick-borne relapsing fever (cave fever): Cave fever, caused by the spirochete Borrelia persica, is transmitted in rural areas by ticks that inhabit animal burrows, cracks in boulders, archeological sites, caves, tombs, and bunkers. Ten percent of the caves in Israel are infested by ticks (55% infested in the lower Galilee). Risk areas include the Negev, the West Bank, the coastal plain, and the northern areas. Treatment, as well as prophylaxis, with tetracycline, is effective.

Leishmaniasis: Focally distributed countrywide. Cutaneous leishmaniasis is present in the Jordan Valley, particularly from the northern Dead Sea region to Massua; other risk areas include the wadis of the Negev Desert (including Keziot), the Arava Valley, and Samaria. Visceral leishmaniasis is reported in the Judean foothills of central Israel and the Galilee Region of northern Israel. Peak transmission of leishmaniasis occurs between April and October. Travelers should take measures to prevent insect (sandfly) bites.

Schistosomiasis: This disease is apparently no longer a threat in Israel. Urinary schistosomiasis was once endemic in the Jordan River, but no recent indigenous cases have been reported.

Rabies: Incidence of rabies in animals, especially foxes, is increasing, but no recent human cases of rabies have been reported. Travelers should seek immediate medical attention for any dog or wild animal bite.

Other illnesses: Anthrax, brucellosis (usually transmitted by raw goat/sheep milk; common cause of fever in humans), echinococcosis (carried by a small percentage of rural dogs; low incidence in humans; more common in northern areas), leptospirosis (human cases frequently reported), tuberculosis, typhoid fever, West Nile fever, and helminthic infections (due to roundworms, hookworms, and whipworms; low incidence).

ITALY

Embassy: 202-328-5500   *Rome*   *GMT +1 hr*

Entry Requirements
- Passport/Visa: Passport required.
- HIV Test: Not required.
- Vaccinations: None required.

Telephone Country Code: 39   **AT&T:** 172-1011   **MCI:** 172-1022

Embassies/Consulates: U.S. Embassy, Rome. Via Veneto 119/A; Tel. (6) 46-741. U.S. Consulate, Florence; Tel. (55) 239-8276 or 217-605.

Hospitals/Doctors: Ospedale S. Camillo de Lellis, Rome (3,461 beds); all specialties available. Medical Diagnostic Center, Rome. Ospedale Maggiore di Milano, Milan; all specialties; 24-hour emergency.

Health Advisory

Travelers' diarrhea: Low risk in major cities, such as Rome, Milan, and Verona, where the water supplies are adequately treated. Higher risk exists in the south and on the islands of Sicily and Sardinia. A quinolone antibiotic is recommended for the treatment of acute diar-

World Medical Guide

rhea. Diarrhea not responding to antibiotic treatment may be due to a parasitic disease such as giardiasis. Amebiasis is uncommon in Italy. Cryptosporidiosis is reported.

Hepatitis: Increased risk of hepatitis A occurs in the south and on the islands of Sicily and Sardinia. All nonimmune travelers should receive hepatitis A vaccine. The overall carrier rate hepatitis B in the general population is estimated at 2.5%. Hepatitis E and C are endemic.

Tick-borne diseases: Lyme disease, tick-borne encephalitis (TBE), and boutonneuse fever (Mediterranean spotted fever) are reported. Risk areas for Lyme disease are limited primarily to northern Italy—along the Ligurian coast, and the Adriatic coast. TBE has been reported around Florence, near the Swiss border and from the Trento area. Boutonneuse fever occurs countrywide in rural areas but is more common along the Ligurian coast and the islands of Sicily and Sardinia. Travelers to all these regions should take measures to prevent tick bites.

Leishmaniasis: Cutaneous and visceral leishmaniasis occur in southern rural areas, including the islands of Sardinia and Sicily and along the Mediterranean coast; risk from visceral leishmaniasis is elevated in Sicily and the Campania Region. Transmission occurs May through November, peaking in July–August. Travelers to risk areas should take measures to prevent insect (sandfly) bites.

Dirofilariasis: Human dirofilariasis reported from the Monferrato area. Other risk areas include Torino, Allessandria, Vercelli, and Pavia. The parasite is transmitted to humans by mosquito bites.

Legionnaire's disease: Six cases of Legionnaire's disease occurred in tourists who visited the Island of Ischia (near Naples) in 1989 and 1990. Source of the bacteria was thought to be contaminated water supplied by three hotels; municipal thermal baths were another possible source of infection.

Rabies: No human cases have recently been reported, but animal rabies occurs in the fox population near the Austrian border.

Other illnesses: Anthrax, brucellosis, echinococcosis (elevated risk in the south and on Sardinia), hemorrhagic fever with renal syndrome, listeriosis, leptospirosis, Q fever, sandfly fever, strongyloidiasis, typhoid fever, tularemia (exposure to wild boar meat and uncooked pork), and tuberculosis.

IVORY COAST (COTE D'IVOIRE)

Embassy: 202-797-0300   *Abidjan*   GMT 0 hrs

Entry Requirements
- Passport/Visa: Valid passport and visa are required.
- HIV Test: Not required.
- Vaccinations: A yellow fever vaccination certificate is required from all travelers more than one year of age arriving from ALL COUNTRIES.

Telephone Country Code: 225

Embassies/Consulates: U.S. Embassy, Abidjan. 5 Rue Jesse Owens; Tel. 21-09-79. Canadian Embassy. Edifice Trade Center; Tel. 32-20-09.

Hospitals/Doctors: Treichville University Hospital, Abidjan (1,500 beds); general medical/surgical facility; most specialties. Polyclinic International St. Ann Marie, Cocody (300 beds); general medical/surgical facility; emergency room; dialysis; heliport. Travelers should contact the U.S. Embassy for additional healthcare referrals.

Health Advisory

Yellow fever: Vaccination is required for entry. This country is in the Yellow Fever Endemic Zone. Yellow fever is not reported active at the present time in this country.

Cholera: This disease is reported active in this country. Although cholera vaccination is not required for entry if arriving directly from the U.S. or Canada, it may be required if arriving from a cholera-infected area, or required for on-going travel to other countries in Latin America, Africa, the Middle East, or Asia. Travelers should consider vaccination (one dose) or a doctor's letter of exemption from vaccination. The risk to travelers of acquiring cholera is considered low. Prevention consists primarily in adhering to safe food and drink guidelines.

World Medical Guide

Malaria: Risk is present year-round throughout this country, including urban areas. Increased risk occurs during and immediately after the rainy seasons (April through July and September through December in the south; April through October in the north). P. falciparum accounts for 90% of cases, followed by P. malariae and P. ovale. Chloroquine-resistant falciparum malaria is reported. Prophylaxis with mefloquine or doxycycline is currently recommended when traveling to malarious areas.

Travelers' diarrhea: Piped water supplies as well as surface water sources may be contaminated or contain excess total dissolved solids (salts). Travelers should observe all food and drink safety precautions. A quinolone antibiotic is recommended for the treatment of acute diarrhea. Diarrhea not responding to treatment with an antibiotic, or chronic diarrhea, may be due to a parasitic disease such as giardiasis, amebiasis, or cryptosporidiosis.

Hepatitis: All susceptible travelers should receive immune globulin or hepatitis A vaccine. Hepatitis E is endemic. The hepatitis B carrier rate in the general population is estimated to exceed 10%. Vaccination against hepatitis B is recommended for healthcare workers and all long-term visitors to this country.

Onchocerciasis: Focally distributed along fast-flowing rivers. Travelers should take measures to prevent blackfly bites.

Schistosomiasis: Urinary schistosomiasis is widely distributed. Major activity occurs in the southeastern (Abidjan, Adzope), central (shores of Lake Kossou), western (Man, Danane), and the northern (Korhogo) areas. Intestinal schistosomiasis is less common and is distributed in the same areas. Travelers should avoid swimming, bathing, or wading in freshwater lakes or streams.

Trypanosomiasis (African sleeping sickness): Endemic, but levels are unclear. Risk reported in central and east-central regions, including Dalao, Vavoua, Bouafle, and Abengourou. Travelers should take measures to prevent insect (tsetse fly) bites.

Meningitis: Northern Ivory Coast borders the sub-Saharan meningitis belt. There is a high incidence of Group A and C meningococcal meningitis. Most recent outbreak occurred in Korhogo vicinity in 1984. Vaccination recommended for travelers having close contact with the indigenous population.

Rabies: Sporadic cases reported countrywide, with increased risk in southeastern department of Abengourou.

AIDS: Heterosexual contact is the predominate mode of transmission. Prevalence of HIV-1 is estimated at 63% in the high-risk urban population. All travelers are cautioned against unsafe sex, unsterile medical or dental injections, and unnecessary blood transfusions.

Other diseases: African tick typhus (transmitted by dog ticks, often in urban areas, and bush ticks), anthrax, brucellosis (from consumption of raw dairy products), cutaneous larval migrans, dengue (low risk; human incidence not known), filariasis (presumably endemic; incidence not known), Lassa fever (virus is present but risk of disease indeterminate), paragonimiasis, toxoplasmosis, tuberculosis (a major health problem), typhoid fever, and intestinal worms (very common) are reported.

JAMAICA

Embassy: 202-452-0660   **Kingston**   **GMT -5 hrs**

Entry Requirements
- If traveling directly from the U.S., Puerto Rico, or the U.S. Virgin Islands, U.S. citizens can enter Jamaica with a certified copy of a U.S. birth certificate or a U.S. passport.
- HIV Test: Not required.
- Vaccinations: A yellow fever vaccination certificate is required from all travelers arriving from infected areas.

Telephone Area Code: 876   **AT&T:** 0-800-872-2883   **MCI:** 800-674-7000

American Express: Stuart's Travel Service, Ltd. 9 Cecelio Avenue, Kingston; Tel. 929-4329.

Embassies/Consulates: U.S. Embassy, Consular Section. 16 Oxford Road, Kingston; Tel. 929-4850. U.S. Consular Agency, Montego Bay; Tel. 952-0160.

World Medical Guide

Hospitals/Doctors: In Kingston: University Hospital (504 beds); general medical/surgical facility; ICU; burn unit; emergency services.

Health Advisory
Malaria: No risk.
Travelers' diarrhea: Low to moderate risk. In urban and resort areas, the hotels and restaurants generally serve reliable food and potable water. Elsewhere, travelers should observe all food and drink safety precautions. A quinolone antibiotic is recommended for the treatment of acute diarrhea. Diarrhea not responding to antibiotic treatment may be due to a parasitic disease such as giardiasis, amebiasis, or cryptosporidiosis.
Hepatitis: Nonimmune travelers should receive hepatitis A vaccine. Hepatitis B is endemic at low levels. Hepatitis E may exist but levels are unclear.
Dengue fever: This mosquito-transmitted viral disease is prevalent in the Caribbean and occurs year-round, especially in coastal and lowland urban areas. All travelers to Jamaica should take measures to prevent insect bites.
Leptospirosis: This spirochetal infection is reported from this country. The risk to tourists, however, is deemed to be low. Travelers should avoid contact with animal urine or water potentially contaminated with animal urine.
Other diseases/health threats: *Angiostrongylus cantonesis*-caused eosinophilic meningitis (outbreak in eight people; transmitted through raw or undercooked vegetables), brucellosis, Chagas' disease (low apparent risk; reduviid bug vectors have been detected on several islands, including Jamaica), histoplasmosis, helminthic infections (ancylostomiasis, ascariasis, strongyloidiasis, and trichuriasis), sexually transmitted diseases, AIDS, tropical spastic paresis (due to HTLV-1; seroprevalence in adult blood donors estimated at 3.5%–5%), toxocariasis, tuberculosis, typhoid fever, viral encephalitis, ciguatera fish toxin poisoning (outbreaks have occurred), and swimming related hazards (jellyfish, spiny sea urchins, and coral).

JAPAN
Embassy: 202-939-6700   *Tokyo*   *GMT +9 hrs*

Entry Requirements
- Passport/Visa: Travelers should contact the closest Japanese Consulate for tourist visa information.
- HIV Test: A 1988 AIDS prevention measure barred entry of HIV-infected foreigners and authorized mandatory testing of those seeking entry who are suspected of being HIV positive.
- Vaccinations: None required.

Telephone Country Code: 81
Embassies/Consulates: U.S. Embassy, Tokyo. 10-5 Alaska 1-chome, Minato-ku. Tel. (3) 3224-5000. U.S. Consulate, Osaka-Kobe; Tel. (6) 315-5900. U.S. Consulate, Sapporo; Tel. (11) 641-1115. U.S. Consulate, Fukuoka; Tel. (92) 751-9331. Canadian Embassy, Tokyo. 3-38 Akasaka, 7-Chome; Tel. (33) 408-2101.

Hospitals/Doctors:
National Hospital Medical Center, Tokyo (1,000 beds); all specialties; 24-hour emergency services; Tel. (03) 202-7181.
St. Luke's International Hospital, Tokyo (359 beds); primary facility for foreign tourists; Tel. (3) 541-5151.
National Nagoya Hospital; most specialties; Tel. (052) 951-1111.
Osaka University Hospital (1,011 beds); most specialties; Tel. (6) 451-0051.
Alan Fair, M.D., John Marshall, M.D., Tokyo Med. & Surg. Clinic; Tel. (33) 436-3028.
Shiun Dong Hsieh, M.D., Tokyo; Tel. (33) 583-2675 or 833-1452 (H).
Beverly Tucker, M.D., Kyoto; Tel. (75) 231-5663.
Sakabe International Clinic, Kyoto; Tel. (075) 231-1624.
Kobe Kasai Hospital; Tel. (078) 871-5201.

World Medical Guide

Health Advisory

Malaria: There is no risk of malaria in Japan.

Travelers' diarrhea: Low risk. Nearly all areas of Japan are supplied with potable water. Many water treatment facilities, however, are in need of modernization. Travelers should drink bottled or treated water unless sure of the potability of water from a particular source. A quinolone antibiotic is recommended for the treatment of diarrhea. Diarrhea not responding to antibiotic treatment may be due to a parasitic disease such as giardiasis, amebiasis, or cryptosporidiosis.

Hepatitis: There is a generally low risk of hepatitis A, which affects less than 1% of people under 25 years of age. All nonimmune travelers, however, should consider receiving the hepatitis A vaccine. The hepatitis B carrier rate in the general population is estimated at 2%.

Japanese encephalitis: Unvaccinated foreigners are at potential risk of illness in rural rice and pig farming areas where the infective culex mosquitoes are most active. Mosquito activity is most intense during the warmer, rainier months (April–November in Okinawa and July–September on the other islands). Highest risk of infection occurs in southeastern Japan; there is negligible risk in northern Hokkaido. Vaccination against Japanese encephalitis is recommended for travelers who will be staying in endemic rural-agricultural areas for two weeks or longer during the peak transmission periods. Travelers to rural areas should also take measures to prevent mosquito bites, especially in the evening when the culex mosquitoes are most active.

Schistosomiasis: Officially eradicated in 1996; no new cases reported since the late 1970s.

Lyme disease: Sporadic cases have been reported from Hokkaido, Honshu, Shikoku, and Kyushu Islands. Hikers and forest workers are at most risk. The dominant species of ticks are

Ixodes persulcatus and *Ixodes ovatus*. The prevalence of Lyme disease spirochetes (*Borrelia burgdorferi*) in these tick species is estimated at 16.6% and 23.6%, respectively. Travelers to wooded, brushy, or forested areas should take measures to prevent tick bites.

Anisakiasis: Raw fish, often consumed as sushi or sashimi, is a potential source of parasitic disease. One such disease, anisakiasis, is transmitted by raw or undercooked saltwater fish, squid, or octopus. Humans are usually infected by eating herring, salmon, cod, mackerel or Pacific red snapper in which infectious larvae are present. Although the sushi bars in Japan are strictly regulated, consumption of raw fish is not without some risk. Each traveler must decide to what extent they wish to be exposed to this potential risk.

Other fish-transmitted helminthic diseases: Paragonimiasis (lung fluke disease). Can be prevented by not eating raw crab or crayfish or the juice of raw crabs or crayfish. Clonorchiasis (an infection of the bile ducts by the liver fluke). The disease is transmitted by raw fish and pickled fish in vinegar (sunomono). Prevent by thoroughly cooking or freezing all freshwater fish prior to consumption. Diphyllobothriasis (fish tapeworm disease). Prevent by not eating raw salmon. Gnathostomiasis (a fish roundworm disease). Prevent by avoiding raw freshwater fish, as well as raw chicken, eels, and frogs.

Scrub typhus: Mite-borne; risk is present in grassy rural areas countrywide; incidence is highest in Kanagawa, Chiba, Miyazaki, Kagoshima Prefectures and in Akita and Niigata regions; greatest risk occurs during May and November.

Other illnesses/hazards: Angiostrongyliasis (occurs mostly in the southwestern islands, including Kyushu Ryukyu), ehrlichiosis (may occur in western Japan), enterohemorrhagic *E. coli* infection (associated with radish sprouts in school lunches), soil-transmitted intestinal helminthic infections (an outbreak of visceral larva migrans due to *Ascaris suum* was reported in Kyushu in 1994), alveolar echinococcosis (reported in Hokkaido), fasciolopsiasis (giant intestinal fluke disease; prevent by thoroughly cooking all aquatic plants and vegetables), Japanese spotted fever, Kawasaki disease, tuberculosis (endemic), and typhoid fever. Air pollution is a major problem in Osaka, Tokyo, and Yokohama.

JORDAN

Embassy: 202-966-2664 *Amman* **GMT +2 hrs**

Entry Requirements
- Travelers can obtain a visa at international ports of entry.
- HIV Test: Not required.
- Vaccinations: Yellow fever vaccination certificate is required if traveling from an infected area and more than 1 year of age.

Telephone Country Code: 962
American Express: International Traders. King Hussein Street; Tel. (6) 666-1014.
Embassies/Consulates: U.S. Embassy, Amman; Tel. (6) 820-101 or 866-121.
Hospitals/Doctors: Ashrifiyah Hospital, Amman (520 beds); most medical specialties; burn unit. King Hussein Medical Center, Amman (600 beds); all specialties; latest state-of-the-art Western medical and surgical equipment. University of Jordan Hospital (400 beds); teaching facility; all specialties.

Health Advisory

Malaria: There is no risk of malaria in this country. No cases reported since 1970.
Travelers' diarrhea: High risk. Piped water supplies are unreliable and may be contaminated. Travelers should observe food and drink safety precautions. Bottled mineral water is available locally. A quinolone antibiotic is recommended for the treatment of acute diarrhea. Diarrhea not responding to treatment with an antibiotic, or chronic diarrhea, may be due to a parasitic disease such as giardiasis, amebiasis or cryptosporidiosis.
Hepatitis: Hepatitis A vaccine is recommended for all nonimmune travelers. Hepatitis E may occur, but endemic levels are unclear. The hepatitis B carrier rate in the general population is estimated at 7%–10%. Vaccination against hepatitis B is recommended for long-term visitors to this country. Hepatitis C is likely endemic.

Leishmaniasis: Cutaneous leishmaniasis is focally distributed countrywide, except in the eastern desert areas. The disease is hyperendemic in the middle and lower Jordan Valley. An outbreak has been reported at Qurayqira in Wadi Araba in southern Jordan. There is a low risk of cutaneous leishmaniasis in northern areas. Historically, visceral leishmaniasis has been reported in the north, but may be more widespread. Travelers to Jordan should take measures to prevent insect (sandfly) bites.

Schistosomiasis: Endemic status is unclear. In 1991, the Ministry of health declared Jordan free of schistosomiasis, but there could be indiginous transmission, especially from irrigation projects. Possible risk areas include the Jordan River and East Ghor canal, the Zarqa River, Yarmouk River, Lake Tiberius, and Jarash Spring. Travelers should avoid swimming or wading in freshwater rivers, ponds, streams, or irrigated areas.

Other illnesses: Cholera (endemic at low levels), Mediterranean spotted fever (boutonneuse fever; occurs regionally), brucellosis (commonly occurs), dengue (historically reported from the Jordan Valley but current data not available), echinococcosis (reported sporadically, especially in northern areas), leptospirosis, rabies (most cases occur in foxes, wolves, and jackals, with spillover into the dog population; rabies occurs sporadically in humans), relapsing fever (tick-borne; caves, rocky shelters, and stone buildings may harbor infected ticks), sandfly fever (foci occur countrywide; transmission highest April–October), tuberculosis, murine typhus (flea-borne), typhoid fever, and helminthic infections (roundworm, hookworm, and whipworm infections are common in rural areas; incidence is estimated at 5%).

KAZAKHSTAN

Embassy of Kazakhstan: 202-333-4507.

U.S. Embassy, Almaty: (7)-3272-633-905

For Health Advisory information, see the Health Advisory for the Caucasus, Central Asia, Siberia, and Far East former USSR on page 261 and 404.

KENYA

Embassy: 202-387-6101   *Nairobi*   *GMT +3 hrs*

Entry Requirements
- A visa, good for 6 months, is required.
- HIV Test: Not required.
- Vaccinations: A yellow fever vaccination certificate is required from all travelers older than 1 year of age arriving from infected areas.
Cholera: A validated vaccination certificate against cholera may be required if a traveler leaves Kenya and tries to enter a country where cholera is endemic. Such countries include Tanzania, Uganda, and other countries in Africa, the Middle East, India, Asia, and Oceania.

Telephone Country Code: 254

Embassies/Consulates: U.S. Embassy, Nairobi. USAID building, The Crescent. Tel: (2) 751-613.

Hospitals/Doctors: The best medical care in Kenya is found in Nairobi, Mombasa, and Kisumu.

Nairobi: Nairobi Hospital, Argwings Kodhen Rd; private hospital; most major specialties. Aga Khan Jubilee Hospital (183 beds); 3rd Parklands Ave; private hospital; most major specialties, including neurosurgery. Kenyatta National Hospital, Nairobi (1,716 beds); all major specialties; overcrowded; inadequate supplies. Not recommended for routine use.

Mombasa: Aga Khan Hospital, Vanga Rd; Tel: 312-953. Mombasa Medical Practice; Tel: 315-661.

Kisumu: Aga Khan Hospital, Otieno Oyoo St; Tel: 43516.

World Medical Guide

Air ambulance services: Flying Doctors Society of Africa, Nairobi; Tel: (2) 501-280; tourist membership available covering emergency air ambulance services. African Air Rescue, Wilson Airport, Nairobi; provides emergency evacuation services throughout East Africa. Tel: (2) 216-842/3/5.

Health Advisory

Yellow fever: Potential for disease outbreaks exist. In 1993, yellow fever was reported active in Rift Valley Province (Baringo and Elgeyo Marakwet Districts). In 1994, 73 cases were confirmed in Rift Valley Province. During 1995, 3 confirmed cases of yellow fever were identified in Baringo, Elgeyo Marakwet, and Nakuru Districts in the Rift Valley Province. Yellow fever vaccination is recommended for travel to rural areas outside the city of Nairobi.

Cholera: This disease is active, especially in southern areas. Although cholera vaccination is not required for entry if arriving directly from the U.S. or Canada, it may be required if arriving from a cholera-infected area, or required for on-going travel to other countries in Latin America, Africa, the Middle East, or Asia. Travelers to this country should consider vaccination (one dose) or a doctor's letter of exemption from vaccination. The risk to travelers of acquiring cholera is low. Prevention consists primarily in strictly adhering to safe food and drink guidelines.

Malaria: This disease occurs year-round with the highest malaria transmission rates during and just after the semiannual rainy seasons, March through May and late September through November. Risk is countrywide below 2,500 meters elevation, including urban areas and game parks. Primary risk areas include Western, Nyanza (Lake Victoria Basin), Coast (including the Tana River Valley and the coastal areas south of Mombasa and Malindi to the Tanzanian border), and southern Eastern Provinces. Seasonal malaria occurs in the game parks along the border with Tanzania. Transmission is limited in arid areas of the Rift Valley, northern Eastern, North Eastern, and Coast Provinces. Heavy rains in 1998, however, resulted in epidemic malaria rates in northeastern Kenya. Malaria may occur in the highland areas of Rift Valley and Western Provinces during and just after periods of exceptionally heavy rainfall. The risk of malaria in Nairobi and in the highland areas above 2,500 meters elevation (e.g., the Aberdare Range, Mt. Kenya, Mt. Elgon) is limited if not negligible. *P. falciparum* causes 85% of cases, followed by *P. malariae* and less frequently by *P. ovale*. Malaria due to *P. vivax* is rare. Chloroquine-resistant falciparum malaria is prevalent, especially in the coastal areas and in western Kenya. Prophylaxis with either mefloquine, malarone, or doxycycline is recommended.

Travelers' diarrhea: Moderate to high risk outside of first-class hotels and resorts. The public water supply in Nairobi is considered potable, but bottled water is recommended for consumption. All water sources outside of major hotels and resorts should be considered potentially contaminated. Travelers should observe food and drink safety precautions. A quinolone antibiotic is recommended for the treatment of acute diarrhea. Diarrhea not responding to antibiotic treatment may be caused by a parasitic disease such as giardiasis, amebiasis, or cryptosporidiosis. About 4% of cases of diarrhea are due to cryptosporidiosis.

Hepatitis: All nonimmune travelers should receive hepatitis A vaccine. The hepatitis B carrier rate in the general population is estimated at 6%. Vaccination against hepatitis B is recommended for nonimmune healthcare workers and long-term visitors to this country. Hepatitis E has not been reported but likely occurs. Hepatitis C is endemic.

Dengue fever: The risk of dengue is considered to be low but outbreaks of disease were reported in 1982 in coastal areas. Dengue has been documented in neighboring Somalia.

Rift Valley, West Nile, Chikungunya,, and O'nyongnyong fevers: These mosquito-transmitted viral illnesses are reported mainly from the coastal areas of Lake Victoria and the Indian Ocean. The risk to tourists is low. An outbreak of Rift Valley fever is recently reported in Northeastern Province. A 1987 serosurvey in Coast Province detected antibody prevalence of 0.9 percent to West Nile fever virus.

Leishmaniasis: Cutaneous leishmaniasis is reported from the highland areas, including the eastern slopes of Mt. Elgon, the Aberdare Range, the Baringo District and Rift Valley Province. Risk areas for visceral leishmaniasis (kala azar) include Rift Valley Province (Baringo,

World Medical Guide

West Potok, and Turkana districts), Eastern Province (Machakos, Kitue, and Meru districts) and North Eastern Province. All travelers to these areas should take measures to prevent sandfly bites.

Schistosomiasis: Urinary schistosomiasis is widely distributed, including the areas along the coastal plain and the lower Tana River Valley (Coast Province), in the Taveta region (extreme southwestern Coast Province), in Kitui District (Eastern Province), and bordering Lake Victoria (Nyanza Province). Intestinal schistosomiasis occurs primarily east of Nairobi, in the Taveta region bordering Tanzania, in the Nyanza Province bordering Lake Victoria, and on the islands of Rusinga and Mfangano. Highest risk areas include Coast Province (for urinary schistosomiasis) and Machakos District, Eastern Province (for intestinal shistosomiasis).

Trypanosomiasis (African sleeping sickness): Sporadic cases (due to *T.b. rhodiense*) are reported, with occasional outbreaks. Disease transmission primarily restricted to Nyanza Province (with a recognized focus in the Lambwe Valley near Lake Victoria) and Western Province (Amukura Hills), extending along the Tanzania border into extreme southwestern Rift Valley Province. In 1996 a tourist acquired sleeping sickness in Masai Mara game preserve. Travelers to these areas should take measures to prevent tsetse fly bites.

Meningitis (meningococcal): Risk is seasonally elevated during the drier months June through February in western areas within the sub-Saharan meningitis belt (Western, Nyanza, and western and northern Rift Valley Provinces). Risk is associated with crowded living conditions and close contact with the indigenous population. Group A usually predominates, but Group C also occurs. Vaccination is recommended for travel during the dry season, although there have been no reports of meningitis in travelers.

Rabies: Risk is increasing in urban areas, including Nairobi. Stray dogs are the main source of rabies transmission. Pre-exposure vaccination is recommended for long-term travel (more than 4 weeks) to this country, especially for travelers going to remote rural areas.

Altitude sickness: Climbers ascending Mt. Kilimanjaro and Mt. Kenya are at risk for acute mountain sickness. All climbers should consider slow ascent as well as prophylaxis with acetazolamide (Diamox). Immediate descent is the treatment of choice for moderate to severe altitude sickness.

AIDS: Heterosexual contact is the predominate means of transmission. Nine percent of the general population is infected with the AIDS virus. HIV prevalence is estimated at up to 85% of the high-risk, sexually active urban population. Unofficial estimates of HIV-infection rates among prostitutes in Nairobi and Mombasa have exceeded 90%. All travelers are cautioned against unsafe sex, unsterile medical or dental injections, and blood transfusions.

Other illnesses/hazards: African tick typhus, anthrax, brucellosis, echinococcosis (highest known prevalence in the world occurs in the Turkana population in northwest Kenya), filariasis (mosquito-borne; endemic in the coastal zone and along the Sabaki River), leptospirosis (associated with rodent-infected areas; reportedly widespread around Kisumu and along the coast), onchocerciasis (last remaining focus was located on southwestern slopes of Mt. Elgon), plague (outbreak occurred in 1990 in Nairobi's Embakasi area), Q fever (due to *Coxiella burnetii*; may be acquired by inhalation of contaminated airborne dust in tribal shacks), toxoplasmosis, syphilis, trachoma, tuberculosis (a major health problem), typhoid fever, and intestinal worms (very common).

Animal hazards: Snakes (vipers, cobras, black mambas, puff adders) are primarily found in the large arid regions of northern Kenya. Other animal hazards include centipedes, scorpions, and black widow spiders. Sea cones, sea urchins, and anemones inhabit the shallow coastal waters of Kenya and may pose a threat to swimmers.

World Medical Guide

KIRIBATI
Tarawa   *GMT +12 hrs*

Entry Requirements
- Passport/Visa: Passport is required.
- HIV Test: Not required.
- Vaccinations: A yellow fever vaccination certificate is required of travelers arriving from infected areas.

Telephone Country Code: 686
Embassies/Consulates: This country consists of 33 atolls and one island scattered over five million square km. Formerly the Gilberts of the British Gilbert and Ellice Islands Colony.
Hospitals/Doctors: Tungaru Central Hospital. Betio Hospital; general medical facility.

Health Advisory
Malaria: No risk.
Hepatitis: Immunization against hepatitis A is recommended.
Typhoid: Immunization is recommended.
Other diseases/health risks: Filariasis, dengue fever, dengue hemorrhagic fever, Japanese encephalitis, helminthic infections, ciguatera poisoning, and poisonous sea snakes.

KYRGYZ REPUBLIC (KYRGYZSTAN)
Embassy of Kyrgyz Republic: 202-338-5141. U.S. Embassy, Bishtek: (7)-3312-223-289

For Health Advisory information, see the Health Advisory for the Caucasus, Central Asia, Siberia, and Far East former USSR on page 261.

LAOS
Embassy: 202-332-6416   *Vientiane*   *GMT +7 hrs*

Entry Requirements
- A visa, good for 30 days, is required.
- HIV Test: Not required.
- Vaccinations: A yellow fever vaccination certificate is required from all travelers arriving from infected areas or Endemic Zones.
  Cholera: The government of Laos requires a valid cholera vaccination certificate for entry. It is recommended that travelers have a cholera vaccination (1 dose) or a doctor's letter of exemption from vaccination.

Embassies/Consulates: U.S. Embassy, Vientiane. Rue Bartholomie; Tel. (21) 212581 or (21) 212582. After hours duty officer's cellular telephone number: (21) 130423.
Doctors/Hospitals: Mahosot Hospital, Vientiane (220 beds); capabilities well below Western standards. Clinique Diplomatique. Pakse Provincial Hospital (160 beds); capabilities well below Western standards.

Health Advisory
Note: Medical and dental capabilities in Laos are extremely limited; pharmaceuticals are in very short supply; water supplies are grossly contaminated in most areas.
Malaria: Risk is present countrywide, but is more prevalent in mountainous and rural areas than in the lowland plains or urban areas. There is no risk of malaria in Vientiane. *P. falciparum* accounts for up to 80% of cases whereas *P. vivax* accounts for 15% of cases and *P. malariae* up to 5%. Vivax malaria may predominate in some areas. Multidrug-resistant falciparum malaria is reported, especially near the border with Thailand. Mefloquine or doxycycline prophylaxis is recommended when traveling to malarious areas.

World Medical Guide

Travelers' diarrhea: Piped water supplies countrywide are frequently untreated and may be grossly contaminated. Travelers should observe all food and drink safety precautions. A quinolone antibiotic is recommended for the treatment of acute diarrhea. Diarrhea not responding to treatment with an antibiotic may be due to a parasitic disease such as giardiasis or amebiasis—or an intestinal virus. Cryptosporidiosis is likely, but not documented.

Hepatitis: All nonimmune travelers should receive hepatitis A vaccine. Hepatitis E has not been reported, but is likely. The hepatitis B carrier rate in the general population is estimated to exceed 10%. Vaccination against hepatitis B is recommended for healthcare workers, corporate employees, expatriates, relief workers, teachers, and others (including family members) who plan an extended visit to this country.

Typhoid fever: High endemicity. Vaccination is recommended.

Dengue fever: Risk is countrywide, year-round, but may be elevated in urban areas, especially during the warmer and wetter months (usually May through October). The *Aedes* mosquitoes, which transmit dengue fever, are more active during the daytime and are present in populous urban areas as well as rural areas. Prevention of dengue consists of taking measures to prevent insect (mosquito) bites.

Japanese encephalitis: Risk is elevated in rural and periurban areas, especially where mosquito-breeding sites and pig farming coexist. Sporadic cases occur throughout the year, but disease transmission is higher during the warmer and wetter months (usually May through October). Vaccination is recommended for travelers planning an extended stay (more than 3–4 weeks) in rural-agricultural areas during the peak transmission season. All travelers should take measures to prevent mosquito bites.

Filariasis: Both the Bancroftian and Malayan varieties are highly endemic in rural and urban areas. Travelers should take personal protection measures against mosquito bites.

Schistosomiasis: Risk is present year-round. Focal distribution occurs along the Mekong River (including Vientiane), and in Louangphrabang and Champasak Provinces. Travelers should avoid swimming, bathing, or wading in freshwater rivers, lakes, ponds, or streams.

Helminthic infections: Soil-transmitted infections (caused by hookworms, roundworms, whipworms, strongyloides) are highly prevalent in most rural areas. Travelers should wear shoes (to prevent the hookworm and strongyloides larvae from penetrating the skin) and food should be thoroughly washed/cooked (to destroy roundworm and whipworm eggs).

Helminthic infections (flukes): Oriental lung fluke disease (paragonimiasis) and liver fluke diseases (clonorchiasis, opisthorchiasis, fascioliasis) are prevalent. Prevention: Travelers should avoid eating raw freshwater fish; raw, salted, or wine-soaked crustacea (freshwater crabs or crayfish); or undercooked water vegetables and plants, especially watercress.

AIDS: HIV is endemic, but levels are not documented.

Other diseases/health threats: Anthrax, chikungunya fever, cholera (endemic; outbreaks occur frequently), echinococcosis, leprosy (highly endemic), leptospirosis, melioidosis, plague, rabies (enzootic at high levels), scrub typhus (mite-borne), tuberculosis (highly endemic) are reported. Animal hazards include snakes (cobras, vipers), spiders (black and brown widow), tigers, leopards, and large leeches. Plant hazards: Bamboo, rattan, and large palm- or fern-like trees, which can cause serious puncture wounds and slow-healing lacerations, are widespread in the forested areas of the country. Regas are large forest trees whose black resinous sap can cause a potent poison ivy–type skin reaction. Stinging nettles, small thorny trees, and many species of euphorbs can also cause skin reactions.

LATVIA

Latvian Embassy: 202-726-8213. U.S. Embassy, Riga: (371)-721-0005

For Health Advisory information, see the Disease Risk Summary for Europe on page 259.

LEBANON

Embassy: 202-939-6300 *Beirut* *GMT +2 hrs*

Entry Requirements
- Passport/Visa: Passport and visa required. Contact the Lebanese embassy for further information.
- HIV Test: Not required.
- Vaccinations: A yellow fever vaccination certificate is required from all travelers older than 1 year arriving from infected areas.

Telephone Country Code: 961 **AT&T:** 426-801

Embassies/Consulates: U.S. Embassy is located in Antelias; (1) 417-774, 415-802, 402-184. Fax: 407-112.

Health Advisory

Malaria: No risk.
Cholera: Sporadic cases.
Travelers' diarrhea: Medium risk. A quinolone antibiotic is recommended for the treatment of acute diarrhea.
Hepatitis: All nonimmune travelers should receive hepatitis A vaccine. The hepatitis B carrier rate in the general population is estimated at 4%. Hepatitis E may occur.
Mediterranean spotted fever: Low risk; may occur, based on serological studies.
Leishmaniasis: Low to absent risk, based on historical patterns.
Schistosomiasis: No transmission reported since 1969.
Other illnesses: Brucellosis, echinococcosis, typhoid fever, rabies (occasional cases), tuberculosis, sandfly fever (presumably endemic at low levels).

LESOTHO

Embassy: 202-797-5533 *Maseru* *GMT +2 hrs*

Entry Requirements
- Passport/Visa: Travelers should possess valid passport. Visa not required.
- HIV Test: Not required.
- Vaccinations: A yellow fever vaccination certificate is required from all travelers older than 1 year arriving from infected areas.

Telephone Country Code: 266

Embassies/Consulates: U.S. Embassy, Maseru; Tel. 312-666/7. Canadian Embassy (South Africa); Tel. [27] 287-062.

Health Advisory

Malaria: Transmission of malaria reportedly does not occur in Lesotho. Risk areas in surrounding South Africa are north of Lesotho.
Travelers' diarrhea: Travelers should observe all food and drink safety precautions. A quinolone antibiotic (Cipro or Floxin) is recommended for the treatment of acute diarrhea. Diarrhea not responding to treatment with an antibiotic, or chronic diarrhea, may be due to a parasitic disease such as giardiasis or amebiasis, and treatment with metronidazole (Flagyl) or tinidazole (Fasigyn) should be considered. All cases of diarrhea should be treated with adequate fluid replacement.
Hepatitis: All susceptible travelers should receive immune globulin prophylaxis or hepatitis A vaccine. The hepatitis B carrier rate in the general population is estimated at 8%. Vaccination against hepatitis B is recommended for healthcare workers and all long-term visitors to this country.
Schistosomiasis: No infected areas are reported in Lesotho. Both urinary and intestinal schistosomiasis, however, occur in eastern and northern regions of neighboring Natal Province of South Africa.

World Medical Guide

Other illnesses/hazards: AIDS (low incidence; HIV prevalence estimated at less than 1%), African tick typhus (contracted from dog ticks—often in urban areas—and from bush ticks), brucellosis, tuberculosis (a major health problem), typhoid fever, and intestinal worms (uncommon).

LIBERIA

Embassy: 202-291-0761   *Monrovia*   *GMT 0 hrs*

Entry Requirements
- Passport/Visa: Valid passport and visa are required. An exit permit is required.
- HIV Test: Not required.
- Vaccinations: A yellow fever vaccination certificate is required from all travelers older than 1 year arriving from ALL COUNTRIES.

Telephone Country Code: 231
Embassies/Consulates: U.S. Embassy, Monrovia. 111 United Nations Drive. Tel. 222-991/2/3/4. Canadian Consulate, Monrovia. EXCHEM Compound. Tel. 223-903.
Hospitals/Doctors: ELWA Mission Hospital, Monrovia (45 beds); 24-hour emergency services. JFK Memorial Hospital, Monrovia (337 beds); general medical/surgical facility. Firestone Plantation Hospital, Monrovia (200 beds); general medical/surgical facility; emergency services. Travelers should contact the U.S. Embassy for physician referrals.

Health Advisory

Yellow fever: This disease is reported active in this country. Yellow fever vaccination is required for entry to Liberia. This country is in the Yellow Fever Endemic Zone. A valid yellow fever vaccination certificate may be required for persons who leave this country and travel to other countries in South America, Africa, the Middle East, or Asia.

Cholera: This disease is active in this country. Although cholera vaccination is not required for entry if arriving directly from the U.S. or Canada, it may be required if arriving from a cholera-infected area, or required for on-going travel to other countries in Latin America, Africa, the Middle East, or Asia. Travelers should consider vaccination (one dose) or a doctor's letter of exemption from vaccination. The risk to travelers of acquiring cholera is considered low. Prevention consists primarily in adhering to safe food and drink guidelines.

Malaria: Transmission occurs countrywide year-round, but is increased during and immediately after the rainy season, April through October. Falciparum malaria accounts for approximately 90% of cases. Other cases are due to the *P. malariae* species, or *P. ovale*. Chloroquine-resistant falciparum malaria has been reported from the northwest (Zorzor) and from Monrovia. Resistance to Fansidar, mefloquine, and quinine has also been reported. Prophylaxis with mefloquine or doxycycline is currently recommended.

Travelers' diarrhea: High risk. All water sources should be considered contaminated. The 3-year civil war has destroyed water treatment and sewage systems. Travelers should strictly observe food and drink precautions. A quinolone antibiotic is recommended for the treatment of acute diarrhea. Diarrhea not responding to treatment with an antibiotic may be due to a parasitic disease such as giardiasis, amebiasis, or cryptosporidiosis.

Hepatitis: High risk. All susceptible travelers should receive hepatitis A vaccine. The hepatitis B carrier rate in the population is estimated to exceed 10%. Vaccination against hepatitis B is recommended for healthcare workers and all long-term visitors to this country.

Leishmaniasis: Low risk. Sporadic cases of cutaneous and visceral leishmaniasis have been reported from neighboring countries. Travelers are advised to take general precautions against insect bites, especially during the night.

Filariasis (Bancroftian variety): Infection rates of up to 37% have been reported from coastal villages, with the highest rates in the eastern county of Maryland. Cases also reported in areas bordering the savanna belt in the north. All travelers should avoid mosquito bites.

Onchocerciasis: Highly endemic in rain forest areas of Grand Bassa County. Foci reported in the west along the St. Paul and Lofa Rivers. Travelers should take personal protection measures against blackfly bites.

Schistosomiasis: Risk is present, primarily in the northwestern and northcentral counties of Lofa, Bong, and Nimba. Infection rates have been highest in Bong County. No transmission occurs in the coastal areas. Travelers should avoid swimming, bathing, or wading in freshwater lakes, ponds, or streams.

Lassa fever: Most cases are reported in the northwestern county of Lofa. Low risk for tourists, but up to 17% of indigenous patients hospitalized with a fever in the Zorzor district in the 1980s were possibly infected with the Lassa fever virus. The virus of Lassa fever is possibly transmitted through infective rodent urine that contaminates food or dust. Travelers can lessen their exposure by avoiding bush areas and the interiors of thatch huts.

Paragonimiasis (lung fluke): Up to 7% infection rates reported from Bong County. Travelers should avoid ingesting raw or undercooked crabs and crayfish.

Trypanosomiasis (sleeping sickness): Sporadic cases have been reported from the northcentral county of Bong. Travelers should take protection measures against tsetse fly bites.

Meningitis: Liberia lies just west of the sub-Saharan meningitis belt. Limited outbreaks reported in Sarwan town, Sinoe County. Vaccination is recommended for travelers who expect to have close contact with the indigenous population.

Rabies: Human cases reported from Monrovia and countrywide, where there are large stray dog populations. Pre-exposure vaccination against rabies (3 doses) is recommended for long-term travelers to this country and for travelers going to remote rural areas if they will be unable to receive antirabies treatment within 24 hours of exposure to a potentially rabid animal such as a dog, cat, or monkey. Pre-exposure vaccination does not preclude the need for additional post-exposure treatment.

AIDS: Prevalence appears to be low, based on limited data.

Other illnesses/hazards: African tick typhus (contracted from dog ticks, often in urban areas, and bush ticks), anthrax, brucellosis, leprosy (up to 2 cases/1,000 population), cutaneous larva migrans, louse-borne relapsing fever, tuberculosis (a major health problem), typhoid fever, typhus, and intestinal worms. Animal hazards include snakes (vipers, mambas, cobras), centipedes, scorpions, and black widow spiders. Potentially harmful marine animals found in the coastal waters of Liberia include Portuguese man-of-war, sea nettle, marine catfish, moonjelly, mauve stinger, marine catfish, eagle ray, scorpionfish, and weeverfish. Swimmers should take sensible precautions to avoid these hazards.

LIBYA

No U.S. Embassy *Tripoli* *GMT +1 hr*

Entry Requirements
- Passport/Visa: A visa is required. U.S. passports no longer valid for travel to Libya without special validation from the State Dept. U.S. citizens should contact:
U.S. Department of State (Att: Mr. Harry Coburn)
1425 K Street, N.W.
Washington, D.C. 20522-1705
- HIV Test: Testing is required for those seeking residence permits. Short-term visitors are exempt. U.S. test results are accepted.
- Vaccinations: A yellow fever vaccination certificate is required for all travelers older than one year arriving from infected areas.

Telephone Country Code: 218

Hospitals/Doctors: Tripoli Central Hospital (1,200 beds); general medical/surgical facility; emergency services; ICU. In Benghazi: Central Hospital (1,200 beds); general medical/surgical facility.

Health Advisory

Malaria: Very low to absent risk of malaria is present from February to August in the valleys and isolated oases in the southwest (Fezzan). There is no malaria risk in urban areas.

Travelers' diarrhea: Moderate to high risk outside of first-class hotels and resorts. Travelers are advised to drink only bottled, boiled, filtered, or treated water and consume only well-

World Medical Guide

cooked food. Most large urban areas have piped water, but supplies are intermittent and delivery systems are subject to contamination. A quinolone antibiotic is recommended for the treatment of acute diarrhea. Diarrhea not responding to antibiotic treatment may be due to a parasitic disease such as giardiasis or amebiasis—or an intestinal virus.

Hepatitis: Hepatitis A vaccine is recommended for all nonimmune travelers. The hepatitis B carrier rate in the general population is estimated at 5%. Vaccination is recommended for all long-term visitors. Hepatitis E is reported.

Leishmaniasis: Low risk of cutaneous leishmaniasis is present. Sporadic cases have been reported from rural villages in the northwest, in the semiarid area extending from Tripoli to the Tunisian border, and from the coast to the plateau of the Jebel Nefusa. No cases have been reported from Tripoli. Visceral leishmaniasis (kala azar) has been reported from the Benghazi region and the northeastern coastal areas. Visceral leishmaniasis tends to be associated with settlements, with dogs as the primary reservoir. Travelers to these regions should take measures to prevent sandfly bites.

Sandfly fever: Significant potential risk is present. Transmission occurs primarily April–October throughout the coastal regions. Travelers to these regions should take measures to prevent sandfly bites.

Schistosomiasis: Risk is present in widespread areas of the southwest, including valleys in the central Fezzan and the Ghat district on the Algerian border. Transmission also occurs in Darnah on the northeastern coast. Cases also reported from Taourga, an oasis located 240 km east of Tripoli. Travelers should avoid swimming or wading in freshwater lakes, irrigation systems, ponds, or streams.

Rabies: Animal rabies occurs throughout this country. Foxes, jackals, and hyenas are the principal animal reservoirs.

Other illnesses: Boutonneuse fever (occurs primarily in coastal areas; contracted from dog ticks, often in suburban areas), brucellosis (risk from raw goat/sheep milk and cheese), echinococcosis (10% of the children in Benghazi infected), plague (outbreaks have occurred near Tobruk), relapsing fever (tick-borne and louse-borne), toxoplasmosis (infection rates as high as 52%), tuberculosis, typhus, and helminthic infections (e.g., roundworm, hookworm disease).

LITHUANIA

Lithuanian Embassy: 202234-5860. U.S. Embassy, Vilnius: (370)-2-223-031

For Health Advisory information, see the Disease Risk Summary for Europe and Russia on page 259.

MADAGASCAR

Embassy: 202-265-5525   *Antananarivo*   *GMT +3 hrs*

Entry Requirements
- A visa is required. Travelers should contact the Embassy of Madagascar for details.
- HIV Test: Not required.
- Vaccinations: A yellow fever vaccination certificate is required from all travelers arriving from, or transiting, infected areas.

Telephone Country Code: 261

Embassies/Consulates: U.S. Embassy, Antananarivo. 14 & 16 Rue Rainitovo, Antsahavola; Tel. (2) 212-57, 200-89, or 207-18.

Hospitals/Doctors: Hospital Befelatnana, Antananarivo (1,300 beds). Fort Dauphin Hospital, Faradofay (80 beds); American Lutheran hospital.

Health Advisory

Malaria: Risk is present year-round in the coastal areas, but transmission is more seasonal in the central highland plateau, occurring primarily November through May. There is minimal risk of malaria in Antananarivo and minimal risk in the towns of Antsirabe,

World Medical Guide

Manjakandriana, and Andramasina. The highest risk of malaria occurs in the eastern coastal areas. Malaria occurs on the high plateau, formerly risk free. Falciparum malaria accounts for approximately 90% of cases. Other cases of malaria are due primarily to the *P. vivax*. Chloroquine-resistant *P. falciparum* is reported. Prophylaxis with mefloquine or doxycycline is currently recommended when traveling to malarious areas.

Travelers' diarrhea: High risk. Water distribution systems are found only in major urban areas and are old and in poor repair. Piped water supplies are frequently contaminated. Travelers should observe all food and drink safety precautions. A quinolone antibiotic is recommended for the treatment of acute diarrhea. Diarrhea not responding to treatment with an antibiotic, or chronic diarrhea, may be due to a parasitic disease such as giardiasis or amebiasis.

Hepatitis: All nonimmune travelers should receive hepatitis A vaccine. Hepatitis E presumably occurs, but incidence is not known. The hepatitis B carrier rate in the general population is estimated at 5%–10%. Vaccination against hepatitis B is recommended for all long-term visitors to this country.

Leishmaniasis: Low risk. Incidence status undetermined.

Schistosomiasis: Widely distributed. Urinary schistosomiasis predominates on the west coast and in the northern regions, while intestinal schistosomiasis predominates in the central and southern coastal zone of Toamasina Province; the coastal zone of Fianarantsoa Province, and inland, in areas at moderate elevations to the south of the central highlands. Risk-free areas include the vicinities of Antsiranana and Antananarivo, and the Presquile Peninsula, including Maroantsetra and Antalaha.

Plague: Up to 1,500 cases of bubonic plague occur annually. In 1997, 18 cases of suspected pneumonic plague, with eight deaths, occurred. The index case was in a remote village 60 miles north of the capital city of Antananarivo. Other cases occurred in the same central highlands area, where plague is endemic. No longer limited to the highland regions, plague has also reappeared in the northwest coastal town of Majunga. Travelers should avoid contact with rodents (and their fleas), sick or dead animals, or patients with the pneumonic form of the disease. Flea precautions include repellents and insecticides. Doxycycline can be used prophylactically if there is risk of exposure. The role for the killed whole-cell vaccine is limited and it does not fully protect against primary pneumonic plague.

AIDS: HIV prevalence appears to be low, even in the high-risk urban population.

Other illnesses/hazards: Brucellosis, filariasis (mosquito-borne; endemic, primarily along the eastern border), leprosy, rabies (dogs main source of human infection), tuberculosis (a major health problem in lower socioeconomic groups), trachoma, typhoid fever, and intestinal worms (very common). Animal hazards include centipedes, scorpions, and black widow spiders. Portuguese man-of-war, sea nettles, sea wasps, stingrays, and several species of poisonous fish are common in the country's coastal waters and are potential hazards to unprotected swimmers.

MADEIRA (PORTUGAL)

GMT 0 hrs

Entry Requirements
- Passport/Visa: A valid passport is required.
- HIV Test: Not required.
- Vaccinations: A yellow fever vaccination certificate is required from all travelers older than 1 year arriving from infected areas.

Telephone Country Code: 351

Health Advisory

Travelers' diarrhea: Medium risk; giardiasis has been reported. Travelers should drink only bottled, boiled, or treated water and avoid undercooked food.

Hepatitis: All nonimmune travelers should receive hepatitis A vaccine.

World Medical Guide

MALAWI

Embassy: 202-797-1103 *Lilongwe* *GMT +2 hrs*

Entry Requirements
- A visa is not required for stays up to 1 year.
- HIV Test: Not required.
- Vaccinations: A yellow fever valid vaccination certificate is required from all travelers older than 1 year arriving from infected areas.

Telephone Country Code: 265

Embassies/Consulates: U.S. Embassy, Area 40, City Center, Lilongwe; Tel. 783-166 or 783-342.

Hospitals/Doctors: Queen Elizabeth Central Hospital, Blantyre (640 beds); general medical/surgical facility. Malamulo Hospital, Blantyre. Likuni Mission Hospital, Lilongwe; recommended as the best local hospital. Adventist Health Centre, Blantyre.

Health Advisory

Yellow fever: Vaccination is recommended for travel outside urban areas. This country is in the Yellow Fever Endemic Zone. A valid vaccination certificate may be required for on-going travel to other countries.

Cholera: This disease is reported active in this country. Although cholera vaccination is not required for entry if arriving directly from the U.S. or Canada, it may be required for on-going travel to other countries in Africa, the Middle East, or Asia. Travelers should consider vaccination (one dose) or getting a doctor's letter of exemption from vaccination. The risk to travelers of acquiring cholera is considered low. Prevention consists primarily in adhering to safe food and drink guidelines.

Malaria: Risk is present year-round throughout this country, including urban areas. Malaria risk is highest along the shores of Lake Malawi where the risk peaks at the end of the rainy season (November through April). Falciparum malaria accounts for approximately 90% of cases. Other cases of malaria are due to the *P. ovale* and *P. malariae* species, rarely *P. vivax*. Chloroquine-resistant falciparum malaria is reported. Prophylaxis with mefloquine or doxycycline is currently recommended when traveling in malarious areas.

Travelers' diarrhea: High risk. There are water treatment systems in some major urban areas, but even treated water should be considered potentially contaminated. Travelers should observe all food and drink safety precautions. A quinolone antibiotic is recommended for the treatment of acute diarrhea. Diarrhea not responding to treatment with an antibiotic, or chronic diarrhea, may be due to a parasitic disease such as giardiasis, amebiasis, or cryptosporidiosis.

Hepatitis: High risk. All nonimmune travelers should receive hepatitis A vaccine. Hepatitis E presumably occurs. The hepatitis B carrier rate in the general population is estimated at 8%. Vaccination against hepatitis B is recommended for all long-term visitors to this country.

Onchocerciasis: A focus of disease activity may exist in the southern Thyolo highlands. Travelers to this area should take measures to prevent insect (blackfly) bites.

Plague: An outbreak of bubonic plague reported in 1997 in southern Malawi with eight cases identified.

Schistosomiasis: An estimated 40%–50% of the population is infected. Risk areas are distributed countrywide with an intense focus along Lake Malawi. Travelers should avoid swimming, bathing, or wading in freshwater lakes, ponds, or streams.

Other illnesses/hazards: African tick typhus, brucellosis (from consumption of raw dairy products), dengue (low risk), echinococcosis, filariasis (may occur along the lower Shire River and along the shores of Lake Malawi), leishmaniasis (risk undetermined; sporadic cases may occur), leptospirosis, meningitis, plague, rabies (transmitted by dogs, hyenas, and jackals), toxoplasmosis, syphilis, tuberculosis (a major health problem), trypanosomiasis (reported from the Kasungu and Vwaza Game Reserves, near the Luangwa Valley of Zambia), trachoma, typhoid fever, and intestinal helminths (very common). Animal hazards include snakes (vipers, cobras), centipedes, scorpions, and black widow spiders.

World Medical Guide

MALAYSIA

Embassy: 202-328-2700 *Kuala Lumpur* *GMT +8 hrs*

Entry Requirements
- Travelers should contact the Embassy of Malaysia for entry requirement information.
- HIV Test: Not presently required.
- Vaccinations: A yellow fever vaccination certificate is required from all travelers older than 1 year arriving from infected areas. A certificate also required of any traveler arriving from any country in the Yellow Fever Endemic Zones.
Cholera: a vaccination certificate may be required for travelers departing Malaysia for any country where cholera is endemic.

Telephone Country Code: 60

Embassies/Consulates: U.S. Embassy, Kuala Lumpur. 376 Jalan Tun Razak; Tel. (3) 248-9011.

Hospitals/Doctors: Subang Jaya Hospital, Kuala Lumpur (244 beds); some specialties; ICU; 24-hour emergency services; used by U.S. Embassy personnel; Tel. 734-1212. Tawakal Hospital; 24-hour emergency service; used by U.S. Embassy personnel. General Hospital, Kuala Lumpur (2,400 beds); used by U.S. Embassy only as an alternative to Subang or Tawakal Hospitals. Penang Adventist Hospital (400 beds); general medical/surgical facility; ICU.

Health Advisory

Cholera: This disease is active. Endemic areas include Sabah, Penang, and Sarawak. Although cholera vaccination is not required for entry if arriving directly from the U.S. or Canada, it may be required if arriving from a cholera-infected area, or required for on-going travel to other countries in Latin America, Africa, the Middle East, or Asia. Travelers should consider vaccination (one dose) or a doctor's letter of exemption from vaccination.

Malaria: Malaria risk is countrywide below 1,700 meters elevation, but is more prevalent in mountainous and rural areas than in lowland regions. Large cities and developed coastal areas are considered malaria free. High risk areas include Perak and Pahang States (peninsular Malaysia) and Sabah and Sarawak. In Sabah and Sarawak the highest risk of transmission is from March through June–July; in peninsular Malaysia the highest risk of transmission is October through January. Falciparum malaria cases outnumber vivax malaria cases 2:1, but in Sarawak, *P. vivax* predominates. Chloroquine-resistant falciparum malaria is reported. The recommended prophylaxis for adult travelers is mefloquine or doxycycline.

Travelers' diarrhea: A quinolone antibiotic is recommended for the treatment of acute diarrhea. Diarrhea not responding to antibiotic treatment may be due to a parasitic disease such as giardiasis or amebiasis—or an intestinal virus.

Hepatitis: All nonimmune travelers should receive hepatitis A vaccine. The hepatitis B carrier rate in the population is estimated at 5%. Vaccination against hepatitis B is recommended for anyone planning an extended visit to this country. Hepatitis E and C are endemic.

Japanese encephalitis: Sporadic cases occur throughout the year. Risk occurs primarily in areas with rice growing and pig farming. Travelers to rural agricultural areas should be vaccinated, especially if travel exceeds 2–4 weeks. All travelers should take measures to prevent mosquito bites.

Nipah virus encephalitis: This recently recognized disease is caused by a virus in the same class as the ebola virus. The symptoms are similar to Japanese encephalitis. One hundred human fatalities were reported in 1999. The virus infects fruit bats (flying foxes) and can be transmitted to pigs. How the virus moves from pigs to humans is still unclear.

Dengue fever: Occurs countrywide, with increased risk in urban and periurban areas. The States most affected are the Federal Territory, Selangor, Perak, Johor, and Panang. Peak infection rates occur in the late monsoon season (October through February in east peninsular Malaysia, Sabah, and Sarawak; July through August in west peninsular Malaysia.) The *Aedes* mosquitoes that transmit dengue and dengue hemorrhagic fever bite during daylight.

World Medical Guide

Filariasis: Malayan and Bancroftian filariasis are endemic countrywide in freshwater swampy areas and inland hilly areas of primary forest, respectively. Moderate risk occurs in rural areas. Travelers should take measures to prevent mosquito bites.

Schistosomiasis: Slight risk of infection in Perak and Pahang States from *Schistosoma malayensis*. The human health significance of this organism is unclear. It may not be pathogenic. Travelers to these areas should avoid swimming or wading in freshwater.

Other illnesses/hazards: Amebiasis, angiostrongyliasis, intestinal helminthic infections (ascariasis, hookworm, strongyloidiasis, trichuriasis), clonorchiasis, paragonimiasis, leptospirosis (countrywide risk, except in urban areas), chikungunya fever, leprosy (moderate to high prevalence), rabies (last reported in 1985), scrub typhus (mite-borne; risk elevated in grassy rural areas), tuberculosis (highly endemic), typhoid fever, and trachoma (highly endemic). Animal hazards include snakes (kraits, vipers, cobras), centipedes, scorpions, and black widow spiders. Other possible hazards include tigers, bears, and wild pigs. Stingrays, sea wasps, cones, jellyfish, the Indo-Pacific man-of-war, spiny sea urchins, and anemones are common in the country's coastal waters and are potentially hazardous to unprotected or careless swimmers.

MALDIVES

Maldives Mission to the U.N.: 212-599-6195

There is no U.S. Embassy in Maldives. Travelers should contact the Consular Section of the American Embassy in Sri Lanka (94) 1-448-007

MALI

Embassy: 202-332-2249   *Bamako*   *GMT 0 hrs*

Entry Requirements
- A valid passport and visa are required. •HIV Test: Not required.
- Vaccinations: A yellow fever vaccination certificate is required from all travelers older than 1 year of age arriving from ALL COUNTRIES.

Telephone Country Code: 223

Embassies/Consulates: U.S. Embassy, Rue Rochester NY & Rue Mohammed V, Bamako; Tel. 225-663.

Doctors/Hospitals: Point G Hospital, Bamako (550 beds); general medical/surgical facility. Centre Medical Interentreprise, Bamako.

Health Advisory

Yellow fever: The Southwestern Region is considered is no longer considered infected by the World Health Organization. The most recent outbreak of yellow fever occurred during late 1987 in the regions of Kayes and Koulikoro. Vaccination is presently required for entry to this country. Southern Mali is in the Yellow Fever Endemic Zone.

Cholera: This disease is active in this country. Although cholera vaccination is not required for entry if arriving directly from the U.S. or Canada, it may be required if arriving from a cholera-infected area, or required for on-going travel to other countries in Latin America, Africa, the Middle East, or Asia. The risk to travelers of acquiring cholera is considered low. Prevention consists primarily in adhering to safe food and drink guidelines.

Malaria: Risk is present year-round countrywide, including urban areas. Risk is increased during and immediately following the rainy season (June–October). The highest risk of malaria occurs in southern Mali, particularly in the southern savanna and central Sahel zones. There is less risk in the northern Saharan region. Falciparum malaria accounts for approximately 85% of cases; *P. malariae* causes most other cases. Chloroquine-resistant falciparum malaria is prevalent, and mefloquine resistance has recently been reported.

Travelers' diarrhea: High risk. Surface water is almost always contaminated and ground water from deep wells commonly brackish. Piped water supplies are either untreated and often contaminated. Travelers should observe all food and drink precautions. A quinolone antibiotic is recommended for the treatment of acute diarrhea. Diarrhea not responding to treatment with an antibiotic may be due to a parasitic disease.

Hepatitis: All nonimmune travelers should receive hepatitis A vaccine. Hepatitis E presumably occurs, but levels are unclear. The hepatitis B carrier rate in the general population is estimated at 9%–18%. Vaccination against hepatitis B is recommended for those planning long-term residence (more than 4 weeks) in this country.

Leishmaniasis: Risk of cutaneous leishmaniasis occurs primarily in rural areas of the southern and central Sahel. Current incidence and distribution data are not available, but sporadic cases have been reported from semi-desert regions, with a major focus in the Nioro District of Kayes Region. Visceral leishmaniasis (kala azar) is currently not reported. All travelers to these regions should take measures to prevent sandfly bites.

Filariasis: Bancroftian filariasis is reported in southern areas. Travelers should take measures to prevent insect (mosquito) bites.

Onchocerciasis: Highly endemic foci are found in the Sikasso and Kayes Regions along rivers where blackflies breed. Travelers should take measures to prevent insect (blackfly) bites.

Schistosomiasis: Prevalence is particularly high in irrigated areas. Urinary schistosomiasis occurs throughout southern Mali, primarily in the upper reaches of the Niger River and the upper basin of the Senegal River. Intestinal schistosomiasis is almost as extensively distributed. A new focus of disease has recently been reported from the Bandiagara and Bankas Districts where the Dogon tribe is located. To prevent schistosomiasis, travelers should avoid swimming, bathing, or wading in freshwater lakes, ponds, or streams.

Trypanosomiasis (African sleeping sickness): There is a low risk of trypanosomiasis in Mali, primarily in the Koulikoro and Sikasso regions. Travelers to these regions should take precautions to prevent tsetse fly bites.

Meningitis: The southern half of Mali lies within the sub-Saharan meningitis belt. Periodic epidemics occur within this country. Most infections are caused by Group A organisms, but Type C also occurs. Vaccination is recommended for travelers who expect to have close, prolonged contact with the indigenous population.

Rabies: Potentially rabid animals include dogs, cats, jackals, and foxes. Human cases occur countrywide from both urban and rural areas, especially following dog bites. Vaccination is recommended for long-term travelers, especially those going to remote areas.

AIDS: HIV prevalence is apparently low in the general population, but as high as 40% of surveyed prostitutes are infected.

Other illnesses/hazards: Anthrax (reported from Kati and Koulikoro Provinces), brucellosis (from consumption of raw dairy products), dracunculiasis (endemic at low levels), dengue (no apparent activity), ehrlichiosis (tick-borne; single case reported in 1992 in a Canadian traveler), echinococcosis, hemorrhagic fever with renal syndrome (level of risk unclear; no human cases reported), Lassa fever, leprosy (4–7 cases/1,000 population in Bamako), relapsing fever (tick-borne and louse-borne), Rift Valley fever, toxoplasmosis, tuberculosis (a major health problem), typhoid fever, and intestinal worms (very common). Animal hazards include snakes (vipers, cobras), centipedes, scorpions, and black widow spiders; crocodiles and hippopotamuses inhabit the rivers of Mali; lions and panthers are the major terrestrial hazards.

World Medical Guide

MALTA

Embassy: 202-462-3611   *Valletta*   *GMT +1 hr*

Entry Requirements
- Passport/Visa: Passport required.
- HIV Test: Not required.
- Vaccinations: A yellow fever vaccination certificate is required for all travelers older than 6 months arriving from infected areas.

Telephone Country Code: 356
Embassies/Consulates: U.S. Embassy, Valletta; Development House, 2nd Floor, St. Anne Street; Tel. 623-653/620-424. Canadian Embassy, Valletta. Demajo House, 103 Archbishop Street; Tel. 233-121/6.
Hospitals/Doctors: Travelers should contact the U.S. Embassy for physician and hospital referrals.

Health Advisory

Traveler's diarrhea: Medium to high risk outside of first-class hotels and resorts. Travelers are advised to drink only bottled, boiled, filtered, or treated water and consume only well-cooked food. All fruit should be peeled prior to consumption. A quinolone antibiotic (Floxin or Cipro) is recommended for the treatment of acute diarrhea. Diarrhea not responding to antibiotic treatment may be due to a parasitic disease such as giardiasis—or an intestinal virus.
Hepatitis: All nonimmune travelers should receive hepatitis A vaccine. The hepatitis B carrier rate in the population is estimated at 1%–2%. Vaccination against hepatitis B is recommended for long-term visitors to this country.

MARSHALL ISLANDS

Embassy: 202-234-5414   *Majuro*

Entry Requirements
- Passport/Visa: No visa required for stays less than 30 days. (Extentible to 90 days.)
- HIV Test: Not required.
- Vaccinations: None required.

Telephone Country Code: 692
Embassies/Consulates: U.S. Embassy, Majuro; Tel: 247-4011.

Health Advisory

See Disease Risk Summary for Oceania. Health care facilities are located only on Majuro and Ebeye.

MARTINIQUE (FRENCH WEST INDIES)

Embassy: 202-944-6000   *Fort-de-France*   *GMT -4 hrs*

Entry Requirements
- Passport/Visa: A valid passport is required. A visa is not required.
- HIV Test: Not required.
- Vaccinations: Yellow fever: A vaccination certificate is required of all travelers older than 1 year arriving from infected areas.

Telephone Country Code: 596
Embassies/Consulates: U.S. Embassy, French Caribbean Dept. 14 Rue Blenac, Martinique; Tel. (596) 631-303.
Hospitals/Doctors: La Maynard Hospital, Fort-de-France Regional Hospital Center (764 beds); general medical/surgical facility; trauma and 24-hour emergency services.

World Medical Guide

Health Advisory

See Disease Risk Summary for the Caribbean.
Travelers' diarrhea: Low to moderate risk. In urban and resort areas, the hotels and restaurants generally serve reliable food and potable water. Elsewhere, travelers should observe all food and drink safety precautions. A quinolone antibiotic (Floxin or Cipro) is recommended for the treatment of acute diarrhea. Diarrhea not responding to antibiotic treatment may be due to a parasitic disease such as giardiasis or amebiasis.
Hepatitis: Low risk to tourists. All nonimmune travelers should receive hepatitis A vaccine.
Dengue fever: Risk is present. This mosquito-transmitted viral disease is prevalent in the Caribbean. Travelers should take measures to prevent insect bites.
Leishmaniasis: Limited risk. Cutaneous and visceral forms of leishmaniasis may be present. Travelers should take measures to avoid insect (sandfly) bites.
Schistosomiasis: Disease due to intestinal schistosomiasis (due to *S. mansoni*) is present on this island, but the risk is deemed to be low. Most snail-infested freshwater foci have been identified and can be avoided. Travelers should avoid swimming, bathing, or wading in freshwater ponds, lakes, or streams unless advised they are safe. Chlorinated swimming pools are considered safe.
Other diseases/health threats: Brucellosis, filariasis (Bancroftian variety; mosquito-borne; may occur in the Lesser Antilles from Trinidad north to Guadeloupe), histoplasmosis, intestinal helminthic infections (ancylostomiasis, ascariasis, strongyloidiasis, and trichuriasis), leptospirosis, sexually transmitted diseases, AIDS, toxocariasis, tuberculosis, typhoid fever, viral encephalitis, ciguatera fish toxin poisoning, and swimming related hazards (jellyfish, spiny sea urchins, and coral).

MAURITANIA

Embassy: 202-232-5700 *Nouakchott* GMT 0 hrs
Entry Requirements
- Passport/Visa: Valid passport and visa are required.
- HIV Test: Not required.
- Vaccinations: A yellow fever vaccination certificate is required from all travelers older than 1 year arriving from ALL COUNTRIES.

Telephone Country Code: 222
Embassies/Consulates: U.S. Embassy, Nouakchott; Tel. 52660. Canadian Embassy (Senegal); Tel. [221] 210-290.
Doctors/Hospitals: National Hospital, Nouakchott (460 beds); general medical/surgical facility; limited specialties.

Health Advisory

Yellow fever: Vaccination is recommended. Southern Mauritania borders the yellow fever endemic zone of Mali, considered "infected" by the World Health Organization.
Cholera: This disease is active in this country. Although cholera vaccination is not required for entry if arriving directly from the U.S. or Canada, it may be required if arriving from a cholera-infected area, or required for on-going travel to other countries in Latin America, Africa, the Middle East, or Asia. Travelers should consider vaccination (one dose) or a doctor's letter of exemption from vaccination. The risk to travelers of acquiring cholera is considered low. Prevention consists primarily in adhering to safe food and drink guidelines.
Malaria: Risk is present countrywide, including urban areas, year-round, particularly along the Senegal River Basin where the risk may be elevated during and immediately after the rainy season (July–September). Limited risk occurs in semidesert and desert areas (north of approximately 20 degrees north latitude). No apparent risk in the extreme desert areas of Dakhlet Nouadhibou, Inchiri, Adrar, Tiris Zemmour, and Hodh el Gharbi Regions. Vivax malaria accounts for 90% of cases. Falciparum malaria accounts for less than 10% of cases. Chloroquine-resistant falciparum malaria was reported for the first time in 1994. Mefloquine or doxycycline prophylaxis is recommended when traveling to malarious areas of Mauritania.

World Medical Guide

Travelers' diarrhea: High risk. All water sources should be considered potentially contaminated. Travelers should observe food and drink safety precautions. A quinolone antibiotic is recommended for the treatment of acute diarrhea. Diarrhea not responding to treatment with an antibiotic, or chronic diarrhea, may be due to a parasitic disease such as giardiasis, amebiasis, or cryptosporidiosis.

Hepatitis: High risk. All nonimmune travelers should receive hepatitis A vaccine. Hepatitis E likely occurs, but data are not available. The hepatitis B carrier rate in the general population is estimated as high as 22%. Vaccination against hepatitis B is recommended for healthcare workers and all long-term visitors to this country.

Dengue fever: Undetermined risk, but probably low. Dengue virus is present in neighboring Senegal.

Leishmaniasis: Sporadic cases of cutaneous leishmaniasis have been reported along the border with Senegal and near the southern border with Mali. Travelers should take measures to prevent insect (sandfly) bites.

Schistosomiasis: Risk is greatest in the south along the Senegal River and extending into the southeast, and a smaller area farther north, around the Adrar mountain range in the vicinity of Atar, in central western Mauritania. Infection rates of urinary schistosomiasis are highest in the south central border regions of Gorgol, Guidimaka, and Hodh el Gharbi. Travelers should avoid swimming, bathing, or wading in freshwater lakes, ponds, or streams.

Rabies: Vaccination against rabies should be considered prior to long-term travel to this region. Vaccination is indicated following the unprovoked bite of a dog or other wild animal.

AIDS: HIV prevalence appears to be low, based on limited data.

Other illnesses/hazards: African tick typhus (may occur), anthrax (incidence data lacking), brucellosis (from consumption of raw dairy products), Crimean-Congo hemorrhagic fever, dracunculiasis, meningococcal meningitis (southern Mauritania borders the sub-Saharan meningitis belt), plague (human incidence data lacking), relapsing fever (tick-borne, louse-borne; may occur), Rift Valley fever, tuberculosis (a major health problem), typhoid fever, and intestinal worms (very common). Animal hazards include snakes (vipers, cobras, adders), centipedes, scorpions, and black widow spiders. Marine hazards include poisonous fishes (weever, scorpion, and toad fishes) and venomous marine invertebrates such as the Portuguese man-of-war, stinging corals, feather hydroids, and sea nettles, anemones, urchins, and sea cucumbers.

MAURITIUS

Embassy: 202-244-1491　　*Port Louis*　　*GMT +4 hrs*

Entry Requirements
- Visa not required for visits up to 6 months.
- HIV Test: Required for foreigners seeking work or permanent residence.
- Vaccinations: A yellow fever vaccination certificate is required from all travelers older than 1 year arriving from infected areas and also from any country in the Yellow Fever Endemic Zones.

Telephone Country Code: 230
Embassies/Consulates: U.S. Embassy, Port Louis. Rogers House, 4th Floor, John Kennedy Street; Tel. 208-9764 through 208-9769.
Hospitals/Doctors: Medical & Surgical Centre.

Health Advisory

Malaria: Risk is present between January and May in rural areas of Pamplemousse, Plaines Wilhelmes, Riviere du Ramparts, Grand Port, and Port Louis Districts. There is no malaria on the island of Rodriguez. Chloroquine-resistant falciparum malaria is reported. Prophylaxis with mefloquine or doxycycline is currently recommended when traveling to malarious areas.

Travelers' diarrhea: High risk. A quinolone antibiotic is recommended for the treatment of acute diarrhea. Diarrhea not responding to treatment with an antibiotic, or chronic diarrhea,

World Medical Guide

may be due to a parasitic disease such as giardiasis or amebiasis, and treatment with metronidazole (Flagyl) or tinidazole (Fasigyn) should be considered. All cases of diarrhea should be treated with adequate fluid replacement.

Hepatitis: All nonimmune travelers should receive hepatitis A vaccine. The hepatitis B carrier rate in the general population is estimated to exceed 10%. Vaccination against hepatitis B is recommended for healthcare workers and all long-term visitors to this country.

Leishmaniasis: Both cutaneous and visceral leishmaniasis are reported. Travelers should take measures to prevent insect (sandfly) bites.

Filariasis: Risk is present throughout this country. Travelers should take measures to prevent insect (mosquito) bites.

Schistosomiasis: Risk is present throughout this country, including urban areas. Travelers should avoid swimming, bathing, or wading in freshwater lakes, ponds, or streams.

Other diseases/health threats: Echinococcosis, leprosy (highly endemic), rabies, tick-borne typhus, syphilis, tuberculosis (highly endemic), and soil-transmitted helminthic disease (ascariasis, hookworm disease, strongyloidiasis) are reported. Animal hazards include snakes (cobras, vipers), spiders (black and brown widow), crocodiles, and leeches. Stingrays, jellyfish, and several species of poisonous fish are common in the country's coastal waters and are potential hazards to unprotected swimmers.

MEXICO

Embassy: 202-736-1000   *Mexico City*   *GMT -6 hrs*

Entry Requirements

- Passport/Visa: Photo identification and proof of citizenship are required for entry by all U.S. citizens. A passport is the best document. A visa is required only for stays exceeding 180 days.
- HIV Test: Not required.
- Vaccinations: A yellow fever vaccination certificate is required from all travelers older than 9 months of age arriving from yellow fever infected areas.

Telephone Country Code: 52   **AT&T:** 95-800-462-4240   **MCI:** 95-800-674-7000

Mexican Government Tourist Office: Washington, DC. Tel. (202) 728-1750.

Embassies/Consulates: U.S. Embassy, Mexico City. Paseo de la Reforma 305, Colonia Cuauhtemoc; Tel. (5) 209-9000. U.S. Consulate, Ciudad Juarez; Tel. (16) 113-000. U.S. Consulate, Guadalajara; Tel. (38) 252-998. U.S. Consulate, Merida; Tel. (99) 255-011. U.S. Consulate, Monterey; Tel. (83) 452-120. U.S. Consulate, Tijuana; Tel. (66) 817-400. U.S. Consular Agency, Acapulco; Tel. (74)-840-300. U.S. Consular Agency, Puerto Vallarta; Tel. (322) 20-069. U.S. Consular Agency, Cancun; (98) 830-272.

Doctors/Hospitals: In Mexico City: John F. Smyth, M.D., Campos Eliseos No. 81 Colonia Polanco; Tel. (5) 545-7861 (office) or (5) 250-0019 (home). The British-American Hospital (160 beds); private hospital; most of the staff are U.S. or British board-certified; specialties include cardiology, ob/gyn, emergency medicine, neurology; Tel. (5) 277-5000.

In Monterrey: Hospital Jose A. Muguerza (1154 beds); private hospital; most specialties, including cardiology, ob/gyn, kidney dialysis; Tel. 460-100.

Dr. Jose Gonzalez University Hospital (704 beds); Tel. 487-926.

In Guadalajara: Civil Hospital (1,000 beds); some specialties; English-speaking, U.S.-trained physicians on staff.

Health Advisory

Malaria: Malaria is endemic in rural areas under 1,000 meters elevation, and is more widespread than most travelers realize. The disease, however, has been eliminated from large urban areas and the major international resorts. The incidence of malaria is highest in the south, including the states of Chiapas, Oaxaca, Guerrero, Quintana Roo, and Campeche, and in Sinaloa State on the Pacific Coast. Lesser-risk areas include Michoacan and Tabasco states. Most cases reported from tourist centers occur in the vicinity of Huatulco Bay (Pochutla region of Oaxaca). *P. vivax* accounts for more than

World Medical Guide

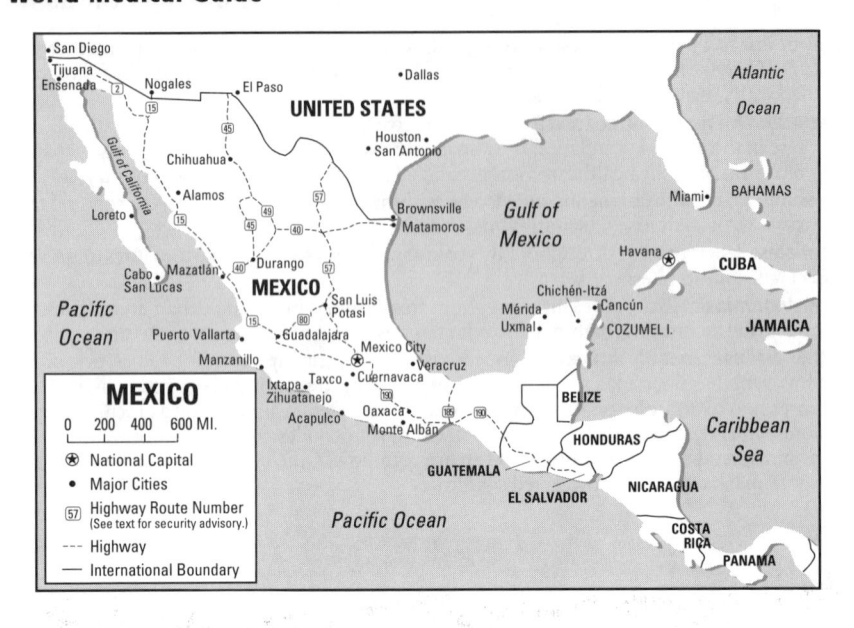

99% of infections, the remainder attributed to *P. falciparum*. No cases of chloroquine-resistant malaria have been reported. Falciparum infections appear to be limited to rain forest areas near the borders with Belize and Guatemala. Malaria precautions are recommended for overnight stays in many rural areas at low altitude, especially in southern Mexico. Persons staying overnight at the following archaeological sites should take consider chloroquine prophylaxis: Palenque, Bonampak, Uxmal, Kabah, Labna, Sayil, Edzna, Coba, and Tulum. Chloroquine is not recommended when visiting major resort areas. In resort areas, mosquito bite prevention measures are considered sufficient, and will help eliminate the risk of dengue fever and leishmaniasis as well as malaria.

Cholera: The risk to travelers of acquiring cholera is low. Vaccination is not routinely recommended. Prevention consists primarily in strictly adhering to safe food and drink guidelines. Although cholera vaccination is not required for entry if arriving directly from the U.S. or Canada, it may be required if arriving from a cholera-infected area, or required for on-going travel to other countries in Latin America, Africa, the Middle East, or Asia. Depending upon their itinerary, travelers should consider vaccination or a doctor's letter of exemption from vaccination.

Travelers' diarrhea: High risk, especially outside major resorts and first-class hotels. Highest risk occurs during the rainy season, May through October. Bacterial organisms, in the following order—*enterotoxigenic E. coli*, campylobacter, salmonella, and shigella—account for more than 80% of cases of travelers' diarrhea. About 10% of cases are caused by viruses (mostly Norwalk virus), and 3%–4% are due to parasites, mainly amebae, giardia, cyclospora, and cryptosporidia. A quinolone antibiotic plus loperamide is recommended for the treatment of acute diarrhea.

Amebiasis: There is a high incidence of amebiasis in Mexico, especially in the southern areas where up to 8.4% of the population is seropositive for *E. histolytica* antibodies. To avoid amebiasis, travelers should drink only safe water and eat only well-cooked food. All fruit should be peeled before eating. Other parasitic diseases include ascariasis, trichiuriasis, and hookworm. None of these infections are common in travelers.

Hepatitis: Hepatitis A is highly endemic. All nonimmune travelers should receive hepatitis A vaccine, especially if planning travel outside the usual resort areas. Hepatitis B: Estimates of the carrier rate in the adult population range from 0.3% to 1.6%, although carrier rates up to 4% have been reported from Chiapas State. Immunization

World Medical Guide

against hepatitis B is not routinely recommended for tourist travel. **Hepatitis E:** Sporadic hepatitis E infections have been reported among visitors to northern Baja, Guerrero, and Morelos States, as well as in the Mexico City and Tijuana. To help prevent hepatitis E, travelers should avoid drinking unsafe water. The consumption of bottled, boiled, or chemically treated water is strongly recommended, especially for pregnant women.

Typhoid fever: Vaccination, which is about 70% effective, is recommended for anyone traveling outside the major tourist areas, and/or for travelers planning to remain in Mexico more than one month. This disease is widespread and more cases of typhoid fever are reported in travelers returning from Mexico than from any other Latin American country. There is increased risk of typhoid from June through October, countrywide. In addition to vaccination, prevention also consists of food and drink precautions.

Dengue fever: Dengue occurs in most areas below 1,200 meters elevation, but recently dengue has been reported in the city of Taxco, 1,700 meters elevation. The risk of dengue is currently greatest in the southern and central Pacific urban coastal areas and in extreme northeastern Mexico. Increased risk may occur during the rainy season, from July through October. This disease is transmitted by the *Aedes aegypti* mosquito, but the Asian "tiger mosquito" (*Aedes albopictus*) may also transmit the virus. All travelers to risk areas below 1,200 meters elevation are advised to take precautions against mosquito bites. A vaccine is not available.

Viral encephalitis: Rare cases of St. Louis encephalitis, Venezuelan equine encephalitis, and eastern and western encephalitis are reported.

Leishmaniasis: Cutaneous leishmaniasis is endemic in rural areas in the southern territory of Quintana Roo, eastern Yucatan, Campeche, eastern Tabasco, Chiapas, Oaxaca, and eastern Veracruz. Mucocutaneous leishmaniasis (espundia) has occurred in Jalisco State, and visceral leishmaniasis (kala azar) has occurred in Guerrero and Morelos States. Diffuse cutaneous leishmaniasis occurs in both the northeast and southeast regions. Mucocutaneous leishmaniasis has occurred in Jalisco State. This disease is transmitted by sandflies, which are most active between sunset and dawn. All travelers should take measures to prevent insect bites, specially in forested areas. Slow- or non-healing skin infections should alert travelers to this possible diagnosis.

Onchocerciasis: This blackfly-transmitted disease is limited to areas along rivers between 600 and 1,500 meters elevation in Chiapas and Oaxaca States. Highest risk is from October through April. Travelers should take measures to prevent insect (blackfly) bites.

Gnathostomiasis: Number of cases appears to be increasing dramatically. This food-borne parasitic disease is acquired through ingesting a parasite found in raw or undercooked freshwater fish (usually eaten in the form of tilapia, or ceviche, a famous Mexican raw fish dish). Endemic areas are found in six states—Sinaloa, Nayarit, Oaxaca, Veracruz, Temaulipas, and Guerrero, which includes the city of Acapulco. All travelers to these regions should avoid ingesting raw freshwater fish.

Chagas' disease: Risk occurs below 1,500 meters elevation in the rural areas of the southern and western states. Most risk is found in those rural-agricultural areas where there are adobe-style huts and houses that potentially harbor the night-biting triatomid (assassin) bugs. Travelers sleeping in such structures should take precautions against nighttime bites. Unscreened blood transfusions are also a source of infection and should be avoided. (Up to 17% of blood donations tested have been seropositive.)

Rabies: Several dozen or more human cases are reported annually. Ninety percent of cases are acquired from contact with rabid dogs, usually in rural areas. Rabid vampire bats reportedly are a problem in Sinaloa State. Travelers should especially avoid stray dogs and seek immediate treatment of any animal bite. Rabies vaccination is especially indicated following the unprovoked bite of a dog, cat, bat, or monkey.

Helminthic infections: Hookworm, roundworm, and whipworm infections, and also strongyloidiasis, are highly prevalent in most rural areas. (Hookworm disease infects up to 90% of some rural villagers.) Travelers should wear shoes to prevent the hookworm and strongyloides larvae from penetrating the skin. All food should be thoroughly cooked to destroy roundworm, whipworm, and pork tapeworm eggs. Pork tapeworm disease is common and can be prevented by eating only thoroughly cooked pork.

World Medical Guide

Environmental pollution: Acute respiratory infections are a common cause of illness in Mexico, probably aggravated by this country's legendary air pollution, about the worst in the world. Extreme conditions can occur in Mexico City and Guadalajara, especially from December to May. Travelers with heart disease, emphysema, and asthma may need to limit or avoid travel to regions with poor air quality. Drinking water in Mexico City and other areas contains high concentrations of lead. Lead is also found in polluted air, leaded paints, in some canned foods and beverages, and leached into beverages stored in lead-glazed pottery.

Tuberculosis: This disease is highly endemic, particularly among the native Indian populations in southern Mexico and Baja California; drug-resistant strains are common.

AIDS: Incidence appears to be increasing rapidly. In 1989, approximately 76% of adult cases were due to bisexual or homosexual contact, 11% to heterosexual contact, and almost 12% to intravenous drug use or blood products.

Seabather's eruption: Reported in Cancun. This condition is caused by sea anemone larvae trapped under the bathing suit. Released toxin causes skin irritation, rash, and fever.

Other diseases/hazards: Anthrax (small outbreaks reported in Zacatecas, central Mexico), brucellosis (90% of cases associated with contact with goats; greatest risk occurs in the northern and central states), coccidiomycosis (endemic in the dry north of Baja California Norte, Sonora and Chihuahua States, and along the Pacific Coast. An outbreak of coccidiomycosis occurred in 1996 in members of a U.S. church group who had visited Tecate, a town in the Sonoran Desert adjacent to the United States-Mexico border), cysticercosis and neurocysticercosis (caused by the ingestion of pork tapeworm eggs; common, especially in Guanajuato and Michocan States), histoplasmosis (contact with bat guano transmits this fungal disease), relapsing fever (tick-borne; endemic in northern and central Mexico), leptospirosis, typhus (both louse- and flea-borne; reported in Chiapas State), and tick-borne rickettsioses (spotted fever group; reported in some rural areas; one case of human monocytic ehrlichiosis reported in Yucatan.)

MICRONESIA (TRUK, YAP, PANAPE, KOSRAE)

Embassy: 202- 544- 2640   *Palikir*   *GMT +11 hrs*

Entry Requirements
- Passport/visa: Passport required. Micronesia is self-governing in free association with the United States. The 600 islands and atolls were formerly part of the U.S. Trust Territory of the Pacific.
- HIV Test: Required of anyone staying over one year.
- Vaccinations: None required.

Telephone Country Code: 691

Health Advisory

Travelers' diarrhea: Low to moderate risk. In urban and resort areas, the hotels and restaurants generally serve reliable food and potable water. Elsewhere, travelers should observe all food and drink safety precautions. A quinolone antibiotic is recommended for the treatment of acute diarrhea.

Hepatitis: Hepatitis A vaccine is recommended for all nonimmune travelers. The hepatitis B carrier rate in parts of Oceania is as high as 15%. Vaccination against hepatitis B is recommended for long-term visitors to this country.

Dengue fever: Sporadic cases and outbreaks are reported. A dengue fever/dengue hemorrhagic fever outbreak occurred in Yap State in 1995. Travelers should take protective measures against mosquito bites.

Japanese encephalitis: Probably not active.

Filariasis: Sporadic cases reported. Travelers should prevent mosquito bites.

World Medical Guide

MOLDOVA
Moldovan Embassy: 202-667-1131. U.S. Embassy, Chisinau: (373)-2-233-772
For Health Advisory information, see the Health Advisory for Russia on page 259.

MONGOLIA
Embassy of Mongolia: 202-333-7117. U.S. Embassy, Ulaanbaatar: (976)-1-329-095.

MONTSERRAT (BRITISH WEST INDIES)
Embassy: 202-462-1340   Plymouth   GMT -4 hrs
Entry Requirements
- Passport/Visa: Visa not required. Montserrat is a French Dependent Territory.
- HIV Test: Not required.
- Vaccinations: No vaccinations are required.

Telephone Area Code: 809
Doctors/Hospitals: Glendon Hospital, Plymouth (67 beds).

Health Advisory
See Disease Risk Summary for the Caribbean.
Travelers' diarrhea: Low to moderate risk. In urban and resort areas, the hotels and restaurants generally serve reliable food and potable water. A quinolone antibiotic is recommended for the treatment of acute diarrhea.
Hepatitis: Low risk to tourists. All nonimmune travelers should receive hepatitis A vaccine.
Dengue fever: Risk is present. This mosquito-transmitted viral disease is prevalent in the Caribbean. Travelers should take measures to prevent insect bites.
Schistosomiasis: This disease is present but the risk is low. Most snail-infested freshwater foci have been identified and can be avoided.
Other diseases/health threats: Intestinal helminthic infections, syphilis, AIDS, toxoplasmosis, tuberculosis, typhoid fever, viral encephalitis, ciguatera fish toxin poisoning (outbreaks have occurred), and swimming related hazards (jellyfish, spiny sea urchins, and coral).

MOROCCO
Embassy: 202-462-7979   Rabat   GMT 0 hrs
Entry Requirements
- Passport/Visa: Valid passport is required. Visa not required.
- HIV Test: Not required.
- Vaccinations: None required.

Telephone Country Code: 212
Embassies/Consulates: U.S. Consulate, Rabat; 8 Blvd. Moulay Yousesef. Tel. (7) 622-65. U.S. Consulate, Casablanca; Tel. 25-45-50. U.S. Consulate, Tangier; Tel. 359-04.
Hospitals/Doctors: Avicenne Hospital, Rabat (850 beds); general medical/surgical facility; blood bank. Clinique Beausejour, Rabat. Croissant Rouge Marocain (Red Cross); Tel. 25-25-21. Dr. A. El Kouhen, Casablanca. Tel: 27-53-43. Dr. Ahmed Mansouri, Marrakesh. Tel. 43-07-54. Clinique California, Tangier; Tel: 388-24/387-22. Hopital Al Kortobi, Tangier; open 24 hours daily for medical emergencies. Tel. 310-73. Joseph Hirt, M.D., Tangier; well-known physician who will make hotel calls. Tel. 357-29.

411

World Medical Guide

Health Advisory

Malaria: Year-round risk, reportedly elevated during the dry season, from May through October, in rural foci located in the central and northern provinces of Beni Mellal, Chaouen, El Kelaa des Srarhna, Khemisset, Khenifra, Khouribga, Larache, Settat, Sidi Kacem, Tanger, Taounate, and Taza. Urban areas are risk-free. Vivax malaria accounts for 99% of cases, with rare P. *malariae* reported.

Travelers' diarrhea: Water sources in Morocco should be considered potentially contaminated. In urban and resort areas, the first-class hotels and restaurants generally serve reliable food and potable water. A quinolone antibiotic is recommended for the treatment of acute diarrhea. Diarrhea not responding to antibiotic treatment may be due to a parasitic disease such as giardiasis, amebiasis, or cryptosporidiosis.

Hepatitis: Hepatitis A vaccine is recommended for nonimmune travelers. Hepatitis E is endemic at a high level. The hepatitis B carrier rate in the population is estimated as high as 6%. Vaccination against hepatitis B is recommended for long-term visitors to this country.

Leishmaniasis: Cutaneous leishmaniasis (CL) is widespread in semiarid rural areas, with increased vector activity June through September, particularly in Er Rachidia, Ouarzazate, and Tata Provinces. CL due to *L. tropica* apparently is distributed countrywide in rural areas, including the High Atlas mountain region (Azilal and Essaouira Provinces), north of the High Atlas Mountains (likely Marrakech Province), and the western part of the Anti-Atlas Mountains (likely Agadir and Tiznit Provinces). *L. infantum* is focally distributed in urban areas throughout Morocco, with the risk greater in northern areas (Al Hoceima, Chaouen, Fes, Meknes, Nador, Taza, and Tetouan Provinces), and possibly in Marrakech Province and the Moyen Atlas mounbtain region. Visceral leishmaniasis (caused by *L. infantum*) is sporadically reported. All travelers should take precautions against sandfly bites in these areas.

Schistosomiasis: Year-round risk, with highest incidence in the summer. Urinary schistosomiasis is widespread, particularly along the wadis and slopes of the Anti- and Haut Atlas Mountains, coastal areas (except for an area on the western coast), in oases, and irrigated agricultural areas. Recognized foci occur in central and southern areas, including Agadir, Beni Mellal, El Kelaa des Srarhna, Er Rachidia, Marrakech, Ouarzazate, Taroudannt, Tata, and Tiznit Provinces. Activity also reported in northern areas, including Kenitra, Nador, and Tanger Provinces. Risk-free areas include the coastal area between Rabat and Essaouira, and the provinces of Fes, Meknes, and Taza.

African tick typhus (boutonneuse fever): Presumed widespread, primarily in rural and suburban coastal areas.

Rabies: Human cases have been reported primarily from the populated northern urban and rural areas. Dogs, jackals, foxes are primary reservoirs of infection.

Other illnesses: AIDS/HIV (endemic at low levels), brucellosis (risk from unpasteurized goat/sheep milk and cheese), cholera, echinococcosis (highly prevalent countrywide), leptospirosis, relapsing fever (tick-borne), sandfly fever (primarily in northern one-half of country), toxoplasmosis (infection rates as high as 52%), trachoma, tuberculosis (a major public health problem), typhoid fever, and intestinal helminthic infections (especially roundworm) are common in rural areas. Scorpion are a major public health problem. Immediate serotherapy is recommended for black scorpion and yellow scorpion stings.

MOZAMBIQUE

Embassy: 202-293-7146 *Maputo* *GMT +2 hrs*

Entry Requirements
- A visa, valid for 30 days, is required. • HIV Test: Not required.
- Vaccinations: A yellow fever vaccination certificate is required from all travelers older than 1 year arriving from infected areas.

Telephone Country Code: 258

Embassies/Consulates: U.S. Embassy, Maputo. Avenida Kenneth Kaunda 193; Tel. (1) 492-797. After hours/emergencies, Tel. (1) 490-723.

Hospitals/Doctors: Travelers should contact the U.S. Embassy for physician referrals.

World Medical Guide

Health Advisory

Yellow fever: Vaccination recommended. No cases are currently reported.
Cholera: This disease is active in this country.
Malaria: High risk is present throughout this country, including urban areas. There is increased malaria risk along the coast and in the lower Zambezi Valley. Outbreaks are reported in Xai-Xai and Maputo. Falciparum malaria accounts for up to 95% of cases. Other cases of malaria are due to the *P. malariae* species, rarely *P. ovale* and *P. vivax*. Chloroquine-resistant falciparum malaria occurs. Prophylaxis with mefloquine or doxycycline is recommended.
Travelers' diarrhea: High risk. Potable water is often in critically short supply. Piped water supplies in urban areas may be grossly contaminated. Travelers should observe all food and drink safety precautions. A quinolone antibiotic is recommended for the treatment of acute diarrhea.
Hepatitis: All nonimmune travelers should receive hepatitis A vaccine. Hepatitis E presumably occurs, but endemic levels are unclear. The hepatitis B carrier rate in the general population is estimated at 11%. Vaccination against hepatitis B is recommended for healthcare workers and all long-term visitors to this country.
Schistosomiasis: Risk of urinary schistosomiasis is reported from all provinces with infection rates up to 60% in some areas. Intestinal schistosomiasis appears almost as widely distributed with major risk areas along the southern coastal plain, the Zambezi Valley, and the vicinity of Lake Malawi. All travelers should avoid swimming, bathing, or wading in freshwater lakes, ponds, or streams.
Trypanosomiasis (sleeping sickness): During the 1980s, approximately 75 cases were reported annually, mostly from Tete Province. All travelers should take precautions against insect (tsetse fly) bites.
Meningitis: Group C meningococcal meningitis outbreak occurred in Maputo in late 1989. Vaccination is recommended for those travelers staying in this country longer than 4 weeks, and those who will have close contact with the indigenous population.
Rabies: Occurs in rural and urban areas, including Maputo. Dogs are the primary source of human infections. Pre-exposure vaccination is recommended for long-term travel (more than 4 weeks) to this country, especially for travelers going to remote areas.
AIDS: Heterosexual contact is the predominate mode of transmission. Lower risk compared to other countries in sub-Saharan Africa. HIV-1 prevalence estimated at 2.6% of the high-risk urban population. All travelers are cautioned against unsafe sex, unsterile medical or dental injections, and unnecessary blood transfusions.
Other illnesses/hazards: African tick typhus, brucellosis, filariasis (mosquito-borne; occurs in northern coastal areas and along the Zambezi River), leishmaniasis (endemic levels unclear; may occur), leprosy, plague (no human cases reported since 1978), Rift Valley fever, tuberculosis (a major health problem), trachoma, typhoid fever, and intestinal worms. Animal hazards include snakes (vipers, cobras, mambas), centipedes, scorpions, and black widow spiders. Stingrays, jellyfish, moon jelly, sea wasps, blue cones, octopi, bat rays and eagle rays, and several species of poisonous fish are common in the country's coastal waters.

NAMIBIA

Embassy: 202-986-0540   *Windhoek*   GMT +2 hrs

Entry Requirements
- A visa not required for tourist or business stays up to 90 days.
- HIV Test: Not required.
- Vaccinations: Yellow fever vaccination certificate is required from travelers older than 1 year arriving from, or transiting through, infected areas, or arriving from any country in the Yellow Fever Endemic Zones.

Telephone Country Code: 264
Embassies/Consulates: U.S. Embassy, Windhoek. 14 Lossen Street; Tel. (61) 221-601.
Doctors/Hospitals: State Hospital, Windhoek (440 beds); general medical/surgical facility; limited burn treatment; emergency services, ICU.

World Medical Guide

Health Advisory
Malaria: Risk occurs primarily from November to May–June, during and just after the rainy season, in the northcentral and northeastern rural regions along the borders with Angola, Zambia, and Botswana, including the Ovamboland, which borders Angola, and the Caprivi strip. Malaria risk has recently extended somewhat into the central plateau and eastern semi-arid areas, but not the coastal desert. Major outbreaks in 1988 affected all areas except the coastal regions. Falciparum malaria accounts for up to 98% of cases countrywide. Chloroquine-resistant falciparum malaria is widespread. Prophylaxis with mefloquine or doxycycline is currently recommended.

Travelers' diarrhea: The water in major urban areas is treated, and in Swakopund, Walvis Bay, and Windhoek, the major hotels and restaurants serve generally safe food and drink. Outside of these areas, all water sources should be considered potentially contaminated. Some surface water in shallow lakes contains dangerously high concentrations of minerals and nitrites and is unsafe for consumption. Travelers should observe all food and drink safety precautions. A quinolone antibiotic is recommended for the treatment of acute diarrhea. Parasitic diseases, such as amebiasis, giardiasis, and cryptosporidiosis, are reported.

Hepatitis: High risk. All nonimmune travelers should receive hepatitis A vaccine. Hepatitis E is endemic, but levels are unclear. The hepatitis B carrier rate in the general population is estimated as high as 15%. Vaccination against hepatitis B is recommended for all long-term visitors to this country.

Leishmaniasis: Sporadic cases of cutaneous leishmaniasis have been reported, primarily from the southern Keetmanshoop-Karasburg-Bethanie vicinity, and also from the central and more northern areas of the inland plateau and escarpment. Travelers should take measures to prevent sandfly bites. Visceral leishmaniasis is not reported.

Schistosomiasis: Risk is present in the northeast along the Angolan border, extending into the Caprivi Strip. Travelers should avoid swimming, bathing, or wading in freshwater lakes, ponds, or streams.

Trypanosomiasis (African sleeping sickness): Sporadic cases have been reported. Travelers should take personal protection measures against insect (tsetse fly) bites, especially in the Okavango delta of the Caprivi Strip.

Poliomyelitis: An outbreak of paralytic polio occurred in the southern region in 1993–1994. All travelers should be fully immunized against this disease.

Plague: Flea-borne; at least 80 cases were reported in late 1990, most from northern areas, particularly the Oshakati/Onandjokwe vicinity of Owambo District.

Rabies: Urban rabies, with dogs the primary source of human infection, occurs mainly in northern areas. Jackals may also be a source of rabies. Travelers should avoid stray dogs and wild animals and seek immediate treatment of any animal bite.

Other illnesses/hazards: African tick typhus, brucellosis, dengue (not reported), relapsing fever (tick-borne; sandy floors of village mud huts provide favorable habitat for these ticks), tuberculosis (a major health problem), trachoma, typhoid fever, typhus, and intestinal worms (very common). Animal hazards include snakes (mambas, adders, vipers, cobras, coral snakes), scorpions, sac spiders, brown widow and black widow spiders.

NAURU

Consulate: 671-649-8300   *Yaren*   *GMT +12 hrs*

Entry Requirements
- Passport/Visa: Passport is required.
- HIV Test: Not required.
- Vaccinations: A yellow fever vaccination certificate is required of travelers arriving from infected areas.

Telephone Country Code: 674

Health Advisory
Travelers' diarrhea: Low to moderate risk. First-class hotels and restaurants generally serve reliable food and potable water. Elsewhere, travelers should observe all food and drink safety precautions. A quinolone antibiotic (Floxin or Cipro) is recommended for the treatment of

414

World Medical Guide

acute diarrhea. Diarrhea not responding to antibiotic treatment may be due to a parasitic disease such as giardiasis or amebiasis.
Hepatitis: Hepatitis A vaccine is recommended for all nonimmune travelers. The hepatitis B carrier rate in the general population of Oceania is estimated at 5.5%–15%. Vaccination against hepatitis B is recommended for long-term visitors to this country.
Filariasis, Japanese encephalitis, dengue fever: Sporadic cases are reported. Travelers should take protective measures against mosquito bites.

NEPAL

Embassy: 202-667-4550 *Kathmandu* *GMT +5¾ hrs*
Entry Requirements
- Passport/Visa: Valid passport and visa are required.
- HIV Test: Not required.
- Vaccinations: A yellow fever vaccination certificate is required from all travelers older than 1 year arriving from infected areas. The *HealthGuide* recommends vaccination if arriving from any country in the Yellow Fever Endemic Zones.

Telephone Country Code: 977
Embassies/Consulates: U.S. Embassy, Kathmandu. Pani Pokhari; Tel. (1) 411-17 or 412-718.
Hospitals/Doctors: Kalimati Clinic, Kathmandu. This facility can supply Japanese encephalitis vaccine. CIWEC Clinic, Kathmandu; offers inoculations and emergency treatment to travelers; rabies vaccine available. Patan Hospital; 24-hour emergency department. United Mission Hospital (100 beds); general medical and surgical facility. Bir Hospital (300 beds); general medical and surgical facility; blood bank.

Health Advisory

Cholera: This disease is active in this country. Although cholera vaccination is not required for entry if arriving directly from the U.S. or Canada, it may be required if arriving from a cholera-infected area, or required for on-going travel to other countries in Latin America, Africa, the Middle East, or Asia. Travelers should consider vaccination (one dose) or a doctor's letter of exemption from vaccination. The risk to travelers of acquiring cholera is considered low. Prevention consists primarily in following safe food and drink guidelines.
Malaria: Risk of transmission primarily occurs in rural areas below 1,200 meters elevation in the Terai plains districts of Bara, Dhanukha, Kapilvastu, Mahotari, Parsa, Rautahat, Rupandehi, and Sarlahi. Highest risk occurs along the Indian border. Malaria occurs year-round in endemic areas but transmission increases during the monsoon season (usually July through October). Kathmandu and the northern Himalayan districts are risk-free. *P. vivax* accounts for 90% of malaria cases countrywide, with *P. falciparum* accounting for the remainder. Chloroquine-resistant *P. falciparum* has been reported, particularly near the Indian border. Mefloquine prophylaxis is recommended when traveling to malarious areas.
Travelers' diarrhea: In Kathmandu, the food and drink in first-class restaurants and hotels are considered generally safe. A high risk of diarrhea is associated with reheated food and blended fruit and yogurt drinks. Potentially contaminated water should be boiled or filtered, especially to remove parasites, such as cryptosporidia, which are not killed by chlorine. The three most common causes of diarrhea in Nepal are *E. coli,* campylobacter, and shigella bacteria. A quinolone antibiotic is recommended for the treatment of acute diarrhea. Diarrhea not responding to treatment with a quinolone may be due to a parasitic disease such as giardiasis, amebiasis, or cryptosporidiosis. Diarrhea caused by cyclospora parasites (cyclosporiasis is common in Nepal—up to 7% of expatriates infected) will respond to treatment with trimethoprim/sulfamethoxazole (co-trimoxazole).
Hepatitis: Hepatitis A is highly endemic and vaccination is recommended for all nonimmune travelers. The carrier rate of the hepatitis B virus in the general population is 1%–6%. Hepatitis B vaccination should be considered by travelers having close, prolonged contact with the indigenous population of this country. Hepatitis E is widespread in Nepal and is usually transmitted by sewage-contaminated ground water. Hepatitis E accounts for the majority (up to 95%) of clinical cases of acute viral hepatitis in adults in Nepal. To reduce the risk of disease, travelers should drink only boiled, bottled, or chemically treated water.

World Medical Guide

Typhoid fever: Highly endemic. There is also a high incidence of paratyphoid fever. Vaccination is recommended for extended travel to this country.

Meningitis: Occurs countrywide, but routine vaccination is no longer recommended by the CDC for visitors to this country.

Japanese encephalitis (JE): Highly endemic in rural areas of the Terai plain and Inner Terai zone, including hills, mountains, and the Kathmandu Valley. Japanese encephalitis is reported year-round but transmission increases between June and October, especially in the southern agricultural areas bordering India, at elevations below 1,000 meters. This raises the question as to whether all resident expatriates and tourists to Kathmandu Valley should receive the vaccine against JE. What is the risk of a foreigner acquiring JE in Nepal? The actual risk is difficult to calculate, as there has not been a single case of JE in a foreigner in Nepal. This doesn't mean that it is not possible for a foreigner to get the disease, but that the actual risk must be extremely low. Short term travelers who will stay in Kathmandu for a week or two and who will go trekking are the lowest risk individuals and do not need to be immunized against JE. Longer term travelers who will reside in Kathmandu particularly in the post-monsoon period from August to October may wish to consider immunization against JE. Foreigners who will be living in known JE endemic areas, such as most of the Terai and long term expatriates who live in Kathmandu particularly in the rural areas of the valley should be immunized against JE. Japanese encephalitis vaccine is available at most travel clinics in the United States and Canada, and also at the Kalimati Clinic in Kathmandu.

Dengue fever: Low apparent risk below 1,000 meters elevation. Although there have been epidemics in neighboring districts of India, dengue is not currently reported in Nepal.

Leishmaniasis: Visceral leishmaniasis (kala azar) occurs year-round, primarily in rural areas in districts of the southeastern Terai region at elevations below 1,000 meters. Districts include Bara, Dhanukha, Jhapa, Mahottari, Makwanpur, Morang, Parsa, Rautahat, Saptari, Sarlahi, Siraha, Sunsari, and Udaipur, adjoining the Indian state of Bihar. Travelers to these districts should take measures to prevent insect (sandfly) bites.

Rabies: This disease is prevalent, especially in Dang district, western Nepal. Annually, about one in 6,000 foreigners in Nepal receive an animal bite for which rabies vaccination is recommended. Dogs account for 76% of bites; monkeys cause 20%. Rabies vaccine and immune globulin are available at the CIWEC Clinic in Kathmandu. All animal bites, especially those inflicted by a dog or monkey, should be examined as soon as possible by a physician who can administer vaccine, if indicated.

Altitude sickness: Risk increases above 2,200 meters elevation. Trekkers to higher altitudes should follow precautions (e.g., gradual ascent) to reduce the risk of acute altitude sickness. Travelers should consider prophylaxis with the drug acetazolamide (Diamox) and remember that the best treatment for altitude sickness is descent.

Other diseases/health threats: Cutaneous myiasis (one dose of ivermectin may be curative), cysticercosis, filariasis (occurs primarily in the southern terai), leprosy (highly prevalent), hookworm disease, AIDS (low incidence; reported primarily in prostitutes who become infected in India), scabies, trachoma (a leading cause of blindness in Nepal), and tuberculosis (highly prevalent; a serious public health problem).

NETHERLANDS

Embassy: 202-483-3176   *The Hague*   *GMT +1 hr*

Entry Requirements
- Passport/Visa: Passport required.
- HIV Test: Not required.
- Vaccinations: None required.

Telephone Country Code: 31   **AT&T:** 06-022-9111   **MCI:** 06-022-9122

Embassies/Consulates: U.S. Embassy, The Hague. Lange Voorhout 102; Tel. (70) 624-911. Canadian Embassy, The Hague. Sophialaan 7; Tel. (70) 614-111.

Hospitals/Doctors: Wilhelmina Gasthuis/Zinnan Gasthuis, Amsterdam (923 beds); coronary care; ICU; emergency unit; first aid. I. C.C. Academish Ziekenhuis, Rotterdam (1,004

World Medical Guide

beds); general medical/surgical facility; all major medical specialties. Academish Zeikenhuis, Utrecht (1,074 beds); all medical specialties including OB/GYN; pediatrics; emergency room; hemodialysis; trauma team. Bronovo Hospital, The Hague.

Health Advisory

Travelers' diarrhea: Low risk. Water is safe throughout The Netherlands.
Hepatitis: Low risk. Hepatitis B accounts for about 20% of all cases of acute viral hepatitis.
Lyme disease and ehrlichiosis: Lyme disease occurs in the southern and eastern parts of The Netherlands. A case of human granulocyctic ehrlichiosis was reported in 1998 from the Gelderland region. Travelers to these areas should take precautions to prevent tick bites.
Swimmers' ear (otitis externa): Large outbreaks occurred in 1994 associated with swimming in recreational freshwater lakes during hot summer months. Infection caused by pseudomonas bacteria infecting the external ear canal. Prevent/treat with Vōsol solution.

NEW CALEDONIA

New Caledonia is a French Overseas Territory. For information, contact the French Embassy: 202-944-6000. There is no U.S. Embassy in New Caledonia. For assistance, contact the U.S. Embassy in Suva, Fiji: (679)-314-466.

For Health Advisory information, see the Disease Risk Summary for Australia and Oceania.

NEW ZEALAND

Embassy: 202-328-4800   **Wellington**   **GMT +12 hrs**

Entry Requirements
- A visa is not required for stays up to 3 months.
- HIV Test: Not required.
- Vaccinations: None required.

Telephone Country Code: 64

Embassies/Consulates: U.S. Embassy, Thorndon, Wellington. 29 Fitzherbert Terrace; Tel. (4) 472-2068. U.S. Consulate, Aukland; Tel. (9) 303-2724. U.S. Consulate, Christchurch; Tel. (3) 379-0040.

Hospitals/Doctors: Medlab. 125 Grafton Rd., Aukland; Tel. (9) 377-8339. Wellington Hospital (959 beds); Tel: (4) 385-5999. Greenlane Hospital (565 beds), Auckland; Tel: (9) 604-106. (3) 640-640. Epsom Medical Center, Aukland; Tel. (9) 794-540. Harold Gray, M.D., Wellington; Tel. (4) 849-675 or 862-124. Larry Skiba, M.D. General Practice & Travel Medicine; 438 Papanui Rd., Christchurch; Tel. (3) 352-9053. Dr. M. Brieseman. Public Health Service Health Link South, Ltd. 10 Oxford TCE, Christchurch, South Island; Tel. (03) 3799-480.

Health Advisory

Travelers' diarrhea: Low risk. Tap water is considered potable countrywide. A quinolone antibiotic is recommended for the treatment of acute diarrhea. Diarrhea not responding to antibiotic treatment may be due to a parasitic disease, such as giardiasis—or an intestinal virus. Amebiasis is endemic at low levels. Cryptosporidiosis presumably is endemic.
Hepatitis: Low risk. Nonimmune travelers should consider hepatitis A vaccination. Hepatitis E has not been reported. The carrier rate of the hepatitis B virus among the general population is 3%, and up to 10% amongst the Maori tribe and Asian/Polynesian residents. Hepatits C is endemic.
Other illnesses/hazards: Leptospirosis, ancylostomiasis, and echinococcosis. In 1994, 133 cases of meningococcal meningitis, with eight deaths, were reported through September. Travelers who expect a prolonged stay in this country should consider immunization.

World Medical Guide

NICARAGUA
Embassy: 202-939-6570   *Managua*   *GMT -6 hrs*

Entry Requirements
- A visa is not required but a tourist card, valid for 30 days, must be obtained.
- HIV Test: Not required.
- Vaccinations: A yellow fever vaccination certificate is required from travelers over 1 year of age coming from infected or endemic areas.

Telephone Country Code: 505 **AT&T:** 174 (02-174 outside Managua)
Embassies/Consulates: U.S. Embassy, Managua; Kilometer 4 1/2 Carretera Sur; Tel. (2) 666-010.
Hospitals/Doctors: Hospital Manolo Morales, Managua (300 beds); general medical/surgical facility; emergency services. Clinica Tiscapa. Hospital Bautista (30 beds); private hospital; 24-hour emergency services; patients must arrange for their own physicians.

Health Advisory

Yellow fever: No cases are currently reported, but vaccination is recommended for travel outside urban areas. Although a vaccination certificate may not be required for entry to this country, one may be required for on-going travel to other countries in Africa, the Middle East, and Asia.

Cholera: This disease is active in this country. Although cholera vaccination is not required for entry if arriving directly from the U.S. or Canada, it may be required if arriving from a cholera-infected area, or required for on-going travel to other countries in Latin America, Africa, the Middle East, or Asia. Travelers should consider vaccination (one dose) or a doctor's letter of exemption from vaccination.

Malaria: Risk is present countrywide below 1,000 meters elevation, except for the centers of major urban areas such as Managua and Leon; risk may be elevated in the northwestern departments of Leon and Chinandega. *P. vivax* accounts for 95% of cases, the remainder due to *P. falciparum*. Chloroquine prophylaxis is recommended in all rural areas.

Travelers' diarrhea: All travelers are advised to consume only bottled, boiled, or treated water unless they are assured of the safety of municipal water supplies. A quinolone antibiotic is recommended for the treatment of acute diarrhea. Diarrhea not responding to treatment with an antibiotic may be due to a parasitic disease such as giardiasis or amebiasis. (A high incidence of amebiasis is reported in Nicaragua. Infection rates of up to 23% have been reported for giardiasis.) Rates for cryptosporidiosis are unclear but probably low.

Hepatitis: Hepatitis A vaccine is recommended for all nonimmune travelers. Hepatitis E is not reported, but could occur. The hepatitis B carrier rate in the general population is estimated at 1.1%. Vaccination against hepatitis B is recommended for long-term visitors.

Dengue fever: A major outbreak occurred in Managua in 1985 with 500,000 cases unofficially reported. The *Aedes* mosquitoes which transmit dengue fever bite during the daytime and are present in populous urban areas as well as resort and rural areas.

Leishmaniasis: Cutaneous leishmaniasis is reported, primarily from the northern, central, and eastern regions, especially around forested areas. Travelers should take measures to prevent insect (sandfly) bites.

Chagas' disease: Reported in Atlantic coastal, western, and central regions under 1,500 meters elevation. Travelers sleeping in adobe-style huts and houses should take precautions against nighttime insect bites.

Rabies: About 4 per year are reported, usually from dog bites.

Leptospirosis: Outbreak of leptospirosis with 13 fatalities due to pulmonary hemorrhage reported in 1995. This disease spread by water or food contaminated by infected animal/rodent urine.

Other diseases: Abdominal angiostrongyliasis, brucellosis, coccidiomycosis, filariasis (possible risk near Lake Managua), measles, syphilis, AIDS (low incidence), tuberculosis, and strongyloidiasis and other helminthic infections.

World Medical Guide

NIGER

Embassy: 202-483-4224 *Niamey* *GMT +1 hr*

Entry Requirements
- A visa is required. Travelers should contact the Embassy of Niger for further information.
- HIV Test: Not required.
- Vaccinations: A yellow fever vaccination certificate is required from all travelers older than 1 year arriving from ALL COUNTRIES.

Telephone Country Code: 227
Embassies/Consulates: U.S. Embassy, Niamey. B.P. 11201; Tel. 722-661 through 722-664.
Hospitals/Doctors: Niamey Central Hospital (790 beds); general medical/surgical facility; some specialties. Gamkalley Hospital, Niamey (20 beds); basic emergency services only.

Health Advisory

Yellow fever: Vaccination is required for entry to this country. This country is in the Yellow Fever Endemic Zone. A vaccination certificate may also be required for on-going travel to other countries in Africa, the Middle East, and Asia.

Cholera: This disease is active in this country. Although cholera vaccination is not required for entry if arriving directly from the U.S. or Canada, cholera vaccination is recommended by Niger, and cholera vaccination may be required for on-going travel to other countries in Latin America, Africa, the Middle East, or Asia. Travelers should consider vaccination (one dose) or a doctor's letter of exemption from vaccination. The risk to travelers of acquiring cholera is low. Prevention consists primarily in adhering to safe food and drink guidelines.

Malaria: Risk is present year-round throughout this country, including urban areas. Risk of malaria is higher in the south than in the northern Saharan areas, especially during and after the rainy season. Falciparum malaria accounts for 85%-90% of cases, followed by *P. malariae* and *P. ovale*. Vivax malaria is rare. Chloroquine-resistant falciparum malaria is reported. Prophylaxis with mefloquine or doxycycline is recommended for travel to malarious areas.

Travelers' diarrhea: High risk. Treated, piped water is available in some major areas, but water supplies are generally not potable. Niger River water is bacterially contaminated. The water in Lake Chad is highly saline. Travelers should observe all food and drink safety precautions. A quinolone antibiotic is recommended for the treatment of acute diarrhea. Diarrhea not responding to treatment with an antibiotic, or chronic diarrhea, may be due to a parasitic disease such as giardiasis, amebiasis, or cryptosporidiosis.

Hepatitis: High risk. All nonimmune travelers should receive hepatitis A vaccine. Hepatitis E presumably occurs, but endemic levels are unclear. The hepatitis B carrier rate in the general population is estimated at 16%-21%. Vaccination against hepatitis B is recommended for all long-term visitors to this country.

Leishmaniasis: Foci of cutaneous leishmaniasis have been reported in southern, central, and western (including the Niamey vicinity) areas, but probably occur throughout Niger. Visceral leishmaniasis has been reported from the Air Mountains, northwestern Agadez Department; isolated cases have been reported from Zinder Department. Travelers should take measures to prevent insect (sandfly) bites.

Schistosomiasis: Urinary schistosomiasis is widely distributed in the Niger River Valley in the southwest, with foci in southcentral Niger along the Nigerian border. Travelers should avoid swimming, bathing, or wading in freshwater lakes, ponds, or streams.

Trypanosomiasis (African sleeping sickness): Historically, cases have occurred on the border with Burkina Fasso, but no cases have been reported since 1980.

Meningitis: Southwestern and southern Niger lie within the sub-Saharan meningitis belt. Outbreaks are reported countrywide, usually during the dry season, November–May. There is increased risk in the southern regions. Vaccination is recommended for travelers who expect to have close contact with the indigenous population for extended periods of time (more than 2–4 weeks).

World Medical Guide

Rabies: Vaccination is recommended for long-term travel (more than 4 weeks) to this country, especially for travelers going to remote rural areas. Dogs, jackals, and foxes are the primary reservoir.

AIDS: Heterosexual contact is the predominate mode of transmission. HIV prevalence in the general population is estimated to be low, but up to 10% of surveyed prostitutes are HIV positive. All travelers are cautioned against unsafe sex, unsterile medical or dental injections, and unnecessary blood transfusions.

Other diseases/hazards: African tick typhus, anthrax, brucellosis (from consumption of raw dairy products), dracunculiasis, filariasis (mosquito-borne; risk occurs in the rural southwest), leprosy, leptospirosis, onchocerciasis (black-fly borne; endemic foci along rivers in the southwest), tuberculosis (a major health problem), and intestinal worms (very common) are reported. Lassa fever has not been confirmed, but the virus is widely distributed throughout West Africa. No cases of Ebola-Marburg virus disease have been reported. Animal hazards include snakes (vipers, cobras, puff adders), scorpions, and black widow spiders; hippopotamuses and crocodiles are found along the banks of the Niger River.

NIGERIA

Embassy: 202-822-1500   *Lagos*   *GMT +1 hr*

Entry Requirements
- A passport and visa are required. Travelers should contact the Embassy of Nigeria for further information. All travelers going to Nigeria are urged to read the Travel Warning, Public Announcement, and Consular Information Sheet issued by the U.S. State Department.
- HIV Test: Foreign nationals from countries that require HIV testing of Nigerians may be required to have an HIV test. Travelers should contact the closest Nigerian consulate or the Nigerian Embassy in Washington, D.C., for further information.
- Vaccinations: A yellow fever vaccination certificate is required from all travelers older than 1 year arriving from infected areas. The State Department advises that a cholera vaccination certificate may be required to enter this country.

Telephone Country Code: 234

Embassies/Consulates: U.S. Embassy, Lagos. 2 Eleke Crescent; Tel. (1) 261-0050. U. S. Embassy office in the new capital city of Abuja is located at 9 Mambilla, Maitanma District; Tel. (9) 523-0916.

Hospitals/Doctors: Lagos General Hospital (2,000 beds); some specialty clinics. University College Hospital, Lagos (822 beds); some specialty clinics. Lagos Clinic. Kelu Specialist Clinic; Tel. Baptist Mission Hospital, 120 km north of Ibadan; general medical/surgical facility. Dr. Oladapo Olatung, travel medicine specialist, Lagos State; can advise on health conditions in Nigeria; attend to travelers' medical needs in Nigeria.

Health Advisory

Yellow fever: This disease is active. Vaccination is recommended. The following states are considered officially infected: Anambra, Bauchi, Bendel, Benue, Cross River, Kaduna, Kwara, Lagos, Niger, Ogun, Ondo, and Plateau. Risk of disease is countrywide. This country is in the Yellow Fever Endemic Zone.

Cholera: This disease is active in this country. Although cholera vaccination is not required for entry if arriving directly from the U.S. or Canada, it may be required if arriving from a cholera-infected area, or required for on-going travel to other countries in Latin America, Africa, the Middle East, or Asia. Travelers should consider vaccination or a doctor's letter of exemption from vaccination. The risk to travelers of acquiring cholera is considered low. Prevention consists primarily in adhering to safe food and drink guidelines.

Malaria: Risk is present year-round countrywide, including urban areas. Risk may be elevated during and just after the rainy seasons (March through July and September through November in the south; May through October north of the Niger-Benin River Valley). *P. falciparum* causes 80% of cases, followed by malaria due to *P. malariae* (15%

World Medical Guide

of cases) and *P. ovale* (5%). Multidrug-resistant falciparum malaria is reported. Mefloquine or doxycycline prophylaxis is currently recommended.

Travelers' diarrhea: High risk. Most of Nigeria's water sources are man-made lakes, rivers, streams, and wells, most of which are contaminated. The water supply in Lagos is pure at the source, but cross contamination with sewage may occur during distribution. Travelers should observe all food and drink safety precautions. A quinolone antibiotic is recommended for the treatment of acute diarrhea. Diarrhea not responding to antibiotics, or chronic diarrhea, may be due to a parasitic disease such as giardiasis, amebiasis, or cryptosporidiosis.

Hepatitis: All nonimmune travelers should receive hepatitis A vaccine. Hepatitis E is likely endemic, but levels are unclear. The hepatitis B carrier rate in the general population is estimated at 8%–11% and 15% in high-risk groups. Vaccination against hepatitis B is recommended for all long-term visitors to this country.

Arboviral fevers: Low risk of dengue (few cases reported, but there is serologic evidence of endemicity). West Nile and Sindbis fevers are moderately to highly endemic. Chikungunya fever may occur in cyclic outbreaks in rural or urban areas. Crimean-Congo hemorrhagic fever occurs in arid savanna grasslands where ticks abound.

Leishmaniasis: A sharp increase in cases of cutaneous leishmaniasis occurred in the north in the 1980s. Visceral leishmaniasis may occur in the northeast.

Onchocerciasis: Widespread along fast-flowing rivers in both savanna and forest zones in parts of all states. Travelers should take measures to prevent blackfly bites.

Filariasis: Major area of Bancroftian filariasis in the south, including the Igwun Basin of Imo State, and the Niger Delta; infection rates up to 26% have been reported. Travelers should take measures to prevent mosquito bites.

Schistosomiasis: High risk areas include the Niger River Basin and Ogun-Oshun River Basin, the southwest (including vicinities of Lagos and Ibadan), the central and northern highlands, and around Lake Chad. Travelers should avoid swimming, bathing, or wading in freshwater lakes, ponds, or streams.

Trypanosomiasis: Foci exist in Gboko vicinity of Benue State (southeastern areas confluent with endemic areas of Cameroon), and the southwestern states of Edo and Delta. Extreme northern areas are tsetse free. Travelers should take measures to prevent tsetse fly bites.

Meningitis: Outbreaks of meningococcal meningitis occurred in 1996 with 2,411 deaths. Vaccination is recommended for travelers who anticipate having close contact with the indigenous population.

Rabies: A public health problem in many rural and urban areas, including Lagos; stray dogs are the primary cause of human infection. Vaccination against rabies should be considered.

AIDS: HIV prevalence estimated at 2.8% of the sexually active urban population. Twenty percent of prostitutes in Lagos are HIV-positive.

Other diseases/hazards: African tick typhus, brucellosis, flea-borne and louse-borne typhus, louse-borne relapsing fever, dracunculiasis (focally endemic), Lassa fever (sporadic outbreaks reported, most recently from Plateau State), leprosy, leptospirosis, loiasis (deer-fly-borne; occurs in southern rain forests and swamp forests), paragonimiasis (19% infection rate in the Igwun Basin), tuberculosis (a major health problem), trachoma, and intestinal worms (very common). Animal hazards include snakes (vipers, cobras, puff adders, mambas), scorpions, brown recluse spider, and black widow spiders; potentially harmful marine animals which occur in the coastal waters of Nigeria include sea wasps, Portuguese man-of-war, rosy anemone, sea urchin, weeverfish, eagle ray, and sea nettle.

World Medical Guide

NORTH KOREA

North Korean Mission to the U.N.: 212-972-3106. No diplomatic relations with the U.S. The Embassy of Sweden is contact in Pyongyang: (850)-2-381-7523
Health Advisory: See South Korea.

NORTHERN MARIANA ISLANDS (U.S.)
SAIPAN, TINIAN, AND ROTA

GMT +11 hrs

Entry Requirements
- Passport/Visa: Not required by U.S. citizens.
- HIV Test: Not required.
- Vaccinations: None required.

Embassies/Consulates: These islands have been a self-governing U.S. territory since 1986.

Health Advisory

Malaria: No risk.
Travelers' diarrhea: Medium risk outside of first-class hotels and resorts. A quinolone antibiotic (e.g., Floxin or Cipro) is recommended for the treatment of acute diarrhea. Diarrhea not responding to antibiotic treatment may be due to a parasitic disease such as giardiasis or amebiasis—or an intestinal virus.
Hepatitis: All nonimmune travelers should receive the hepatitis A vaccine. The hepatitis B carrier rate in the general population is estimated at 10%. Vaccination against hepatitis B is recommended for all healthcare workers and long-term visitors.
Filariasis, Japanese encephalitis, dengue fever: Sporadic cases and outbreaks are reported. Travelers to this region should take protective measures against mosquito bites.

NORWAY

Embassy: 202-333-6000   Oslo   *GMT +1 hr*

Entry Requirements
- Tourist visa not required.
- HIV Test: Not required.
- Vaccinations: None required.

Telephone Country Code: 47   **AT&T:** 800-190-11   **MCI:** 800-199-12
Embassies/Consulates: U.S. Embassy, Oslo. Drammensveien 18; Tel. (22) 448-550.
Hospitals/Doctors: Riks Hospital, Oslo (1,185 beds); all specialties; Tel. (2) 867-010. Ullevaal Hospital, Oslo; all specialties. Tel. (2) 118-080.

Health Advisory

Travelers' diarrhea: Very low risk of bacterial or parasitic-caused diarrhea.
Tick-borne diseases: Tick-borne encephalitis occurs in scattered areas in extreme southern and western Norway, especially around Bergen. Lyme disease occurs and is transmitted by ticks in brushy areas and forests in the southern coastal areas at elevations below 1,500 meters.
Other diseases: Hemorrhagic fever with renal syndrome, tularemia.

World Medical Guide

OMAN
Embassy: 202-387-1980   *Muscat*   *GMT +4 hrs*

Entry Requirements
- A 6-month, multiple entry tourist visa is available, valid for two years.
- HIV Test: Required for work permit. U.S. test not accepted.
- Vaccinations: A yellow fever and cholera vaccination certificate is required from all travelers older than 1 year arriving from infected areas.

Telephone Country Code: 968
Embassies & Consulates: American Embassy, Muscat; Jameat A'Duwal Al Arabiya Street; Tel. 698-989 and 699-049.

Health Advisory

Malaria: Risk is present year-round countrywide below 2,000 meters elevation, peaking seasonally from November through April. Risk is greatest in the coastal and foothill areas of Dhahira, South and North Batinah (coastal plain north of the Seeb International Airport, to the northern border with the United Arab Emirates.), and Dakhilya; risk is lower in Muscat, Al Woustah, Sharqiya, and Musandam. The risk of malaria is lowest in Dhofar. The capital area around Muscat and the southern Dhofar region are risk-free. Countrywide, *P. falciparum* causes approximately 96% of cases of malaria, *P. vivax* the remainder. Chloroquine-resistant falciparum malaria may account for 20% of cases. Fansidar-resistant malaria is reported. Travelers to risk areas are advised to take mefloquine or doxycycline prophylaxis.

Travelers' diarrhea: First-class hotels and restaurants in Muscat generally serve reliable food and potable water. Travelers are advised, however, to drink only bottled, boiled, or treated water and consume only well-cooked food. A quinolone antibiotic is recommended for the treatment of acute diarrhea. Diarrhea not responding to antibiotic treatment may be due to a parasitic disease such as giardiasis, cryptosporidiosis, or amebiasis.

Hepatitis: Hepatitis A vaccine is recommended for all nonimmune travelers. Hepatitis E has not been reported, but likely occurs. Hepatitis B is moderately endemic.

Leishmaniasis: Presumably widespread and focally distributed countrywide. Transmission presumably occurs during April through October, peaking during July through September. Both cutaneous and visceral leishmaniasis may be present in endemic areas. Visceral leishmaniasis is known to occur in focal rural foothill and mountainous areas in Sharqiyah and Dhahirah Regions. Travelers should take protective measures against sandfly bites.

Schistosomiasis: Risk areas for intestinal schistosomiasis occur in southern coastal areas of the Dhofar (Zufar) Governate (near Arazat, Mirbat, Taqah, and Salalah). "Swimmer's itch" (cercarial dermatitis) due probably to noninvasive animal schistosomes is reported after exposure in freshwater pools in Wadi Darbat. Travelers should avoid swimming or wading in freshwater rivers, ponds, streams, or irrigated areas.

Rabies: Occurs very sporadically in stray dogs; rarely reported in humans.

Other illnesses/hazards: Boutonneuse fever, brucellosis (usually transmitted by raw goat/sheep milk, especially in the southern Dhofar region), dengue (endemic status unclear; probably not active), echinococcosis (carried by stray dogs; reported sporadically, especially in northern areas), filariasis (cases of Bancroftian filariasis are reported annually), leptospirosis, myiasis (due to larvae of the sheep nasal botfly; a case of ophthalmic myiasis has been reported, with fly maggots infecting the superficial periocular tissue), onchocerciasis (historically reported from southern areas; may occur), rabies (foxes are the main reservoir, with spillover into the dog population), relapsing fever (tick-borne), sandfly fever (viral; mosquito-borne), typhus (flea-borne and louse-borne), tuberculosis, helminthic infections (roundworm, hookworm, and whipworm infections are common in rural areas; incidence is estimated at 5%). Centipedes, scorpions, black widow spiders inhabit the dry interior regions of Oman. Sea urchins and marine rays inhabit the coastal waters of Oman and could pose a hazard to swimmers.

World Medical Guide

PAKISTAN

Embassy: 203-939-6200   *Islamabad*   *GMT +5 hrs*

Entry Requirements
- Passport/Visa: Valid passport and visa are required.
- HIV Test: Test required if staying more than 1 year.
- Vaccinations: A yellow fever vaccination certificate is required from all travelers older than 1 year arriving from any country any part of which is infected. A certificate is also required if arriving from any country in the Yellow Fever Endemic Zones.
Cholera: A vaccination certificate is required if arriving from any country any part of which is infected.

Telephone Country Code: 92

Embassies/Consulates: U.S. Embassy, Islamabad, Diplomatic Enclave, Ramna 5; Tel. (51) 826-161. The Consular Section is located separately in the USAID building, 18 Sixth Avenue, Ramna 5; Tel. (51) 824-071.

Hospitals/Doctors: Jinnah Central Hospital, Karachi (800 beds); government hospital; all specialties. Seventh Day Adventist Hospital, Karachi (120 beds); private hospital; most specialties. United Christian Hospital, Lahore. Khyber Medical Center, Peshawar.

Health Advisory

Cholera: This disease is not officially reported as active in this country, but cases do occur. The vaccine-resistant Bengal strain of cholera has been reported. Although cholera vaccination is not required for entry if arriving directly from the U.S. or Canada, it may be required if arriving from a cholera-infected area, or required for on-going travel to other countries in Latin America, Africa, the Middle East, or Asia.

Malaria: Malaria is endemic throughout the Indus Basin (Punjab in the east, Sind in the south), along the Gulf of Oman (Baluchistan) and in the Northwest Frontier Province. Punjab is the most malarious area. Transmission occurs in rural areas up to 2,000 meters elevation and in the valleys up to 3,500 meters in the Gilgit Agency in the north. Transmission also occurs in the urban areas in the south (including the perimeter of Karachi). Urban areas in the north (Islamabad) and the east (Lahore) are at much lower risk, but not risk free, since transmission occurs at the fringes. *P. falciparum* causes 77% of malaria in Baluchistan and Sind Province, 33% in Punjab Province, and 15% in NW Frontier Province; *P. vivax* causes the remainder. Chloroquine-resistant *P. falciparum* has been reported in Punjab. Mefloquine or doxycycline prophylaxis is recommended when traveling to risk areas.

Travelers' diarrhea: High risk. Although urban areas usually have water treatment facilities, central distribution systems, and public taps, none of the water in Pakistan should be considered potable. Piped water supplies are frequently untreated and may be grossly contaminated. A quinolone antibiotic is recommended for the treatment of acute diarrhea. Diarrhea not responding to treatment with an antibiotic, or chronic diarrhea, may be due to a parasitic disease such as giardiasis, amebiasis, or cryptosporidiosis.

Hepatitis: All nonimmune travelers should receive hepatitis A vaccine. The hepatitis B carrier rate in the general population is estimated at 5%–10%. Hepatitis B vaccination is recommended for those people (teachers, relief workers, Peace Corps volunteers, etc.) who will have prolonged close contact with the indigenous population There is a very high incidence of hepatitis E in this country. An explosive waterborne epidemic of hepatitis E occurred in Islamabad in 1994 and outbreaks have occurred in Karachi and Sargodha. All travelers should avoid drinking water that may be virus-contaminated (e.g., untreated well water, tap water, or ground water). Hepatitis C is endemic.

Typhoid fever: Highly endemic. Risk is elevated during the warmer months, June–August, especially in urban areas. Immunization against typhoid fever is recommended.

Japanese encephalitis: Low risk. A few cases have been reported near Karachi.

Dengue fever: Outbreaks of this mosquito-transmitted disease, including dengue hemorrhagic fever, have been serologically and virologically confirmed since 1994.
Leishmaniasis: Cutaneous leishmaniasis occurs sporadically in the urban and semirural areas at the margin of the deserts, especially in the west, in Baluchistan. Visceral leishmaniasis occurs primarily in northern areas (northern Punjab Province and the Northwest Frontier Province), at elevations between 2,000 and 6,000 meters. Travelers to these regions should protect themselves against sandfly bites. The most intense sandfly-biting activity is April through October.
Rabies: Human cases (more than 100 per year) usually occur sporadically in rural villages or on the outskirts of larger cities. Travelers should seek immediate treatment of any animal bite, especially by a dog. Pre-exposure vaccination against rabies (3 doses) should be considered prior to long-term travel to this region.
Other diseases/health threats: Anthrax, brucellosis (human cases associated with occupational exposure to livestock), Crimean-Congo hemorrhagic fever (transmitted by ticks; sporadic outbreaks occur), chikungunya fever (rare outbreaks occur), dracunculiasis (focally endemic in NW Frontier, Punjab, Sind Provinces), echinococcosis, filariasis (Bancroftian filariasis occurs in the southern Indus delta), leprosy (widespread among lower socioeconomic groups), leptospirosis (rare in humans), Indian tick typhus (boutonneuse fever, reported sporadically), melioidosis (sporadic cases), sandfly fever (highly endemic below 1,800 meters elevation; risk is higher in nondesert areas of Pakistan), West Nile fever (mosquito-transmitted; absent during winter), soil-transmitted intestinal worms (ascarid and hookworm widespread, especially in rural areas), syphilis (moderate incidence), AIDS (spreading rapidly), trachoma (widespread in western rural areas), tuberculosis (highly endemic in rural areas), typhoid fever, West Nile fever, and typhus (both murine and scrub typhus occur).

PALAU

Representative: 202-624-7793   *Koror*   *GMT +9 hrs*

Entry Requirements
- Passport/Visa: Not required for U.S. citizens. U.S. Embassy, Palau; Tel: (680) 920-990.
- HIV Test: Not required.
- Vaccinations: None required.

Health Advisory

Malaria: No risk.
Travelers' diarrhea: Medium risk. A quinolone antibiotic (Cipro or Floxin) is recommended for the treatment of diarrhea.
Hepatitis: All nonimmune travelers should receive hepatitis A vaccine. The hepatitis B carrier rate in the general population is approximately 15 percent. Vaccination against hepatitis B is recommended for all healthcare workers and long-term visitors.
Filariasis, Japanese encephalitis, dengue fever: Sporadic cases and outbreaks are reported. Travelers should take protective measures against mosquito bites.

World Medical Guide

PANAMA

Embassy: 202-483-1407 **Panama City** **GMT -5 hrs**

Entry Requirements
- U.S. citizens must have a passport or proof of citizenship. A tourist card or visa is required.
- HIV Test: Not required.
- Vaccinations: None required.

Telephone Country Code: 507 **AT&T:** 109 **MCI:** 108

Embassies/Consulates: U.S. Embassy, Consular Section, Panama City. 40th St. & Balboa Ave; Tel. 225-6988.

Hospitals/Doctors: Gorgas Army Hospital, Panama City. Centro Medico Paitilla (180 beds; private). General medical/surgical facility; CAT scan, emergency services. Clinica San Fernando (150 beds); private hospital; general medical/surgical facility; CAT scan, trauma unit. Tel. 61-6666. Hospital Samaritano, Colon.

Health Advisory

Yellow fever: This country is in the Yellow Fever Endemic Zone. Vaccination is recommended for travel to rural areas. No cases reported since the 1940s.

Cholera: This disease is active in this country. Although cholera vaccination is not required for entry if arriving directly from the U.S. or Canada, it may be required if arriving from a cholera-infected area, or required for on-going travel to other countries in Latin America, Africa, the Middle East, or Asia.

Malaria: Focally endemic. Low-level risk exists year-round in rural areas of eastern (Darien and San Blas) and western (Bocas Del Toro, Chiriqui, and Veraguas) provinces. Areas immediately adjacent to the Panama Canal and all major urban areas are probably risk free. Outbreaks reported from both western (including the provinces of Bocas del Toro—near the border with Costa Rica, Chiriqui, and Veraguas) and eastern (Darien Province) areas. Vivax malaria predominates; with falciparum malaria accounting for 3% to 28% of all cases. Chloroquine-resistant *P. falciparum* has been reported in all malarious areas east of the Panama Canal and in the vicinity of Gatun Lake west of the Canal, as well as in the extreme northwest, near the border with Costa Rica. Mefloquine or doxycycline prophylaxis is recommended when traveling to any rural malarious area.

Travelers' diarrhea: Variable risk. All water sources outside major hotels should be considered potentially contaminated. A quinolone antibiotic is recommended for the treatment of diarrhea. Diarrhea not responding to antibiotic therapy may be due to a parasitic disease such as amebiasis or giardiasis. Cryptosporidiosis may occur.

Hepatitis: Hepatitis A vaccine is recommended for nonimmune travelers. Hepatitis E status is unclear. The hepatitis B carrier rate in the general population is estimated at 0.7% to 1.4%. Vaccination against hepatitis B is recommended for long-term travelers.

Dengue fever: Endemic year-round, countrywide, with risk elevated during the rainier months (usually May through December). All travelers, however, should take measures to prevent mosquito bites.

Leishmaniasis: Scattered cases of cutaneous leishmaniasis occur countrywide in rural areas, but most cases are reported from the western or west-central areas. Visceral leishmaniasis not reported. All travelers should take measures to prevent sandfly bites.

Chagas' disease: Chagas' disease occurs at low levels in most rural areas of Panama, including the former Canal Zone.

Other diseases: Cysticercosis, filariasis (may occur in the extreme northeast), histoplasmosis (from exposure to bat guano), leptospirosis, mansonellosis (increased incidence in northwestern Darien), measles, paragonimiasis (from raw freshwater crabs or crayfish), rabies (currently a minor threat to humans; dogs account for most human exposure), tick-borne rickettsioses (spotted fever group), toxoplasmosis (usually transmitted by infective cat feces), tuberculosis (incidence declining), typhoid fever, viral encephalitis, and intestinal helminth infections, including strongyloidiasis, are reported.

World Medical Guide

PAPUA NEW GUINEA
***Embassy:** 202-745-3680   **Port Moresby**   GMT +10 hrs*
Entry Requirements
- Passport/Visa: Passport and visa required. A 30-day tourist visa can be obtained on arrival in Port Moresby.
- HIV Test: Test required for a work permit or anyone seeking residency.
- Vaccinations: A yellow fever vaccination certificate is required from all travelers older than 1 year arriving from infected areas.

Telephone Country Code: 675
Embassies/Consulates: U.S. Embassy, Port Moresby. Armit Street; Tel. 211-445/594/054.
Hospitals/Doctors: Port Moresby General Hospital (700 beds); Jacobi Medical Center, Port Moresby. General Hospital, Madanng (280 beds); general medical facility; x-ray, laboratory. Base Hospital, Lae (297 beds); x-ray, pharmacy, laboratory.

Health Advisory

Malaria: Highly endemic. Risk is present countrywide (including urban areas) year-round at elevations below 1,800 meters; elevated risk occurs along coastal areas and in the lowlands, especially during the wetter months, December through February. *P. falciparum* accounts for 77% of cases, followed by *P. vivax*. Up to 5% of malaria cases are caused by *P. malariae*. Chloroquine- and Fansidar-resistant falciparum malaria are widespread, and mefloquine-resistant *P. falciparum* has been reported. *P. vivax* strains resistant to chloroquine and primaquine have also been reported.

Travelers' diarrhea: Medium to high risk outside of first-class hotels and resorts. Travelers are advised to drink only bottled, boiled, filtered, or treated water and consume only well-cooked food. All fruit should be peeled prior to consumption. A quinolone antibiotic is recommended for the treatment of acute diarrhea. Diarrhea not responding to antibiotic treatment may be due to a parasitic disease such as giardiasis, amebiasis, or cryptosporidiosis.

Hepatitis: Hepatitis A vaccine is recommended for all travelers not immune to hepatitis A. The hepatitis B carrier rate in the general population varies from 5% to 25%, depending on the group studied. Vaccination against hepatitis B is recommended for healthcare workers and should be considered by long-term visitors to this country.

Dengue fever: Countrywide risk except for the deep mountain interior over 1,000 meters elevation. Urban areas and low-lying rural areas are considered at higher risk from December through February and May through September, the monsoon seasons. The *Aedes* mosquito, which transmits dengue, bites during the daytime and is present in populous urban areas as well as resort and rural areas. Prevention of dengue consists of taking protective measures against mosquito bites.

Filariasis: Bancroftian filariasis is highly endemic in coastal and low-lying regions and some islands off the mainland. All travelers should take measures to avoid mosquito bites.

Japanese encephalitis: Low risk. Endemic status uncertain, but this disease occurs in neighboring Irian Jaya. Vaccination against Japanese encephalitis is recommended for travelers who will be staying in rural-agricultural endemic areas more than several weeks. All travelers should take protective measures against mosquito bites, especially in the evening.

Rabies: There is no rabies reported from Papua New Guinea.

Other illnesses/hazards: Angiostrongyliasis, brucellosis (low incidence), hydatid disease, helminthic infections (ascariasis, hookworm disease, and strongyloidiasis are highly endemic in urban and rural areas), paragonimiasis, leprosy (highly endemic), Lyme disease, leptospirosis, melioidosis, Ross River fever (mosquito-borne; low incidence), epidemic typhus (louse-borne; low endemicity), scrub typhus (mite-borne; risk elevated in grassy rural areas; low endemicity), tuberculosis (highly endemic), typhoid fever, and yaws. Animal hazards include snakes, centipedes, scorpions, red back spiders, mouse spiders. Bites by taipans (the world's deadliest snake) are responsible for 80% of snake bites in the Central Province and the National Capital District of Papua New Guinea. Other possible hazards include crocodiles, tigers, panthers, bears, wild pigs, and wild cattle. Large leeches, which are not poison-

World Medical Guide

ous but inflict slow-healing, easily infected bites, are abundant in the swamps and streams of this country. Stingrays, sea wasps, the Indo-Pacific man-of-war, and poisonous sea cones are common in the country's coastal waters and are potentially hazardous to unprotected or careless swimmers. Fatal tetrodotoxin poisoning has occurred after the consumption of porcupine fish.

Crime/personal security: Crime and personal security are serious concerns on Papua New Guinea. All travelers should obtain a Papua New Guinea Consular Information Sheet from the U.S. State Department prior to departure.

PARAGUAY

Embassy: 202-483-6960   *Asuncion*   *GMT -4 hrs*

Entry Requirements
- A valid passport is required. No visa is required for a 3-month stay.
- HIV Test: Not required.
- Vaccinations: Yellow fever. No certificate is required to enter this country. A yellow fever vaccination certificate is required from travelers leaving Paraguay destined to countries in the Yellow Fever Endemic Zones. Travelers to this country should carefully consult their itinerary.

Telephone Country Code: 595
Embassies/Consulates: U.S. Embassy, Asuncion. 1776 Mariscal Lopez Avenue; Tel. (21) 213-715.
Hospitals/Doctors: Adventist Hospital, Asunscion (35 beds); general medical; emergency and ICU units; physicians on 24-hr call. Migone Hospital, Asuncion (30 beds); general medical facility; emergency and ICU units; physicians on 24-hr call. Instituto Paraguayo de Diagnostico.

Health Advisory

Yellow fever: No risk.
Malaria: Risk is present in rural areas on Alto Parana (90% of cases), Amambay, and Canandiyu Departments along the southeastern border with Brazil and in the central departments of Caaguazu and San Pedro. Urban areas and Iguassu Falls vicinity are risk free. Vivax malaria accounts for 94%–99% of cases. Chloroquine prophylaxis is recommended for travel to rural malarious areas.
Travelers' diarrhea: Moderate risk. In ten large urban areas, including the capital city of Asuncion, piped water is supplied and is considered safe for consumption. Travelers, nevertheless, should carefully follow food and drink precautions, especially outside urban areas. A quinolone antibiotic is recommended for the treatment of diarrhea. Diarrhea not responding to treatment with an antibiotic may be due to a parasitic disease such as giardiasis or amebiasis. Giardiasis infection rates up to 45% have been reported in school children. Cryptosporidiosis may occur.
Hepatitis: All nonimmune travelers should receive the hepatitis A vaccine prior to visiting this country. Hepatitis E has not been reported but could occur. The hepatitis B carrier rate in the general population is estimated at less than 1%. Vaccination against hepatitis B is recommended for anyone planning an extended visit to this country.
Leishmaniasis: Highly endemic in rural areas in the departments of Alto Parana, Amambay, Caaguazu, Caazapa, Canendiyu, Guaira, and San Pedro. The highest incidence occurs in Caaguazu Department. Seventy-five percent of cases are cutaneous, the remainder mucocutaneous. Travelers should take measures to prevent insect (sandfly) bites.
Schistosomiasis: This disease is not reported in Paraguay but exists in adjacent areas of Brazil along the Parana River.
Dengue fever: Endemic, but levels are unclear. Risk occurs primarily during the warmer months (November–April), especially in urban areas. An outbreak occurred in the Asuncion area in 1989. Precautions against mosquito bites are advised.

World Medical Guide

Chagas' disease: Widely distributed in nearly all rural areas. Risk occurs primarily in Conception, San Pedro, Cordillera, and Paraguari Departments in areas where there are adobe-style huts and houses. These structures often harbor the night-biting triatomid (assassin) bugs which are responsible for transmitting Chagas' disease. Travelers sleeping in such structures should take precautions against nighttime bites. Unscreened blood transfusions are also a source of infection and should be avoided.

Hantavirus pulmonary syndrome: Seventeen cases of hantavirus pulmonary syndrome occurred in western Paraguay in 1995. This is a semiarid, thorn-scrub savannah region which experienced a 10-fold increase in rainful in the spring of 1995, favoring an increase in the virus-carrying rodent population. Transmission of hantavirus is from aerosolized rodent droppings. Travelers should avoid, if possible, rodent-infested dwellings.

AIDS: Relatively low prevalence of HIV in the general population. 26% of male prostitutes are reported HIV positive.

Other diseases: Anthrax, brucellosis, coccidiomycosis, leptospirosis, measles, rabies (a relatively minor public health problem), tuberculosis (relatively high incidence, especially among Amerindian children), Venezuelan equine encephalitis, and strongyloidiasis and other helminthic infections are reported. Animal hazards include snakes (vipers, coral snakes), centipedes, scorpions, black widow spiders, brown recluse spiders, banana spiders, and wolf spiders. Species of carnivorous fish occur in the freshwaters of Paraguay.

PERU

Embassy: 202-833-9860   **Lima**   **GMT -5 hrs**

Entry Requirements
- No visa is required for tourist visits up to 90 days.
- HIV Test: Not required.
- Vaccinations: A yellow fever vaccination certificate is required of travelers 6 months or older arriving from infected areas. Peru recommends vaccination for those who intend to visit any rural area of the country.

Telephone Country Code: 51   **AT&T:** 191   **MCI:** 001-190

Embassies/Consulates: U.S. Embassy, Lima. Avenida la Encalada, Block Seventeen, Monterrico; Tel. (1) 434-3000. After hours: Tel. 434-3032. U.S. Consular agency, Cuzco. Avenida Tullumayo 125; Tel. (84) 23-9451. Travelers should contact the Embassy for updated information on travel and security within Peru.

Hospitals/Doctors: British American Hospital, Lima (100 beds); general medical/surgical facility; ambulance service; Tel. (14) 403-570 or 41-7570. Clinica Pardo, Cuzco.

Travel Advisory
Additional travel information is available through the South American Explorers' Club. They can be contacted in the United States at 800-274-0568. In Lima: Avenida Portugal 146, Brena (suburb of Lima); Telephone (14) 314480. Or write to South American Explorers' Club, Casilla #3714, Lima 100, Peru.

Health Advisory
Yellow fever: This disease is active in this country. Vaccination is recommended for all travelers more than 9 months of age who travel outside urban areas. Infected areas are the Departments of Amazonas, Ancash, Ayacucho, Cuzco, Huanuco, Junin, Loreto, Madre de Dios, Pasco, Puno, San Martin, and Ucayall. Most cases occur at elevations of 400 to 1,000 meters, with increased risk December–June. This country is in the Yellow Fever Endemic Zone. Although yellow fever vaccination may not be required for entry into this country, it may be required for on-going travel to other countries in Latin America, Africa, the Middle East, or Asia.

429

World Medical Guide

Cholera: This disease is endemic in this country and is associated with poor sanitary conditions. Although *V. cholerae* 01 remains susceptible to tetracycline and doxycycline, acute diarrhea should initially be treated with a quinolone (See Travelers' Diarrhea, below). Although cholera vaccination is not required for entry if arriving directly from the U.S. or Canada, it may be required if arriving from a cholera-infected area, or required for on-going travel to other countries in Latin America, Africa, the Middle East, or Asia.

Malaria: Since the early 1990s, malaria has increased dramatically in Peru, but there is no risk to travelers who will only visit the urban center of Lima, the coastal areas south of Lima, or the highland tourist areas (Cuzco, Machu Picchu, Lake Titacaca). Malaria is focally endemic year-round in rural areas below 1,500 meters elevation in eastern, northeastern, and northwestern Peru, especially along the border with Ecuador. Foci may also occur in some coastal areas. Malaria infection rates may exceed 25% in some areas of the northeastern lowlands (especially in the Amazonian Department of Loreto) and along the northwestern border with Ecuador. These areas have been been the foci of a major increase in malaria cases. Countrywide, vivax malaria predominates, but falciparum malaria now accounts for 30% of all malaria cases in Peru and 67% of cases in Loretto. Sporadic cases of vivax malaria have occurred in the southeastern and northern suburbs of Lima. Chloroquine- and Fansidar-resistant *P. falciparum* is reported. Antimalarial chemoprophylaxis with mefloquine, doxycycline, or Malarone is recommended for travelers going to rural areas of the provinces bordering Brazil and Ecuador, as well as Piura and Tumbes departments. For travelers to other parts of Peru, chloroquine is currently recommended.

Travelers' diarrhea: High risk outside first-class hotels and resorts. Travelers should observe strict food and drink precautions. This includes consuming only bottled, boiled, or chemically treated water consumed without ice. Food should be thoroughly cooked and consumed while still hot. Salads should be avoided. All fruit should be peeled by the traveler. Travelers should strictly avoid raw or undercooked fish or shellfish, especially ceviche. The most common causes of acute diarrhea in adults are *Vibrio cholera* (53%), shigella species (4.8%), and salmonella species (2.7%). The best predictor of cholera is severe watery diarrhea and dehydration. A quinolone antibiotic is recommended for the treatment of acute diarrhea. Diarrhea not responding to treatment with an antibiotic may be due to a parasitic disease such as giardiasis, amebiasis, cryptosporidiosis, or cyclosporiasis.

Hepatitis: All nonimmune travelers should receive hepatitis A vaccine. Hepatitis E is endemic. The hepatitis B carrier rate in the general population is approximately 1.4%. Risk of hepatitis B is increased in the Amazon Basin and the southern Andes where the carrier rate of the virus is as high as 15%. Vaccination against hepatitis B is recommended for long-term visitors to this country.

Typhoid fever: The risk of typhoid is higher than in most other Latin American countries. Typhoid vaccination is recommended for persons who stay more than one week in this country.

Dengue fever: Occurs year-round primarily in northern coastal and eastern lowland urban areas. Scattered outbreaks reported. All travelers are advised to take measures to prevent mosquito bites.

Arboviral fevers (other than dengue fever and yellow fever): Oropouche fever (vectored by biting midges; mostly reported in northern Amazon lowlands), eastern equine encephalitis (primarily in northern Amazon lowlands, usually October through May), Mayaro virus fever (mosquito-borne; occurs east of the Andes; cases in tourists have occurred).

Leishmaniasis: This disease is a major public health problem in Peru. Cutaneous leishmaniasis is endemic in Andean and inter-Andean valleys and foothills of Peru between the northern border of the country and latitude of 13° S (approximate latitude of Cuzco) within an altitude range up to 3,000 meters above sea level. Mucosal leishmaniasis is endemic in the tropical rainforests at lower altitudes. Visceral leishmaniasis (kala-azar) does not occur. All travelers to endemic areas in the Andes mountains and the tropical rainforests should take measures to prevent sand fly bites.

Chagas' disease: Widely distributed in rural areas, mostly in the southern one-half and northern one-fourth of the country. Forty percent of Peruvians are considered at risk. Chagas' disease occurs primarily in rural-agricultural areas where there are adobe-style huts and houses. These structures often harbor the night-biting triatomid (assassin) bugs which

World Medical Guide

are responsible for transmitting Chagas' disease. Travelers sleeping in such structures should take precautions against nighttime bites. Unscreened blood transfusions are also a source of infection and should be avoided.

Rabies: High risk, relative to other South American countries. Cases of human rabies, transmitted by dogs, has increased but the exact incidence of human rabies is not known. Two outbreaks of rabies, transmitted by vampire bats, claimed 40 lives. Vaccination against rabies is recommended for long-term travelers and for travelers to remote rural areas.

AIDS: Lower incidence than in other Latin American countries, such as Brazil. Prevalence of HIV in the blood donor population of Lima is 0.7% to 1.4%. HIV seroprevalence is 30% among male homosexuals/bisexuals and 8.3% among female prostitutes (1987-1994).

Altitude sickness: Risk is present in the Sierra region of central Peru which contains the Andes mountain ranges (average elevations 2,743 meters to 5,791 meters). The city of Cuzco is at 3,500 meters elevation. Travelers to high elevations should consider acetazolamide (Diamox) prophylaxis to reduce their risk of acute mountain sickness. Travelers arriving at high altitudes should spend several days acclimatizing and restricting strenuous activity.

Other diseases/hazards: Brucellosis, bartonellosis (Oroyo fever; sandfly-transmitted; usually occurs in remote Andean villages between 500 and 3,000 meters levation. Recent cases have been reported from lower elevations in the Pomabamba Valley), coccidiomycosis (endemic in the Amazonian lowlands), cysticercosis (residents of rural, endemic areas of Peru have a disease prevalence of 8%), cyclosporiasis, diphyllobothriasis (tapeworm infection from raw marine fish), echinococcosis (major health problem in central Andean areas), fascioliasis (liver fluke disease; acquired by consumption of raw aquatic plants; risk elevated in Amazonian lowlands), hantaviral disease (including hemorrhagic fever with renal syndrome and hantaviral pulmonary syndrome), leptospirosis, Lyme disease (may occur), paragonimiasis (from ingestion of raw freshwater crabs and crayfish), plague (flea-borne; focally-endemic in rural areas of Ancash, Cajamarca, Lambayeque, La Libertad, and Piura Departments), tuberculosis (a serious public health problem), strongyloidiasis and other helminthic infections, tick-borne relapsing fever, and typhus (flea- and louse-borne) are reported. Animal hazards include snakes, centipedes, scorpions, black widow spiders, brown recluse spiders, banana spiders, and wolf spiders. Nearly all snakes in Peru are found in the Montana region. Fatal bushmaster envenomations have occurred and ecotourists (e.g., birders) should have access to antivenin and air ambulance evacuation to Lima. Electric eels and piranha may be found in the country's fresh waters. Crocodiles and alligators are abundant. Portuguese man-of-war, sea wasps, and stingrays are found in the coastal waters of Peru and could be a hazard to swimmers.

PHILIPPINES

Embassy: 202-467-9300   *Manila*   *GMT +8 hrs*

Entry Requirements
- Travelers should contact the Embassy of the Philippines for entry information.
- HIV Test: Applicants for permanent residence must be tested.
- Vaccinations: A yellow fever vaccination certificate is required from all travelers older than 1 year arriving from infected areas or from any country in the Endemic Zones.
Cholera: A valid vaccination certificate may be required if arriving from an infected area.

Telephone Country Code: 63
Embassies/Consulates: U.S. Embassy, Manila. 1201 Roxas Boulevard; Tel. (2) 521-7116, ext. 2246. U.S. Consular Agency, Cebu City, Cebu; Tel: (32) 231-1261.
Hospitals/Doctors: Makati Medical Center, Manila (300 beds); most specialties; 24-hour ambulance and emergency services and ICU. University of Santo Tomas Hospital, Manila.

Health Advisory

Cholera: This disease is active in this country. Travelers to this country should consider vaccination or a doctor's letter of exemption from vaccination.

World Medical Guide

Malaria: Year-round risk, countrywide, excluding the islands of Bohol, Catanduanes, Cebu, and Leyte, the plains of the islands of Negros and Panay, and the city of Manila and other urban centers. Risk occurs primarily in the forested foothills and rolling terrain below 1,000 meters elevation in those rural areas rarely visited by tourists. Most malaria transmission occurs during and just after the monsoon season, May through November. *P. falciparum* accounts for 63% of malaria reported countrywide. Chloroquine-resistant falciparum malaria is common. Mefloquine prophylaxis is advised for travel to risk areas.

Travelers' diarrhea: High risk outside of first-class hotels and resorts. Travelers are advised to drink only bottled, boiled, filtered, or treated water and consume only well-cooked food. All fruit should be peeled prior to consumption. A quinolone antibiotic is recommended for the treatment of acute diarrhea. Diarrhea not responding to antibiotic treatment may be due to a parasitic disease such as giardiasis, amebiasis, or cryptosporidiosis.

Hepatitis: Hepatitis A is endemic and the vaccine is recommended for all nonimmune travelers. Hepatitis E is endemic at moderate levels. The hepatitis B carrier rate in the general population is estimated at 13%. Vaccination against hepatitis B is recommended for long-term visitors to this country. Hepatitis C is endemic.

Japanese encephalitis: Year-round risk, with peak transmission during the monsoon season (usually May through November) in rice-farming areas, especially on Luzon and Mindanao, with high endemicity in extreme southern Luzon, Negros, Cebu, and the Catanduanes Island. Vaccination against Japanese encephalitis is recommended for travelers who will be staying in rural-agricultural endemic areas for more than 3–4 weeks. In addition, all travelers should take personal protection measures against mosquito bites, especially in the evening when the culex mosquitoes are active.

Dengue fever: Endemic at high levels, countrywide. Year-round risk, especially in urban areas. Peak infection rates occur during the wetter months, May through November. The *Aedes* mosquitoes, which transmit dengue, bite during the daytime and are present in populous urban areas as well as resort and rural areas. Prevention of dengue consists of taking daytime protective measures against mosquito bites.

Filariasis: Bancroftian and Malayan forms of the disease are transmitted by mosquitoes in rural areas. Disease is endemic on Luzon, Leyte, Marinduque, Mindanao, Mindoro, Palawan, Samar, and Sulu. Travelers to these islands should take measures to prevent insect bites.

Schistosomiasis: Risk exists year-round. *S. japonicum* is distributed widely in southern Luzon, Leyte, Samar, Mindanao, and the east coast of Mindoro and Bohol Islands. All travelers to these areas should avoid swimming in freshwater lakes, ponds, or streams.

Rabies: About 200 human rabies cases a year are reported. Travelers should seek immediate treatment of any animal bite, especially those inflicted by a dog.

Helminthic infections: Soil-transmitted infections (caused by hookworms, roundworms, and Strongyloides) are prevalent in most rural areas. Travelers should wear shoes (to prevent the hookworm and Strongyloides larvae from penetrating the skin) and food should be thoroughly washed/cooked (to destroy roundworm eggs).

Other helminthic infections: Paragonimiasis (oriental lung fluke disease), fascioliasis, clonorchiasis (liver fluke disease), and gnathostomiasis are prevalent. Capillariasis and opisthorchiasis are endemic. Anisakiasis is reported from ingesting raw saltwater fish such as tuna and mackerel. Angiostrongyliasis is transmitted by raw prawns, fish, land crabs, or contaminated leafy vegetables. Travelers should avoid eating raw freshwater or saltwater fish and shellfish, wild watercress salad, or aquatic plants.

Other illnesses/hazards: AIDS/HIV (incidence probably higher than officially reported), chikungunya fever (year-round; reported from urban and village areas of central and southern islands), leptospirosis (risk elevated end of monsoon season, peaking early dry season), murine typhus (flea-borne), scrub typhus (mite-borne; risk elevated in grassy rural areas below 3,000 meters elevation on Leyte, Samar, Mindoro, Luzon, Negros, Panay, Palawan, Cebu, and Mindanao), tuberculosis (highly endemic), and typhoid fever. Animal hazards include snakes (cobras), centipedes, scorpions, and black widow spiders. Stingrays, jellyfish, nettles, sea cucumbers, sea wasps (potentially fatal), urchins, anemones, and the Indo-Pacific man-of-war are common in the country's coastal waters and are potentially hazardous to unprotected or careless swimmers.

World Medical Guide

POLAND

Embassy: 202-232-4517 *Warsaw* *GMT +1 hr*

Entry Requirements
- No visa required for stays up to 90 days.
- HIV Test: Testing required for foreign students intending to remain in Poland more than a few weeks; U.S. test results not accepted.
- Vaccinations: None required.

Telephone Country Code: 48 **AT&T:** 0-010-480-0111 **MCI:** 0-01-04-800-222

Embassies/Consulates: U.S. Embassy, Warsaw. Aleje Ujazdowskle 29/31; Tel. (2) 628-3041. U.S. Consulate, Krakow; Tel. (12) 221-400.

Hospitals/Doctors: State Hospital #1, Warsaw (1,500 beds); most major specialties; ICU; staff includes 200 physicians. Medical Academy, Gdansk (1,000 beds); most specialties; ICU.

Health Advisory

Travelers' diarrhea: Water and water distribution systems are unreliable. Surface water is polluted with organic, industrial, and agricultural waste/runoff. All drinking water should preferably be bottled, boiled, filtered, or chemically treated. A quinolone antibiotic is recommended for the treatment of acute diarrhea. Diarrhea not responding to treatment with an antibiotic may be due to a parasitic disease such as giardiasis. Amebiasis and cryptosporidiosis are reported.

Hepatitis: Hepatitis A vaccine is recommended for all nonimmune travelers. Hepatitis E may occur, but has not been reported. The hepatitis B carrier rate in the general population is estimated at 0.2% to 1.2%.

Tick-borne diseases: Lyme disease and tick-borne encephalitis (TBE) are reported. Lyme disease is reported sporadically. Risk is elevated in the Warmia and the Mazury Lake Region, Western Pomerania, the Bialowieza National Forest, and the Carpathian Mountain Forest. The incidence of TBE is low. The tick vector is distributed widely in brushy, wooded areas throughout most of Poland. Increased risk is present in the northern forested areas around Gdansk south and eastward to the Russian border, including the areas around Bialystock, the forested lands around Warsaw, Lodz, and Lukow, and along the border with Czechoslovakia south of Wroclaw.

Other illnesses/hazards: Brucellosis, cysticercosis (regionally enzootic), echinococcosis (regionally enzootic), hemorrhagic fever with renal syndrome, leptospirosis, rabies (enzootic in foxes; rare in humans), trichinosis (elevated risk in eastern Poland), and typhoid fever.

Air pollution: Severe air pollution occurs in most industrial areas.

PORTUGAL

Embassy: 202-332-3007 *Lisbon* *GMT 0 hrs*

Entry Requirements
- Passport/Visa: A valid passport is required.
- HIV Test: Not required.
- Vaccinations: A yellow fever vaccination certificate is required from travelers more than 1 year of age coming from infected areas; this requirement applies only to travelers arriving in or destined for the Azores or Madeira Islands. However, no certificate is required from transit passengers on the islands of Funchal, Porto Santo, or Santa Maria.

Telephone Country Code: 351 **AT&T:** 05017-1-288 **MCI:** 05-017-1234

Embassies/Consulates: U.S. Embassy, Lisbon. Avenida das Forcas Armadas; Tel. (1)726-6600 Canadian Embassy, Lisbon. Rua Rosa Araujo 2, 6th floor; Tel. (1)563-821.

Hospitals/Doctors: Santa Maria Hospital, Lisbon (1,384 beds); most medical specialties, including eye surgery and ENT; Tel. (1) 797-5171 or 797-8035. The British Hospital, Lisbon; Tel. (1) 602-020 or 678-161. Antonia Meyrelles do Souto, M.D., Lisbon; Tel. (1) 570-217.

World Medical Guide

Health Advisory
Malaria: There is no risk of malaria in Portugal.
Travelers'diarrhea: Medium risk; most sections of major cities have piped, potable water. In rural areas, water supplies may be contaminated. A quinolone antibiotic is recommended for the treatment of acute diarrhea.
Hepatitis: All nonimmune travelers should receive hepatitis A vaccine. The carrier rate of the hepatitis B virus in the general population is estimated at 1.3%—high for western Europe. Vaccination should be considered by long-term visitors.
Leishmaniasis: Cases of cutaneous leishmaniasis are rare but reported sporadically. Visceral leishmaniasis (VL) is said to be increasing. Eighty percent of cases of VL occur in the Douro River Basin in the districts of Real, Braganca, Viseau, and Gaurda. Travelers should take measures to prevent sandfly bites.
Boutonneuse fever: Countrywide incidence below 1,000 meters elevation, especially in the Mediterranean coastal areas. Travelers should avoid close contact with dogs, which are carriers of the infective brown dog tick.
Rabies: No risk; Portugal is currently rabies free.
Other illnesses: Amebiasis and giardiasis (endemic), schistosomiasis (may occur in the Algarve Province in the extreme south), ehrlichiosis, echinococcosis, fascioliasis (infection rates of 2% to 7% reported from northern rural communities), leptospirosis, tick-borne relapsing fever, and typhoid fever.

PUERTO RICO AND U.S. VIRGIN ISLANDS
San Juan　　　　　　　　　　　　　　　　　GMT -4 hrs

Entry Requirements
- A passport recommended for United States travelers.
- HIV Test: Not required.
- Vaccinations: None required.

Telephone Area Code: 787
Hospitals/Doctors: Ashford Presbyterian Hospital, San Juan; Tel. 721-2160. Dwight Santiago, M.D. Ashford Medical Center; Tel. 722-5513 or 843-4588.

Health Advisory
See Disease Risk Summary for the Caribbean.
Travelers' diarrhea: Low to moderate risk. In urban and resort areas, the hotels and restaurants generally serve reliable food and potable water.
Hepatitis: Low to moderate risk. Nonimmune travelers should receive hepatitis A vaccine.
Dengue fever: Risk is present year-round. Highest incidence reported in the vicinity of Yanes. All travelers to Puerto Rico should take measures to prevent insect (mosquito) bites.
Schistosomiasis: Risk of intestinal schistosomiasis is focally present throughout Puerto Rico. Seventeen of 79 municipalities tested have seroprevalence rates averaging 10%. The highest exposure (seroprevalence) rates occur around Jayuya (38.5%) and Naguabo (36.4%). Travelers should avoid swimming or wading in freshwater ponds, lakes, or streams.
Other diseases/health threats: Bancroftian filariasis (mosquito-borne; may be a threat; travelers should prevent insect bites), intestinal helminthic infections (ancylostomiasis, ascariasis, strongyloidiasis, and trichuriasis), rabies, sexually transmitted diseases, AIDS, typhoid fever, viral encephalitis, ciguatera fish toxin poisoning, and swimming related hazards (jellyfish, spiny sea urchins, and coral).

World Medical Guide

QATAR

Embassy: 202-274-1600 *Doha* *GMT +3 hrs*

Entry Requirements
- Ten-year, multiple entry visa is available. Travelers should contact the Qatar Embassy in Washington for further details.
- HIV Test: Required for work permit or student visa.
- Vaccinations: A yellow fever vaccination certificate is required from all travelers arriving from infected areas.

Telephone Country Code: 974   **AT&T:** 0800-011-77   **MCI:** 0800-012-77
Embassies/Consulates: U.S. Embassy, Doha; 149 Ali Bin Ahmed Street, Farig Bin Omran; Tel. 864-701/7022/703.
Hospitals/Doctors: Hamad Hospital, Doha (600 beds); major referral center; all specialties; well-equipped and staffed.

Health Advisory

Malaria: There is no risk of malaria in this country.
Travelers' diarrhea: Water is obtained almost exclusively from desalination plants. The high mineral content of underground water makes it unsuitable for drinking. A quinolone antibiotic is recommended for the treatment of acute diarrhea. Diarrhea not responding to antibiotic treatment may be due to a parasitic disease such as giardiasis or amebiasis.
Hepatitis: Hepatitis A vaccine is recommended for all nonimmune travelers. Hepatitis E has not been reported, but may occur. The hepatitis B carrier rate in the general population is estimated at 2%. Vaccination against hepatitis B is recommended for healthcare workers and should be considered by long-term visitors to this country.
Leishmaniasis: Both cutaneous and visceral leishmaniasis may be present in endemic areas.
Other illnesses: Brucellosis (usually transmitted by raw dairy products), rabies (occurs rarely in stray dogs), trachoma, tuberculosis (low incidence), typhoid fever, soil-transmitted helminthic infections (roundworm, hookworm, and whipworm infections are common in rural areas; incidence is estimated at less than 5%).
Environmental: Raw sewage is pumped directly into the Persian Gulf, and beaches are considered contaminated.

ROMANIA

Embassy: 202-232-4747 *Bucharest* *GMT +2 hrs*

Entry Requirements
- Visa: A visa is required for stays greater than 30 days. Travelers should call the Romanian Embassy for further information.
- HIV Test: Not required.
- Vaccinations: None required.

Telephone Country Code: 40   **AT&T:** 01-800-4288   **MCI:** 01-800-1800
Embassies/Consulates: U.S. Embassy, Bucharest. Strada Tudor Arghezi 7-9; Tel. (1) 210-4042.
Hospitals/Doctors: Cantacuzina Hospital, Bucharest (1,200 beds); most specialties. Travelers should contact the U.S. Consular Section at Strada Filipescu No. 26 (Tel. 210-4042) for physician referrals.

Health Advisory

Travelers' diarrhea: High risk outside of first-class hotels and resorts. Water in the larger cities, but not rural areas, is generally potable. Travelers are advised to drink only bottled, boiled, filtered, or treated water and consume only well-cooked food. All fruit should be peeled prior to consumption. A quinolone antibiotic is recommended for the treatment of acute diarrhea. Diarrhea not responding to antibiotic treatment may be due to a parasitic disease such as giardiasis, amebiasis, or cryptosporidiosis—or an intestinal virus such as rotavirus.

World Medical Guide

Cholera: Sporadic cases are reported, especially from Tulcea, Braila, and Constanta counties and along the Danube River. Infections associated with the consumption of raw seafood have been reported along the Black Sea coast.

Hepatitis: All nonimmune travelers should receive hepatitis A vaccine. The hepatitis B carrier rate in the general population is estimated at up to 9%—the highest in Europe. Vaccination against hepatitis B is recommended for anyone planning an extended visit to this country. There is also increased risk of transmission of hepatitis B from medical injections that are administered with unclean needles and syringes.

Tick-borne diseases: Lyme disease, Central European tick-borne encephalitis, and boutonneuse fever are reported. The ticks that transmit these diseases (*Ixodes ricinus*) are found in brushy, wooded areas throughout the country. There is higher risk of tick-borne encephalitis in the Tulcea District and in Transylvania at the base of the Carpathian Mountains and Transylvanian Alps. Boutonneuse fever is endemic along the Black Sea coast.

Viral encephalitis: An outbreak of mosquito-transmitted West Nile encephalitis occurred in 1996 in the lower Danube valley and Bucharest.

AIDS: High incidence reported, especially in children and newborns—more cases, in fact, than have been reported cumulatively in all other European countries. Most cases occur in the Bucharest and Constanta areas. There is risk of transmission of HIV from unclean needles and syringes, as well as from contaminated blood transfusions. All travelers are cautioned against receiving unnecessary medical or dental injections and blood transfusions, and travelers are advised to carry their own sterile needles and syringes in case a medical injection is necessary.

Other illnesses: Anthrax, brucellosis (enzootic at low levels, particularly in sheep, goats, and cattle; human cases usually due to consumption of unpasteurized milk or milk products), echinococcosis (stray dogs in urban and rural areas commonly infected; human cases reported sporadically), hemorrhagic fever with renal syndrome (similar to hantavirus syndrome; disease transmitted by rodent excreta), leptospirosis, rabies (enzootic in foxes, wolves, and wild canids; rare in humans), trichinosis (from raw or undercooked pork), tuberculosis (highest reported incidence in Europe), typhoid fever, typhus (murine and louse-borne), and helminthic infections (roundworm, hookworm, and whipworm infections, and strongyloidiasis).

RUSSIA
HEALTH ADVISORY ALSO INCLUDES: ARMENIA, AZERBAIJAN, THE BALTIC STATES, BELARUS, UKRAINE, GEORGIA, AND MOLDOVA

Embassy: 202-939-8918   *Moscow*   *GMT +3 hrs*

Entry Requirements
- Passport/Visa: A valid passport, visa, and exit permit required. Strict customs regulations may apply. For updated information for travel to Russia, travelers should contact the Russian Embassy in Washington.
- HIV Test: HIV testing is required for foreigners staying more than 3 months. U.S. test result is currently acceptable.
- Vaccinations: None required. Tetanus/diphtheria immunization is recommended.

Telephone Country Code: 7   **AT&T:** 155-5042   **MCI:** 8-10-800-497-7222

Embassies/Consulates: U.S. Embassy, Moscow. Novinskiy Bulvar 19/23. Tel. (095) 252-2451. After hours: Tel. (095) 956-4422.

Hospitals/Doctors: Ambulance services: dial 03 countrywide. Kremlin Hospital, Moscow; all specialties; reportedly among the best in Russia.

American Medical Center (Moscow and St. Petersburg). American-owned, western-quality health-care clinics offer family practice and 24-hour emergency care. They primarily serve tourists, student groups, and corporate executives. In Moscow (1, Grokholsky Pereulok), Tel. (095) 933-7700; in St. Petersburg (10, Serpukhovskaya Street), Tel. (812) 326-1730. Membership plan is available. Travelers in the United States should call 877-952-6262 or 617-262-5301 for information.

World Medical Guide

Travelers not receiving care at one of the above clinics should contact the U.S. Embassy in case of serious illness. Health care in Russia and the countries of the former Soviet Union is seriously deficient by Western standards. All travelers should consider purchasing a travel insurance policy with telephone assistance and medical evacuation capabilities. Chapter 16 lists numerous companies that offer assistance policies.

Health Advisory

Cholera: This disease is currently reported active in Dagestan, a republic within the Russian Federation. Travelers to this area are advised to avoid street vendor food and consume only bottled, boiled, or chemically treated water. All travelers should observe strict food and drink safety precautions.

Malaria: Transmission currently is limited to the warmer months of May through September. Risk likely is limited to the southwest, particularly areas bordering Georgia, Azerbaijan, and the coastal areas of the Black and Caspian Seas. All cases appear to be vivax malaria.

Travelers' diarrhea: High risk outside of first-class hotels. All water supplies in Russia are suspect, including municipal tap water, which may be untreated and grossly contaminated. Travelers should consume only bottled water, or boiled or chemically treated water. Travelers should observe strict food and drink safety precautions. A quinolone antibiotic is recommended for the treatment of acute diarrhea. Diarrhea not responding to treatment with an antibiotic may be due to a parasitic disease, especially giardiasis. Outbreaks of giardiasis and cryptosporidiosis are reported from many urban areas throughout Russia. Amebiasis occurs focally countrywide but is more common in the south.

Hepatitis: All nonimmune travelers should receive hepatitis A vaccine. Hepatitis E accounts for up to 18% of acute hepatitis in the south. The hepatitis B carrier rate in the general population of Russia is estimated at 3.8%. Vaccination against hepatitis B is recommended for anyone planning an extended visit to this country. Many cases of hepatitis B are transmitted by unsterilized needles, syringes, and surgical instruments. Blood supplies may be contaminated with hepatitis B and C viruses.

Diphtheria: An epidemic diphtheria began in 1990 in the Russian Federation has spread extensively, involving all countries of the former Soviet Union. Seventy percent of cases have occurred in persons older than 15 years. All travelers to Russia and the NIS, especially adults, should be fully immunized against this disease. (The CDC estimates that 20% to 60% of Americans older than 20 years lack sufficient immunity to diphtheria.) Diphtheria vaccine in the United States is widely available and is administered in combination with the tetanus toxoid vaccine (Td vaccine).

Typhoid fever: Travelers to rural areas or those planning long stays should receive typhoid vaccine. A marked increase in typhoid fever has occurred in Tajikistan and Turkmenistan.

Lyme disease: Occurs focally in rural forested areas with the highest incidence in the Ural Mountains area. Risk presumably also occurs in the northwest and central areas.

Tick-borne encephalitis (TBE): Tick-borne encephalitis is transmitted from the Baltics to the Crimea by ixodid ticks. Peak transmission period is April through October. Risk is present primarily in rural brushy and forested areas below 1,500 meters elevation. Highly enzootic foci occur throughout the Urals and much of the northern, forested mountainous areas, including suburban "forests" bordering large cities. Highest number of indigenous cases are reported from the south-central areas, including Altay, Kemerovo, Novosibirsk Oblasts, and Krasnoyarsk Kray. Co-infection with Lyme disease is increasing. Travelers to endemic areas should take measures to prevent tick bites.

Boutonneuse fever: Tick-borne; reported most commonly in the Black Sea coastal areas of the Caucasus, Transcaucasus, and the Crimea, and along the Caspian Sea coastline.

Crimean-Congo hemorrhagic fever: Reported mostly from southern areas, but outbreaks have occurred in some areas of Rostov Oblast (near the sea of Azov), April through November. Risk areas are rural steppe, savannah, semi-desert, and foothill/low mountain habitats below 2,000 meters elevation.

Arboviral diseases: Karelian fever (mosquito-borne; most cases occur July–September in the Karelian region); Tahjna virus fever (mosquito-borne; occurs sporadically from the Baltic region north to the Kolsky Peninsula); sandfly fever (sandfly-borne; limited to Moldova and

437

World Medical Guide

the Crimea); dengue fever (mosquito-borne; cases previously reported from extreme southern regions); West Nile fever (mosquito-borne; virus reportedly circulates in the Volga Delta region from May–September); Sindbis virus fever (detected in the Volga Delta, July–August).

Leishmaniasis: Risk for cutaneous leishmaniasis primarily limited to southern regions, including portions of Georgia Republic and the southern Ukraine, below 1,300 meters elevation. Visceral leishmaniasis is confined to areas along the southeastern coast of the Black Sea, the southeastern and southwestern coasts of the Caspian Sea and the border areas of Georgia and Azerbaijan. Travelers to these regions should take measures to prevent sandfly bites.

AIDS/HIV: AIDS cases are increasing and an epidemic may be in the making. The reasons include 1) an increase in IV drug abuse, 2) an increase in prostitution and sexual promiscuity, 3) an increase in sexually transmitted diseases, 4) decreased availability of sterile needles and syringes, and 5) no education or prevention programs.

Other illnesses/hazards: Anthrax (sporadic human cases occur, related to exposure to livestock in rural areas, especially southern areas), brucellosis, echinococcosis (in southern and northeastern areas. *Echinococcus multilocularis* associated with reindeer culture in north), legionellosis, leptospirosis (a particular problem in fish-breeding areas of Rostov Province; extensive outbreaks have occurred in east central areas), North Asian tick typhus (also called Siberian tick typhus; occurs in the steppe areas bordering Kazakhstan, Georgia, and Azerbaijan; risk elevated May–June), opisthorchiasis (acquired from consumption of raw freshwater fish; reported from western European Russia), plague (flea-borne; usually occurs as isolated cases or small outbreaks in semi-arid areas of the southern republics of Azerbaijan, Armenia, and Georgia), rabies, rickettsialpox, tick-borne relapsing fever (may occur south of 55 degrees north latitude), trichinosis (greatest risk in western Belarus and the Ukraine), tularemia ("rabbit fever"; risk may be elevated in the north), tuberculosis (40% rise in cases since 1995; incidence in Moscow has doubled since 1991), and helminthic infections (roundworm, hookworm, and whipworm infections and strongyloidiasis) reported, especially from the Transcaucasus, especially Azerbaijan.

RWANDA

Embassy: 202-232-2882   **Kigali**   GMT +2 hrs

Entry Requirements
- Passport/Visa: Valid passport and visa are required.
- HIV Test: Not required.
- Vaccinations: A yellow fever vaccination certificate is required from all travelers older than 1 year of age arriving from ALL COUNTRIES.
  Cholera: Vaccination is not officially required, but is advised.

Telephone Country Code: 250
Embassies/Consulates: U.S. Embassy, Kigali. Boulevard de la Revolution; Tel. 75601, 72126.
Hospitals/Doctors: Kigali Central Hospital (450 beds); general medical services.

World Medical Guide

Health Advisory
Yellow fever: Vaccination is required for entry. This disease is not currently active.
Cholera: This disease is reported active in this country. Cholera vaccination certificate may be required if arriving from an infected area or for on-going travel to other countries. Travelers should consider vaccination or obtaining a doctor's letter of exemption from vaccination. Furazolidone or a quinolone is the antibiotic of choice for treatment.
Malaria: Risk is present throughout this country, including urban areas. Risk may be less in the northwest prefecture of Ruhengeri. *P. falciparum* accounts for approximately 90% of cases. Remainder of cases are due to the *P. ovale* and *P. malariae* species, rarely *P. vivax*. Chloroquine-resistant falciparum malaria is reported. Prophylaxis with mefloquine or doxycycline is currently recommended.
Travelers' diarrhea: High risk. Water supplies, even in Kigali, may be contaminated. Travelers should observe all food and drink safety precautions. A quinolone antibiotic is recommended for the treatment of acute diarrhea.
Hepatitis: High risk. All susceptible travelers should receive hepatitis A vaccine. The hepatitis B carrier rate in the general population is estimated to exceed 10%. Vaccination is recommended for healthcare and relief workers.
Schistosomiasis: Intestinal schistosomiasis occurs along Lake Kivu and in the northwest around Lakes Bulera and Ruhondu, with risk also in Byumba, Kigali, and Butare prefectures. Travelers to these regions should avoid swimming, bathing, or wading in freshwater lakes, ponds, or streams.
Trypanosomiasis (African sleeping sickness): Sporadic cases occur; risk areas include Akagera Game Park, in the northeast, and Nasho Lake vicinity (east of Kigali).
Other illnesses/hazards: AIDS (HIV prevalence is 24.4%–30% among pregnant women in Kigali), African tick typhus, brucellosis, echinococcosis, filariasis, leishmaniasis (transmission occurs year-round), meningitis, plague, rabies (transmitted primarily by dogs), louse-borne relapsing fever and typhus fever (primarily in highlands), Rift Valley fever, tuberculosis (a major health problem), trachoma, typhoid fever, and intestinal worms.

ST. BARTHELEMY (FRENCH WEST INDIES)
Embassy: 202-944-6000   *Gustavia*   GMT -4 hrs
Entry Requirements
- Passport/Visa: Visa not required. Visitors arriving by air are required to show return or ongoing ticket. This island, often called "St. Barts," is a dependency of Guadeloupe, which in turn is a Department of France.
- HIV Test: Not required.
- Vaccinations: None required.

Telephone Country Code: 590
Doctors/Hospitals: Gustavia Clinic (staffed by 5 physicians and 3 dentists); Tel. 27-60-35.

Health Advisory
See Disease Risk Summary for the Caribbean.
Travelers' diarrhea: Low to moderate risk. In urban and resort areas, the hotels and restaurants generally serve reliable food and potable water. Elsewhere, travelers should observe all food and drink safety precautions. A quinolone antibiotic (Floxin or Cipro) is recommended for the treatment of acute diarrhea. Diarrhea not responding to antibiotic treatment may be due to a parasitic disease such as giardiasis or amebiasis.
Hepatitis: Low risk to tourists. All nonimmune travelers should receive hepatitis A vaccine.
Dengue fever: This mosquito-transmitted viral disease is prevalent in the Caribbean. Travelers should take measures to prevent insect bites.
Other diseases/health threats: Typhoid fever, viral encephalitis, ciguatera fish toxin poisoning (outbreaks have occurred), and swimming related hazards (jellyfish, spiny sea urchins, and coral).

World Medical Guide

ST. KITTS & NEVIS

Embassy: 202-833-355   *Basseterre*   *GMT -4 hrs*

Entry Requirements
- Passport/Visa: Visa not required. These islands have been independent of Britain since 1983.
- HIV Test: Not required.
- Vaccinations: A yellow fever vaccination certificate is required from travelers over 6 months of age coming from infected or endemic areas.

Telephone Area Code: 80   **AT&T:** 1-800-872-2881
Doctors/Hospitals: Joseph N. France Hospital, Basseterre (164 beds); general medical/surgical facility; emergency room.

Health Advisory
See Disease Risk Summary for the Caribbean.
Travelers' diarrhea: Low to moderate risk. In urban and resort areas, the hotels and restaurants generally serve reliable food and potable water. Elsewhere, travelers should observe all food and drink safety precautions. A quinolone antibiotic (Floxin or Cipro) is recommended for the treatment of acute diarrhea.
Hepatitis: Low risk to tourists. All nonimmune travelers should receive hepatitis A vaccine.
Dengue fever: This mosquito-transmitted viral disease is prevalent in the Caribbean. Travelers should take measures to prevent insect bites.
Other diseases/health threats: Typhoid fever, viral encephalitis, ciguatera fish toxin poisoning (outbreaks have occurred), and swimming related hazards (jellyfish, spiny sea urchins, and coral).

SAINT LUCIA

Embassy: 202-463-3550   *Castries*   *GMT -4 hrs*

Entry Requirements
- Passport/Visa: A passport is required for entry.
- HIV Test: Not required.
- Vaccinations: A vaccination certificate is required of all travelers older than 1 year arriving from infected areas.

Telephone Country Code: 809
Electricity/Plugs: AC 50 Hz, 220 volts; plug type G. Adaptors and transformer necessary for U.S.-made appliances.
Embassies/Consulates: Canadian High Commission (Barbados); Tel. (809) 429-3550.
Doctors/Hospitals: Victoria Hospital, Castries (211 beds); general medical/surgical facility;.

Health Advisory
See Disease Risk Summary for the Caribbean.
Travelers' diarrhea: Low to moderate risk. In urban and resort areas, the hotels and restaurants generally serve reliable food and potable water. Elsewhere, travelers should observe all food and drink safety precautions. A quinolone antibiotic (Floxin or Cipro) is recommended for the treatment of acute diarrhea. Diarrhea not responding to antibiotic treatment may be due to a parasitic disease such as giardiasis or amebiasis.
Hepatitis: Low risk to tourists. All nonimmune travelers should receive hepatitis A vaccine.
Dengue fever: This mosquito-transmitted viral disease is prevalent in the Caribbean. Travelers should take measures to prevent insect bites.
Schistosomiasis: Disease due to intestinal schistosomiasis (caused by *S. mansoni*) is present on this island, but is of limited risk. Most snail-infested freshwater foci have been identified and can be avoided. Risk areas include Cul de Sac River Valley (south of Castries), the Roseau Valley, and around Soufriere and Riche Fond. Travelers should avoid swimming or wading in freshwater ponds, lakes, or streams in these areas.

World Medical Guide

Other diseases/health threats: Brucellosis, filariasis (mosquito-borne; low apparent risk; may occur in the Lesser Antilles from Trinidad north to Guadeloupe), Chagas' disease (low apparent risk; reduviid bug vectors have been detected on several other islands), histoplasmosis, helminthic infections (ancylostomiasis, ascariasis, strongyloidiasis, and trichuriasis), leptospirosis (skin contact with water or moist soil contaminated with the urine of infected animals), syphilis, AIDS, tuberculosis, typhoid fever (St. Lucia had the highest incidence reported in the Caribbean in 1987 (36 cases per 100,000 population), viral encephalitis, ciguatera fish toxin poisoning, and swimming related hazards (jellyfish, spiny sea urchins, and coral).

SAINT MAARTEN (NETH. ANTILLES)

Embassy: 202-244-5300   *Philipsburg*   *GMT -4 hrs*

Entry Requirements
- Passport/Visa: Visa not required. Saint Maarten is part of the Netherland Antilles.
- HIV Test: Not required.
- Vaccinations: None required.

Telephone Country Code: 599   **AT&T:** 001-800-872-2881   **MCI:** 001-800-950-1022

Doctors/Hospitals: St. Maarten Medical Center, Philipsburg (57 beds); new multispecialty clinic and hospital (opened in 1992); 24-hr. emergency coverage; 3-bed ICU; hemodialysis (2 units); Tel. (5) 31111. Ambulance; Tel. 22111. To call St. Martin Medical Center from French St. Martin, travelers should dial (93)-25685.

Health Advisory

See Disease Risk Summary for the Caribbean.

Travelers' diarrhea: Low to moderate risk. A quinolone antibiotic (Floxin or Cipro) is recommended for the treatment of acute diarrhea.

Hepatitis: Low risk to tourists. All nonimmune travelers should receive hepatitis A vaccine.

Dengue fever: This mosquito-transmitted viral disease is prevalent in the Caribbean. Travelers should take measures to prevent insect bites.

Other diseases/health threats: Typhoid fever, viral encephalitis, ciguatera fish toxin poisoning (outbreaks have occurred), and swimming related hazards (jellyfish, spiny sea urchins, and coral).

SAINT MARTIN (FRENCH WEST INDIES)

Embassy: 202-944-6000   *Marigot*   *GMT -4 hrs*

Entry Requirements
- Passport/Visa: Visa not required. Saint Martin is a French Dependent Territory.
- HIV Test: Not required.
- Vaccinations: None required.

Telephone Country Code: 590

Doctors/Hospitals: Hopital de Marigot (55 beds); general medical/surgical facility; physicians on call 24 hours.

See Disease Risk Summary for the Caribbean.

Health Advisory

Malaria: No risk.

Travelers' diarrhea: Low to moderate risk. In urban and resort areas, the hotels and restaurants generally serve reliable food and potable water. Elsewhere, travelers should observe all food and drink safety precautions. A quinolone antibiotic (Floxin or Cipro) is recommended for the treatment of acute diarrhea.

Hepatitis: Low risk to tourists. All nonimmune travelers should receive hepatitis A vaccine.

Dengue fever: This mosquito-transmitted viral disease is prevalent in the Caribbean. Travelers should take measures to prevent insect bites.

Other diseases/health threats: Typhoid fever, viral encephalitis, ciguatera fish toxin poisoning (outbreaks have occurred), and swimming related hazards (jellyfish, spiny sea urchins, and coral).

World Medical Guide

SAINT VINCENT AND THE GRENADINES
(INCLUDES MUSTIQUE AND BEQUIA)

Embassy: 202-462-7806 *Kingstown* *GMT -4 hrs*

Entry Requirements
- Passport/Visa: Visa not required.
- HIV Test: Not required.
- Vaccinations: A vaccination certificate is required of all travelers older than 1 year arriving from infected areas.

Telephone Area Code: 809
Doctors/Hospitals: General Hospital, Kingstown (204 beds); general medical/surgical facility; Tel. 456-1185.

Health Advisory

See Disease Risk Summary for the Caribbean.
Travelers' diarrhea: Low to moderate risk. In urban and resort areas, the hotels and restaurants generally serve reliable food and potable water. Elsewhere, travelers should observe all food and drink safety precautions. A quinolone antibiotic (Floxin or Cipro) is recommended for the treatment of acute diarrhea. Diarrhea not responding to antibiotic treatment may be due to a parasitic disease such as giardiasis or amebiasis.
Hepatitis: Low risk to tourists. All nonimmune travelers should receive hepatitis A vaccine.
Dengue fever: This mosquito-transmitted viral disease is prevalent in the Caribbean. Travelers should take measures to prevent insect bites.
Other diseases/health threats: Brucellosis, filariasis (Bancroftian variety; mosquito-borne; may occur in the Lesser Antilles from Trinidad north to Guadeloupe), histoplasmosis, intestinal helminthic infections (ancylostomiasis, ascariasis, strongyloidiasis, and trichuriasis), leptospirosis, sexually transmitted diseases, AIDS, tuberculosis, typhoid fever, viral encephalitis, ciguatera fish toxin poisoning, and swimming related hazards (jellyfish, spiny sea urchins, and coral).

AMERICAN SAMOA
Pago Pago

Entry Requirements
- Passport/Visa: Passport required. American Samoa consists of seven islands and atolls that are a U.S. territory.
- HIV Test: Not required.
- Vaccinations: A yellow fever vaccination certificate is required from travelers over 6 months of age coming from infected or endemic areas.

Telephone Country Code: 684

Health Advisory

Malaria: No risk.
Travelers' diarrhea: Low to moderate risk. In urban and resort areas, the hotels and restaurants generally serve reliable food and potable water. Elsewhere, travelers should observe all food and drink safety precautions. A quinolone antibiotic (Floxin or Cipro) is recommended for the treatment of acute diarrhea. Diarrhea not responding to antibiotic treatment may be due to a parasitic disease such as giardiasis or amebiasis—or an intestinal virus.
Hepatitis: All nonimmune travelers should receive hepatitis A vaccine prior to visiting this country. The hepatitis B carrier rate in the general population is estimated at 5.5%. Vaccination against hepatitis B is recommended for all healthcare workers and should be considered by anyone planning an extended visit to this country.
Filariasis, Japanese encephalitis, dengue fever: Sporadic cases and outbreaks are reported. Travelers should take protective measures against mosquito bites.

World Medical Guide

SAMOA (WESTERN)

UN Mission: 212-599- 6196   Apia   GMT -11 hrs

Entry Requirements
- Passport/Visa: Passport required.
- HIV Test: Not required.
- Vaccinations: A yellow fever vaccination certificate is required from travelers over 6 months of age coming from infected or endemic areas.

Telephone Country Code: 685
Hospitals/Doctors: National Hospital (335 beds); general medical facility; emergency room.
Embassies & Consulates: U.S. Embassy, Apia; Tel: 21631.

Health Advisory

Malaria: No risk.
Travelers' diarrhea: Moderate risk outside of first-class hotels and resorts. Travelers should drink only bottled, boiled, or treated water. Food should be eaten well cooked. A quinolone antibiotic (Floxin or Cipro) is recommended for the treatment of acute diarrhea. Diarrhea not responding to antibiotic treatment may be due to a parasitic disease such as giardiasis or amebiasis—or an intestinal virus.
Hepatitis: Hepatitis A vaccine is recommended for all nonimmune travelers. The hepatitis B carrier rate in the general population is estimated at 10%. Vaccination against hepatitis B is recommended for healthcare workers and should be considered by long-term visitors to this country.
Dengue fever: Most risk occurs during rainy season months. Travelers should take protective measures against mosquito bites.
Filariasis: Malayan filariasis occurs in this country. Travelers should take protective measures against mosquito bites.

SAO TOME & PRINCIPE

Permanent Mission: 212-697-4211   Sao Tome   GMT 0 hrs

Entry Requirements
- Passport/Visa: Valid passport and visa are required.
- HIV Test: Not required.
- Vaccinations: A yellow fever vaccination certificate is required from all travelers older than 1 year arriving from ALL COUNTRIES.

U.S. Embassy: The U.S. Ambassador based in Gabon is accredited to Sao Tome on a non-resident basis.

Health Advisory

Yellow fever: Vaccination is required for entry. No recent yellow fever cases are reported. This country is in the Yellow Fever Endemic Zone. A valid yellow fever vaccination certificate may be required for travel to other countries in South America, Africa, the Middle East, or Asia.
Cholera: This disease is active in this country. Although cholera vaccination is not required for entry if arriving directly from the U.S. or Canada, it may be required if arriving from a cholera-infected area, or required for on-going travel to other countries in Latin America, Africa, the Middle East, or Asia. Travelers should consider vaccination (one dose) or a doctor's letter of exemption from vaccination. The risk to travelers of acquiring cholera is considered low. Prevention consists primarily in adhering to safe food and drink guidelines.
Malaria: Risk is present year-round throughout this country, including urban areas. Falciparum malaria accounts for 87% of cases. Chloroquine-resistant falciparum malaria is reported. Prophylaxis with mefloquine or doxycycline is currently recommended when traveling to malarious areas of this country.

World Medical Guide

Travelers' diarrhea: High risk. Piped water supplies should be considered potentially contaminated. Travelers should observe all food and drink safety precautions. A quinolone antibiotic is recommended for the treatment of acute diarrhea. Diarrhea not responding to treatment with an antibiotic, or chronic diarrhea, may be due to a parasitic disease such as giardiasis, amebiasis, or cryptosporidiosis.

Hepatitis: High risk. All susceptible travelers should receive hepatitis A vaccine or immune globulin prophylaxis. The hepatitis B carrier rate in the general population is estimated to exceed 10%. Vaccination against hepatitis B is recommended for healthcare workers and all long-term visitors to this country. No data is currently available on hepatitis E.

Schistosomiasis: Widely distributed throughout the island of Sao Tome. The major risk area is in the northeast between the Rio Grande and Manuel Jorge Rivers, including the capital and environs, the surrounding Agua Grande District, and the adjacent part of Mezoxi District. Travelers should avoid swimming, bathing, or wading in freshwater lakes, ponds, or streams.

Arboviral fevers: Data are not available to indicate if arboviral fevers such as chikungunya, West Nile, Crimean-Congo hemorrhagic fever, and dengue are transmitted on the islands.

AIDS: Incidence is presumed low, but widespread surveys have not been done.

Other illnesses/hazards: Data on filariasis, loiasis, onchocerciasis, leishmaniasis, intestinal helminthic diseases, and rabies not available, but these diseases are presumed to occur. Tuberculosis and typhoid fever are considered to be endemic.

SAUDI ARABIA

Embassy: 202-342-3800   *Riyadh*   *GMT +3 hrs*

Entry Requirements
- Passport/Visa: A valid passport and visa are required. No tourist visas are issued.
- HIV Test: Required for applicants for work visas. Travelers should contact the Saudi Embassy for further details.
- Vaccinations: A yellow fever vaccination certificate is required from all travelers arriving from, or transiting through, any country any part of which is infected with yellow fever. Meningococcal meningitis: A vaccination certificate issued within the past 2 years is required. This certificate must be issued no less than 3 weeks before the date of arrival.

Telephone Country Code: 966   **AT&T:** 1-800-10   **MCI:** 1-800-11

Embassies/Consulates: U.S. Embassy, Collector Road M, Riyadh. Diplomatic Quarter; Tel. (1) 488-3800. U.S. Consulate, Dhahran; Tel. (3) 891-3200. U.S. Cosulate, Jeddah; Tel. (2) 667-0080.

Hospitals/Doctors: King Faisal Specialist Hospital, Riyadh (400 beds); all specialties; ambulance service and helipad; rated best medical facility in Saudi Arabia. Aramco Hospital, Dhahran (361 beds); private accredited hospital; most specialties; one of the best medical facilities in the country.

Health Advisory

Malaria: Transmission of this disease occurs year-round in the southern areas, with increased risk October through April. Risk exists up to 2,000 meters elevation in rural and urban areas of the Tihama coastal region, and the Asir highlands in the southwest (Jizan, Asir, and Al Bahah provinces). Risk in the western provinces (Makkah and Al Madinah) is limited to rural valley foci in the Hijaz mountains, and along the Red Sea coast. Urban areas in the western provinces are risk-free, as are all other parts of the country (Riyadh, Ar'ar, Al Jawf, Al Qurayyah, Tabuk, At Taif). There is no malaria in the urban areas of Jedda, Mecca, Medina, and Taif. The most intense malaria transmission occurs in the southwestern provinces where *P. falciparum* accounts for 85% of the cases; *P. vivax* accounts for the remainder. Two cases of chloroquine-resistant falciparum malaria have been reported in the southwest. Chloroquine resistance has been confirmed in adjacent areas in Yemen. Prophylaxis with chloroquine is still currently recommended when traveling to malarious areas of this country.

World Medical Guide

Travelers' diarrhea: Water is supplied via potable water distribution systems in all major urban areas of Saudi Arabia and is safe for drinking. Outside of major urban areas all travelers should drink only boiled, bottled, or treated/filtered water. All food should be well cooked. A quinolone antibiotic is recommended for the treatment of acute diarrhea. Diarrhea not responding to antibiotic treatment may be due to a parasitic disease such as giardiasis or amebiasis—or an intestinal virus (Rotavirus or Norwalk virus).

Hepatitis: Hepatitis A vaccine is recommended for all nonimmune travelers. Hepatitis E is likely, but no data currently available. The hepatitis B carrier rate in the general population is estimated at 8%–10%. Vaccination against hepatitis B is recommended for healthcare workers and should be considered by long-term visitors to this country.

Dengue fever: Low risk of potential disease in the eastern coastal areas where the *Aedes* mosquito is found. No current data available. Travelers to this area should take measures to prevent mosquito bites.

Meningitis: Sporadic cases occur, as well as small outbreaks, usually related to pilgrimages to Mecca where crowded conditions promote disease transmission. The CDC recommends that all travelers to Saudi Arabia be vaccinated against meningococcal meningitis.

Leishmaniasis: Transmission of cutaneous leishmaniasis caused by *L. major* occurs year-round (peaking from July through September) in the oases of the eastern and central emirates. A hyperendemic focus may exist near the Al-Hofuf oasis. Transmission of cutaneous leishmaniasis caused by *L. tropica* occurs primarily in the mountains of western emirates (cases were reported among American military personnel stationed in eastern Saudi Arabia during Operation Desert Storm). Transmission of visceral leishmaniasis (kala azar) occurs year-round and is restricted to the southwestern Asir region. Travelers should take measures to prevent sandfly bites.

Sandfly fever: Moderate to highly endemic. Foci may occur throughout the country, with elevated risk (April through October) in village and periurban areas. All travelers should take precautions against sandfly bites between dusk and dawn.

Schistosomiasis: Risk is present in the western (in wadis and cisterns) and central (in oases) emirates. Intestinal schistosomiasis foci occur in the central (Hail, Riyadh), northern (Al Jawf), northwestern (Tabuk, Medina), midwestern (Makkah, Al Bahah), and the highlands of the southwestern (Jiazan) and midwestern (Makkah) emirates. In these areas, all travelers should avoid swimming or wading in freshwater ponds, lakes, streams, cisterns, aqueducts, or irrigated areas.

Crimean-Congo hemorrhagic fever: Virus circulates in rural agricultural areas. A small number of human cases are reported sporadically. This disease is usually transmitted by ticks and occasionally by exposure to infected animals (usually sheep, goats, or cattle that have been slaughtered). Low risk to most travelers. All travelers, however, should take precautions to prevent tick bites or exposure to freshly slaughtered meat.

Rabies: Human cases are very sporadic, usually occurring in northern and eastern rural areas. Most animal rabies is in foxes with spillover into the stray dog population. Travelers should seek immediate treatment of any animal bite. Rabies vaccination is indicated following the unprovoked bite of a dog or fox. Bites by other animals should be considered on an individual basis.

Other illnesses: AIDS (very low prevalence; officially attributed to blood transfusions), brucellosis, echinococcosis (carried by stray dogs, especially in rural and agricultural areas), onchocerciasis (black-fly-borne; confined to the southwestern Arabian peninsula in focally endemic area), plague (flea-borne; no cases reported recently, but enzootic foci exist in the Asir region of the southwestern Arabian peninsula and along the Tigris-Euphrates river extending to Kuwait), Q fever, sandfly fever (transmission primarily April through October), trachoma (highly endemic), tuberculosis (moderate prevalence in rural areas among lower socio-economic groups), typhoid fever, flea-borne typhus (sporadic cases occur in eastern areas), and soil-transmitted helminthic infections (roundworm, hookworm, and whipworm).

Snake bite hazards: Risk of carpet viper bites (usually nonfatal in adults) reported from lowland areas of the Asir region in southern Saudi Arabia.

World Medical Guide

SENEGAL

Embassy: 202-234-0540   *Dakar*   *GMT 0 hrs*

Entry Requirements
- Visa not required for stays less than 90 days. Onward/return ticket required.
- HIV Test: Not required.
- Vaccinations: A yellow fever vaccination certificate is required from all travelers over 1 year of age arriving from infected areas or from any country in the Yellow Fever Endemic Zones that they have transited in the preceding 6 days.

Telephone Country Code: 221
Embassies/Consulates: U.S. Embassy, Dakar. Avenue Jean XXIII; Tel. 23-42-96.
Doctors/Hospitals: CTO Trauma Care Facility, Dakar (160 beds); general medical/surgical facility; trauma; orthopedics. Dantec Hospital, Dakar (190 beds); general medical/surgical facility; trauma. Hospitale Principale, Dakar (650 beds); cardiothoracic surgery; orthopedics.

Health Advisory

Cholera: This disease is active in this country. Although cholera vaccination is not required for entry if arriving directly from the U.S. or Canada, it may be required if arriving from a cholera-infected area, or required for on-going travel to other countries in Latin America, Africa, the Middle East, or Asia.

Yellow fever: No cases of yellow fever are currently reported, but an outbreak occurred in 1995 in the central part of the country in the Koungheul area. Vaccination is recommended for any person over age 9 months who travels outside urban areas.

Malaria: Risk is present year-round throughout this country, including Dakar and other urban areas. There is less risk in the Cap Vert vicinity and northern Sahel regions from January through July. Risk is highest in the central and southern areas of this country, but is also increasing in the north due to the construction of dams which afford mosquito breeding sites. Risk is elevated during and immediately after the rainy season (May–October in the south and July–September in the north). *P. falciparum* accounts for 90% of malaria cases. Chloroquine-resistant falciparum malaria is reported. Prophylaxis with mefloquine or doxycycline is currently recommended when traveling to malarious areas.

Travelers' diarrhea: The cities of Dakar, Saint-Louis, Kaolack, Thies, and Ziguinchor have municipal water systems and public taps, but these systems may be contaminated. Travelers should observe all food and drink safety precautions. A quinolone antibiotic is recommended for the treatment of acute diarrhea. Diarrhea not responding to treatment with an antibiotic, or chronic diarrhea, may be due to a parasitic disease such as giardiasis, amebiasis, or cryptosporidiosis.

Hepatitis: All nonimmune travelers should receive hepatitis A vaccine. Hepatitis E is endemic but the level is unclear; 20% of hospitalized acute infectious hepatitis cases in Dakar during 1990 were HEV antibody positive. The hepatitis B carrier rate in the general population is estimated as high as 18%. Vaccination against hepatitis B is recommended for all long-term visitors to this country.

Leishmaniasis: Risk of cutaneous leishmaniasis occurs in the northwest (Keur Moussa in the Theis Region) and has been reported in the northeast along the Mauritanian border. Sporadic cases occur annually among Peace Corps volunteers stationed countrywide. Visceral leishmaniasis has not been reported.

Schistosomiasis: Risk of urinary schistosomiasis is present in the Senegal River Valley along the Mauritanian border; in the west-central regions of Dakar, Thies, Diourbel, and Fatick; and in the southwestern and southcentral areas. Intestinal schistosomiasis occurs in scattered areas. Travelers should avoid swimming, bathing, or wading in freshwater lakes, ponds, or streams.

AIDS: Heterosexual contact is the predominate mode of transmission. HIV-1 prevalence estimated at 2.3% of the high-risk urban population while HIV-2 prevalence is reported at 10% of the high-risk urban population. Unofficially, up to 40% of prostitutes are HIV-positive. All travelers are cautioned against unsafe sex, unsterile medical or dental injections, and unnecessary blood transfusions.

World Medical Guide

Other diseases: African tick typhus, brucellosis (from consumption of raw dairy products), chikungunya fever (endemic; reported in cyclic outbreaks), dengue (low risk; there is serological evidence of viral activity), dracunculiasis (endemic along the eastern border with Mali and Mauritania), West Nile fever, Rift Valley fever, Crimean-Congo hemorrhagic fever (tick-borne), filariasis (mosquito-borne), Lassa fever (slight risk may occur in the southeast near the border with Mali), leprosy, leptospirosis, meningitis, murine typhus (flea-borne), onchocerciasis (black-fly-borne; contracted near fast-flowing rivers), rabies, tick-borne relapsing fever, trypanosomiasis (no new cases of sleeping sickness since 1978), tuberculosis (a major health problem), and intestinal worms.

SEYCHELLES
Permanent Mission to the U.N.: 212-687-9766. No U.S. Embassy in Seychelles. Contact U.S. Embassy, Mauritius: (230)-208-9534

SERBIA & MONTENEGRO
Embassy of the Federal Republic of Jugoslavia: 202--462-6566. U.S. Embassy, Belgrade: (381)-11-645-655
For Health Advisory information, see the Disease Risk Summary for Europe on page 259.

SIERRA LEONE
Embassy: 202-939-9261   Freetown   GMT 0 hrs

Entry Requirements
- Passport/Visa: Valid passport and visa are required.
- HIV Test: Not required.
- Vaccinations: A yellow fever vaccination certificate is required from all travelers over 1 year of age arriving from infected areas.

Telephone Country Code: 232
Embassies/Consulates: U.S. Embassy, Freetown. Corner Walpole & Siaka Stevens; Tel. 26481. Canadian Embassy (Nigeria); Tel. [234] 612-382.
Hospitals/Doctors: Connaught Hospital, Freetown (240 beds); overcrowded, understaffed facility lacking modern equipment.

Health Advisory

Cholera: This disease is active. Although cholera vaccination is not required for entry if arriving directly from the U.S. or Canada, it may be required if arriving from a cholera-infected area, or required for on-going travel to other countries in Latin America, Africa, the Middle East, or Asia.

Yellow fever: This disease is active in the Kenema District. Vaccination is recommended. This country is in the Yellow Fever Endemic Zone. Although a vaccination certificate may not be required for entry to this country, one may be required for on-going travel to other countries in Africa, the Middle East, and Asia.

Malaria: Risk is present year-round throughout this country, including urban areas. Increased risk occurs during and immediately after the rainy season (May through November). Falciparum malaria accounts for 80% of cases, the rest due to *P. malariae* or *P. ovale*. Chloroquine-resistant falciparum malaria is reported. Prophylaxis with mefloquine or doxycycline is currently recommended when traveling to malarious areas of this country.

Travelers' diarrhea: High risk outside of urban areas. In the Freetown area, chlorinated water from the Cuma Valley Dam is piped directly to the consumer. Travelers should observe all food and drink safety precautions. A quinolone antibiotic is recommended for the treatment of acute diarrhea. Diarrhea not responding to treatment with an antibiotic, or chronic diarrhea, may be due to a parasitic disease such as giardiasis, amebiasis, or cryptosporidiosis.

World Medical Guide

Hepatitis: All susceptible travelers should receive immune globulin prophylaxis or hepatitis A vaccine. Hepatitis E may be endemic. The hepatitis B carrier rate in the general population is estimated to exceed 10%. Vaccination against hepatitis B is recommended for healthcare workers and all long-term visitors to this country.
Leishmaniasis: Risk is undetermined, but probably is low. Outbreaks of cutaneous leishmaniasis have occurred in nearby Senegal.
Onchocerciasis: Widely distributed, except for the coastal plain and the Freetown peninsula. Travelers should take precautions to prevent insect (blackfly) bites, especially near fast-flowing rivers, where blackflies breed.
Schistosomiasis: Risk is year-round. Foci of urinary schistosomiasis are distributed primarily in the eastern and central areas. Intestinal schistosomiasis is less prevalent but has the same distribution pattern. Travelers should avoid swimming, bathing, or wading in freshwater lakes, ponds, or streams.
Trypanosomiasis (African sleeping sickness): Current incidence and risk data are not currently available. Sporadic cases were reported during the early 1980s. Travelers should take precautions to prevent insect (tsetse fly) bites.
Lassa fever: Risk is countrywide, particularly in Eastern Province (Kailahun and Kenema Districts). There is increased risk during the dry season, February through April. Lassa fever is a common cause of fever and deafness, reportedly accounting for 10% to 16% of all adult medical admissions in two rural hospitals during the late 1970s. Transmission of the virus is from contact with dust or food contaminated with infected rodent urine. Household sanitary measures and rodenticides should reduce or eliminate risk.
Rabies: Risk of exposure, especially from stray dogs, occurs in urban and rural areas. Pre-exposure vaccination against rabies (3 doses) should be considered for long-term travel to this region. This is especially true for travelers going to remote rural areas if they will be unable to receive antirabies treatment within 24 hours of exposure to a potentially rabid animal.
AIDS: Surveys during the early 1990s in Freetown found HIV prevalences of 28% and 7% among prostitutes and blood donors, respectively. All travelers are cautioned against unsafe sex, unsterile medical or dental injections, and unnecessary blood transfusions.
Other diseases: African tick typhus (transmitted by dog ticks, often in urban areas, and bush ticks), anthrax, brucellosis (from consumption of raw dairy products), dengue (low risk), Bancroftian filariasis (mosquito-borne), leprosy (1 case/1,000 population), leptospirosis, tuberculosis (a major health problem), and intestinal helminths (very common) are reported.

SINGAPORE

Embassy: 202-537-3100 *Singapore* *GMT +8 hrs*

Entry Requirements
- Visa not required for tourist/business stays up to 30 days.
- HIV Test: Not required.
- Vaccinations: A yellow fever vaccination certificate is required from all travelers older than 1 year arriving from any country any part of which is infected. A certificate is also required of any traveler arriving from, or transiting through, any country in the Yellow Fever Endemic Zones.

Telephone Country Code: 65
Embassies/Consulates: U.S. Embassy, Singapore. 27 Napier; Tel. 476-9100.
Hospitals/Doctors: Mt. Elizabeth Hospital (485 beds); all specialties; emergency, burn, trauma units; considered one of the best hospitals in SE Asia; Tel. 737-2666.
Gleneagles Hospital; used by U.S. Embassy personnel; Tel. 63-7222.

Health Advisory
Cholera: This disease is not currently active in this country. Although cholera vaccination is not required for entry if arriving directly from the U.S. or Canada, it may be required if arriving from a cholera-infected area, or required for on-going travel to other countries in Latin America, Africa, the Middle East, or Asia.

World Medical Guide

Malaria: There is no risk of malaria in Singapore.
Travelers' diarrhea: Low risk. Tap water in Singapore is potable. A quinolone antibiotic is recommended for the treatment of acute diarrhea. Diarrhea not responding to antibiotic treatment may be due to a parasitic disease such as giardiasis, amebiasis, or cryptosporidiosis—or an intestinal virus.
Hepatitis: Hepatitis A vaccine is recommended for all nonimmune travelers. Hepatitis E and C are endemic. The hepatitis B carrier rate in the general population is estimated at 5%. Vaccination against hepatitis B is recommended for long-term visitors to this country.
Japanese encephalitis: Low risk, but cases are reported year-round. Peak transmission occurs during April. Vaccination against Japanese encephalitis is recommended for travelers visiting rural-agricultural endemic areas for periods exceeding 2-4 weeks, especially during the peak transmission period. All travelers should take personal protection measures against mosquito bites, especially in the evening.
Dengue fever: Seasonal outbreaks occur with risk elevated from May through September, countrywide. The disease is more common in urban areas where the *Aedes* mosquitoes have many breeding sites. All persons should take daytime protective measures against mosquito bites. A vaccine is not available.
Filariasis: Low risk; both the Bancroftian and Malayan forms occur and are transmitted by a variety of mosquitoes. Travelers should take protective measures against insect bites.
Other diseases/hazards: Leptospirosis (low risk), cholera, helminthic infections (ascariasis, ancylostomiasis, hookworm, clonorchiasis, opisthorchiasis, and taeniasis; low endemicity), hemorrhagic fever with renal syndrome (a few cases reported), melioidosis (rare), scrub typhus, and tuberculosis. Stingrays, poisonous fish, sea anemones, the Indo-China man-o'-war, and the very dangerous sea wasp are found along the coral reefs that fringe Singapore. Swimmers should take sensible precautions to avoid these hazards.

SLOVAK REPUBLIC

Embassy of the Slovak Republic: 202-965-5160. U.S. Embassy, Bratislava: (421)-7-330-0861
For Health Advisory information, see the Disease Risk Summary for Europe on page 259.

SLOVENIA

Slovenian Embassy: 202-667-5363. U.S. Embassy, Ljubljana: (386)-61-301-427
For Health Advisory information, see the Disease Risk Summary for Europe on page 259.

SOLOMON ISLANDS

U.N. Mission: 212-599-6192   *Honiara*   **GMT +11 hrs**
Entry Requirements
- Passport/Visa: Passport and visa required. Visas obtained through the Australian Embassy (800-242-2878) or the New Zealand Embassy (202-328-4800).
- HIV Test: Not required.
- Vaccination: A yellow fever vaccination certificate is required from travelers over 1 year of age arriving from infected or endemic areas.

Telephone Country Code: 677
Embassies/Consulates: There is no U.S. Embassy or diplomatic post in the Solomon Islands. There is a volunteer American warden in Honiara who has general information and can provide assistance, for example with passports; contact B.J.S. Industries Limited; Tel. (677) 22-393. Consular assistance for U.S. citizens is provided by the U.S. Embassy in Port Moresby, Papua New Guinea; Tel. (675)-321-1455.

449

World Medical Guide

Hospitals/Doctors: Island Medical Clinic, Honiara. Central Hospital (158 beds); general medical facility; x-ray, pharmacy, laboratory. Ambulance; Tel. 22200. Ato'ifi Adventist Hospital (91 beds); general medical facility; x-ray, pharmacy. The U.S. Peace Corps (Tel. 21612) or Embassy can also be contacted for a physician recommendation.

Health Advisory

Malaria: Risk is present countrywide, including urban areas. Falciparum malaria predominates 2:1 over vivax malaria. Multidrug-resistant falciparum malaria occurs, and chloroquine- and Fansidar-resistant falciparum malaria are widespread. The recommended prophylaxis for adult travelers is mefloquine, 250 mg weekly, or doxycycline, 100 mg daily.

Travelers' diarrhea: Medium risk. All tap water should be considered unsafe. Travelers are advised to drink only bottled, boiled, or treated water. A quinolone antibiotic is recommended for the treatment of acute diarrhea.

Hepatitis: All nonimmune travelers should receive hepatitis A vaccine prior to visiting this country. Hepatitis B is hyperendemic in this country, with a carrier rate of 20% in certain population groups. Vaccination against hepatitis B is recommended for all healthcare workers and should be considered by anyone planning an extended visit to this country.

Filariasis, Japanese encephalitis: Bancroftian filariasis is endemic. Sporadic cases and outbreaks of Japanese encephalitis are reported. All travelers should take protective measures against mosquito bites.

Dengue fever: Urban areas and low-lying rural areas are considered at high risk of dengue outbreaks during the rainy season months, December–January to May–June. The *Aedes* mosquito, which transmits dengue, bites during the daytime and is present in populous urban areas as well as resort and rural areas. Prevention of dengue consists of taking protective measures against mosquito bites.

Other diseases/health hazards: Hookworm is endemic. Travelers are advised to wear shoes/sandals to prevent transmission of the hookworm larvae through the soles of the feet. There is a low risk of scrub typhus during the rainy seasons. Travelers walking through grassy areas should protect themselves from chigger mites. Centipedes, scorpions, and large black ants may be encountered by hikers and "bush walkers."

SOMALIA

Embassy: 202-342-1575   *Mogadishu*   GMT +3 hrs

Entry Requirements

- Passport/Visa: Valid passport and visa are required.
- HIV Test: Not required.
- Vaccinations: A yellow fever vaccination certificate is required from all travelers arriving from infected areas.
  Cholera: A vaccination certificate is required if arriving from infected areas.

Embassies/Consulates: U.S. Embassy, Mogadishu. Corso Primo Luglio; Tel. 20811.

Doctors/Hospitals: The local medical facilities are inadequate. The State Department recommends evacuating personnel to Nairobi, Kenya, in lieu of using Somali hospitals.

Health Advisory

Yellow fever: This country lies within the Yellow Fever Endemic Zone. Although yellow fever has not been reported, vaccination is recommended.

Cholera: Although cholera vaccination is not officially required for entry if arriving directly from the U.S. or Canada, it may be required unofficially, or be required for on-going travel to other countries in Africa, the Middle East, Asia, or Latin America. Travelers to this country should consider vaccination or getting a doctor's letter of exemption from vaccination. The risk to travelers of acquiring cholera is considered to be low.

Malaria: Risk is present year-round throughout this country, including urban areas. Risk of transmission is highest in July and December, after the semiannual rains. The risk of malaria is greater in the south, particularly along the Shabeelle and Juba River valleys. There is limited malaria risk in the city center of Mogadishu. Falciparum malaria accounts for 95% of

World Medical Guide

cases countrywide, but in 106 U.S. marines returning from Somalia in 1993 *P. vivax* accounted for 87% of cases. Prophylaxis with mefloquine or doxycycline is currently recommended when traveling to malarious areas. (Note: 2 cases of mefloquine-resistant *P. falciparum* malaria were reported in U.S. troops stationed in Somalia.)

Travelers' diarrhea: High risk. All water supplies are potentially contaminated. Travelers should observe all food and drink safety precautions. A quinolone antibiotic is recommended for the treatment of acute diarrhea. Diarrhea not responding to antibiotic treatment may be due to a parasitic disease such as giardiasis or amebiasis.

Hepatitis: High risk. All nonimmune travelers should receive hepatitis A vaccine. The hepatitis B carrier rate in the general population is estimated as high as 19%. Vaccination against hepatitis B is recommended for healthcare workers and all long-term visitors to this country. Hepatitis E outbreaks have been reported in refugee camps and is a hazard to healthcare and relief workers.

Leishmaniasis: A hyperendemic focus of visceral leishmaniasis (kala azar) persists along the Shabeelle River in the Giohar District in southern Somalia. Cutaneous leishmaniasis has not been reported but may occur in southern Somalia near the borders with Kenya and Ethiopia.

Schistosomiasis: Year-round risk of urinary schistosomiasis, primarily in the valleys of the Giuba and Shabeelle Rivers in southern Somalia. Travelers to these areas should avoid bathing, wading, or swimming in freshwater lakes, ponds, or streams.

Dengue fever: Moderate risk. Thirty-three cases of dengue were reported in American personnel in Somalia in 1992; the virus is estimated to have caused 17% of febrile illness in U.S. troops previously stationed in this country.

Arboviral fevers: Chikungunya fever, Rift Valley fever, West Nile fever, and sandfly fever may occur. Rift Valley fever outbreak reported in 1998.

Other illnesses/hazards: African tick typhus, brucellosis, echinococcosis, filariasis (occurs in southern Somalia, in the area between Kenya and the Indian Ocean), histoplasmosis (common), leptospirosis (high incidence), meningitis, Q fever, rabies (transmitted primarily by dogs but also by foxes, cats, camels, donkeys, hyenas, badgers, and jackals), tick-borne relapsing fever (endemic), tuberculosis (a major health problem), trachoma, typhoid fever, epidemic typhus (louse-borne; increased risk in those having contact with refugees), murine typhus (flea-borne), and intestinal worms.

SOUTH AFRICA

Embassy: 202-966-1650   *Pretoria*   *GMT +2 hrs*

Entry Requirements
- Visa: Travelers should contact the South African Embassy in Washington for information.
- HIV Test: Not required.
- Vaccinations: A yellow fever vaccination certificate is required from all travelers older than 1 year of age arriving from a country any part of which is infected or from any country in the Yellow Fever Endemic Zones.

Telephone Country Code: 27   **AT&T Access:** 0-800-99-0123

Embassies/Consulates: U.S. Embassy, Pretoria. 877 Pretorious Street; Tel. (12) 342-1048. U.S. Consulate, Johannesburg; Tel. (11) 331-1681. Provides most consular services for Americans in the Pretoria area. U.S. Consulate, Cape Town; Tel; (21) 214-280. U.S. Consulate, Durban; Tel. (31) 304-4737.

Hospitals/Doctors: Gu Rankuwa Hospital, Pretoria (2,000 beds); all specialties, including hemodialysis capability. Groote Schuur Hospital, Capetown (1,350 beds); all specialties, including cardiovascular surgery, hemodialysis. Barabwanath Hospital, Johannesburg (2,640 beds); all specialties, including neurosurgery, hemodialysis, ICU.

Health Advisory

Malaria: Risk is present year-round, primarily in the northeastern areas of Transvaal Province bordering Botswana, Mozambique, and Zimbabwe, including the game parks. Malaria risk is also present along, and inland from, the KwaZulu/Natal coast north of 29 degrees south

World Medical Guide

latitude (Tugela River). Peak transmission occurs March through May. Since the late 1980s, risk areas have extended south of the Tugela River in Natal Province, and malaria may occur in northern Cape Province along sections of the Orange and Molopo Rivers following extreme flooding. Risk (relatively low for tourists who take mosquito precautions) is present in Kruger National Park, especially during April. Falciparum malaria accounts for up to 99% of cases. Chloroquine-resistant *P. falciparum* is reported in coastal areas north of Richard's Bay and in the northern Transvaal. Prophylaxis with mefloquine or doxycycline is currently recommended when traveling to malarious areas.

Travelers' diarrhea: Low to moderate risk in urban areas. Cities and townships have municipal water systems which supply water to hotels and homes. Tap water safety is variable. Travelers, especially outside urban areas, should observe food and drink safety precautions. A quinolone antibiotic is recommended for the treatment of acute diarrhea. Diarrhea not responding to antibiotic treatment may be due to a parasitic disease such as giardiasis, amebiasis, or cryptosporidiosis.

Hepatitis: Hepatitis A is highly endemic. All nonimmune travelers should receive the hepatitis A vaccine. Hepatitis E is endemic at low levels. The hepatitis B carrier rate in the general population is variable and is as high as 15% in some population groups. Hepatitis C is endemic.

West Nile, Sindbis, and Chikungunya fevers: Sporadic outbreaks occur, primarily in Central Cape Province, and eastern and southern Transvaal during warmer months. Travelers should take measures to prevent insect (mosquito) bites.

Dengue fever: Low risk; currently not endemic.

Crimean-Congo hemorrhagic fever: Sporadic human cases reported. Viral infection may occur following exposure to infected ticks, animals, or humans.

Schistosomiasis: Risk is present primarily in the warmer months (October–April) in the northeast and the eastern coastal area, generally below 1,500 meters elevation. Foci of urinary schistosomiasis are distributed over large areas of the northeast (including Kruger National Park), KwaZulu/Natal Province, and along the coastal areas of Eastern Cape Province as far south as Humansdorp. Risk areas for intestinal schistosomiasis occur in the lowveld of Eastern and Northern Transvaal Provinces and sporadically in coastal areas of KwaZulu/Natal Province. There is also risk along the lower Orange River in Northern Cape Province bordering Namibia. Travelers to these areas should avoid swimming, bathing, or wading in freshwater lakes, ponds, or streams.

Plague: No human cases have been reported since 1982. Known areas of risk include the northern and western borders with Lesotho and in Mount Zebra National Park north of Port Elizabeth. Vaccination against plague is recommended only for persons who may be occupationally exposed to wild rodents (anthropologists, archaeologists, medical personnel, and missionaries).

Meningitis: Low risk. South Africa is south of the sub-Saharan meningitis belt. Long-term visitors who expect to have close contact with the indigenous population should consider vaccination.

Rabies: Case reports are highest in KwaZulu/Natal Province and Eastern Transvaal, and attributed to an increasing stray and wild dog population. Vaccination should be considered for prolonged travel (more than 3–4 weeks) to these areas.

AIDS: Heterosexual contact is now the predominate mode of transmission. All travelers are cautioned against unsafe sex, unsterile medical or dental injections, and unnecessary blood transfusions.

Air pollution: Emissions from coal-fired power stations in the highveld east of Pretoria combine with stagnant air masses to produce dangerous levels of photochemical pollutants.

Other diseases/health threats: African tick typhus (focally distributed, including periurban areas near Johannesburg; cases reported among travelers; may be due also to *R. africae* transmitted by ticks of cattle and game as well as *R. conorii transmitted by dogs*), brucellosis, leishmaniasis (low to negligible risk), leptospirosis, trachoma (high incidence in northern Transvaal), tuberculosis (highly endemic in Western Cape), typhoid fever, and helminthic

World Medical Guide

disease (ascariasis, hookworm disease, strongyloidiasis in lower socioeconomic populations) are reported. Animal hazards include snakes (cobras, mambas, adders, vipers), spiders (black and brown widow); Stingrays, jellyfish, and several species of poisonous fish are common in the country's coastal waters and are potential hazards to unprotected swimmers.

SOUTH KOREA

Embassy: 202-939-5660   *Seoul*   *GMT +9 hrs*

Entry Requirements
- Passport/Visa: Passport required. Tourist card and visa can be obtained on arrival.
- HIV Test: Required for stays over 90 days by foreigners working as entertainers.
- Vaccinations: None required.

Telephone Country Code: 82
Embassies/Consulates: U.S. Embassy, Seoul. 82 Sejong-Ro, Chongro-ku; Tel. (2) 397-4114. U.S. Consulate, Pusan; Tel. (51) 246-7791.
Hospitals/Doctors: International Clinic-Asan Medical Center, Seoul. Tel. (2) 224-5001/5002. Largest medical center in South Korea with over 220 medical and surgical specialists, many of them U.S.- and Canadian-Board Certified. VIP suites are available. Haseong E. Yew, M.D. is the Director of the International Clinic. Kangbuk Samsung Hospital, Seoul. Modern, with English-speaking staff; used by expatriate community.

Health Advisory

Malaria: Low risk. The U.S. military has reported cases of vivax malaria in soldiers stationed near the DMZ. Malaria is not considered a threat to tourists and prophylaxis is not currently recommended for travelers.
Travelers' diarrhea: Medium to high risk outside of first-class hotels and resorts. Travelers are advised to drink only bottled, boiled, filtered, or treated water and consume only well-cooked food. All fruit should be peeled prior to consumption. A quinolone antibiotic is recommended for the treatment of acute diarrhea. Diarrhea not responding to antibiotic treatment may be due to a parasitic disease such as giardiasis, amebiasis, or cryptosporidiosis.
Hepatitis: All nonimmune travelers should receive hepatitis A vaccine prior to visiting this country. The hepatitis B carrier rate in the general population is estimated at 6%–9%. Vaccination against hepatitis B is recommended for anyone planning an extended visit to this country. Hepatitis C is endemic.
Dengue fever: No apparent risk.
Japanese encephalitis (JE): Risk is present, but at low levels. There is no risk of JE in Seoul. Cases of Japanese encephalitis have been reported in the southwest during the transmission season, June through October. Vaccination is recommended for travelers who will be staying in rural-agricultural endemic areas longer than 2–3 weeks during the peak transmission season. All travelers to rural areas should take measures to prevent mosquito bites.
Hemorrhagic fever with renal syndrome (HFRS): Year-round risk, countrywide. Elevated risk is associated with dusty, dry conditions and peak rodent populations. The virus (hantavirus) that causes HFRS is transmitted by infected rodent secretions (e.g., excreta) and virus-carrying dust particles. Most cases occur from October through December, associated with peak human activity in rodent-infected areas during harvest.
Helminthic infections: Low risk of ascariasis and hookworm disease. Anisakiasis, fascioliasis, fasciolopsiasis, paragonimiasis, and clonorchiasis are endemic. Travelers should avoid eating uncooked water plants and raw or undercooked seafood and shellfish, including Ke Jang (raw crab in soy sauce).
Other illnesses/hazards: Filariasis (low risk occurs in southern coastal provinces, especially Cheju-do), leptospirosis (elevated risk associated with areas of stagnant water and muddy soils), rabies (extremely rare), murine typhus (flea-borne), scrub typhus (mite-borne; risk elevated in grassy rural areas; 90% occur October–December), tuberculosis (highly endemic), typhoid fever, and acute hemorrhagic conjunctivitis. Animal hazards include centipedes and black widow spiders. Lynxes, bears, and wild boars may be encountered in remote areas.

World Medical Guide

SPAIN AND ANDORRA

Embassy of Spain: 202-728-2330
Andorran Mission to the U.N.: 212-750-8064

Entry Requirements
- A visa is not required for tourist or business stays of up to 3 months.
- HIV Test: Not required.
- Vaccinations: None required.

Telephone Country Code: 34   **AT&T:** 900-99-00-11   **MCI:** 900-99-0014
Embassies/Consulates: U.S. Embassy, Madrid. Serrano 75. Tel. (1) 577-4000. U.S. Consulate, Barcelona; Tel. (3) 280-2227. For Andorra, contact the consulate in Barcelona.
Hospitals/Doctors: Ciudad Sanitaria de la Paz, Madrid (2,346 beds); all specialties. Unidad Medica Anglo-Americana. Hospital Clinico y Provincal, Barcelona (1,001 beds); all specialties, including cardiology.

Health Advisory

Travelers' diarrhea: Medium risk. Urban water supplies are considered potable, but travelers are advised to consume only bottled, boiled, or treated water. Giardiasis, amebiasis, and cryptosporidiosis are endemic.
Hepatitis: Hepatitis A vaccine is recommended for nonimmune travelers. The hepatitis B carrier rate in the general population varies from approximately 1% in the northwest to more than 3% in the southeast Mediterranean areas. Vaccination against hepatitis B is not routinely recommended for travel to Spain. Hepatitis E is endemic, but levels are unclear.
Typhoid fever: Higher risk than in other major European countries. Risk may be elevated during summer months. Vaccination is recommended for visits exceeding 3–4 weeks or for travel in rural areas.
Lyme disease: Typical Lyme borreliosis occurs in northern Spain where *Ixodes ricinus* ticks are prevalent. In southern Spain (where *Ixodes ricinus* ticks are rare), *Ornithodorus erraticus* ticks transmit an atypical Lyme disease (a relapsing fever without a rash) caused by a related *Borrelia* organism. Travelers should take precautions against ticks.
Mediterranean spotted fever (Boutonneuse fever): Risk areas include the southern Mediterranean coast, the west-central and northern provinces (except areas bordering the Bay of Biscay), and the Balearic Islands (Majorca, Menorca, and Ibiza). The Canary Islands are risk free. Ninety-five percent of cases result from contact with tick-carrying dogs.
Typhus: A fatal case of flea-borne typhus (also called endemic typhus or murine typhus; illness is caused by *Rickettsia typhi* organisms) reported in 1994 in a British tourist visiting the Costa del Sol. Infection with *Rickettsia typhi* is widespread in southern Europe but most cases are mild or subclinical.
Leishmaniasis: Risk of cutaneous and visceral leishmaniasis occurs in rural areas of central Spain, the south (Andalucia), the east (Catalonia and Valencia), and the Balearic Islands. Travelers should take measures to prevent sandfly bites. Sandflies bite predominantly between dusk and dawn.
Rabies: Spain is currently rabies-free.
Other diseases: Brucellosis, echinococcosis, fascioliasis, legionellosis (outbreaks associated with resort hotel spas and hot tubs; reported in Granada and Majorca), leptospirosis, trichinosis, tick-borne relapsing fever, tuberculosis, and intestinal helminth infections are reported.

World Medical Guide

SRI LANKA

Embassy: 202-483-4025 *Colombo* *GMT +5½ hrs*

Entry Requirements
- A tourist visa is granted on arrival and is valid for 90 days.
- HIV Test: Not required.
- Vaccinations: A yellow fever vaccination certificate is required from all travelers older than 1 year arriving from infected areas.
A cholera vaccination certificate is required if arriving from infected areas.

Telephone Country Code: 94

Embassies/Consulates: U.S. Embassy, Colombo. 210 Galle Road; Tel. (1) 448-007. After hours: Tel. (1) 447-355. Tel. (1) 595-841.

Hospitals/Doctors: Sri Jayewardhanapura Hospital, Colombo (1,001 beds); ICU; emergency services. Lakeside Medical Center, Kandy; Tel. 23-466.

Health Advisory

Cholera: This disease may be active in this country. The risk to travelers of acquiring cholera is very low. Prevention consists primarily in following strict adherence to safe food and drink guidelines.

Malaria: Occurs countrywide, including urban areas, below 800 meters elevation. Colombo is free of malaria. The northern one-half and southeastern quadrant are highly malarious, especially around Anuradhapura. Malaria is less common in the Jaffna Peninsula or the southwestern areas because mosquito breeding sites are scarce. Falciparum malaria accounts for up to 30% of cases, vivax the rest. Chloroquine- and Fansidar-resistant falciparum malaria reported. Mefloquine or doxycycline prophylaxis are recommended in malarious areas.

Travelers' diarrhea: All water supplies in Sri Lanka, including piped city water supplies, are potentially contaminated. Travelers should observe strict food and drink safety precautions. A quinolone antibiotic is recommended for the treatment of acute diarrhea. Giardiasis, amebiasis, and cryptosporidiosis occur.

Hepatitis: Hepatitis A vaccination is recommended for all nonimmune travelers. The carrier rate of the hepatitis B virus in the general population is estimated at 1%. Vaccination against hepatitis B is recommended for all long-term visitors to this country. Hepatitis E is likely but incidence is unclear.

Japanese encephalitis: Sporadic cases occur year-round, but there have also been recent explosive epidemics in the region around Anuradhapura, due to increased mosquito breeding sites. JE vaccination is recommended for extended travel (more than 4 weeks) in rural-agricultural areas. All travelers should take measures to prevent mosquito bites.

Dengue fever: Risk is year-round below 1,000 meters elevation, especially in urban areas. The *Aedes* mosquitoes, which transmit dengue fever, bite during the daytime. Prevention of dengue consists of taking measures to prevent mosquito bites.

Leishmaniasis: This disease is not endemic at this time in Sri Lanka.

Filariasis: Bancroftian filariasis is endemic in both urban and rural areas of the southwestern coast. All travelers should take measures to prevent mosquito bites.

Rabies: Risk is present, but declining. Stray dogs transmit most cases of human rabies. Preexposure rabies vaccination should be considered prior to extended travel in this country.

Other diseases/health threats: Anthrax, chikungunya fever, echinococcosis, hemorrhagic fever with renal syndrome, leptospirosis, tuberculosis (moderately endemic), typhoid fever, and soil-transmitted helminthic infections (due to roundworms, hookworms, and whipworms) are reported. Animal hazards include snakes (kraits, cobras, coral snakes, vipers), spiders (black widow and red-backed), leopards, bears, and wild pigs. Stingrays, sea wasps, starfish, and marine invertebrates (cones, jellyfish, nettles, urchins, anemones) are common in the country's coastal waters and are potential hazards to unprotected swimmers.

World Medical Guide

SUDAN

Embassy: 202-338-8565   **Khartoum**   **GMT +2 hrs**

Entry Requirements
- Passport/Visa: A valid passport and visa are required.
- HIV Test: Not required.
- Vaccinations: A valid yellow fever vaccination certificate is required from all travelers older than 1 year of age arriving from infected areas or from any country in the Yellow Fever Endemic Zones. A vaccination certificate may also be required to leave Sudan.
  Cholera: A cholera vaccination certificate may be required of travelers arriving from infected areas.

Telephone Country Code: Operator-assisted calls only.
Embassies/Consulates: U.S. Embassy/Khartoum. Sharia Ali Abdul Latif; Tel. (11) 74700. Canadian Embassy (Ethiopia); Tel. [251] (1) 151-100.
Hospitals/Doctors: Khartoum Civil Hospital (795 beds); general medical facility; some specialty services.

Health Advisory

Yellow fever: This disease is active in this country (south of 12° north latitude). Vaccination is recommended for all travelers. Sudan is in the Yellow Fever Endemic Zone. A valid vaccination certificate may be required for on-going travel to other countries.

Cholera: This disease is active in this country, but not officially reported. Although cholera vaccination is not officially required for entry if arriving directly from the U.S. or Canada, it may be unofficially required for entry, or required for on-going travel to other countries in Africa, the Middle East, or Asia. Travelers should consider vaccination or getting a doctor's letter of exemption from vaccination.

Malaria: Risk is present year-round throughout this country, including all urban areas. Increased risk occurs during and after the rainy season, June through October, especially in southern Sudan. There is less malaria risk in the desert areas of the extreme north and northwest. Falciparum malaria accounts for approximately 84% of cases. Other cases of malaria are due to the *P. vivax* (9%–20%) and *P. malariae* species (7%), rarely *P. ovale*. Chloroquine-resistant falciparum malaria is reported. Prophylaxis with mefloquine or doxycycline is currently recommended when traveling to malarious areas.

Travelers' diarrhea: High risk. Water supplies are frequently untreated and may be bacterially contaminated. Travelers should observe all food and drink safety precautions. A quinolone antibiotic is recommended for the treatment of acute diarrhea. Diarrhea not responding to antibiotic treatment, or chronic diarrhea, may be due to a parasitic disease such as giardiasis, amebiasis, or cryptosporidiosis. Amebiasis is common and the giardia carrier rate in children is reported as high as 69%. Rotavirus is also a common cause of diarrhea in children.

Hepatitis: High risk. All nonimmune travelers should receive hepatitis A vaccine. The hepatitis B carrier rate in the general population is estimated at 12%–19%. Vaccination against hepatitis B is recommended. Hepatitis E outbreaks have been reported from Khartoum, and elsewhere.

Dengue fever: Mosquito-borne. Reported primarily from the coastal regions. Other arboviral infections include sandfly fever (widespread), Rift Valley fever, Crimean-Congo hemorrhagic fever (tick-borne), and West Nile fever.

Leishmaniasis: An epidemic of visceral leishmaniasis (kala azar) is afflicting the Nuer and Dinka tribes in southern Sudan. Kala azar also reported from the Upper Blue Nile, Blue Nile, and Kassala Provinces, and Eastern Equatoria, Darfur, and Kordofan Districts. Outbreaks have also occurred north of Khartoum along the Nile River.

Cutaneous leishmaniasis: Risk is widespread. Endemic areas for cutaneous leishmaniasis include Darfur, Kordofan, and other provinces of central Sudan, and north of Khartoum, along the Nile River. Travelers to all regions should take measures to prevent insect (sandfly) bites.

World Medical Guide

Schistosomiasis: Risk is widespread, especially in the major irrigation systems in the Gezira area between the Blue and White Nile Rivers. Travelers should avoid swimming, bathing, or wading in freshwater lakes, ponds, or streams.

Trypanosomiasis (African sleeping sickness): The Gambian form of this illness occurs in southern Sudan, primarily in Western and Equatoria Provinces. Rhodesian sleeping sickness may occur in areas adjacent to Ethiopia and in areas adjacent to Uganda. Increased risk occurs during the dry season. Travelers should take measures to prevent tsetse fly bites.

Meningitis: Sudan lies within the sub-Saharan meningitis belt. Increased risk in central and southern regions. Vaccination is recommended for travelers who will have close, prolonged contact with the indigenous population.

Rabies: Risk of dog-transmitted rabies in Khartoum and elsewhere, including rural areas. Rabies vaccination is recommended prior to long-term travel (more than 4 weeks) to this country.

Other illnesses/hazards: AIDS (low prevalence), African tick typhus, brucellosis, dracunculiasis, Ebola-Marburg virus disease (risk may be elevated in southern areas), echinococcosis (high prevalence in the south), filariasis (mosquito-borne; reported from the Nuba Mountains around Kadogli in Kurdufan Province), loiasis (deer-fly-borne; confined to rain forests and nearby savanna of Western Equatoria Province in the southwest), leprosy (high incidence in the Nuba Mountains and the provinces of Southern Darfur, Bahr el Ghazal, Western and Eastern Equatoria), leptospirosis, onchocerciasis (high prevalence along rivers in southwestern Sudan), relapsing fever (louse-borne and tick-borne), toxoplasmosis, tuberculosis (a major health problem), trachoma, typhoid fever, typhus (flea-borne and louse-borne), and helminthic infections (intestinal worms; very common). Animal hazards include snakes (vipers, cobras), centipedes, scorpions, and black widow spiders.

SURINAME

Embassy: 202-244-7488   *Paramaribo*   *GMT -3 hrs*

Entry Requirements
- A visa is required.
- HIV Test: Not required.
- Vaccinations: A yellow fever vaccination certificate is required of all travelers arriving from infected areas.

Telephone Country Code: 597   **AT&T:** 156

Embassies/Consulates: U.S. Embassy, Paramaribo. Dr. Sophie Redmondstraat 129; Tel. 477-881.

Hospitals/Doctors: St. Vincentius, Paramaribo (320 beds); private hospital; 4-bed ICU. University Hospital (425 beds); government hospital; 5-bed ICU. Medical Clinic, Paramaribo.

Health Advisory

Yellow fever: Vaccination is recommended for all travelers going to rural areas. This country is in the Yellow Fever Endemic Zone. A valid yellow fever certificate may be required for on-going travel to certain other countries in Latin America, Africa, the Middle East, and Asia.

Cholera: This disease is active in this country. Although cholera vaccination is not required for entry if arriving directly from the U.S. or Canada, it may be required if arriving from a cholera-infected area, or required for on-going travel to other countries in Latin America, Africa, the Middle East, or Asia. Travelers should consider vaccination or a doctor's letter of exemption from vaccination. The risk to travelers of acquiring cholera is considered low.

Malaria: Risk is present year-round. Elevated risk occurs along the upper Marowijne River in the east, and in the southern interior. Only the city of Paramaribo, a narrow strip along the Atlantic coast, and areas of the interior above 1,300 meters elevation are considered risk-free. Falciparum malaria accounts for 80%–90% of cases, the remainder being due to *P. vivax*. Chloroquine- and Fansidar-resistant falciparum malaria are reported. Chemoprophylaxis with mefloquine or doxycycline is currently recommended in malarious areas.

Travelers' diarrhea: High risk. All water sources outside of Paramaribo should be considered contaminated. Travelers should strictly observe food and drink precautions. A qui-

World Medical Guide

nolone antibiotic is recommended for the treatment of acute diarrhea. Diarrhea not responding to treatment with an antibiotic may be due to a parasitic disease such as giardiasis, amebiasis, or cryptosporidiosis—or an intestinal virus.

Hepatitis: All nonimmune travelers should receive the hepatitis A vaccine. Hepatitis E has not been reported but could occur. The hepatitis B carrier rate in the general population is estimated at 2%–3%. Vaccination against hepatitis B is recommended for anyone planning an extended visit to this country. Hepatitis C is likely.

Dengue fever: Limited dengue transmission occurs, primarily in the Paramaribo area. Outbreaks occur at irregular intervals, particularly in urban areas. The *Aedes* mosquitoes, which transmit dengue fever, bite primarily during the daytime and are present in populous urban areas as well as resort and rural areas. All travelers should take measures to prevent mosquito bites.

Arboviral encephalitis: At least six distinct viruses causing encephalitis have been detected in Suriname. The area of greatest risk occurs in the savanna region located 20 to 40 km inland from the coastal strip. All travelers to these inland regions should take measures to prevent mosquito bites.

Leishmaniasis: Cutaneous leishmaniasis ("bush yaws"), as well as mucocutaneous leishmaniasis, occurs primarily in the forested areas of the interior. Travelers should take measures to prevent insect (sandfly) bites.

Schistosomiasis: Risk is present year-round, but elevated during the height of the rainy season (May–June). Infected areas are found in the northern coastal strip from the Commewijne River west to the Nickerie River, with risk of infection apparently highest in Suriname and Saramacca Districts. Travelers should avoid swimming in freshwater lakes, ponds, or streams.

Rabies: Reported in animals, especially dogs and cats, but no human rabies cases have been officially reported since the 1970s. Travelers, however, should seek immediate treatment of any animal bite. Rabies vaccination is usually indicated following the unprovoked bite of a dog, cat, bat, or monkey.

Other diseases/hazards: Filariasis (risk may occur in urbanized areas of Brokopondo, Commewijne, and Suriname Districts and in the city of Paramaribo), brucellosis, Chagas' disease (incidence data lacking; northern rural areas may be higher risk), fungal infections (e.g., histoplasmosis, coccidiomycosis), leprosy (incidence is declining), leptospirosis, AIDS (incidence data lacking due to inadequate surveillance), tuberculosis (moderately endemic), and strongyloidiasis and other helminthic infections. (Incidence of hookworm is reported as high as 40%.) Animal hazards include snakes (vipers), centipedes, scorpions, black widow spiders, brown recluse spiders, banana spiders, and wolf spiders. Electric eels and piranha may be found in the country's fresh waters. Portuguese man-of-war, sea wasps, and stingrays are found in the coastal waters of Suriname and could be a hazard to swimmers.

SWAZILAND

Embassy: 202-362-6683   *Mbabane*   *GMT +2 hrs*

Entry Requirements
- Tourist card or transit visa should be obtained upon arrival. Visa not required for stays up to 60 days.
- HIV Test: Not required.
- Vaccinations: A yellow fever vaccination certificate is required of travelers arriving from endemic areas.

Telephone Country Code: 268

Embassies/Consulates: U.S. Embassy, Mbabane. Central Bank Building, Warner Street; Tel. 464-41.

Hospitals/Doctors: Mbabane Clinic (26 beds); general medical facility; x-ray and small laboratory. Tel. 2425 or 2886.

Health Advisory

Cholera: This disease is active in this country. Although cholera vaccination is not required for entry if arriving directly from the U.S. or Canada, it may be required if arriving from a cholera-infected area, or required for on-going travel to other countries in

Africa, the Middle East, Asia, or Latin America. Travelers to this country should consider vaccination (one dose) or a doctor's letter of exemption from vaccination. The risk to travelers of acquiring cholera is very low. Prevention consists primarily in following strict adherence to safe food and drink guidelines.

Malaria: Malaria is absent in most of the country. Risk is present in the northern and eastern grassland and plain areas of Bordergate, Lomahasha, Mhlume, and Tshaneni. Falciparum malaria accounts for 99% of cases. Because chloroquine- and Fansidar resistant falciparum malaria are widespread in these areas, mefloquine or doxycycline prophylaxis is recommended.

Travelers' diarrhea: High risk. Piped water supplies are frequently untreated and may be grossly contaminated. Travelers should observe food and drink safety precautions. A quinolone antibiotic (Cipro or Floxin) is recommended for the treatment of acute diarrhea. Diarrhea not responding to treatment with an antibiotic, or chronic diarrhea, may be due to a parasitic disease such as giardiasis or amebiasis, and treatment with metronidazole (Flagyl) or tinidazole (Fasigyn) should be considered. All cases of diarrhea should be treated with adequate fluid replacement.

Hepatitis: High risk. All nonimmune travelers should receive hepatitis A vaccine. The hepatitis B carrier rate in the general population is estimated at 14%. Vaccination against hepatitis B is recommended for healthcare workers and all long-term visitors to this country.

Schistosomiasis: Risk areas for urinary schistosomiasis are primarily in middleveld and lowveld areas. Intestinal schistosomiasis is found only in lowveld areas. Travelers are advised to avoid swimming or wading in freshwater ponds, lakes, or streams in these areas.

Other illnesses/hazards: African tick typhus (contracted from dog ticks—often in urban areas—and from bush ticks), brucellosis, leprosy, syphilis, tuberculosis (a major health problem), trachoma, typhoid fever, and intestinal worms (very common). Animal hazards include snakes (vipers, cobras), centipedes, scorpions, and black widow spiders.

SWEDEN

Embassy: 202-944-5600   *Stockholm*   GMT 0 hrs

Entry Requirements
- Passport/Visa: A valid passport is required.
- HIV Test: Not required.
- Vaccinations: None required.

Telephone Country Code: 46   **AT&T:** 020-795-611   **MCI:** 020-795-922

Embassies/Consulates: U.S. Embassy, Stockholm. Strandvagen 101; Tel. (8) 783-5300. Canadian High Commission, Stockholm. Tegelbacken 4, 7th Floor; Tel. (8) 237-920.

Hospitals/Doctors: Karolinska Hospital, Stockholm (1,654 beds); all specialties; Tel: (8) 729-2000. Sahlgrenska Hospital, Goteborg (1,979 beds); all specialties, Tel: (31) 60-1000.

Health Advisory

Travelers' diarrhea: Low risk. Municipal piped water is potable. A quinolone antibiotic is recommended for the treatment of acute diarrhea.

Hepatitis: Low risk. Nonimmune travelers, however, should consider hepatitis A vaccination. The hepatitis B carrier rate in the general population is less than 1%. Hepatitis B vaccination is not routinely recommended for travel to Sweden.

Lyme disease: This disease is very common in southern Sweden. Ten to 30% of *Ixodes ricinus* ticks in endemic areas are infected with spirochetes. Greatest risk occurs in the forests of the southern coastal areas below 1,500 meters elevation. Travelers to rural areas, especially during May–November, should take measures to prevent tick bites.

Tick-borne encephalitis: Risk is present from the forested areas around Uppsala down to Kristianstad, including the islands of Gotland and Oland, and in the wooded areas around Goteborg.

Other illnesses: Hemorrhagic fever with renal syndrome (human cases usually in young adults exposed to dried or aerosolized rodent excreta), Karelian fever (mosquito-transmitted; endemic in rural areas of southern and coastal provinces), leptospirosis, and tularemia.

World Medical Guide

SWITZERLAND

Embassy: 202-745-7900   Bern   GMT +1 hr

Entry Requirements
- A valid passport is required.
- HIV Test: Not required.
- Vaccinations: None required.

Telephone Country Code: 41   **AT&T:** 0800-890-011   **MCI:** 0800-890-222
Embassies/Consulates: U.S. Embassy: Jubilaeumstrasse 93, Bern. Tel. (31) 357-7011. U.S. consular agency (part-time), Geneva: American Center of Geneva, World Trade Center II, Geneva Airport, Route de la Bois; Tel. (22) 798-1605 or 798-1615.
Hospitals/Doctors: SOS Medecins Cite Calvin, Geneva. Tel; 748-4950 (24-hr. hotel/house calls). Hopital Cantonal, 24 Rue Michel-du-Crest, Geneva (1,800 beds); major university teaching hospital; all specialties. In Geneva, you can telephone 144 for any medical problem. You will be connected to a triage center that can summon an ambulance, if necessary—or send a doctor to your hotel. They can also refer you to a 24-hour walk-in clinic (called "permanence medical" in French) closest to you. One such clinic is Permanence Medical Vermont at 9A, Rue de Vermont; Tel: 734-5150. University Hospital, Zurich (1,200 beds); all specialties; Tel: (1) 257-1111.

Health Advisory

Travelers' diarrhea: Minimal risk, but streams, lakes, and other sources of raw water may be contaminated. Bottled water is recommended in the Lugano/Locarno regions. Giardiasis and cryptosporidiosis have been reported from this country but the risk to the traveler is considered low.

Lyme disease: The incidence of Lyme disease in Switzerland is among the highest in Europe, but the risk to the average tourist is low. Risk occurs primarily in wooded, forested areas below 1,500 meters elevation in an area extending from Lake Geneva in the west to Lake Bodensee in the northeast. Risk may be elevated on the northern Swiss plateau. Up to 50% of *Ixodes ricinus* ticks in some regions are infected. Ticks are most active May–October.

Tick-borne encephalitis (TBE): This viral illness is transmitted by the same tick (*Ixodes ricinus*) that transmits Lyme disease. Transmission primarily occurs May–October, with the highest risk June–August. Ticks are found primarily in brushy and/or wooded areas of central and northern Switzerland. Most reported cases of TBE (40–50/year) occur in the vicinity of Zurich (especially to the north, in Schaffhausen) and Bern (Thun and Biel), and on the northern Swiss plateau. Prevention: Travelers to rural areas should use measures to prevent tick bites. Vaccination against TBE is recommended only for persons who have higher-than-average exposure to ticks. Such persons include foresters and agricultural workers, as well as some hikers and campers.

Hepatitis: Low risk. Nonimmune travelers should, however, consider hepatitis A immunization. The carrier rate of the hepatitis B virus in the general population is less than 1%. Vaccination against hepatitis B is not routinely recommended for travel to this country. Hepatitis E has not been reported but could occur.

Rabies: No recent human cases have been reported. Rabies occurs primarily in the fox population in the northwest of this country, but the incidence is declining.

Acute mountain sickness (AMS): Travelers ascending rapidly to alpine elevations over 8,000 feet are subject to altitude sickness. Diamox (acetazolamide) may be useful for prevention or treatment, especially for persons who will be climbing and sleeping at high altitudes. Descent to a lower altitude is imperative if symptoms of AMS are moderate to severe.

Other illnesses: Brucellosis, boutonneuse fever (tick-borne; may occur in southern areas), diphyllobothriasis (a tapeworm infection acquired from raw fish; may occur in Lake Maggiore), hemorrhagic fever with renal syndrome, listeriosis (may be transmitted by contaminated soft cheeses), leptospirosis, echinococcosis (risk may occur in the northwest), AIDS (among the highest rates in Europe), and legionellosis (sporadic cases).

World Medical Guide

SYRIA (SYRIAN ARAB REPUBLIC)
Embassy: 202-232-6313   *Damascus*   *GMT +2 hrs*

Entry Requirements
- Passport/Visa: Valid passport and visa required.
- HIV Test: Testing required for students and anyone staying more than 1 year. Contact the Syrian Embassy (202-232-6313) for further details.
- Vaccinations: A yellow fever vaccination certificate is required from all travelers arriving from infected areas.

Telephone Country Code: 963
Embassies/Consulates: U.S. Embassy, Damascus. Abu Rumaneh, Al Mansur Street, No. 2; Tel. (11) 333-052/332-557.
Doctors/Hospitals: Mu'assat University Hospital, Damascus (850 beds); all specialties; emergency and trauma services. Social Insurance Foundation Hospital, Damascus (400 beds); specializes in emergency, trauma, and occupational medicine. National Hospital, Aleppo (482 beds); general medical facility.

Health Advisory

Malaria: Transmission occurs from May through October, peaking in July and August, below 1,100 meters elevation in rural areas (except As Suwayda and Dayr az Zawr Provinces), particularly in the northern provinces bordering Turkey and Iraq. Urban areas are generally risk free. Ninety-nine percent of malaria cases are vivax, 1% falciparum. Low level of risk in endemic areas. Chloroquine prophylaxis is recommended for travel to the lower river valleys of northeast Syria.

Travelers' diarrhea: Medium-high risk outside of first-class hotels. Water distribution systems may be contaminated. Travelers should drink only bottled, boiled, or treated water. All food should be well cooked. Shigellosis is common in this country. Cases of amebiasis and giardiasis occur, even among the higher socio-economic classes. A quinolone antibiotic is recommended for the treatment of acute diarrhea. Diarrhea not responding to antibiotic treatment may be due to a parasitic disease such as giardiasis or amebiasis—or an intestinal virus.

Hepatitis: Hepatitis A vaccine is recommended for all nonimmune travelers. The hepatitis B carrier rate in the general population is estimated at 3%–4%. Vaccination against hepatitis B is recommended for healthcare workers and should be considered by long-term visitors to this country.

Leishmaniasis: Cases of cutaneous leishmaniasis occur in the steppe region, which is the transitional area between the fertile river valleys and the southeastern desert area. There is no apparent risk of visceral leishmaniasis. Travelers to this country should take measures to prevent insect (sandfly) bites.

Schistosomiasis: Urinary schistosomiasis is found in the basins of the Euphrates and Bolikh Rivers to the Iraqi border in the northeast. Travelers should avoid swimming or wading in freshwater streams, ponds, or irrigated areas.

Rabies: Human cases occur sporadically (about 10 cases per year). Jackals, foxes, and stray dogs constitute the main animal reservoir of rabies in this country. Travelers should avoid stray animals and seek immediate medical attention of any animal bite.

Other illnesses: Anthrax, boutonneuse fever (may occur), brucellosis, echinococcosis (carried by stray dogs; reported sporadically), relapsing fever (tick-borne; reported frequently), sandfly fever (may occur), trachoma, tuberculosis, typhoid fever, and helminthic infections (roundworm, whipworm, and dwarf tapeworm infections are common in rural areas; estimated prevalence is low).

World Medical Guide

TAIWAN

Economic Representative: 202-895-1800   Taipei   GMT +8 hrs

Entry Requirements
- A visa is not required for stays up to 2 weeks.
- HIV Test: Required for those staying more than 3 months or applying for work or residency.
- Vaccinations: A yellow fever vaccination certificate is required from all travelers older than 1 year arriving from infected or endemic areas.

Telephone Country Code: 886
Embassies/Consulates: The American Institute. No. 7 Lane 134, Hsin Yi Road, Section 3, Taipei; Tel. (2) 709-2000. After hours: Tel. (2) 709-2013.
Hospitals/Doctors: Taiwan Adventist Hospital, Taipei; used by American Institute (Embassy) personnel; Tel. 771-8151.

Health Advisory

Malaria: There is currently no risk of malaria on Taiwan. Officially eradicated in 1965.
Travelers' diarrhea: Medium to high risk outside of first-class hotels. Travelers are advised to drink only bottled, boiled, filtered, or treated water and consume only well-cooked food. Taiwan's water sources are deteriorating from demands of a rapidly growing population. Diarrhea not responding to antibiotic treatment may be due to a parasitic disease such as giardiasis, amebiasis, or cryptosporidiosis.
Hepatitis: All nonimmune travelers should receive hepatitis A vaccine prior to visiting this country. Hepatitis E is endemic. The hepatitis B carrier rate in pregnant women is 11%–14%. Vaccination against hepatitis B is recommended for anyone planning an extended visit to this country. Hepatitis C is endemic.
Dengue fever: Countrywide risk, year-round. The incidence of dengue is higher in the warmer, wetter months (April–October), especially in the southwestern coastal counties and islands. The mosquitoes which transmit dengue are most active during the day in populous urban areas, as well as resort and rural areas. Prevention of dengue consists of taking protective measures against mosquito bites.
Japanese encephalitis (JE): Confirmed cases occur sporadically all over the island throughout the year. The epidemic period occurs anually from May through October, with the highest transmission rate during June. Vaccination is recommended for travelers who will be staying in rural-agricultural endemic areas longer than 3–4 weeks, especially from May through October. In addition, all travelers should take measures to prevent mosquito bites.
Clonorchiasis: Enzootic countrywide with recognized foci in Miao-li in northern, Sun-moon in central, and Mei-nung in southern Taiwan. Travelers should avoid eating raw or undercooked freshwater fish.
Other illnesses/hazards: Angiostrongyliasis (enzootic in mountainous, remote areas of southern and eastern Taiwan; associated with ingesting raw seafood, snails, vegetables), capillariasis, fasciolopsiasis, filariasis (endemic on the Pescadores, Kinmen, and Matsu Islands), hand, foot and mouth disease (usually caused by coxsackie virus; outbreaks are common; risk primarily to children, but has not been reported in travelers), hookworm disease, leishmaniasis (not endemic), leptospirosis, Lyme disease (spirochetes have been isolated from rodents; a case of human Lyme disease has been reported, but disease prevalence is unknown), paragonimiasis, scrub typhus (countrywide; risk may be elevated on Penghu, Kinmen, Matsu, and Orchid Islands; transmitted primarily in mountainous, wooded, grassy areas, or cleared forest and scrub brush-type areas), flea-borne typhus (sporadic cases reported), tuberculosis (highly endemic), typhoid fever, and acute hemorrhagic conjunctivitis. Animal hazards include snakes (coral, krait, viper), centipedes, scorpions, and black widow spiders. Several species of poisonous fishes (stone, puffer, scorpion, zebra), as well as jellyfish, anemones, nettles, urchins, and sea cucumbers are found in the coastal waters around Taiwan and are potential hazards to swimmers.

World Medical Guide

TAJIKSTAN
Visa issued by Russian Embassy, Consular Division: 202-939-8907
U.S. Embassy, Dushanbe: (7)-3772-210-356
For Health Advisory information, see the Health Advisory for the Caucasus, Central Asia, Siberia, and Far East former USSR on page 261.

TANZANIA
Embassy: 202-939-6125   *Dar es Salaam*   *GMT +3 hrs*
Entry Requirements
- Visa: Travelers should contact the Tanzanian Embassy for entry information.
- HIV Test: Not required.
- Yellow fever. A vaccination certificate is required from all travelers older than 1 year of age arriving from infected areas or from any country in the Yellow Fever Endemic Zones. This includes travelers arriving from Kenya and Uganda.
Cholera: Vaccination may be required for entry if arriving from an endemic area.

Telephone Country Code: 255
Embassies/Consulates: U.S. Embassy, Dar es Salaam. 36 Laibon Road (off Ali Hassan Mwinyi Road); Tel. (51) 666-010 through 5.
Doctors/Hospitals: Muhimbili Hospital, Dar es Salaam (1,000 beds); general medical/surgical facility; orthopedics.

Health Advisory

Yellow fever: Vaccination recommended. No cases reported recently, but this country is in the Yellow Fever Endemic Zone. A valid yellow fever vaccination certificate may be required for persons who leave this country and travel to other countries in Africa, the Middle East, Asia, or Latin America.

Cholera: This disease is active in this country. Although cholera vaccination is not required for entry if arriving directly from the U.S. or Canada, it may be required if arriving from a cholera-infected area, or required for on-going travel to other countries in Latin America, Africa, the Middle East, or Asia. Travelers to this country should consider vaccination or a doctor's letter of exemption from vaccination.

Malaria: High risk is present throughout this country, including urban areas, the highland areas below 2,000 meters elevation, and the islands of Zanzibar and Pemba. Risk of malaria is increased during and just after the rainy seasons (November through December and March through May). Risk has also been increasing in high plateau areas, previously considered areas of limited risk. *P. falciparum* accounts for over 90% of cases; the rest are due to *P. malariae* (up to 10%) and *P. ovale* (1%). Chloroquine-resistant *P. falciparum* is prevalent. Antimalarial prophylaxis with either mefloquine or doxycycline is recommended. All travelers to Tanzania should also take stringent measures to prevent mosquito bites, especially in the evening when mosquito activity is highest.

Travelers' diarrhea: Potential risk in all areas. Multidrug-resistant shigellosis is reported. Several cities have water treatment facilities, but piped water supplies are frequently untreated and may be contaminated. Travelers should observe food and drink safety precautions. A quinolone antibiotic is recommended for the treatment of acute diarrhea. Diarrhea not responding to antibiotic treatment may be due to a parasitic disease such as giardiasis, amebiasis, or cryptosporidiosis.

Hepatitis: All nonimmune travelers should receive hepatitis A vaccine. The hepatitis B carrier rate in the general population is estimated at 4%. Vaccination against hepatitis B is recommended for healthcare workers and all long-term visitors to this country. Hepatitis E is endemic, likely at high levels. Hepatitis C is endemic.

Leishmaniasis: Risk is estimated to be low. A few cases of cutaneous leishmaniasis have been reported from northern areas.

World Medical Guide

Filariasis: Bancroftian filariasis (mosquito-borne) is reported along the coast, including Pemba and Zanzibar, and also reported south of Lake Victoria, north of Lake Nyasa, and in the vicinity of Lake Tanganyika.

Onchocerciasis: Black-fly borne; risk area extends from the Usambara mountains in the northeast to Lake Nyasa in the south. Travelers to these areas should take measures to prevent insect (blackfly) bites.

Schistosomiasis: This disease is focally distributed country-wide. Major risk areas include the shores of Lake Victoria, Tanga and Kigoma Districts, and the Lake Rukwa area. Urban transmission occurs in Dar es Salaam. Schistosomiasis is transmitted on Zanzibar and Pemba Islands. Travelers should avoid swimming or wading in freshwater lakes, ponds, or streams.

Trypanosomiasis (African sleeping sickness): Foci of disease persist in Arusha, Kigoma, Lindi, Mtwara, Rukwa, Tabora, and Ziwa Magharibi Regions. There may be risk in Mbeya. Annual cases have increased in Kigoma Region during the 1990s. Travelers to these areas should take protective measures against insect bites.

Meningitis: Outbreaks of Groups A and C meningococcal meningitis are reported. Risk is year-round and country-wide. Higher risk areas include the northern part of the Arusha Region (bordering Kenya) and the northern and central regions (including Mwanza, Mara, Arusha, Kilimanjaro, Tanga, Dar es Salaam, Morogoro, Dodoma, and Tabora). Over 4500 cases of meningitis reported during 1992, but none occurred in travelers. Vaccination, however, is recommended for all travelers to this country, especially if they will be having close contact with the native population.

Rabies: Human cases are frequently reported. Stray dogs in both rural and urban areas are mainly responsible for transmission.

AIDS: Heterosexual transmission is the predominate means of transmission. HIV prevalence estimated at 50% of the high-risk and 16% of the low-risk urban populations, as of 1996. All travelers are cautioned against unsafe sex, unsterile medical or dental injections, and blood transfusions.

Other illnesses/hazards: Anthrax, African tick typhus, brucellosis, Chikungunya fever (explosive urban outbreaks have occurred), dengue (no recent reports), echinococcosis (high incidence in the Masai of northern areas), leptospirosis, Lyme disease (risk unclear; one case reported in a Peace Corps volunteer), leprosy, onchocerciasis (black-fly-borne; from Usambara Mountains south to Lake Nyasa and Ruvuma Region), plague (hundreds of cases reported annually, mostly from the Lushoto District), relapsing fever (louse- and tick-borne), toxoplasmosis, tuberculosis (a major health problem), trachoma, typhoid fever (endemic at moderate to high levels), and intestinal worms (very common). Animal hazards include snakes (vipers, cobras), centipedes, scorpions, and black widow spiders.

World Medical Guide

THAILAND
Embassy: 202-4944-3600 *Bangkok* *GMT +7 hrs*

Entry Requirements
- Passport/Visa: A valid passport is required.
- HIV Test: "Those suspected of carrying AIDS" may be denied entry. Travelers should contact the Thai Embassy in Washington for further information and advice.
- Vaccinations: A yellow fever vaccination certificate is required if arriving from infected areas or from countries in the Yellow Fever Endemic Zones in Africa and South America.

Telephone Country Code: 66

Embassies/Consulates: U.S. Embassy (consular section), Bangkok. 95 Wireless Road; Tel. (2) 205-4000. U.S. Consulate, Chiang Mai. 387 Vidhayanond Road; Tel. (53) 252-629.

Hospitals/Doctors:
Bangkok—Bangkok General Hospital & Heart Institute; Tel. (2) 318-0066 to 0077. Phyathai Hospital; often used by expatriates; Tel. 245-2621-8. Siriraj University Hospital, Bangkok; extensive neurosurgical, cardiovascular, and trauma capability; Tel. 411-0241. Tel. 252-0570. Samitivej Hospital. This is a luxurious hospital located in an expatriate neighborhood; highly recommended for its excellent care. Tel. 392-0010 to 0011. Bangkok/Pattaya Hospital (southeast of Bangkok); Tel. 384-277-55 or 384-277-515. Bangkla Baptist Hospital (Bangkla Chacheungsao); Tel. 038-541-033.

Chiang Mai—McCormick Hospital; well set-up to treat foreigners; Tel. 241-107. Chiang Mai Ram Hospital; the most modern of all hospitals in Chiang Mai, with many US-trained physicians. Lanna Hospital; especially well-known for its OB/GYN services

Health Advisory

Malaria: Although malaria is the seventh-ranking cause of death in Thailand (1994), this disease rarely occurs in people visiting the usual tourist sites in Thailand. There is no risk of malaria in Bangkok and other major urban areas (Chiangmai, Chiangrai) or the large coastal resort cities (Phuket, Pattaya, Haadya, and Sonkhla). Malaria is mostly eradicated from urban areas and the plains, but there is risk of malaria in the forested foothills, jungles, rubber plantations, and fruit orchards. Major malaria risk areas include southeastern Thailand along the Thai-Cambodian border, western and northwestern Thailand along the Thai-Burmese border, as well and the southern border with Malaysia. The highest incidence of malaria occurs in the border provinces of Tak, Trat, Chanthaburi, Kanchanaburi, Mae Hong Son, Prachuap Khiri Khan, Prachin Buri, Ratchaburi, and Sisaket. There is no malaria in the rain forests immediately adjacent to Chiangmai, but trekkers venturing deeper into the foothills and rain forest or staying overnight in huts of hill tribes should take antimalarial prophylaxis and protect themselves against mosquito bites, especially between dusk and dawn when mosquito activity is highest. Countrywide, *Plasmodium falciparum* causes about 65% of malaria, *P. vivax* about 34%. *P. malariae* causes less than 1% of cases. There is a high incidence of multidrug-resistant falciparum malaria, especially in the forested border areas. *P. falciparum* resistance to standard treatment doses of mefloquine runs as high as 50%. Travelers to malarious areas should take doxycycline, 100 mg daily. The best alternative prophylactic regimen is proguanil, 200 mg daily, plus sulfisoxazole (Gantrisan), 2 gm daily. The current treatment of uncomplicated falciparum malaria acquired in Thailand is either a 7-day course of quinine plus tetracycline or mefloquine combined with a 3-day course of an artemisinin deriviative (artesunate or artemether).

Travelers' diarrhea: Moderate risk. In urban and resort areas, the better hotels and restaurants generally serve reliable food and potable water. Elsewhere, travelers should observe all food and drink safety precautions. *Campylobacter jejeuni* causes most cases of bacterial diarrhea. Cholera is reported sporadically. A quinolone antibiotic or azithromycin is recommended for the treatment of acute diarrhea. (Azithromycin may be more effective since quinolone-resistant campylobacter is reported in this country). Diarrhea not responding to antibiotic treatment may be due to a parasitic disease such as giardiasis, amebiasis, cryptosporidiosis, or cyclosporiasis.

World Medical Guide

Hepatitis: Hepatitis A vaccine is recommended for all nonimmune travelers. Hepatitis E is endemic, with seropositivity rates of 9–22% in adults. The hepatitis B carrier rate in the general population is estimated at 9–10%. Vaccination against hepatitis B is recommended for long-term visitors to this country. Hepatitis C is endemic.

Dengue fever: Highly endemic; peak infection rates occur in the late monsoon season. Dengue occurs more commonly in urban than in rural areas. Epidemics of dengue hemorrhagic fever is a protracted problem in Bangkok. The *Aedes* mosquitoes, which transmit dengue, bite during the daytime. Travelers should take measures to prevent mosquito bites.

Filariasis: Both the Malayan and Bancroftian varieties occur in scattered areas—the southern peninsular coastal provinces, the central provinces of Sisaket and Surin, and the forested areas along the Thailand–Burma border. Travelers should prevent mosquito bites.

Japanese encephalitis: Highly endemic, especially in the central and northern provinces; sporadic cases occur in the south. Elevated risk occurs in rural and periurban areas where pig farming and mosquito-breeding sites coexist. There is also risk of infection in the suburban areas of major cities. Highest risk in the south occurs during the rainy and early dry season; in the north, during late summer and autumn. Vaccination is recommended for travelers who will be staying in rural-agricultural endemic areas longer than 2–3 weeks during the peak transmission season. In addition, all travelers should take measures to prevent mosquito bites, especially in the evening. The Regional Medical Officer of the American Embassy currently recommends JE vaccination for all expatriate Americans.

Schistosomiasis: There is potential risk of schistosomiasis, albeit minimal, in the southern province of Nakhon Si Thammarat, where intermediate snail hosts exist. To be safe, travelers should avoid swimming or wading in freshwater lakes, ponds, or streams in these areas.

Rabies: There is a high incidence of dog rabies in Thailand and human cases are reported frequently, especially in central Thailand. Rabies, however, is rare among tourists—but there is risk. Rabid, stray dogs are common in Bangkok (where 3–4% of dogs may be infected) as well as other urban and rural areas. No one should pet or pick up any stray animals. All children should be warned to avoid contact with unknown animals. Travelers to rural areas should be vaccinated if they will be unable to receive antirabies treatment within 24 hours of exposure to a potentially rabid animal such as a dog, a cat, or a monkey. The State Department recommends vaccination for all expatriate corporate employees and their families, especially the children. A rabies clinic is operated by the Queen Saovabha Institute/Thai Red Cross Society Hospital in Bangkok. Tel: (2) 252-6117.

AIDS: An explosive increase of HIV infection has occurred in commercial sex workers, of whom 14–72% are now seropositive. The majority of patients are heterosexual. Thailand now has the highest number of officially-reported AIDS cases in Southeast Asia. Blood used for transfusion in Thailand is checked for the AIDS virus.

Other illnesses/hazards: Angiostrongyliasis (primarily in north-northeastern provinces; associated with eating raw seafood, snails, or vegetables), anisakias reported in 1993, anthrax (low endemicity; occurs in rural areas), capillariasis (associated with eating raw fish), Chikungunya fever (rare but intense, focal outbreaks reported in Nongkai and Nakornsri-thamaraj in 1995), capillariasis (associated with eating raw fish), gnathostomiasis (human cases associated with eating raw freshwater fish or poultry), helminthic infections (ascariasis, hookworm disease, and strongyloidiasis are highly endemic in urban and rural areas), leptospirosis (high rates during the rainy season), melioidosis (highest risk in northeastern Thailand where it is the most common cause of community-acquired pneumonia), opisthorchiasis and clonorchiasis (liver fluke diseases; transmitted by raw seafood; travelers should especially avoid "Koi Pla"— uncooked freshwater fish), opisthorchiasis (enzootic at high levels in northern and northeastern provinces; associated with eating koi-pla—chopped raw fish), paragonimiasis (lung fluke disease; endemic in central, north, and northeastern Thailand, including Chiang Rai; travelers should avoid raw freshwater crabs), murine typhus (flea-borne), scrub typhus (drug-resistant scrub typhus reported near Changmai), toxoplasmosis, tuberculosis (highly endemic), and typhoid fever. Animal hazards include snakes (kraits, vipers, cobras), centipedes, scorpions, and black widow spiders. Other possible hazards include tigers, leopards, crocodiles, pythons, poisonous

World Medical Guide

toads and frogs, and large, aggressive lizards. Stingrays, jellyfish, and several species of poisonous fish (puffer, goblin, stone, toad, scorpion, pig, porcupine, and box fish) are common in the country's coastal waters and are potentially hazardous to unprotected or careless swimmers.
Accidents: Bangkok is sometimes called "the gridlock city" because of its chaotic traffic. The traffic is left hand (as in England) and there is a high incidence of accidents and pedestrian injury. All drivers should be alert, and seat belts should be worn at all times.

THE GAMBIA

Embassy: 202-785-1399   *Banjul*   *GMT 0 hrs*
Entry Requirements
- A visa is required.
- HIV Test: Not required.
- Vaccinations: A yellow fever vaccination certificate is required from travelers older than 1 year arriving from endemic or infected areas.

Telephone Country Code: 220
Embassies/Consulates: U.S. Embassy, Banjul. Fajara, Kairaba Avenue; Tel. 392-856 or 392-858.
Hospitals/Doctors: Royal Victoria Hospital (255 beds), Banjul; general medical facility.

Health Advisory

Yellow fever: This disease is active in this country, with the Upper River Division considered "infected" by the WHO. No cases of yellow fever have been reported recently. Vaccination is recommended for travel to this country. This country is in the Yellow Fever Endemic Zone. A valid yellow fever vaccination certificate may be required for travel to other countries in South America, Africa, the Middle East, or Asia.
Cholera: No cases officially reported, but travelers should consider vaccination (one dose) or getting a doctor's letter of exemption from vaccination. Cholera vaccine gives only brief, incomplete protection and is not routinely recommended for travelers in good health. Prevention consists primarily in adhering to safe food and drink guidelines.
Malaria: Risk is present year-round throughout this country, including urban areas. Risk is elevated during and immediately after the rainy season, June through October. Falciparum malaria accounts for approximately 85% of cases, followed by malaria due to *P. malariae* and *P. ovale* parasites. Chloroquine-resistant falciparum malaria is reported. Prophylaxis with mefloquine or doxycycline is currently recommended when traveling to malarious areas.
Travelers' diarrhea: Water in Banjul is treated and distributed through a piped system; nevertheless, all water sources, including tap water, should be considered contaminated. Travelers should observe all food and drink precautions. A quinolone antibiotic is recommended for the treatment of acute diarrhea. Diarrhea not responding to treatment with an antibiotic may be due to a parasitic disease such as giardiasis, amebiasis, or cryptosporidiosis.
Hepatitis: High risk. All nonimmune travelers should receive hepatitis A vaccine. Hepatitis E is likely, but the level is unclear. The hepatitis B carrier rate in the general population is 10%–35%. Hepatitis B vaccination is recommended for all long-term travelers.
Leishmaniasis: Risk undetermined. Sporadic cases of cutaneous and visceral leishmaniasis were reported in the early 1980s in the Farafenni and Banjul vicinities. Current data not available. Travelers should take measures to prevent insect (sandfly) bites.
Schistosomiasis: Risk of urinary schistosomiasis is distributed along the Gambia River. Intestinal schistosomiasis has been reported in the extreme southwestern corner of the Gambia, including the Banjul vicinity. All travelers should avoid swimming, bathing, or wading in freshwater lakes, ponds, or streams.
AIDS: Heterosexual contact is the predominate mode of transmission. HIV prevalence is estimated at 29% in the high-risk urban population. All travelers are cautioned against unsafe sex, unsterile medical or dental injections, and unnecessary blood transfusions.

World Medical Guide

Other Illnesses/Hazards: African tick typhus (contracted from dog ticks, often in urban areas, and bush ticks), brucellosis, Chikungunya fever (epidemics may be explosive), cutaneous larva migrans, echinococcosis, filariasis (mosquito-borne), hemorrhagic fever with renal syndrome, leprosy (up to 0.8 cases/1,000 population), leptospirosis, meningitis, onchocerciasis (black-fly-borne; transmitted near fast-flowing rivers), rabies, tick-borne relapsing fever, trachoma, trypanosomiasis (endemic, but level is unclear; sporadic cases reported in the early 1980s indicates low-level transmission occurs), tuberculosis (a major health problem), typhoid fever, and intestinal worms (very common).

TOGO

Embassy: 202-234-4212   *Lome*   *GMT 0 hrs*

Entry Requirements
- Passport/Visa: Travelers should possess valid passport. Visa not required.
- HIV Test: Not required.
- Vaccinations: A yellow fever vaccination certificate is required from all travelers older than 1 year of age arriving from ALL COUNTRIES. Cholera: The State Department reports that a cholera vaccination certificate may also be required for entry into Togo.

Telephone Country Code: 228

Embassies/Consulates: U.S. Embassy, Lome. Rue Pelletier Caventou & Rue Vouban; Tel. 2991. Canadian Embassy (Ghana); Tel. [233] 228-555.

Hospitals/Doctors: Tokoin National Hospital, Lome (650 beds); general medical/surgical facility; trauma unit; ENT. Hospital Baptiste Biblique Adeta; well-equipped medical/surgical facility. Travelers should contact the U.S. Embassy for additional physician referrals.

Health Advisory

Yellow fever: Vaccination is recommended for all travelers over 9 months of age who plan to travel outside urban areas. This country is in the Yellow Fever Endemic Zone and a valid yellow fever vaccination certificate may be required for entry to other countries.

Malaria: Risk is present throughout this country, including urban areas. Falciparum malaria accounts for approximately 85% of cases. Most other cases of malaria are due to the *P. malariae* and *P. ovale* species. Chloroquine-resistant falciparum malaria is reported. Mefloquine or doxycycline prophylaxis is currently recommended. Protection against mosquito bites is essential.

Travelers' diarrhea: High risk. Safe water is available in only a few urban areas where there are treatment plants and piped distribution systems. These systems are subject to contamination. Travelers should observe all food and drink safety precautions. A quinolone antibiotic (Cipro or Floxin) is recommended for the treatment of acute diarrhea. Diarrhea not responding to treatment with an antibiotic, or chronic diarrhea, may be due to a parasitic disease such as giardiasis or amebiasis, and treatment with metronidazole (Flagyl) or tinidazole (Fasigyn) should be considered. All cases of diarrhea should be treated with adequate fluid replacement.

Hepatitis: High risk. All susceptible travelers should receive immune globulin prophylaxis or hepatitis A vaccine. The hepatitis B carrier rate in the general population is estimated to exceed 10%. Vaccination against hepatitis B is recommended for healthcare workers and all long-term visitors to this country.

Schistosomiasis: Risk is present in eastern, central, and northern areas, but transmission reportedly does not occur within 100 km of the Atlantic coast. Travelers should avoid swimming or wading in freshwater lakes, ponds, or streams.

Meningitis: Togo lies within the sub-Saharan meningitis belt. Sporadic outbreaks of meningococcal meningitis occur, especially in the northern and central areas. Vaccination is recommended for travelers staying in these regions longer than 4 weeks who will have close contact with the indigenous population.

World Medical Guide

AIDS: Heterosexual transmission is the predominate means of transmission. Current infection rates of high-risk groups is presently not available. All travelers are cautioned against unsafe sex, unsterile medical or dental injections, and unnecessary blood transfusions.

Other illnesses/hazards: African tick typhus (contracted from dog ticks, often in urban areas, and bush ticks), anthrax, brucellosis (from consumption of raw dairy products), filariasis (mosquito-borne), Lassa fever, leishmaniasis (sporadic cases have previously been reported), leprosy (up to 1.3 cases/1,000 population), onchocerciasis (black-fly-borne; transmitted near fast-flowing rivers), toxoplasmosis, syphilis, tuberculosis (a major health problem), typhoid fever, and intestinal helminths (very common). Animal hazards include snakes (vipers, cobras), centipedes, scorpions, and black widow spiders.

TONGA

Consulate: 415-781-0365   *Nuku'alofa*   *GMT +13 hrs*

Entry Requirements
- Passport/Visa: A visa is required only for visits exceeding 30 days.
- HIV Test: Not required.
- Vaccinations: A yellow fever vaccination certificate is required from all travelers coming from infected or endemic areas.

Telephone Country Code: 676

Embassies/Consulates: The nearest U.S. Embassy is in Suva, Fiji; Tel. [679] 314-466.

Hospitals/Doctors: Vaiola Hospital, Nuku'alofa (202 beds); general medical/surgical facility; emergency room. Ngu Hospital, Neiafu (61 beds); limited medical and surgical services.

Health Advisory

Malaria: No risk.

Hepatitis: All nonimmune travelers should receive hepatitis A vaccine. The hepatitis B carrier rate in the general population exceeds 10 percent. Vaccination against hepatitis B is recommended for all healthcare workers and long-term visitors.

Travelers' diarrhea: Low to medium risk: The tap water in Nuku'alofa is potable, but travelers are advised to consume only boiled or bottled water unless assured the water has been adequately treated. A quinolone antibiotic is recommended for the treatment of diarrhea.

Cholera: This water-borne diarrheal disease occurs sporadically in Oceania. Rare cases of cholera have occurred in this country but there is little, if any, danger to tourists.

Filariasis, Japanese encephalitis, Ross River fever, dengue fever: Sporadic cases and outbreaks are reported. Travelers should take protective measures against mosquito bites.

Animal hazards: Stingrays, poisonous fish, various sharks, sea anemones, corals and jellyfish are hazards to swimmers. Tropical centipedes can inflict painful stings if touched. Common sense is usually adequate to avoid these hazards.

TRINIDAD & TOBAGO

Embassy: 202-467-6490   *Port-of-Spain*   *GMT -4 hrs*

Entry Requirements
- Passport/Visa: A visa is not required for visits up to 3 months.
- HIV Test: Not required.
- Vaccinations: A yellow fever vaccination certificate is required from travelers over one year of age arriving from infected or endemic areas.

Telephone Area Code: 809

Embassies/Consulates: U.S. Embassy, Port-of-Spain, 15 Queen's Park; Tel. 622-6372. Canadian High Commission, Port-of-Spain, 72 South Quay Street; Tel. 623-4787.

Hospitals/Doctors: In Port-of-Spain: General Hospital (882 beds); general medical and surgical facility; neurosurgery, orthopedics.

World Medical Guide

Health Advisory

Yellow fever: This disease has been reported active in the jungle regions of Trinidad and vaccination is advised for all travelers older than 9 months of age who plan travel outside of urban areas. No human cases of yellow fever have been reported since 1980. This country is in the Yellow Fever Endemic Zone. Although a vaccination certificate may not be required for entry to this country, one may be required for on-going travel to other countries in Latin America, Africa, the Middle East, or Asia.

Malaria: An outbreak of vivax malaria has been reported in southwestern Trinidad, in the town of Icacos. Travelers to this region should consider chloroquine prophylaxis and take measures to prevent mosquito bites.

Travelers' diarrhea: Low to moderate risk. In urban and resort areas, the hotels and restaurants generally serve reliable food and potable water. Elsewhere, travelers should observe all food and drink safety precautions. A quinolone antibiotic is recommended for the treatment of acute diarrhea. Diarrhea not responding to antibiotic treatment may be due to a parasitic disease such as giardiasis or amebiasis.

Hepatitis: All nonimmune travelers should receive hepatitis A vaccine. Long-stay travelers or healthcare workers should be immunized against hepatitis B.

Dengue fever: This mosquito-transmitted viral disease is prevalent in the Caribbean. Major outbreaks of dengue have previously occurred on Trinidad. Travelers should take measures to prevent insect (mosquito) bites. The *Aedes* mosquitoes, which transmit dengue, bite primarily during the daytime and are present in populous urban areas as well as resort and rural areas.

Leishmaniasis: Low apparent risk. The disease, however, has been reported historically. Travelers should take measures to prevent insect (sandfly) bites.

Chagas' disease: Low apparent risk. Disease may be transmitted in rural-agricultural areas where there are the adobe-style huts and houses that can potentially harbor the night-biting triatomid (assassin) bugs. Travelers sleeping in such structures should take precautions against nighttime bites.

Leptospirosis: This spirochetal infection is reported from this country. Travelers should avoid contact with animal urine or water potentially contaminated with animal urine.

Rabies: Animal rabies was reported in 1987. The potential of transmission to humans exists. Travelers should especially avoid stray dogs and seek immediate treatment of any wild animal bite. Rabies vaccination is especially indicated following the unprovoked bite of a dog, cat, vampire bat, or monkey.

Other diseases/health threats: Brucellosis, filariasis (Bancroftian variety; mosquito-borne; may occur in the Lesser Antilles from Trinidad north to Guadeloupe), histoplasmosis, intestinal helminthic infections (ancylostomiasis, ascariasis, strongyloidiasis, and trichuriasis), sexually transmitted diseases, AIDS, tuberculosis, typhoid fever, viral encephalitis, ciguatera fish toxin poisoning, and swimming related hazards (jellyfish, spiny sea urchins, and coral).

TUNISIA

Embassy: 202-862-1850   *Tunis*   *GMT +1 hr*

Entry Requirements
- Passport/Visa: Passport is required.
- HIV Test: Not required.
- Vaccinations: A yellow fever vaccination certificate is required from all travelers arriving from infected areas.

Telephone Country Code: 216

Embassies/Consulates: U.S. Embassy, Tunis. 144 Avenue de la Liberte; Tel: (1) 782-566. Canadian High Commission, Tunis. 3 Rue de Senegal, Place Palestine; Tel: (1) 286-577.

Hospitals/Doctors: Charles Nicolle Hospital, Tunis (756 beds); general medical/surgical facility; Habib Thameur Hospital (555 beds); general medical/surgical facility; Hadi Chakar Hospital, Tunis (870 beds); general medical/surgical facility.

World Medical Guide

Health Advisory

Malaria: Low risk. Indigenous malaria has not occurred since 1978 but foci of vivax malaria activity may still exist. Travelers should take measures to prevent mosquito bites and seek medical attention for any unexplained illness accompanied by chills, fever, and headache.

Travelers' diarrhea: High risk. Piped water in Tunis is not consistently potable. In most other large urban areas, and all rural areas, water supplies are not considered potable. Travelers should observe food and drink safety precautions. A quinolone antibiotic (Cipro or Floxin) is recommended for the treatment of acute diarrhea. Diarrhea not responding to treatment with an antibiotic, or chronic diarrhea, may be due to a parasitic disease such as giardiasis or amebiasis—or an intestinal virus.

Hepatitis: Immune globulin or hepatitis A vaccine is recommended for all susceptible travelers. The hepatitis B carrier rate in the general population is estimated at 4.6%. Vaccination against hepatitis B is recommended for healthcare workers and should be considered by long-term visitors to this country.

Sandfly fever: Disease risk is present in the northern, central, and southeastern areas of the country. Transmission occurs primarily April–October, when sandfly activity is highest.

Leishmaniasis: Cutaneous leishmaniasis is reported from northern, central (primarily Qafsah, Sidi Bu Zayd, and Safaqis Governorates), and the southeastern areas. Visceral leishmaniasis (kala-azar) occurs in the northern half of Tunisia, primarily northeast, including the outskirts of Tunis. All travelers should take measures to prevent insect (sandfly) bites.

Schistosomiasis: Low risk. Foci include oases in Qafsah and Qabis Governorates and in the village of Hadjeb El Aioun, 120 miles south of Tunis. Travelers should avoid swimming or wading in freshwater lakes, ponds, irrigation ditches, or streams in these areas.

Rabies: Human cases reported year-round. Vaccination is recommended for long-term travelers to this country, especially children. Wild animal reservoir of rabies virus is primarily foxes, jackals, and hyenas.

Other illnesses: Boutonneuse fever (African tick typhus; distribution is widespread; contracted from dog ticks, often in suburban areas), brucellosis (risk from raw goat/sheep milk and cheese), echinococcosis (a major health problem in central Tunisia), leptospirosis, trachoma, tuberculosis, typhoid fever, soil-transmitted helminthic infections (roundworm, hookworm) are common in rural areas.

TURKEY

Embassy: 202-659-8200   *Ankara*   *GMT +2 hrs*

Entry Requirements

- Passport/Visa: A tourist visa is required and can be purchased at the airport upon arrival.
- HIV Test: There is no formal testing requirement, but screening 75 centers, most of them located at border checkpoints and tourist areas, have been established.
- Vaccinations: None required.

Telephone Country Code: 90   **AT&T:** 00-800-12277   **MCI:** 00-8001-1177

Embassies/Consulates: U.S. Embassy, Ankara. 110 Ataturk Boulevard; Tel. (312) 468-6110. U.S. Consulate, Istanbul. Tel. (212) 251-3602.

Hospitals/Doctors: Admiral Bristol (American) Hospital, Istanbul; private; most specialties; Tel. (0212) 231-4050. International Hospital, Istanbul; private; most specialties; Tel. (0212) 663-3000. Volkan Korten, MD. Director of Travel Medicine and Infectious Diseases, Academic Hospital, Istanbul (private; most specialties, including travel medicine); Tel. (0216) 492-4750 or (0216) 327-4142. Hacettepe University Hospital (Tel. 312-310-3545) is considered the best health center in Ankara. Bayindir Hospital, Ankara; private; most specialties; Considered the best private hospital in Ankara.

Health Advisory

Malaria: Cases are reported countrywide, but the majority are reported from southern and eastern Turkey, particularly along the Mediterranean coast, including Diyarbakir and Siirt Provinces, and the provinces bordering Syria, Iraq, and Iran. Transmission occurs up to 1,500

World Medical Guide

meters elevation in endemic areas, primarily between February–November, peaking in June and July. There is no risk of malaria in the major cities such as Istanbul and Ankara. Vivax malaria accounts for 100% of cases. Chloroquine prophylaxis recommended in risk areas.

Travelers' diarrhea: High risk outside of resorts and first-class hotels. Contamination of existing municipal water systems is common. A quinolone antibiotic is recommended for the treatment of acute diarrhea. Giardiasis and amebiasis are common.

Hepatitis: Hepatitis A vaccine is recommended for all nonimmune travelers. Waterborne epidemics of hepatitis E is endemic, but levels are unclear. The hepatitis B carrier rate in the general population is estimated at 6%–10%. Vaccination against hepatitis B is recommended for all long-term visitors to this country.

Typhoid fever: Vaccination recommended for travel to rural areas exceeding 2-3 weeks.

Leishmaniasis: Cutaneous leishmaniasis is common in the southeastern region of Turkey and the Tigris-Euphrates Basin. Visceral leishmaniasis (kala azar) occurs along the Aegean coast, the Mediterranean coast, the Sea of Marmara coast, and the Black Sea coast. Travelers should take measures to prevent insect (sandfly) bites.

Schistosomiasis: There is no risk of schistosomiasis at the present time. Potential for transmission, however, occurs in the southern-most areas of the Belikh branch of the Euphrates River (near the Syrian border), where snail vectors are present.

Rabies: Human cases are frequently reported and are usually due to contact with rabid stray dogs. Travelers should seek immediate treatment following the unprovoked bite of a dog, cat, or fox. Bites by other animals should be considered on an individual basis.

Other illnesses: Brucellosis, Mediterranean spotted fever (boutonneuse fever; this tick-borne encephalitis occurs in the western and southern regions), brucellosis (usually transmitted by raw goat or sheep milk), cholera (sporadic cases, as well as large-scale outbreaks), cutaneous larva migrans, echinococcosis (human cases reported sporadically, especially in northern and northeastern areas), tick-borne encephalitis (sporadic cases reported; presumed risk in brushy, forested western and northern regions), leprosy (low prevalence), plague (flea-borne; low risk of transmission may exist in the southeast near Syria and Iraq, in the northeast near Iran, and in central Anatolia), murine typhus (flea-borne), North Asian tick typhus (in areas bordering the former Soviet Union), sandfly fever (transmission occurs predominantly from April through October), tuberculosis, typhoid fever (endemic, with frequent outbreaks), and helminthic infections (roundworm, hookworm, and whipworm) infections are common in rural areas.

TURKS & CAICOS

Embassy: 202-462-1340   *GMT -5 hrs*

Entry Requirements
- Passport/Visa: Visa not required. Turks & Caicos is a British Dependent Territory.
- HIV Test: Not required.
- Vaccinations: None required.

Telephone Area Code: 809

Doctors/Hospitals: General Hospital, Cockburn Town (32 beds); limited medical and surgical services.

Health Advisory

See Disease Risk Summary for the Caribbean.

Travelers' diarrhea: Low to medium risk. Travelers should drink bottled or treated water and carry a quinolone antibiotic for the treatment of more severe diarrhea.

Dengue fever: This mosquito-transmitted viral disease is prevalent in the Caribbean. Travelers should take measures to prevent insect bites.

World Medical Guide

TURKMENISTAN
Entry Requirements: *Embassy of Turkmenistan: 202-588-1500.*
U.S. Embassy, Ashgabat: *(9)-9312-511-306*
For Health Advisory information, see the Health Advisory for the Caucasus, Central Asia, Siberia, and Far East former USSR on page 261.

TUVALU
Funafuti   *GMT +12 hrs*

Entry Requirements
- Passport/Visa: A visa is not required.
- HIV Test: Not required.
- Vaccinations: None required.

Hospitals/Doctors
Princess Margaret Hospital, Funafuti. Tel: 752.

Health Advisory
Malaria: No risk.
Hepatitis: All nonimmune travelers should receive hepatitis A vaccine. The hepatitis B carrier rate in the general population exceeds 10 percent. Vaccination against hepatitis B is recommended for all healthcare workers and long-term visitors.
Filariasis, Japanese encephalitis, dengue fever: Sporadic cases and outbreaks are reported. Travelers should take protective measures against mosquito bites.
Marine hazards: Stingrays, poisonous fish, sea anemones, corals and jellyfish are hazards to swimmers.

UGANDA
Embassy: 202-726-7100   *Kampala*   *GMT +3 hrs*

Entry Requirements
- Passport/Visa: Valid passport and visa are required.
- HIV Test: Not required.
- Vaccinations: A yellow fever vaccination certificate is required from all travelers older than 1 year arriving from infected areas or from any country in the Yellow Fever Endemic Zones.
  Cholera: Vaccination recommended to avoid possible delays at the border.

Telephone Country Code: 256
Embassies/Consulates: U.S. Embassy, Kampala. Parliament Avenue; Tel. (41) 259-791/2/3/5. Canadian High Commission (Kenya); Tel. [254] (2) 334-033.
Hospitals/Doctors: Mulago General Hospital, Kampala (1,080 beds); general medical facility; no anesthesiology. Nsambya Hospital, Kampala (370 beds); general medical/surgical facility.

473

World Medical Guide

Health Advisory

Yellow fever: Vaccination is recommended. No cases have been reported recently, but this country is in the Yellow Fever Endemic Zone. A valid yellow fever vaccination certificate will be required if arriving from Kenya (where yellow fever is active).

Cholera: This disease is active in this country. Although cholera vaccination is not required for entry if arriving directly from the U.S. or Canada, it may be required if arriving from a cholera-infected area, or required for on-going travel to other countries in Latin America, Africa, the Middle East, or Asia. The risk to travelers of acquiring cholera is considered low. Prevention consists primarily in following strict adherence to safe food and drink guidelines.

Malaria: Risk is present year-round throughout this country, including urban areas. Falciparum malaria accounts for approximately 80% of cases. Other cases of malaria are due to the *P. malariae* species, followed by *P. ovale* and (rarely) *P. vivax*. Chloroquine-resistant falciparum malaria is reported. Prophylaxis with mefloquine or doxycycline is currently recommended for travel to this country.

Travelers' diarrhea: High risk. Supplies of potable water are inadequate to meet the needs of the population. Piped water supplies may be grossly contaminated. Travelers should observe food and drink safety precautions. A quinolone antibiotic (Floxin or Cipro) is recommended for the treatment of acute diarrhea. Diarrhea not responding to treatment with an antibiotic, or chronic diarrhea, may be due to a parasitic disease such as giardiasis or amebiasis, and treatment with metronidazole or tinidazole should be considered.

Hepatitis: High risk. All nonimmune travelers should receive hepatitis A vaccine. The hepatitis B carrier rate in the general population is estimated at 10%. Vaccination against hepatitis B is recommended for all long-term visitors to this country.

Schistosomiasis: Intestinal schistosomiasis occurs primarily in the northwest and along the northern shore of Lake Victoria. Urinary schistosomiasis is confined to northern central Uganda, north of Lake Kyoga. Travelers should avoid swimming or wading in freshwater lakes, ponds, or streams.

Filariasis, onchocerciasis, loiasis: Sporadic cases are reported. Travelers to this country are advised to take protective measures against blackflies.

Leishmaniasis: Visceral leishmaniasis occurs in the northeast province of Karamoja. Sporadic cases of cutaneous leishmaniasis are reported from the Mt. Elgon vicinity. Travelers should take protective measures against insect (sandfly) bites.

Trypanosomiasis (African sleeping sickness): Prevalent in scattered areas countrywide. Major risk of disease presumably persists in the southeast (extending from the northern shore of Lake Victoria and Lake Kyoga), with foci of gambiense disease primarily in northwestern and north central areas (along the White Nile and the Sudanese border). All travelers to these regions should take measures to prevent tsetse fly bites.

Meningitis: Risk is present. An outbreak of meningococcal meningitis began in Kampala in 1989 and extended to other provinces. Vaccination against meningococcal disease is advised, especially for those who expect close, prolonged contact with the indigenous population.

Rabies: Increased incidence of rabies was reported in Kampala and Karamoja Province in 1986. Rabies vaccination is recommended for persons planning an extended stay in this country.

Plague: Three hundred cases were reported from Nebbi District in Western Province in 1986. Vaccination against plague should be considered by persons who may be occupationally exposed to wild rodents. Prophylaxis with tetracycline or doxycycline can be considered in lieu of vaccination.

AIDS: Promiscuous heterosexual contact is the predominate mode of transmission. HIV-1 prevalence is estimated at up to 86% of the high-risk urban population. All travelers are cautioned against unsafe sex, unsterile medical or dental injections, and unnecessary blood transfusions.

Other illnesses/hazards: African tick typhus (contracted from dog ticks—often in urban areas—and from bush ticks), brucellosis, chikungunya fever, Crimean-Congo hemorrhagic fever (cases reported from Entebbe), dengue (not reported recently), echinococcosis, leprosy, leptospirosis, louse-borne typhus, toxoplasmosis, syphilis, tuberculosis (a major health problem), trachoma, typhoid fever, and intestinal worms (very common). Animal hazards include snakes (vipers, cobras), centipedes, scorpions, and black widow spiders.

World Medical Guide

UKRAINE

Embassy: 202-333-0606   *GMT +3 hrs*

Entry Requirements
- Passport/Visa: A valid passport, visa, and exit permit required. Strict customs regulations may apply. For updated information for travel to Ukraine, travelers should contact the Embassy of Ukraine in Washington.
- HIV Test: HIV testing is required for foreigners staying more than 3 months. U.S. test result is currently acceptable.
- Vaccinations: None required. Tetanus/diphtheria immunization is recommended.

Telephone Country Code: 380
Embassies/Consulates: U.S. Embassy, Kiev. Vulitsa Yuria Kotsubinskoho 10. Tel. (44) 244-7343, 244-7345, 244-7349. After hours: (44) 216-3805

Health Advisory

Malaria: There is no risk of malaria in Ukraine.

Cholera: This disease is officially reported "not active", but all travelers should follow safe food and drink guidelines to prevent possible infection. Sporadic cases of cholera are seen throughout the year.

Hepatitis: All nonimmune travelers should receive hepatitis A vaccine. The hepatitis B carrier rate in the general population of Russia is estimated at 5%–7%. Vaccination against hepatitis B is recommended for anyone planning an extended visit to this country. Many cases of hepatitis B are transmitted by unsterilized needles, syringes, and surgical instruments. Hepatitis E accounts for up to 18% of hepatitis in the Volga Delta region, but less than 1% regionwide. Blood supplies may be contaminated with hepatitis B and C viruses.

Diphtheria: An epidemic diphtheria began in 1990 in the Russian Federation has spread extensively, involving all countries of the former Soviet Union. Seventy percent of cases have occurred in persons older than 15 years. All travelers to Ukraine, especially adults, should be fully immunized. Diphtheria vaccine in the United States is widely available and is administered in combination with the tetanus toxoid vaccine (Td vaccine).

Typhoid fever: Travelers to rural areas or those planning long stays should receive typhoid vaccine. A marked increase in typhoid fever has occurred in Tajikistan and Turkmenistan.

Lyme disease: Occurs focally in rural forested areas primarily in the mid-south to the Baltic region eastward, and north to 65 degrees north latitude. Up to 35% of ticks tested in Estonia were infected with borrelia spirochetes. The vector ticks (*Ixodes ricinus, I. persulcatus*) are most abundant and active from May through August. Up to 60% of ticks may be infected.

Tick-borne encephalitis (TBE): Tick-borne encephalitis is transmitted from the Baltics to the Crimea by ixodid ticks. Peak transmission period is April through October. Risk is present primarily in rural brushy and forested areas below 1,500 meters elevation—especially in suburban "forests" bordering large cities. TBE is usually known as "Central European tick-borne encephalitis" west of the Urals. Increased incidence reported in the Perm-Sverlovsk areas (central Urals) in the 1990s. Travelers to rural areas should take measures to prevent tick bites.

Boutonneuse fever: Tick-borne; reported most commonly in the Black Sea coastal areas of the Caucus, Transcaucasus, and the Crimea, and along the Caspian Sea coastline.

Crimean-Congo hemorrhagic fever: Also known as Central Asian hemorrhagic fever. Tick-borne (*Hyalomma asiaticum, H. marginatum*). Reported mostly from southern areas, but outbreaks have occurred in some areas of Rostov Oblast (near the sea of Azov), April through November. Risk areas are rural steppe, savannah, semi-desert, and foothill/low mountain habitats below 2,000 meters elevation.

Arboviral diseases: Karelian fever (mosquito-borne; most cases occur July–September in the Karelian region); Tahjna virus fever (mosquito-borne; occurs sporadically from the Baltic region north to the Kolsky Peninsula); sandfly fever (sandfly-borne; limited to Moldova and the Crimea); dengue fever (mosquito-borne; cases previously reported from extreme southern regions); West Nile fever (mosquito-borne; virus reportedly circulates in the Volga Delta region from May–September); Sindbis virus fever (detected in the Volga Delta, July–August).

475

World Medical Guide

Leishmaniasis: Risk for cutaneous leishmaniasis primarily limited to southern regions, including portions of Georgia Republic and the southern Ukraine, below 1,300 meters elevation. Visceral leishmaniasis is confined to areas of the Transcaucasus. Travelers to these regions should take measures to prevent sandfly bites.

AIDS/HIV: AIDS cases are increasing and an epidemic may be in the making. The reasons include 1) an increase in IV drug abuse, 2) an increase in prostitution and sexual promiscuity, 3) an increase in sexually transmitted diseases, 4) decreased availablity of sterile needles and syringes, and 5) no education or prevention programs.

Other illnesses/hazards: Anthrax, brucellosis, echinococcosis (sheep and reindeer are hosts; dog feces are infective), legionellosis, leptospirosis (a particular problem in fish-breeding areas of Rostov Province; extensive outbreaks have occurred in east central areas), North Asian (Siberian) tick typhus (occurs in the steppe areas bordering Kazakhstan, Georgia, and Azerbaijan; risk elevated May–June), plague (flea-borne; usually occurs as isolated cases or small outbreaks in semi-arid areas of the southern republics of Azerbaijan, Armenia, and Georgia), rabies, rickettsialpox, tick-borne relapsing fever (may occur south of 55 degrees north latitude), trichinosis (greatest risk in western Belarus and the Ukraine), tularemia ("rabbit fever"; risk may be elevated in the north), tuberculosis (40% rise in cases since 1995; incidence in Moscow has doubled since 1991), and helminthic infections (roundworm, hookworm, and whipworm infections and strongyloidiasis) reported, especially from the Transcaucaus, especially Azerbaijan.

UNITED ARAB EMIRATES

Embassy: 202-338-6500   *Abu Dhabi*   *GMT +4 hrs*

Entry Requirements
- A passport and visa are required. Tourist visa must be obtained by hotel or sponsor. Sponsor must meet traveler at airport.
- HIV Test: Applicants for work and residence (more than 30 days) are tested upon arrival. Contact the UAE Embassy in Washington (202-338-6500) for further details.
- Vaccinations: A yellow fever vaccination certificate is required of all travelers arriving from infected areas.

Telephone Country Code: 971   **AT&T:** 800-121   **MCI:** 800-111

Embassies/Consulates: U.S. Embassy, Abu Dhabi. Al Sudan Street; Tel. (2) 436-691. U.S. Consulate General: Tel. (4) 313-115.

Hospitals/Doctors: Mafraq, Abu Dhabi (520 beds); most specialties; burn unit; ambulance service; helipad. Dubai Hospital (635 beds); major referral facility; ambulance service; helipad. Raship Hospital, Dubai (500 beds); emergency/trauma facility; ambulance; helipad.

Health Advisory

Malaria: Risk is confined to the northeastern UAE, primarily north and east of Dubayy; primary risk areas occur in coastal and/or foothill regions (up to 2,000 meters elevation) along the Gulf of Oman and bordering Oman, including Al Ayan Oasis. Cases are reported year-round, and the incidence increases from May to July. Most of the country (Dubai, Sharjah, Ajman, Umm al Qaiwan, the Emirate of Abu Dhabi, and the west coast) is malaria free. Vivax malaria accounts for 60%-75% of cases. Chloroquine is advised in malarious areas.

Travelers' diarrhea: Moderate risk. A quinolone antibiotic is recommended for the treatment of acute diarrhea. Giardiasis and amebiasis are commonly reported.

Hepatitis A: Low risk in Abu Dhabi and Dubai due to improved levels of sanitation. Hepatitis A vaccine is recommended for all nonimmune travelers to this country. The hepatitis B carrier rate in the general population is estimated at 2%. Vaccination against hepatitis B is recommended for long-term visitors. Hepatitis E has not been reported but likely occurs.

Leishmaniasis: Endemic. There is a low risk of cutaneous and visceral leishmaniasis.

Rabies: Animal rabies occurs in foxes and sporadically in stray dogs. There have been no recently reported cases of human rabies.

Other illnesses: Boutonneuse fever, brucellosis, dengue fever (not active), Crimean-Congo hemorrhagic fever (reported in abattoir workers), filariasis, meningitis, schistosomiasis (not reported), relapsing fever (tick-borne), tuberculosis (prevalence is low), typhoid fever, helminthic infections (roundworm, hookworm, and whipworm) are reported; incidence is very low.

World Medical Guide

UNITED KINGDOM

Embassy: 202-462-1340 **London** **GMT 0 hrs**

Entry Requirements
- Passport/Visa: A visa not required for U.S. citizens.
- HIV Test: Not required.
- Vaccinations: None required.

Telephone Country Code: 44

Embassies/Consulates: U.S. Embassy, London. 24/31 Grosvenor Square, W1; Tel. (071)-499-9000.

Health Advisory

Travelers' diarrhea: Low risk. Tap water is considered potable.

Hepatitis: Low risk. Nonimmune travelers, however, should consider hepatitis A vaccination. The hepatitis B carrier rate in the general population is less than 1%. Hepatitis B vaccination is not routinely recommended for travel to this country.

Traffic alert: Travelers should look to their right when crossing streets; traffic is left-sided and four to five pedestrian fatalities occur annually when tourists are struck by cars.

Lyme disease and tick-borne diseases: The incidence of Lyme disease in the UK is ten-fold less than in other European countries. Outbreaks of Lyme disease have been reported in heavily forested rural areas and in parts of Scotland. Recently, the tick that transmits Lyme disease has been found in parks within the city of London. Tick-borne fever of sheep occurs in upland areas of the UK and the infectious agent (*Ehrlichia phagocytophila*) also causes human granulocytic ehrlichiosis.

Other illnesses: An outbreak of enterohemorrhagic *E. coli* infection, associated with meat products, was reported in late 1996 in Scotland.

UNITED STATES

Washington, DC **GMT -5 hrs, -4 hrs (Apr–Oct)**

Entry Requirements
- Passport/Visa: A passport is required. Travelers should check visa requirements.
- HIV Test: Not required for tourists.
- Vaccinations: None required.

Telephone Country Code: 1

Canadian Embassy: 501 Pennsylvania Ave., N.W., Washington, D.C. 20001. Tel. (202)-682-1740.

Health Advisory

Travelers' diarrhea: Low risk nationwide. Tap water from municipal water systems is potable.

Food-borne disease: Low risk nationwide. Sporadic cases of food-borne illness, usually due to salmonella or campylobacter, are reported. Raw eggs and chicken are often the source of salmonellosis outbreaks. Outbreaks of bloody diarrhea caused by *E. coli* O157:H7 in undercooked hamburger meat have been reported from several states. Mexican cheese, imported to California, has transmitted listeriosis. Cholera, transmitted by contaminated shellfish (crab, shrimp, raw oysters), occurs sporadically along the Gulf of Mexico (Texas, Louisiana). Gastroenteritis, due to *Vibrio* species, salmonella, or campylobacter, has been reported after the consumption of contaminated oysters in Louisiana, Maryland, North Carolina, Florida, and Mississippi. Ciguatera fish poisoning is occasionally reported from Hawaii and Florida.

Hepatitis: Low risk nationwide of hepatitis A. Up to 3.1% of Alaskan natives are chronic carriers of the hepatitis B virus.

Giardiasis: Occurs primarily in wilderness areas of the Rocky Mountains and the Pacific Northwest. Pockets of disease occur elsewhere. Nationwide distribution of risk, however, is not precisely delineated. Campers and hikers are advised to boil or filter drinking water.

World Medical Guide

Tick-borne diseases: Lyme disease occurs in the Middle Atlantic states, the Northeast, the upper Midwest, and the northern Pacific Coast region. Babesiosis occurs in the Nantucket region and was recently reported in Wisconsin. A new *Babesia* strain has appeared in Washington State. Human monocytic ehrlichiosis occurs in the southcentral and southeastern United States. Human granulocytic ehrlichiosis is reported from Minnesota, Wisconsin, California, and the northeastern United States.

Dengue fever: Locally-acquired cases are reported in southern Texas where the *Aedes aegypti* and *Aedes albopictus* mosquitoes are common.

Leishmaniasis: Transmission of this disease has been reported in southern Texas. Travelers should take measurses to avoid insect (sandfly) bites.

Legionnaire's disease: Outbreaks reported on cruise ships departing U.S. ports. Disease transmission related to being in or near shipboard whirlpool spas.

Viral encephalitis: Cases recently reported in Arkansas, Texas, Massachusetts, Florida, Georgia, and South Carolina. Viral encephalitis is commonly spread by culex mosquitoes, but the *Aedes albopictus* mosquito ("Asian tiger mosquito") is also known to transmit the virus.

Rabies: During 1995, a total of four cases of human rabies were documented in the United States, all caused by bats. Of the 25 cases since 1981 in which people contracted rabies in this country, 22 involved strains that could have come only from bats. Only one of these patients was aware of having been bitten. The number of cases of animal rabies in the United States is increasing. Raccoon rabies is endemic in the southeastern and Middle Atlantic states and is increasing in the northeastern United States. In northcentral and southcentral United States, and California, skunk rabies predominates. Along the U.S.-Mexican border, rabies transmitted by dogs and coyotes is a potential threat to humans. In Alaska, the arctic and red fox are primarily infected. Bats *anywhere* in the United States should be considered potentially rabid. Travelers should seek immediate treatment for any unprovoked animal bite, particularly if from a raccoon, fox, skunk, or bat. Other wild animals that rarely transmit rabies include groundhogs, wolves, bobcats, and black bears. No cases of wild animal rabies have been reported from the states of Washington, Idaho, Utah, Nevada, or Colorado.

Leptospirosis: Reported most frequently from Hawaii and Puerto Rico. Most transmission occurs from immersion in freshwater streams or in association with surface water sports.

Hantavirus pulmonary syndrome (HPS): Sporadic cases of HPS, a severe cardio-pulmonary illness first identified in 1993 in the southwestern United States, continue to occur. HPS has now been identified in 24 states. New Mexico, Arizona, and California have the most cases, but HPS has also been reported in Rhode Island. Transmission of the virus is through aerosolized rodent urine or secondary aerosolization of dried rodent excreta.

URUGUAY

Embassy: 202-331-1313 *Montevideo* *GMT -3 hrs*

Entry Requirements
- Passport/Visa: A valid passport is required.
- HIV Test: Not required.
- Vaccinations: None required.

Telephone Country Code: 598   **AT&T:** 00-0410

Embassies/Consulates: U.S. Embassy, Montevideo. Lauro Muller No. 1776. Tel. 40-90-51 or 40-91-26. Canadian Embassy (Argentina). Tel. 54 (1) 312-9081/88.

Hospitals/Doctors: Hospital Britanico, Montevideo (120 beds); commonly used by U.S. Embassy personnel; Tel. (2) 800-020/800-909.

Health Advisory

Yellow fever: No risk.
Malaria: No risk.
Travelers' diarrhea: Low to moderate risk. All water sources outside of Montevideo should be considered potentially contaminated. Beaches close to Montevideo may be contaminated by sewage. Travelers should observe food and drink precautions. A quinolone antibiotic is recommended for the treatment of diarrhea. Diarrhea not respond-

World Medical Guide

ing to treatment with an antibiotic may be due to a parasitic disease such as giardiasis, amebiasis, or cryptosporidiosis.
Hepatitis: High risk of hepatitis A. All nonimmune travelers should receive hepatitis A vaccine. The carrier rate of the hepatitis B virus in the general population is under 1%; hepatitis B vaccination is not routinely recommended.
Dengue fever: Not currently reported. The risk to travelers appears minimal, but dengue has been reported in neighboring Paraguay.
Chagas' disease: Reported in all rural areas of Uruguay except the Atlantic coast areas. Areas with high incidence include the Departments of Artigas, Rivera, Salto, and Tacuarembo. Risk occurs in those rural-agricultural areas where there are adobe-style huts and houses that potentially harbor the night-biting triatomid (assassin) bugs. Travelers sleeping in such structures should take precautions against nighttime bites.
Rabies: There is no risk of rabies in Uruguay.
Other diseases: Anthrax (human cases reported frequently), brucellosis, echinococcosis (up to 1.4% of rural human population may be infected), AIDS (fewer than 200 cases reported), measles (extensive outbreaks reported), meningitis (sporadic small outbreaks occur), tuberculosis (low incidence), strongyloidiasis and other helminthic infections, and trichinosis (3% of the population infected).

UZBEKISTAN

Contact Russian Embassy, Consular Division: 202-939-8907 for visa information. U.S. Embassy, Consular Section, Tashkent: (7)-3712-772-231
For Health Advisory information, see the Health Advisory for the Caucasus, Central Asia, Siberia, and Far East former USSR on page 261.

VANUATU

U.N. Mission: 212-593-0144/0215   Port-Vila   *GMT +11–12 hrs*
Entry Requirements
- Visa: 30-day visas are issued. Contact the Embassy of Australia (800-242-2878) or the Embassy of New Zealand (202-328-4800) for more information.
- HIV Test: Not required.
- Vaccinations: None required.

Telephone Country Code: 678
Embassies/consulates: There is no U.S. Embassy in Vanuatu. Assistance for U.S. citizens is provided by the American Embassy in Port Moresby, Papua New Guinea. Tel. [675]-321-1445. Fax: [675]-321-1593.
Hospitals/Doctors: Bougainville House, Port Villa. Vila Central Hospital (100 beds); X-ray, pharmacy, laboratory. Basic services only. Lenakel Hospital (50 beds); basic services only. X-ray; small laboratory.

Health Advisory
Malaria: There is a generally high risk of malaria throughout this country, including urban areas. There is no malaria on Futuna Island. *P. falciparum* accounts for 62.1% of cases, *P. vivax* the remainder. Chloroquine- and Fansidar-resistant falciparum malaria are reported. Chloroquine-resistant vivax malaria is also confirmed. Mefloquine or doxycycline prophylaxis is recommended for travel to this country. All travelers should take personal protection measures to prevent mosquito bites, especially between dusk and dawn—the time when the malaria-carrying *Anopheles* mosquitoes are most active. Anti-insect precautions are especially important in the northern islands, where mosquito activity is highest.
Travelers' diarrhea: Medium risk. The drinking water in this country is collected in ground catchment systems, and water supplies should be considered potentially contaminated. All travelers are advised to drink only bottled, boiled, or treated water unless assured that the local tap water has been treated. (The tap water in Vila is considered safe.) Standard safe food

479

World Medical Guide

precautions should also be observed. A quinolone antibiotic (Cipro or Floxin) is recommended for the treatment of acute diarrhea. Diarrheal illness not responding to antibiotic treatment may be due to giardiasis, which is moderately endemic in this country.

Typhoid fever: An outbreak of typhoid fever occurred in 1987. The risk of typhoid is low for tourists. Vaccination is recommended only for long-term visitors to this country. All travelers to this country should follow safe food and water guidelines. The risk of typhoid is increased during the rainy season, when ground water may become contaminated.

Hepatitis: All nonimmune travelers should receive hepatitis A vaccine. The hepatitis B carrier rate in the general population is estimated to exceed 10%. Vaccination against hepatitis B is recommended for all nonimmune long-term visitors to this country.

Insect-borne diseases: Filariasis, Japanese encephalitis, and dengue occur sporadically, with occasional outbreaks reported. Travelers should take personal protective measures against mosquito bites. Long-term visitors should consider vaccination against Japanese encephalitis.

Scrub typhus: There is a low incidence of scrub typhus reported from this country. Travelers walking through grassy areas should protect themselves from chigger mites by using a deet-containing skin repellent and permethrin-treated clothing.

VENEZUELA

Embassy: 202-342-2214   *Caracas*   *GMT -4 hrs*

Entry Requirements
- A tourist card and multiple entry visa are available. Contact the Embassy of Venezuela.
- HIV Test: Not required.
- Vaccinations: No vaccinations are required to visit this country.

Telephone Country Code: 58   **AT&T:** 80-011-120   **MCI:** 800-1114-0

Embassies/Consulates: U.S. Embassy, Caracas. Calle Suspure and Calle F, Colinas de Valle Arriba; Tel. (2) 977-2011.

Hospitals/Doctors: Centro Medico La Floresta, Caracas (40+ beds); modern, high-quality private facility; some specialties; ICU and emergency services. Hospital Universitario de Caracas (1,200 beds); most specialties; emergency services.

Health Advisory

Yellow fever: Vaccination is recommended for all travelers who visit rural areas. In October 1998, Venezuela reported an outbreak of yellow fever among the Yanomani Indians in the Parima region within Alto Orinoco County in the State of Amazonas. In 1999, an American tourist traveled to the rainforests of southern Venezuela (Amazonas State) and died from yellow fever shortly after returning to the United States. Although a vaccination certificate is not required to enter this country, one may be required for on-going travel to other countries in Latin America, Africa, the Middle East, and Asia.

Cholera: This disease is active in this country. Although cholera vaccination is not required for entry if arriving directly from the U.S. or Canada, it may be required if arriving from a cholera-infected area, or required for on-going travel to other countries in Latin America, Africa, the Middle East, or Asia. The risk to travelers of acquiring cholera is considered to be low. Prevention consists primarily in adhering to safe food and drink guidelines.

Malaria: Risk is present year-round in most rural areas below 600 meters elevation. Risk of malaria is highest in the western, southern, and eastern border areas. Risk is highest in Bolivar and Sucre States. Most north-central areas, including the Federal District and the states of Aragua, Carabobo, Cojedes, Miranda, and Yaracuy, are risk-free. This includes the major cities and resort areas of northern Venezuela. Elevated risk in most malarious areas occurs with the early months of the rainy season (which usually extends from late May through November); however, in the Orinoco Basin, the period of elevated risk may begin with the onset of the dry season. Nationwide, *P. vivax* accounts for about 75% of all cases, varying from 40% in Bolivar State to 99% in Sucre State. A few cases caused by *P. malariae* occur. Chloroquine-resistant falciparum malaria probably occurs in most malarious areas. Mefloquine or doxycycline prophylaxis is currently recommended for travel to malarious areas.

World Medical Guide

Travelers' diarrhea: High risk outside of Merida, Caracas, Maracaibo, and resort areas. A quinolone antibiotic is recommended for the treatment of acute diarrhea. Diarrhea not responding to antibiotic treatment may be due to amebiasis, giardiasis, or cryptosporidiosis. Infection rates of 18% for giardiasis, and 11% for cryptosporidiosis, are reported.

Hepatitis: All nonimmune travelers should receive hepatitis A vaccine prior to visiting this country. Hepatitis E is endemic, but levels are unclear. The carrier rate of the hepatitis B virus in the general population is estimated at 2% to 3%, but rates as high as 31% have been found in some aboriginal populations (e.g., the Yucpa Indians in Zulia State). Vaccination against hepatitis B is recommended for anyone planning an extended visit to this country. Hepatitis C is endemic.

Dengue fever: Year-round risk in coastal and lowland urban areas. Outbreaks of dengue occur regularly in central and northern Venezuela, including Caracas. The *Aedes aegypti* mosquitoes, which transmit dengue fever, bite primarily during the daytime and are present in populous urban areas as well as resort and rural areas. All travelers should take protective measures against mosquito bites.

Venezuelan equine encephalitis: Mosquito-borne; highest risk located in northwestern areas, primarily Zulia State. All travelers should take protective measures against mosquito bites to prevent transmission of this viral disease.

Leishmaniasis: Cutaneous leishmaniasis (CL) is widespread in rural areas under 2,000 meters elevation, especially in rural west-central areas. Transmission of CL has been reported at elevations as high as 2,500 meters in the Andes. Except for a focus in northern Bolivar State, visceral leishmaniasis is primarily limited to northwestern and northern areas under 500 meters elevation. All travelers to risk areas should take measures to prevent insect (sandfly) bites, whixh occur primarily during the night.

Onchocerciasis: Risk occurs along fast-flowing rivers at elevations up to 1,000 meters in the northcentral, northeast, and southern regions. Up to 90% of the population is infected in some southern regions. Travelers to these areas should take measures to prevent insect (blackfly) bites.

Filariasis: Limited risk of mosquito-transmitted Bancroftian filariasis in coastal areas. Mansonellosis, another type of filariasis, transmitted by blackflies, is endemic in Amazonas Federal Territory. Travelers to these regions should take measures to prevent insect bites.

Schistosomiasis: Risk is present year-round. Risk areas are limited to north-central Venezuela, including the Federal District (but not Caracas) and the surrounding states of Aragua, Carabobo, Guarico, and Miranda. Travelers should avoid swimming in freshwater lakes, ponds, or streams. Risk may be elevated in periurban areas.

Chagas' disease: This disease is endemic to rural areas in the northern one-half of Venezuela. An extensive outbreak occurred in Guarico State in 1986. In some areas up to 50% of the population has been exposed. Chagas' disease is among the top 10 causes of death in Venezuelans over age 45. Risk occurs in those rural-agricultural areas where there are adobe-style huts and houses that potentially harbor the night-biting triatomid (assassin) bugs. Travelers sleeping in such structures should take precautions against nighttime bites. Unscreened blood transfusions are also a source of infection and should be avoided.

Meningitis: From January to March 1994, 22 cases and six deaths due to invasive Type C meningococcal disease were reported from Caracas. None of the cases occurred in relation to tourist areas, and there are no special recommendations for meningococcal polysaccharide vaccine (A/C/Y/W-135) at this time.

Rabies: Relatively low risk. Travelers should especially avoid stray dogs and seek immediate treatment of any animal bite. Rabies vaccination is indicated following the unprovoked bite of a dog, cat, vampire bat, or monkey. Bites by other animals should be evaluated on an individual basis. Pre-exposure vaccination against rabies is recommended for long-term travelers to this country and for travelers going to remote rural areas.

Other diseases/hazards: AIDS/HIV (endemic; seroprevalence increasing rapidly among women), angiostrongyliasis, brucellosis, echinococcosis, fascioliasis, leptospirosis, mansonellosis, paragonimiasis, tuberculosis, typhoid fever, Venezuelan hemorrhagic fever, and helminthic diseases (due to hookworm, roundworm, whipworm, and strongyloides) are reported. Animal hazards include snakes (vipers), centipedes, scorpions, black widow spiders, brown recluse spiders, banana spiders, and wolf spiders. Portuguese man-of-war, sea wasps, and stingrays are found in the coastal waters of Venezuela and could be a hazard to swimmers.

World Medical Guide

VIETNAM

Embassy: 202-861-0737　　　　Hanoi　　　　GMT +7 hrs

Entry Requirements
- Passport/Visa: Passport and visa are required.
- HIV Test: Not required.
- Vaccinations: A yellow fever vaccination certificate is required of all travelers older than 1 year arriving from infected areas.

Telephone Country Code: 84
Embassies/Consulates: U.S. Embassy, Hanoi: 7 Lang Ha, Dong Da District. Tel. (4) 431-500.
Doctors/Hospitals: Bach Mai Hospital, Hanoi (1,200 beds); general medical facility. Ho Chi Minh City Hospital (Saigon). Cho Ray Hospital. Czech Friendship Hospital, Haiphong.

Health Advisory

Cholera: This disease is active in this country.
Malaria: Countrywide risk below 1,400 meters elevation. Attack rates are highest in the rural mountainous areas, followed by the central plains and the lowland deltas, respectively. Elevated risk occurs during the warmer rainy months, May through October. The risk of malaria in urban areas is low. *P. falciparum* causes 70%–75% of cases countrywide, but *P. vivax* may cause 75% of cases in some coastal areas. *P. malariae* causes 5%, or less, of cases. Multidrug-resistant falciparum malaria is reported. Mefloquine or doxycycline prophylaxis advised for travelers visiting malarious areas.
Travelers' diarrhea: Urban and rural water pollution is widespread. All water supplies should be considered potentially contaminated. Travelers should observe food and drink safety precautions. A quinolone antibiotic is recommended for the treatment of diarrhea. Diarrhea not responding to treatment with an antibiotic, or chronic diarrhea, may be due to a parasitic disease such as giardiasis, amebiasis, or cryptosporidiosis.
Hepatitis: All nonimmune travelers should receive hepatitis A vaccine prior to visiting this country. The overall hepatitis B carrier rate in the general population is estimated to exceed 12%. Outbreaks of Hepatitis E have been reported. Hepatitis C is endemic
Dengue fever: Occurs year-round, with peak transmission in the warmer rainy season, April–October in the north and June–December in the south. Elevated risk occurs throughout the Red River Delta and Mekong Delta, and the coastal district and provincial capitals of central Vietnam. Incidence is low in remote, mountainous regions. All travelers are advised to take precautions against mosquito bites.
Japanese encephalitis: Risk is present in rural and periurban lowland areas countrywide. Peak transmission in the subtropical north occurs during the monsoon season, June–July. In the tropical south, disease risk is year-round but peak levels occur June–July. Travelers to rural areas (especially where there is pig rearing and rice farming) should consider vaccination.
Schistosomiasis: Endemic status unclear. Risk may occur along the Mekong Delta. Travelers should avoid swimming or wading in freshwater lakes, ponds, streams, or irrigation ditches.
Other illnesses/hazards: AIDS/HIV (endemic at low, but increasing, levels), anthrax, angiostrongyliasis (from eating raw snails, slugs, or vegetables), helminthic infections (ascariasis, hookworm disease, strongyloidiasis), other helminthic infections (clonorchiasis, fasciolopsiasis, and paragonimiasis), filariasis (Bancroftian filariasis endemic throughout southern Vietnam; Malayan filariasis is endemic in the Red River Delta in northern Vietnam), leptospirosis, leprosy (moderately high levels), melioidosis (endemic countrywide), meningitis (endemic), plague (339 cases reported in 1994, mostly from the central highlands, but may occur countrywide), rabies (transmitted by feral dogs; highly enzootic in rural and urban areas), typhus (louse-borne and flea-borne), scrub typhus (mite-borne; risk elevated in mountainous, wooded southeastern areas), tuberculosis (highly endemic), typhoid fever, and trachoma (widespread). Animal hazards include snakes (vipers, cobras, kraits), scorpions, and black widow spiders. Other hazards include crocodiles, pythons, and large, aggressive lizards, poisonous frogs and toads, all abundant in and near swamps and rivers; tigers, leopards, bears, and wild pigs are found in the forested and hilly regions of the country. Stingrays, jellyfish, and several species of poisonous fish are common in the country's coastal waters and are potentially hazardous to swimmers.

World Medical Guide

WALLIS & FUTUNA (FRANCE)

GMT +12 hrs

Entry Requirements
- HIV Test: Not required.
- Vaccinations: None required.

Hospitals/Doctors
Wallis Hospital (85 beds); general medical facility; pharmacy, x-ray, laboratory.

Health Advisory

Malaria: No risk.
Hepatitis: All nonimmune travelers should receive hepatitis A vaccine. The hepatitis B carrier rate in the general population exceeds 10 percent. Vaccination against hepatitis B is recommended for all healthcare workers and long-term visitors to this country.
Travelers' diarrhea: Medium risk. Water supplies should be considered potentially contaminated, and travelers are advised to drink only bottled, boiled, or treated water, unless assured that the local water is safe. Standard safe food precautions should also be observed.
Typhoid fever: Risk is low, but long-term travelers should consider vaccination. All travelers should observe safe food and water guidelines.
Insect-borne diseases: Filariasis, Japanese encephalitis, Ross River fever, and dengue are potential risks. All travelers should take personal protective measures against mosquito and insect bites. Long-term visitors should consider vaccination against Japanese encephalitis.

YEMEN (REPUBLIC OF YEMEN)

Embassy: 202-965-4760   *Sanaa*   *GMT +3 hrs*

Entry Requirements
- A 30-day visa is available. Visitor's visa requires letter of invitation.
- HIV Test: Not required.
- Vaccinations: A yellow fever vaccination certificate is recommended and is required of all travelers arriving from infected areas. A cholera certificate is recommended.

Telephone Country Code: 967
Embassies/Consulates: U.S. Embassy, Sanaa; Dhahr Himyar Zone, Sheraton Hotel District. Tel. (1) 238-843 through 852.
Hospitals/Doctors: Caution—Travelers should use hospitals for emergency situations only; care is well below Western standards.

Health Advisory

Malaria: Transmission occurs year-round, with risk elevated October through March in endemic areas up to 2,000 meters elevation. Risk areas include rural and urban locales in foothill and coastal areas, including Socotra. Elevated risk occurs in irrigated agricultural areas and near wadis. Aden City (although cases are occasionally reported from suburban areas), high mountain areas, and northern and eastern desert regions, including Sanaa, are risk-free. Mefloquine or doxycycline prophylaxis is recommended for travel to malarious areas.
Travelers' diarrhea: High risk. Well water usually is contaminated. Piped water supplies are potentially contaminated. Bottled water or carbonated soft drinks are available and generally safe. Travelers should observe food and drink safety precautions. A quinolone antibiotic is recommended for the treatment of acute diarrhea. Giardiasis and amebiasis are reported.
Hepatitis: Hepatitis A vaccine is recommended for all nonimmune travelers. Hepatitis E has not been reported but likely occurs. The hepatitis B carrier rate in the general population is estimated at 10%–15%. Vaccination against hepatitis B is recommended for long-term visitors to this country.
Leishmaniasis: Cutaneous leishmaniasis commonly occurs in semirural villages of the Asir mountains. Visceral leishmaniasis occurs sporadically in rural areas, usually in the foothill region or the Asir mountains, at elevations between 400 and 1,500 meters. Travelers to these areas should take measures to prevent insect (sandfly) bites.

483

World Medical Guide

Onchocerciasis: Blackfly-borne. Probably occurs throughout the length of Yemen, in wadis flowing into the Gulf of Aden and the Red Sea; known to be endemic in all westward-flowing permanent streams (wadis) between the northern Wadi Surdud (Al Hudaydah Province) and the southern Wadi Ghayl (Taiz Province) at elevations of 300 to 1,200 meters; cases have been reported from Al Hudafdah to Taiz, mostly in Al Barh between Mokha and Taiz. All travelers to these regions should take measures to prevent insect (blackfly) bites.

Schistosomiasis: High potential risk. Transmission occurs year-round. Focally distributed (commonly associated with wadis, oases, aqueducts, cisterns, and irrigation canals) in urban and rural locales, particularly in foothill and highland areas; only Marib and Al Bayda are risk-free. Primary recognized risk areas occur in Ibb, Taiz, and Sanaa Provinces.

Rabies: High potential risk due to large population of stray dogs. Human cases are reported frequently. Rabies vaccination is indicated following the unprovoked bite of a dog, cat, jackal, or fox.

Other illnesses: Filariasis (mosquito-borne; sporadically reported), brucellosis (human cases usually related to exposure to unpasteurized dairy products, especially raw goat/sheep milk or milk products), cholera, dengue fever (low-level transmission may occur in coastal regions), dracunculiasis (endemic in Al Hudaydah Province, with cases reported from Sadah Province), echinococcosis (reported sporadically in humans), plague (flea-borne; last outbreak in 1969 Sadah Province; cases were also reported in the 1980s), flea-borne typhus, louse-borne typhus, louse- and flea-borne relapsing fever, trachoma, tuberculosis, and helminthic infections (roundworm, hookworm, and whipworm—common in rural areas).

YUGOSLAVIA

Embassy: 202-462-6566   *Belgrade*   *GMT +1 hr*

Entry Requirements
- Passport/Visa: A valid passport and visa are required. Travelers should contact the Yugoslavian Embassy in Washington (202-462-3884) for details.
- HIV Test: Not required.
- Vaccinations: None required.

Telephone Country Code: 38

Embassies/Consulates: U.S. Embassy, Belgrade. Kneza Milosa 50; Tel. (11) 645-655.

Hospitals/Doctors: Univerzitetski Klinicki Centar, Belgrade; Tel: 444-2222. University Hospital, Belgrade; ICU has latest equipment. Teaching Hospital, Zagreb; Tel. 276-693. Contact the U.S. Embassy for additional referrals and telephone numbers.

Health Advisory

Malaria: No risk. Yugoslavia was declared malaria free in 1974.

Travelers' diarrhea: High risk. Drinking water in Belgrade is considered safe, but water elsewhere should be considered contaminated, especially in smaller urban areas, and rural areas. A quinolone antibiotic is recommended for the treatment of acute diarrhea. Diarrhea not responding to treatment with an antibiotic, or chronic diarrhea, may be due to a parasitic disease such as giardiasis, amebiasis, or cryptosporidiosis.

Hepatitis: Hepatitis A vaccine is recommended for all nonimmune travelers. The hepatitis B carrier rate in the general population is estimated at up to 4%. Vaccination against hepatitis B is recommended for healthcare and relief workers and should be considered by long-term visitors to this country.

Tick-borne diseases: Tick-borne viral encephalitis (TBE) occurs primarily in two forested areas: (1) in northern areas between the Sava and Drava Rivers (especially in Slovenia, in the Ljubljana area) and in northwest Croatia, north of Zagreb; and (2) in smaller pockets along the Adriatic coast, near Split and north of Dubrovnik. The tick vector that transmits TBE (*Ixodes ricinus*) also transmits Lyme disease. Ticks are abundant from March to September, with peak activity occurring in April and May. All travelers should take measures to prevent tick bites in these areas.

World Medical Guide

Leishmaniasis: Both cutaneous and visceral leishmaniasis are reported, but risk is low. Transmission of leishmaniasis occurs primarily May through October with the highest prevalence of cutaneous leishmaniasis on the islands and along the Dalmatian coast. Visceral leishmaniasis occurs more focally, especially in southeastern Serbia and also along the Dalmation coast. Travelers to these areas should take measures to prevent sandfly bites.

Sandfly fever: Risk period is primarily May through October along the Adriatic coast from Istria to Dubrovnik and from Mali Losinj to Korcula on the islands. Travelers to these areas should avoid sandfly bites. West Nile, Sindbis, and Tahnya virus fevers (mosquito-borne; reported in the border regions of Slovenia and Serbia).

Hemorrhagic fever with renal syndrome (HFRS): During the last seven years, more than 35 severe cases of HFRS have been identified in Slovenia. Transmission of the virus results from inhalation or contact with virus excreted or secreted in rodent urine, saliva, or feces. Exposure to virus can occur, e.g., when cleaning out a rodent-infested dwelling.

Rabies: Animal rabies occurs mostly in foxes, sporadically in dogs and cats; human cases occur, but are rare.

Other illnesses: Boutonneuse fever (infrequently reported), brucellosis (usually transmitted by raw goat/sheep milk), Crimean-Congo hemorrhagic fever (occurs especially in areas where ticks are found), echinococcosis (carried by stray dogs; reported sporadically, especially in southwestern areas—Montenegro, Dalmatia, Serbia), leptospirosis, relapsing fever (tick-borne), trichinosis, tuberculosis, tularemia (human cases are uncommon), typhoid fever (consider vaccination), typhus (louse-borne), and soil-transmitted helminthic infections (roundworm, hookworm, and whipworm) are common in rural areas.

DEMOCRATIC REPUBLIC OF CONGO (ZAIRE)

Embassy: 202-234-7690   *Kinshasa*   GMT +2 hrs

Entry Requirements
- A visa is required. Travelers should contact the Embassy of the Democrtaic Republic of Congo for further information.
- HIV Test: Not required.
- Vaccinations: A yellow fever vaccination certificate is required from all travelers older than 1 year of age arriving from ALL COUNTRIES.

Telephone Country Code: 243
Embassies/Consulates: U.S. Embassy, Kinshasa. 310 Avenue des Aviateures; Tel. (12) 21532 or 21628. U.S. Consular Section; Tel. (12) 21532. The Embassy's cellular telephone number is (88) 43608. Cellular telephone access may be more reliable.
Hospitals/Doctors: Centre Medico-Chirurgical, Kinshasa. Mama Yemo Hospital (2,000 beds); general medical/surgical facility; some specialties.

Health Advisory

Yellow fever: This disease is considered active in this country, north of 10° south latitude. Yellow fever vaccination is required and is also recommended for all travelers. This country is in the Yellow Fever Endemic Zone.

Cholera: This disease is active in this country. Although cholera vaccination is not officially required for entry, it may be unofficially required, or required for on-going travel to other countries in Africa, the Middle East, or Asia. Travelers should consider vaccination (one dose) or getting a doctor's letter of exemption from vaccination. The risk to travelers of acquiring cholera is considered low. Prevention consists primarily in adhering to safe food and drink guidelines.

Malaria: Risk is present year-round countrywide under 1,800 meters elevation, including urban areas. Falciparum malaria accounts for approximately 95% of cases. *P. malariae* species is the next most common cause of malaria. Other cases of malaria are due to the *P. ovale* and, rarely, the *P. vivax* species. Chloroquine-resistant falciparum malaria is reported. Prophylaxis with mefloquine or doxycycline is recommended when traveling to malarious areas.

485

World Medical Guide

Travelers' diarrhea: High risk. In urban areas, about 50% of the population has access to potable water. Piped water supplies may be contaminated. Travelers should observe all food and drink safety precautions. A quinolone antibiotic is recommended for the treatment of acute diarrhea. Diarrhea not responding to treatment with an antibiotic, or chronic diarrhea, may be due to a parasitic disease such as giardiasis, amebiasis, or cryptosporidiosis.

Hepatitis: High risk. All nonimmune travelers should receive hepatitis A vaccine. Hepatitis E has not been reported but presumably occurs. The hepatitis B carrier rate in the general population is estimated at 15%. Vaccination against hepatitis B is recommended for long-term visitors to this country.

Leishmaniasis: Risk undetermined, but probably low. Sporadic cases of visceral leishmaniasis have been diagnosed in the northwest, on the fringe of the equatorial forest, and in the southeast, in the savanna belt. No cases of cutaneous leishmaniasis have recently been reported. Travelers should take personal protection measures against insect (sandfly) bites.

Onchocerciasis: Widespread risk, especially along fast-flowing rivers in the regions of Haut-Zaire, Kasai-Oriental, Kasai-Occidental, central and southern Equator, the forest zone of Maniema in Kivu, and western Bas-Zaire. Travelers to these regions should take measures to prevent insect (blackfly) bites.

Schistosomiasis: High risk. Intestinal schistosomiasis occurs primarily in four geographical regions: the northern border along the Kibali-Uele Rivers and tributaries; the eastern border from Lake Mobuto to Lake Tanganyika; the Lualaba basin of Shaba region; and the area between Kinshasa and the Atlantic coast. High-risk area of urinary schistosomiasis occurs in the extreme southeast tip of Democrtaic Republic of Congo. Travelers to these areas should avoid swimming, bathing, or wading in freshwater lakes or ponds.

Trypanosomiasis (sleeping sickness): Risk has surged during the 1990s due to decreased tsetse fly control programs associated with civil unrest. Areas of disease risk (gambiense disease) include the western border region, the extreme northeast, and the southwest (including Bas Zaire Region), extending in a band across southcentral areas of this country. High transmission levels exist along the Congo River and the Bandundu and Equateur regions. Foci of the Rhodesian form of sleeping sickness may occur in eastern Democrtaic Republic of Congo. Travelers should take measures to prevent insect (tsetse fly) bites.

Ebola virus hemorrhagic fever: An outbreak of this disease is reported in Kikwit (approximately 250 miles southeast of Kinshasa) and the surrounding areas within Bandundu Province. The disease is transmitted primarily by contaminated injections and close personal contact with severely ill patients. Transmission usually occurs by direct contact with infected blood, secretions, organs, or semen. Persons in the incubation period are not considered to be significant risks. Although the risk of acquiring Ebola virus hemorrhagic fever infection is very low under normal circumstances, tourist travel to the above mentioned areas should currently be avoided.

Plague: Widespread enzootic foci presumably occur in rural and urban areas, particularly in northeastern areas. In Iruti Subregion and the Haut-Zaire Region, increased incidence reported during 1991–1992. Travelers should avoid close contact with rodents. Tetracycline or doxycycline are effective prophylactic antibiotics.

Rabies: Urban rabies, transmitted primarily by stray dogs, reported from Kinshasa and Lisala, and elsewhere. Vaccination is recommended for long-term travel (more than 4 weeks) to this country, especially for travelers going to remote rural areas.

AIDS: Heterosexual contact is the predominate mode of transmission. HIV-1 prevalence estimated at 38% of the high-risk urban population. All travelers are cautioned against unsafe sex, unsterile medical or dental injections, and unnecessary blood transfusions.

Other illnesses/hazards: African tick typhus (risk elevated in eastern areas), brucellosis (from consumption of raw dairy products), chikungunya fever, Crimean-Congo hemorrhagic fever (tick-borne; sporadic cases occur), dengue (not recently reported), echinococcosis, filariasis (mosquito-borne), loiasis (deer fly–borne), Lyme disease, meningitis, toxoplasmosis, syphilis, tuberculosis (a major health problem), trachoma, typhoid fever, yellow fever (no recent cases), and intestinal helminths (very common). Animal hazards include snakes (vipers, cobras), centipedes, scorpions, and black widow spiders.

World Medical Guide

ZAMBIA

Embassy: 202-265-9717　　*Lusaka*　　*GMT +2 hrs*

Entry Requirements
- A Visa is required.
- HIV Test: Not required.
- Vaccinations: No vaccinations are required.

Telephone Country Code: 260
Embassies/Consulates: U.S. Embassy, Lusaka. Corner of Independence & United Nations Avenues; Tel. (1) 250-955.
Hospitals/Doctors: University Teaching Hospital, Lusaka (1,500 beds).

Health Advisory

Yellow fever: Risk may be present in northwestern forest areas. Vaccination is recommended for travel outside urban areas. This country is in the Yellow Fever Endemic Zone. A valid vaccination certificate may be required for on-going travel to other countries.

Cholera: This disease has been reported active. Although cholera vaccination is not required for entry if arriving directly from the U.S. or Canada, it may be required for on-going travel to other countries in Africa, the Middle East, or Asia. Travelers should consider vaccination (one dose) or getting a doctor's letter of exemption from vaccination. The risk to travelers of acquiring cholera is considered low. Prevention consists primarily in adhering to safe food and drink guidelines.

Malaria: Risk is present year-round in the Zambezi Valley, including urban areas, but seasonal in the rest of the country, primarily from November through June (during and just after the rainy season). Incidence has been increasing in Copperbelt Province and Southern Province. Falciparum malaria accounts for approximately 90% of cases. Other cases of malaria are due to the *P. ovale* and *P. malariae* species, and sometimes *P. vivax*. Chloroquine-resistant falciparum malaria is reported. Prophylaxis with mefloquine or doxycycline is currently recommended when traveling to malarious areas.

Travelers' diarrhea: Public water supplies are filtered and chlorinated. In Lusaka and Kabwe, water is obtained from deep bore holes and is treated. Water in these cities is considered potable. All other water sources in the country should be considered potentially contaminated. Travelers should observe all food and drink safety precautions. A quinolone antibiotic (Cipro or Floxin) is recommended for the treatment of acute diarrhea. Diarrhea not responding to treatment with an antibiotic, or chronic diarrhea, may be due to a parasitic disease such as giardiasis or amebiasis, and treatment with metronidazole (Flagyl) or tinidazole (Fasigyn) should be considered. All cases of diarrhea should be treated with adequate fluid replacement.

Hepatitis: High risk. All nonimmune travelers should receive hepatitis A vaccination. Hepatitis E presumably occurs, based on regional data. The hepatitis B carrier rate in the general population is estimated at 13%–14%. Vaccination against hepatitis B is recommended for healthcare workers and all long-term visitors to this country.

Leishmaniasis: Low, but undetermined, risk. Cases of visceral leishmaniasis probably occur, but rarely. Travelers should take measures to prevent insect (sandfly) bites.

Onchocerciasis: Cases are reported near Choma in the Southern Province, perhaps the southernmost limit of transmission of this disease in Africa. Travelers should take precautions against insect (blackfly) bites.

Filariasis (Bancroftian): Risk may occur in northern areas. Travelers should take precautions against mosquito bites.

Schistosomiasis: Urinary schistosomiasis is endemic in all provinces. Intestinal schistosomiasis is less widely distributed, with major foci in Northern Province, Luapula Province (including Lake Mweru vicinity), Lusaka vicinity, and Southern Province (including the shores of Lake Kariba). All travelers should avoid swimming, bathing, or wading in freshwater lakes, ponds, or streams.

Dengue and other arboviral fevers: Dengue has not been reported recently from this region. Outbreaks of chikungunya fever have been reported from Zambia.

World Medical Guide

Trypanosomiasis (African sleeping sickness): Risk persists in the northern areas, particularly in the Luangwa Valley and Kafue National Park. One-third of rural areas countrywide are infested with tsetse flies. Travelers should take personal protection measures against insect (tsetse fly) bites.
Rabies: Dogs are the primary source of human exposure. Outbreaks in cattle have been reported, primarily in the rural areas of Southern Province. Travelers should seek immediate treatment of any animal bite. Rabies vaccination should be considered by long-term travelers to this region. This is especially true for travelers going to remote rural areas.
Plague: Ninety cases of bubonic plague were reported in 1996 in Namwala District. No cases of the pulmonary form of the disease were reported, and there are no restrictions for travelers visiting this country.
AIDS: Heterosexual transmission is the predominate means of transmission. HIV-1 prevalence estimated at 54% of the high-risk urban population. All travelers are cautioned against unsafe sex, unsterile medical or dental injections, and unnecessary blood transfusions.
Other illnesses/hazards: African tick typhus (contracted from dog ticks, often in urban areas, and bush ticks), brucellosis, chikungunya fever, leprosy (1.5 cases/1,000 population; incidence is decreasing), relapsing fever (tick-borne), toxoplasmosis, syphilis, tuberculosis (a major health problem), typhoid fever, and intestinal worms (very common). Animal hazards include snakes (vipers, cobras), centipedes, scorpions, and black widow spiders.

ZIMBABWE

Embassy: 202-332-7100   *Harare*   *GMT +2 hrs*

Entry Requirements
- Travelers should contact the Embassy of Zimbabwe for entry requirements.
- HIV Test: Not required.
- Vaccinations: A yellow fever vaccination certificate is required from all travelers older than 1 year arriving from an infected area.

Telephone Country Code: 263
Embassies/Consulates: U.S. Embassy, Harare. 172 Herbert Chitepo Avenue; Tel. (4) 794-521.
Hospitals/Doctors: Parirenyatwa Hospital, Harare (900 beds); emergency services; intensive care and burn units. Mpilo Central Hospital. Bulawayo (600 beds); general medical facility. The Avenues Clinic, Harare.

Health Advisory

Cholera: This disease is active in this country. Although cholera vaccination is not required for entry if arriving directly from the U.S. or Canada, it may be required if arriving from a cholera-infected area, or required for on-going travel to other countries in Africa, the Middle East, Asia, or Latin America. Travelers to this country should consider vaccination or a doctor's letter of exemption from vaccination.
Malaria: Year-round transmission occurs in the low-lying areas of the Zambezi Valley in the north (border area with Zambia) and the Sabi-Limpopo system in the south, but transmission is seasonal in the rest of the country below 1,200 meters elevation, occurring primarily from November through June (during and just after the warm wet months of November and March). The central plateau (stretching from the southwest to the northeast, with elevations from 1,200 to 1,500 meters, including Harare City) is essentially risk free. Malaria is especially endemic in the Zambezi Valley. Epidemics have occurred in the Matabeleland North and northern Midlands Provinces. Falciparum malaria accounts for approximately 98% of cases countrywide. Other cases of malaria are usually due to the *P. malariae*. Chloroquine-resistant falciparum malaria is reported. Prophylaxis with mefloquine or doxycycline is currently recommended when traveling to malarious areas. Malaria prophylaxis is especially recommended for travel to Victoria Falls.
Travelers' diarrhea: Water in major urban systems is chlorinated and checked for potability. In Harare, water is chemically treated with flocculents and clarifiers and is sand-filtered. Out-

World Medical Guide

side major urban areas, travelers should observe all food and drink safety precautions. A quinolone antibiotic is recommended for the treatment of acute diarrhea. Diarrhea not responding to treatment with an antibiotic, or chronic diarrhea, may be due to a parasitic disease such as giardiasis or amebiasis.

Hepatitis: Hepatitis A is highly endemic. Vaccination is ercommended for all nonimmune travelers. Hepatitis E is endemic, but levels are unclear. The hepatitis B carrier rate in the general population is estimated at 8%–10%. Vaccination against hepatitis B is recommended for all long-term visitors to this country. Hepatitis c is endemic.

Chikungunya fever, West Nile fever, Rift Valley fever: Explosive outbreaks of chikungunya fever have occurred in urban areas, but most cases are in rural regions. West Nile and Sinbis fevers are endemic in neighboring South Africa. Dengue fever is not reported. All travelers should take measures to prevent insect bites.

Schistosomiasis: Peak transmission of urinary schistosomiasis occurs in the northeast during the hot, dry season (September–October). Transmission is year-round in the Zambezi Valley, the shores of Lake Kariba and the southeast lowveld. Intestinal schistosomiasis occurs primarily in the north and east. Travelers are advised to avoid swimming or wading in freshwater lakes, ponds, or streams.

Meningitis: Low risk. Zimbabwe is south of the sub-Saharan meningitis belt. Long-term visitors who expect to have close contact with the indigenous population should, however, consider vaccination.

Trypanosomiasis (African sleeping sickness): Risk areas presumably exist in the northern Zambezi River drainage area, including the Lake Kariba vicinity. Outbreaks along the border with Mozambique were reported in the 1980s. Travelers should take measures to prevent insect (tsetse fly) bites.

Plague: Sporadic cases have occurred in the northwest, and north of Harare. Vaccination against plague is recommended only for persons who may be occupationally exposed to wild rodents (e.g., anthropologists, archaeologists, medical personnel, and missionaries).

Rabies: Sporadic human cases are reported, with dogs and jackals as the primary source of exposure. Most cases occur in Matabeleland North and South Provinces, which have been declared "rabies areas." Rabies vaccination is recommended for persons planning an extended stay (more than 4 weeks).

Other illnesses/hazards: African tick typhus (contracted from dog ticks—often in urban areas—and bush ticks), brucellosis (from consumption of raw dairy products), Crimean-Congo hemorrhagic fever (tick-borne), leishmaniasis (low risk), leptospirosis, tuberculosis (a major health problem), typhoid fever, and intestinal worms (very common). Animal hazards include snakes (vipers, cobras), centipedes, scorpions, and black widow spiders.

Index

A

AARP Medigap insurance, for travel 227
Access America International, insurance 232
Accidental death and disability insurance 230
Acetazolamide (Diamox) 209
  for hypercapnic, hypoxemic travelers 22
Acupressure bands, for sea sickness 60
Acute mountain sickness (AMS) 205
AEAInternational /SOS, travel insurance 231
Afghanistan 303
Afrin (oxymetazoline) for air travel 63
AIDS 197
Air ambulance companies, State Dept. listing 235
Air Ambulance International 235
Air ambulance transport 234
Air Security International 6
Airport magnetometers, safety with implanted defib 22
Albania 304
Albendazole 166
  for ascariasis 164
  for capillariasis 164
  for cysticercosis 166
  for strongyloidiasis 165
Algeria 304
Altitude sickness
  in children 214, 277
  in South America 341, 352, 431
Ambien (zolpidem tartrate), for jet lag 56
Amblyomma americanum 146–147, 148
Amebiasis 152
Amebic dysentery 153
American Citizens Services 6
American Express Platinum Card, for medical assist 221

American Express, travel insurance 232
American Hospital in Paris 223
American Society of Tropical Medicine & Hygiene 8
  Web site 9
Amoxicillin, for Lyme disease 176
Amphotericin B, for leishmaniasis 140
AMS treatment options 213
Ancylostomiasis 164
Angola 306
Anisakiasis 165
Antibiotics
  for treating travelers' diarrhea 84
  during pregnancy 264
  in children 272
Antigua & Barbuda 307
Antimalarial drugs
  use during pregnancy 257
Antivert (meclizine) 61
Argentina 308
Armenia 308
Armenia, health advisory 436
Artemether 114
Artemisinin 113
Artesunate 114
Aruba 309
Ascariasis 164
Assist Travel Assistance, insurance 232
Assistance for Canadians Overseas 12
AT&T Language Line 20
Atovaquone/proguanil (Malarone) 107
  during pregnancy 257
  for treatment 258
  for children 275
Australia 310
Austria 311
AVAXIM (Aventis) 36
Azerbaijan 312
Azithromycin
  for cholera 155
  for sexually transmitted diseases 204
  for shigellosis 158
  for travelers' diarrhea 85
  during pregnancy 259, 264
  in children 273
  for typhoid fever 156
Azores 312

Index **491**

B

Babesiosis 147, 148
Bacillary dysentery (shigellosis) 158
Bahamas 312
Bahrain 313
Balkan States 345
Baltic States 398, 436
Bangladesh 313
Barbados 314
Bartonellosis (Oroya fever) 341
BayRab, rabies immune globulin 170
BCG vaccine 43
Beef tapeworm disease 165
Belarus 315
Belgium 315
Belize 315
Benin 316
Benznidazole (Ragonil®, Roche) 136
Bhutan 317
Bilharzia 160
Boiling water, for purification 74
Bolivia 318
Bonaire 320
Bosnia & Herzegovina 320
Botswana 320
BRAT diet, for treating dehydration 90
Brazil 321
British Virgin Islands 323
Brown dog tick 148
Brucellosis 166
Brunei Darussalam 324
Bulgaria 324
Bureau of Consular Affairs 7, 19
Burkina Faso 325
Burma 327
Burundi 328
Business travel 239
Byelarus 436

C

Cabin air, in airliners 63
Caffeine, and dehydration 59
Calabar swelling 138
Cambodia 329
Cameroon 330
Canada 332
Capillariasis 164, 300

Care Flight-Air Critical Care 235
Caribbean, Disease Risk Summary 284
CDC Hepatitis Branch 186
CDC Travelers' Health Information 9
Cefixime, for travelers' diarrhea 15
    during pregnancy 265
    use in children 274
cefotaxime (Claforan), for
    meningitis 159
Ceftin (cefuroxime)
    for Lyme disease 176
Ceftriaxone
    for Lyme disease 176
    for meningitis 159
    for PID and gonorrhea 204
    for typhoid fever 156
Centers for Disease Control
    Parasitic Disease Branch
        telephone numbers for
        advice 140
    Travelers' Health Information 9
Central African Republic 333
CeraLyte, for rehydration 89
Chad 334
Chagas' disease 135
Chancroid 203
Chickenpox vaccine 32, 47
Childhood immunization schedule 53
Children and travel 267
Chile 336
China 337
Chlorine, to purify water 75
Chloroquine-resistant P. vivax 103
Cholera 154
Cholera vaccine 33
Christmas Island (Australia) 343
Chronic diarrhea, causes of 78
Chrysops biting fly 138
Ciguatera poisoning 171
Ciprofloxacin
    eye drops, to treat corneal ulcers 16
    for travelers' diarrhea 84, 273
Clonorchiasis 162, 300
Clostridium difficile 153
Co-artmether (Riamet) 114
Colombia 340
Colorado tick fever 147
Combivax-HB vaccine 183

Commercial airliners, and medical transport 233
Comoros Islands 342
Congo 342
Contact lenses, and corneal ulcers 16
and ciprofloxacin eye drops 25
Cook Islands (New Zealand) 344
Coronary artery bypass surgery
and trekking 217
travel after 21
Costa Rica 344
Croatia 345
Cryptosporidiosis 67, 78
Cuba 346
Culturgrams 10
Cyclospora, and chronic diarrhea 152
Cyclospora cayetanensis 78
Cyprus 347
Cysticercosis 165
Czechoslovakia 347

D

Decompression chambers, worldwide listing 11
Deep vein thrombosis 64
(traveler's thrombosis)
prevention with low molecular weight heparin 65
DEET repellents 118
to prevent schistosomiasis 162
DEET toxicity/safety 119
Dehydration
from travelers' diarrhea 88
oral rehydration solutions 87
Demand-release iodine resin element and thyroid disease 76
Dengue fever 130
Dengue hemorrhagic fever 132
Dengue shock syndrome
diagnosis and treatment 132
Denmark 348
Department of State
American Citizens Services 6
Bureau of Consular Affairs 7
Web site address for key officers of foreign posts 7
Dermacentor andersoni 148

Dermacentor variabilis 148
DIA-PAK
kits for diabetic supplies 23
Diabetes 189
Dialysis clinics, worldwide listing 11
Diarrhea, chronic 78
Diethylcarbamazine (DEC)
for filariasis 137
for loiasis (Loa loa) 139
Diphtheria vaccine 34
Diphyllobothriasis (fish tapeworm disease) 165
Dirofilariasis 296
Disease Risk Summaries 289
Australia and Oceania 302
Central America 282
China and the Indian sub-Continent 297
Europe and Russia 289, 291
Japan, Korea, and Taiwan 301
Mexico 282
North Africa 292
South America 286
Southeast Asia 299
the Caribbean 282
Disinfecting water, methods 74
Divers' Alert Network 19
scuba diving insurance 232
Djibouti 348
Doctors and hospitals abroad 19
Dominica 349
Dominican Republic 350
Doxycycline
for brucellosis 167
for chlamydia 204
for ehrlichiosis 147
for Lyme disease 175, 176
for malaria prophylaxis 104
for malaria treatment 111
for Mediterranean spotted fever 145
for scrub typhus 143
for sexually transmitted diseases 204
to prevent leptospirosis 168
to prevent plague 144
to treat plague 145
Dramamine 61

Drugs, use during pregnancy 259
DTaP vaccine 34
Dukoral
    oral cholera vaccine 33
Dysentery 78
    causes of 78

E

Ear infections, and air travel 63
EarPlanes 16, 63
Ecuador 350
Egypt 352
Ehrlichiosis 146
El Salvador 354
Emergency dental kit 25
Engerix-B vaccine 183
England (see United Kingdom) 477
EPAXAL 36
Epi-Pen (emergency epinephrine) 15
Erythema migrans 174
Espundia 141
Estonia 355
Ethiopia 355
Eustachian tube, during flight 62
Excedrin PM, for jet lag 57
Exercise and pregnancy 262
EZY DOSE syringe, for dehydration 91

F

Fansidar
    for malaria treatment 111
    for self treatment 115
Fascioliasis 163, 300, 340
Fasciolopsiasis 163, 300, 340
Fever
    evaluation in travelers 26
    post-travel evaluation 27
Fiji 357
Filariasis 136
    prophylaxis with DEC 139
Finland 357
Flumadine (Rimantidine) 39
fluroquinolones, to treat diarrhea 84
Flying Doctors Society 236
Flying, during pregnancy 263
Food safety 68
Food-based rehydration solutions 89

Foot care for travel 25
Foreign hospitals
    assessing capabilities 222
Foreign physicians 222
Former Yugoslav Republic of
    Macedonia 417
France 358
French Guiana 359
French Polynesia 360
Fugu poisoning 171
Fungal skin infections 16
Furazolidone (Furoxone) 85
    in children
        for travelers' diarrhea 274
    in pregnancy
        for travelers' diarrhea 265

G

Gabon 361
Gamow bag, for AMS 212
Gatorade, for rehydration 88
Gay bowel syndrome 203
Georgia 361
Georgia, former Soviet Union 436
Gerber's Rice Cereal, to treat
    dehydration 90
German Air Rescue 236
Germany 362
Ghana 363
Giardiasis 67, 151
Giardiasis, and filter removal 67
Global Assist hotline 221
Global Med-Net 19
Glucose, to promote water
    absorption 88
Going International (video on overseas
    living) 245
Gonorrhea 203
Great Britain (see United
    Kingdom) 477
Grenada 365
Guadeloupe 366
Guam 366
Guatemala 367
Guinea 368
Guinea-Bissau 369
Guyana 370

H

Haemophilus influenzae type b, vaccine 35
Haiti 371
Halcion (triazolam) 56
  for altitude sickness 206
  for jet lag 56
Halofantrine 110
Health Canada web site 10
Health Information for International Travel (CDC) 10
Hemolytic-uremic syndrome 67
Hemorrhagic fever with renal syndrome 143
Heparin (Lovenox)
  to prevent travelers' thrombosis 65
Hepatitis 179
  type A 179
  type B 181
  type C 184
  type D 179
  type E 186
Hepatitis A vaccine 35, 46, 180
  dosage schedule 49
  for children 181
Hepatitis B
  high-risk countries 182
  immune globulin (HBIG) 183
  serological tests for 183
  vaccine 183
Hepatitis B vaccine 36
Hepatitis E, and water purifiers 73
Heterophyiasis 353
Hetrazan (diethylcarbamazine) 137
Hib vaccine 35
High Altitude Medicine Guide 212
High altitude pulmonary edema 212
Hismanal 16
HIV, and the traveler 25, 197
HIV testing, on the Internet 241
HIV testing requirements
  Internet listing, country requirements 20
HMOs
  and approving medical transport 233
HMOs, and travel insurance 227

Honduras 372
Hong Kong 373
Hookworm disease 164
Hotel doctors 220
Houston, Dr. Charles
  advice for climbers with heart disease 217
Humalog insulin pen 192
Human granulocytic ehrlichiosis 146
Human monocytic ehrlichiosis 146
Hungary 374
Hydroxychloroquine 102

I

IAMAT 10, 11, 19, 221
Iceland 374
Immune globulin, for hepatitis E 186
Immune globulin, for travel 46
Immune globulin, use with hepatitis A vaccine 180
Immunizations
  during pregnancy 255
  for HIV-positive travelers 51
  infancy & childhood 53, 268
Imodium (loperamide) 83
Imogam, rabies immune globulin 170
Imovax rabies vaccine 169
Impetigo, and spread of hepatitis 183
India 375
Indonesia 378
Influenza, antiviral agents for 39
Insulin dose adjustment
  during air travel 193
Insulin lispro 192
Interferon
  for hepatitis 185
International driver's permit 21
International Medical Group (IMG)
  travel insurance 231
International Pharmacy Organization 19
International Society of Travel Medicine (ISTM) 9
International SOS 253
Internet, health information via 9
Intestinal fluke disease 163
Intron-A, for hepatitis C 185

Iodine
   and thyroid dysfunction 76
   residual concentration in treated water 76
Iodine tablets 75
Iodoquinol 153
Iran 380
Iraq 381
Ireland 382
Israel 382
Italy 384
Ivermectin 138
   for onchocerciasis 138
   for strongyloidiasis 165
Ivory Coast (Cote d'Ivoire) 385

J

Jamaica 386
Japan 387
Japanese encephalitis 132
Japanese encephalitis vaccine 38
Jet lag 55
   diets 55
   light exposure 55
Jordan 389

K

Kala azar 140
Katayama fever 160
Kazakhstan 297, 390
Kenya 390
Ketoconazole
   for leishmaniasis 142
Kidnapping and terrorism
   advice for avoiding 6, 242
Kids on the Go! newsletter 11
Kiribati 393
Kiribati (formerly Gilbert Islands) 393
Kroll Information Services 6
Kyrgystan 297
Kyrgyz Republic (Kyrgystan) 393

L

L-tryptophan, for jet lag 57
Laboratory tests, for fever in travelers 30

Lampit (nifurtimox)
   for Chagas' disease 136
Laos 393
Latvia 394
Leishamiasis 139
Leptospirosis 167
Lesotho 395
Levofloxacin 15, 84
Liberia 396
Libya 397
Lithuania 398
Liver fluke diseases 162
Liver fluke parasite, in Canada 332
Loiasis 138
Lone Star tick 148
Loperamide 84
Lost passport overseas 18
Lovenox, for travelers' thrombosis 65
Lung fluke disease 163
Lyme disease 147, 173
   PCR test for 178
   treatment of 175
Lyme disease vaccine 38

M

Madagascar 398
Madeira 399
Malaria 93
   and pregnancy 257
   in children
      treatment/prevention 275
   prophylaxis 101
   self-treatment 115
   treatment 108
      by oral route 112
Malarone 110
Malawi 400
Malaysia 401
Mali 402
Malta 404
Marshall Islands 404
Martinique 404
Mauritania 405
Mauritius 406
Measles vaccine 40
Measles/mumps/rubella vaccine 47

Mebendazole 164
   for ancylostomiasis (hookworm
      disease 164
   for ascariasis 164
   for capillariasis 164
   for trichuriasis 163
MedEscort International 24
Medic Alert 19
Medical care overseas 219
Medical Information for Americans
   Traveling Abroad 12
Medicare HMOs, and foreign
   travel 228
Medicare, paying doctors abroad 227
Medigap insurance, for travelers 227
Mediterranean spotted fever 144
Mefloquine 103
   for infants & children 104
   use during pregnany 104
Melatonin, for jet lag 55
Meningococcal meningitis 158
Meningococcal vaccine 40
Metronidazole 86
   for amebiasis 153
   for giardiasis 152
Mexico 407
Micronesia 410
Microwave ovens
   and safe food 69
Moldova 411, 436
Montserrat 411
Morocco 411
Mosquito nets
   Indoor Travel Tent 126
Mosquitoes
   and transmission of HIV 117
Motion sickness 59
Mozambique 412
Mt. Kilimanjaro, and AMS 209
Mutachol, oral cholera vaccine 33

N

Nalidixic acid (Negram), for travelers'
   diarrhea 15
Namibia 413
Nauru 414
Nepal 415

Netherlands 416
New Caledonia 417
New World leishmaniasis
   mucocutaneous leishmaniasis 141
New Zealand 417
Nicaragua 418
Nifurtimox (Lampit) 136
Niger 419
Nigeria 420
North Korea 404, 422
Northern Mariana Islands (U.S.) 422
Norway 422

O

Obstetrical emergencies, during
   travel 253
Ofloxacin
   for sexually-transmitted
      diseases 204
   for travelers' diarrhea 84, 273
   for typhoid fever 156
      short course for children 156
Old World leishmaniasis 140
Oman 423
Onchocerciasis 139
Opisthorchiasis 163
Oral rehydration therapy 87
Oral rehydration solutions 89
Oxygen, for altitude sickness 214

P

Pakistan 424
Palau 425
Panama 426
Papua New Guinea 427
Paragonimiasis 163, 300
Paraguay 428
Parasitic Disease Branch
   CDC assistance hotlines 140
   drugs for leishmaniasis 140
Parasitic Disease Drug Service, of the
   CDC 140
Passport Plus 18
Paying, for medical care abroad 223
PCR test, for Lyme disease 178
Pelvic inflammatory disease 203
Penicillin G, for meningitis 159
Pentostam 141

Pentostam, for leishmaniasis 140
Pepto-Bismol, for travelers'
    diarrhea 80, 82
    use in children 272
Permethrin 124
    application to clothing 125
Personal Physicians
    Worldwide 19, 221, 252
Personal safety guidelines
    during travel abroad 5
Pertussis 41
Peru 429
Phenergan (promethazine) 61
Philippines 431
Physical exam, in travelers with
    fever 30
Physicians abroad, how to locate 220
Pinkerton Global Intelligence 6
Plant-derived insect repellents 123
Plaquenil (hydroxychloroquine) 102
Poland 433
Polio vaccine 41, 47
Pork tapeworm disease 165
Portugal 433
Praziquantel 165
    for beef tapeworm disease 165
    for fish tapeworm disease 165
    for intesrtinal fluke disease 163
    for liver fluke diseases 162
    for pork tapeworm disease 166
    for schistosomiasis 162
Pregnancy and travel 251
Pretravel medical consultation 24
Primaquine 110
    for malaria prophylaxis 107
    treatment of vivax malaria 107
Primaquine-resistant P. vivax 108
Pristine, water purifier 75
Pro-Som (estazolam), for jet lag 56
    for altitude sickness 206
Proguanil 106
Proguanil/sulfonamide
    prophylaxis for falciparum
        malaria 101
Puerto Rico 434
Pufferfish poisoning 171
Purification devices (water) 76

Q

Qatar 435
Qinghaosu, for malaria 113
Quick ORS formula 89
Quinidine, for malaria 113
Quinine 111
Quinolones
    for ehrlichiosis 147
    for pregnant women 86
    for salmonellosis 157
    for sexually transmitted
        diseases 204
    for travelers' diarrhea 84
    for typhoid fever 155
    single-dose treatment of
        cholera 155

R

Rabies 168
Rabies immune globulin 169
Rabies vaccine, accelerated
    schedule 169
Ragonil (benznidazole)
    for Chagas' disease 136
Regional Security Officer, U.S.
    Embassies 7
Relapsing (cave) fever, in Israel 384
Relapsing fever 142
Relenza (Zanamivir) 39
Rennie, Dr. Drummond, advice for
    trekkers 217
Repellents 118
    list of available products
        with DEET concentrations 121
Restoril (temazepam) 56
    for altitude sickness 206
    for jet lag 56
Riamet (co-artemether) 114
Ribavirin
    for Crimean-Congo hemorrhagic
        fever 145
    for hepatitis C 185
    for tick encephalitis 145
Rifamycins, for ehrlichiosis 147
Rift Valley fever 142

Risk reduction companies
   Ackerman Group 6
   Air Security International 6
   Kroll Information Services 6
   Pinkerton Global Intelligence 6
Risks of travel
   accidents 3
   illness & fatalities 3
   personal safety 5
Rocky Mountain spotted fever 147
Rocky Mountain wood tick 148
Romania 435
Ross River fever 357
Roundworm diseases 163
Russia & the Commonwealth States 436
Rwanda 438

S

Safe restaurants
   how to evaluate 70
Safe travel tips 242
Saint Lucia 440
Saint Martin (Saint Maarten) 441
Saint Vincent/Grenadines 442
Salmonellosis 157
Samoa (Western) 443
Sandfly fever 142
Sao Tome & Principe 443
Saudi Arabia 444
Schistosomiasis 160
Scombroid poisoning 170
SCOPACE (scopolamine) 16, 60
Scuba diving insurance 232
Seafood toxins 171
Senegal 446
Serbia & Montengro 447
Sexually transmitted diseases 203
   treatment during pregnancy 204
Seychelles 447
Shigella dysenteriae, and treatment with quinolone 85
Shigellosis 78, 158
Shoreland's Travel Health Online 11
Short wave radios 244
Sierra Leone 447
Singapore 448
Sinusitis, and air flight 63

Sleeping pills, and altitude sickness 206
Slovak Republic 449
Slovak Republic (see Czech Republic) 347
Slovenia 449
Sodium cotransport, and rehydration 88
Solomon Islands 449
Somalia 450
Sonata (Zaleplon) 56
Sonata (zaleplon) 16
South Africa 451
South Korea 453
Spain 454
Sri Lanka 455
St. Barthelemy (St. Bart's) 439
St. Kitts & Nevis 440
State Department travel warnings 7
State Dept.. *See* Department of State
Sterile needles and syringes 15
   kits for travelers 17, 241
Stibogluconate (Pentostam), for leishmaniasis 140
Stress, and business travel 243
Stress management for overseas living 250
Stromectol (ivermectin) 138
Strongyloidiasis 164
Sudan 456
Sudden illness abroad, coping with 224
Suprax, for travelers' diarrhea 15
Suriname 457
Survival Kit for Overseas Living 245
Swaziland 458
Sweden 459
Swiss Air Rescue 236
Switzerland 460
Symmetrel (Amantadine) 39
Syphilis 203
Syria 461

T

Tadjikistan 297
Taenia saginata 165
Taenia solium 165
Taiwan 462
Tajikstan 463

Tamiflu (Oseltamivir) 39
Tanzania 463
Tapeworm diseases 165
Tetanus/diphtheria, for travel 47
Tetracycline
    for malaria treatment 111
    for Mediterranean spotted fever 145
    for relapsing fever 142
    to prevent plague 144
    to treat plague 145
Thailand 465
Thallium-201 SPECT testing
    after CABG surgery 217
    pretravel cardiac evaluation 22
The Baltic States, hea;lth advisory 436
The Gambia 467
The Safe Travel Book 242
Thomas W. Snyder & Co., travel insurance 232
Tick paralysis 147
Tick-borne encephalitis 145
Ticks (in USA) 148
    American dog tick 148
    brown dog tick 148
    deer tick 148
    Lone Star tick 148
    relapsing fever ticks 148
    Rocky Mountain wood tick 148
    western deer tick 148
Togo 468
Tonga 469
Toxic shellfish poisoning 171
Trachoma, in Africa
    treatment with azithromycin 295
TransDerm Scop, for motion sickness 16, 60
Travel, after heart attack 21
Travel and pregnancy 251
Travel clinics, finding on Internet 9
Travel Guard International 232
Travel insurance 227
Travel insurance, for pregnant travelers 253
Travel Medicine, Inc. 9, 17
Traveler's checks 20
Travelers' clinics, types of 8

Travelers' diarrhea 77
    antibiotics, during pregnancy 264
    antibiotics, for children 86, 272
    oral rehydration treatment 87
    rehydration of infants & children 91
    treatment summary 87
Traveling Nurses' Network 24
TravMed, travel insurance 231
Triazolam (Halcion) 56
    for jet lag 56
    improving altitude performance 206
Trichinosis 166
Trichuriasis 163
Triclabendazole 163
    for fascioliasis 163
    for lung fluke disease (paragonimiasis) 163
Trimethoprim/sulfamethoxazole
    for brucellosis 167
    for cholera 155
    for cyclosporiasis 86, 274
    for travelers' diarrhea 85, 274
Trinidad & Tobago 469
Trip interruption insurance 230
Trip preparation checklists 14
Tularemia 147
Tunisia 470
Turkey 471
Turkmenistan 297, 473
Turks & Caicos 472
Tuvalu 473
Tylenol PM, for jet lag 57
Typhoid fever 155
    treatment with azithromycin 156
    treatment with cephalosporins 156
    treatment with quinolones 156
    typhoid vaccine 44, 47

U

U.S. Embassies & Consulates 12
    Internet listing 12
Uganda 473
Ukraine 436
Ultrathon 17, 121
United Arab Emirates 476

United Kingdom 477
United States
  health advisory for 477
Uruguay 478
Uzbekistan 297, 479

V

Vaccinations, for international travel
  indications, dosage, precautions,
  Table 2.2 48
Vaccinations, for travel 31
  during pregnancy 255
  for children 267
  for the HIV-positive traveler 51
  influenza 37
  summary of recommendations 46
Vaccines 31, 32, 35
  BCG, for TB 43
  for children 268
  hepatitis A 35, 180
  hepatitis B 36, 183
  Japanese encephalitis 38, 133
  Lyme disease 38, 177
  measles/mumps/rubella 47
  pertussis (whooping cough) 41
  plague 144
  rabies 42, 169
  tetanus/diphtheria 47
  tick-borne encephalitis 145
  yellow fever 44, 130
Vanuatu 479
VAQTA 46, 180
  immunization schedule 49
Varicella (chickenpox) 47
Varicella (chickenpox) vaccine 32
Venezuela 480
ViCPS typhoid vaccine 269
Vietnam 482
Viruses, and water filters 72

W

Wallis & Futuna 483
Water disinfection methods 73
Water, for jet lag 58
Weil's disease 167
Western deer tick 148

Western Union Money Transfer
  service 20
Whipworm disease (trichuriasis) 163
WHO International Travel &
  Vaccination Requirement 12
Wood tick 148
World Health Organization,
  rehydration formula 89
World Weather Guide (book) 17
WorldCare Travel Assistance 232
Worldwide Assistance Services,
  Inc. 231, 253
Wright & Co. 232

Y

Yellow fever 129
Yellow Fever Endemic Zones 44
Yellow fever vaccine 44
Yemen (Yemen Arab Republic) 483
Yugoslavia 484

Z

Zaire 485
Zaleplon (Sonata), for jet leg 16
Zambia 487
Zimbabwe 488
Zyrtec 16
  for mosquito bite reactions 126

International Road Signs

Left Bend (Right if reversed)	Double Bend	Dangerous Bend	Crossroads
Dangerous Crossroad	Narrowing Road	Danger	Rough Road
School Crossing	Pedestrian Crossing	Men at Work	Railroad Crossing
Slippery Road	Loose Gravel	Falling Rocks	Light Signals
No Entry	No U Turn	Road Closed	No Passing
Speed Limit	Quiet Zone	Do Not Enter	No Turns In Directions Indicated

Appears in red on actual signs